OSGi Service Platform, Service Compendium Release 4, Version 4.2

OSGi Service Platform
Service Compendium

Release 4, Version 4.2
August 2009

OSGi Alliance / aQute Publishing

Publisher

aQute Publishing
9c, Avenue St. Drézéry
34160 Beaulieu
FRANCE
http://www.aQute.biz

ISBN 978-90-79350-05-6   aQute Publishing

Legal Notice

The publisher is not responsible for he use which might be made of the following information.

Trademarks

Feedback

This specification can be downloaded from the OSGi Alliance web site:

```
http://www.osgi.org
```

Comments about this specification can be mailed to:

```
speccomments@mail.osgi.org
```

Disclaimer

This is a reprinted copy of the OSGi Service Platform Core Specification, Release 4, Version 4.2. To fit the book size, this document had to be reformatted. In the unlikely case of any discrepancies between the original document and this book, the original document overrides this book. The original document can be downloaded from http://www.osgi.org

OSGi Specification License, Version 1.0

The OSGi Alliance ("OSGi Alliance") hereby grants you a fully-paid, non-exclusive, non-transferable, worldwide, limited license (without the right to sublicense), under the OSGi Alliance's applicable intellectual property rights to view, download, and reproduce the OSGi Specification ("Specification") which follows this License Agreement ("Agreement"). You are not authorized to create any derivative work of the Specification. The OSGi Alliance also grants you a perpetual, non-exclusive, worldwide, fully paid-up, royalty free, limited license (without the right to sublicense) under any applicable copyrights, to create and/or distribute an implementation of the Specification that: (i) fully implements the Specification including all its required interfaces and functionality; (ii) does not modify, subset, superset or otherwise extend the OSGi Name Space, or include any public or protected packages, classes, Java interfaces, fields or methods within the OSGi Name Space other than those required and authorized by the Specification. An implementation that does not satisfy limitations (i)-(ii) is not considered an implementation of the Specification, does not receive the benefits of this license, and must not be described as an implementation of the Specification. An implementation of the Specification must not claim to be a compliant implementation of the Specification unless it passes the OSGi Alliance Compliance Tests for the Specification in accordance with OSGi Alliance processes. "OSGi Name Space" shall mean the public class or interface declarations whose names begin with "org.osgi" or any recognized successors or replacements thereof.

THE SPECIFICATION IS PROVIDED "AS IS," AND THE OSGi ALLIANCE, ITS MEMBERS AND ANY OTHER AUTHORS MAKE NO REPRESENTATIONS OR WARRANTIES, EXPRESS OR IMPLIED, INCLUDING, BUT NOT LIMITED TO, WARRANTIES OF MERCHANTABILITY, FITNESS FOR A PARTICULAR PURPOSE, NON-INFRINGEMENT, OR TITLE; THAT THE CONTENTS OF THE SPECIFICATION ARE SUITABLE FOR ANY PURPOSE; NOR THAT THE IMPLEMENTATION OF SUCH CONTENTS WILL NOT INFRINGE ANY THIRD PARTY PATENTS, COPYRIGHTS, TRADEMARKS OR OTHER RIGHTS. THE OSGi ALLIANCE, ITS MEMBERS AND ANY OTHER AUTHORS WILL NOT BE LIABLE FOR ANY DIRECT, INDIRECT, SPECIAL, INCIDENTAL OR CONSEQUENTIAL DAMAGES ARISING OUT OF ANY USE OF THE SPECIFICATION OR THE PERFORMANCE OR IMPLEMENTATION OF THE CONTENTS THEREOF.

The name and trademarks of the OSGi Alliance or any other Authors may NOT be used in any manner, including advertising or publicity pertaining to the Specification or its contents without specific, written prior permission. Title to copyright in the Specification will at all times remain with the Authors.

No other rights are granted by implication, estoppel or otherwise.

Table Of Contents

116 Application Admin Specification   357

117 DMT Admin Service Specification   387

119 Monitor Admin Service Specification   487

703   Position Specification   643

704   Measurement and State Specification   647

999   Execution Environment Specification   661

1 Introduction

This compendium contains the specifications of all OSGi services.

1.1 Reader Level

This specification is written for the following audiences:

- Application developers
- Framework and system service developers (system developers)
- Architects

This specification assumes that the reader has at least one year of practical experience in writing Java programs. Experience with embedded systems and server-environments is a plus. Application developers must be aware that the OSGi environment is significantly more dynamic than traditional desktop or server environments.

System developers require a *very* deep understanding of Java. At least three years of Java coding experience in a system environment is recommended. A Framework implementation will use areas of Java that are not normally encountered in traditional applications. Detailed understanding is required of class loaders, garbage collection, Java 2 security, and Java native library loading.

Architects should focus on the introduction of each subject. This introduction contains a general overview of the subject, the requirements that influenced its design, and a short description of its operation as well as the entities that are used. The introductory sections require knowledge of Java concepts like classes and interfaces, but should not require coding experience.

Most of these specifications are equally applicable to application developers and system developers.

1.2 Version Information

This document specifies OSGi Service Platform Release 4, Version 4.2. This specification is backward compatible.

Components in this specification have their own specification version, independent of the OSGi Service Platform, Release 4, Version 4.2 specification. The following table summarizes the packages and specification versions for the different subjects.

Table 1.1   Packages and versions

Item	Package	Version
101 Log Service Specification	org.osgi.service.log	Version 1.3
102 Http Service Specification	org.osgi.service.http	Version 1.2
103 Device Access Specification	org.osgi.service.device	Version 1.1
104 Configuration Admin Service Specification	org.osgi.service.cm	Version 1.3
105 Metatype Service Specification	org.osgi.service.metatype	Version 1.1
106 Preferences Service Specification	org.osgi.service.prefs	Version 1.1
107 User Admin Service Specification	org.osgi.service.useradmin	Version 1.1
108 Wire Admin Service Specification	org.osgi.service.wireadmin	Version 1.0
109 IO Connector Service Specification	org.osgi.service.io	Version 1.0
110 Initial Provisioning	org.osgi.service.provisioning	Version 1.2
111 UPnP™ Device Service Specification	org.osgi.service.upnp	Version 1.1

Table 1.1 *Packages and versions*

Item	Package	Version
112 Declarative Services Specification	org.osgi.service.component	Version 1.1
113 Event Admin Service Specification	org.osgi.service.event	Version 1.2
114 Deployment Admin Specification	org.osgi.service.deploymentadmin org.osgi.service. deploymentadmin.spi	Version 1.1
115 Auto Configuration Specification		Version 1.2
116 Application Admin Specification	org.osgi.service.application	Version 1.1
117 DMT Admin Service Specification	info.dmtree info.dmtree.notification info.dmtree.notification.spi info.dmtree.registry info.dmtree.security info.dmtree.spi	Version 1.0
119 Monitor Admin Service Specification	org.osgi.service.monitor	Version 1.0
120 Foreign Application Access Specification	org.osgi.application	Version 1.0
121 Blueprint Container Specification	org.osgi.blueprint.container org.osgi.blueprint.reflect	Version 1.0
701 Tracker Specification	org.osgi.util.tracker	Version 1.4
702 XML Parser Service Specification	org.osgi.util.xml	Version 1.0
703 Position Specification	org.osgi.util.position	Version 1.0
704 Measurement and State Specification	org.osgi.util.measurement	Version 1.0
999 Execution Environment Specification		Version 1.3

When a component is represented in a bundle, a version attribute is needed in the declaration of the Import-Package or Export-Package manifest headers.

1.3 Changes

- Added Chapter 13, Remote Services
- Added Chapter 121, Blueprint Container Specification

1.4 References

[1] *Bradner, S., Key words for use in RFCs to Indicate Requirement Levels*
http://www.ietf.org/rfc/rfc2119.txt, March 1997.

[2] *OSGi Specifications*
http://www.osgi.org/Specifications/HomePage

13   Remote Services

Version 1.0

The OSGi framework provides a *local* service registry for bundles to communicate through service objects, where a service is an object that one bundle registers and another bundle gets. A *distribution provider* can use this loose coupling between bundles to *export* a registered service by creating a *endpoint*. Vice versa, the distribution provider can create a *proxy* that accesses an endpoint and then registers this proxy as an *imported* service. A Framework can contain multiple distribution providers simultaneously, each independently importing and exporting services.

An endpoint is a communications access mechanisms to a service in another framework, a (web) service, another process, or a queue or topic destination, etc., requiring some protocol for communications. The constellation of the mapping between services and endpoints as well as their communication characteristics is called the *topology*. A common case for distribution providers is to be present on multiple frameworks importing and exporting services; effectively distributing the service registry.

The local architecture for remote services is depicted in Figure 13.1 on page 3.

The local architecture for remote services is depicted in Figure 13.1 on page 3.

Figure 13.1   *Remote Services Architecture*

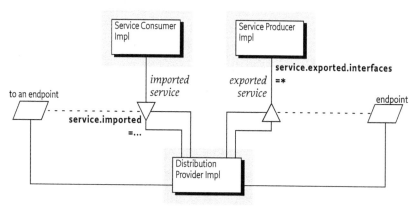

Local services imply in-VM call semantics. Many of these semantics cannot be supported over a communications connection, or require special configuration of the communications connection. It is therefore necessary to define a mechanism for bundles to convey their assumptions and requirements to the distribution provider. This chapter defines a number of service properties that a distribution provider can use to establish a topology while adhering to the given constraints.

13.1   The Fallacies

General abstractions for distributed systems have been tried before and often failed. Well known are the fallacies described in [2] *The Fallacies of Distributed Computing Explained*:

- The network is reliable
- Latency is zero
- Bandwidth is infinite
- The network is secure
- Topology doesn't change

- There is one administrator
- Transport cost is zero
- The network is homogeneous

Most fallacies represent non-functional trade-offs that should be considered by administrators, their decisions can then be reflected in the topology. For example, in certain cases limited bandwidth is acceptable and the latency in a datacenter is near zero. However, the reliability fallacy is the hardest because it intrudes into the application code. If a communication channel is lost, the application code needs to take specific actions to recover from this failure.

This reliability aspect is also addressed with OSGi services because services are dynamic. Failures in the communications layer can be mapped to the unregistration of the imported service. OSGi bundles are already well aware of these dynamics, and a number of programming models have been developed to minimize the complexity of writing these dynamic applications.

13.2 Remote Service Properties

This section introduces a number of properties that participating bundles can use to convey information to the distribution provider according to this Remote Service specification. These properties are listed alphabetically in Table 13.1. The scenarios that these properties are used in are discussed in later sections.

Table 13.1   Remote Service Properties

Service Property Name	Type	Description
remote.configs.supported	String+	Registered by the distribution provider on one of its services to indicate the supported configuration types. See *Configuration Types* on page 10 and *Dependencies* on page 12.
remote.intents.supported	String+	Registered by the distribution provider on one of its services to indicate the vocabulary of implemented intents. See *Dependencies* on page 12.
service.exported.configs	String+	A list of configuration types that should be used to export the service. Each configuration type represents the configuration parameters for an endpoint. A distribution provider should create an endpoint for each configuration type that it supports. See *Configuration Types* on page 10 for more details.
service.exported.intents	String+	A list of *intents* that the distribution provider must implement to distribute the service. Intents listed in this property are reserved for intents that are critical for the code to function correctly, for example, ordering of messages. These intents should not be configurable. For more information about intents, see *Intents* on page 8.

Table 13.1   *Remote Service Properties*

Service Property Name	Type	Description
service.exported.intents.extra	String+	This property is merged with the service.exported.intents property before the distribution provider interprets the listed intents; it has therefore the same semantics but the property should be configurable so the administrator can choose the intents based on the topology. Bundles should therefore make this property configurable, for example through the Configuration Admin service. See *Intents* on page 8.
service.exported.interfaces	String+	Setting this property marks this service for export. It defines the interfaces under which this service can be exported. This list must be a subset of the types listed in the objectClass service property. The single value of an asterisk ('*', \u002A) indicates all interfaces in the registration's objectClass property and ignore the classes. It is strongly recommended to only export interfaces and not concrete classes due to the complexity of creating proxies for some type of concrete classes. See *Registering a Service for Export* on page 7.
service.imported	*	Must be set by a distribution provider to any value when it registers the endpoint proxy as an imported service. A bundle can use this property to filter out imported services.
service.imported.configs	String+	The configuration information used to import this service, as described in service.exported.configs. Any associated properties for this configuration types must be properly mapped to the importing system. For example, a URL in these properties must point to a valid resource when used in the importing framework.

If multiple configuration types are listed in this property, then they must be synonyms for exactly the same remote endpoint that is used to export this service. |

Table 13.1   *Remote Service Properties*

Service Property Name	Type	Description

service.intents	String+	A list of intents that this service implements. This property has a dual purpose:
		
		• A bundle can use this service property to notify the distribution provider that these intents are already implemented by the exported service object.
		• A distribution provider must use this property to convey the combined intents of:
		  • The exporting service, and
		  • The intents that the exporting distribution provider adds.
		  • The intents that the importing distribution provider adds.
		
		To export a service, a distribution provider must expand any qualified intents. Both the exporting and importing distribution providers must recognize all intents before a service can be distributed. See *Intents* on page 8.

service.pid	String+	Services that are exported should have a service.pid property. The service.pid (PID) is a unique persistent identity for the service, the PID is defined in *Persistent Identifier (PID)* on page 129 of the Core specification. This property enables a distribution provider to associate persistent proprietary data with a service registration.

The properties and their treatment by the distribution provider is depicted in *Distribution Service Properties* on page 6.

Figure 13.2   *Distribution Service Properties*

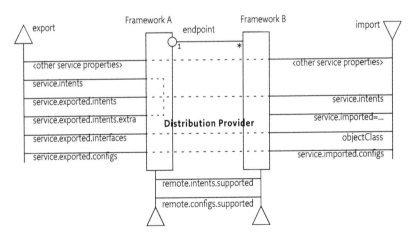

| 13.2.1 | **Registering a Service for Export** |

A distribution provider should create one or more endpoints for an exported service when the following conditions are met:

- The service has the service property service.exported.interfaces set.
- All intents listed in service.exported.intents, service.exported.intents.extra and service.intents are part of the distributed provider's vocabulary
- None of the intents are mutually exclusive.
- The distribution provider can use the configuration types in service.exported.configs to create one or more endpoints.

The endpoint must at least implement all the intents that are listed in the service.exported.intents and service.exported.intents.extra properties.

The configuration types listed in the service.exported.configs can contain *alternatives* and/or *synonyms*. Alternatives describe different endpoints for the same service while a synonym describes a different configuration type for the same endpoint.

A distribution provider should create an endpoint for each of the configuration types it supports; these configuration types should be alternatives. Synonyms are allowed, but each synonym should be supported by only one distribution provider.

If no configuration types are recognized, the distribution provider should create an endpoint with a default configuration type except when one of the listed configuration types is <<nodefault>>.

For more information about the configuration types, see further *Configuration Types* on page 10.

| 13.2.2 | **Getting an Imported Service** |

An imported service must be a normal service, there are therefore no special rules for getting it. An imported service has a number of additional properties that must be set by the distribution provider.

If the endpoint for an exported service is imported as an OSGi service in another framework, then the following properties must be treated as special.

- service.imported – Must be set to some value.
- service.intents – This must be the combination of the following:
  - The service.intents property on the exported service
  - The service.exported.intents and service.exported.intents.extra properties on the exported service
  - Any additional intents implemented by the distribution providers on both sides.
- service.imported.configs – Contains the configuration types that can be used to import this service. The types listed in this property must be *synonymous*, that is, they must refer to exactly the same endpoint that is exporting the service. See *Configuration Types* on page 10.
- service.exported.* – Properties starting with service.exported. must not be set on the imported service.
- service.exported.interfaces – This property must not be set, its content is reflected in the objectClass property.

All other *public* service properties (not starting with a dot ('.' \u002E)) must be listed on the imported service if they use the basic service property types. If the service property cannot be communicated because, for example, it uses a type that can not be marshalled by the distribution provider then the distribution provider must ignore this property.

The service.imported property indicates that a service is an imported service. If this service property is set to any value, then the imported service is a proxy for an endpoint. If a bundle wants to filter out imported services, then it can add the following filter:

```
(&(!(service.imported=*)) <previous filter>)
```

Distribution providers can also use the *Service Hooks Specification* on page 315 of the core specification to hide services from specific bundles.

On Demand Import

The Service Hooks specification, see *Service Hooks Specification* on page 315 of the core specification, allows a distribution provider to detect when a bundle is listening for specific services. Bundles can request imported services with specific intents by building an appropriate filter. The distribution provider can use this information to import a service on demand.

The following example creates a Service Tracker that is interested in an imported service.

```
Filter f = context.createFilter(
    "(&(objectClasss=com.acme.Foo)"
  +    "(service.intents=confidentiality))"
);
ServiceTracker tracker =
   new ServiceTracker(context, f, null );
tracker.open();
```

Such a Service Tracker will inform the Listener Hook and will give it the filter expression. If the distribution provider has registered such a hook, it will be informed about the need for an imported com.acme.Foo service that has a confidentiality intent. It can then use some proprietary means to find a service to import that matches the given object class and intent.

How the distribution provider finds an appropriate endpoint is out of scope for this specification.

13.3 Intents

An intent is a name for an abstract distribution capability. An intent can be *implemented* by a service; this can then be reflected in the service.intents property. An intent can also *constrain* the possible communication mechanisms that a distribution provider can choose to distribute a service. This is reflected in the service.export.intents and service.exported.intents.extra properties.

The purpose of the intents is to have a *vocabulary* that is shared between distribution aware bundles and the distribution provider. This vocabulary allows the bundles to express constraints on the export of their services as well as providing information on what intents are implemented by a service.

Intents have the following syntax

```
intent    ::= token | qualified
qualified ::= token ( '.' token )*
```

Qualified intents use a dotted notation to provide additional details but fully imply their prefixes. For example:

```
confidentiality.message.body
```

This example, can be *expanded* into confidentiality, confidentiality.message, and confidentiality.message.body. Qualified intents can be used to provide additional details how an intent is achieved. However, a distribution provider must expand any qualified intents into its prefixes.

The concept of intents is derived from the [4] *SCA Policy Framework specification.* When designing a vocabulary for a distribution provider it is recommended to closely follow the vocabulary of intents defined in the SCA Policy Framework.

13.4   General Usage

13.4.1   Call by Value

Normal service semantics are call-by-reference. An object passed as an argument in a service call is a direct reference to that object. Any changes to this object will be shared on both sides of the service registry.

Distributed services are different. Arguments are normally passed by value, which means that a copy is sent to the remote system, changes to this value are not reflected in the originating framework. When using distributed services, call-by-value should always be assumed by all participants in the distribution chain.

13.4.2   Data Fencing

Services are syntactically defined by their Java interfaces. When exposing a service over a remote protocol, typically such an interface is mapped to a protocol-specific interface definition. For example, in CORBA the Java interfaces would be converted to a corresponding IDL definition. This mapping does not always result in a complete solution.

Therefore, for many practical distributed applications it will be necessary to constrain the possible usage of data types in service interfaces. A distribution provider must at least support interfaces (not classes) that only use the basic types as defined for the service properties. These are the primitive types and their wrappers as well as arrays and collections. See *Filter Syntax* on page 33 of the Core Specification for a list of service property types.

Distribution providers will in general provide a richer set of types that can be distributed.

13.4.3   Remote Services Life Cycle

If a distribution provider has distributed a service, it must closely track any modifications on the exported service. If there is a corresponding imported service, it must closely match any modified service properties in the way that was specified for the registration. If the exported service is unregistered, the endpoint must be withdrawn as soon as possible. If there is a corresponding imported service, then this imported service must also be unregistered expediently.

13.4.4   Runtime

An imported service is just like any other service and can be used as such. However, certain non-functional characteristics of this service can differ significantly from what is normal for an in-VM object call. Many of these characteristics can be mapped to the normal service operations. That is, if the connection fails in any way, the service can be unregistered. According to the standard OSGi contract, this means that the users of that service must perform the appropriate cleanup to prevent stale references.

13.4.5   Exceptions

It is impossible to guarantee that a service is not used when it is no longer valid. Even with the synchronous callbacks from the Service Listeners, there is always a finite window where a service can be used while the underlying implementation has failed. In a distributed environment, this window can actually be quite large for an imported service.

Such failure situations must be exposed to the application code that uses a failing imported service. In these occasions, the distribution provider must notify the application by throwing a Service Exception, or subclass thereof, with the reason REMOTE. The Service Exception is a Runtime Exception, it can be handled higher up in the call chain. The cause of this Service Exception must be the Exception that caused the problem.

A distribution provider should log any problems with the communications layer to the Log Service, if available.

13.5   Configuration Types

An exported service can have a service.exported.configs service property. This property lists configuration types for endpoints that are provided for this service. Each type provides a specification that defines how the configuration data for one or more endpoints is provided. For example, a hypothetical configuration type could use a service property to hold a URL for the RMI naming registry.

Configuration types that are not defined by the OSGi Alliance should use a name that follows the reverse internet domain name scheme defined in Java Language Specification for Java packages. For example, com.acme.wsdl would be the proprietary way for the ACME company to specify a WSDL configuration type.

13.5.1   Configuration Type Properties

The service.exported.configs and service.imported.configs use the configuration types in very different ways. That is, the service.imported.configs property is not a copy of the service.exported.configs as the name might seem to imply.

An exporting service can list its desired configuration types in the service.exported.configs property. This property is potentially seen and interpreted by multiple distribution providers. Each of these providers can independently create endpoints from the configuration types. In principle, the service.exported.configs lists *alternatives* for a single distribution provider and can list *synonyms* to support alternative distribution providers. If only one of the synonyms is useful, there is an implicit assumption that when the service is exported, only one of the synonyms should be supported by the installed distribution providers. If it is detected that this assumption is violated, then an error should be logged and the conflicting configuration is further ignored.

The interplay of synonyms and alternatives is depicted in Table 13.2. In this table, the first columns on the left list different combinations of the configuration types in the service.exported.configs property. The next two columns list two distribution providers that each support an overlapping set of configuration types. The x's in this table indicate if a configuration type or distribution provider is active in a line. The description then outlines the issues, if any. It is assumed in this table that hypothetical configuration types net.rmi and com.rmix map to an identical endpoint, just like net.soap and net.soapx..

Table 13.2   Synonyms and Alternatives in Exported Configurations

net.rmi	com.rmix	net.soap	com.soapx	<<nodefault>>	Distribution Provider A Supports: net.rmi com.rmix com.soapx	Distribution Provider B Supports net.rmi net.soap	Description
x			x		x		*Ok*, A will create an endpoint for the RMI and SOAP alternatives.
x					x	x	*Configuration error.* There is a clash for net.rmi because A and B can both create an endpoint for the same configuration. It is likely that one will fail.
		x	x		x		*Ok*, exported on com.soapx by A, the net.soap is ignored.
		x	x		x	x	*Synonym error* because A and B export to same SOAP endpoint, it is likely that one will fail.
	x	x			x	x	*Ok*, two alternative endpoints over RMI (by A) and SOAP (by B) are created. This is a typical use case.
		x	x		x		*Ok.* Synonyms are used to allow frameworks that have either A or B installed. In this case A exports over SOAP.
		x	x			x	*Ok.* Synonyms are used to allow frameworks that have either A or B installed. In this case B exports.
					x		*Ok.* A creates an endpoint with default configuration type.
					x	x	*Ok.* Both A and B each create an endpoint with their default configuration type.
				x	x		*Ok.* No endpoint is created.
x	x					x	Provider B does not recognize the configuration types it should therefore use a default configuration type.

To summarize, the following rules apply for a single distribution provider:

- Only configuration types that are supported by this distribution provider must be used. All other configuration types must be ignored.
- All of the supported configuration types must be *alternatives*, that is, they must map to different endpoints. Synonyms for the same distribution provider should be logged as errors.
- If a configuration type results in an endpoint that is already in use, then an error should be logged. It is likely then that another distribution provider already had created that endpoint.

An export of a service can therefore result in multiple endpoints being created. For example, a service can be exported over RMI as well as SOAP. Creating an endpoint can fail, in that case the distribution provider must log this information in the Log Service, if available, and not export the service to that endpoint. Such a failure can, for example, occur when two configuration types are synonym and multiple distribution providers are installed that supporting this type.

On the importing side, the service.imported.configs property lists configuration types that must refer to the same endpoint. That is, it can list alternative configuration types for this endpoint but all configuration types must result in the same endpoint.

For example, there are two distribution providers installed at the exporting and importing frameworks. Distribution provider A supports the hypothetical configuration type net.rmi and net.soap. Distribution provider B supports the hypothetical configuration type net.smart. A service is registered that list all three of those configuration types.

Distribution provider A will create two endpoints, one for RMI and one for SOAP. Distribution provider B will create one endpoint for the smart protocol. The distribution provider A knows how to create the configuration data for the com.acme.rmi configuration type as well and can therefore create a synonymous description of the endpoint in that configuration type. It will therefore set the imported configuration type for the RMI endpoint to:

```
service.imported.configs = net.rmi, com.acme.rmi
net.rmi.url = rmi://172.25.25.109:1099/service-id/24
com.acme.rmi.address = 172.25.25.109
com.acme.rmi.port = 1099
com.acme.rmi.path = service-id/24
```

Figure 13.3   *Relation between imported and exported configuration types*

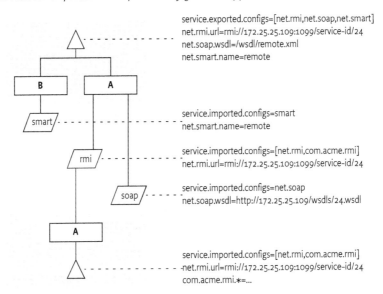

13.5.2   Dependencies

A bundle that uses a configuration type has an implicit dependency on the distribution provider. To make this dependency explicit, the distribution provider must register a service with the following properties:

- remote.intents.supported – (String+) The vocabulary of the given distribution provider.

- remote.configs.supported – (String+) The configuration types that are implemented by the distribution provider.

A bundle that depends on the availability of specific intents or configuration types can create a service dependency on an anonymous service with the given properties. The following filter is an example of depending on a hypothetical net.rmi configuration type:

    (remote.configs.supported=net.rmi)

13.6 Security

The distribution provider will be required to invoke methods on any exported service. This implies that it must have the combined set of permissions of all methods it can call. It also implies that the distribution provider is responsible for ensuring that a bundle that calls an imported service is not granted additional permissions through the fact that the distribution provider will call the exported service, not the original invoker.

The actual mechanism to ensure that bundles can get additional permissions through the distribution is out of scope for this specification. However, distribution providers should provide mechanisms to limit the set of available permissions for a remote invocation, preferably on a small granularity basis.

One possible means is to use the getAccessControlContext method on the Conditional Permission Admin service to get an Access Control Context that is used in a doPrivileged block where the invocation takes place. The getAccessControlContext method takes a list of signers which could represent the remote bundles that cause an invocation. How these are authenticated is up to the distribution provider.

A distribution provider is a potential attack point for intruders. Great care should be taken to properly setup the permissions or topology in an environment that requires security.

13.6.1 Limiting Exports and Imports

Service registration and getting services is controlled through the ServicePermission class. This permission supports a filter based constructor that can assert service properties. This facility can be used to limit bundles from being able to register exported services or get imported services if they are combined with Conditional Permission Admin's ALLOW facility. The following example shows how all bundles except from www.acme.com are denied the registration and getting of distributed services.

```
DENY {
    [...BundleLocationCondition("http://www.acme.com/*" "!")]
    (...ServicePermission "(service.imported=*)" "GET" )
    (...ServicePermission "(service.exported.interfaces=*)"
                          "REGISTER" )
}
```

13.7 References

[1]   *OSGi Core Specifications*
       http://www.osgi.org/Specifications/HomePage

[2]   *The Fallacies of Distributed Computing Explained*
       http://www.rgoarchitects.com/Files/fallacies.pdf

[3]   *Service Component Architecture (SCA)*
       http://www.oasis-opencsa.org/

[4]   *SCA Policy Framework specification*
       http://www.oasis-open.org/committees/sca-policy/

101 Log Service Specification

Version 1.3

101.1 Introduction

The Log Service provides a general purpose message logger for the OSGi Service Platform. It consists of two services, one for logging information and another for retrieving current or previously recorded log information.

This specification defines the methods and semantics of interfaces which bundle developers can use to log entries and to retrieve log entries.

Bundles can use the Log Service to log information for the Operator. Other bundles, oriented toward management of the environment, can use the Log Reader Service to retrieve Log Entry objects that were recorded recently or to receive Log Entry objects as they are logged by other bundles.

101.1.1 Entities

- *LogService* – The service interface that allows a bundle to log information, including a message, a level, an exception, a ServiceReference object, and a Bundle object.
- *LogEntry* - An interface that allows access to a log entry in the log. It includes all the information that can be logged through the Log Service and a time stamp.
- *LogReaderService* - A service interface that allows access to a list of recent LogEntry objects, and allows the registration of a LogListener object that receives LogEntry objects as they are created.
- *LogListener* - The interface for the listener to LogEntry objects. Must be registered with the Log Reader Service.

Figure 101.1   *Log Service Class Diagram org.osgi.service.log package*

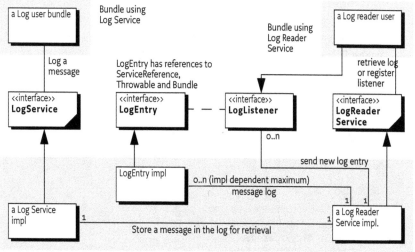

101.2   The Log Service Interface

The LogService interface allows bundle developers to log messages that can be distributed to other bundles, which in turn can forward the logged entries to a file system, remote system, or some other destination.

The LogService interface allows the bundle developer to:

- Specify a message and/or exception to be logged.
- Supply a log level representing the severity of the message being logged. This should be one of the levels defined in the LogService interface but it may be any integer that is interpreted in a user-defined way.
- Specify the Service associated with the log requests.

By obtaining a LogService object from the Framework service registry, a bundle can start logging messages to the LogService object by calling one of the LogService methods. A Log Service object can log any message, but it is primarily intended for reporting events and error conditions.

The LogService interface defines these methods for logging messages:

- log(int, String) – This method logs a simple message at a given log level.
- log(int, String, Throwable) – This method logs a message with an exception at a given log level.
- log(ServiceReference, int, String) – This method logs a message associated with a specific service.
- log(ServiceReference, int, String, Throwable) – This method logs a message with an exception associated with a specific service.

While it is possible for a bundle to call one of the log methods without providing a ServiceReference object, it is recommended that the caller supply the ServiceReference argument whenever appropriate, because it provides important context information to the operator in the event of problems.

The following example demonstrates the use of a log method to write a message into the log.

```
logService.log(
    myServiceReference,
    LogService.LOG_INFO,
    "myService is up and running"
);
```

In the example, the myServiceReference parameter identifies the service associated with the log request. The specified level, LogService.LOG_INFO, indicates that this message is informational.

The following example code records error conditions as log messages.

```
try {
    FileInputStream fis = new FileInputStream("myFile");
    int b;
    while ( (b = fis.read()) != -1 ) {
        ...
    }
    fis.close();
}
catch ( IOException exception ) {
    logService.log(
        myServiceReference,
        LogService.LOG_ERROR,
        "Cannot access file",
        exception );
}
```

Notice that in addition to the error message, the exception itself is also logged. Providing this information can significantly simplify problem determination by the Operator.

101.3 Log Level and Error Severity

The log methods expect a log level indicating error severity, which can be used to filter log messages when they are retrieved. The severity levels are defined in the LogService interface.

Callers must supply the log levels that they deem appropriate when making log requests. The follow-

Table 101.1   Log Levels

Level	Descriptions
LOG_DEBUG	Used for problem determination and may be irrelevant to anyone but the bundle developer.
LOG_ERROR	Indicates the bundle or service may not be functional. Action should be taken to correct this situation.
LOG_INFO	May be the result of any change in the bundle or service and does not indicate a problem.
LOG_WARNING	Indicates a bundle or service is still functioning but may experience problems in the future because of the warning condition.

ing table lists the log levels.

101.4 Log Reader Service

The Log Reader Service maintains a list of LogEntry objects called the *log*. The Log Reader Service is a service that bundle developers can use to retrieve information contained in this log, and receive notifications about LogEntry objects when they are created through the Log Service.

The size of the log is implementation-specific, and it determines how far into the past the log entries go. Additionally, some log entries may not be recorded in the log in order to save space. In particular, LOG_DEBUG log entries may not be recorded. Note that this rule is implementation-dependent. Some implementations may allow a configurable policy to ignore certain LogEntry object types.

The LogReaderService interface defines these methods for retrieving log entries.

- getLog() – This method retrieves past log entries as an enumeration with the most recent entry first.
- addLogListener(LogListener) – This method is used to subscribe to the Log Reader Service in order to receive log messages as they occur. Unlike the previously recorded log entries, all log messages must be sent to subscribers of the Log Reader Service as they are recorded.
  A subscriber to the Log Reader Service must implement the LogListener interface.
  After a subscription to the Log Reader Service has been started, the subscriber's LogListener.logged method must be called with a LogEntry object for the message each time a message is logged.

The LogListener interface defines the following method:

- logged(LogEntry) – This method is called for each LogEntry object created. A Log Reader Service implementation must not filter entries to the LogListener interface as it is allowed to do for its log. A LogListener object should see all LogEntry objects that are created.

The delivery of LogEntry objects to the LogListener object should be done asynchronously.

101.5 Log Entry Interface

The LogEntry interface abstracts a log entry. It is a record of the information that was passed when an event was logged, and consists of a superset of information which can be passed through the LogService methods. The LogEntry interface defines these methods to retrieve information related to LogEntry objects:

- getBundle() – This method returns the Bundle object related to a LogEntry object.
- getException() – This method returns the exception related to a LogEntry object. In some implementations, the returned exception may not be the original exception. To avoid references to a bundle defined exception class, thus preventing an uninstalled bundle from being garbage collected, the Log Service may return an exception object of an implementation defined Throwable subclass. This object will attempt to return as much information as possible, such as the message and stack trace, from the original exception object .
- getLevel() – This method returns the severity level related to a LogEntry object.
- getMessage() – This method returns the message related to a LogEntry object.
- getServiceReference() –This method returns the ServiceReference object of the service related to a LogEntry object.
- getTime() – This method returns the time that the log entry was created.

101.6 Mapping of Events

Implementations of a Log Service must log Framework-generated events and map the information to LogEntry objects in a consistent way. Framework events must be treated exactly the same as other logged events and distributed to all LogListener objects that are associated with the Log Reader Service. The following sections define the mapping for the three different event types: Bundle, Service, and Framework.

101.6.1 Bundle Events Mapping

A Bundle Event is mapped to a LogEntry object according to Table 101.2, "Mapping of Bundle Events to Log Entries," on page 18.

Table 101.2   *Mapping of Bundle Events to Log Entries*

Log Entry method	Information about Bundle Event
getLevel()	LOG_INFO
getBundle()	Identifies the bundle to which the event happened. In other words, it identifies the bundle that was installed, started, stopped, updated, or uninstalled. This identification is obtained by calling getBundle() on the BundleEvent object.
getException()	null
getServiceReference()	null
getMessage()	The message depends on the event type:
	• INSTALLED – "BundleEvent INSTALLED"
	• STARTED – "BundleEvent STARTED"
	• STOPPED – "BundleEvent STOPPED"
	• UPDATED – "BundleEvent UPDATED"
	• UNINSTALLED – "BundleEvent UNINSTALLED"
	• RESOLVED – "BundleEvent RESOLVED"
	• UNRESOLVED – "BundleEvent UNRESOLVED"

101.6.2   **Service Events Mapping**

A Service Event is mapped to a LogEntry object according to Table 101.3, "Mapping of Service Events to Log Entries," on page 19.

Table 101.3   *Mapping of Service Events to Log Entries*

Log Entry method	Information about Service Event
getLevel()	LOG_INFO, except for the ServiceEvent.MODIFIED event. This event can happen frequently and contains relatively little information. It must be logged with a level of LOG_DEBUG.
getBundle()	Identifies the bundle that registered the service associated with this event. It is obtained by calling getServiceReference().getBundle() on the ServiceEvent object.
getException()	null
getServiceReference()	Identifies a reference to the service associated with the event. It is obtained by calling getServiceReference() on the ServiceEvent object.
getMessage()	This message depends on the actual event type. The messages are mapped as follows: • REGISTERED – "ServiceEvent REGISTERED" • MODIFIED – "ServiceEvent MODIFIED" • UNREGISTERING – "ServiceEvent UNREGISTERING"

101.6.3   **Framework Events Mapping**

A Framework Event is mapped to a LogEntry object according to Table 101.4, "Mapping of Framework Event to Log Entries," on page 19.

Table 101.4   *Mapping of Framework Event to Log Entries*

Log Entry method	Information about Framework Event
getLevel()	LOG_INFO, except for the FrameworkEvent.ERROR event. This event represents an error and is logged with a level of LOG_ERROR.
getBundle()	Identifies the bundle associated with the event. This may be the system bundle. It is obtained by calling getBundle() on the FrameworkEvent object.
getException()	Identifies the exception associated with the error. This will be null for event types other than ERROR. It is obtained by calling getThrowable() on the FrameworkEvent object.
getServiceReference()	null
getMessage()	This message depends on the actual event type. The messages are mapped as follows: • STARTED – "FrameworkEvent STARTED" • ERROR – "FrameworkEvent ERROR" • PACKAGES_REFRESHED – "FrameworkEvent PACKAGES REFRESHED" • STARTLEVEL_CHANGED – "FrameworkEvent STARTLEVEL CHANGED" • WARNING – "FrameworkEvent WARNING" • INFO – "FrameworkEvent INFO"

101.6.4   **Log Events**

Log events must be delivered by the Log Service implementation to the Event Admin service (if present) asynchronously under the topic:

```
org/osgi/service/log/LogEntry/<event type>
```

The logging level is used as event type:

```
LOG_ERROR
LOG_WARNING
LOG_INFO
LOG_DEBUG
LOG_OTHER (when event is not recognized)
```

The properties of a log event are:

- bundle.id – (Long) The source bundle's id.
- bundle.symbolicName – (String) The source bundle's symbolic name. Only set if not null.
- bundle – (Bundle) The source bundle.
- log.level – (Integer) The log level.
- message – (String) The log message.
- timestamp – (Long) The log entry's timestamp.
- log.entry – (LogEntry) The LogEntry object.

If the log entry has an associated Exception:

- exception.class – (String) The fully-qualified class name of the attached exception. Only set if the getExceptionmethod returns a non-null value.
- exception.message – (String) The message of the attached Exception. Only set if the Exception message is not null.
- exception – (Throwable) The Exception returned by the getException method.

If the getServiceReference method returns a non-null value:

- service – (ServiceReference) The result of the getServiceReference method.
- service.id – (Long) The id of the service.
- service.pid – (String) The service's persistent identity. Only set if the service.pid service property is not null.
- service.objectClass – (String[]) The object class of the service object.

101.7 Security

The Log Service should only be implemented by trusted bundles. This bundle requires ServicePermission[LogService|LogReaderService, REGISTER]. Virtually all bundles should get ServicePermission[LogService, GET]. The ServicePermission[LogReaderService, GET] should only be assigned to trusted bundles.

101.8 org.osgi.service.log

Log Service Package Version 1.3.

Bundles wishing to use this package must list the package in the Import-Package header of the bundle's manifest. For example:

```
Import-Package: org.osgi.service.log; version="[1.3,2.0)"
```

101.8.1 Summary

- *LogEntry* - Provides methods to access the information contained in an individual Log Service log entry.
- *LogListener* - Subscribes to LogEntry objects from the LogReaderService.
- *LogReaderService* - Provides methods to retrieve LogEntry objects from the log.
- *LogService* - Provides methods for bundles to write messages to the log.

101.8.2   public interface LogEntry

Provides methods to access the information contained in an individual Log Service log entry.

A LogEntry object may be acquired from the LogReaderService.getLog method or by registering a LogListener object.

See Also   LogReaderService.getLog, LogListener

Concurrency   Thread-safe

101.8.2.1   public Bundle getBundle( )

□ Returns the bundle that created this LogEntry object.

Returns   The bundle that created this LogEntry object; null if no bundle is associated with this LogEntry object.

101.8.2.2   public Throwable getException( )

□ Returns the exception object associated with this LogEntry object.

In some implementations, the returned exception may not be the original exception. To avoid references to a bundle defined exception class, thus preventing an uninstalled bundle from being garbage collected, the Log Service may return an exception object of an implementation defined Throwable subclass. The returned object will attempt to provide as much information as possible from the original exception object such as the message and stack trace.

Returns   Throwable object of the exception associated with this LogEntry;null if no exception is associated with this LogEntry object.

101.8.2.3   public int getLevel( )

□ Returns the severity level of this LogEntry object.

This is one of the severity levels defined by the LogService interface.

Returns   Severity level of this LogEntry object.

See Also   LogService.LOG_ERROR, LogService.LOG_WARNING, LogService.LOG_INFO, LogService.LOG_DEBUG

101.8.2.4   public String getMessage( )

□ Returns the human readable message associated with this LogEntry object.

Returns   String containing the message associated with this LogEntry object.

101.8.2.5   public ServiceReference getServiceReference( )

□ Returns the ServiceReference object for the service associated with this LogEntry object.

Returns   ServiceReference object for the service associated with this LogEntry object; null if no ServiceReference object was provided.

101.8.2.6   public long getTime( )

□ Returns the value of currentTimeMillis() at the time this LogEntry object was created.

Returns   The system time in milliseconds when this LogEntry object was created.

See Also   System.currentTimeMillis()

101.8.3   public interface LogListener
extends EventListener

Subscribes to LogEntry objects from the LogReaderService.

A LogListener object may be registered with the Log Reader Service using the LogReaderService.addLogListener method. After the listener is registered, the logged method will be called for each LogEntry object created. The LogListener object may be unregistered by calling the LogReaderService.removeLogListener method.

See Also   LogReaderService, LogEntry, LogReaderService. addLogListener (LogListener), LogReaderService. removeLogListener (LogListener)

Concurrency   Thread-safe

101.8.3.1   **public void logged(LogEntry entry)**

entry   A LogEntry object containing log information.

☐ Listener method called for each LogEntry object created.

As with all event listeners, this method should return to its caller as soon as possible.

See Also   LogEntry

101.8.4   public interface LogReaderService

Provides methods to retrieve LogEntry objects from the log.

There are two ways to retrieve LogEntry objects:

- The primary way to retrieve LogEntry objects is to register a LogListener object whose LogListener.logged method will be called for each entry added to the log.
- To retrieve past LogEntry objects, the getLog method can be called which will return an Enumeration of all LogEntry objects in the log.

See Also   LogEntry, LogListener, LogListener. logged (LogEntry)

Concurrency   Thread-safe

101.8.4.1   **public void addLogListener(LogListener listener)**

listener   A LogListener object to register; the LogListener object is used to receive LogEntry objects.

☐ Subscribes to LogEntry objects.

This method registers a LogListener object with the Log Reader Service. The LogListener.logged(LogEntry) method will be called for each LogEntry object placed into the log.

When a bundle which registers a LogListener object is stopped or otherwise releases the Log Reader Service, the Log Reader Service must remove all of the bundle's listeners.

If this Log Reader Service's list of listeners already contains a listener l such that (l==listener), this method does nothing.

See Also   LogListener, LogEntry, LogListener. logged (LogEntry)

101.8.4.2   **public Enumeration getLog( )**

☐ Returns an Enumeration of all LogEntry objects in the log.

Each element of the enumeration is a LogEntry object, ordered with the most recent entry first. Whether the enumeration is of all LogEntry objects since the Log Service was started or some recent past is implementation-specific. Also implementation-specific is whether informational and debug LogEntry objects are included in the enumeration.

Returns   An Enumeration of all LogEntry objects in the log.

101.8.4.3   **public void removeLogListener(LogListener listener)**

listener   A LogListener object to unregister.

☐ Unsubscribes to LogEntry objects.

This method unregisters a LogListener object from the Log Reader Service.

If listener is not contained in this Log Reader Service's list of listeners, this method does nothing.

See Also   LogListener

101.8.5   public interface LogService

Provides methods for bundles to write messages to the log.

LogService methods are provided to log messages; optionally with a ServiceReference object or an exception.

Bundles must log messages in the OSGi environment with a severity level according to the following hierarchy:

1 LOG_ERROR
2 LOG_WARNING
3 LOG_INFO
4 LOG_DEBUG

Concurrency   Thread-safe

101.8.5.1   public static final int LOG_DEBUG = 4

A debugging message (Value 4).

This log entry is used for problem determination and may be irrelevant to anyone but the bundle developer.

101.8.5.2   public static final int LOG_ERROR = 1

An error message (Value 1).

This log entry indicates the bundle or service may not be functional.

101.8.5.3   public static final int LOG_INFO = 3

An informational message (Value 3).

This log entry may be the result of any change in the bundle or service and does not indicate a problem.

101.8.5.4   public static final int LOG_WARNING = 2

A warning message (Value 2).

This log entry indicates a bundle or service is still functioning but may experience problems in the future because of the warning condition.

101.8.5.5   public void log(int level, String message)

level   The severity of the message. This should be one of the defined log levels but may be any integer that is interpreted in a user defined way.

message   Human readable string describing the condition or null.

☐   Logs a message.

The ServiceReference field and the Throwable field of the LogEntry object will be set to null.

See Also   LOG_ERROR, LOG_WARNING, LOG_INFO, LOG_DEBUG

101.8.5.6   public void log(int level, String message, Throwable exception)

level   The severity of the message. This should be one of the defined log levels but may be any integer that is interpreted in a user defined way.

message The human readable string describing the condition or null.

exception The exception that reflects the condition or null.

    ☐ Logs a message with an exception.

The ServiceReference field of the LogEntry object will be set to null.

See Also LOG_ERROR, LOG_WARNING, LOG_INFO, LOG_DEBUG

101.8.5.7   **public void log(ServiceReference sr, int level, String message)**

sr The ServiceReference object of the service that this message is associated with or null.

level The severity of the message. This should be one of the defined log levels but may be any integer that is interpreted in a user defined way.

message Human readable string describing the condition or null.

    ☐ Logs a message associated with a specific ServiceReference object.

The Throwable field of the LogEntry will be set to null.

See Also LOG_ERROR, LOG_WARNING, LOG_INFO, LOG_DEBUG

101.8.5.8   **public void log(ServiceReference sr, int level, String message, Throwable exception)**

sr The ServiceReference object of the service that this message is associated with.

level The severity of the message. This should be one of the defined log levels but may be any integer that is interpreted in a user defined way.

message Human readable string describing the condition or null.

exception The exception that reflects the condition or null.

    ☐ Logs a message with an exception associated and a ServiceReference object.

See Also LOG_ERROR, LOG_WARNING, LOG_INFO, LOG_DEBUG

102   **Http Service Specification**

Version 1.2

102.1   **Introduction**

An OSGi Service Platform normally provides users with access to services on the Internet and other networks. This access allows users to remotely retrieve information from, and send control to, services in an OSGi Service Platform using a standard web browser.

Bundle developers typically need to develop communication and user interface solutions for standard technologies such as HTTP, HTML, XML, and servlets.

The Http Service supports two standard techniques for this purpose:

- *Registering servlets* – A servlet is a Java object which implements the Java Servlet API. Registering a servlet in the Framework gives it control over some part of the Http Service URI name-space.
- *Registering resources* – Registering a resource allows HTML files, image files, and other static resources to be made visible in the Http Service URI name-space by the requesting bundle.

Implementations of the Http Service can be based on:

- [1] *HTTP 1.0 Specification RFC-1945*
- [2] *HTTP 1.1 Specification RFC-2616*

Alternatively, implementations of this service can support other protocols if these protocols can conform to the semantics of the javax.servlet API. This additional support is necessary because the Http Service is closely related to [3] *Java Servlet Technology.* Http Service implementations must support at least version 2.1 of the Java Servlet API.

102.1.1   **Entities**

This specification defines the following interfaces which a bundle developer can implement collectively as an Http Service or use individually:

- HttpContext – Allows bundles to provide information for a servlet or resource registration.
- HttpService – Allows other bundles in the Framework to dynamically register and unregister resources and servlets into the Http Service URI name-space.
- NamespaceException – Is thrown to indicate an error with the caller's request to register a servlet or resource into the Http Service URI name-space.

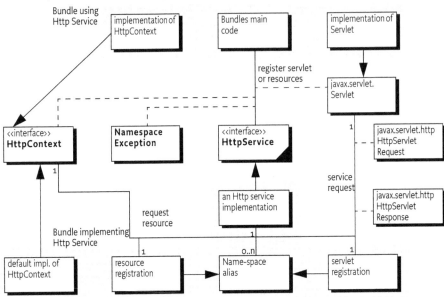

102.2   **Registering Servlets**

javax.servlet.Servlet objects can be registered with the Http Service by using the HttpService interface. For this purpose, the HttpService interface defines the method registerServlet(String,
javax.servlet.Servlet,Dictionary,HttpContext).

For example, if the Http Service implementation is listening to port 80 on the machine
www.acme.com and the Servlet object is registered with the name "/servlet", then the Servlet
object's service method is called when the following URL is used from a web browser:

    http://www.acme.com/servlet?name=bugs

All Servlet objects and resource registrations share the same name-space. If an attempt is made to register a resource or Servlet object under the same name as a currently registered resource or Servlet
object, a NamespaceException is thrown. See *Mapping HTTP Requests to Servlet and Resource Registrations* on page 29 for more information about the handling of the Http Service name-space.

Each Servlet registration must be accompanied with an HttpContext object. This object provides the
handling of resources, media typing, and a method to handle authentication of remote requests. See
Authentication on page 32.

For convenience, a default HttpContext object is provided by the Http Service and can be obtained
with createDefaultHttpContext(). Passing a null parameter to the registration method achieves the
same effect.

Servlet objects require a ServletContext object. This object provides a number of functions to access
the Http Service Java Servlet environment. It is created by the implementation of the Http Service for
each unique HttpContext object with which a Servlet object is registered. Thus, Servlet objects registered with the same HttpContext object must also share the same ServletContext object.

Servlet objects are initialized by the Http Service when they are registered and bound to that specific
Http Service. The initialization is done by calling the Servlet object's Servlet.init(ServletConfig)
method. The ServletConfig parameter provides access to the initialization parameters specified
when the Servlet object was registered.

Therefore, the same Servlet instance must not be reused for registration with another Http Service, nor can it be registered under multiple names. Unique instances are required for each registration.

The following example code demonstrates the use of the registerServlet method:

```
Hashtable initparams = new Hashtable();
initparams.put( "name", "value" );

Servlet myServlet = new HttpServlet() {
   String     name = "<not set>";

   public void init( ServletConfig config ) {
      this.name = (String)
         config.getInitParameter( "name" );
   }

   public void doGet(
      HttpServletRequest req,
      HttpServletResponse rsp
   ) throws IOException {
      rsp.setContentType( "text/plain" );
      req.getWriter().println( this.name );
   }
};

getHttpService().registerServlet(
   "/servletAlias",
   myServlet,
   initparams,
   null // use default context
);
// myServlet has been registered
// and its init method has been called. Remote
// requests are now handled and forwarded to
// the servlet.
...
getHttpService().unregister("/servletAlias");
// myServlet has been unregistered and its
// destroy method has been called
```

This example registers the servlet, myServlet, at alias: /servletAlias. Future requests for http://www.acme.com/servletAlias maps to the servlet, myServlet, whose service method is called to process the request. (The service method is called in the HttpServlet base class and dispatched to a doGet, doPut, doPost, doOptions, doTrace, or doDelete call depending on the HTTP request method used.)

102.3 Registering Resources

A resource is a file containing images, static HTML pages, sounds, movies, applets, etc. Resources do not require any handling from the bundle. They are transferred directly from their source--usually the JAR file that contains the code for the bundle--to the requestor using HTTP.

Resources could be handled by Servlet objects as explained in *Registering Servlets* on page 26. Transferring a resource over HTTP, however, would require very similar Servlet objects for each bundle. To prevent this redundancy, resources can be registered directly with the Http Service via the HttpService interface. This HttpService interface defines the registerResources(String,String,HttpContext) method for registering a resource into the Http Service URI name-space.

The first parameter is the external alias under which the resource is registered with the Http Service. The second parameter is an internal prefix to map this resource to the bundle's name-space. When a request is received, the HttpService object must remove the external alias from the URI, replace it with the internal prefix, and call the getResource(String) method with this new name on the associated HttpContext object. The HttpContext object is further used to get the MIME type of the resource and to authenticate the request.

Resources are returned as a java.net.URL object. The Http Service must read from this URL object and transfer the content to the initiator of the HTTP request.

This return type was chosen because it matches the return type of the java.lang.Class.getResource(String resource) method. This method can retrieve resources directly from the same place as the one from which the class was loaded – often a package directory in the JAR file of the bundle. This method makes it very convenient to retrieve resources from the bundle that are contained in the package.

The following example code demonstrates the use of the register Resources method:

```
package com.acme;
...
HttpContext context = new HttpContext() {
    public boolean handleSecurity(
        HttpServletRequest request,
        HttpServletResponse response
    ) throws IOException {
        return true;
    }

    public URL getResource(String name) {
        return getClass().getResource(name);
    }

    public String getMimeType(String name) {
        return null;
    }
};

getHttpService().registerResources (
    "/files",
    "www",
    context
);
...
getHttpService().unregister("/files");
```

This example registers the alias /files on the Http Service. Requests for resources below this name-space are transferred to the HttpContext object with an internal name of www/<name>. This example uses the Class.get
Resource(String) method. Because the internal name does not start with a
"/", it must map to a resource in the "com/acme/www" directory of the JAR file. If the internal name

did start with a "/", the package name would not have to be prefixed and the JAR file would be searched from the root. Consult the java.lang.Class.getResource(String) method for more information.

In the example, a request for http://www.acme.com/files/myfile.html must map to the name "com/acme/www/myfile.html" which is in the bundle's JAR file.

More sophisticated implementations of the getResource(String) method could filter the input name, restricting the resources that may be returned or map the input name onto the file system (if the security implications of this action are acceptable).

Alternatively, the resource registration could have used a default HttpContext object, as demonstrated in the following call to registerResources:

```
getHttpService().registerResources(
    "/files",
    "/com/acme/www",
    null
);
```

In this case, the Http Service implementation would call the createDefaultHttpContext() method and use its return value as the HttpContext argument for the registerResources method. The default implementation must map the resource request to the bundle's resource, using Bundle.getResource(String). In the case of the previous example, however, the internal name must now specify the full path to the directory containing the resource files in the JAR file. No automatic prefixing of the package name is done.

The getMimeType(String) implementation of the default HttpContext object should rely on the default mapping provided by the Http Service by returning null. Its handleSecurity(HttpServletRequest,HttpServletResponse) may implement an authentication mechanism that is implementation-dependent.

102.4   Mapping HTTP Requests to Servlet and Resource Registrations

When an HTTP request comes in from a client, the Http Service checks to see if the requested URI matches any registered aliases. A URI matches only if the path part of the URI is exactly the same string. Matching is case sensitive.

If it does match, a matching registration takes place, which is processed as follows:

1. If the registration corresponds to a servlet, the authorization is verified by calling the handleSecurity method of the associated HttpContext object. See *Authentication* on page 32. If the request is authorized, the servlet must be called by its service method to complete the HTTP request.

2. If the registration corresponds to a resource, the authorization is verified by calling the handleSecurity method of the associated HttpContext object. See *Authentication* on page 32. If the request is authorized, a target resource name is constructed from the requested URI by substituting the alias from the registration with the internal name from the registration if the alias is not "/". If the alias is "/", then the target resource name is constructed by prefixing the requested URI with the internal name. An internal name of "/" is considered to have the value of the empty string ("") during this process.

3. The target resource name must be passed to the getResource method of the associated HttpContext object.

4. If the returned URL object is not null, the Http Service must return the contents of the URL to the client completing the HTTP request. The translated target name, as opposed to the original requested URI, must also be used as the argument to HttpContext.getMimeType.

5. If the returned URL object is null, the Http Service continues as if there was no match.

6. If there is no match, the Http Service must attempt to match sub-strings of the requested URI to registered aliases. The sub-strings of the requested URI are selected by removing the last "/" and everything to the right of the last "/".

The Http Service must repeat this process until either a match is found or the sub-string is an empty string. If the sub-string is empty and the alias "/" is registered, the request is considered to match the alias "/". Otherwise, the Http Service must return HttpServletResponse.SC_NOT_FOUND(404) to the client.

For example, an HTTP request comes in with a request URI of "/fudd/bugs/foo.txt", and the only registered alias is "/fudd". A search for "/fudd/bugs/foo.txt" will not match an alias. Therefore, the Http Service will search for the alias "/fudd/bugs" and the alias "/fudd". The latter search will result in a match and the matched alias registration must be used.

Registrations for identical aliases are not allowed. If a bundle registers the alias "/fudd", and another bundle tries to register the exactly the same alias, the second caller must receive a NamespaceException and its resource or servlet must *not* be registered. It could, however, register a similar alias – for example, "/fudd/bugs", as long as no other registration for this alias already exists.

The following table shows some examples of the usage of the name-space.

Table 102.1   Examples of Name-space Mapping

Alias	Internal Name	URI	getResource Parameter
/	(empty string)	/fudd/bugs	/fudd/bugs
/	/	/fudd/bugs	/fudd/bugs
/	/tmp	/fudd/bugs	/tmp/fudd/bugs
/fudd	(empty string)	/fudd/bugs	/bugs
/fudd	/	/fudd/bugs	/bugs
/fudd	/tmp	/fudd/bugs	/tmp/bugs
/fudd	tmp	/fudd/bugs/x.gif	tmp/bugs/x.gif
/fudd/bugs/x.gif	tmp/y.gif	/fudd/bugs/x.gif	tmp/y.gif

102.5   The Default Http Context Object

The HttpContext object in the first example demonstrates simple implementations of the HttpContext interface methods. Alternatively, the example could have used a default HttpContext object, as demonstrated in the following call to registerServlet:

```
getHttpService().registerServlet(
   "/servletAlias",
   myServlet,
   initparams,
   null
);
```

In this case, the Http Service implementation must call createDefault HttpContext and use the return value as the HttpContext argument.

If the default HttpContext object, and thus the ServletContext object, is to be shared by multiple servlet registrations, the previous servlet registration example code needs to be changed to use the same default HttpContext object. This change is demonstrated in the next example:

```
HttpContext defaultContext =
    getHttpService().createDefaultHttpContext();

getHttpService().registerServlet(
    "/servletAlias",
    myServlet,
    initparams,
    defaultContext
);

// defaultContext can be reused
// for further servlet registrations
```

102.6 Multipurpose Internet Mail Extension (MIME) Types

MIME defines an extensive set of headers and procedures to encode binary messages in US-ASCII mails. For an overview of all the related RFCs, consult [4] *MIME Multipurpose Internet Mail Extension.*

An important aspect of this extension is the type (file format) mechanism of the binary messages. The type is defined by a string containing a general category (text, application, image, audio and video, multipart, and message) followed by a "/" and a specific media type, as in the example, "text/html" for HTML formatted text files. A MIME type string can be followed by additional specifiers by separating key=value pairs with a ';'. These specifiers can be used, for example, to define character sets as follows:

```
text/plan ; charset=iso-8859-1
```

The Internet Assigned Number Authority (IANA) maintains a set of defined MIME media types. This list can be found at [5] *Assigned MIME Media Types.* MIME media types are extendable, and when any part of the type starts with the prefix "x-", it is assumed to be vendor-specific and can be used for testing. New types can be registered as described in [6] *Registration Procedures for new MIME media types.*

HTTP bases its media typing on the MIME RFCs. The "Content-Type" header should contain a MIME media type so that the browser can recognize the type and format the content correctly.

The source of the data must define the MIME media type for each transfer. Most operating systems do not support types for files, but use conventions based on file names, such as the last part of the file name after the last ".". This extension is then mapped to a media type.

Implementations of the Http Service should have a reasonable default of mapping common extensions to media types based on file extensions.

Table 102.2   *Sample Extension to MIME Media Mapping*

Extension	MIME media type	Description
.jpg .jpeg	image/jpeg	JPEG Files
.gif	image/gif	GIF Files
.css	text/css	Cascading Style Sheet Files
.txt	text/plain	Text Files
.wml	text/vnd.wap.wml	Wireless Access Protocol (WAP) Mark Language

Table 102.2   Sample Extension to MIME Media Mapping

Extension	MIME media type	Description
.htm .html	text/html	Hyper Text Markup Language
.wbmp	image/vnd.wap.wbmp	Bitmaps for WAP

Only the bundle developer, however, knows exactly which files have what media type. The HttpContext interface can therefore be used to map this knowledge to the media type. The HttpContext class has the following method for this: getMimeType(String).

The implementation of this method should inspect the file name and use its internal knowledge to map this name to a MIME media type.

Simple implementations can extract the extension and look up this extension in a table.

Returning null from this method allows the Http Service implementation to use its default mapping mechanism.

102.7   Authentication

The Http Service has separated the authentication and authorization of a request from the execution of the request. This separation allows bundles to use available Servlet sub-classes while still providing bundle specific authentication and authorization of the requests.

Prior to servicing each incoming request, the Http Service calls the handleSecurity(javax.servlet.http.HttpServletRequest,javax.servlet.http.HttpServletResponse) method on the HttpContext object that is associated with the request URI. This method controls whether the request is processed in the normal manner or an authentication error is returned.

If an implementation wants to authenticate the request, it can use the authentication mechanisms of HTTP. See [7] *RFC 2617: HTTP Authentication: Basic and Digest Access Authentication.* These mechanisms normally interpret the headers and decide if the user identity is available, and if it is, whether that user has authenticated itself correctly.

There are many different ways of authenticating users, and the handleSecurity method on the HttpContext object can use whatever method it requires. If the method returns true, the request must continue to be processed using the potentially modified HttpServletRequest and HttpServletResponse objects. If the method returns false, the request must *not* be processed.

A common standard for HTTP is the basic authentication scheme that is not secure when used with HTTP. Basic authentication passes the password in base 64 encoded strings that are trivial to decode into clear text. Secure transport protocols like HTTPS use SSL to hide this information. With these protocols basic authentication is secure.

Using basic authentication requires the following steps:

1. If no Authorization header is set in the request, the method should set the WWW-Authenticate header in the response. This header indicates the desired authentication mechanism and the realm. For example, WWW-Authenticate: Basic realm="ACME".
    The header should be set with the response object that is given as a parameter to the handleSecurity method. The handleSecurity method should set the status to HttpServletResponse.SC_UNAUTHORIZED (401) and return false.

2. Secure connections can be verified with the ServletRequest.getScheme() method. This method returns, for example, "https" for an SSL connection; the handleSecurity method can use this and other information to decide if the connection's security level is acceptable. If not, the handleSecurity method should set the status to HttpServletResponse.SC_FORBIDDEN (403) and return false.

3. Next, the request must be authenticated. When basic authentication is used, the Authorization header is available in the request and should be parsed to find the user and password. See [7] *RFC 2617: HTTP Authentication: Basic and Digest Access Authentication* for more information. If the user cannot be authenticated, the status of the response object should be set to HttpServletResponse.SC_UNAUTHORIZED (401) and return false.

4. The authentication mechanism that is actually used and the identity of the authenticated user can be of interest to the Servlet object. Therefore, the implementation of the handleSecurity method should set this information in the request object using the ServletRequest.setAttribute method. This specification has defined a number of OSGi-specific attribute names for this purpose:

   - AUTHENTICATION_TYPE - Specifies the scheme used in authentication. A Servlet may retrieve the value of this attribute by calling the HttpServletRequest.getAuthType method. This attribute name is org.osgi.service.http.authentication.type.
   - REMOTE_USER - Specifies the name of the authenticated user. A Servlet may retrieve the value of this attribute by calling the HttpServletRequest.getRemoteUser method. This attribute name is org.osgi.service.http.authentication.remote.user.
   - AUTHORIZATION - If a User Admin service is available in the environment, then the handleSecurity method should set this attribute with the Authorization object obtained from the User Admin service. Such an object encapsulates the authentication of its remote user. A Servlet may retrieve the value of this attribute by calling ServletRequest.getAttribute(HttpContext.AUTHORIZATION). This header name is org.osgi.service.useradmin.authorization.

5. Once the request is authenticated and any attributes are set, the handleSecurity method should return true. This return indicates to the Http Service that the request is authorized and processing may continue. If the request is for a Servlet, the Http Service must then call the service method on the Servlet object.

102.8 Security

This section only applies when executing in an OSGi environment which is enforcing Java permissions.

102.8.1 Accessing Resources in Bundles

The Http Service must be granted AdminPermission[*,RESOURCE] so that bundles may use a default HttpContext object. This is necessary because the implementation of the default HttpContext object must call Bundle.getResource to access the resources of a bundle and this method requires the caller to have AdminPermission[bundle,RESOURCE].

Any bundle may access resources in its own bundle by calling Class.getResource. This operation is privileged. The resulting URL object may then be passed to the Http Service as the result of a HttpContext.getResource call. No further permission checks are performed when accessing bundle resource URL objects, so the Http Service does not need to be granted any additional permissions.

102.8.2 Accessing Other Types of Resources

In order to access resources that were not registered using the default HttpContext object, the Http Service must be granted sufficient privileges to access these resources. For example, if the getResource method of the registered HttpContext object returns a file URL, the Http Service requires the corresponding FilePermission to read the file. Similarly, if the getResource method of the registered HttpContext object returns an HTTP URL, the Http Service requires the corresponding SocketPermission to connect to the resource.

Therefore, in most cases, the Http Service should be a privileged service that is granted sufficient permission to serve any bundle's resources, no matter where these resources are located. Therefore, the Http Service must capture the AccessControlContext object of the bundle registering resources or a servlet, and then use the captured AccessControlContext object when accessing resources returned by the registered HttpContext object. This situation prevents a bundle from registering resources that it does not have permission to access.

Therefore, the Http Service should follow a scheme like the following example. When a resource or servlet is registered, it should capture the context.

```
AccessControlContext acc =
    AccessController.getContext();
```

When a URL returned by the getResource method of the associated HttpContext object is called, the Http Service must call the getResource method in a doPrivileged construct using the AccessControlContext object of the registering bundle:

```
AccessController.doPrivileged(
    new PrivilegedExceptionAction() {
        public Object run() throws Exception {
            ...
        }
    }, acc);
```

The Http Service must only use the captured AccessControlContext when accessing resource URL objects. Servlet and HttpContext objects must use a doPrivileged construct in their implementations when performing privileged operations.

102.9 Configuration Properties

If the Http Service does not have its port values configured through some other means, the Http Service implementation should use the following properties to determine the port values upon which to listen.

The following OSGi environment properties are used to specify default HTTP ports:

- org.osgi.service.http.port – This property specifies the port used for servlets and resources accessible via HTTP. The default value for this property is 80.
- org.osgi.service.http.port.secure – This property specifies the port used for servlets and resources accessible via HTTPS. The default value for this property is 443.

102.10 org.osgi.service.http

Http Service Package Version 1.2.

Bundles wishing to use this package must list the package in the Import-Package header of the bundle's manifest. For example:

```
Import-Package: org.osgi.service.http; version="[1.2,2.0)"
```

102.10.1 Summary

- *HttpContext* - This interface defines methods that the Http Service may call to get information about a registration.
- *HttpService* - The Http Service allows other bundles in the OSGi environment to dynamically register resources and servlets into the URI namespace of Http Service.
- *NamespaceException* - A NamespaceException is thrown to indicate an error with the caller's request to register a servlet or resources into the URI namespace of the Http Service.

102.10.2   public interface HttpContext

This interface defines methods that the Http Service may call to get information about a registration.

Servlets and resources may be registered with an HttpContext object; if no HttpContext object is specified, a default HttpContext object is used. Servlets that are registered using the same HttpContext object will share the same ServletContext object.

This interface is implemented by users of the HttpService.

102.10.2.1   public static final String AUTHENTICATION_TYPE = "org.osgi.service.http.authentication.type"

HttpServletRequest attribute specifying the scheme used in authentication. The value of the attribute can be retrieved by HttpServletRequest.getAuthType. This attribute name is org.osgi.service.http.authentication.type.

Since 1.1

102.10.2.2   public static final String AUTHORIZATION = "org.osgi.service.useradmin.authorization"

HttpServletRequest attribute specifying the Authorization object obtained from the org.osgi.service.useradmin.UserAdmin service. The value of the attribute can be retrieved by HttpServletRequest.getAttribute(HttpContext.AUTHORIZATION). This attribute name is org.osgi.service.useradmin.authorization.

Since 1.1

102.10.2.3   public static final String REMOTE_USER = "org.osgi.service.http.authentication.remote.user"

HttpServletRequest attribute specifying the name of the authenticated user. The value of the attribute can be retrieved by HttpServletRequest.getRemoteUser. This attribute name is org.osgi.service.http.authentication.remote.user.

Since 1.1

102.10.2.4   public String getMimeType(String name)

name determine the MIME type for this name.

  ☐ Maps a name to a MIME type. Called by the Http Service to determine the MIME type for the name. For servlet registrations, the Http Service will call this method to support the ServletContext method getMimeType. For resource registrations, the Http Service will call this method to determine the MIME type for the Content-Type header in the response.

Returns MIME type (e.g. text/html) of the name or null to indicate that the Http Service should determine the MIME type itself.

102.10.2.5   public URL getResource(String name)

name the name of the requested resource

  ☐ Maps a resource name to a URL.

Called by the Http Service to map a resource name to a URL. For servlet registrations, Http Service will call this method to support the ServletContext methods getResource and getResourceAsStream. For resource registrations, Http Service will call this method to locate the named resource. The context can control from where resources come. For example, the resource can be mapped to a file in the bundle's persistent storage area via bundleContext.getDataFile(name).toURL() or to a resource in the context's bundle via getClass().getResource(name)

Returns URL that Http Service can use to read the resource or null if the resource does not exist.

102.10.2.6   public boolean handleSecurity(HttpServletRequest request, HttpServletResponse response) throws IOException

request the HTTP request

response the HTTP response

□ Handles security for the specified request.

The Http Service calls this method prior to servicing the specified request. This method controls whether the request is processed in the normal manner or an error is returned.

If the request requires authentication and the Authorization header in the request is missing or not acceptable, then this method should set the WWW-Authenticate header in the response object, set the status in the response object to Unauthorized(401) and return false. See also RFC 2617: *HTTP Authentication: Basic and Digest Access Authentication* (available at http://www.ietf.org/rfc/rfc2617.txt).

If the request requires a secure connection and the getScheme method in the request does not return 'https' or some other acceptable secure protocol, then this method should set the status in the response object to Forbidden(403) and return false.

When this method returns false, the Http Service will send the response back to the client, thereby completing the request. When this method returns true, the Http Service will proceed with servicing the request.

If the specified request has been authenticated, this method must set the AUTHENTICATION_TYPE request attribute to the type of authentication used, and the REMOTE_USER request attribute to the remote user (request attributes are set using the setAttribute method on the request). If this method does not perform any authentication, it must not set these attributes.

If the authenticated user is also authorized to access certain resources, this method must set the AUTHORIZATION request attribute to the Authorization object obtained from the org.osgi.service.useradmin.UserAdmin service.

The servlet responsible for servicing the specified request determines the authentication type and remote user by calling the getAuthType and getRemoteUser methods, respectively, on the request.

Returns true if the request should be serviced, false if the request should not be serviced and Http Service will send the response back to the client.

Throws IOException – may be thrown by this method. If this occurs, the Http Service will terminate the request and close the socket.

102.10.3   public interface HttpService

The Http Service allows other bundles in the OSGi environment to dynamically register resources and servlets into the URI namespace of Http Service. A bundle may later unregister its resources or servlets.

See Also HttpContext

102.10.3.1   public HttpContext createDefaultHttpContext( )

□ Creates a default HttpContext for registering servlets or resources with the HttpService, a new HttpContext object is created each time this method is called.

The behavior of the methods on the default HttpContext is defined as follows:

- getMimeType- Does not define any customized MIME types for the Content-Type header in the response, and always returns null.
- handleSecurity- Performs implementation-defined authentication on the request.
- getResource- Assumes the named resource is in the context bundle; this method calls the context bundle's Bundle.getResource method, and returns the appropriate URL to access the resource. On a Java runtime environment that supports permissions, the Http Service needs to be granted org.osgi.framework.AdminPermission[*,RESOURCE].

Returns a default HttpContext object.

Since 1.1

102.10.3.2   **public void registerResources(String alias, String name, HttpContext context) throws NamespaceException**

alias   name in the URI namespace at which the resources are registered

name   the base name of the resources that will be registered

context   the HttpContext object for the registered resources, or null if a default HttpContext is to be created and used.

☐ Registers resources into the URI namespace.

The alias is the name in the URI namespace of the Http Service at which the registration will be mapped. An alias must begin with slash ('/') and must not end with slash ('/'), with the exception that an alias of the form "/" is used to denote the root alias. The name parameter must also not end with slash ('/') with the exception that a name of the form "/" is used to denote the root of the bundle. See the specification text for details on how HTTP requests are mapped to servlet and resource registrations.

For example, suppose the resource name /tmp is registered to the alias /files. A request for /files/foo.txt will map to the resource name /tmp/foo.txt.

```
httpservice.registerResources("/files", "/tmp", context);
```

The Http Service will call the HttpContext argument to map resource names to URLs and MIME types and to handle security for requests. If the HttpContext argument is null, a default HttpContext is used (see createDefaultHttpContext).

Throws   NamespaceException – if the registration fails because the alias is already in use.

IllegalArgumentException – if any of the parameters are invalid

102.10.3.3   **public void registerServlet(String alias, Servlet servlet, Dictionary initparams, HttpContext context) throws ServletException, NamespaceException**

alias   name in the URI namespace at which the servlet is registered

servlet   the servlet object to register

initparams   initialization arguments for the servlet or null if there are none. This argument is used by the servlet's ServletConfig object.

context   the HttpContext object for the registered servlet, or null if a default HttpContext is to be created and used.

☐ Registers a servlet into the URI namespace.

The alias is the name in the URI namespace of the Http Service at which the registration will be mapped.

An alias must begin with slash ('/') and must not end with slash ('/'), with the exception that an alias of the form "/" is used to denote the root alias. See the specification text for details on how HTTP requests are mapped to servlet and resource registrations.

The Http Service will call the servlet's init method before returning.

```
httpService.registerServlet("/myservlet", servlet, initparams, context);
```

Servlets registered with the same HttpContext object will share the same ServletContext. The Http Service will call the context argument to support the ServletContext methods getResource, getResourceAsStream and getMimeType, and to handle security for requests. If the context argument is null, a default HttpContext object is used (see createDefaultHttpContext).

Throws   NamespaceException – if the registration fails because the alias is already in use.

javax.servlet.ServletException – if the servlet's init method throws an exception, or the given servlet object has already been registered at a different alias.

IllegalArgumentException – if any of the arguments are invalid

102.10.3.4   **public void unregister(String alias)**

alias   name in the URI name-space of the registration to unregister

□   Unregisters a previous registration done by registerServlet or registerResources methods.

After this call, the registered alias in the URI name-space will no longer be available. If the registration was for a servlet, the Http Service must call the destroy method of the servlet before returning.

If the bundle which performed the registration is stopped or otherwise "unget"s the Http Service without calling unregister then Http Service must automatically unregister the registration. However, if the registration was for a servlet, the destroy method of the servlet will not be called in this case since the bundle may be stopped. unregister must be explicitly called to cause the destroy method of the servlet to be called. This can be done in the BundleActivator.stop method of the bundle registering the servlet.

Throws   IllegalArgumentException – if there is no registration for the alias or the calling bundle was not the bundle which registered the alias.

102.10.4   public class NamespaceException
extends Exception

A NamespaceException is thrown to indicate an error with the caller's request to register a servlet or resources into the URI namespace of the Http Service. This exception indicates that the requested alias already is in use.

102.10.4.1   **public NamespaceException(String message)**

message   the detail message

□   Construct a NamespaceException object with a detail message.

102.10.4.2   **public NamespaceException(String message, Throwable cause)**

message   The detail message.

cause   The nested exception.

□   Construct a NamespaceException object with a detail message and a nested exception.

102.10.4.3   **public Throwable getCause( )**

□   Returns the cause of this exception or null if no cause was set.

Returns   The cause of this exception or null if no cause was set.

Since   1.2

102.10.4.4   **public Throwable getException( )**

□   Returns the nested exception.

This method predates the general purpose exception chaining mechanism. The getCause() method is now the preferred means of obtaining this information.

Returns   The result of calling getCause().

102.10.4.5   **public Throwable initCause(Throwable cause)**

cause   The cause of this exception.

□   Initializes the cause of this exception to the specified value.

Returns   This exception.

Throws   IllegalArgumentException – If the specified cause is this exception.

IllegalStateException – If the cause of this exception has already been set.

Since 1.2

102.11   References

[1]   *HTTP 1.0 Specification RFC-1945*
       http://www.ietf.org/rfc/rfc1945.txt, May 1996

[2]   *HTTP 1.1 Specification RFC-2616*
       http://www.ietf.org/rfc/rfc2616.txt, June 1999

[3]   *Java Servlet Technology*
       http://java.sun.com/products/servlet/index.html

[4]   *MIME Multipurpose Internet Mail Extension*
       http://www.mhonarc.org/~ehood/MIME/MIME.html

[5]   *Assigned MIME Media Types*
       http://www.iana.org/assignments/media-types

[6]   *Registration Procedures for new MIME media types*
       http://www.ietf.org/rfc/rfc2048.txt

[7]   *RFC 2617: HTTP Authentication: Basic and Digest Access Authentication*
       http://www.ietf.org/rfc/rfc2617.txt

103   Device Access Specification

Version 1.1

103.1   Introduction

A Service Platform is a meeting point for services and devices from many different vendors: a meeting point where users add and cancel service subscriptions, newly installed services find their corresponding input and output devices, and device drivers connect to their hardware.

In an OSGi Service Platform, these activities will dynamically take place while the Framework is running. Technologies such as USB and IEEE 1394 explicitly support plugging and unplugging devices at any time, and wireless technologies are even more dynamic.

This flexibility makes it hard to configure all aspects of an OSGi Service Platform, particularly those relating to devices. When all of the possible services and device requirements are factored in, each OSGi Service Platform will be unique. Therefore, automated mechanisms are needed that can be extended and customized, in order to minimize the configuration needs of the OSGi environment.

The Device Access specification supports the coordination of automatic detection and attachment of existing devices on an OSGi Service Platform, facilitates hot-plugging and -unplugging of new devices, and downloads and installs device drivers on demand.

This specification, however, deliberately does not prescribe any particular device or network technology, and mentioned technologies are used as examples only. Nor does it specify a particular device discovery method. Rather, this specification focuses on the attachment of devices supplied by different vendors. It emphasizes the development of standardized device interfaces to be defined in device categories, although no such device categories are defined in this specification.

103.1.1   Essentials

*   *Embedded Devices* – OSGi bundles will likely run in embedded devices. This environment implies limited possibility for user interaction, and low-end devices will probably have resource limitations.
*   *Remote Administration* – OSGi environments must support administration by a remote service provider.
*   *Vendor Neutrality* – OSGi-compliant driver bundles will be supplied by different vendors; each driver bundle must be well-defined, documented, and replaceable.
*   *Continuous Operation* – OSGi environments will be running for extended periods without being restarted, possibly continuously, requiring stable operation and stable resource consumption.
*   *Dynamic Updates* – As much as possible, driver bundles must be individually replaceable without affecting unrelated bundles. In particular, the process of updating a bundle should not require a restart of the whole OSGi Service Platform or disrupt operation of connected devices.

A number of requirements must be satisfied by Device Access implementations in order for them to be OSGi-compliant. Implementations must support the following capabilities:

*   *Hot-Plugging* – Plugging and unplugging of devices at any time if the underlying hardware and drivers allow it.
*   *Legacy Systems* – Device technologies which do not implement the automatic detection of plugged and unplugged devices.
*   *Dynamic Device Driver Loading* – Loading new driver bundles on demand with no prior device-specific knowledge of the Device service.

- *Multiple Device Representations* – Devices to be accessed from multiple levels of abstraction.
- *Deep Trees* – Connections of devices in a tree of mixed network technologies of arbitrary depth.
- *Topology Independence* – Separation of the interfaces of a device from where and how it is attached.
- *Complex Devices* – Multifunction devices and devices that have multiple configurations.

103.1.2   Operation

This specification defines the behavior of a device manager (which is *not* a service as might be expected). This device manager detects registration of Device services and is responsible for associating these devices with an appropriate Driver service. These tasks are done with the help of Driver Locator services and the Driver Selector service that allow a device manager to find a Driver bundle and install it.

103.1.3   Entities

The main entities of the Device Access specification are:

- *Device Manager* – The bundle that controls the initiation of the attachment process behind the scenes.
- *Device Category* – Defines how a Driver service and a Device service can cooperate.
- *Driver* – Competes for attaching Device services of its recognized device category. See *Driver Services* on page 47.
- *Device* – A representation of a physical device or other entity that can be attached by a Driver service. See *Device Services* on page 43.
- *DriverLocator* – Assists in locating bundles that provide a Driver service. See *Driver Locator Service* on page 53.
- *DriverSelector* – Assists in selecting which Driver service is best suited to a Device service. See *The Driver Selector Service* on page 55.

Figure 103.1 show the classes and their relationships.

Figure 103.1   *Device Access Class Overview*

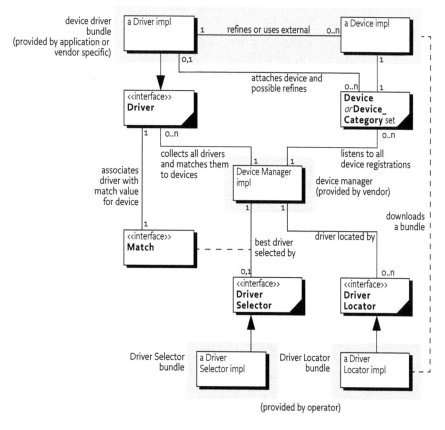

103.2   **Device Services**

A Device service represents some form of a device. It can represent a hardware device, but that is not a requirement. Device services differ widely: some represent individual physical devices and others represent complete networks. Several Device services can even simultaneously represent the same physical device at different levels of abstraction. For example:

- A USB network.
- A device attached on the USB network.
- The same device recognized as a USB to Ethernet bridge.
- A device discovered on the Ethernet using Salutation.
- The same device recognized as a simple printer.
- The same printer refined to a PostScript printer.

A device can also be represented in different ways. For example, a USB mouse can be considered as:

- A USB device which delivers information over the USB bus.
- A mouse device which delivers x and y coordinates and information about the state of its buttons.

Each representation has specific implications:

- That a particular device is a mouse is irrelevant to an application which provides management of USB devices.
- That a mouse is attached to a USB bus or a serial port would be inconsequential to applications that respond to mouse-like input.

Device services must belong to a defined *device category*, or else they can implement a generic service which models a particular device, independent of its underlying technology. Examples of this type of implementation could be Sensor or Actuator services.

A device category specifies the methods for communicating with a Device service, and enables inter-operability between bundles that are based on the same underlying technology. Generic Device services will allow inter-operability between bundles that are not coupled to specific device technologies.

For example, a device category is required for the USB, so that Driver bundles can be written that communicate to the devices that are attached to the USB. If a printer is attached, it should also be available as a generic Printer service defined in a Printer service specification, indistinguishable from a Printer service attached to a parallel port. Generic categories, such as a Printer service, should also be described in a Device Category.

It is expected that most Device service objects will actually represent a physical device in some form, but that is not a requirement of this specification. A Device service is represented as a normal service in the OSGi Framework and all coordination and activities are performed upon Framework services. This specification does not limit a bundle developer from using Framework mechanisms for services that are not related to physical devices.

103.2.1 Device Service Registration

A Device service is defined as a normal service registered with the Framework that either:

- Registers a service object under the interface org.osgi.service.Device with the Framework, or
- Sets the DEVICE_CATEGORY property in the registration. The value of DEVICE_CATEGORY is an array of String objects of all the device categories that the device belongs to. These strings are defined in the associated device category.

If this document mentions a Device service, it is meant to refer to services registered with the name org.osgi.service.device.Device *or* services registered with the DEVICE_CATEGORY property set.

When a Device service is registered, additional properties may be set that describe the device to the device manager and potentially to the end users. The following properties have their semantics defined in this specification:

- DEVICE_CATEGORY – A marker property indicating that this service must be regarded as a Device service by the device manager. Its value is of type String[], and its meaning is defined in the associated device category specification.
- DEVICE_DESCRIPTION – Describes the device to an end user. Its value is of type String.
- DEVICE_SERIAL – A unique serial number for this device. If the device hardware contains a serial number, the driver bundle is encouraged to specify it as this property. Different Device services representing the same physical hardware at different abstraction levels should set the same DEVICE_SERIAL, thus simplifying identification. Its value is of type String.
- service.pid – Service Persistent ID (PID), defined in org.osgi.framework.Constants. Device services should set this property. It must be unique among all registered services. Even different abstraction levels of the same device must use different PIDs. The service PIDs must be reproducible, so that every time the same hardware is plugged in, the same PIDs are used.

103.2.2 Device Service Attachment

When a Device service is registered with the Framework, the device manager is responsible for finding a suitable Driver service and instructing it to attach to the newly registered Device service. The Device service itself is passive: it only registers a Device service with the Framework and then waits until it is called.

The actual communication with the underlying physical device is not defined in the Device interface because it differs significantly between different types of devices. The Driver service is responsible for attaching the device in a device type-specific manner. The rules and interfaces for this process must be defined in the appropriate device category.

If the device manager is unable to find a suitable Driver service, the Device service remains unattached. In that case, if the service object implements the Device interface, it must receive a call to the noDriverFound() method. The Device service can wait until a new driver is installed, or it can unregister and attempt to register again with different properties that describe a more generic device or try a different configuration.

103.2.2.1 Idle Device Service

The main purpose of the device manager is to try to attach drivers to idle devices. For this purpose, a Device service is considered *idle* if no bundle that itself has registered a Driver service is using the Device service.

103.2.2.2 Device Service Unregistration

When a Device service is unregistered, no immediate action is required by the device manager. The normal service of unregistering events, provided by the Framework, takes care of propagating the unregistration information to affected drivers. Drivers must take the appropriate action to release this Device service and perform any necessary cleanup, as described in their device category specification.

The device manager may, however, take a device unregistration as an indication that driver bundles may have become idle and are thus eligible for removal. It is therefore important for Device services to unregister their service object when the underlying entity becomes unavailable.

103.3 Device Category Specifications

A device category specifies the rules and interfaces needed for the communication between a Device service and a Driver service. Only Device services and Driver services of the same device category can communicate and cooperate.

The Device Access service specification is limited to the attachment of Device services by Driver services, and does *not* enumerate different device categories.

Other specifications must specify a number of device categories before this specification can be made operational. Without a set of defined device categories, no inter-operability can be achieved.

Device categories are related to a specific device technology, such as USB, IEEE 1394, JINI, UPnP, Salutation, CEBus, Lonworks, and others. The purpose of a device category specification is to make all Device services of that category conform to an agreed interface, so that, for example, a USB Driver service of vendor A can control Device services from vendor B attached to a USB bus.

This specification is limited to defining the guidelines for device category definitions only. Device categories may be defined by the OSGi organization or by external specification bodies – for example, when these bodies are associated with a specific device technology.

103.3.1 Device Category Guidelines

A device category definition comprises the following elements:

- An interface that all devices belonging to this category must implement. This interface should lay out the rules of how to communicate with the underlying device. The specification body may define its own device interfaces (or classes) or leverage existing ones. For example, a serial port device category could use the javax.comm.SerialPort interface which is defined in [1] *Java Communications API*.

When registering a device belonging to this category with the Framework, the interface or class name for this category must be included in the registration.

- A set of service registration properties, their data types, and semantics, each of which must be declared as either MANDATORY or OPTIONAL for this device category.
- A range of match values specific to this device category. Matching is explained later in *The Device Attachment Algorithm* on page 56.

103.3.2 Sample Device Category Specification

The following is a partial example of a fictitious device category:

```
public interface /* com.acme.widget.*/ WidgetDevice {
    int MATCH_SERIAL           = 10;
    int MATCH_VERSION          =  8;
    int MATCH_MODEL            =  6;
    int MATCH_MAKE             =  4;
    int MATCH_CLASS            =  2;
    void sendPacket( byte [] data );
    byte [] receivePacket( long timeout );
}
```

Devices in this category must implement the interface com.acme.widget.WidgetDevice to receive attachments from Driver services in this category.

Device properties for this fictitious category are defined in table Table 103.1.

Table 103.1   Example Device Category Properties, M=Mandatory, O=Optional

Property name	M/O	Type	Value
DEVICE_CATEGORY	M	String[]	{"Widget"}
com.acme.class	M	String	A class description of this device. For example "audio", "video", "serial", etc. An actual device category specification should contain an exhaustive list and define a process to add new classes.
com.acme.model	M	String	A definition of the model. This is usually vendor specific. For example "Mouse".
com.acme.manufacturer	M	String	Manufacturer of this device, for example "ACME Widget Division".
com.acme.revision	O	String	Revision number. For example, "42".
com.acme.serial	O	String	A serial number. For example "SN6751293-12-2112/A".

103.3.3 Match Example

Driver services and Device services are connected via a matching process that is explained in *The Device Attachment Algorithm* on page 56. The Driver service plays a pivotal role in this matching process. It must inspect the Device service (from its ServiceReference object) that has just been registered and decide if it potentially could cooperate with this Device service.

It must be able to answer a value indicating the quality of the match. The scale of this match value must be defined in the device category so as to allow Driver services to match on a fair basis. The scale must start at least at 1 and go upwards.

Driver services for this sample device category must return one of the match codes defined in the com.acme.widget.WidgetDevice interface or Device.MATCH_NONE if the Device service is not recognized. The device category must define the exact rules for the match codes in the device category specification. In this example, a small range from 2 to 10 (MATCH_NONE is 0) is defined for WidgetDevice devices. They are named in the WidgetDevice interface for convenience and have the following semantics.

Table 103.2   Sample Device Category Match Scale

Match name	Value	Description
MATCH_SERIAL	10	An exact match, including the serial number.
MATCH_VERSION	8	Matches the right class, make model, and version.
MATCH_MODEL	6	Matches the right class and make model.
MATCH_MAKE	4	Matches the make.
MATCH_CLASS	2	Only matches the class.

A Driver service should use the constants to return when it decides how closely the Device service matches its suitability. For example, if it matches the exact serial number, it should return MATCH_SERIAL.

103.4   Driver Services

A Driver service is responsible for attaching to suitable Device services under control of the device manager. Before it can attach a Device service, however, it must compete with other Driver services for control.

If a Driver service wins the competition, it must attach the device in a device category-specific way. After that, it can perform its intended functionality. This functionality is not defined here nor in the device category; this specification only describes the behavior of the Device service, not how the Driver service uses it to implement its intended functionality. A Driver service may register one or more new Device services of another device category or a generic service which models a more refined form of the device.

Both refined Device services as well as generic services should be defined in a Device Category. See *Device Category Specifications* on page 45.

103.4.1   Driver Bundles

A Driver service is, like *all* services, implemented in a bundle, and is recognized by the device manager by registering one or more Driver service objects with the Framework.

Such bundles containing one or more Driver services are called *driver bundles*. The device manager must be aware of the fact that the cardinality of the relationship between bundles and Driver services is 1:1...*.

A driver bundle must register *at least* one Driver service in its BundleActivator.start implementation.

103.4.2   Driver Taxonomy

Device Drivers may belong to one of the following categories:

- Base Drivers (Discovery, Pure Discovery and Normal)
- Refining Drivers
- Network Drivers
- Composite Drivers
- Referring Drivers
- Bridging Drivers

- Multiplexing Drivers
- Pure Consuming Drivers

This list is not definitive, and a Driver service is not required to fit into one of these categories. The purpose of this taxonomy is to show the different topologies that have been considered for the Device Access service specification.

Figure 103.2   *Legend for Device Driver Services Taxonomy*

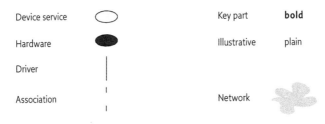

103.4.2.1   Base Drivers

The first category of device drivers are called *base drivers* because they provide the lowest-level representation of a physical device. The distinguishing factor is that they are not registered as Driver services because they do not have to compete for access to their underlying technology.

Figure 103.3   *Base Driver Types*

Base drivers discover physical devices using code not specified here (for example, through notifications from a device driver in native code) and then register corresponding Device services.

When the hardware supports a discovery mechanism and reports a physical device, a Device service is then registered. Drivers supporting a discovery mechanism are called *discovery base drivers*.

An example of a discovery base driver is a USB driver. Discovered USB devices are registered with the Framework as a generic USB Device service. The USB specification (see [2] *USB Specification*) defines a tightly integrated discovery method. Further, devices are individually addressed; no provision exists for broadcasting a message to all devices attached to the USB bus. Therefore, there is no reason to expose the USB network itself; instead, a discovery base driver can register the individual devices as they are discovered.

Not all technologies support a discovery mechanism. For example, most serial ports do not support detection, and it is often not even possible to detect whether a device is attached to a serial port.

Although each driver bundle should perform discovery on its own, a driver for a non-discoverable serial port requires external help – either through a user interface or by allowing the Configuration Admin service to configure it.

It is possible for the driver bundle to combine automatic discovery of Plug and Play-compliant devices with manual configuration when non-compliant devices are plugged in.

103.4.2.2   Refining Drivers

The second category of device drivers are called *refining drivers*. Refining drivers provide a refined view of a physical device that is already represented by another Device service registered with the Framework. Refining drivers register a Driver service with the Framework. This Driver service is used by the device manager to attach the refining driver to a less refined Device service that is registered as a result of events within the Framework itself.

Figure 103.4   *Refining Driver Diagram*

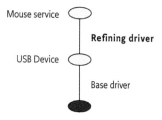

An example of a refining driver is a mouse driver, which is attached to the generic USB Device service representing a physical mouse. It then registers a new Device service which represents it as a Mouse service, defined elsewhere.

The majority of drivers fall into the refining driver type.

103.4.2.3   Network Drivers

An Internet Protocol (IP) capable network such as Ethernet supports individually addressable devices and allows broadcasts, but does not define an intrinsic discovery protocol. In this case, the entire network should be exposed as a single Device service.

Figure 103.5   *Network Driver diagram*

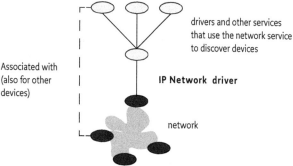

103.4.2.4   Composite Drivers

Complex devices can often be broken down into several parts. Drivers that attach to a single service and then register multiple Device services are called *composite drivers*. For example, a USB speaker containing software-accessible buttons can be registered by its driver as two separate Device services: an Audio Device service and a Button Device service.

Figure 103.6   *Composite Driver structure*

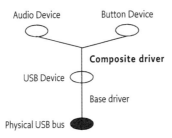

This approach can greatly reduce the number of interfaces needed, as well as enhance reusability.

103.4.2.5   **Referring Drivers**

A referring driver is actually not a driver in the sense that it controls Device services. Instead, it acts as an intermediary to help locate the correct driver bundle. This process is explained in detail in *The Device Attachment Algorithm* on page 56.

A referring driver implements the call to the attach method to inspect the Device service, and decides which Driver bundle would be able to attach to the device. This process can actually involve connecting to the physical device and communicating with it. The attach method then returns a String object that indicates the DRIVER_ID of another driver bundle. This process is called a referral.

For example, a vendor ACME can implement one driver bundle that specializes in recognizing all of the devices the vendor produces. The referring driver bundle does not contain code to control the device – it contains only sufficient logic to recognize the assortment of devices. This referring driver can be small, yet can still identify a large product line. This approach can drastically reduce the amount of downloading and matching needed to find the correct driver bundle.

103.4.2.6   **Bridging Drivers**

A bridging driver registers a Device service from one device category but attaches it to a Device service from another device category.

Figure 103.7   *Bridging Driver Structure*

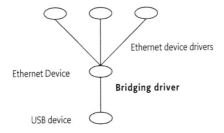

For example, USB to Ethernet bridges exist that allow connection to an Ethernet network through a USB device. In this case, the top level of the USB part of the Device service stack would be an Ethernet Device service. But the same Ethernet Device service can also be the bottom layer of an Ethernet layer of the Device service stack. A few layers up, a bridge could connect into yet another network.

The stacking depth of Device services has no limit, and the same drivers could in fact appear at different levels in the same Device service stack. The graph of drivers-to-Device services roughly mirrors the hardware connections.

103.4.2.7   **Multiplexing Drivers**

A *multiplexing driver* attaches a number of Device services and aggregates them in a new Device service.

Figure 103.8   *Multiplexing Driver Structure*

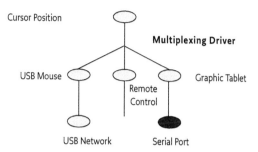

For example, assume that a system has a mouse on USB, a graphic tablet on a serial port, and a remote control facility. Each of these would be registered as a service with the Framework. A multiplexing driver can attach all three, and can merge the different positions in a central Cursor Position service.

103.4.2.8   **Pure Consuming Drivers**

A *pure consuming driver* bundle will attach to devices without registering a refined version.

Figure 103.9   *Pure Consuming Driver Structure*

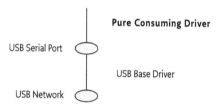

For example, one driver bundle could decide to handle all serial ports through javax.comm instead of registering them as services. When a USB serial port is plugged in, one or more Driver services are attached, resulting in a Device service stack with a Serial Port Device service. A pure consuming driver may then attach to the Serial Port Device service and register a new serial port with the javax.comm.* registry instead of the Framework service registry. This registration effectively transfers the device from the OSGi environment into another environment.

103.4.2.9   **Other Driver Types**

It should be noted that any bundle installed in the OSGi environment may get and use a Device service without having to register a Driver service.

The following functionality is offered to those bundles that do register a Driver service and conform to the this specification:

- The bundles can be installed and uninstalled on demand.
- Attachment to the Device service is only initiated after the winning the competition with other drivers.

103.4.3   Driver Service Registration

Drivers are recognized by registering a Driver service with the Framework. This event makes the device manager aware of the existence of the Driver service. A Driver service registration must have a DRIVER_ID property whose value is a String object, uniquely identifying the driver to the device manager. The device manager must use the DRIVER_ID to prevent the installation of duplicate copies of the same driver bundle.

Therefore, this DRIVER_ID must:

- Depend only on the specific behavior of the driver, and thus be independent of unrelated aspects like its location or mechanism of downloading.
- Start with the reversed form of the domain name of the company that implements it: for example, com.acme.widget.1.1.
- Differ from the DRIVER_ID of drivers with different behavior. Thus, it must *also* be different for each revision of the same driver bundle so they may be distinguished.

When a new Driver service is registered, the Device Attachment Algorithm must be applied to each idle Device service. This requirement gives the new Driver service a chance to compete with other Driver services for attaching to idle devices. The techniques outlined in *Optimizations* on page 59 can provide significant shortcuts for this situation.

As a result, the Driver service object can receive match and attach requests before the method which registered the service has returned.

This specification does not define any method for new Driver services to *steal* already attached devices. Once a Device service has been attached by a Driver service, it can only be released by the Driver service itself.

103.4.4 Driver Service Unregistration

When a Driver service is unregistered, it must release all Device services to which it is attached. Thus, *all* its attached Device services become idle. The device manager must gather all of these idle Device services and try to re-attach them. This condition gives other Driver services a chance to take over the refinement of devices after the unregistering driver. The techniques outlined in *Optimizations* on page 59 can provide significant shortcuts for this situation.

A Driver service that is installed by the device manager must remain registered as long as the driver bundle is active. Therefore, a Driver service should only be unregistered if the driver bundle is stopping, an occurrence which may precede its being uninstalled or updated. Driver services should thus not unregister in an attempt to minimize resource consumption. Such optimizations can easily introduce race conditions with the device manager.

103.4.5 Driver Service Methods

The Driver interface consists of the following methods:

- match(ServiceReference) – This method is called by the device manager to find out how well this Driver service matches the Device service as indicated by the ServiceReference argument. The value returned here is specific for a device category. If this Device service is of another device category, the value Device.MATCH_NONE must be returned. Higher values indicate a better match. For the exact matching algorithm, see *The Device Attachment Algorithm* on page 56.
  Driver match values and referrals must be deterministic, in that repeated calls for the same Device service must return the same results so that results can be cached by the device manager.
- attach(ServiceReference) – If the device manager decides that a Driver service should be attached to a Device service, it must call this method on the Driver service object. Once this method is called, the Device service is regarded as attached to that Driver service, and no other Driver service must be called to attach to the Device service. The Device service must remain *owned* by the Driver service until the Driver bundle is stopped. No unattach method exists.
  The attach method should return null when the Device service is correctly attached. A referring driver (see *Referring Drivers* on page 50) can return a String object that specifies the DRIVER_ID of a driver that can handle this Device service. In this case, the Device service is not attached and the device manager must attempt to install a Driver service with the same DRIVER_ID via a Driver Locator service. The attach method must be deterministic as described in the previous method.

103.4.6   Idle Driver Bundles

An idle Driver bundle is a bundle with a registered Driver service, and is not attached to any Device service. Idle Driver bundles are consuming resources in the OSGi Service Platform. The device manager should uninstall bundles that it has installed and which are idle.

103.5   Driver Locator Service

The device manager must automatically install Driver bundles, which are obtained from Driver Locator services, when new Device services are registered.

A Driver Locator service encapsulates the knowledge of how to fetch the Driver bundles needed for a specific Device service. This selection is made on the properties that are registered with a device: for example, DEVICE_CATEGORY and any other properties registered with the Device service registration.

The purpose of the Driver Locator service is to separate the mechanism from the policy. The decision to install a new bundle is made by the device manager (the mechanism), but a Driver Locator service decides which bundle to install and from where the bundle is downloaded (the policy).

Installing bundles has many consequences for the security of the system, and this process is also sensitive to network setup and other configuration details. Using Driver Locator services allows the Operator to choose a strategy that best fits its needs.

Driver services are identified by the DRIVER_ID property. Driver Locator services use this particular ID to identify the bundles that can be installed. Driver ID properties have uniqueness requirements as specified in *Device Service Registration* on page 44. This uniqueness allows the device manager to maintain a list of Driver services and prevent unnecessary installs.

An OSGi Service Platform can have several different Driver Locator services installed. The device manager must consult all of them and use the combined result set, after pruning duplicates based on the DRIVER_ID values.

103.5.1   The DriverLocator Interface

The DriverLocator interface allows suitable driver bundles to be located, downloaded, and installed on demand, even when completely unknown devices are detected.

It has the following methods:

- findDrivers(Dictionary) – This method returns an array of driver IDs that potentially match a service described by the properties in the Dictionary object. A driver ID is the String object that is registered by a Driver service under the DRIVER_ID property.
- loadDriver(String) – This method returns an InputStream object that can be used to download the bundle containing the Driver service as specified by the driver ID argument. If the Driver Locator service cannot download such a bundle, it should return null. Once this bundle is downloaded and installed in the Framework, it must register a Driver service with the DRIVER_ID property set to the value of the String argument.

103.5.2   A Driver Example

The following example shows a very minimal Driver service implementation. It consists of two classes. The first class is SerialWidget. This class tracks a single WidgetDevice from *Sample Device Category Specification* on page 46. It registers a javax.comm.SerialPort service, which is a general serial port specification that could also be implemented from other device categories like USB, a COM port, etc. It is created when the SerialWidgetDriver object is requested to attach a WidgetDevice by the device manager. It registers a new javax.comm.SerialPort service in its constructor.

The org.osgi.util.tracker.ServiceTracker is extended to handle the Framework events that are needed to simplify tracking this service. The removedService method of this class is overridden to unregister the SerialPort when the underlying WidgetDevice is unregistered.

```
package com.acme.widget;
import org.osgi.service.device.*;
import org.osgi.framework.*;
import org.osgi.util.tracker.*;

class SerialWidget extends ServiceTracker
    implements javax.comm.SerialPort,
       org.osgi.service.device.Constants {
    ServiceRegistration        registration;

    SerialWidget( BundleContext c, ServiceReference r ) {
        super( c, r, null );
        open();
    }

    public Object addingService( ServiceReference ref ) {
        WidgetDevice dev = (WidgetDevice)
            context.getService( ref );
        registration = context.registerService(
            javax.comm.SerialPort.class.getName(),
            this,
            null );
        return dev;
    }

    public void removedService( ServiceReference ref,
        Object service ) {
        registration.unregister();
        context.ungetService(ref);
    }
    ... methods for javax.comm.SerialPort that are
    ... converted to underlying WidgetDevice
}
```

A SerialWidgetDriver object is registered with the Framework in the Bundle Activator start method under the Driver interface. The device manager must call the match method for each idle Device service that is registered. If it is chosen by the device manager to control this Device service, a new SerialWidget is created that offers serial port functionality to other bundles.

```
public class SerialWidgetDriver implements Driver {
    BundleContext           context;

    String      spec =
          "(&"
        +" (objectclass=com.acme.widget.WidgetDevice)"
        +" (DEVICE_CATEGORY=WidgetDevice)"
        +" (com.acme.class=Serial)"
        + ")";

    Filter    filter;
```

```
        SerialWidgetDriver( BundleContext context )
          throws Exception {
          this.context = context;
          filter = context.createFilter(spec);
        }
        public int match( ServiceReference d ) {
          if ( filter.match( d ) )
            return WidgetDevice.MATCH_CLASS;
          else
            return Device.MATCH_NONE;
        }
        public synchronized String attach(ServiceReference r){
          new SerialWidget( context, r );
        }
      }
```

103.6   The Driver Selector Service

The purpose of the Driver Selector service is to customize the selection of the best Driver service from a set of suitable Driver bundles. The device manager has a default algorithm as described in *The Device Attachment Algorithm* on page 56. When this algorithm is not sufficient and requires customizing by the operator, a bundle providing a Driver Selector service can be installed in the Framework. This service must be used by the device manager as the final arbiter when selecting the best match for a Device service.

The Driver Selector service is a singleton; only one such service is recognized by the device manager. The Framework method BundleContext.getServiceReference must be used to obtain a Driver Selector service. In the erroneous case that multiple Driver Selector services are registered, the service.ranking property will thus define which service is actually used.

A device manager implementation must invoke the method select(ServiceReference,Match[]). This method receives a Service Reference to the Device service and an array of Match objects. Each Match object contains a link to the ServiceReference object of a Driver service and the result of the match value returned from a previous call to Driver.match. The Driver Selector service should inspect the array of Match objects and use some means to decide which Driver service is best suited. The index of the best match should be returned. If none of the Match objects describe a possible Driver service, the implementation must return DriverSelector.SELECT_NONE (-1).

103.7   Device Manager

Device Access is controlled by the device manager in the background. The device manager is responsible for initiating all actions in response to the registration, modification, and unregistration of Device services and Driver services, using Driver Locator services and a Driver Selector service as helpers.

The device manager detects the registration of Device services and coordinates their attachment with a suitable Driver service. Potential Driver services do not have to be active in the Framework to be eligible. The device manager must use Driver Locator services to find bundles that might be suitable for the detected Device service and that are not currently installed. This selection is done via a DRIVER_ID property that is unique for each Driver service.

The device manager must install and start these bundles with the help of a Driver Locator service. This activity must result in the registration of one or more Driver services. All available Driver services, installed by the device manager and also others, then participate in a bidding process. The Driver service can inspect the Device service through its ServiceReference object to find out how well this Driver service matches the Device service.

If a Driver Selector service is available in the Framework service registry, it is used to decide which of the eligible Driver services is the best match.

If no Driver Selector service is available, the highest bidder must win, with tie breaks defined on the service.ranking and service.id properties. The selected Driver service is then asked to attach the Device service.

If no Driver service is suitable, the Device service remains idle. When new Driver bundles are installed, these idle Device services must be reattached.

The device manager must reattach a Device service if, at a later time, a Driver service is unregistered due to an uninstallation or update. At the same time, however, it should prevent superfluous and non-optimal reattachments. The device manager should also garbage-collect driver bundles it installed which are no longer used.

The device manager is a singleton. Only one device manager may exist, and it must have no public interface.

103.7.1 Device Manager Startup

To prevent race conditions during Framework startup, the device manager must monitor the state of Device services and Driver services immediately when it is started. The device manager must not, however, begin attaching Device services until the Framework has been fully started, to prevent superfluous or non-optimal attachments.

The Framework has completed starting when the FrameworkEvent.STARTED event has been published. Publication of that event indicates that Framework has finished all its initialization and all bundles are started. If the device manager is started after the Framework has been initialized, it should detect the state of the Framework by examining the state of the system bundle.

103.7.2 The Device Attachment Algorithm

A key responsibility of the device manager is to attach refining drivers to idle devices. The following diagram illustrates the device attachment algorithm.

Figure 103.10   *Device Attachment Algorithm*

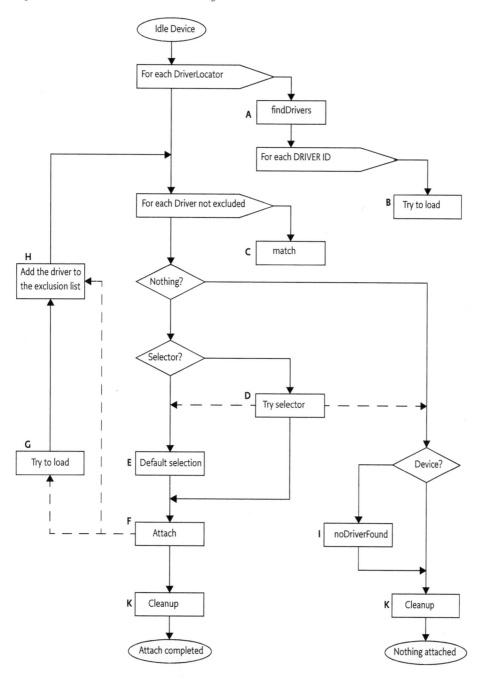

103.7.3
Table 103.3

Legend
Driver attachment algorithm

Step	Description
A	DriverLocator.findDrivers is called for each registered Driver Locator service, passing the properties of the newly detected Device service. Each method call returns zero or more DRIVER_ID values (identifiers of particular driver bundles).
	If the findDrivers method throws an exception, it is ignored, and processing continues with the next Driver Locator service. See *Optimizations* on page 59 for further guidance on handling exceptions.
B	For each found DRIVER_ID that does not correspond to an already registered Driver service, the device manager calls DriverLocator.loadDriver to return an InputStream containing the driver bundle. Each call to loadDriver is directed to one of the Driver Locator services that mentioned the DRIVER_ID in step A. If the loadDriver method fails, the other Driver Locator objects are tried. If they all fail, the driver bundle is ignored.
	If this method succeeds, the device manager installs and starts the driver bundle. Driver bundles must register their Driver services synchronously during bundle activation.
C	For each Driver service, except those on the exclusion list, call its Driver.match method, passing the ServiceReference object to the Device service.
	Collect all successful matches – that is, those whose return values are greater than Device.MATCH_NONE – in a list of active matches. A match call that throws an exception is considered unsuccessful and is not added to the list.
D	If there is a Driver Selector service, the device manager calls the DriverSelector.select method, passing the array of active Match objects.
	If the Driver Selector service returns the index of one of the Match objects from the array, its associated Driver service is selected for attaching the Device service. If the Driver Selector service returns DriverSelector.SELECT_NONE, no Driver service must be considered for attaching the Device service.
	If the Driver Selector service throws an exception or returns an invalid result, the default selection algorithm is used.
	Only one Driver Selector service is used, even if there is more than one registered in the Framework. See *The Driver Selector Service* on page 55.
E	The winner is the one with the highest match value. Tie breakers are respectively: • Highest service.ranking property. • Lowest service.id property.
F	The selected Driver service's attach method is called. If the attach method returns null, the Device service has been successfully attached. If the attach method returns a String object, it is interpreted as a referral to another Driver service and processing continues at G. See *Referring Drivers* on page 50.
	If an exception is thrown, the Driver service has failed, and the algorithm proceeds to try another Driver service after excluding this one from further consideration at Step H.

Table 103.3   *Driver attachment algorithm*

Step	Description
G	The device manager attempts to load the referred driver bundle in a manner similar to Step B, except that it is unknown which Driver Locator service to use. Therefore, the loadDriver method must be called on each Driver Locator service until one succeeds (or they all fail). If one succeeds, the device manager installs and starts the driver bundle. The driver bundle must register a Driver service during its activation which must be added to the list of Driver services in this algorithm.
H	The referring driver bundle is added to the exclusion list. Because each new referral adds an entry to the exclusion list, which in turn disqualifies another driver from further matching, the algorithm cannot loop indefinitely. This list is maintained for the duration of this algorithm. The next time a new Device service is processed, the exclusion list starts out empty.
I	If no Driver service attached the Device service, the Device service is checked to see whether it implements the Device interface. If so, the noDriverFound method is called. Note that this action may cause the Device service to unregister and possibly a new Device service (or services) to be registered in its place. Each new Device service registration must restart the algorithm from the beginning.
K	Whether an attachment was successful or not, the algorithm may have installed a number of driver bundles. The device manager should remove any idle driver bundles that it installed.

103.7.4   Optimizations

Optimizations are explicitly allowed and even recommended for an implementation of a device manager. Implementations may use the following assumptions:

- Driver match values and referrals must be deterministic, in that repeated calls for the same Device service must return the same results.
- The device manager may cache match values and referrals. Therefore, optimizations in the device attachment algorithm based on this assumption are allowed.
- The device manager may delay loading a driver bundle until it is needed. For example, a delay could occur when that DRIVER_ID's match values are cached.
- The results of calls to DriverLocator and DriverSelector methods are not required to be deterministic, and must not be cached by the device manager.
- Thrown exceptions must not be cached. Exceptions are considered transient failures, and the device manager must always retry a method call even if it has thrown an exception on a previous invocation with the same arguments.

103.7.5   Driver Bundle Reclamation

The device manager may remove driver bundles it has installed at any time, provided that all the Driver services in that bundle are idle. This recommended practice prevents unused driver bundles from accumulating over time. Removing driver bundles too soon, however, may cause unnecessary installs and associated delays when driver bundles are needed again.

If a device manager implements driver bundle reclamation, the specified matching algorithm is not guaranteed to terminate unless the device manager takes reclamation into account.

For example, assume that a new Device service triggers the attachment algorithm. A driver bundle recommended by a Driver Locator service is loaded. It does not match, so the Device service remains idle. The device manager is eager to reclaim space, and unloads the driver bundle. The disappearance of the Driver service causes the device manager to reattach idle devices. Because it has not kept a record of its previous activities, it tries to reattach the same device, which closes the loop.

On systems where the device manager implements driver bundle reclamation, all refining drivers should be loaded through Driver Locator services. This recommendation is intended to prevent the device manager from erroneously uninstalling pre-installed driver bundles that cannot later be reinstalled when needed.

The device manager can be updated or restarted. It cannot, however, rely on previously stored information to determine which driver bundles were pre-installed and which were dynamically installed and thus are eligible for removal. The device manager may persistently store cachable information for optimization, but must be able to cold start without any persistent information and still be able to manage an existing connection state, satisfying all of the requirements in this specification.

103.7.6 Handling Driver Bundle Updates

It is not straightforward to determine whether a driver bundle is being updated when the UNREGISTER event for a Driver service is received. In order to facilitate this distinction, the device manager should wait for a period of time after the unregistration for one of the following events to occur:

- A BundleEvent.UNINSTALLED event for the driver bundle.
- A ServiceEvent.REGISTERED event for another Driver service registered by the driver bundle.

If the driver bundle is uninstalled, or if neither of the above events are received within the allotted time period, the driver is assumed to be inactive. The appropriate waiting period is implementation-dependent and will vary for different installations. As a general rule, this period should be long enough to allow a driver to be stopped, updated, and restarted under normal conditions, and short enough not to cause unnecessary delays in reattaching devices. The actual time should be configurable.

103.7.7 Simultaneous Device Service and Driver Service Registration

The device attachment algorithm may discover new driver bundles that were installed outside its direct control, which requires executing the device attachment algorithm recursively. However, in this case, the appearance of the new driver bundles should be queued until completion of the current device attachment algorithm.

Only one device attachment algorithm may be in progress at any moment in time.

The following example sequence illustrates this process when a Driver service is registered:

- Collect the set of all idle devices.
- Apply the device attachment algorithm to each device in the set.
- If no Driver services were registered during the execution of the device attachment algorithm, processing terminates.
- Otherwise, restart this process.

103.8 Security

The device manager is the only privileged bundle in the Device Access specification and requires the org.osgi.framework.AdminPermission with the LIFECYCLE action to install and uninstall driver bundles.

The device manager itself should be free from any knowledge of policies and should not actively set bundle permissions. Rather, if permissions must be set, it is up to the Management Agent to listen to synchronous bundle events and set the appropriate permissions.

Driver Locator services can trigger the download of any bundle, because they deliver the content of a bundle to the privileged device manager and could potentially insert a Trojan horse into the environment. Therefore, Driver Locator bundles need the ServicePermission[DriverLocator, REGISTER] to register Driver Locator services, and the operator should exercise prudence in assigning this ServicePermission.

Bundles with Driver Selector services only require ServicePermission[DriverSelector, REGISTER] to register the DriverSelector service. The Driver Selector service can play a crucial role in the selection of a suitable Driver service, but it has no means to define a specific bundle itself.

103.9 org.osgi.service.device

Device Access Package Version 1.1.

Bundles wishing to use this package must list the package in the Import-Package header of the bundle's manifest. For example:

```
Import-Package: org.osgi.service.device; version="[1.1,2.0)"
```

103.9.1 Summary

- *Constants* - This interface defines standard names for property keys associated with Device and Driver services.
- *Device* - Interface for identifying device services.
- *Driver* - A Driver service object must be registered by each Driver bundle wishing to attach to Device services provided by other drivers.
- *DriverLocator* - A Driver Locator service can find and load device driver bundles given a property set.
- *DriverSelector* - When the device manager detects a new Device service, it calls all registered Driver services to determine if anyone matches the Device service.
- *Match* - Instances of Match are used in the DriverSelector.select method to identify Driver services matching a Device service.

103.9.2 public interface Constants

This interface defines standard names for property keys associated with Device and Driver services.

The values associated with these keys are of type java.lang.String, unless otherwise stated.

See Also Device, Driver

Since 1.1

103.9.2.1 public static final String DEVICE_CATEGORY = "DEVICE_CATEGORY"

Property (named "DEVICE_CATEGORY") containing a human readable description of the device categories implemented by a device. This property is of type String[]

Services registered with this property will be treated as devices and discovered by the device manager

103.9.2.2 public static final String DEVICE_DESCRIPTION = "DEVICE_DESCRIPTION"

Property (named "DEVICE_DESCRIPTION") containing a human readable string describing the actual hardware device.

103.9.2.3 public static final String DEVICE_SERIAL = "DEVICE_SERIAL"

Property (named "DEVICE_SERIAL") specifying a device's serial number.

103.9.2.4   **public static final String DRIVER_ID = "DRIVER_ID"**

Property (named "DRIVER_ID") identifying a driver.

A DRIVER_ID should start with the reversed domain name of the company that implemented the driver (e.g., com.acme), and must meet the following requirements:

- It must be independent of the location from where it is obtained.
- It must be independent of the DriverLocator service that downloaded it.
- It must be unique.
- It must be different for different revisions of the same driver.

This property is mandatory, i.e., every Driver service must be registered with it.

103.9.3   public interface Device

Interface for identifying device services.

A service must implement this interface or use the Constants.DEVICE_CATEGORY registration property to indicate that it is a device. Any services implementing this interface or registered with the DEVICE_CATEGORY property will be discovered by the device manager.

Device services implementing this interface give the device manager the opportunity to indicate to the device that no drivers were found that could (further) refine it. In this case, the device manager calls the noDriverFound method on the Device object.

Specialized device implementations will extend this interface by adding methods appropriate to their device category to it.

See Also   Driver

Concurrency   Thread-safe

103.9.3.1   **public static final int MATCH_NONE = 0**

Return value from Driver.match indicating that the driver cannot refine the device presented to it by the device manager. The value is zero.

103.9.3.2   **public void noDriverFound( )**

□ Indicates to this Device object that the device manager has failed to attach any drivers to it.

If this Device object can be configured differently, the driver that registered this Device object may unregister it and register a different Device service instead.

103.9.4   public interface Driver

A Driver service object must be registered by each Driver bundle wishing to attach to Device services provided by other drivers. For each newly discovered Device object, the device manager enters a bidding phase. The Driver object whose match method bids the highest for a particular Device object will be instructed by the device manager to attach to the Device object.

See Also   Device, DriverLocator

Concurrency   Thread-safe

103.9.4.1   **public String attach(ServiceReference reference) throws Exception**

reference   the ServiceReference object of the device to attach to

□ Attaches this Driver service to the Device service represented by the given ServiceReference object.

A return value of null indicates that this Driver service has successfully attached to the given Device service. If this Driver service is unable to attach to the given Device service, but knows of a more suitable Driver service, it must return the DRIVER_ID of that Driver service. This allows for the implementation of referring drivers whose only purpose is to refer to other drivers capable of handling a given Device service.

After having attached to the Device service, this driver may register the underlying device as a new service exposing driver-specific functionality.

This method is called by the device manager.

Returns null if this Driver service has successfully attached to the given Device service, or the DRIVER_ID of a more suitable driver

Throws Exception – if the driver cannot attach to the given device and does not know of a more suitable driver

103.9.4.2 **public int match(ServiceReference reference) throws Exception**

reference the ServiceReference object of the device to match

☐ Checks whether this Driver service can be attached to the Device service. The Device service is represented by the given ServiceReference and returns a value indicating how well this driver can support the given Device service, or Device.MATCH_NONE if it cannot support the given Device service at all.

The return value must be one of the possible match values defined in the device category definition for the given Device service, or Device.MATCH_NONE if the category of the Device service is not recognized.

In order to make its decision, this Driver service may examine the properties associated with the given Device service, or may get the referenced service object (representing the actual physical device) to talk to it, as long as it ungets the service and returns the physical device to a normal state before this method returns.

A Driver service must always return the same match code whenever it is presented with the same Device service.

The match function is called by the device manager during the matching process.

Returns value indicating how well this driver can support the given Device service, or Device.MATCH_NONE if it cannot support the Device service at all

Throws Exception – if this Driver service cannot examine the Device service

103.9.5 **public interface DriverLocator**

A Driver Locator service can find and load device driver bundles given a property set. Each driver is represented by a unique DRIVER_ID.

Driver Locator services provide the mechanism for dynamically downloading new device driver bundles into an OSGi environment. They are supplied by providers and encapsulate all provider-specific details related to the location and acquisition of driver bundles.

See Also Driver

Concurrency Thread-safe

103.9.5.1 **public String[] findDrivers(Dictionary props)**

props the properties of the device for which a driver is sought

☐ Returns an array of DRIVER_ID strings of drivers capable of attaching to a device with the given properties.

The property keys in the specified Dictionary objects are case-insensitive.

Returns array of driver DRIVER_ID strings of drivers capable of attaching to a Device service with the given properties, or null if this Driver Locator service does not know of any such drivers

103.9.5.2   **public InputStream loadDriver(String id) throws IOException**

id the DRIVER_ID of the driver that needs to be installed.

□ Get an InputStream from which the driver bundle providing a driver with the giving DRIVER_ID can be installed.

Returns An InputStream object from which the driver bundle can be installed or null if the driver with the given ID cannot be located

Throws IOException – the input stream for the bundle cannot be created

103.9.6   public interface DriverSelector

When the device manager detects a new Device service, it calls all registered Driver services to determine if anyone matches the Device service. If at least one Driver service matches, the device manager must choose one. If there is a Driver Selector service registered with the Framework, the device manager will ask it to make the selection. If there is no Driver Selector service, or if it returns an invalid result, or throws an Exception, the device manager uses the default selection strategy.

Since 1.1

Concurrency Thread-safe

103.9.6.1   **public static final int SELECT_NONE = -1**

Return value from DriverSelector.select, if no Driver service should be attached to the Device service. The value is -1.

103.9.6.2   **public int select(ServiceReference reference, Match[] matches)**

reference the ServiceReference object of the Device service.

matches the array of all non-zero matches.

□ Select one of the matching Driver services. The device manager calls this method if there is at least one driver bidding for a device. Only Driver services that have responded with nonzero (not Device.MATCH_NONE) match values will be included in the list.

Returns index into the array of Match objects, or SELECT_NONE if no Driver service should be attached

103.9.7   public interface Match

Instances of Match are used in the DriverSelector.select method to identify Driver services matching a Device service.

See Also DriverSelector

Since 1.1

Concurrency Thread-safe

103.9.7.1   **public ServiceReference getDriver( )**

□ Return the reference to a Driver service.

Returns ServiceReference object to a Driver service.

103.9.7.2   **public int getMatchValue( )**

□ Return the match value of this object.

Returns the match value returned by this Driver service.

103.10   References

[1]   *Java Communications API*
http://java.sun.com/products/javacomm

[2]   *USB Specification*
http://www.usb.org

[3]   *Universal Plug and Play*
http://www.upnp.org

[4]   *Jini, Service Discovery and Usage*
http://www.jini.org/resources/

104 Configuration Admin Service Specification

Version 1.3

104.1 Introduction

The Configuration Admin service is an important aspect of the deployment of an OSGi Service Platform. It allows an Operator to set the configuration information of deployed bundles.

Configuration is the process of defining the configuration data of bundles and assuring that those bundles receive that data when they are active in the OSGi Service Platform.

Figure 104.1   *Configuration Admin Service Overview*

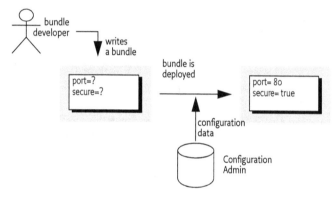

104.1.1 Essentials

The following requirements and patterns are associated with the Configuration Admin service specification:

- *Local Configuration* – The Configuration Admin service must support bundles that have their own user interface to change their configurations.
- *Reflection* – The Configuration Admin service must be able to deduce the names and types of the needed configuration data.
- *Legacy* – The Configuration Admin service must support configuration data of existing entities (such as devices).
- *Object Oriented* – The Configuration Admin service must support the creation and deletion of instances of configuration information so that a bundle can create the appropriate number of services under the control of the Configuration Admin service.
- *Embedded Devices* – The Configuration Admin service must be deployable on a wide range of platforms. This requirement means that the interface should not assume file storage on the platform. The choice to use file storage should be left to the implementation of the Configuration Admin service.
- *Remote versus Local Management* – The Configuration Admin service must allow for a remotely managed OSGi Service Platform, and must not assume that configuration information is stored

locally. Nor should it assume that the Configuration Admin service is always done remotely. Both implementation approaches should be viable.

- *Availability* – The OSGi environment is a dynamic environment that must run continuously (24/7/365). Configuration updates must happen dynamically and should not require restarting of the system or bundles.
- *Immediate Response* – Changes in configuration should be reflected immediately.
- *Execution Environment* – The Configuration Admin service will not require more than an environment that fulfills the minimal execution requirements.
- *Communications* – The Configuration Admin service should not assume "always-on" connectivity, so the API is also applicable for mobile applications in cars, phones, or boats.
- *Extendability* – The Configuration Admin service should expose the process of configuration to other bundles. This exposure should at a minimum encompass initiating an update, removing certain configuration properties, adding properties, and modifying the value of properties potentially based on existing property or service values.
- *Complexity Trade-offs* – Bundles in need of configuration data should have a simple way of obtaining it. Most bundles have this need and the code to accept this data. Additionally, updates should be simple from the perspective of the receiver.
Trade-offs in simplicity should be made at the expense of the bundle implementing the Configuration Admin service and in favor of bundles that need configuration information. The reason for this choice is that normal bundles will outnumber Configuration Admin bundles.

104.1.2 Operation

This specification is based on the concept of a Configuration Admin service that manages the configuration of an OSGi Service Platform. It maintains a database of Configuration objects, locally or remote. This service monitors the service registry and provides configuration information to services that are registered with a service.pid property, the Persistent IDentity (PID), and implement one of the following interfaces:

- *Managed Service* – A service registered with this interface receives its *configuration dictionary* from the database or receives null when no such configuration exists or when an existing configuration has never been updated.
- *Managed Service Factory* – Services registered with this interface receive several configuration dictionaries when registered. The database contains zero or more configuration dictionaries for this service. Each configuration dictionary is given sequentially to the service.

The database can be manipulated either by the Management Agent or bundles that configure themselves.

Other parties can provide Configuration Plugin services. Such services participate in the configuration process. They can inspect the configuration dictionary and modify it before it reaches the target service.

104.1.3 Entities

- *Configuration information* – The information needed by a bundle before it can provide its intended functionality.
- *Configuration dictionary* – The configuration information when it is passed to the target service. It consists of a Dictionary object with a number of properties and identifiers.
- *Configuring Bundle* – A bundle that modifies the configuration information through the Configuration Admin service. This bundle is either a management bundle or the bundle for which the configuration information is intended.
- *Configuration Target* – The target (bundle or service) that will receive the configuration information. For services, there are two types of targets: ManagedServiceFactory or ManagedService objects.
- *Configuration Admin Service* – This service is responsible for supplying configuration target bundles with their configuration information. It maintains a database with configuration infor-

mation, keyed on the service.pid of configuration target services. These services receive their configuration dictionary or dictionaries when they are registered with the Framework.
Configurations can be modified or extended using Configuration Plugin services before they
reach the target bundle.

- *Managed Service* – A Managed Service represents a client of the Configuration Admin service, and
  is thus a configuration target. Bundles should register a Managed Service to receive the configuration data from the Configuration Admin service. A Managed Service adds one or more unique
  service.pid service registration properties as a primary key for the configuration information.
- *Managed Service Factory* – A Managed Service Factory can receive a number of configuration dictionaries from the Configuration Admin service, and is thus also a configuration target service. It
  should register with one or more service.pid strings and receives zero or more configuration dictionaries. Each dictionary has its own PID.
- *Configuration Object* – Implements the Configuration interface and contains the configuration dictionary for a Managed Service or one of the configuration dictionaries for a Managed Service
  Factory. These objects are manipulated by configuring bundles.
- *Configuration Plugin* Services – Configuration Plugin services are called before the configuration
  dictionary is given to the configuration targets. The plug-in can modify the configuration dictionary, which is passed to the Configuration Target.

Figure 104.2   Configuration Admin Class Diagram org.osgi.service.cm

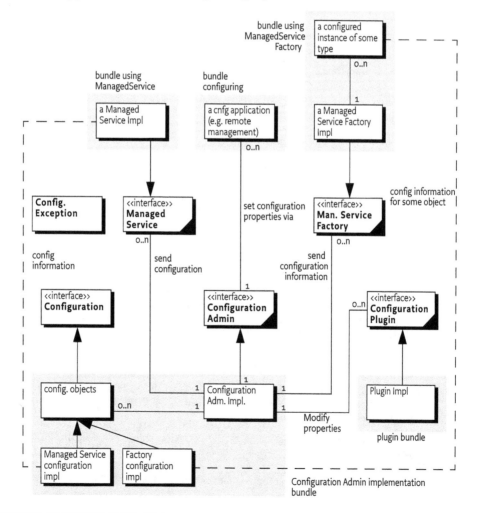

104.2 Configuration Targets

One of the more complicated aspects of this specification is the subtle distinction between the ManagedService and ManagedServiceFactory classes.

Both receive configuration information from the Configuration Admin service and are treated similarly in most respects. Therefore, this specification refers to *configuration targets* when the distinction is irrelevant.

The difference between these types is related to the cardinality of the configuration dictionary. A Managed Service is used when an existing entity needs a configuration dictionary. Thus, a one-to-one relationship always exists between the configuration dictionary and the entity.

A Managed Service Factory is used when part of the configuration is to define *how many instances are required.* A management bundle can create, modify, and delete any number of instances for a Managed Service Factory through the Configuration Admin service. Each instance is configured by a single Configuration object. Therefore, a Managed Service Factory can have multiple associated Configuration objects.

Figure 104.3   *Differentiation of ManagedService and ManagedServiceFactory Classes*

To summarize:

- A *Managed Service* must receive a single configuration dictionary when it is registered or when its configuration is modified.
- A *Managed Service Factory* must receive from zero to *n* configuration dictionaries when it registers, depending on the current configuration. The Managed Service Factory is informed of configuration dictionary changes: modifications, creations, and deletions.

104.3 The Persistent Identity

A crucial concept in the Configuration Admin service specification is the Persistent IDentity (PID) as defined in the Framework's service layer. Its purpose is to act as a primary key for objects that need a configuration dictionary. The name of the service property for PID is defined in the Framework in org.osgi.framework.Constants.SERVICE.PID.

The Configuration Admin service requires the use of PIDs with Managed Service and Managed Service Factory registrations because it associates its configuration data with PIDs.

PIDs must be unique for each service, though a service can register with multiple PIDs. A bundle must not register multiple configuration target services with the same PID. If that should occur, the Configuration Admin service must:

- Send the appropriate configuration data to all services registered under that PID from that bundle only.
- Report an error in the log.
- Ignore duplicate PIDs from other bundles and report them to the log.

104.3.1	**PID Syntax**

PIDs are intended for use by other bundles, not by people, but sometimes the user is confronted with a PID. For example, when installing an alarm system, the user needs to identify the different components to a wiring application. This type of application exposes the PID to end users.

PIDs should follow the symbolic-name syntax, which uses a very restricted character set. The following sections, define some schemes for common cases. These schemes are not required, but bundle developers are urged to use them to achieve consistency.

104.3.1.1	**Local Bundle PIDs**

As a convention, descriptions starting with the bundle identity and a dot (.) are reserved for a bundle. As an example, a PID of "65.536" would belong to the bundle with a bundle identity of 65.

104.3.1.2	**Software PIDs**

Configuration target services that are singletons can use a Java package name they own as the PID (the reverse domain name scheme) as long as they do not use characters outside the basic ASCII set. As an example, the PID named com.acme.watchdog would represent a Watchdog service from the ACME company.

104.3.1.3	**Devices**

Devices are usually organized on buses or networks. The identity of a device, such as a unique serial number or an address, is a good component of a PID. The format of the serial number should be the same as that printed on the housing or box, to aid in recognition.

Table 104.1   *Schemes for Device-Oriented PID Names*

Bus	Example	Format	Description
USB	USB.0123-0002-9909873	idVendor (hex 4) idProduct (hex 4) iSerialNumber (decimal)	Universal Serial Bus. Use the standard device descriptor.
IP	IP.172.16.28.21	IP nr (dotted decimal)	Internet Protocol
802	802-00:60:97:00:9A:56	MAC address with: separators	IEEE 802 MAC address (Token Ring, Ethernet,...)
ONE	ONE.06-00000021E461	Family (hex 2) and serial number including CRC (hex 6)	1-wire bus of Dallas Semiconductor
COM	COM.krups-brewer-12323	serial number or type name of device	Serial ports

104.4 The Configuration Object

A Configuration object contains the configuration dictionary, which is a set of properties that configure an aspect of a bundle. A bundle can receive Configuration objects by registering a configuration target service with a PID service property. See *The Persistent Identity* on page 70 for more information about PIDs.

During registration, the Configuration Admin service must detect these configuration target services and hand over their configuration dictionary via a callback. If this configuration dictionary is subsequently modified, the modified dictionary is handed over to the configuration target again with the same callback.

The Configuration object is primarily a set of properties that can be updated by a Management Agent, user interfaces on the OSGi Service Platform, or other applications. Configuration changes are first made persistent, and then passed to the target service via a call to the updated method in the ManagedServiceFactory or ManagedService class.

A Configuration object must be uniquely bound to a Managed Service or Managed Service Factory. This implies that a bundle must not register a Managed Service Factory with a PID that is the same as the PID given to a Managed Service.

104.4.1   Location Binding

When a Configuration object is created by either getConfiguration or createFactoryConfiguration, it becomes bound to the location of the calling bundle. This location is obtained with the associated bundle's getLocation method.

Location binding is a security feature that assures that only management bundles can modify configuration data, and other bundles can only modify their own configuration data. A SecurityException is thrown if a bundle other than a Management Agent bundle attempts to modify the configuration information of another bundle.

If a Managed Service is registered with a PID that is already bound to another location, the normal callback to ManagedService.updated must not take place.

The two argument versions of getConfiguration and createFactoryConfiguration take a location String as their second argument. These methods require the correct permission, and they create Configuration objects bound to the specified location, instead of the location of the calling bundle. These methods are intended for management bundles.

The creation of a Configuration object does not in itself initiate a callback to the target.

A null location parameter may be used to create Configuration objects that are not bound. In this case, the objects become bound to a specific location the first time that they are used by a bundle. When this dynamically bound bundle is subsequently uninstalled, the Configuration object's bundle location must be set to null again so it can be bound again later.

A management bundle may create a Configuration object before the associated Managed Service is registered. It may use a null location to avoid any dependency on the actual location of the bundle which registers this service. When the Managed Service is registered later, the Configuration object must be bound to the location of the registering bundle, and its configuration dictionary must then be passed to ManagedService.updated.

104.4.2   Configuration Properties

A configuration dictionary contains a set of properties in a Dictionary object. The value of the property must be the same type as the set of types specified in the OSGi Core Specification in *Figure 3.8 Primary property types*.

The name or key of a property must always be a String object, and is not case-sensitive during look up, but must preserve the original case. The format of a property name should be:

```
property-name ::= public | private
public        ::= symbolic-name // See 1.3.2
private       ::= '.' symbolic-name
```

Properties can be used in other subsystems that have restrictions on the character set that can be used. The symbolic-name production uses a very minimal character set.

Bundles must not use nested vectors or arrays, nor must they use mixed types. Using mixed types or nesting makes it impossible to use the meta typing specification. See *Metatype Service Specification* on page 105.

104.4.3　**Property Propagation**

A configuration target should copy the public configuration properties (properties whose name does not start with a '.' or \u002E) of the Dictionary object argument in updated(Dictionary) into the service properties on any resulting service registration.

This propagation allows the development of applications that leverage the Framework service registry more extensively, so compliance with this mechanism is advised.

A configuration target may ignore any configuration properties it does not recognize, or it may change the values of the configuration properties before these properties are registered as service properties. Configuration properties in the Framework service registry are not strictly related to the configuration information.

Bundles that follow this recommendation to propagate public configuration properties can participate in horizontal applications. For example, an application that maintains physical location information in the Framework service registry could find out where a particular device is located in the house or car. This service could use a property dedicated to the physical location and provide functions that leverage this property, such as a graphic user interface that displays these locations.

Bundles performing service registrations on behalf of other bundles (e.g. OSGi Declarative Services) should propagate all public configuration properties and not propagate private configuration properties.

104.4.4　**Automatic Properties**

The Configuration Admin service must automatically add a number of properties to the configuration dictionary. If these properties are also set by a configuring bundle or a plug-in, they must always be overridden before they are given to the target service. See *Configuration Plugin* on page 84,Therefore, the receiving bundle or plug-in can assume that the following properties are defined by the Configuration Admin service and not by the configuring bundle:

- service.pid – Set to the PID of the associated Configuration object.
- service.factoryPid – Only set for a Managed Service Factory. It is then set to the PID of the associated Managed Service Factory.
- service.bundleLocation – Set to the location of the bundle that can use this Configuration object. This property can only be used for searching, it may not appear in the configuration dictionary returned from the getProperties method due to security reasons, nor may it be used when the target is updated.

Constants for some of these properties can be found in org.osgi.framework.Constants. These system properties are all of type String.

104.4.5　**Equality**

Two different Configuration objects can actually represent the same underlying configuration. This means that a Configuration object must implement the equals and hashCode methods in such a way that two Configuration objects are equal when their PID is equal.

104.5　Managed Service

A Managed Service is used by a bundle that needs one configuration dictionary and is thus associated with one Configuration object in the Configuration Admin service.

A bundle can register any number of ManagedService objects, but each must be identified with its own PID or PIDs.

A bundle should use a Managed Service when it needs configuration information for the following:

- *A Singleton* – A single entity in the bundle that needs to be configured.

- *Externally Detected Devices* – Each device that is detected causes a registration of an associated ManagedService object. The PID of this object is related to the identity of the device, such as the address or serial number.

104.5.1 Singletons

When an object must be instantiated only once, it is called a *singleton*. A singleton requires a single configuration dictionary. Bundles may implement several different types of singletons if necessary.

For example, a Watchdog service could watch the registry for the status and presence of services in the Framework service registry. Only one instance of a Watchdog service is needed, so only a single configuration dictionary is required that contains the polling time and the list of services to watch.

104.5.2 Networks

When a device in the external world needs to be represented in the OSGi Environment, it must be detected in some manner. The Configuration Admin service cannot know the identity and the number of instances of the device without assistance. When a device is detected, it still needs configuration information in order to play a useful role.

For example, a 1-Wire network can automatically detect devices that are attached and removed. When it detects a temperature sensor, it could register a Sensor service with the Framework service registry. This Sensor service needs configuration information specifically for that sensor, such as which lamps should be turned on, at what temperature the sensor is triggered, what timer should be started, in what zone it resides, and so on. One bundle could potentially have hundreds of these sensors and actuators, and each needs its own configuration information.

Each of these Sensor services should be registered as a Managed Service with a PID related to the physical sensor (such as the address) to receive configuration information.

Other examples are services discovered on networks with protocols like Jini, UPnP, and Salutation. They can usually be represented in the Framework service registry. A network printer, for example, could be detected via UPnP. Once in the service registry, these services usually require local configuration information. A Printer service needs to be configured for its local role: location, access list, and so on.

This information needs to be available in the Framework service registry whenever that particular Printer service is registered. Therefore, the Configuration Admin service must remember the configuration information for this Printer service.

This type of service should register with the Framework as a Managed Service in order to receive appropriate configuration information.

104.5.3 Configuring Managed Services

A bundle that needs configuration information should register one or more ManagedService objects with a PID service property. If it has a default set of properties for its configuration, it may include them as service properties of the Managed Service. These properties may be used as a configuration template when a Configuration object is created for the first time. A Managed Service optionally implements the MetaTypeProvider interface to provide information about the property types. See *Meta Typing* on page 87.

When this registration is detected by the Configuration Admin service, the following steps must occur:

- The configuration stored for the registered PID must be retrieved. If there is a Configuration object for this PID, it is sent to the Managed Service with updated(Dictionary).
- If a Managed Service is registered and no configuration information is available, the Configuration Admin service must call updated(Dictionary) with a null parameter.

- If the Configuration Admin service starts *after* a Managed Service is registered, it must call updated(Dictionary) on this service as soon as possible. For this reason, a Managed Service must always get a callback when it registers *and* the Configuration Admin service is started.

The updated(Dictionary) callback from the Configuration Admin service to the Managed Service must take place asynchronously. This requirement allows the Managed Service to finish its initialization in a synchronized method without interference from the Configuration Admin service callback.

Care should be taken not to cause deadlocks by calling the Framework within a synchronized method.

Figure 104.4   *Managed Service Configuration Action Diagram*

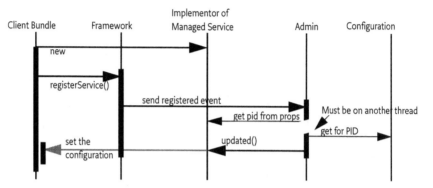

The updated method may throw a ConfigurationException. This object must describe the problem and what property caused the exception.

104.5.4   Race Conditions

When a Managed Service is registered, the default properties may be visible in the service registry for a short period before they are replaced by the properties of the actual configuration dictionary. Care should be taken that this visibility does not cause race conditions for other bundles.

In cases where race conditions could be harmful, the Managed Service must be split into two pieces: an object performing the actual service and a Managed Service. First, the Managed Service is registered, the configuration is received, and the actual service object is registered. In such cases, the use of a Managed Service Factory that performs this function should be considered.

104.5.5   Examples of Managed Service

Figure 104.5 shows a Managed Service configuration example. Two services are registered under the ManagedService interface, each with a different PID.

Figure 104.5   *PIDs and External Associations*

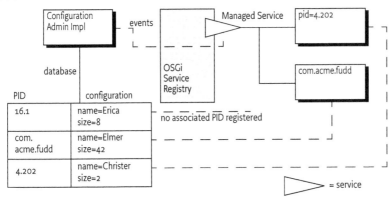

The Configuration Admin service has a database containing a configuration record for each PID. When the Managed Service with service.pid = com.acme.fudd is registered, the Configuration Admin service will retrieve the properties name=Elmer and size=42 from its database. The properties are stored in a Dictionary object and then given to the Managed Service with the updated(Dictionary) method.

104.5.5.1   **Configuring A Console Bundle**

In this example, a bundle can run a single debugging console over a Telnet connection. It is a single-ton, so it uses a ManagedService object to get its configuration information: the port and the network name on which it should register.

```
class SampleManagedService implements ManagedService {
    Dictionary              properties;
    ServiceRegistration     registration;
    Console                 console;

    public synchronized void start(
        BundleContext context ) throws Exception {
        properties = new Hashtable();
        properties.put( Constants.SERVICE_PID,
            "com.acme.console" );
        properties.put( "port",  new Integer(2011) );

        registration = context.registerService(
            ManagedService.class.getName(),
            this,
            properties
        );
    }

    public synchronized void updated( Dictionary np ) {
        if ( np != null ) {
            properties = np;
            properties.put(
                Constants.SERVICE_PID, "com.acme.console" );
        }

        if (console == null)
            console = new Console();
```

```
                    int port = ((Integer)properties.get("port"))
                      .intValue();

                    String network = (String) properties.get("network");
                    console.setPort(port, network);
                    registration.setProperties(properties);
                }
                ... further methods
            }
```

104.5.6   Deletion

When a Configuration object for a Managed Service is deleted, the Configuration Admin service must call updated(Dictionary) with a null argument on a thread that is different from that on which the Configuration.delete was executed. This deletion must send out a Configuration Event CM_DELETED to any registered Configuration Listener services after the updated method is called with a null.

104.6   Managed Service Factory

A Managed Service Factory is used when configuration information is needed for a service that can be instantiated multiple times. When a Managed Service Factory is registered with the Framework, the Configuration Admin service consults its database and calls updated(String,Dictionary) for each associated Configuration object. It passes the identifier of the instance, which can be used as a PID, as well as a Dictionary object with the configuration properties.

A Managed Service Factory is useful when the bundle can provide functionality a number of times, each time with different configuration dictionaries. In this situation, the Managed Service Factory acts like a *class* and the Configuration Admin service can use this Managed Service Factory to *instantiate instances* for that *class*.

In the next section, the word *factory* refers to this concept of creating *instances* of a function defined by a bundle that registers a Managed Service Factory.

104.6.1   When to Use a Managed Service Factory

A Managed Service Factory should be used when a bundle does not have an internal or external entity associated with the configuration information but can potentially be instantiated multiple times.

104.6.1.1   Example Email Fetcher

An email fetcher program displays the number of emails that a user has – a function likely to be required for different users. This function could be viewed as a *class* that needs to be *instantiated* for each user. Each instance requires different parameters, including password, host, protocol, user id, and so on.

An implementation of the Email Fetcher service should register a ManagedServiceFactory object. In this way, the Configuration Admin service can define the configuration information for each user separately. The Email Fetcher service will only receive a configuration dictionary for each required instance (user).

104.6.1.2   Example Temperature Conversion Service

Assume a bundle has the code to implement a conversion service that receives a temperature and, depending on settings, can turn an actuator on and off. This service would need to be instantiated many times depending on where it is needed. Each instance would require its own configuration information for the following:

- Upper value
- Lower value
- Switch Identification
- ...

Such a conversion service should register a service object under a ManagedServiceFactory interface. A configuration program can then use this Managed Service Factory to create instances as needed. For example, this program could use a Graphic User Interface (GUI) to create such a component and configure it.

104.6.1.3   Serial Ports

Serial ports cannot always be used by the OSGi Device Access specification implementations. Some environments have no means to identify available serial ports, and a device on a serial port cannot always provide information about its type.

Therefore, each serial port requires a description of the device that is connected. The bundle managing the serial ports would need to instantiate a number of serial ports under the control of the Configuration Admin service, with the appropriate DEVICE_CATEGORY property to allow it to participate in the Device Access implementation.

If the bundle cannot detect the available serial ports automatically, it should register a Managed Service Factory. The Configuration Admin service can then, with the help of a configuration program, define configuration information for each available serial port.

104.6.2   Registration

Similar to the Managed Service configuration dictionary, the configuration dictionary for a Managed Service Factory is identified by a PID. The Managed Service Factory, however, also has a *factory* PID, which is the PID of the associated Managed Service Factory. It is used to group all Managed Service Factory configuration dictionaries together.

When a Configuration object for a Managed Service Factory is created (ConfigurationAdmin.createFactoryConfiguration), a new unique PID is created for this object by the Configuration Admin service. The scheme used for this PID is defined by the Configuration Admin service and is unrelated to the factory PID.

When the Configuration Admin service detects the registration of a Managed Service Factory, it must find all configuration dictionaries for this factory and must then sequentially call ManagedServiceFactory.updated(String,Dictionary) for each configuration dictionary. The first argument is the PID of the Configuration object (the one created by the Configuration Admin service) and the second argument contains the configuration properties.

The Managed Service Factory should then create any artifacts associated with that factory. Using the PID given in the Configuration object, the bundle may register new services (other than a Managed Service) with the Framework, but this is not required. This may be necessary when the PID is useful in contexts other than the Configuration Admin service.

The receiver must *not* register a Managed Service with this PID because this would force two Configuration objects to have the same PID. If a bundle attempts to do this, the Configuration Admin service should log an error and must ignore the registration of the Managed Service.

The Configuration Admin service must guarantee that no race conditions exist between initialization, updates, and deletions.

Figure 104.6   *Managed Service Factory Action Diagram*

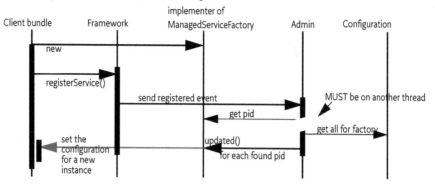

A Managed Service Factory has only one update method: updated(String,Dictionary). This method can be called any number of times as Configuration objects are created or updated.

The Managed Service Factory must detect whether a PID is being used for the first time, in which case it should create a new *instance*, or a subsequent time, in which case it should update an existing instance.

The Configuration Admin service must call updated(String,Dictionary) on a thread that is different from the one that executed the registration. This requirement allows an implementation of a Managed Service Factory to use a synchronized method to assure that the callbacks do not interfere with the Managed Service Factory registration.

The updated(String,Dictionary) method may throw a ConfigurationException object. This object describes the problem and what property caused the problem. These exceptions should be logged by a Configuration Admin service.

104.6.3   Deletion

If a configuring bundle deletes an instance of a Managed Service Factory, the deleted(String) method is called. The argument is the PID for this instance. The implementation of the Managed Service Factory must remove all information and stop any behavior associated with that PID. If a service was registered for this PID, it should be unregistered.

Deletion will asynchronously send out a Configuration Event CM_DELETED to all registered Configuration Listener services.

104.6.4   Managed Service Factory Example

Figure 104.7 highlights the differences between a Managed Service and a Managed Service Factory. It shows how a Managed Service Factory implementation receives configuration information that was created before it was registered.

- A bundle implements an EMail Fetcher service. It registers a ManagedServiceFactory object with PID=com.acme.email.
- The Configuration Admin service notices the registration and consults its database. It finds three Configuration objects for which the factory PID is equal to com.acme.email. It must call updated(String,Dictionary) for each of these Configuration objects on the newly registered ManagedServiceFactory object.
- For each configuration dictionary received, the factory should create a new instance of a EMailFetcher object, one for erica (PID=16.1), one for anna (PID=16.3), and one for elmer (PID=16.2).
- The EMailFetcher objects are registered under the Topic interface so their results can be viewed by an online display.
  If the EMailFetcher object is registered, it may safely use the PID of the Configuration object because the Configuration Admin service must guarantee its suitability for this purpose.

Figure 104.7   *Managed Service Factory Example*

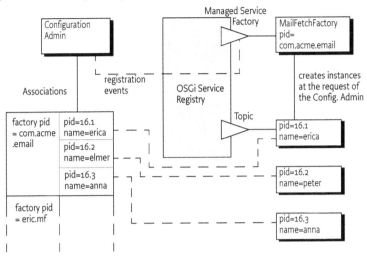

104.6.5   Multiple Consoles Example

This example illustrates how multiple consoles, each of which has its own port and interface can run simultaneously. This approach is very similar to the example for the Managed Service, but highlights the difference by allowing multiple consoles to be created.

```
class ExampleFactory implements ManagedServiceFactory {
    Hashtable consoles = new Hashtable();
    BundleContext context;
    public void start( BundleContext context )
        throws Exception {
        this.context = context;
        Hashtable local = new Hashtable();
        local.put(Constants.SERVICE_PID,"com.acme.console");
        context.registerService(
            ManagedServiceFactory.class.getName(),
            this,
            local );
    }

    public void updated( String pid, Dictionary config ){
        Console console = (Console) consoles.get(pid);
        if (console == null) {
            console = new Console(context);
            consoles.put(pid, console);
        }

        int port = getInt(config, "port", 2011);
        String network = getString(
            config,
            "network",
            null /*all*/
        );
        console.setPort(port, network);
    }
```

```
            public void deleted(String pid) {
              Console console = (Console) consoles.get(pid);
              if (console != null) {
                consoles.remove(pid);
                console.close();
              }
            }
          }
        }
```

104.7 Configuration Admin Service

The ConfigurationAdmin interface provides methods to maintain configuration data in an OSGi environment. This configuration information is defined by a number of Configuration objects associated with specific configuration targets. Configuration objects can be created, listed, modified, and deleted through this interface. Either a remote management system or the bundles configuring their own configuration information may perform these operations.

The ConfigurationAdmin interface has methods for creating and accessing Configuration objects for a Managed Service, as well as methods for managing new Configuration objects for a Managed Service Factory.

104.7.1 Creating a Managed Service Configuration Object

A bundle can create a new Managed Service Configuration object with ConfigurationAdmin.getConfiguration. No create method is offered because doing so could introduce race conditions between different bundles trying to create a Configuration object for the same Managed Service. The getConfiguration method must atomically create and persistently store an object if it does not yet exist.

Two variants of this method are:

- getConfiguration(String) – This method is used by a bundle with a given location to configure its *own* ManagedService objects. The argument specifies the PID of the targeted service.
- getConfiguration(String,String) – This method is used by a management bundle to configure *another* bundle. Therefore, this management bundle needs the right permission. The first argument is the PID and the second argument is the location identifier of the targeted ManagedService object.

All Configuration objects have a method, getFactoryPid(), which in this case must return null because the Configuration object is associated with a Managed Service.

Creating a new Configuration object must *not* initiate a callback to the Managed Service updated method.

104.7.2 Creating a Managed Service Factory Configuration Object

The ConfigurationAdmin class provides two methods to create a new instance of a Managed Service Factory:

- createFactoryConfiguration(String) – This method is used by a bundle with a given location to configure its own ManagedServiceFactory objects. The argument specifies the PID of the targeted ManagedServiceFactory object. This *factory PID* can be obtained from the returned Configuration object with the getFactoryPid() method.
- createFactoryConfiguration(String,String)– This method is used by a management bundle to configure another bundle's ManagedServiceFactory object. The first argument is the PID and the second is the location identifier of the targeted ManagedServiceFactory object. The *factory PID* can be obtained from the returned Configuration object with getFactoryPid method.

Creating a new factory configuration must *not* initiate a callback to the Managed Service Factory updated method until the properties are set in the Configuration object with the update method.

104.7.3 Accessing Existing Configurations

The existing set of Configuration objects can be listed with listConfigurations(String). The argument is a String object with a filter expression. This filter expression has the same syntax as the Framework Filter class. For example:

```
(&(size=42)(service.factoryPid=*osgi*))
```

The filter function must use the properties of the Configuration objects and only return the ones that match the filter expression.

A single Configuration object is identified with a PID and can be obtained with getConfiguration(String).

If the caller has the right permission, then all Configuration objects are eligible for search. In other cases, only Configuration objects bound to the calling bundle's location must be returned.

null is returned in both cases when an appropriate Configuration object cannot be found.

104.7.3.1 Updating a Configuration

The process of updating a Configuration object is the same for Managed Services and Managed Service Factories. First, listConfigurations(String) or getConfiguration(String) should be used to get a Configuration object. The properties can be obtained with Configuration.getProperties. When no update has occurred since this object was created, getProperties returns null.

New properties can be set by calling Configuration.update. The Configuration Admin service must first store the configuration information and then call a configuration target's updated method: either the ManagedService.updated or ManagedServiceFactory.updated method. If this target service is not registered, the fresh configuration information must be given to the target when the configuration target service registers.

The update method calls in Configuration objects are not executed synchronously with the related target service updated method. This method must be called asynchronously. The Configuration Admin service, however, must have updated the persistent storage before the update method returns.

The update method must also asynchronously send out a Configuration Event CM_UPDATED to all registered Configuration Listeners.

104.7.4 Deletion

A Configuration object that is no longer needed can be deleted with Configuration.delete, which removes the Configuration object from the database. The database must be updated before the target service updated method is called.

If the target service is a Managed Service Factory, the factory is informed of the deleted Configuration object by a call to ManagedServiceFactory.deleted. It should then remove the associated *instance*. The ManagedServiceFactory.deleted call must be done asynchronously with respect to Configuration.delete.

When a Configuration object of a Managed Service is deleted, ManagedService.updated is called with null for the properties argument. This method may be used for clean-up, to revert to default values, or to unregister a service.

The update method must also asynchronously send out a Configuration Event CM_DELETED to all registered Configuration Listeners.

104.7.5   Updating a Bundle's Own Configuration

The Configuration Admin service specification does not distinguish between updates via a Management Agent and a bundle updating its own configuration information (as defined by its location). Even if a bundle updates its own configuration information, the Configuration Admin service must callback the associated target service updated method.

As a rule, to update its own configuration, a bundle's user interface should *only* update the configuration information and never its internal structures directly. This rule has the advantage that the events, from the bundle implementation's perspective, appear similar for internal updates, remote management updates, and initialization.

104.8   Configuration Events

Configuration Admin can update interested parties of changes in its repository. The model is based on the white board pattern where a Configuration Listener service is registered with the service registry. The Configuration Listener service will receive ConfigurationEvent objects if important changes take place. The Configuration Admin service must call the ConfigurationListener. configuration-Event(ConfigurationEvent) method with such an event. This method should be called asynchronously, and on another thread, than the call that caused the event. Configuration Events must be delivered in order for each listener as they are generated. The way events must be delivered is the same as described in *Delivering Events* on page 116 of the Core specification.

The ConfigurationEvent object carries a factory PID (getFactoryPid()) and a PID (getPid()). If the factory PID is null, the event is related to a Managed Service Configuration object, else the event is related to a Managed Service Factory Configuration object.

The ConfigurationEvent object can deliver the following events from the getType() method:

- CM_DELETED – The Configuration object is deleted.
- CM_UPDATED – The Configuration object is updated.

The Configuration Event also carries the ServiceReference object of the Configuration Admin service that generated the event.

104.8.1   Event Admin Service and Configuration Change Events

Configuration events must delivered asynchronously by the Configuration Admin implementation, if present. The topic of a configuration event must be:

```
org/osgi/service/cm/ConfigurationEvent/<event type>
```

Event type can be any of the following:

```
CM_UPDATED
CM_DELETED
```

The properties of a configuration event are:

- cm.factoryPid – (String) The factory PID of the associated Configuration object, if the target is a Managed Service Factory. Otherwise not set.
- cm.pid – (String) The PID of the associated Configuration object.
- service – (ServiceReference) The Service Reference of the Configuration Admin service.
- service.id – (Long) The Configuration Admin service's ID.
- service.objectClass – (String[]) The Configuration Admin service's object class (which must include org.osgi.service.cm.ConfigurationAdmin)
- service.pid – (String) The Configuration Admin service's persistent identity

104.9   Configuration Plugin

The Configuration Admin service allows third-party applications to participate in the configuration process. Bundles that register a service object under a ConfigurationPlugin interface can process the configuration dictionary just before it reaches the configuration target service.

Plug-ins allow sufficiently privileged bundles to intercept configuration dictionaries just *before* they must be passed to the intended Managed Service or Managed Service Factory but *after* the properties are stored. The changes the plug-in makes are dynamic and must not be stored. The plug-in must only be called when an update takes place while it is registered and there is a valid dictionary. The plugin is not called when a configuration is deleted.

The ConfigurationPlugin interface has only one method: modifyConfiguration(ServiceReference, Dictionary). This method inspects or modifies configuration data.

All plug-ins in the service registry must be traversed and called before the properties are passed to the configuration target service. Each Configuration Plugin object gets a chance to inspect the existing data, look at the target object, which can be a ManagedService object or a ManagedServiceFactory object, and modify the properties of the configuration dictionary. The changes made by a plug-in must be visible to plugins that are called later.

ConfigurationPlugin objects should not modify properties that belong to the configuration properties of the target service unless the implications are understood. This functionality is mainly intended to provide functions that leverage the Framework service registry. The changes made by the plugin should normally not be validated. However, the Configuration Admin must ignore changes to the automatic properties as described in *Automatic Properties* on page 73.

For example, a Configuration Plugin service may add a physical location property to a service. This property can be leveraged by applications that want to know where a service is physically located. This scenario could be carried out without any further support of the service itself, except for the general requirement that the service should propagate the public properties it receives from the Configuration Admin service to the service registry.

Figure 104.8   *Order of Configuration Plugin Services*

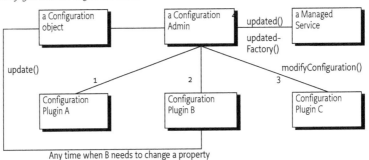

104.9.1   Limiting The Targets

A ConfigurationPlugin object may optionally specify a cm.target registration property. This value is the PID of the configuration target whose configuration updates the ConfigurationPlugin object wants to intercept.

The ConfigurationPlugin object must then only be called with updates for the configuration target service with the specified PID. For a factory target service, the factory PID is used and the plugin will see all instances of the factory. Omitting the cm.target registration property means that it is called for *all* configuration updates.

104.9.2   **Example of Property Expansion**

Consider a Managed Service that has a configuration property service.to with the value (objectclass=com.acme.Alarm). When the Configuration Admin service sets this property on the target service, a ConfigurationPlugin object may replace the (objectclass=com.acme.Alarm) filter with an array of existing alarm systems' PIDs as follows:

> ID "service. to=[32434,232,12421,1212]"

A new Alarm Service with service.pid=343 is registered, requiring that the list of the target service be updated. The bundle which registered the Configuration Plugin service, therefore, wants to set the to registration property on the target service. It does *not* do this by calling ManagedService.updated directly for several reasons:

- In a securely configured system, it should not have the permission to make this call or even obtain the target service.
- It could get into race conditions with the Configuration Admin service if it had the permissions in the previous bullet. Both services would compete for access simultaneously.

Instead, it must get the Configuration object from the Configuration Admin service and call the update method on it.

The Configuration Admin service must schedule a new update cycle on another thread, and some-time in the future must call ConfigurationPlugin.modifyProperties. The ConfigurationPlugin object could then set the service.to property to [32434,232,12421,1212, 343]. After that, the Configuration Admin service must call updated on the target service with the new service.to list.

104.9.3   **Configuration Data Modifications**

Modifications to the configuration dictionary are still under the control of the Configuration Admin service, which must determine whether to accept the changes, hide critical variables, or deny the changes for other reasons.

The ConfigurationPlugin interface must also allow plugins to detect configuration updates to the service via the callback. This ability allows them to synchronize the configuration updates with transient information.

104.9.4   **Forcing a Callback**

If a bundle needs to force a Configuration Plugin service to be called again, it must fetch the appropriate Configuration object from the Configuration Admin service and call the update() method (the no parameter version) on this object. This call forces an update with the current configuration dictionary so that all applicable plug-ins get called again.

104.9.5   **Calling Order**

The order in which the ConfigurationPlugin objects are called must depend on the service.cmRanking configuration property of the ConfigurationPlugin object. Table 104.2 shows the usage of the service.cmRanking property for the order of calling the Configuration Plugin services.

Table 104.2   service.cmRanking *Usage For Ordering*

service.cmRanking value	Description
< 0	The Configuration Plugin service should not modify properties and must be called before any modifications are made.

Table 104.2   service.cmRanking *Usage For Ordering*

service.cmRanking value	Description
>= 0 && <= 1000	The Configuration Plugin service modifies the configuration data. The calling order should be based on the value of the service.cmRanking property.
> 1000	The Configuration Plugin service should not modify data and is called after all modifications are made.

104.10 Remote Management

This specification does not attempt to define a remote management interface for the Framework. The purpose of this specification is to define a minimal interface for bundles that is complete enough for testing.

The Configuration Admin service is a primary aspect of remote management, however, and this specification must be compatible with common remote management standards. This section discusses some of the issues of using this specification with [1] *DMTF Common Information Model* (CIM) and [2] *Simple Network Management Protocol* (SNMP), the most likely candidates for remote management today.

These discussions are not complete, comprehensive, or normative. They are intended to point the bundle developer in relevant directions. Further specifications are needed to make a more concrete mapping.

104.10.1 Common Information Model

Common Information Model (CIM) defines the managed objects in [4] *Interface Definition Language* (IDL) language, which was developed for the Common Object Request Broker Architecture (CORBA).

The data types and the data values have a syntax. Additionally, these syntaxes can be mapped to XML. Unfortunately, this XML mapping is very different from the very applicable [3] *XSchema* XML data type definition language. The Framework service registry property types are a proper subset of the CIM data types.

In this specification, a Managed Service Factory maps to a CIM class definition. The primitives create, delete, and set are supported in this specification via the ManagedServiceFactory interface. The possible data types in CIM are richer than those the Framework supports and should thus be limited to cases when CIM classes for bundles are defined.

An important conceptual difference between this specification and CIM is the naming of properties. CIM properties are defined within the scope of a class. In this specification, properties are primarily defined within the scope of the Managed Service Factory, but are then placed in the registry, where they have global scope. This mechanism is similar to LDAP, see [5] *Understanding and Deploying LDAP Directory services*, in which the semantics of the properties are defined globally and a class is a collection of globally defined properties.

This specification does not address the non-Configuration Admin service primitives such as notifications and method calls.

104.10.2 Simple Network Management Protocol

The Simple Network Management Protocol (SNMP) defines the data model in ASN.1. SNMP is a rich data typing language that supports many types that are difficult to map to the data types supported in this specification. A large overlap exists, however, and it should be possible to design a data type that is applicable in this context.

The PID of a Managed Service should map to the SNMP Object IDentifier (OID). Managed Service Factories are mapped to tables in SNMP, although this mapping creates an obvious restriction in data types because tables can only contain scalar values. Therefore, the property values of the Configuration object would have to be limited to scalar values.

Similar scope issues as seen in CIM arise for SNMP because properties have a global scope in the service registry.

SNMP does not support the concept of method calls or function calls. All information is conveyed as the setting of values. The SNMP paradigm maps closely to this specification.

This specification does not address non-Configuration Admin primitives such as traps.

104.11 Meta Typing

This section discusses how the Metatype specification is used in the context of a Configuration Admin service.

When a Managed Service or Managed Service Factory is registered, the service object may also implement the MetaTypeProvider interface.

If the Managed Service or Managed Service Factory object implements the MetaTypeProvider interface, a management bundle may assume that the associated ObjectClassDefinition object can be used to configure the service.

The ObjectClassDefinition and AttributeDefinition objects contain sufficient information to automatically build simple user interfaces. They can also be used to augment dedicated interfaces with accurate validations.

When the Metatype specification is used, care should be taken to match the capabilities of the metatype package to the capabilities of the Configuration Admin service specification. Specifically:

- The metatype specification must describe nested arrays and vectors or arrays/vectors of mixed type.

This specification does not address how the metatype is made available to a management system due to the many open issues regarding remote management.

104.12 Security

104.12.1 Configuration Permission

The Configuration Permission provides a bundle with the authority to configure other bundles. All bundles implicitly have the permission to manage configurations that are bound to their own location.

The Configure Permission has only a single action and the target must always be ∗. The action is:

- CONFIGURE – This action grants a bundle the authority to manage configurations for any other bundle.

The ∗ wildcard for the actions parameter is supported.

104.12.2 Permissions Summary

Configuration Admin service security is implemented using Service Permission and Configuration Permission. The following table summarizes the permissions needed by the Configuration Admin bundle itself, as well as the typical permissions needed by the bundles with which it interacts.

Configuration Admin:

```
ServicePermission[ ..ConfigurationAdmin, REGISTER ]
ServicePermission[ ..ManagedService, GET ]
ServicePermission[ ..ManagedServiceFactory, GET ]
ServicePermission[ ..ConfigurationPlugin, GET ]
ConfigurationPermission[ *, CONFIGURE ]
AdminPermission[ *, METADATA ]
```

Managed Service:

```
ServicePermission[ ..ConfigurationAdmin, GET ]
ServicePermission[ ..ManagedService, REGISTER ]
```

Managed Service Factory:

```
ServicePermission[ ..ConfigurationAdmin, GET ]
ServicePermission[ ..ManagedServiceFactory, REGISTER ]
```

Configuration Plugin:

```
ServicePermission[ ..ConfigurationPlugin, REGISTER ]
```

Configuration Listener:

```
ServicePermission[ ..ConfigurationListener, REGISTER ]
```

The Configuration Admin service must have ServicePermission[ConfigurationAdmin, REGISTER]. It will also be the only bundle that needs the ServicePermission[ManagedService | ManagedServiceFactory |Configur ationPlugin, GET]. No other bundle should be allowed to have GET permission for these interfaces. The Configuration Admin bundle must also hold ConfigurationPermission[*,CONFIGURE].

Bundles that can be configured must have the ServicePermission[ManagedService | ManagedServiceFactory, REGISTER]. Bundles registering ConfigurationPlugin objects must have ServicePermission[ConfigurationPlugin, REGISTER]. The Configuration Admin service must trust all services registered with the ConfigurationPlugin interface. Only the Configuration Admin service should have ServicePermission[Configur ationPlugin, GET].

If a Managed Service or Managed Service Factory is implemented by an object that is also registered under another interface, it is possible, although inappropriate, for a bundle other than the Configuration Admin service implementation to call the updated method. Security-aware bundles can avoid this problem by having their updated methods check that the caller has ConfigurationPermission[*, CONFIGURE].

Bundles that want to change their own configuration need ServicePermission[ConfigurationAdmin, GET]. A bundle with ConfigurationPermission[*,CONFIGURE]is allowed to access and modify any Configuration object.

Pre-configuration of bundles requires ConfigurationPermission[*,CONFIGURE] because the methods that specify a location require this permission.

104.12.3 Forging PIDs

A risk exists of an unauthorized bundle forging a PID in order to obtain and possibly modify the configuration information of another bundle. To mitigate this risk, Configuration objects are generally *bound* to a specific bundle location, and are not passed to any Managed Service or Managed Service Factory registered by a different bundle.

Bundles with the required permission can create Configuration objects that are not bound. In other words, they have their location set to null. This can be useful for pre-configuring bundles before they are installed without having to know their actual locations.

In this scenario, the Configuration object must become bound to the first bundle that registers a Managed Service (or Managed Service Factory) with the right PID.

A bundle could still possibly obtain another bundle's configuration by registering a Managed Service with the right PID before the victim bundle does so. This situation can be regarded as a denial-of-service attack, because the victim bundle would never receive its configuration information. Such an attack can be avoided by always binding Configuration objects to the right locations. It can also be detected by the Configuration Admin service when the victim bundle registers the correct PID and two equal PIDs are then registered. This violation of this specification should be logged.

104.12.4   Configuration and Permission Administration

Configuration information has a direct influence on the permissions needed by a bundle. For example, when the Configuration Admin Bundle orders a bundle to use port 2011 for a console, that bundle also needs permission for listening to incoming connections on that port.

Both a simple and a complex solution exist for this situation.

The simple solution for this situation provides the bundle with a set of permissions that do not define specific values but allow a range of values. For example, a bundle could listen to ports above 1024 freely. All these ports could then be used for configuration.

The other solution is more complicated. In an environment where there is very strong security, the bundle would only be allowed access to a specific port. This situation requires an atomic update of both the configuration data and the permissions. If this update was not atomic, a potential security hole would exist during the period of time that the set of permissions did not match the configuration.

The following scenario can be used to update a configuration and the security permissions:

1   Stop the bundle.
2   Update the appropriate Configuration object via the Configuration Admin service.
3   Update the permissions in the Framework.
4   Start the bundle.

This scenario would achieve atomicity from the point of view of the bundle.

104.13   Configurable Service

Both the Configuration Admin service and the org.osgi.framework.Configurable interface address configuration management issues. It is the intention of this specification to replace the Framework interface for configuration management.

The Framework Configurable mechanism works as follows. A registered service object implements the Configurable interface to allow a management bundle to configure that service. The Configurable interface has only one method: getConfigurationObject(). This method returns a Java Bean. Beans can be examined and modified with the java.reflect or java.bean packages.

This scheme has the following disadvantages:

- *No factory* – Only registered services can be configured, unlike the Managed Service Factory that configures any number of services.
- *Atomicity* – The beans or reflection API can only modify one property at a time and there is no way to tell the bean that no more modifications to the properties will follow. This limitation complicates updates of configurations that have dependencies between properties.
  This specification passes a Dictionary object that sets all the configuration properties atomically.
- *Profile* – The Java beans API is linked to many packages that are not likely to be present in OSGi environments. The reflection API may be present but is not simple to use.
  This specification has no required libraries.
- *User Interface support* – UI support in beans is very rudimentary when no AWT is present.
  The associated Metatyping specification does not require any external libraries, and has extensive support for UIs including localization.

104.14   Changes

- Removed the sending of a CM_UPDATED event for the creation of a Configuration object and for the updating of a target.
- Introduced public and private properties for propagation. See *Property Propagation* on page 73.
- Made the use of the factory pid for cm.target Configuration Plugin service explicit. See *Limiting The Targets* on page 84.
- Clarified that the plugins do not receive a callback for configuration deletions.
- It is allowed to register a service with multiple PIDs

104.15   org.osgi.service.cm

Configuration Admin Package Version 1.3.

Bundles wishing to use this package must list the package in the Import-Package header of the bundle's manifest. For example:

```
Import-Package: org.osgi.service.cm; version="[1.3,2.0)"
```

104.15.1   Summary

- *Configuration* - The configuration information for a ManagedService or ManagedServiceFactory object.
- *ConfigurationAdmin* - Service for administering configuration data.
- *ConfigurationEvent* - A Configuration Event.
- *ConfigurationException* - An Exception class to inform the Configuration Admin service of problems with configuration data.
- *ConfigurationListener* - Listener for Configuration Events.
- *ConfigurationPermission* - Indicates a bundle's authority to configure bundles.
- *ConfigurationPlugin* - A service interface for processing configuration dictionary before the update.
- *ManagedService* - A service that can receive configuration data from a Configuration Admin service.
- *ManagedServiceFactory* - Manage multiple service instances.

104.15.2   public interface Configuration

The configuration information for a ManagedService or ManagedServiceFactory object. The Configuration Admin service uses this interface to represent the configuration information for a ManagedService or for a service instance of a ManagedServiceFactory.

A Configuration object contains a configuration dictionary and allows the properties to be updated via this object. Bundles wishing to receive configuration dictionaries do not need to use this class - they register a ManagedService or ManagedServiceFactory. Only administrative bundles, and bundles wishing to update their own configurations need to use this class.

The properties handled in this configuration have case insensitive String objects as keys. However, case is preserved from the last set key/value.

A configuration can be *bound* to a bundle location (Bundle.getLocation()). The purpose of binding a Configuration object to a location is to make it impossible for another bundle to forge a PID that would match this configuration. When a configuration is bound to a specific location, and a bundle with a different location registers a corresponding ManagedService object or ManagedServiceFactory object, then the configuration is not passed to the updated method of that object.

If a configuration's location is null, it is not yet bound to a location. It will become bound to the location of the first bundle that registers a ManagedService or ManagedServiceFactory object with the corresponding PID.

The same Configuration object is used for configuring both a Managed Service Factory and a Managed Service. When it is important to differentiate between these two the term "factory configuration" is used.

104.15.2.1   **public void delete( ) throws IOException**

□ Delete this Configuration object. Removes this configuration object from the persistent store. Notify asynchronously the corresponding Managed Service or Managed Service Factory. A ManagedService object is notified by a call to its updated method with a null properties argument. A ManagedServiceFactory object is notified by a call to its deleted method.

Also initiates an asynchronous call to all ConfigurationListeners with a ConfigurationEvent.CM_DELETED event.

Throws   IOException – If delete fails

IllegalStateException – if this configuration has been deleted

104.15.2.2   **public boolean equals(Object other)**

other   Configuration object to compare against

□ Equality is defined to have equal PIDs Two Configuration objects are equal when their PIDs are equal.

Returns   true if equal, false if not a Configuration object or one with a different PID.

104.15.2.3   **public String getBundleLocation( )**

□ Get the bundle location. Returns the bundle location to which this configuration is bound, or null if it is not yet bound to a bundle location.

Returns   location to which this configuration is bound, or null.

Throws   IllegalStateException – If this Configuration object has been deleted.

SecurityException – If the caller does not have ConfigurationPermission[*,CONFIGURE].

104.15.2.4   **public String getFactoryPid( )**

□ For a factory configuration return the PID of the corresponding Managed Service Factory, else return null.

Returns   factory PID or null

Throws   IllegalStateException – if this configuration has been deleted

104.15.2.5   **public String getPid( )**

□ Get the PID for this Configuration object.

Returns   the PID for this Configuration object.

Throws   IllegalStateException – if this configuration has been deleted

104.15.2.6   **public Dictionary getProperties( )**

□ Return the properties of this Configuration object. The Dictionary object returned is a private copy for the caller and may be changed without influencing the stored configuration. The keys in the returned dictionary are case insensitive and are always of type String.

If called just after the configuration is created and before update has been called, this method returns null.

Returns   A private copy of the properties for the caller or null. These properties must not contain the "service.bundleLocation" property. The value of this property may be obtained from the getBundleLocation method.

Throws   IllegalStateException – if this configuration has been deleted

104.15.2.7   **public int hashCode( )**

□ Hash code is based on PID. The hashcode for two Configuration objects must be the same when the Configuration PID's are the same.

Returns hash code for this Configuration object

104.15.2.8   **public void setBundleLocation(String bundleLocation)**

bundleLocation a bundle location or null

□ Bind this Configuration object to the specified bundle location. If the bundleLocation parameter is null then the Configuration object will not be bound to a location. It will be set to the bundle's location before the first time a Managed Service/Managed Service Factory receives this Configuration object via the updated method and before any plugins are called. The bundle location will be set persistently.

Throws IllegalStateException – If this configuration has been deleted.

SecurityException – If the caller does not have ConfigurationPermission[*,CONFIGURE].

104.15.2.9   **public void update(Dictionary properties) throws IOException**

properties the new set of properties for this configuration

□ Update the properties of this Configuration object. Stores the properties in persistent storage after adding or overwriting the following properties:

• "service.pid" : is set to be the PID of this configuration.
• "service.factoryPid" : if this is a factory configuration it is set to the factory PID else it is not set.

These system properties are all of type String.

If the corresponding Managed Service/Managed Service Factory is registered, its updated method must be called asynchronously. Else, this callback is delayed until aforementioned registration occurs.

Also initiates an asynchronous call to all ConfigurationListeners with a ConfigurationEvent.CM_UPDATED event.

Throws IOException – if update cannot be made persistent

IllegalArgumentException – if the Dictionary object contains invalid configuration types or contains case variants of the same key name.

IllegalStateException – if this configuration has been deleted

104.15.2.10   **public void update( ) throws IOException**

□ Update the Configuration object with the current properties. Initiate the updated callback to the Managed Service or Managed Service Factory with the current properties asynchronously.

This is the only way for a bundle that uses a Configuration Plugin service to initiate a callback. For example, when that bundle detects a change that requires an update of the Managed Service or Managed Service Factory via its ConfigurationPlugin object.

Throws IOException – if update cannot access the properties in persistent storage

IllegalStateException – if this configuration has been deleted

See Also ConfigurationPlugin

104.15.3   public interface ConfigurationAdmin

Service for administering configuration data.

The main purpose of this interface is to store bundle configuration data persistently. This information is represented in Configuration objects. The actual configuration data is a Dictionary of properties inside a Configuration object.

There are two principally different ways to manage configurations. First there is the concept of a Managed Service, where configuration data is uniquely associated with an object registered with the service registry.

Next, there is the concept of a factory where the Configuration Admin service will maintain 0 or more Configuration objects for a Managed Service Factory that is registered with the Framework.

The first concept is intended for configuration data about "things/services" whose existence is defined externally, e.g. a specific printer. Factories are intended for "things/services" that can be created any number of times, e.g. a configuration for a DHCP server for different networks.

Bundles that require configuration should register a Managed Service or a Managed Service Factory in the service registry. A registration property named service.pid (persistent identifier or PID) must be used to identify this Managed Service or Managed Service Factory to the Configuration Admin service.

When the ConfigurationAdmin detects the registration of a Managed Service, it checks its persistent storage for a configuration object whose service.pid property matches the PID service property (service.pid) of the Managed Service. If found, it calls ManagedService.updated method with the new properties. The implementation of a Configuration Admin service must run these call-backs asynchronously to allow proper synchronization.

When the Configuration Admin service detects a Managed Service Factory registration, it checks its storage for configuration objects whose service.factoryPid property matches the PID service property of the Managed Service Factory. For each such Configuration objects, it calls the ManagedServiceFactory.updated method asynchronously with the new properties. The calls to the updated method of a ManagedServiceFactory must be executed sequentially and not overlap in time.

In general, bundles having permission to use the Configuration Admin service can only access and modify their own configuration information. Accessing or modifying the configuration of another bundle requires ConfigurationPermission[*,CONFIGURE].

Configuration objects can be *bound* to a specified bundle location. In this case, if a matching Managed Service or Managed Service Factory is registered by a bundle with a different location, then the Configuration Admin service must not do the normal callback, and it should log an error. In the case where a Configuration object is not bound, its location field is null, the Configuration Admin service will bind it to the location of the bundle that registers the first Managed Service or Managed Service Factory that has a corresponding PID property. When a Configuration object is bound to a bundle location in this manner, the Configuration Admin service must detect if the bundle corresponding to the location is uninstalled. If this occurs, the Configuration object is unbound, that is its location field is set back to null.

The method descriptions of this class refer to a concept of "the calling bundle". This is a loose way of referring to the bundle which obtained the Configuration Admin service from the service registry. Implementations of ConfigurationAdmin must use a org.osgi.framework.ServiceFactory to support this concept.

104.15.3.1 **public static final String SERVICE_BUNDLELOCATION = "service.bundleLocation"**

Configuration property naming the location of the bundle that is associated with a a Configuration object. This property can be searched for but must not appear in the configuration dictionary for security reason. The property's value is of type String.

Since 1.1

104.15.3.2   **public static final String SERVICE_FACTORYPID = "service.factoryPid"**

Configuration property naming the Factory PID in the configuration dictionary. The property's value is of type String.

Since 1.1

104.15.3.3   **public Configuration createFactoryConfiguration(String factoryPid) throws IOException**

factoryPid PID of factory (not null).

□ Create a new factory Configuration object with a new PID. The properties of the new Configuration object are null until the first time that its Configuration.update(Dictionary) method is called.

It is not required that the factoryPid maps to a registered Managed Service Factory.

The Configuration object is bound to the location of the calling bundle.

Returns A new Configuration object.

Throws IOException – if access to persistent storage fails.

SecurityException – if caller does not have ConfigurationPermission[*,CONFIGURE] and factoryPid is bound to another bundle.

104.15.3.4   **public Configuration createFactoryConfiguration(String factoryPid, String location) throws IOException**

factoryPid PID of factory (not null).

location A bundle location string, or null.

□ Create a new factory Configuration object with a new PID. The properties of the new Configuration object are null until the first time that its Configuration.update(Dictionary) method is called.

It is not required that the factoryPid maps to a registered Managed Service Factory.

The Configuration is bound to the location specified. If this location is null it will be bound to the location of the first bundle that registers a Managed Service Factory with a corresponding PID.

Returns a new Configuration object.

Throws IOException – if access to persistent storage fails.

SecurityException – if caller does not have ConfigurationPermission[*,CONFIGURE].

104.15.3.5   **public Configuration getConfiguration(String pid, String location) throws IOException**

pid Persistent identifier.

location The bundle location string, or null.

□ Get an existing Configuration object from the persistent store, or create a new Configuration object.

If a Configuration with this PID already exists in Configuration Admin service return it. The location parameter is ignored in this case.

Else, return a new Configuration object. This new object is bound to the location and the properties are set to null. If the location parameter is null, it will be set when a Managed Service with the corresponding PID is registered for the first time.

Returns An existing or new Configuration object.

Throws IOException – if access to persistent storage fails.

SecurityException – if the caller does not have ConfigurationPermission[*,CONFIGURE].

104.15.3.6   **public Configuration getConfiguration(String pid) throws IOException**

pid persistent identifier.

☐ Get an existing or new Configuration object from the persistent store. If the Configuration object for this PID does not exist, create a new Configuration object for that PID, where properties are null. Bind its location to the calling bundle's location.

Otherwise, if the location of the existing Configuration object is null, set it to the calling bundle's location.

Returns an existing or new Configuration matching the PID.

Throws IOException – if access to persistent storage fails.

SecurityException – if the Configuration object is bound to a location different from that of the calling bundle and it has no ConfigurationPermission[*,CONFIGURE].

104.15.3.7   **public Configuration[] listConfigurations(String filter) throws IOException, InvalidSyntaxException**

filter A filter string, or null to retrieve all Configuration objects.

☐ List the current Configuration objects which match the filter.

Only Configuration objects with non-null properties are considered current. That is, Configuration.getProperties() is guaranteed not to return null for each of the returned Configuration objects.

Normally only Configuration objects that are bound to the location of the calling bundle are returned, or all if the caller has ConfigurationPermission[*,CONFIGURE].

The syntax of the filter string is as defined in the org.osgi.framework.Filter class. The filter can test any configuration properties including the following:

- service.pid-String- the PID under which this is registered
- service.factoryPid-String- the factory if applicable
- service.bundleLocation-String- the bundle location

The filter can also be null, meaning that all Configuration objects should be returned.

Returns All matching Configuration objects, or null if there aren't any.

Throws IOException – if access to persistent storage fails

InvalidSyntaxException – if the filter string is invalid

104.15.4   **public class ConfigurationEvent**

A Configuration Event.

ConfigurationEvent objects are delivered to all registered ConfigurationListener service objects. ConfigurationEvents must be asynchronously delivered in chronological order with respect to each listener.

A type code is used to identify the type of event. The following event types are defined:

- CM_UPDATED
- CM_DELETED

Security Considerations. ConfigurationEvent objects do not provide Configuration objects, so no sensitive configuration information is available from the event. If the listener wants to locate the Configuration object for the specified pid, it must use ConfigurationAdmin.

See Also ConfigurationListener

Since 1.2

104.15.4.1   **public static final int CM_DELETED = 2**

A Configuration has been deleted.

This ConfigurationEvent type that indicates that a Configuration object has been deleted. An event is fired when a call to Configuration.delete() successfully deletes a configuration.

The value of CM_DELETED is 2.

104.15.4.2   **public static final int CM_UPDATED = 1**

A Configuration has been updated.

This ConfigurationEvent type that indicates that a Configuration object has been updated with new properties. An event is fired when a call to Configuration.update(Dictionary) successfully changes a configuration.

The value of CM_UPDATED is 1.

104.15.4.3   **public ConfigurationEvent(ServiceReference reference, int type, String factoryPid, String pid)**

reference   The ServiceReference object of the Configuration Admin service that created this event.

type   The event type. See getType.

factoryPid   The factory pid of the associated configuration if the target of the configuration is a ManagedService-Factory. Otherwise null if the target of the configuration is a ManagedService.

pid   The pid of the associated configuration.

☐   Constructs a ConfigurationEvent object from the given ServiceReference object, event type, and pids.

104.15.4.4   **public String getFactoryPid( )**

☐   Returns the factory pid of the associated configuration.

Returns   Returns the factory pid of the associated configuration if the target of the configuration is a Managed-ServiceFactory. Otherwise null if the target of the configuration is a ManagedService.

104.15.4.5   **public String getPid( )**

☐   Returns the pid of the associated configuration.

Returns   Returns the pid of the associated configuration.

104.15.4.6   **public ServiceReference getReference( )**

☐   Return the ServiceReference object of the Configuration Admin service that created this event.

Returns   The ServiceReference object for the Configuration Admin service that created this event.

104.15.4.7   **public int getType( )**

☐   Return the type of this event.

The type values are:

· CM_UPDATED
· CM_DELETED

Returns   The type of this event.

104.15.5   public class ConfigurationException
extends Exception

An Exception class to inform the Configuration Admin service of problems with configuration data.

104.15.5.1   **public ConfigurationException(String property, String reason)**

property   name of the property that caused the problem, null if no specific property was the cause *reason*   reason for failure

☐ Create a ConfigurationException object.

104.15.5.2   **public ConfigurationException(String property, String reason, Throwable cause)**

property   name of the property that caused the problem, null if no specific property was the cause

reason   reason for failure

cause   The cause of this exception.

☐ Create a ConfigurationException object.

Since   1.2

104.15.5.3   **public Throwable getCause( )**

☐ Returns the cause of this exception or null if no cause was set.

Returns   The cause of this exception or null if no cause was set.

Since   1.2

104.15.5.4   **public String getProperty( )**

☐ Return the property name that caused the failure or null.

Returns   name of property or null if no specific property caused the problem

104.15.5.5   **public String getReason( )**

☐ Return the reason for this exception.

Returns   reason of the failure

104.15.5.6   **public Throwable initCause(Throwable cause)**

cause   The cause of this exception.

☐ Initializes the cause of this exception to the specified value.

Returns   This exception.

Throws   IllegalArgumentException – If the specified cause is this exception.

IllegalStateException – If the cause of this exception has already been set.

Since   1.2

104.15.6   **public interface ConfigurationListener**

Listener for Configuration Events. When a ConfigurationEvent is fired, it is asynchronously delivered to a ConfigurationListener.

ConfigurationListener objects are registered with the Framework service registry and are notified with a ConfigurationEvent object when an event is fired.

ConfigurationListener objects can inspect the received ConfigurationEvent object to determine its type, the pid of the Configuration object with which it is associated, and the Configuration Admin service that fired the event.

Security Considerations. Bundles wishing to monitor configuration events will require ServicePermission[ConfigurationListener,REGISTER] to register a ConfigurationListener service.

Since   1.2

104.15.6.1   **public void configurationEvent(ConfigurationEvent event)**

event   The ConfigurationEvent.

☐ Receives notification of a Configuration that has changed.

104.15.7 public final class ConfigurationPermission extends BasicPermission

Indicates a bundle's authority to configure bundles. This permission has only a single action: CONFIGURE.

Since 1.2

Concurrency Thread-safe

104.15.7.1 public static final String CONFIGURE = "configure"

The action string configure.

104.15.7.2 public ConfigurationPermission(String name, String actions)

name Name must be "*".

actions configure (canonical order).

☐ Create a new ConfigurationPermission.

104.15.7.3 public boolean equals(Object obj)

obj The object being compared for equality with this object.

☐ Determines the equality of two ConfigurationPermission objects.

Two ConfigurationPermission objects are equal.

Returns true if obj is equivalent to this ConfigurationPermission; false otherwise.

104.15.7.4 public String getActions( )

☐ Returns the canonical string representation of the ConfigurationPermission actions.

Always returns present ConfigurationPermission actions in the following order: CONFIGURE

Returns Canonical string representation of the ConfigurationPermission actions.

104.15.7.5 public int hashCode( )

☐ Returns the hash code value for this object.

Returns Hash code value for this object.

104.15.7.6 public boolean implies(Permission p)

p The target permission to check.

☐ Determines if a ConfigurationPermission object "implies" the specified permission.

Returns true if the specified permission is implied by this object; false otherwise.

104.15.7.7 public PermissionCollection newPermissionCollection( )

☐ Returns a new PermissionCollection object suitable for storing ConfigurationPermissions.

Returns A new PermissionCollection object.

104.15.8 public interface ConfigurationPlugin

A service interface for processing configuration dictionary before the update.

A bundle registers a ConfigurationPlugin object in order to process configuration updates before they reach the Managed Service or Managed Service Factory. The Configuration Admin service will detect registrations of Configuration Plugin services and must call these services every time before it calls the ManagedService or ManagedServiceFactoryupdated method. The Configuration Plugin service thus has the opportunity to view and modify the properties before they are passed to the Managed Service or Managed Service Factory.

Configuration Plugin (plugin) services have full read/write access to all configuration information. Therefore, bundles using this facility should be trusted. Access to this facility should be limited with ServicePermission[ConfigurationPlugin,REGISTER]. Implementations of a Configuration Plugin service should assure that they only act on appropriate configurations.

The Integerservice.cmRanking registration property may be specified. Not specifying this registration property, or setting it to something other than an Integer, is the same as setting it to the Integer zero. The service.cmRanking property determines the order in which plugins are invoked. Lower ranked plugins are called before higher ranked ones. In the event of more than one plugin having the same value of service.cmRanking, then the Configuration Admin service arbitrarily chooses the order in which they are called.

By convention, plugins with service.cmRanking< 0 or service.cmRanking > 1000 should not make modifications to the properties.

The Configuration Admin service has the right to hide properties from plugins, or to ignore some or all the changes that they make. This might be done for security reasons. Any such behavior is entirely implementation defined.

A plugin may optionally specify a cm.target registration property whose value is the PID of the Managed Service or Managed Service Factory whose configuration updates the plugin is intended to intercept. The plugin will then only be called with configuration updates that are targeted at the Managed Service or Managed Service Factory with the specified PID. Omitting the cm.target registration property means that the plugin is called for all configuration updates.

104.15.8.1   **public static final String CM_RANKING = "service.cmRanking"**

A service property to specify the order in which plugins are invoked. This property contains an Integer ranking of the plugin. Not specifying this registration property, or setting it to something other than an Integer, is the same as setting it to the Integer zero. This property determines the order in which plugins are invoked. Lower ranked plugins are called before higher ranked ones.

Since 1.2

104.15.8.2   **public static final String CM_TARGET = "cm.target"**

A service property to limit the Managed Service or Managed Service Factory configuration dictionaries a Configuration Plugin service receives. This property contains a String[] of PIDs. A Configuration Admin service must call a Configuration Plugin service only when this property is not set, or the target service's PID is listed in this property.

104.15.8.3   **public void modifyConfiguration(ServiceReference reference, Dictionary properties)**

reference reference to the Managed Service or Managed Service Factory

properties The configuration properties. This argument must not contain the "service.bundleLocation" property. The value of this property may be obtained from the Configuration.getBundleLocation method.

☐ View and possibly modify the a set of configuration properties before they are sent to the Managed Service or the Managed Service Factory. The Configuration Plugin services are called in increasing order of their service.cmRanking property. If this property is undefined or is a non-Integer type, 0 is used.

This method should not modify the properties unless the service.cmRanking of this plugin is in the range 0 <= service.cmRanking <= 1000.

If this method throws any Exception, the Configuration Admin service must catch it and should log it.

104.15.9 public interface ManagedService

A service that can receive configuration data from a Configuration Admin service.

A Managed Service is a service that needs configuration data. Such an object should be registered with the Framework registry with the service.pid property set to some unique identifier called a PID.

If the Configuration Admin service has a Configuration object corresponding to this PID, it will callback the updated() method of the ManagedService object, passing the properties of that Configuration object.

If it has no such Configuration object, then it calls back with a null properties argument. Registering a Managed Service will always result in a callback to the updated() method provided the Configuration Admin service is, or becomes active. This callback must always be done asynchronously.

Else, every time that either of the updated() methods is called on that Configuration object, the ManagedService.updated() method with the new properties is called. If the delete() method is called on that Configuration object, ManagedService.updated() is called with a null for the properties parameter. All these callbacks must be done asynchronously.

The following example shows the code of a serial port that will create a port depending on configuration information.

```
class SerialPort implements ManagedService {

    ServiceRegistration registration;
    Hashtable configuration;
    CommPortIdentifier id;

    synchronized void open(CommPortIdentifier id,
    BundleContext context) {
      this.id = id;
      registration = context.registerService(
        ManagedService.class.getName(),
        this,
        getDefaults()
      );
    }

    Hashtable getDefaults() {
      Hashtable defaults = new Hashtable();
      defaults.put( "port", id.getName() );
      defaults.put( "product", "unknown" );
      defaults.put( "baud", "9600" );
      defaults.put( Constants.SERVICE_PID,
        "com.acme.serialport." + id.getName() );
      return defaults;
    }

    public synchronized void updated(
      Dictionary configuration  ) {
      if ( configuration ==
null
  )
```

```
      registration.setProperties( getDefaults() );
    else {
      setSpeed( configuration.get("baud") );
      registration.setProperties( configuration );
    }
  }
  ...
}
```

As a convention, it is recommended that when a Managed Service is updated, it should copy all the properties it does not recognize into the service registration properties. This will allow the Configuration Admin service to set properties on services which can then be used by other applications.

104.15.9.1   **public void updated(Dictionary properties) throws ConfigurationException**

properties   A copy of the Configuration properties, or null. This argument must not contain the "service.bundle-Location" property. The value of this property may be obtained from the Configuration.getBundleLocation method.

☐   Update the configuration for a Managed Service.

When the implementation of updated(Dictionary) detects any kind of error in the configuration properties, it should create a new ConfigurationException which describes the problem. This can allow a management system to provide useful information to a human administrator.

If this method throws any other Exception, the Configuration Admin service must catch it and should log it.

The Configuration Admin service must call this method asynchronously which initiated the callback. This implies that implementors of Managed Service can be assured that the callback will not take place during registration when they execute the registration in a synchronized method.

Throws   ConfigurationException – when the update fails

104.15.10   public interface ManagedServiceFactory

Manage multiple service instances. Bundles registering this interface are giving the Configuration Admin service the ability to create and configure a number of instances of a service that the implementing bundle can provide. For example, a bundle implementing a DHCP server could be instantiated multiple times for different interfaces using a factory.

Each of these *service instances* is represented, in the persistent storage of the Configuration Admin service, by a factory Configuration object that has a PID. When such a Configuration is updated, the Configuration Admin service calls the ManagedServiceFactory updated method with the new properties. When updated is called with a new PID, the Managed Service Factory should create a new factory instance based on these configuration properties. When called with a PID that it has seen before, it should update that existing service instance with the new configuration information.

In general it is expected that the implementation of this interface will maintain a data structure that maps PIDs to the factory instances that it has created. The semantics of a factory instance are defined by the Managed Service Factory. However, if the factory instance is registered as a service object with the service registry, its PID should match the PID of the corresponding Configuration object (but it should **not** be registered as a Managed Service!).

An example that demonstrates the use of a factory. It will create serial ports under command of the Configuration Admin service.

```
class SerialPortFactory
  implements ManagedServiceFactory {
  ServiceRegistration registration;
```

```
                    Hashtable ports;
                    void start(BundleContext context) {
                      Hashtable properties = new Hashtable();
                      properties.put( Constants.SERVICE_PID,
                        "com.acme.serialportfactory" );
                      registration = context.registerService(
                        ManagedServiceFactory.class.getName(),
                        this,
                        properties
                      );
                    }
                    public void updated( String pid,
                      Dictionary properties ) {
                      String portName = (String) properties.get("port");
                      SerialPortService port =
                        (SerialPort) ports.get( pid );
                      if ( port == null ) {
                        port = new SerialPortService();
                        ports.put( pid, port );
                        port.open();
                      }
                      if ( port.getPortName().equals(portName) )
                        return;
                      port.setPortName( portName );
                    }
                    public void deleted( String pid ) {
                      SerialPortService port =
                        (SerialPort) ports.get( pid );
                      port.close();
                      ports.remove( pid );
                    }
                    ...
                  }
```

104.15.10.1   public void deleted(String pid)

pid the PID of the service to be removed

☐ Remove a factory instance. Remove the factory instance associated with the PID. If the instance was registered with the service registry, it should be unregistered.

If this method throws any Exception, the Configuration Admin service must catch it and should log it.

The Configuration Admin service must call this method asynchronously.

104.15.10.2   public String getName( )

☐ Return a descriptive name of this factory.

Returns the name for the factory, which might be localized

104.15.10.3   public void updated(String pid, Dictionary properties) throws ConfigurationException

pid The PID for this configuration.

properties A copy of the configuration properties. This argument must not contain the service.bundleLocation" property. The value of this property may be obtained from the Configuration.getBundleLocation method.

□ Create a new instance, or update the configuration of an existing instance. If the PID of the Configuration object is new for the Managed Service Factory, then create a new factory instance, using the configuration properties provided. Else, update the service instance with the provided properties.

If the factory instance is registered with the Framework, then the configuration properties should be copied to its registry properties. This is not mandatory and security sensitive properties should obviously not be copied.

If this method throws any Exception, the Configuration Admin service must catch it and should log it.

When the implementation of updated detects any kind of error in the configuration properties, it should create a new ConfigurationException which describes the problem.

The Configuration Admin service must call this method asynchronously. This implies that implementors of the ManagedServiceFactory class can be assured that the callback will not take place during registration when they execute the registration in a synchronized method.

Throws ConfigurationException – when the configuration properties are invalid.

104.16   References

[1] *DMTF Common Information Model*
     http://www.dmtf.org

[2] *Simple Network Management Protocol*
     RFCs http://directory.google.com/Top/Computers/Internet/Protocols/SNMP/RFCs

[3] *XSchema*
     http://www.w3.org/TR/xmlschema-0/

[4] *Interface Definition Language*
     http://www.omg.org

[5] *Understanding and Deploying LDAP Directory services*
     Timothy Howes et. al. ISBN 1-57870-070-1, MacMillan Technical publishing.

105   Metatype Service Specification

Version 1.1

105.1   Introduction

The Metatype specification defines interfaces that allow bundle developers to describe attribute types in a computer readable form using so-called *metadata*.

The purpose of this specification is to allow services to specify the type information of data that they can use as arguments. The data is based on *attributes*, which are key/value pairs like properties.

A designer in a type-safe language like Java is often confronted with the choice of using the language constructs to exchange data or using a technique based on attributes/properties that are based on key/value pairs. Attributes provide an escape from the rigid type-safety requirements of modern programming languages.

Type-safety works very well for software development environments in which multiple programmers work together on large applications or systems, but often lacks the flexibility needed to receive structured data from the outside world.

The attribute paradigm has several characteristics that make this approach suitable when data needs to be communicated between different entities which "speak" different languages. Attributes are uncomplicated, resilient to change, and allow the receiver to dynamically adapt to different types of data.

As an example, the OSGi Service Platform Specifications define several attribute types which are used in a Framework implementation, but which are also used and referenced by other OSGi specifications such as the *Configuration Admin Service Specification* on page 67. A Configuration Admin service implementation deploys attributes (key/value pairs) as configuration properties.

The Meta Type Service provides a unified access point to the Meta Type information that is associated with bundles. This Meta Type information can be defined by an XML resource in a bundle (OSGI-INF/metatype directories must be scanned for any XML resources), or it can be obtained from Managed Service or Managed Service Factory services that are implemented by a bundle.

105.1.1   Essentials

- *Conceptual model* – The specification must have a conceptual model for how classes and attributes are organized.
- *Standards* – The specification should be aligned with appropriate standards, and explained in situations where the specification is not aligned with, or cannot be mapped to, standards.
- *Remote Management* – Remote management should be taken into account.
- *Size* – Minimal overhead in size for a bundle using this specification is required.
- *Localization* – It must be possible to use this specification with different languages at the same time. This ability allows servlets to serve information in the language selected in the browser.
- *Type information* – The definition of an attribution should contain the name (if it is required), the cardinality, a label, a description, labels for enumerated values, and the Java class that should be used for the values.
- *Validation* – It should be possible to validate the values of the attributes.

105.1.2   Entities

- *Meta Type Service* – A service that provides a unified access point for meta type information.
- *Attribute* – A key/value pair.

- *PID* – A unique persistent ID, defined in configuration management.
- *Attribute Definition* – Defines a description, name, help text, and type information of an attribute.
- *Object Class Definition* – Defines the type of a datum. It contains a description and name of the type plus a set of AttributeDefinition objects.
- *Meta Type Provider* – Provides access to the object classes that are available for this object. Access uses the PID and a locale to find the best ObjectClassDefinition object.
- *Meta Type Information* – Provides meta type information for a bundle.

Figure 105.1   Class Diagram Meta Type Service, org.osgi.service.metatype

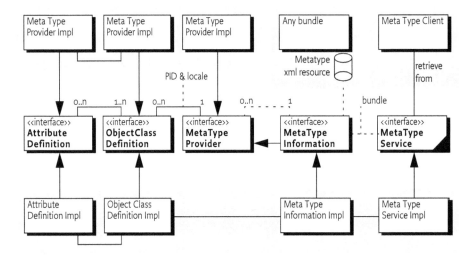

105.1.3   Operation

The Meta Type service defines a rich dynamic typing system for properties. The purpose of the type system is to allow reasonable User Interfaces to be constructed dynamically.

The type information is normally carried by the bundles themselves. Either by implementing the MetaTypeProvider interface or by carrying one or more XML resources in that define a number of Meta Types in the OSGI-INF/metatype directories. Additionally, a Meta Type service could have other sources.

The Meta Type Service provides unified access to Meta Types that are carried by the resident bundles. The Meta Type Service collects this information from the bundles and provides uniform access to it. A client can requests the Meta Type Information associated with a particular bundle. The MetaTypeInformation object provides a list of ObjectClassDefinition objects for a bundle. These objects define all the information for a specific *object class*. An object class is a some descriptive information and a set of named attributes (which are key/value pairs).

Access to Object Class Definitions is qualified by a locale and a Persistent IDentity (PID). This specification does not specify what the PID means. One application is OSGi Configuration Management where a PID is used by the Managed Service and Managed Service Factory services. In general, a PID should be regarded as the name of a variable where an Object Class Definition defines its type.

105.2   Attributes Model

The Framework uses the LDAP filter syntax for searching the Framework registry. The usage of the attributes in this specification and the Framework specification closely resemble the LDAP attribute model. Therefore, the names used in this specification have been aligned with LDAP. Consequently, the interfaces which are defined by this Specification are:

- AttributeDefinition
- ObjectClassDefinition
- MetaTypeProvider

These names correspond to the LDAP attribute model. For further information on ASN.1-defined attributes and X.500 object classes and attributes, see [2] *Understanding and Deploying LDAP Directory services.*

The LDAP attribute model assumes a global name-space for attributes, and object classes consist of a number of attributes. So, if an object class inherits the same attribute from different parents, only one copy of the attribute must become part of the object class definition. This name-space implies that a given attribute, for example cn, should *always* be the common name and the type must always be a String. An attribute cn cannot be an Integer in another object class definition. In this respect, the OSGi approach towards attribute definitions is comparable with the LDAP attribute model.

105.3   Object Class Definition

The ObjectClassDefinition interface is used to group the attributes which are defined in AttributeDefinition objects.

An ObjectClassDefinition object contains the information about the overall set of attributes and has the following elements:

- A name which can be returned in different locales.
- A global name-space in the registry, which is the same condition as LDAP/X.500 object classes. In these standards the OSI Object Identifier (OID) is used to uniquely identify object classes. If such an OID exists, (which can be requested at several standard organizations, and many companies already have a node in the tree) it can be returned here. Otherwise, a unique id should be returned. This id can be a Java class name (reverse domain name) or can be generated with a GUID algorithm. All LDAP-defined object classes already have an associated OID. It is strongly advised to define the object classes from existing LDAP schemes which provide many preexisting OIDs. Many such schemes exist ranging from postal addresses to DHCP parameters.
- A human-readable description of the class.
- A list of attribute definitions which can be filtered as required, or optional. Note that in X.500 the mandatory or required status of an attribute is part of the object class definition and not of the attribute definition.
- An icon, in different sizes.

105.4   Attribute Definition

The AttributeDefinition interface provides the means to describe the data type of attributes.

The AttributeDefinition interface defines the following elements:

- Defined names (final ints) for the data types as restricted in the Framework for the attributes, called the syntax in OSI terms, which can be obtained with the getType() method.
- AttributeDefinition objects should use and ID that is similar to the OID as described in the ID field for ObjectClassDefinition.
- A localized name intended to be used in user interfaces.

- A localized description that defines the semantics of the attribute and possible constraints, which should be usable for tooltips.
- An indication if this attribute should be stored as a unique value, a Vector, or an array of values, as well as the maximum cardinality of the type.
- The data type, as limited by the Framework service registry attribute types.
- A validation function to verify if a possible value is correct.
- A list of values and a list of localized labels. Intended for popup menus in GUIs, allowing the user to choose from a set.
- A default value. The return type of this is a String[ ]. For cardinality = zero, this return type must be an array of one String object. For other cardinalities, the array must not contain more than the absolute value of *cardinality* String objects. In that case, it may contain 0 objects.

105.5   Meta Type Service

The Meta Type Service provides unified access to Meta Type information that is associated with a Bundle. It can get this information through the following means:

- *Meta Type Resource* – A bundle can provide one ore more XML resources that are contained in its JAR file. These resources contain and XML definition of meta types as well as to what PIDs these Meta Types apply. These XML resources must reside in the OSGI-INF/metatype directories of the bundle (including any fragments).
- *ManagedService[Factory] objects* – As defined in the configuration management specification, ManagedService and ManagedServiceFactory service objects can optionally implement the MetaTypeProvider interface. The Meta Type Service will only search for MetaTypeProvider objects if no meta type resources are found in the bundle.

Figure 105.2   *Sources for Meta Types*

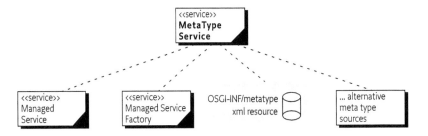

This model is depicted in Figure 105.2.

The Meta Type Service can therefore be used to retrieve meta type information for bundles which contain Meta Type resources or which provide their own MetaTypeProvider objects. The MetaTypeService interface has a single method:

- getMetaTypeInformation(Bundle) – Given a bundle, it must return the Meta Type Information for that bundle, even if there is no meta type information available at the moment of the call.

The returned MetaTypeInformation object maintains a map of PID to ObjectClassDefinition objects. The map is keyed by locale and PID. The list of maintained PIDs is available from the MetaTypeInformation object with the following methods:

- getPids() – PIDs for which Meta Types are available.
- getFactoryPids() – PIDs associated with Managed Service Factory services.

These methods and their interaction with the Meta Type resource are described in *Use of the Designate Element* on page 114.

The MetaTypeInformation interface extends the MetaTypeProvider interface. The MetaTypeProvider interface is used to access meta type information.It supports locale dependent information so that the text used in AttributeDefinition and ObjectClassDefinition objects can be adapted to different locales.

Which locales are supported by the MetaTypeProvider object are defined by the implementer or the meta type resources.The list of available locales can be obtained from the MetaTypeProvider object.

The MetaTypeProvider interface provides the following methods:

- getObjectClassDefinition(String,String) – Get access to an ObjectClassDefinition object for the given PID. The second parameter defines the locale.
- getLocales() – List the locales.that are available.

Locale objects are represented in String objects because not all profiles support Locale. The String holds the standard Locale presentation of:

```
locale = language ( '_' country ( '_' variation?) )?
language ::= < defined by ISO 3166 >
country  ::= < defined by ISO 639 >
```

For example, en, nl_BE, en_CA_posix are valid locales. The use of null for locale indicates that java.util.Locale.getDefault() must be used.

The Meta Type Service implementation class is the main class. It registers the org.osgi.service.metatype.MetaTypeService service and has a method to get a MetaTypeInformation object for a bundle.

Following is some sample code demonstrating how to print out all the Object Class Definitions and Attribute Definitions contained in a bundle:

```java
void printMetaTypes( MetaTypeService mts, Bundle b ) {
  MetaTypeInformation mti =
    mts.getMetaTypeInformation(b);
  String [] pids = mti.getPids();
  String [] locales = mti.getLocales();

  for ( int locale = 0; locale<locales.length; locale++ ) {
    System.out.println("Locale " + locales[locale] );
    for (int i=0; i< pids.length; i++) {
      ObjectClassDefinition ocd =
        mti.getObjectClassDefinition(pids[i], null);
      AttributeDefinition[] ads =
        ocd.getAttributeDefinitions(
          ObjectClassDefinition.ALL);
      for (int j=0; j< ads.length; j++) {
        System.out.println("OCD="+ocd.getName()
          + "AD="+ads[j].getName());
      }
    }
  }
}
```

105.6   Using the Meta Type Resources

A bundle that wants to provide meta type resources must place these resources in the OSGI-INF/ metatype directory. The name of the resource must be a valid JAR path. All resources in that directory must be meta type documents. Fragments can contain additional meta type resources in the same directory and they must be taken into account when the meta type resources are searched. A meta type resources must be encoded in UTF-8.

The MetaType Service must support localization of the

- name
- icon
- description
- label attributes

The localization mechanism must be identical using the same mechanism as described in the Core module layer, section *Localization* on page 68, using the same property resource. However, it is possible to override the property resource in the meta type definition resources with the localization attribute of the MetaData element.

The Meta Type Service must examine the bundle and its fragments to locate all localization resources for the localization base name. From that list, the Meta Type Service derives the list of locales which are available for the meta type information. This list can then be returned by MetaTypeInformation.getLocales method. This list can change at any time because the bundle could be refreshed. Clients should be prepared that this list changes after they received it.

105.6.1   XML Schema of a Meta Type Resource

This section describes the schema of the meta type resource. This schema is not intended to be used during runtime for validating meta type resources. The schema is intended to be used by tools and external management systems.

The XML namespace for meta type documents must be:

```
http://www.osgi.org/xmlns/metatype/v1.1.0
```

The namespace abbreviation should be metatype. I.e. the following header should be:

```
<metatype:MetaData
    xmlns:metatype=
        "http://www.osgi.org/xmlns/metatype/v1.1.0"
    xmlns:xsi="http://www.w3.org/2001/XMLSchema-instance"
    >
```

The file can be found in the osgi.jar file that can be downloaded from the www.osgi.org web site.

Figure 105.3   *XML Schema Instance Structure (Type name = Element name)*

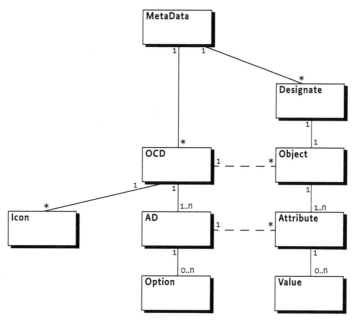

The element structure of the XML file is:

```
MetaData   ::= OCD* Designate*

OCD        ::= AD+  Icon ?
AD         ::= Option*

Designate  ::= Object
Object     ::= Attribute *

Attribute  ::= Value *
```

The different elements are described in Table 105.1.

Table 105.1   *XML Schema for Meta Type resources*

Attribute	Deflt	Type	Method	Description
MetaData				Top Element
localization		string		Points to the Properties file that can localize this XML. See *Localization* on page 68 of the Core book.
OCD				Object Class Definition
name	<>	string	getName()	A human readable name that can be localized.
description			getDescription()	A human readable description of the Object Class Definition that can be localized.
id	<>		getID()	A unique id, cannot be localized.

Table 105.1 *XML Schema for Meta Type resources*

Attribute	Deflt	Type	Method	Description
Designate				An association between one PID and an Object Class Definition. This element *designates* a PID to be of a certain *type*.
pid	<>	string		The PID that is associated with an OCD. This can be a reference to a factory or singleton configuration object. See *Use of the Designate Element* on page 114.
factoryPid		string		If the factoryPid attribute is set, this Designate element defines a factory configuration for the given factory, if it is not set or empty, it designates a singleton configuration. See *Use of the Designate Element* on page 114.
bundle		string		Location of the bundle that implements the PID. This binds the PID to the bundle. I.e. no other bundle using the same PID may use this designation. In a Meta Type resource this field may be set to an wildcard (\u002A, "∗") to indicate the bundle where the resource comes from. This is an optional attribute but can be mandatory in certain usage schemes, like for example the Autoconf Resource Processor.
optional	false	boolean		If true, then this Designate element is optional, errors during processing must be ignored.
merge	false	boolean		If the PID refers to an existing variable, then merge the properties with the existing properties if this attribute is true. Otherwise, replace the properties.
AD				Attribute Definition
name		string	getName()	A localizable name for the Attribute Definition. description
description		string	getDescription()	A localizable description for the Attribute Definition.
id			getID()	The unique ID of the Attribute Definition.

Table 105.1   *XML Schema for Meta Type resources*

Attribute	Deflt	Type	Method	Description
type		string	getType()	The type of an attribute is an enumeration of the different scalar types. The string is mapped to one of the constants on the AttributeDefinition interface. Valid values, which are defined in the Scalar type, are:

```
String   ↔   STRING
Long     ↔   LONG
Double   ↔   DOUBLE
Float    ↔   FLOAT
Integer  ↔   INTEGER
Byte     ↔   BYTE
Char     ↔   CHARACTER
Boolean  ↔   BOOLEAN
Short    ↔   SHORT
```

Attribute	Deflt	Type	Method	Description
cardinality	o		getCardinality()	The number of elements an instance can take. Positive numbers describe an array ([]) and negative numbers describe a Vector object.
min		string	validate(String)	A validation value. This value is not directly available from the AttributeDefinition interface. However, the validate(String) method must verify this. The semantics of this field depend on the type of this Attribute Definition.
max		string	validate(String)	A validation value. Similar to the min field.
default		string	getDefaultValue()	The default value. A default is an array of String objects. The XML attribute must contain a comma delimited list. If the comma must be represented, it must be escaped with a back slash ('\' \u005c). A back slash can be included with two backslashes. White spaces around the command and after/before an XML element must be ignored. For example: dflt="a\,b,b\,c, c\\,d" => ["a,b", "b,c", "c\", "d"]
required	true	boolean		Required attributes
Option				One option label/value for the options in an AD.
label	<>	string	getOptionLabels()	The label
value	<>	string	getOptionValues()	The value
Icon				An icon definition.

Table 105.1   XML Schema for Meta Type resources

Attribute	Deflt	Type	Method	Description
resource	<>	string	getIcon(int)	The resource is a URL. The base URL is assumed to be the XML file with the definition. I.e. if the XML is a resource in the JAR file, then this URL can reference another resource in that JAR file using a relative URL.
size	<>	string	getIcon(int)	The number of pixels of the icon, maps to the size parameter of the getIcon(int) method.
Object				A definition of an instance.
ocdref	<>	string		A reference to the id attribute of an OCD element. I.e. this attribute defines the OCD type of this object.
Attribute				A value for an attribute of an object.
adref	<>	string		A reference to the id of the AD in the OCD as referenced by the parent Object.
content		string		The content of the attributes. If this is an array, the content must be separated by commas (',' \u002C). Commas must be escaped as described at the default attribute of the AD element. See default on page 113.
Value				Holds a single value. This element can be repeated multiple times under an Attribute

105.6.2   Use of the Designate Element

For the MetaType Service, the Designate definition is used to declare the available PIDs and factory PIDs; the Attribute elements are never used by the MetaType service.

The getPids() method returns an array of PIDs that were specified in the pid attribute of the Object elements. The getFactoryPids() method returns an array of the factoryPid attributes. For factories, the related pid attribute is ignored because all instances of a factory must share the same meta type.

The following example shows a metatype reference to a singleton configuration and a factory configuration.

```
<Designate pid="com.acme.designate.1">
    <Object ocdref="com.acme.designate"./>
</Designate>
<Designate factoryPid="com.acme.designate.factory"
    bundle="*">
    <Object ocdref="com.acme.designate"/>
</Designate>
```

Other schemes can embed the Object element in the Designate element to define actual instances for the Configuration Admin service. In that case the pid attribute must be used together with the factoryPid attribute. However, in that case an aliasing model is required because the Configuration Admin service does not allow the creator to choose the Configuration object's PID.

105.6.3   Example Meta Data File

This example defines a meta type file for a Person record, based on ISO attribute types. The ids that are used are derived from ISO attributes.

```
<?xml version="1.0" encoding="UTF-8"?>
<MetaData
  xmlns=
     "http://www.osgi.org/xmlns/metatype/v1.1.0"
   localization="person">
 <OCD name="%person" id="2.5.6.6"
     description="%Person Record">
    <AD name="%sex" id="2.5.4.22" type="Integer">
       <Option label="%male" value="1"/>
       <Option label="%female" value="0"/>
    </AD>
    <AD name="%sn" id="2.5.4.4" type="String"/>
    <AD name="%cn" id="2.5.4.3" type="String"/>
    <AD name="%seeAlso" id="2.5.4.34" type="String"
        cardinality="8" default="http://www.google.com,
              http://www.yahoo.com"/>
    <AD name="%telNumber" id="2.5.4.20" type="String"/>
 </OCD>

 <Designate pid="com.acme.addressbook">
  <Object ocdref="2.5.6.6"/>
 </Designate>
</MetaData>
```

Translations for this file, as indicated by the localization attribute must be stored in the root directory (e.g. person_du_NL.properties). The default localization base name for the properties is OSGI-INF/l10n/bundle, but can be overridden by the manifest Bundle-Localization header and the localization attribute of the Meta Data element. The property files have the base name of person. The Dutch, French and English translations could look like:

```
person_du_NL.properties:
person=Persoon
person\ record=Persoons beschrijving
cn=Naam
sn=Voornaam
seeAlso=Zie ook
telNumber=Tel. Nummer
sex=Geslacht
male=Mannelijk
female=Vrouwelijk

person_fr.properties
person=Personne
person\ record=Description de la personne
cn=Nom
sn=Surnom
seeAlso=Reference
telNumber=Tel.
sex=Sexe
male=Homme
female=Femme
```

```
person_en_US.properties
person=Person
person\ record=Person Record
cn=Name
sn=Sur Name
seeAlso=See Also
telNumber=Tel.
sex=Sex
male=Male
female=Female
```

105.7 Object

The OCD element can be used to describe the possible contents of a Dictionary object. In this case, the attribute name is the key. The Object element can be used to assign a value to a Dictionary object.

For example:

```
<Designate pid="com.acme.b">
    <Object ocdref="b">
        <Attribute adref="foo" content="Zaphod Beeblebrox"/>
        <Attribute adref="bar">
            <Value>1</Value>
            <Value>2</Value>
            <Value>3</Value>
            <Value>4</Value>
            <Value>5</Value>
        </Attribute>
    </Object>
</Designate>
```

105.8 XML Schema

```
<?xml version="1.0" encoding="UTF-8"?>
<schema xmlns="http://www.w3.org/2001/XMLSchema"
    xmlns:metatype="http://www.osgi.org/xmlns/metatype/v1.1.0"
    targetNamespace="http://www.osgi.org/xmlns/metatype/v1.1.0"
    version="1.1.0">

    <element name="MetaData" type="metatype:Tmetadata" />

    <complexType name="Tmetadata">
        <sequence>
            <element name="OCD" type="metatype:Tocd" minOccurs="0"
                maxOccurs="unbounded" />
            <element name="Designate" type="metatype:Tdesignate"
                minOccurs="0" maxOccurs="unbounded" />
            <any namespace="##other" processContents="lax" minOccurs="0"
                maxOccurs="unbounded" />
        </sequence>
        <attribute name="localization" type="string" use="optional" />
        <anyAttribute />
    </complexType>

    <complexType name="Tocd">
        <sequence>
            <element name="AD" type="metatype:Tad" minOccurs="1"
                maxOccurs="unbounded" />
            <element name="Icon" type="metatype:Ticon" minOccurs="0"
                maxOccurs="1" />
            <any namespace="##other" processContents="lax" minOccurs="0"
                maxOccurs="unbounded" />
```

```
        </sequence>
        <attribute name="name" type="string" use="required" />
        <attribute name="description" type="string" use="optional" />
        <attribute name="id" type="string" use="required" />
        <anyAttribute />
    </complexType>

    <complexType name="Tad">
        <sequence>
            <element name="Option" type="metatype:Toption" minOccurs="0"
                maxOccurs="unbounded" />
            <any namespace="##other" processContents="lax" minOccurs="0"
                maxOccurs="unbounded" />
        </sequence>
        <attribute name="name" type="string" use="optional" />
        <attribute name="description" type="string" use="optional" />
        <attribute name="id" type="string" use="required" />
        <attribute name="type" type="metatype:Tscalar" use="required" />
        <attribute name="cardinality" type="int" use="optional"
            default="0" />
        <attribute name="min" type="string" use="optional" />
        <attribute name="max" type="string" use="optional" />
        <attribute name="default" type="string" use="optional" />
        <attribute name="required" type="boolean" use="optional"
            default="true" />
        <anyAttribute />
    </complexType>

    <complexType name="Tobject">
        <sequence>
            <element name="Attribute" type="metatype:Tattribute"
                minOccurs="0" maxOccurs="unbounded" />
            <any namespace="##other" processContents="lax" minOccurs="0"
                maxOccurs="unbounded" />
        </sequence>
        <attribute name="ocdref" type="string" use="required" />
        <anyAttribute />
    </complexType>

    <complexType name="Tattribute">
        <sequence>
            <element name="Value" type="string" minOccurs="0"
                maxOccurs="unbounded" />
            <any namespace="##other" processContents="lax" minOccurs="0"
                maxOccurs="unbounded" />
        </sequence>
        <attribute name="adref" type="string" use="required" />
        <attribute name="content" type="string" use="optional" />
        <anyAttribute />
    </complexType>

    <complexType name="Tdesignate">
        <sequence>
            <element name="Object" type="metatype:Tobject" minOccurs="1"
                maxOccurs="1" />
            <any namespace="##any" processContents="lax" minOccurs="0"
                maxOccurs="unbounded" />
        </sequence>
        <attribute name="pid" type="string" use="required" />
        <attribute name="factoryPid" type="string" use="optional" />
        <attribute name="bundle" type="string" use="optional" />
        <attribute name="optional" type="boolean" default="false"
            use="optional" />
        <attribute name="merge" type="boolean" default="false"
            use="optional" />
        <anyAttribute />
    </complexType>

    <simpleType name="Tscalar">
        <restriction base="string">
            <enumeration value="String" />
            <enumeration value="Long" />
            <enumeration value="Double" />
            <enumeration value="Float" />
            <enumeration value="Integer" />
```

```
        <enumeration value="Byte" />
        <enumeration value="Char" />
        <enumeration value="Boolean" />
        <enumeration value="Short" />
    </restriction>
</simpleType>

<complexType name="Toption">
    <sequence>
        <any namespace="##any" processContents="lax" minOccurs="0"
            maxOccurs="unbounded" />
    </sequence>
    <attribute name="label" type="string" use="required" />
    <attribute name="value" type="string" use="required" />
    <anyAttribute />
</complexType>

<complexType name="Ticon">
    <sequence>
        <any namespace="##any" processContents="lax" minOccurs="0"
            maxOccurs="unbounded" />
    </sequence>
    <attribute name="resource" type="string" use="required" />
    <attribute name="size" type="positiveInteger" use="required" />
    <anyAttribute />
</complexType>

<attribute name="must-understand" type="boolean">
    <annotation>
        <documentation xml:lang="en">
            This attribute should be used by extensions to documents
            to require that the document consumer understand the
            extension.
        </documentation>
    </annotation>
</attribute>
</schema>
```

105.9 Limitations

The OSGi MetaType specification is intended to be used for simple applications. It does not, therefore, support recursive data types, mixed types in arrays/vectors, or nested arrays/vectors.

105.10 Related Standards

One of the primary goals of this specification is to make metatype information available at run-time with minimal overhead. Many related standards are applicable to metatypes; except for Java beans, however, all other metatype standards are based on document formats (e.g. XML). In the OSGi Service Platform, document format standards are deemed unsuitable due to the overhead required in the execution environment (they require a parser during run-time).

Another consideration is the applicability of these standards. Most of these standards were developed for management systems on platforms where resources are not necessarily a concern. In this case, a metatype standard is normally used to describe the data structures needed to control some other computer via a network. This other computer, however, does not require the metatype information as it is *implementing* this information.

In some traditional cases, a management system uses the metatype information to control objects in an OSGi Service Platform. Therefore, the concepts and the syntax of the metatype information must be mappable to these popular standards. Clearly, then, these standards must be able to describe objects in an OSGi Service Platform. This ability is usually not a problem, because the metatype languages used by current management systems are very powerful.

105.11   Security Considerations

Special security issues are not applicable for this specification.

105.12   Changes

- Updated schema to 1.1

105.13   org.osgi.service.metatype

Metatype Package Version 1.1.

Bundles wishing to use this package must list the package in the Import-Package header of the bundle's manifest. For example:

```
Import-Package: org.osgi.service.metatype; version="[1.1,2.0)"
```

105.13.1   Summary

- *AttributeDefinition* - An interface to describe an attribute.
- *MetaTypeInformation* - A MetaType Information object is created by the MetaTypeService to return meta type information for a specific bundle.
- *MetaTypeProvider* - Provides access to metatypes.
- *MetaTypeService* - The MetaType Service can be used to obtain meta type information for a bundle.
- *ObjectClassDefinition* - Description for the data type information of an objectclass.

105.13.2   public interface AttributeDefinition

An interface to describe an attribute.

An AttributeDefinition object defines a description of the data type of a property/attribute.

105.13.2.1   public static final int BIGDECIMAL = 10

The BIGDECIMAL (10) type. Attributes of this type should be stored as BigDecimal, Vector with BigDecimal or BigDecimal[] objects depending on getCardinality().

Deprecated As of 1.1.

105.13.2.2   public static final int BIGINTEGER = 9

The BIGINTEGER (9) type. Attributes of this type should be stored as BigInteger, Vector with BigInteger or BigInteger[] objects, depending on the getCardinality() value.

Deprecated As of 1.1.

105.13.2.3   public static final int BOOLEAN = 11

The BOOLEAN (11) type. Attributes of this type should be stored as Boolean, Vector with Boolean or boolean[] objects depending on getCardinality().

105.13.2.4   public static final int BYTE = 6

The BYTE (6) type. Attributes of this type should be stored as Byte, Vector with Byte or byte[] objects, depending on the getCardinality() value.

105.13.2.5   public static final int CHARACTER = 5

The CHARACTER (5) type. Attributes of this type should be stored as Character, Vector with Character or char[] objects, depending on the getCardinality() value.

105.13.2.6 **public static final int DOUBLE = 7**

The DOUBLE (7) type. Attributes of this type should be stored as Double, Vector with Double or double[] objects, depending on the getCardinality() value.

105.13.2.7 **public static final int FLOAT = 8**

The FLOAT (8) type. Attributes of this type should be stored as Float, Vector with Float or float[] objects, depending on the getCardinality() value.

105.13.2.8 **public static final int INTEGER = 3**

The INTEGER (3) type. Attributes of this type should be stored as Integer, Vector with Integer or int[] objects, depending on the getCardinality() value.

105.13.2.9 **public static final int LONG = 2**

The LONG (2) type. Attributes of this type should be stored as Long, Vector with Long or long[] objects, depending on the getCardinality() value.

105.13.2.10 **public static final int SHORT = 4**

The SHORT (4) type. Attributes of this type should be stored as Short, Vector with Short or short[] objects, depending on the getCardinality() value.

105.13.2.11 **public static final int STRING = 1**

The STRING (1) type.

Attributes of this type should be stored as String, Vector with String or String[] objects, depending on the getCardinality() value.

105.13.2.12 **public int getCardinality( )**

□ Return the cardinality of this attribute. The OSGi environment handles multi valued attributes in arrays ([]) or in Vector objects. The return value is defined as follows:

```
x = Integer.MIN_VALUE    no limit, but use Vector
x < 0                    -x = max occurrences, store in Vector
x > 0                     x = max occurrences, store in array []
x = Integer.MAX_VALUE    no limit, but use array []
x = 0                     1 occurrence required
```

Returns The cardinality of this attribute.

105.13.2.13 **public String[] getDefaultValue( )**

□ Return a default for this attribute. The object must be of the appropriate type as defined by the cardinality and getType(). The return type is a list of String objects that can be converted to the appropriate type. The cardinality of the return array must follow the absolute cardinality of this type. E.g. if the cardinality = 0, the array must contain 1 element. If the cardinality is 1, it must contain 0 or 1 elements. If it is -5, it must contain from 0 to max 5 elements. Note that the special case of a 0 cardinality, meaning a single value, does not allow arrays or vectors of 0 elements.

Returns Return a default value or null if no default exists.

105.13.2.14 **public String getDescription( )**

□ Return a description of this attribute. The description may be localized and must describe the semantics of this type and any constraints.

Returns The localized description of the definition.

105.13.2.15   **public String getID( )**

☐ Unique identity for this attribute. Attributes share a global namespace in the registry. E.g. an attribute cn or commonName must always be a String and the semantics are always a name of some object. They share this aspect with LDAP/X.500 attributes. In these standards the OSI Object Identifier (OID) is used to uniquely identify an attribute. If such an OID exists, (which can be requested at several standard organisations and many companies already have a node in the tree) it can be returned here. Otherwise, a unique id should be returned which can be a Java class name (reverse domain name) or generated with a GUID algorithm. Note that all LDAP defined attributes already have an OID. It is strongly advised to define the attributes from existing LDAP schemes which will give the OID. Many such schemes exist ranging from postal addresses to DHCP parameters.

Returns The id or oid

105.13.2.16   **public String getName( )**

☐ Get the name of the attribute. This name may be localized.

Returns The localized name of the definition.

105.13.2.17   **public String[] getOptionLabels( )**

☐ Return a list of labels of option values.

The purpose of this method is to allow menus with localized labels. It is associated with getOptionValues. The labels returned here are ordered in the same way as the values in that method.

If the function returns null, there are no option labels available.

This list must be in the same sequence as the getOptionValues() method. I.e. for each index i in getOptionLabels, i in getOptionValues() should be the associated value.

For example, if an attribute can have the value male, female, unknown, this list can return (for dutch) new String[] { "Man", "Vrouw", "Onbekend" }.

Returns A list values

105.13.2.18   **public String[] getOptionValues( )**

☐ Return a list of option values that this attribute can take.

If the function returns null, there are no option values available.

Each value must be acceptable to validate() (return "") and must be a String object that can be converted to the data type defined by getType() for this attribute.

This list must be in the same sequence as getOptionLabels(). I.e. for each index i in getOptionValues, i in getOptionLabels() should be the label.

For example, if an attribute can have the value male, female, unknown, this list can return new String[] { "male", "female", "unknown" }.

Returns A list values

105.13.2.19   **public int getType( )**

☐ Return the type for this attribute.

Defined in the following constants which map to the appropriate Java type. STRING,LONG,INTEGER, CHAR,BYTE,DOUBLE,FLOAT, BOOLEAN.

Returns The type for this attribute.

105.13.2.20   **public String validate(String value)**

value The value before turning it into the basic data type

❑ Validate an attribute in String form. An attribute might be further constrained in value. This method will attempt to validate the attribute according to these constraints. It can return three different values:

```
null          No validation present
" "           No problems detected
"..."         A localized description of why the value is wrong
```

Returns null, "", or another string

105.13.3 public interface MetaTypeInformation extends MetaTypeProvider

A MetaType Information object is created by the MetaTypeService to return meta type information for a specific bundle.

Since 1.1

105.13.3.1 public Bundle getBundle( )

❑ Return the bundle for which this object provides meta type information.

Returns Bundle for which this object provides meta type information.

105.13.3.2 public String[] getFactoryPids( )

❑ Return the Factory PIDs (for ManagedServiceFactories) for which ObjectClassDefinition information is available.

Returns Array of Factory PIDs.

105.13.3.3 public String[] getPids( )

❑ Return the PIDs (for ManagedServices) for which ObjectClassDefinition information is available.

Returns Array of PIDs.

105.13.4 public interface MetaTypeProvider

Provides access to metatypes.

105.13.4.1 public String[] getLocales( )

❑ Return a list of available locales. The results must be names that consists of language [_ country [_ variation]] as is customary in the Locale class.

Returns An array of locale strings or null if there is no locale specific localization can be found.

105.13.4.2 public ObjectClassDefinition getObjectClassDefinition(String id, String locale)

id The ID of the requested object class. This can be a pid or factory pid returned by getPids or getFactoryPids.

locale The locale of the definition or null for default locale.

❑ Returns an object class definition for the specified id localized to the specified locale.

The locale parameter must be a name that consists of language["_" country["_" variation]] as is customary in the Locale class. This Locale class is not used because certain profiles do not contain it.

Returns A ObjectClassDefinition object.

Throws IllegalArgumentException – If the id or locale arguments are not valid

105.13.5   public interface MetaTypeService

The MetaType Service can be used to obtain meta type information for a bundle. The MetaType Service will examine the specified bundle for meta type documents to create the returned MetaTypeInformation object.

If the specified bundle does not contain any meta type documents, then a MetaTypeInformation object will be returned that wrappers any ManagedService or ManagedServiceFactory services registered by the specified bundle that implement MetaTypeProvider. Thus the MetaType Service can be used to retrieve meta type information for bundles which contain a meta type documents or which provide their own MetaTypeProvider objects.

Since 1.1

105.13.5.1   public static final String METATYPE_DOCUMENTS_LOCATION = "OSGI-INF/metatype"

Location of meta type documents. The MetaType Service will process each entry in the meta type documents directory.

105.13.5.2   public MetaTypeInformation getMetaTypeInformation(Bundle bundle)

bundle The bundle for which meta type information is requested.

☐ Return the MetaType information for the specified bundle.

Returns A MetaTypeInformation object for the specified bundle.

105.13.6   public interface ObjectClassDefinition

Description for the data type information of an objectclass.

105.13.6.1   public static final int ALL = -1

Argument for getAttributeDefinitions(int).

ALL indicates that all the definitions are returned. The value is -1.

105.13.6.2   public static final int OPTIONAL = 2

Argument for getAttributeDefinitions(int).

OPTIONAL indicates that only the optional definitions are returned. The value is 2.

105.13.6.3   public static final int REQUIRED = 1

Argument for getAttributeDefinitions(int).

REQUIRED indicates that only the required definitions are returned. The value is 1.

105.13.6.4   public AttributeDefinition[] getAttributeDefinitions(int filter)

filter ALL,REQUIRED,OPTIONAL

☐ Return the attribute definitions for this object class.

Return a set of attributes. The filter parameter can distinguish between ALL,REQUIRED or the OPTIONAL attributes.

Returns An array of attribute definitions or null if no attributes are selected

105.13.6.5   public String getDescription( )

☐ Return a description of this object class. The description may be localized.

Returns The description of this object class.

105.13.6.6   **public InputStream getIcon(int size) throws IOException**

size   Requested size of an icon, e.g. a 16x16 pixels icon then size = 16

☐   Return an InputStream object that can be used to create an icon from.

Indicate the size and return an InputStream object containing an icon. The returned icon maybe larger or smaller than the indicated size.

The icon may depend on the localization.

Returns   An InputStream representing an icon or null

Throws   IOException – If the InputStream cannot be returned.

105.13.6.7   **public String getID( )**

☐   Return the id of this object class.

ObjectDefintion objects share a global namespace in the registry. They share this aspect with LDAP/X.500 attributes. In these standards the OSI Object Identifier (OID) is used to uniquely identify object classes. If such an OID exists, (which can be requested at several standard organisations and many companies already have a node in the tree) it can be returned here. Otherwise, a unique id should be returned which can be a java class name (reverse domain name) or generated with a GUID algorithm. Note that all LDAP defined object classes already have an OID associated. It is strongly advised to define the object classes from existing LDAP schemes which will give the OID for free. Many such schemes exist ranging from postal addresses to DHCP parameters.

Returns   The id of this object class.

105.13.6.8   **public String getName( )**

☐   Return the name of this object class. The name may be localized.

Returns   The name of this object class.

105.14   References

[1]   *LDAP.*
       http://en.wikipedia.org/wiki/Lightweight_Directory_Access_Protocol

[2]   *Understanding and Deploying LDAP Directory services*
       Timothy Howes et. al. ISBN 1-57870-070-1, MacMillan Technical publishing.

106   Preferences Service Specification

Version 1.1

106.1   Introduction

Many bundles need to save some data persistently--in other words, the data is required to survive the stopping and restarting of the bundle, Framework and OSGi Service Platform. In some cases, the data is specific to a particular user. For example, imagine a bundle that implements some kind of game. User specific persistent data could include things like the user's preferred difficulty level for playing the game. Some data is not specific to a user, which we call *system* data. An example would be a table of high scores for the game.

Bundles which need to persist data in an OSGi environment can use the file system via org.osgi.framework.BundleContext.getDataFile. A file system, however, can store only bytes and characters, and provides no direct support for named values and different data types.

A popular class used to address this problem for Java applications is the java.util.Properties class. This class allows data to be stored as key/value pairs, called *properties*. For example, a property could have a name com.acme.fudd and a value of elmer. The Properties class has rudimentary support for storage and retrieving with its load and store methods. The Properties class, however, has the following limitations:

- Does not support a naming hierarchy.
- Only supports String property values.
- Does not allow its content to be easily stored in a back-end system.
- Has no user name-space management.

Since the Properties class was introduced in Java 1.0, efforts have been undertaken to replace it with a more sophisticated mechanism. One of these efforts is this Preferences Service specification.

106.1.1   Essentials

The focus of this specification is simplicity, not reliable access to stored data. This specification does *not* define a general database service with transactions and atomicity guarantees. Instead, it is optimized to deliver the stored information when needed, but it will return defaults, instead of throwing an exception, when the back-end store is not available. This approach may reduce the reliability of the data, but it makes the service easier to use, and allows for a variety of compact and efficient implementations.

This API is made easier to use by the fact that many bundles can be written to ignore any problems that the Preferences Service may have in accessing the back-end store, if there is one. These bundles will mostly or exclusively use the methods of the Preferences interface which are not declared to throw a BackingStoreException.

This service only supports the storage of scalar values and byte arrays. It is not intended for storing large data objects like documents or images. No standard limits are placed on the size of data objects which can be stored, but implementations are expected to be optimized for the handling of small objects.

A hierarchical naming model is supported, in contrast to the flat model of the Properties class. A hierarchical model maps naturally to many computing problems. For example, maintaining information about the positions of adjustable seats in a car requires information for each seat. In a hierarchy, this information can be modeled as a node per seat.

A potential benefit of the Preferences Service is that it allows user specific preferences data to be kept in a well defined place, so that a user management system could locate it. This benefit could be useful for such operations as cleaning up files when a user is removed from the system, or to allow a user's preferences to be cloned for a new user.

The Preferences Service does *not* provide a mechanism to allow one bundle to access the preferences data of another. If a bundle wishes to allow another bundle to access its preferences data, it can pass a Preferences or PreferencesService object to that bundle.

The Preferences Service is not intended to provide configuration management functionality. For information regarding Configuration Management, refer to the *Configuration Admin Service Specification* on page 67.

106.1.2   Entities

The PreferencesService is a relatively simple service. It provides access to the different roots of Preferences trees. A single system root node and any number of user root nodes are supported. Each *node* of such a tree is an object that implements the Preferences interface.

This Preferences interface provides methods for traversing the tree, as well as methods for accessing the properties of the node. This interface also contains the methods to flush data into persistent storage, and to synchronize the in-memory data cache with the persistent storage.

All nodes except root nodes have a parent. Nodes can have multiple children.

Figure 106.1   *Preferences Class Diagram*

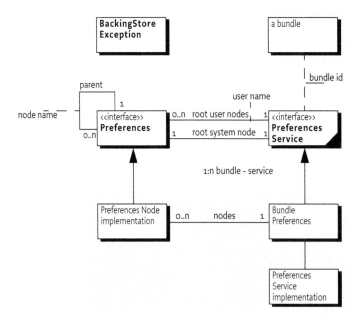

106.1.3   Operation

The purpose of the Preferences Service specification is to allow bundles to store and retrieve properties stored in a tree of nodes, where each node implements the Preferences interface. The PreferencesService interface allows a bundle to create or obtain a Preferences tree for system properties, as well as a Preferences tree for each user of the bundle.

This specification allows for implementations where the data is stored locally on the service platform or remotely on a back-end system.

106.2   Preferences Interface

Preferences is an interface that defines the methods to manipulate a node and the tree to which it belongs. A Preferences object contains:

- A set of properties in the form of key/value pairs.
- A parent node.
- A number of child nodes.

106.2.1   Hierarchies

A valid Preferences object always belongs to a *tree*. A tree is identified by its root node. In such a tree, a Preferences object always has a single parent, except for a root node which has a null parent.

The root node of a tree can be found by recursively calling the parent() method of a node until null is returned. The nodes that are traversed this way are called the *ancestors* of a node.

Each Preferences object has a private name-space for child nodes. Each child node has a name that must be unique among its siblings. Child nodes are created by getting a child node with the node(String) method. The String argument of this call contains a path name. Path names are explained in the next section.

Child nodes can have child nodes recursively. These objects are called the *descendants* of a node.

Descendants are automatically created when they are obtained from a Preferences object, including any intermediate nodes that are necessary for the given path. If this automatic creation is not desired, the nodeExists(String) method can be used to determine if a node already exists.

Figure 106.2   *Categorization of nodes in a tree*

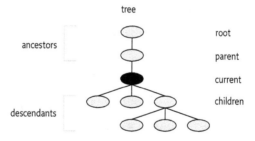

106.2.2   Naming

Each node has a name relative to its parent. A name may consist of Unicode characters except for the forward slash ("/"). There are no special names, like ".." or ".".

Empty names are reserved for root nodes. Node names that are directly created by a bundle must *always* contain at least one character.

Preferences node names and property keys are *case sensitive*: for example, "org.osgi" and "oRg.oSgI" are two distinct names.

The Preferences Service supports different roots, so there is no absolute root for the Preferences Service. This concept is similar to the Windows Registry that also supports a number of roots.

A path consists of one or more node names, separated by a slash ("/"). Paths beginning with a "/" are called *absolute path*s while other paths are called *relative paths*. Paths cannot end with a "/" except for the special case of the root node which has absolute path "/".

Path names are always associated with a specific node; this node is called the current node in the following descriptions. Paths identify nodes as follows.

- *Absolute path* – The first "/" is removed from the path, and the remainder of the path is interpreted as a relative path from the tree's root node.
- *Relative path* –
    - If the path is the empty string, it identifies the current node.
    - If the path is a name (does not contain a "/"), then it identifies the child node with that name.
    - Otherwise, the first name from the path identifies a child of the current node. The name and slash are then removed from the path, and the remainder of the path is interpreted as a relative path from the child node.

106.2.3 Tree Traversal Methods

A tree can be traversed and modified with the following methods:

- childrenNames()– Returns the names of the child nodes.
- parent() – Returns the parent node.
- removeNode() – Removes this node and all its descendants.
- node(String) – Returns a Preferences object, which is created if it does not already exist. The parameter is an absolute or relative path.
- nodeExists(String) – Returns true if the Preferences object identified by the path parameter exists.

106.2.4 Properties

Each Preferences node has a set of key/value pairs called properties. These properties consist of:

- *Key* – A key is a String object and *case sensitive*.
- The name-space of these keys is separate from that of the child nodes. A Preferences node could have both a child node named fudd and a property named fudd.
- *Value* – A value can always be stored and retrieved as a String object. Therefore, it must be possible to encode/decode all values into/from String objects (though it is not required to store them as such, an implementation is free to store and retrieve the value in any possible way as long as the String semantics are maintained). A number of methods are available to store and retrieve values as primitive types. These methods are provided both for the convenience of the user of the Preferences interface, and to allow an implementation the option of storing the values in a more compact form.

All the keys that are defined in a Preferences object can be obtained with the keys() method. The clear() method can be used to clear all properties from a Preferences object. A single property can be removed with the remove(String) method.

106.2.5 Storing and Retrieving Properties

The Preferences interface has a number of methods for storing and retrieving property values based on their key. All the put* methods take as parameters a key and a value. All the get* methods take as parameters a key and a default value.

- put(String,String), get(String,String)
- putBoolean(String,boolean), getBoolean(String,boolean)
- putInt(String,int), getInt(String,int)
- putLong(String,long), getLong(String,long)
- putFloat(String,float), getFloat(String,float)

- putDouble(String,double), getDouble(String,double)
- putByteArray(String,byte[]), getByteArray(String,byte[])

The methods act as if all the values are stored as String objects, even though implementations may use different representations for the different types. For example, a property can be written as a String object and read back as a float, providing that the string can be parsed as a valid Java float object. In the event of a parsing error, the get* methods do not raise exceptions, but instead return their default parameters.

106.2.6 Defaults

All get* methods take a default value as a parameter. The reasons for having such a default are:

- When a property for a Preferences object has not been set, the default is returned instead. In most cases, the bundle developer does not have to distinguish whether or not a property exists.
- A *best effort* strategy has been a specific design choice for this specification. The bundle developer should not have to react when the back-end store is not available. In those cases, the default value is returned without further notice.
  Bundle developers who want to assure that the back-end store is available should call the flush or sync method. Either of these methods will throw a BackingStoreException if the back-end store is not available.

106.3 Concurrency

This specification specifically allows an implementation to modify Preferences objects in a back-end store. If the back-end store is shared by multiple processes, concurrent updates may cause differences between the back-end store and the in-memory Preferences objects.

Bundle developers can partly control this concurrency with the flush() and sync() method. Both methods operate on a Preferences object.

The flush method performs the following actions:

- Stores (makes persistent) any ancestors (including the current node) that do not exist in the persistent store.
- Stores any properties which have been modified in this node since the last time it was flushed.
- Removes from the persistent store any child nodes that were removed from this object since the last time it was flushed.
- Flushes all existing child nodes.

The sync method will first flush, and then ensure that any changes that have been made to the current node and its descendents in the back-end store (by some other process) take effect. For example, it could fetch all the descendents into a local cache, or it could clear all the descendents from the cache so that they will be read from the back-end store as required.

If either method fails, a BackingStoreException is thrown.

The flush or sync methods provide no atomicity guarantee. When updates to the same back-end store are done concurrently by two different processes, the result may be that changes made by different processes are intermingled. To avoid this problem, implementations may simply provide a dedicated section (or name-space) in the back-end store for each OSGi environment, so that clashes do not arise, in which case there is no reason for bundle programmers to ever call sync.

In cases where sync is used, the bundle programmer needs to take into account that changes from different processes may become intermingled, and the level of granularity that can be assumed is the individual property level. Hence, for example, if two properties need to be kept in lockstep, so that one should not be changed without a corresponding change to the other, consider combining them into a single property, which would then need to be parsed into its two constituent parts.

106.4   PreferencesService Interface

The PreferencesService is obtained from the Framework's service registry in the normal way. Its purpose is to provide access to Preferences root nodes.

A Preferences Service maintains a system root and a number of user roots. User roots are automatically created, if necessary, when they are requested. Roots are maintained on a per bundle basis. For example, a user root called elmer in one bundle is distinct from a user root with the same name in another bundle. Also, each bundle has its own system root. Implementations should use a ServiceFactory service object to create a separate PreferencesService object for each bundle.

The precise description of *user* and *system* will vary from one bundle to another. The Preference Service only provides a mechanism, the bundle may use this mechanism in any desired way.

The PreferencesService interface has the following methods to access the system root and user roots:

- getSystemPreferences() – Return a Preferences object that is the root of the system preferences tree.
- getUserPreferences(String) – Return a Preferences object associated with the user name that is given as argument. If the user does not exist, a new root is created atomically.
- getUsers() – Return an array of the names of all the users for whom a Preferences tree exists.

106.5   Cleanup

The Preferences Service must listen for bundle uninstall events, and remove all the preferences data for the bundle that is being uninstalled. The Preferences Service must use the bundle id for the association and not the location.

It also must handle the possibility of a bundle getting uninstalled while the Preferences Service is stopped. Therefore, it must check on startup whether preferences data exists for any bundle which is not currently installed. If it does, that data must be removed.

106.6   org.osgi.service.prefs

Preferences Service Package Version 1.1.

Bundles wishing to use this package must list the package in the Import-Package header of the bundle's manifest. For example:

```
Import-Package: org.osgi.service.prefs; version="[1.1,2.0)"
```

106.6.1   Summary

- *BackingStoreException* - Thrown to indicate that a preferences operation could not complete because of a failure in the backing store, or a failure to contact the backing store.
- *Preferences* - A node in a hierarchical collection of preference data.
- *PreferencesService* - The Preferences Service.

106.6.2   public class BackingStoreException
extends Exception

Thrown to indicate that a preferences operation could not complete because of a failure in the backing store, or a failure to contact the backing store.

106.6.2.1   public BackingStoreException(String message)

message   The detail message.

  ❑ Constructs a BackingStoreException with the specified detail message.

106.6.2.2   **public BackingStoreException(String message, Throwable cause)**

message The detail message.

cause The cause of the exception. May be null.

  ❑ Constructs a BackingStoreException with the specified detail message.

Since 1.1

106.6.2.3   **public Throwable getCause( )**

  ❑ Returns the cause of this exception or null if no cause was set.

Returns The cause of this exception or null if no cause was set.

Since 1.1

106.6.2.4   **public Throwable initCause(Throwable cause)**

cause The cause of this exception.

  ❑ Initializes the cause of this exception to the specified value.

Returns This exception.

Throws IllegalArgumentException – If the specified cause is this exception.

   IllegalStateException – If the cause of this exception has already been set.

Since 1.1

106.6.3 public interface Preferences

A node in a hierarchical collection of preference data.

This interface allows applications to store and retrieve user and system preference data. This data is stored persistently in an implementation-dependent backing store. Typical implementations include flat files, OS-specific registries, directory servers and SQL databases.

For each bundle, there is a separate tree of nodes for each user, and one for system preferences. The precise description of "user" and "system" will vary from one bundle to another. Typical information stored in the user preference tree might include font choice, and color choice for a bundle which interacts with the user via a servlet. Typical information stored in the system preference tree might include installation data, or things like high score information for a game program.

Nodes in a preference tree are named in a similar fashion to directories in a hierarchical file system. Every node in a preference tree has a *node name* (which is not necessarily unique), a unique *absolute path name*, and a path name *relative* to each ancestor including itself.

The root node has a node name of the empty String object (""). Every other node has an arbitrary node name, specified at the time it is created. The only restrictions on this name are that it cannot be the empty string, and it cannot contain the slash character ('/').

The root node has an absolute path name of "/". Children of the root node have absolute path names of "/" + *‹node name›*. All other nodes have absolute path names of *‹parent's absolute path name›* + "/" + *‹node name›*. Note that all absolute path names begin with the slash character.

A node *n*'s path name relative to its ancestor *a* is simply the string that must be appended to *a*'s absolute path name in order to form *n*'s absolute path name, with the initial slash character (if present) removed. Note that:

- No relative path names begin with the slash character.
- Every node's path name relative to itself is the empty string.

- Every node's path name relative to its parent is its node name (except for the root node, which does not have a parent).
- Every node's path name relative to the root is its absolute path name with the initial slash character removed.

Note finally that:

- No path name contains multiple consecutive slash characters.
- No path name with the exception of the root's absolute path name end in the slash character.
- Any string that conforms to these two rules is a valid path name.

Each Preference node has zero or more properties associated with it, where a property consists of a name and a value. The bundle writer is free to choose any appropriate names for properties. Their values can be of type String,long,int,boolean, byte[],float, or double but they can always be accessed as if they were String objects.

All node name and property name comparisons are case-sensitive.

All of the methods that modify preference data are permitted to operate asynchronously; they may return immediately, and changes will eventually propagate to the persistent backing store, with an implementation-dependent delay. The flush method may be used to synchronously force updates to the backing store.

Implementations must automatically attempt to flush to the backing store any pending updates for a bundle's preferences when the bundle is stopped or otherwise ungets the Preferences Service.

The methods in this class may be invoked concurrently by multiple threads in a single Java Virtual Machine (JVM) without the need for external synchronization, and the results will be equivalent to some serial execution. If this class is used concurrently *by multiple JVMs* that store their preference data in the same backing store, the data store will not be corrupted, but no other guarantees are made concerning the consistency of the preference data.

106.6.3.1   **public String absolutePath( )**

☐ Returns this node's absolute path name. Note that:

- Root node - The path name of the root node is "/".
- Slash at end - Path names other than that of the root node may not end in slash ('/').
- Unusual names -"." and ".." have *no* special significance in path names.
- Illegal names - The only illegal path names are those that contain multiple consecutive slashes, or that end in slash and are not the root.

Returns this node's absolute path name.

106.6.3.2   **public String[] childrenNames( ) throws BackingStoreException**

☐ Returns the names of the children of this node. (The returned array will be of size zero if this node has no children and not null!)

Returns the names of the children of this node.

Throws BackingStoreException – if this operation cannot be completed due to a failure in the backing store, or inability to communicate with it.

IllegalStateException – if this node (or an ancestor) has been removed with the removeNode() method.

106.6.3.3   **public void clear( ) throws BackingStoreException**

☐ Removes all of the properties (key-value associations) in this node. This call has no effect on any descendants of this node.

Throws BackingStoreException – if this operation cannot be completed due to a failure in the backing store, or inability to communicate with it.

IllegalStateException – if this node (or an ancestor) has been removed with the removeNode() method.

See Also   remove (String)

106.6.3.4   **public void flush( ) throws BackingStoreException**

☐   Forces any changes in the contents of this node and its descendants to the persistent store.

Once this method returns successfully, it is safe to assume that all changes made in the subtree rooted at this node prior to the method invocation have become permanent.

Implementations are free to flush changes into the persistent store at any time. They do not need to wait for this method to be called.

When a flush occurs on a newly created node, it is made persistent, as are any ancestors (and descendants) that have yet to be made persistent. Note however that any properties value changes in ancestors are *not* guaranteed to be made persistent.

Throws   BackingStoreException – if this operation cannot be completed due to a failure in the backing store, or inability to communicate with it.

IllegalStateException – if this node (or an ancestor) has been removed with the removeNode() method.

See Also   sync ()

106.6.3.5   **public String get(String key, String def)**

key   key whose associated value is to be returned.

def   the value to be returned in the event that this node has no value associated with key or the backing store is inaccessible.

☐   Returns the value associated with the specified key in this node. Returns the specified default if there is no value associated with the key, or the backing store is inaccessible.

Returns   the value associated with key, or def if no value is associated with key.

Throws   IllegalStateException – if this node (or an ancestor) has been removed with the removeNode() method.

NullPointerException – if key is null. (A null default *is* permitted.)

106.6.3.6   **public boolean getBoolean(String key, boolean def)**

key   key whose associated value is to be returned as a boolean.

def   the value to be returned in the event that this node has no value associated with key or the associated value cannot be interpreted as a boolean or the backing store is inaccessible.

☐   Returns the boolean value represented by the String object associated with the specified key in this node. Valid strings are "true", which represents true, and "false", which represents false. Case is ignored, so, for example, "TRUE" and "False" are also valid. This method is intended for use in conjunction with the putBoolean method.

Returns the specified default if there is no value associated with the key, the backing store is inaccessible, or if the associated value is something other than "true" or "false", ignoring case.

Returns   the boolean value represented by the String object associated with key in this node, or null if the associated value does not exist or cannot be interpreted as a boolean.

Throws   NullPointerException – if key is null.

IllegalStateException – if this node (or an ancestor) has been removed with the removeNode() method.

See Also   get (String, String), putBoolean (String, boolean)

106.6.3.7   **public byte[] getByteArray(String key, byte[] def)**

key key whose associated value is to be returned as a byte[] object.

def the value to be returned in the event that this node has no value associated with key or the associated value cannot be interpreted as a byte[] type, or the backing store is inaccessible.

☐ Returns the byte[] value represented by the String object associated with the specified key in this node. Valid String objects are *Base64* encoded binary data, as defined in RFC 2045 (http:// www.ietf.org/rfc/rfc2045.txt) , Section 6.8, with one minor change: the string must consist solely of characters from the *Base64 Alphabet*; no newline characters or extraneous characters are permitted. This method is intended for use in conjunction with the putByteArray method.

Returns the specified default if there is no value associated with the key, the backing store is inaccessible, or if the associated value is not a valid Base64 encoded byte array (as defined above).

Returns the byte[] value represented by the String object associated with key in this node, or def if the associated value does not exist or cannot be interpreted as a byte[].

Throws NullPointerException – if key is null. (A null value for def*is* permitted.)

IllegalStateException – if this node (or an ancestor) has been removed with the removeNode() method.

See Also get(String,String), putByteArray(String,byte[])

106.6.3.8   **public double getDouble(String key, double def)**

key key whose associated value is to be returned as a double value.

def the value to be returned in the event that this node has no value associated with key or the associated value cannot be interpreted as a double type or the backing store is inaccessible.

☐ Returns the double value represented by the String object associated with the specified key in this node. The String object is converted to a double value as by Double.parseDouble(String). Returns the specified default if there is no value associated with the key, the backing store is inaccessible, or if Double.parseDouble(String) would throw a NumberFormatException if the associated value were passed. This method is intended for use in conjunction with the putDouble method.

Returns the double value represented by the String object associated with key in this node, or def if the associated value does not exist or cannot be interpreted as a double type.

Throws IllegalStateException – if this node (or an ancestor) has been removed with the the removeNode() method.

NullPointerException – if key is null.

See Also putDouble(String,double), get(String,String)

106.6.3.9   **public float getFloat(String key, float def)**

key key whose associated value is to be returned as a float value.

def the value to be returned in the event that this node has no value associated with key or the associated value cannot be interpreted as a float type or the backing store is inaccessible.

☐ Returns the float value represented by the String object associated with the specified key in this node. The String object is converted to a float value as by Float.parseFloat(String). Returns the specified default if there is no value associated with the key, the backing store is inaccessible, or if Float.parseFloat(String) would throw a NumberFormatException if the associated value were passed. This method is intended for use in conjunction with the putFloat method.

Returns the float value represented by the string associated with key in this node, or def if the associated value does not exist or cannot be interpreted as a float type.

Throws IllegalStateException – if this node (or an ancestor) has been removed with the removeNode() method.

NullPointerException – if key is null.

See Also putFloat(String, float), get(String, String)

106.6.3.10   **public int getInt(String key, int def)**

key key whose associated value is to be returned as an int.

def the value to be returned in the event that this node has no value associated with key or the associated value cannot be interpreted as an int or the backing store is inaccessible.

☐ Returns the int value represented by the String object associated with the specified key in this node. The String object is converted to an int as by Integer.parseInt(String). Returns the specified default if there is no value associated with the key, the backing store is inaccessible, or if Integer.parseInt(String) would throw a NumberFormatException if the associated value were passed. This method is intended for use in conjunction with the putInt method.

Returns the int value represented by the String object associated with key in this node, or def if the associated value does not exist or cannot be interpreted as an int type.

Throws NullPointerException – if key is null.

IllegalStateException – if this node (or an ancestor) has been removed with the removeNode() method.

See Also putInt(String, int), get(String, String)

106.6.3.11   **public long getLong(String key, long def)**

key key whose associated value is to be returned as a long value.

def the value to be returned in the event that this node has no value associated with key or the associated value cannot be interpreted as a long type or the backing store is inaccessible.

☐ Returns the long value represented by the String object associated with the specified key in this node. The String object is converted to a long as by Long.parseLong(String). Returns the specified default if there is no value associated with the key, the backing store is inaccessible, or if Long.parseLong(String) would throw a NumberFormatException if the associated value were passed. This method is intended for use in conjunction with the putLong method.

Returns the long value represented by the String object associated with key in this node, or def if the associated value does not exist or cannot be interpreted as a long type.

Throws NullPointerException – if key is null.

IllegalStateException – if this node (or an ancestor) has been removed with the removeNode() method.

See Also putLong(String, long), get(String, String)

106.6.3.12   **public String[] keys( ) throws BackingStoreException**

☐ Returns all of the keys that have an associated value in this node. (The returned array will be of size zero if this node has no preferences and not null!)

Returns an array of the keys that have an associated value in this node.

Throws BackingStoreException – if this operation cannot be completed due to a failure in the backing store, or inability to communicate with it.

IllegalStateException – if this node (or an ancestor) has been removed with the removeNode() method.

106.6.3.13   **public String name( )**

☐ Returns this node's name, relative to its parent.

Returns this node's name, relative to its parent.

106.6.3.14   **public Preferences node(String pathName)**

pathName the path name of the Preferences object to return.

☐ Returns a named Preferences object (node), creating it and any of its ancestors if they do not already exist. Accepts a relative or absolute pathname. Absolute pathnames (which begin with '/') are interpreted relative to the root of this node. Relative pathnames (which begin with any character other than '/') are interpreted relative to this node itself. The empty string ("") is a valid relative pathname, referring to this node itself.

If the returned node did not exist prior to this call, this node and any ancestors that were created by this call are not guaranteed to become persistent until the flush method is called on the returned node (or one of its descendants).

Returns the specified Preferences object.

Throws IllegalArgumentException – if the path name is invalid.

IllegalStateException – if this node (or an ancestor) has been removed with the removeNode() method.

NullPointerException – if path name is null.

See Also flush()

106.6.3.15   **public boolean nodeExists(String pathName) throws BackingStoreException**

pathName the path name of the node whose existence is to be checked.

☐ Returns true if the named node exists. Accepts a relative or absolute pathname. Absolute pathnames (which begin with '/') are interpreted relative to the root of this node. Relative pathnames (which begin with any character other than '/') are interpreted relative to this node itself. The pathname "" is valid, and refers to this node itself.

If this node (or an ancestor) has already been removed with the removeNode() method, it *is* legal to invoke this method, but only with the pathname ""; the invocation will return false. Thus, the idiom p.nodeExists("") may be used to test whether p has been removed.

Returns true if the specified node exists.

Throws BackingStoreException – if this operation cannot be completed due to a failure in the backing store, or inability to communicate with it.

IllegalStateException – if this node (or an ancestor) has been removed with the removeNode() method and pathname is not the empty string ("").

IllegalArgumentException – if the path name is invalid (i.e., it contains multiple consecutive slash characters, or ends with a slash character and is more than one character long).

106.6.3.16   **public Preferences parent( )**

☐ Returns the parent of this node, or null if this is the root.

Returns the parent of this node.

Throws IllegalStateException – if this node (or an ancestor) has been removed with the removeNode() method.

106.6.3.17   **public void put(String key, String value)**

key key with which the specified value is to be associated.

value value to be associated with the specified key.

◻ Associates the specified value with the specified key in this node.

Throws NullPointerException – if key or value is null.

IllegalStateException – if this node (or an ancestor) has been removed with the removeNode() method.

106.6.3.18   **public void putBoolean(String key, boolean value)**

key key with which the string form of value is to be associated.

value value whose string form is to be associated with key.

◻ Associates a String object representing the specified boolean value with the specified key in this node. The associated string is "true" if the value is true, and "false" if it is false. This method is intended for use in conjunction with the getBoolean method.

Implementor's note: it is *not* necessary that the value be represented by a string in the backing store. If the backing store supports boolean values, it is not unreasonable to use them. This implementation detail is not visible through the Preferences API, which allows the value to be read as a boolean (with getBoolean) or a String (with get) type.

Throws NullPointerException – if key is null.

IllegalStateException – if this node (or an ancestor) has been·removed with the removeNode() method.

See Also getBoolean(String,boolean),get(String,String)

106.6.3.19   **public void putByteArray(String key, byte[] value)**

key key with which the string form of value is to be associated.

value value whose string form is to be associated with key.

◻ Associates a String object representing the specified byte[] with the specified key in this node. The associated String object the *Base64* encoding of the byte[], as defined in RFC 2045 (http:// www.ietf.org/rfc/rfc2045.txt), Section 6.8, with one minor change: the string will consist solely of characters from the *Base64 Alphabet*; it will not contain any newline characters. This method is intended for use in conjunction with the getByteArray method.

Implementor's note: it is *not* necessary that the value be represented by a String type in the backing store. If the backing store supports byte[] values, it is not unreasonable to use them. This implementation detail is not visible through the Preferences API, which allows the value to be read as an byte[] object (with getByteArray) or a String object (with get).

Throws NullPointerException – if key or value is null.

IllegalStateException – if this node (or an ancestor) has been removed with the removeNode() method.

See Also getByteArray(String,byte[]),get(String,String)

106.6.3.20   **public void putDouble(String key, double value)**

key key with which the string form of value is to be associated.

value value whose string form is to be associated with key.

◻ Associates a String object representing the specified double value with the specified key in this node. The associated String object is the one that would be returned if the double value were passed to Double.toString(double). This method is intended for use in conjunction with the getDouble method

Implementor's note: it is *not* necessary that the value be represented by a string in the backing store. If the backing store supports double values, it is not unreasonable to use them. This implementation detail is not visible through the Preferences API, which allows the value to be read as a double (with getDouble) or a String (with get) type.

Throws NullPointerException – if key is null.

IllegalStateException – if this node (or an ancestor) has been removed with the removeNode() method.

See Also getDouble(String, double)

106.6.3.21   **public void putFloat(String key, float value)**

key key with which the string form of value is to be associated.

value value whose string form is to be associated with key.

☐ Associates a String object representing the specified float value with the specified key in this node. The associated String object is the one that would be returned if the float value were passed to Float.toString(float). This method is intended for use in conjunction with the getFloat method.

Implementor's note: it is *not* necessary that the value be represented by a string in the backing store. If the backing store supports float values, it is not unreasonable to use them. This implementation detail is not visible through the Preferences API, which allows the value to be read as a float (with getFloat) or a String (with get) type.

Throws NullPointerException – if key is null.

IllegalStateException – if this node (or an ancestor) has been removed with the removeNode() method.

See Also getFloat(String, float)

106.6.3.22   **public void putInt(String key, int value)**

key key with which the string form of value is to be associated.

value value whose string form is to be associated with key.

☐ Associates a String object representing the specified int value with the specified key in this node. The associated string is the one that would be returned if the int value were passed to Integer.toString(int). This method is intended for use in conjunction with getInt method.

Implementor's note: it is *not* necessary that the property value be represented by a String object in the backing store. If the backing store supports integer values, it is not unreasonable to use them. This implementation detail is not visible through the Preferences API, which allows the value to be read as an int (with getInt or a String (with get) type.

Throws NullPointerException – if key is null.

IllegalStateException – if this node (or an ancestor) has been removed with the removeNode() method.

See Also getInt(String, int)

106.6.3.23   **public void putLong(String key, long value)**

key key with which the string form of value is to be associated.

value value whose string form is to be associated with key.

☐ Associates a String object representing the specified long value with the specified key in this node. The associated String object is the one that would be returned if the long value were passed to Long.toString(long). This method is intended for use in conjunction with the getLong method.

Implementor's note: it is *not* necessary that the value be represented by a String type in the backing store. If the backing store supports long values, it is not unreasonable to use them. This implementation detail is not visible through the Preferences API, which allows the value to be read as a long (with getLong or a String (with get) type.

Throws NullPointerException – if key is null.

IllegalStateException – if this node (or an ancestor) has been removed with the removeNode() method.

See Also getLong(String, long)

106.6.3.24   **public void remove(String key)**

key key whose mapping is to be removed from this node.

☐ Removes the value associated with the specified key in this node, if any.

Throws IllegalStateException – if this node (or an ancestor) has been removed with the removeNode() method.

See Also get(String, String)

106.6.3.25   **public void removeNode( ) throws BackingStoreException**

☐ Removes this node and all of its descendants, invalidating any properties contained in the removed nodes. Once a node has been removed, attempting any method other than name(),absolutePath() or nodeExists("") on the corresponding Preferences instance will fail with an IllegalStateException. (The methods defined on Object can still be invoked on a node after it has been removed; they will not throw IllegalStateException.)

The removal is not guaranteed to be persistent until the flush method is called on the parent of this node.

Throws IllegalStateException – if this node (or an ancestor) has already been removed with the removeNode() method.

BackingStoreException – if this operation cannot be completed due to a failure in the backing store, or inability to communicate with it.

See Also flush()

106.6.3.26   **public void sync( ) throws BackingStoreException**

☐ Ensures that future reads from this node and its descendants reflect any changes that were committed to the persistent store (from any VM) prior to the sync invocation. As a side-effect, forces any changes in the contents of this node and its descendants to the persistent store, as if the flush method had been invoked on this node.

Throws BackingStoreException – if this operation cannot be completed due to a failure in the backing store, or inability to communicate with it.

IllegalStateException – if this node (or an ancestor) has been removed with the removeNode() method.

See Also flush()

106.6.4   public interface PreferencesService

The Preferences Service.

Each bundle using this service has its own set of preference trees: one for system preferences, and one for each user.

A PreferencesService object is specific to the bundle which obtained it from the service registry. If a bundle wishes to allow another bundle to access its preferences, it should pass its PreferencesService object to that bundle.

106.6.4.1   **public Preferences getSystemPreferences( )**

☐ Returns the root system node for the calling bundle.

Returns The root system node for the calling bundle.

106.6.4.2   **public Preferences getUserPreferences(String name)**

name The user for which to return the preference root node.

☐ Returns the root node for the specified user and the calling bundle.

Returns The root node for the specified user and the calling bundle.

106.6.4.3   **public String[] getUsers( )**

☐ Returns the names of users for which node trees exist.

Returns The names of users for which node trees exist.

106.7   References

[1] *JSR 10 Preferences API*
     http://www.jcp.org/jsr/detail/10.jsp

[2] *RFC 2045 Base 64 encoding*
     http://www.ietf.org/rfc/rfc2045.txt

107 User Admin Service Specification

Version 1.1

107.1 Introduction

OSGi Service Platforms are often used in places where end users or devices initiate actions. These kinds of actions inevitably create a need for authenticating the initiator. Authenticating can be done in many different ways, including with passwords, one-time token cards, bio-metrics, and certificates.

Once the initiator is authenticated, it is necessary to verify that this principal is authorized to perform the requested action. This authorization can only be decided by the operator of the OSGi environment, and thus requires administration.

The User Admin service provides this type of functionality. Bundles can use the User Admin service to authenticate an initiator and represent this authentication as an Authorization object. Bundles that execute actions on behalf of this user can use the Authorization object to verify if that user is authorized.

The User Admin service provides authorization based on who runs the code, instead of using the Java code-based permission model. See [1] *The Java Security Architecture for JDK 1.2*. It performs a role similar to [2] *Java Authentication and Authorization Service*.

107.1.1 Essentials

- *Authentication* – A large number of authentication schemes already exist, and more will be developed. The User Admin service must be flexible enough to adapt to the many different authentication schemes that can be run on a computer system.
- *Authorization* – All bundles should use the User Admin service to authenticate users and to find out if those users are authorized. It is therefore paramount that a bundle can find out authorization information with little effort.
- *Security* – Detailed security, based on the Framework security model, is needed to provide safe access to the User Admin service. It should allow limited access to the credentials and other properties.
- *Extensibility* – Other bundles should be able to build on the User Admin service. It should be possible to examine the information from this service and get real-time notifications of changes.
- *Properties* – The User Admin service must maintain a persistent database of users. It must be possible to use this database to hold more information about this user.
- *Administration* – Administering authorizations for each possible action and initiator is time-consuming and error-prone. It is therefore necessary to have mechanisms to group end users and make it simple to assign authorizations to all members of a group at one time.

107.1.2 Entities

This Specification defines the following User Admin service entities:

- *UserAdmin* – This interface manages a database of named roles which can be used for authorization and authentication purposes.
- *Role* – This interface exposes the characteristics shared by all roles: a name, a type, and a set of properties.

- *User* – This interface (which extends Role) is used to represent any entity which may have credentials associated with it. These credentials can be used to authenticate an initiator.
- *Group* – This interface (which extends User) is used to contain an aggregation of named Role objects (Group or User objects).
- *Authorization* – This interface encapsulates an authorization context on which bundles can base authorization decisions.
- *UserAdminEvent* – This class is used to represent a role change event.
- *UserAdminListener* – This interface provides a listener for events of type UserAdminEvent that can be registered as a service.
- *UserAdminPermission* – This permission is needed to configure and access the roles managed by a User Admin service.
- *Role.USER_ANYONE* – This is a special User object that represents *any* user, it implies all other User objects. It is also used when a Group is used with only basic members. The Role.USER_ANYONE is then the only required member.

Figure 107.1   *User Admin Service*, org.osgi.service.useradmin

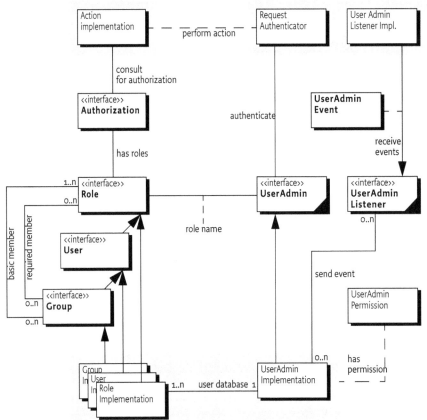

107.1.3   Operation

An Operator uses the User Admin service to define OSGi Service Platform users and configure them with properties, credentials, and *roles*.

A Role object represents the initiator of a request (human or otherwise). This specification defines two types of roles:

- *User* – A User object can be configured with credentials, such as a password, and properties, such as address, telephone number, and so on.
- *Group* – A Group object is an aggregation of *basic* and *required* roles. Basic and required roles are used in the authorization phase.

An OSGi Service Platform can have several entry points, each of which will be responsible for authenticating incoming requests. An example of an entry point is the Http Service, which delegates authentication of incoming requests to the handleSecurity method of the HttpContext object that was specified when the target servlet or resource of the request was registered.

The OSGi Service Platform entry points should use the information in the User Admin service to authenticate incoming requests, such as a password stored in the private credentials or the use of a certificate.

A bundle can determine if a request for an action is authorized by looking for a Role object that has the name of the requested action.

The bundle may execute the action if the Role object representing the initiator *implies* the Role object representing the requested action.

For example, an initiator Role object *X* implies an action Group object *A* if:

- *X* implies at least one of *A*'s basic members, and
- *X* implies all of *A*'s required members.

An initiator Role object *X* implies an action User object *A* if:

- *A* and *X* are equal.

The Authorization class handles this non-trivial logic. The User Admin service can capture the privileges of an authenticated User object into an Authorization object. The Authorization.hasRole method checks if the authenticate User object has (or implies) a specified action Role object.

For example, in the case of the Http Service, the HttpContext object can authenticate the initiator and place an Authorization object in the request header. The servlet calls the hasRole method on this Authorization object to verify that the initiator has the authority to perform a certain action. See *Authentication* on page 32.

107.2 Authentication

The authentication phase determines if the initiator is actually the one it says it is. Mechanisms to authenticate always need some information related to the user or the OSGi Service Platform to authenticate an external user. This information can consist of the following:

- A secret known only to the initiator.
- Knowledge about cards that can generate a unique token.
- Public information like certificates of trusted signers.
- Information about the user that can be measured in a trusted way.
- Other specific information.

107.2.1 Repository

The User Admin service offers a repository of Role objects. Each Role object has a unique name and a set of properties that are readable by anyone, and are changeable when the changer has the UserAdminPermission. Additionally, User objects, a sub-interface of Role, also have a set of private protected properties called credentials. Credentials are an extra set of properties that are used to authenticate users and that are protected by UserAdminPermission.

Properties are accessed with the Role.getProperties() method and credentials with the User.getCredentials()method. Both methods return a Dictionary object containing key/value pairs. The keys are String objects and the values of the Dictionary object are limited to String or byte[ ] objects.

This specification does not define any standard keys for the properties or credentials. The keys depend on the implementation of the authentication mechanism and are not formally defined by OSGi specifications.

The repository can be searched for objects that have a unique property (key/value pair) with the method UserAdmin.getUser(String,String). This makes it easy to find a specific user related to a specific authentication mechanism. For example, a secure card mechanism that generates unique tokens could have a serial number identifying the user. The owner of the card could be found with the method

```
User owner = useradmin.getUser(
    "secure-card-serial", "132456712-1212" );
```

If multiple User objects have the same property (key *and* value), a null is returned.

There is a convenience method to verify that a user has a credential without actually getting the credential. This is the User.hasCredential(String,Object) method.

Access to credentials is protected on a name basis by UserAdminPermission. Because properties can be read by anyone with access to a User object, UserAdminPermission only protects change access to properties.

107.2.2   Basic Authentication

The following example shows a very simple authentication algorithm based on passwords.

The vendor of the authentication bundle uses the property "com.acme.basic-id" to contain the name of a user as it logs in. This property is used to locate the User object in the repository. Next, the credential "com.acme.password" contains the password and is compared to the entered password. If the password is correct, the User object is returned. In all other cases a SecurityException is thrown.

```
public User authenticate(
    UserAdmin ua, String name, String pwd )
  throws SecurityException {
  User user = ua.getUser("com.acme.basicid",
    username);
  if (user == null)
    throw new SecurityException( "No such user" );

  if (!user.hasCredential("com.acme.password", pwd))
    throw new SecurityException(
      "Invalid password" );
  return user;
}
```

107.2.3   Certificates

Authentication based on certificates does not require a shared secret. Instead, a certificate contains a name, a public key, and the signature of one or more signers.

The name in the certificate can be used to locate a User object in the repository. Locating a User object, however, only identifies the initiator and does not authenticate it.

1. The first step to authenticate the initiator is to verify that it has the private key of the certificate.

2. Next, the User Admin service must verify that it has a User object with the right property, for example "com.acme.certificate"="Fudd".

3. The next step is to see if the certificate is signed by a trusted source. The bundle could use a central list of trusted signers and only accept certificates signed by those sources. Alternatively, it could require that the certificate itself is already stored in the repository under a unique key as a byte[] in the credentials.

4. In any case, once the certificate is verified, the associated User object is authenticated.

107.3   Authorization

The User Admin service authorization architecture is a *role-based model*. In this model, every action that can be performed by a bundle is associated with a *role*. Such a role is a Group object (called group from now on) from the User Admin service repository. For example, if a servlet could be used to activate the alarm system, there should be a group named AlarmSystemActivation.

The operator can administrate authorizations by populating the group with User objects (users) and other groups. Groups are used to minimize the amount of administration required. For example, it is easier to create one Administrators group and add administrative roles to it rather than individually administer all users for each role. Such a group requires only one action to remove or add a user as an administrator.

The authorization decision can now be made in two fundamentally different ways:

An initiator could be allowed to carry out an action (represented by a Group object) if it implied any of the Group object's members. For example, the AlarmSystemActivation Group object contains an Administrators and a Family Group object:

```
Administrators            = { Elmer, Pepe, Bugs }
Family                    = { Elmer, Pepe, Daffy }

AlarmSystemActivation     = { Administrators, Family }
```

Any of the four members Elmer, Pepe, Daffy, or Bugs can activate the alarm system.

Alternatively, an initiator could be allowed to perform an action (represented by a Group object) if it implied *all* the Group object's members. In this case, using the same AlarmSystemActivation group, only Elmer and Pepe would be authorized to activate the alarm system, since Daffy and Bugs are *not* members of *both* the Administrators and Family Group objects.

The User Admin service supports a combination of both strategies by defining both a set of *basic members* (any) and a set of *required members* (all).

```
Administrators  = { Elmer, Pepe, Bugs }
Family          = { Elmer, Pepe, Daffy }

AlarmSystemActivation
   required     = { Administrators }
   basic        = { Family }
```

The difference is made when Role objects are added to the Group object. To add a basic member, use the Group.addMember(Role) method. To add a required member, use the Group.addRequiredMember(Role) method.

Basic members define the set of members that can get access and required members reduce this set by requiring the initiator to *imply* each required member.

A User object implies a Group object if it implies the following:

- *All* of the Group's required members, and
- At *least* one of the Group's basic members

A User object always implies itself.

If only required members are used to qualify the implication, then the standard user Role.USER_ANYONE can be obtained from the User Admin service and added to the Group object. This Role object is implied by anybody and therefore does not affect the required members.

107.3.1   The Authorization Object

The complexity of authorization is hidden in an Authorization class. Normally, the authenticator should retrieve an Authorization object from the User Admin service by passing the authenticated User object as an argument. This Authorization object is then passed to the bundle that performs the action. This bundle checks the authorization with the Authorization.hasRole(String) method. The performing bundle must pass the name of the action as an argument. The Authorization object checks whether the authenticated user implies the Role object, specifically a Group object, with the given name. This is shown in the following example.

```
public void activateAlarm(Authorization auth) {
    if ( auth.hasRole( "AlarmSystemActivation" ) ) {
        // activate the alarm
        ...
    }
    else throw new SecurityException(
        "Not authorized to activate alarm" );
}
```

107.3.2   Authorization Example

This section demonstrates a possible use of the User Admin service. The service has a flexible model and many other schemes are possible.

Assume an Operator installs an OSGi Service Platform. Bundles in this environment have defined the following action groups:

```
AlarmSystemControl
InternetAccess
TemperatureControl
PhotoAlbumEdit
PhotoAlbumView
PortForwarding
```

Installing and uninstalling bundles could potentially extend this set. Therefore, the Operator also defines a number of groups that can be used to contain the different types of system users.

```
Administrators
Buddies
Children
Adults
Residents
```

In a particular instance, the Operator installs it in a household with the following residents and buddies:

```
Residents:        Elmer, Fudd, Marvin, Pepe
Buddies:          Daffy, Foghorn
```

First, the residents and buddies are assigned to the system user groups. Second, the user groups need to be assigned to the action groups.

The following tables show how the groups could be assigned.

Table 107.1   *Example Groups with Basic and Required Members*

Groups	Elmer	Fudd	Marvin	Pepe	Daffy	Foghorn
Residents	Basic	Basic	Basic	Basic	-	-
Buddies	-	-	-	-	Basic	Basic
Children	-	-	Basic	Basic	-	-
Adults	Basic	Basic	-	-	-	-
Administrators	Basic	-	-	-	-	-

Table 107.2   *Example Action Groups with their Basic and Required Members*

Groups	Residents	Buddies	Children	Adults	Admin
AlarmSystemControl	Basic	-	-	-	Required
InternetAccess	Basic	-	-	Required	-
TemperatureControl	Basic	-	-	Required	-
PhotoAlbumEdit	Basic	-	Basic	Basic	-
PhotoAlbumView	Basic	Basic	-	-	-
PortForwarding	Basic	-	-	-	Required

107.4 Repository Maintenance

The UserAdmin interface is a straightforward API to maintain a repository of User and Group objects. It contains methods to create new Group and User objects with the createRole(String,int) method. The method is prepared so that the same signature can be used to create new types of roles in the future. The interface also contains a method to remove a Role object.

The existing configuration can be obtained with methods that list all Role objects using a filter argument. This filter, which has the same syntax as the Framework filter, must only return the Role objects for which the filter matches the properties.

Several utility methods simplify getting User objects depending on their properties.

107.5 User Admin Events

Changes in the User Admin service can be determined in real time. Each User Admin service implementation must send a UserAdminEvent object to any service in the Framework service registry that is registered under the UserAdminListener interface. This event must be send asynchronously from the cause of the event. The way events must be delivered is the same as described in *Delivering Events* on page 116 of the Core specification.

This procedure is demonstrated in the following code sample.

```
class Listener implements UserAdminListener {
    public void roleChanged( UserAdminEvent event ) {
        ...
    }
}
public class MyActivator
    implements BundleActivator {
```

```
      public void start( BundleContext context ) {
        context. registerService(
          UserAdminListener.class.getName(),
          new Listener(), null );
      }
      public void stop( BundleContext context ) {}
    }
```

It is not necessary to unregister the listener object when the bundle is stopped because the Framework automatically unregisters it. Once registered, the UserAdminListener object must be notified of all changes to the role repository.

107.5.1 Event Admin and User Admin Change Events

User admin events must be delivered asynchronously to the Event Admin service by the implementation, if present. The topic of a User Admin Event is:

org/osgi/service/useradmin/UserAdmin/<event type>

The following event types are supported:

```
ROLE_CREATED
ROLE_CHANGED
ROLE_REMOVED
```

All User Admin Events must have the following properties:

- event – (UserAdminEvent) The event that was broadcast by the User Admin service.
- role – (Role) The Role object that was created, modified or removed.
- role.name – (String) The name of the role.
- role.type – (Integer) One of ROLE, USER or GROUP.
- service – (ServiceReference) The Service Reference of the User Admin service.
- service.id – (Long) The User Admin service's ID.
- service.objectClass – (String[]) The User Admin service's object class (which must include org.osgi.service.useradmin.UserAdmin)
- service.pid – (String) The User Admin service's persistent identity

107.6 Security

The User Admin service is related to the security model of the OSGi Service Platform, but is complementary to the [1] *The Java Security Architecture for JDK 1.2*. The final permission of most code should be the intersection of the Java 2 Permissions, which are based on the code that is executing, and the User Admin service authorization, which is based on the user for whom the code runs.

107.6.1 UserAdminPermission

The User Admin service defines the UserAdminPermission class that can be used to restrict bundles in accessing credentials. This permission class has the following actions:

- changeProperty – This permission is required to modify properties. The name of the permission is the prefix of the property name.
- changeCredential – This action permits changing credentials. The name of the permission is the prefix of the name of the credential.
- getCredential – This action permits getting credentials. The name of the permission is the prefix of the credential.

If the name of the permission is "admin", it allows the owner to administer the repository. No action is associated with the permission in that case.

Otherwise, the permission name is used to match the property name. This name may end with a ".*" string to indicate a wildcard. For example, com.acme.*matches com.acme.fudd.elmer and com.acme.bugs.

107.7   Relation to JAAS

At a glance, the Java Authorization and Authentication Service (JAAS) seems to be a very suitable model for user administration. The OSGi organization, however, decided to develop an independent User Admin service because JAAS was not deemed applicable. The reasons for this include dependency on J2SE version 1.3 ("JDK 1.3") and existing mechanisms in the previous OSGi Service Gateway 1.0 specification.

107.7.1   JDK 1.3 Dependencies

The authorization component of JAAS relies on the java.security.DomainCombiner interface, which provides a means to dynamically update the ProtectionDomain objects affiliated with an AccessControlContext object.

This interface was added in JDK 1.3. In the context of JAAS, the SubjectDomainCombiner object, which implements the DomainCombiner interface, is used to update ProtectionDomain objects. The permissions of ProtectionDomain objects depend on where code came from and who signed it, with permissions based on who is running the code.

Leveraging JAAS would have resulted in user-based access control on the OSGi Service Platform being available only with JDK 1.3, which was not deemed acceptable.

107.7.2   Existing OSGi Mechanism

JAAS provides a pluggable authentication architecture, which enables applications and their underlying authentication services to remain independent from each other.

The Http Service already provides a similar feature by allowing servlet and resource registrations to be supported by an HttpContext object, which uses a callback mechanism to perform any required authentication checks before granting access to the servlet or resource. This way, the registering bundle has complete control on a per-servlet and per-resource basis over which authentication protocol to use, how the credentials presented by the remote requestor are to be validated, and who should be granted access to the servlet or resource.

107.7.3   Future Road Map

In the future, the main barrier of 1.3 compatibility will be removed. JAAS could then be implemented in an OSGi environment. At that time, the User Admin service will still be needed and will provide complementary services in the following ways:

- The authorization component relies on group membership information to be stored and managed outside JAAS. JAAS does not manage persistent information, so the User Admin service can be a provider of group information when principals are assigned to a Subject object.
- The authorization component allows for credentials to be collected and verified, but a repository is needed to actually validate the credentials.

In the future, the User Admin service can act as the back-end database to JAAS. The only aspect JAAS will remove from the User Admin service is the need for the Authorization interface.

107.8   org.osgi.service.useradmin

User Admin Package Version 1.1.

Bundles wishing to use this package must list the package in the Import-Package header of the bundle's manifest. For example:

```
Import-Package: org.osgi.service.useradmin; version="[1.1,2.0)"
```

107.8.1 Summary

- *Authorization* - The Authorization interface encapsulates an authorization context on which bundles can base authorization decisions, where appropriate.
- *Group* - A named grouping of roles (Role objects).
- *Role* - The base interface for Role objects managed by the User Admin service.
- *User* - A User role managed by a User Admin service.
- *UserAdmin* - This interface is used to manage a database of named Role objects, which can be used for authentication and authorization purposes.
- *UserAdminEvent* - Role change event.
- *UserAdminListener* - Listener for UserAdminEvents.
- *UserAdminPermission* - Permission to configure and access the Role objects managed by a User Admin service.

107.8.2 public interface Authorization

The Authorization interface encapsulates an authorization context on which bundles can base authorization decisions, where appropriate.

Bundles associate the privilege to access restricted resources or operations with roles. Before granting access to a restricted resource or operation, a bundle will check if the Authorization object passed to it possess the required role, by calling its hasRole method.

Authorization contexts are instantiated by calling the UserAdmin.getAuthorization method.

Trusting Authorization objects

There are no restrictions regarding the creation of Authorization objects. Hence, a service must only accept Authorization objects from bundles that has been authorized to use the service using code based (or Java 2) permissions.

In some cases it is useful to use ServicePermission to do the code based access control. A service basing user access control on Authorization objects passed to it, will then require that a calling bundle has the ServicePermission to get the service in question. This is the most convenient way. The OSGi environment will do the code based permission check when the calling bundle attempts to get the service from the service registry.

Example: A servlet using a service on a user's behalf. The bundle with the servlet must be given the ServicePermission to get the Http Service.

However, in some cases the code based permission checks need to be more fine-grained. A service might allow all bundles to get it, but require certain code based permissions for some of its methods.

Example: A servlet using a service on a user's behalf, where some service functionality is open to anyone, and some is restricted by code based permissions. When a restricted method is called (e.g., one handing over an Authorization object), the service explicitly checks that the calling bundle has permission to make the call.

107.8.2.1 public String getName( )

☐ Gets the name of the User that this Authorization context was created for.

Returns The name of the User object that this Authorization context was created for, or null if no user was specified when this Authorization context was created.

107.8.2.2 public String[] getRoles( )

☐ Gets the names of all roles implied by this Authorization context.

Returns The names of all roles implied by this Authorization context, or null if no roles are in the context. The predefined role user.anyone will not be included in this list.

107.8.2.3   **public boolean hasRole(String name)**

name The name of the role to check for.

□ Checks if the role with the specified name is implied by this Authorization context.

Bundles must define globally unique role names that are associated with the privilege of accessing restricted resources or operations. Operators will grant users access to these resources, by creating a Group object for each role and adding User objects to it.

Returns true if this Authorization context implies the specified role, otherwise false.

**107.8.3   public interface Group
extends User**

A named grouping of roles (Role objects).

Whether or not a given Authorization context implies a Group object depends on the members of that Group object.

A Group object can have two kinds of members: *basic* and *required*. A Group object is implied by an Authorization context if all of its required members are implied and at least one of its basic members is implied.

A Group object must contain at least one basic member in order to be implied. In other words, a Group object without any basic member roles is never implied by any Authorization context.

A User object always implies itself.

No loop detection is performed when adding members to Group objects, which means that it is possible to create circular implications. Loop detection is instead done when roles are checked. The semantics is that if a role depends on itself (i.e., there is an implication loop), the role is not implied.

The rule that a Group object must have at least one basic member to be implied is motivated by the following example:

```
group foo
  required members: marketing
  basic members: alice, bob
```

Privileged operations that require membership in "foo" can be performed only by "alice" and "bob", who are in marketing.

If "alice" and "bob" ever transfer to a different department, anybody in marketing will be able to assume the "foo" role, which certainly must be prevented. Requiring that "foo" (or any Group object for that matter) must have at least one basic member accomplishes that.

However, this would make it impossible for a Group object to be implied by just its required members. An example where this implication might be useful is the following declaration: "Any citizen who is an adult is allowed to vote." An intuitive configuration of "voter" would be:

```
group voter
  required members: citizen, adult
    basic members:
```

However, according to the above rule, the "voter" role could never be assumed by anybody, since it lacks any basic members. In order to address this issue a predefined role named "user.anyone" can be specified, which is always implied. The desired implication of the "voter" group can then be achieved by specifying "user.anyone" as its basic member, as follows:

```
group voter
   required members: citizen, adult
      basic members: user.anyone
```

107.8.3.1   **public boolean addMember(Role role)**

role   The role to add as a basic member.

☐   Adds the specified Role object as a basic member to this Group object.

Returns   true if the given role could be added as a basic member, and false if this Group object already contains a Role object whose name matches that of the specified role.

Throws   SecurityException – If a security manager exists and the caller does not have the UserAdminPermission with name admin.

107.8.3.2   **public boolean addRequiredMember(Role role)**

role   The Role object to add as a required member.

☐   Adds the specified Role object as a required member to this Group object.

Returns   true if the given Role object could be added as a required member, and false if this Group object already contains a Role object whose name matches that of the specified role.

Throws   SecurityException – If a security manager exists and the caller does not have the UserAdminPermission with name admin.

107.8.3.3   **public Role[] getMembers( )**

☐   Gets the basic members of this Group object.

Returns   The basic members of this Group object, or null if this Group object does not contain any basic members.

107.8.3.4   **public Role[] getRequiredMembers( )**

☐   Gets the required members of this Group object.

Returns   The required members of this Group object, or null if this Group object does not contain any required members.

107.8.3.5   **public boolean removeMember(Role role)**

role   The Role object to remove from this Group object.

☐   Removes the specified Role object from this Group object.

Returns   true if the Role object could be removed, otherwise false.

Throws   SecurityException – If a security manager exists and the caller does not have the UserAdminPermission with name admin.

107.8.4   public interface Role

The base interface for Role objects managed by the User Admin service.

This interface exposes the characteristics shared by all Role classes: a name, a type, and a set of properties.

Properties represent public information about the Role object that can be read by anyone. Specific UserAdminPermission objects are required to change a Role object's properties.

Role object properties are Dictionary objects. Changes to these objects are propagated to the User Admin service and made persistent.

Every User Admin service contains a set of predefined Role objects that are always present and cannot be removed. All predefined Role objects are of type ROLE. This version of the org.osgi.service.useradmin package defines a single predefined role named "user.anyone", which is inherited by any other role. Other predefined roles may be added in the future. Since "user.anyone" is a Role object that has properties associated with it that can be read and modified. Access to these properties and their use is application specific and is controlled using UserAdminPermission in the same way that properties for other Role objects are.

107.8.4.1   **public static final int GROUP = 2**

The type of a Group role.

The value of GROUP is 2.

107.8.4.2   **public static final int ROLE = 0**

The type of a predefined role.

The value of ROLE is 0.

107.8.4.3   **public static final int USER = 1**

The type of a User role.

The value of USER is 1.

107.8.4.4   **public static final String USER_ANYONE = "user.anyone"**

The name of the predefined role, user.anyone, that all users and groups belong to.

Since 1.1

107.8.4.5   **public String getName( )**

☐ Returns the name of this role.

Returns The role's name.

107.8.4.6   **public Dictionary getProperties( )**

☐ Returns a Dictionary of the (public) properties of this Role object. Any changes to the returned Dictionary will change the properties of this Role object. This will cause a UserAdminEvent object of type UserAdminEvent.ROLE_CHANGED to be broadcast to any UserAdminListener objects.

Only objects of type String may be used as property keys, and only objects of type String or byte[] may be used as property values. Any other types will cause an exception of type IllegalArgumentException to be raised.

In order to add, change, or remove a property in the returned Dictionary, a UserAdminPermission named after the property name (or a prefix of it) with action changeProperty is required.

Returns Dictionary containing the properties of this Role object.

107.8.4.7   **public int getType( )**

☐ Returns the type of this role.

Returns The role's type.

107.8.5   public interface User
extends Role

A User role managed by a User Admin service.

In this context, the term "user" is not limited to just human beings. Instead, it refers to any entity that may have any number of credentials associated with it that it may use to authenticate itself.

In general, User objects are associated with a specific User Admin service (namely the one that created them), and cannot be used with other User Admin services.

A User object may have credentials (and properties, inherited from the Role class) associated with it. Specific UserAdminPermission objects are required to read or change a User object's credentials.

Credentials are Dictionary objects and have semantics that are similar to the properties in the Role class.

107.8.5.1   **public Dictionary getCredentials( )**

☐   Returns a Dictionary of the credentials of this User object. Any changes to the returned Dictionary object will change the credentials of this User object. This will cause a UserAdminEvent object of type UserAdminEvent.ROLE_CHANGED to be broadcast to any UserAdminListeners objects.

Only objects of type String may be used as credential keys, and only objects of type String or of type byte[] may be used as credential values. Any other types will cause an exception of type IllegalArgumentException to be raised.

In order to retrieve a credential from the returned Dictionary object, a UserAdminPermission named after the credential name (or a prefix of it) with action getCredential is required.

In order to add or remove a credential from the returned Dictionary object, a UserAdminPermission named after the credential name (or a prefix of it) with action changeCredential is required.

Returns   Dictionary object containing the credentials of this User object.

107.8.5.2   **public boolean hasCredential(String key, Object value)**

key   The credential key.

value   The credential value.

☐   Checks to see if this User object has a credential with the specified key set to the specified value.

If the specified credential value is not of type String or byte[], it is ignored, that is, false is returned (as opposed to an IllegalArgumentException being raised).

Returns   true if this user has the specified credential; false otherwise.

Throws   SecurityException – If a security manager exists and the caller does not have the UserAdminPermission named after the credential key (or a prefix of it) with action getCredential.

107.8.6   **public interface UserAdmin**

This interface is used to manage a database of named Role objects, which can be used for authentication and authorization purposes.

This version of the User Admin service defines two types of Role objects: "User" and "Group". Each type of role is represented by an int constant and an interface. The range of positive integers is reserved for new types of roles that may be added in the future. When defining proprietary role types, negative constant values must be used.

Every role has a name and a type.

A User object can be configured with credentials (e.g., a password) and properties (e.g., a street address, phone number, etc.).

A Group object represents an aggregation of User and Group objects. In other words, the members of a Group object are roles themselves.

Every User Admin service manages and maintains its own namespace of Role objects, in which each Role object has a unique name.

107.8.6.1   **public Role createRole(String name, int type)**

name The name of the Role object to create.

type The type of the Role object to create. Must be either a Role.USER type or Role.GROUP type.

☐ Creates a Role object with the given name and of the given type.

   If a Role object was created, a UserAdminEvent object of type UserAdminEvent.ROLE_CREATED is broadcast to any UserAdminListener object.

Returns The newly created Role object, or null if a role with the given name already exists.

Throws IllegalArgumentException – if type is invalid.

   SecurityException – If a security manager exists and the caller does not have the UserAdminPermission with name admin.

107.8.6.2   **public Authorization getAuthorization(User user)**

user The User object to create an Authorization object for, or null for the anonymous user.

☐ Creates an Authorization object that encapsulates the specified User object and the Role objects it possesses. The null user is interpreted as the anonymous user. The anonymous user represents a user that has not been authenticated. An Authorization object for an anonymous user will be unnamed, and will only imply groups that user.anyone implies.

Returns the Authorization object for the specified User object.

107.8.6.3   **public Role getRole(String name)**

name The name of the Role object to get.

☐ Gets the Role object with the given name from this User Admin service.

Returns The requested Role object, or null if this User Admin service does not have a Role object with the given name.

107.8.6.4   **public Role[] getRoles(String filter) throws InvalidSyntaxException**

filter The filter criteria to match.

☐ Gets the Role objects managed by this User Admin service that have properties matching the specified LDAP filter criteria. See org.osgi.framework.Filter for a description of the filter syntax. If a null filter is specified, all Role objects managed by this User Admin service are returned.

Returns The Role objects managed by this User Admin service whose properties match the specified filter criteria, or all Role objects if a null filter is specified. If no roles match the filter, null will be returned.

Throws InvalidSyntaxException – If the filter is not well formed.

107.8.6.5   **public User getUser(String key, String value)**

key The property key to look for.

value The property value to compare with.

☐ Gets the user with the given property key-value pair from the User Admin service database. This is a convenience method for retrieving a User object based on a property for which every User object is supposed to have a unique value (within the scope of this User Admin service), such as for example a X.500 distinguished name.

Returns A matching user, if *exactly* one is found. If zero or more than one matching users are found, null is returned.

107.8.6.6   **public boolean removeRole(String name)**

name The name of the Role object to remove.

☐ Removes the Role object with the given name from this User Admin service and all groups it is a member of.

If the Role object was removed, a UserAdminEvent object of type UserAdminEvent.ROLE_REMOVED is broadcast to any UserAdminListener object.

Returns true If a Role object with the given name is present in this User Admin service and could be removed, otherwise false.

Throws SecurityException – If a security manager exists and the caller does not have the UserAdminPermission with name admin.

107.8.7 public class UserAdminEvent

Role change event.

UserAdminEvent objects are delivered asynchronously to any UserAdminListener objects when a change occurs in any of the Role objects managed by a User Admin service.

A type code is used to identify the event. The following event types are defined: ROLE_CREATED type, ROLE_CHANGED type, and ROLE_REMOVED type. Additional event types may be defined in the future.

See Also UserAdmin, UserAdminListener

107.8.7.1 public static final int ROLE_CHANGED = 2

A Role object has been modified.

The value of ROLE_CHANGED is 0x00000002.

107.8.7.2 public static final int ROLE_CREATED = 1

A Role object has been created.

The value of ROLE_CREATED is 0x00000001.

107.8.7.3 public static final int ROLE_REMOVED = 4

A Role object has been removed.

The value of ROLE_REMOVED is 0x00000004.

107.8.7.4 public UserAdminEvent(ServiceReference ref, int type, Role role)

ref The ServiceReference object of the User Admin service that generated this event.

type The event type.

role The Role object on which this event occurred.

☐ Constructs a UserAdminEvent object from the given ServiceReference object, event type, and Role object.

107.8.7.5 public Role getRole( )

☐ Gets the Role object this event was generated for.

Returns The Role object this event was generated for.

107.8.7.6 public ServiceReference getServiceReference( )

☐ Gets the ServiceReference object of the User Admin service that generated this event.

Returns The User Admin service's ServiceReference object.

107.8.7.7   **public int getType( )**

☐ Returns the type of this event.

The type values are ROLE_CREATED type, ROLE_CHANGED type, and ROLE_REMOVED type.

Returns The event type.

107.8.8   public interface UserAdminListener

Listener for UserAdminEvents.

UserAdminListener objects are registered with the Framework service registry and notified with a UserAdminEvent object when a Role object has been created, removed, or modified.

UserAdminListener objects can further inspect the received UserAdminEvent object to determine its type, the Role object it occurred on, and the User Admin service that generated it.

See Also UserAdmin, UserAdminEvent

107.8.8.1   **public void roleChanged(UserAdminEvent event)**

event The UserAdminEvent object.

☐ Receives notification that a Role object has been created, removed, or modified.

107.8.9   public final class UserAdminPermission
extends BasicPermission

Permission to configure and access the Role objects managed by a User Admin service.

This class represents access to the Role objects managed by a User Admin service and their properties and credentials (in the case of User objects).

The permission name is the name (or name prefix) of a property or credential. The naming convention follows the hierarchical property naming convention. Also, an asterisk may appear at the end of the name, following a ".", or by itself, to signify a wildcard match. For example: "org.osgi.security.protocol.*" or "*" is valid, but "*protocol" or "a*b" are not valid.

The UserAdminPermission with the reserved name "admin" represents the permission required for creating and removing Role objects in the User Admin service, as well as adding and removing members in a Group object. This UserAdminPermission does not have any actions associated with it.

The actions to be granted are passed to the constructor in a string containing a list of one or more comma-separated keywords. The possible keywords are: changeProperty, changeCredential, and getCredential. Their meaning is defined as follows:

```
action
changeProperty    Permission to change (i.e., add and remove)
                  Role object properties whose names start with
                  the name argument specified in the constructor.
changeCredential  Permission to change (i.e., add and remove)
                  User object credentials whose names start
                  with the name argument specified in the constructor.
getCredential     Permission to retrieve and check for the
                  existence of User object credentials whose names
                  start with the name argument specified in the
                  constructor.
```

The action string is converted to lowercase before processing.

Following is a PermissionInfo style policy entry which grants a user administration bundle a number of UserAdminPermission object:

```
(org.osgi.service.useradmin.UserAdminPermission "admin")
(org.osgi.service.useradmin.UserAdminPermission "com.foo.*" "changeProperty,get-
Credential,changeCredential")
(org.osgi.service.useradmin.UserAdminPermission "user.*", "changeProperty,
changeCredential")
```

The first permission statement grants the bundle the permission to perform any User Admin service operations of type "admin", that is, create and remove roles and configure Group objects.

The second permission statement grants the bundle the permission to change any properties as well as get and change any credentials whose names start with com.foo..

The third permission statement grants the bundle the permission to change any properties and credentials whose names start with user.. This means that the bundle is allowed to change, but not retrieve any credentials with the given prefix.

The following policy entry empowers the Http Service bundle to perform user authentication:

```
grant codeBase "${jars}http.jar" {
  permission org.osgi.service.useradmin.UserAdminPermission
    "user.password", "getCredential";
};
```

The permission statement grants the Http Service bundle the permission to validate any password credentials (for authentication purposes), but the bundle is not allowed to change any properties or credentials.

Concurrency Thread-safe

107.8.9.1   **public static final String ADMIN = "admin"**

The permission name "admin".

107.8.9.2   **public static final String CHANGE_CREDENTIAL = "changeCredential"**

The action string "changeCredential".

107.8.9.3   **public static final String CHANGE_PROPERTY = "changeProperty"**

The action string "changeProperty".

107.8.9.4   **public static final String GET_CREDENTIAL = "getCredential"**

The action string "getCredential".

107.8.9.5   **public UserAdminPermission(String name, String actions)**

name the name of this UserAdminPermission

actions the action string.

☐ Creates a new UserAdminPermission with the specified name and actions. name is either the reserved string "admin" or the name of a credential or property, and actions contains a comma-separated list of the actions granted on the specified name. Valid actions are changeProperty, changeCredential, and getCredential.

Throws IllegalArgumentException – If name equals "admin" and actions are specified.

107.8.9.6   **public boolean equals(Object obj)**

     obj the object to be compared for equality with this object.

     ❑ Checks two UserAdminPermission objects for equality. Checks that obj is a UserAdminPermission, and has the same name and actions as this object.

   Returns true if obj is a UserAdminPermission object, and has the same name and actions as this UserAdminPermission object.

107.8.9.7   **public String getActions( )**

     ❑ Returns the canonical string representation of the actions, separated by comma.

   Returns the canonical string representation of the actions.

107.8.9.8   **public int hashCode( )**

     ❑ Returns the hash code value for this object.

   Returns A hash code value for this object.

107.8.9.9   **public boolean implies(Permission p)**

     p the permission to check against.

     ❑ Checks if this UserAdminPermission object "implies" the specified permission.

        More specifically, this method returns true if:

- *p* is an instanceof UserAdminPermission,
- *p*'s actions are a proper subset of this object's actions, and
- *p*'s name is implied by this object's name. For example, "java.*" implies "java.home".

   Returns true if the specified permission is implied by this object; false otherwise.

107.8.9.10   **public PermissionCollection newPermissionCollection( )**

     ❑ Returns a new PermissionCollection object for storing UserAdminPermission objects.

   Returns a new PermissionCollection object suitable for storing UserAdminPermission objects.

107.8.9.11   **public String toString( )**

     ❑ Returns a string describing this UserAdminPermission object. This string must be in PermissionInfo encoded format.

   Returns The PermissionInfo encoded string for this UserAdminPermission object.

   See Also org.osgi.service.permissionadmin.PermissionInfo.getEncoded

107.9   References

[1]   *The Java Security Architecture for JDK 1.2*
       Version 1.0, Sun Microsystems, October 1998

[2]   *Java Authentication and Authorization Service*
       http://java.sun.com/javase/technologies/security/

108   Wire Admin Service Specification

Version 1.0

108.1   Introduction

The Wire Admin service is an administrative service that is used to control a wiring topology in the OSGi Service Platform. It is intended to be used by user interfaces or management programs that control the wiring of services in an OSGi Service Platform.

The Wire Admin service plays a crucial role in minimizing the amount of context-specific knowledge required by bundles when used in a large array of configurations. The Wire Admin service fulfills this role by dynamically *wiring* services together. Bundles participate in this wiring process by registering services that produce or consume data. The Wire Admin service *wires* the services that produce data to services which consume data.

The purpose of wiring services together is to allow configurable cooperation of bundles in an OSGi Service Platform. For example, a temperature sensor can be connected to a heating module to provide a controlled system.

The Wire Admin service is a very important OSGi configuration service and is designed to cooperate closely with the Configuration Admin service, as defined in *Configuration Admin Service Specification* on page 67.

108.1.1   Wire Admin Service Essentials

- *Topology Management* – Provide a comprehensive mechanism to link data-producing components with data-consuming components in an OSGi environment.
- *Configuration Management* – Contains configuration data in order to allow either party to adapt to the special needs of the wire.
- *Data Type Handling* – Facilitate the negotiation of the data type to be used for data transfer between producers of data and consumers of data. Consumers and producers must be able to handle multiple data types for data exchanges using a preferred order.
- *Composites* – Support producers and consumers that can handle a large number of data items.
- *Security* – Separate connected parties from each other. Each party must not be required to hold the service object of the other party.
- *Simplicity* – The interfaces should be designed so that both parties, the Producer and the Consumer services, should be easy to implement.

108.1.2   Wire Admin Service Entities

- *Producer* – A service object that generates information to be used by a Consumer service.
- *Consumer* – A service object that receives information generated by a Producer service.
- *Wire* – An object created by the Wire Admin service that defines an association between a Producer service and a Consumer service. Multiple Wire objects can exist between the same Producer and Consumer pair.
- *WireAdmin* – The service that provides methods to create, update, remove, and list Wire objects.
- *WireAdminListener* – A service that receives events from the Wire Admin service when the Wire object is manipulated or used.

- *WireAdminEvent* – The event that is sent to a WireAdminListener object, describing the details of what happened.
- *Configuration Properties* – Properties that are associated with a Wire object and that contain identity and configuration information set by the administrator of the Wire Admin service.
- *PID* – The Persistent IDentity as defined in the Configuration Admin specification.
- *Flavors* – The different data types that can be used to exchange information between Producer and Consumer services.
- *Composite Producer/Consumer* – A Producer/Consumer service that can generate/accept different kinds of values.
- *Envelope* – An interface for objects that can identify a value that is transferred over the wire. Envelope objects contain also a scope name that is used to verify access permissions.
- *Scope* – A set of names that categorizes the kind of values contained in Envelope objects for security and selection purposes.
- *Basic Envelope* – A concrete implementation of the Envelope interface.
- *WirePermission* – A Permission sub-class that is used to verify if a Consumer service or Producer service has permission for specific scope names.
- *Composite Identity* – A name that is agreed between a composite Consumer and Producer service to identify the kind of objects that they can exchange.

Figure 108.1   *Class Diagram, org.osgi.service.wireadmin*

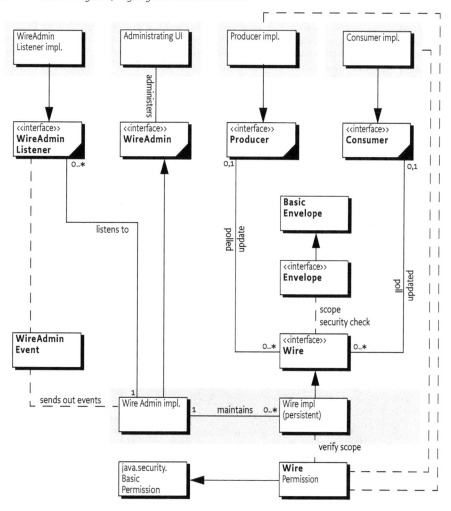

108.1.3   Operation Summary

The Wire Admin service maintains a set of persistent Wire objects. A Wire object contains a Persistent IDentity (PID) for a Consumer service and a PID for a Producer service. (Wire objects can therefore be created when the Producer or Consumer service is not registered.)

If both those Producer and Consumer services are registered with the Framework, they are connected by the Wire Admin service. The Wire Admin service calls a method on each service object and provides the list of Wire objects to which they are connected.

When a Producer service has new information, it should send this information to each of the connected Wire objects. Each Wire object then must check the filtering and security. If both filtering and security allow the transfer, the Producer service should inform the associated Consumer service with the new information. The Consumer services can also poll a Wire object for an new value at any time.

When a Consumer or Producer service is unregistered from the OSGi Framework, the other object in the association is informed that the Wire object is no longer valid.

Administrative applications can use the Wire Admin service to create and delete wires. These changes are immediately reflected in the current topology and are broadcast to Wire Admin Listener services.

Figure 108.2   *An Example Wiring Scheme in an OSGi Environment*

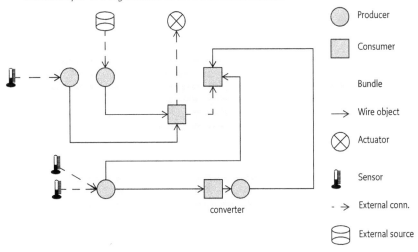

108.2   Producer Service

A Producer is a service that can produce a sequence of data objects. For example, a Producer service can produce, among others, the following type of objects:

- Measurement objects that represent a sensor measurement such as temperature, movement, or humidity.
- A String object containing information for user consumption, such as headlines.
- A Date object indicating the occurrence of a periodic event.
- Position information.
- Envelope objects containing status items which can be any type.

108.2.1   Producer Properties

A Producer service must be registered with the OSGi Framework under the interface name org.osgi.service.wireadmin.Producer. The following service properties must be set:

- service.pid – The value of this property, also known as the PID, defines the Persistent IDentity of a service. A Producer service must always use the same PID value whenever it is registered. The PID value allows the Wire Admin service to consistently identify the Producer service and create a persistent Wire object that links a Producer service to a Consumer service. See [1] *Design Patterns* specification for the rules regarding PIDs.

- wireadmin.producer.flavors – The value of this property is an array of Class objects (Class[]) that are the classes of the objects the service can produce. See *Flavors* on page 176 for more information about the data type negotiation between Producer and Consumer services.

- wireadmin.producer.filters – This property indicates to the Wire Admin service that this Producer service performs its own update filtering, meaning that the consumer can limit the number of update calls with a filter expression. This does not modify the data; it only determines whether an update via the wire occurs. If this property is not set, the Wire object must filter according to the description in *Composite objects* on page 170. This service registration property does not need to have a specific value.

- wireadmin.producer.scope – Only for a composite Producer service, a list of scope names that define the scope of this Producer service, as explained in *Scope* on page 171.
- wireadmin.producer.composite – List the composite identities of Consumer services with which this Producer service can interoperate. This property is of type String[]. A composite Consumer service can inter-operate with a composite Producer service when there is at least one name that occurs in both the Consumer service's array and the Producer service's array for this property.

108.2.2 Connections

The Wire Admin service connects a Producer service and a Consumer service by creating a Wire object. If the Consumer and Producer services that are bound to a Wire object are registered with the Framework, the Wire Admin service must call the consumersConnected(Wire[]) method on the Producer service object. Every change in the Wire Admin service that affects the Wire object to which a Producer service is connected must result in a call to this method. This requirement ensures that the Producer object is informed of its role in the wiring topology. If the Producer service has no Wire objects attached when it is registered, the Wire Admin service must always call consumersConnected(null). This situation implies that a Producer service can assume it always gets called back from the Wire Admin service when it registers.

108.2.3 Producer Example

The following example shows a clock producer service that sends out a Date object every second.

```java
public class Clock extends Thread implements Producer {
    Wire                wires[];
    BundleContext       context;
    boolean             quit;

    Clock( BundleContext context ) {
        this.context = context;
        start();
    }
    public synchronized void run() {
        Hashtable p = new Hashtable();
        p.put( org.osgi.service.wireadmin.WireConstants.
                    WIREADMIN_PRODUCER_FLAVORS,
                new Class[] { Date.class } );
        p.put( org.osgi.framework.Constants.SERVICE_PID,
            "com.acme.clock" );
        context.registerService(
            Producer.class.getName(),this,p );

        while( ! quit )
        try {
            Date  now = new Date();
            for( int i=0; wires!=null && i<wires.length; i++ )
                wires[i].update( now );
            wait( 1000 );
        }
        catch( InterruptedException ie) {
            /* will recheck quit */
        }
    }
    public void synchronized consumersConnected(Wire wires[])
    {
        this.wires = wires;
```

```
    }
    public Object polled(Wire wire) { return new Date(); }
    ...
}
```

108.2.4 Push and Pull

Communication between Consumer and Producer services can be initiated in one of the following ways.

- The Producer service calls the update(Object) method on the Wire object. The Wire object implementation must then call the updated(Wire,Object) method on the Consumer service, if the filtering allows this.

- The Consumer service can call poll() on the Wire object. The Wire object must then call polled(Wire) on the Producer object. Update filtering must not apply to polling.

108.2.5 Producers and Flavors

Consumer services can only understand specific data types, and are therefore restricted in what data they can process. The acceptable object classes, the flavors, are communicated by the Consumer service to the Wire Admin service using the Consumer service's service registration properties. The method getFlavors() on the Wire object returns this list of classes. This list is an ordered list in which the first class is the data type that is the most preferred data type supported by the Consumer service. The last class is the least preferred data type. The Producer service must attempt to convert its data into one of the data types according to the preferred order, or will return null from the poll method to the Consumer service if none of the types are recognized.

Classes cannot be easily compared for equivalence. Sub-classes and interfaces allow classes to masquerade as other classes. The Class.isAssignableFrom(Class) method verifies whether a class is type compatible, as in the following example:

```
Object polled(Wire wire) {
    Class clazzes[] = wire.getFlavors();
    for ( int i=0; i<clazzes.length; i++ ) {
        Class clazz = clazzes[i];
        if ( clazz.isAssignableFrom( Date.class ) )
            return new Date();
        if ( clazz.isAssignableFrom( String.class) )
            return new Date().toString();
    }
    return null;
}
```

The order of the if statements defines the preferences of the Producer object. Preferred data types are checked first. This order normally works as expected but in rare cases, sub-classes can change it. Normally, however, that is not a problem.

108.3 Consumer Service

A Consumer service is a service that receives information from one or more Producer services and is wired to Producer services by the Wire Admin service. Typical Consumer services are as follows:

- The control of an actuator, such as a heating element, oven, or electric shades
- A display
- A log
- A state controller such as an alarm system

108.3.1 Consumer Properties

A Consumer service must be registered with the OSGi Framework under the interface name org.osgi.service.wireadmin.Consumer. The following service properties must be set:

- service.pid – The value of this property, also known as the PID, defines the Persistent IDentity of a service. A Consumer service must always use the same PID value whenever it is registered. The PID value allows the Wire Admin service to consistently identify the Consumer service and create a persistent Wire object that links a Producer service to a Consumer service. See the Configuration Admin specification for the rules regarding PIDs.
- wireadmin.consumer.flavors – The value of this property is an array of Class objects (Class[]) that are the acceptable classes of the objects the service can process. See *Flavors* on page 176 for more information about the data type negotiation between Producer and Consumer services.
- wireadmin.consumer.scope – Only for a composite Consumer service, a list of scope names that define the scope of this Consumer service, as explained in *Scope* on page 171.
- wireadmin.consumer.composite – List the composite identities of Producer services that this Consumer service can interoperate with. This property is of type String[]. A composite Consumer service can interoperate with a composite Producer service when at least one name occurs in both the Consumer service's array and the Producer service's array for this property.

108.3.2 Connections

When a Consumer service is registered and a Wire object exists that associates it to a registered Producer service, the producersConnected(Wire[]) method is called on the Consumer service.

Every change in the Wire Admin service that affects a Wire object to which a Consumer service is connected must result in a call to the producersConnected(Wire[]) method. This rule ensures that the Consumer object is informed of its role in the wiring topology. If the Consumer service has no Wire objects attached, the argument to the producersConnected(Wire[]) method must be null. This method must also be called when a Producer service registers for the first time and no Wire objects are available.

108.3.3 Consumer Example

For example, a service can implement a Consumer service that logs all objects that are sent to it in order to allow debugging of a wiring topology.

```
public class LogConsumer implements Consumer {
    public LogConsumer( BundleContext context ) {
        Hashtable    ht = new Hashtable();
        ht.put(
            Constants.SERVICE_PID, "com.acme.logconsumer" );
        ht.put( WireConstants.WIREADMIN_CONSUMER_FLAVORS,
            new Class[] { Object.class } );
        context.registerService( Consumer.class.getName(),
            this, ht );
    }
    public void updated( Wire wire, Object o ) {
        getLog().log( LogService.LOG_INFO, o.toString() );
    }
    public void producersConnected( Wire [] wires) {}
    LogService getLog() { ... }
}
```

108.3.4   Polling or Receiving a Value

When the Producer service produces a new value, it calls the update(Object) method on the Wire object, which in turn calls the updated(Wire,Object) method on the Consumer service object. When the Consumer service needs a value immediately, it can call the poll() method on the Wire object which in turn calls the polled(Wire) method on the Producer service.

If the poll() method on the Wire object is called and the Producer is unregistered, it must return a null value.

108.3.5   Consumers and Flavors

Producer objects send objects of different data types through Wire objects. A Consumer service object should offer a list of preferred data types (classes) in its service registration properties. The Producer service, however, can still send a null object or an object that is not of the preferred types. Therefore, the Consumer service must check the data type and take the appropriate action. If an object type is incompatible, then a log message should be logged to allow the operator to correct the situation.

The following example illustrates how a Consumer service can handle objects of type Date, Measurement, and String.

```
void process( Object in ) {
   if ( in instanceof Date )
      processDate( (Date) in );
   else if ( in instanceof Measurement )
      processMeasurement( (Measurement) in );
   else if ( in instanceof String )
      processString( (String) in );
   else
      processError( in );
}
```

108.4   Implementation issues

The Wire Admin service can call the consumersConnected or producersConnected methods during the registration of the Consumer or Producer service. Care should be taken in this method call so that no variables are used that are not yet set, such as the ServiceRegistration object that is returned from the registration. The same is true for the updated or polled callback because setting the Wire objects on the Producer service causes such a callback from the consumersConnected or producersConnected method.

A Wire Admin service must call the producersConnected and consumersConnected method asynchronously from the registrations, meaning that the Consumer or Producer service can use synchronized to restrict access to critical variables.

When the Wire Admin service is stopped, it must disconnect all connected consumers and producers by calling producersConnected and consumersConnected with a null for the wires parameter.

108.5   Wire Properties

A Wire object has a set of properties (a Dictionary object) that configure the association between a Consumer service and a Producer service. The type and usage of the keys, as well as the allowed types for the values are defined in *Configuration Properties* on page 72.

The Wire properties are explained in Table 108.1.

Table 108.1   Standard Wire Properties

Constant	Description
WIREADMIN_PID	The value of this property is a unique Persistent IDentity as defined in chapter 104 *Configuration Admin Service Specification.* This PID must be automatically created by the Wire Admin service for each new Wire object.
WIREADMIN_PRODUCER_PID	The value of the property is the PID of the Producer service.
WIREADMIN_CONSUMER_PID	The value of this property is the PID of the Consumer service.
WIREADMIN_FILTER	The value of this property is an OSGi filter string that is used to control the update of produced values.
	This filter can contain a number of attributes as explained in *Wire Flow Control* on page 173.

The properties associated with a Wire object are not limited to the ones defined in Table 108.1. The Dictionary object can also be used for configuring *both* Consumer services and Producer services. Both services receive the Wire object and can inspect the properties and adapt their behavior accordingly.

108.5.1   Display Service Example

In the following example, the properties of a Wire object, which are set by the Operator or User, are used to configure a Producer service that monitors a user's email account regularly and sends a message when the user has received email. This WireMail service is illustrated as follows:

```
public class WireMail extends Thread
   implements Producer {
   Wire                wires[];
   BundleContext       context;
   boolean             quit;

   public void start( BundleContext context ) {
      Hashtable          ht = new Hashtable();
      ht.put( Constants.SERVICE_PID, "com.acme.wiremail" );
      ht.put( WireConstants.WIREADMIN_PRODUCER_FLAVORS,
         new Class[] { Integer.class } );
      context.registerService( this,
         Producer.class.getName(),
         ht );
   }
   public synchronized void  consumersConnected(
      Wire wires[] ) {
      this.wires = wires;
   }
   public Object polled( Wire wire  ) {
      Dictionary              p = wire.getProperties();
      // The password should be
      // obtained from User Admin Service
      int n = getNrMails(
         p.get( "userid" ),
         p.get( "mailhost" ) );
      return new Integer( n );
   }
   public synchronized void run() {
```

```
       while ( !quit )
       try {
          for ( int i=0; wires != null && i<wires.length; i++ )
             wires[i].update( polled( wires[i] ) );

          wait( 150000 );
       }
       catch( InterruptedException e ) { break; }
    }
    ...
}
```

108.6   Composite objects

A Producer and/or Consumer service for each information item is usually the best solution. This solution is not feasible, however, when there are hundreds or thousands of information items. Each registered Consumer or Producer service carries the overhead of the registration, which may overwhelm a Framework implementation on smaller platforms.

When the size of the platform is an issue, a Producer and a Consumer service should abstract a larger number of information items. These Consumer and Producer services are called *composite*.

Figure 108.3   *Composite Producer Example*

Composite Producer and Consumer services should register respectively the WIREADMIN_PRODUCER_COMPOSITE and WIREADMIN_CONSUMER_COMPOSITE *composite identity* property with their service registration. These properties should contain a list of composite identities. These identities are not defined here, but are up to a mutual agreement between the Consumer and Producer service. For example, a composite identity could be MOST-1.5 or GSM-Phase2-Terminal. The name may follow any scheme but will usually have some version information embedded. The composite identity properties are used to match Consumer and Producer services with each other during configuration of the Wire Admin service. A Consumer and Producer service should inter-operate when at least one equal composite identity is listed in both the Producer and Consumer composite identity service property.

Composite producers/consumers must identify the *kind* of objects that are transferred over the Wire object, where *kind* refers to the intent of the object, not the data type. For example, a Producer service can represent the status of a door-lock and the status of a window as a boolean. If the status of the window is transferred as a boolean to the Consumer service, how would it know that this boolean represents the window and not the door-lock?

To avoid this confusion, the Wire Admin service includes an Envelope interface. The purpose of the Envelope interface is to associate a value object with:

- An identification object
- A scope name

Figure 108.4   *Envelope*

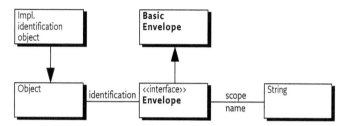

108.6.1   Identification

The Envelope object's identification object is used to identify the value carried in the Envelope object. Each unique kind of value must have its own unique identification object. For example, a left-front-window should have a different identification object than a rear-window.

The identification is of type Object. Using the Object class allows String objects to be used, but also makes it possible to use more complex objects. These objects can convey information in a way that is mutually agreed between the Producer and Consumer service. For example, its type may differ depending on each kind of value so that the *Visitor* pattern, see [1] *Design Patterns*, can be used. Or it may contain specific information that makes the Envelope object easier to dispatch for the Consumer service.

108.6.2   Scope

The scope name is a String object that *categorizes* the Envelope object. The scope name is used to limit the kind of objects that can be exchanged between composite Producer and Consumer services, depending on security settings.

The name-space for this scope should be mutually agreed between the Consumer and Producer services a priori. For the Wire Admin service, the scope name is an opaque string. Its syntax is specified in *Scope name syntax* on page 173.

Both composite Producer and Consumer services must add a list of their supported scope names to the service registration properties. This list is called the *scope* of that service. A Consumer service must add this scope property with the name of WIREADMIN_CONSUMER_SCOPE, a Producer service must add this scope property with the name WIREADMIN_PRODUCER_SCOPE. The type of this property must be a String[] object.

Not registering this property by the Consumer or the Producer service indicates to the Wire Admin service that any Wire object connected to that service must return null for the Wire.getScope() method. This case must be interpreted by the Consumer or Producer service that no scope verification is taking place. Secure Producer services should not produce values for this Wire object and secure Consumer services should not accept values.

It is also allowed to register with a *wildcard*, indicating that all scope names are supported. In that case, the WIREADMIN_SCOPE_ALL (which is String[] { "*" }) should be registered as the scope of the service. The Wire object's scope is then fully defined by the other service connected to the Wire object.

The following example shows how a scope is registered.

```
static String [] scope = { "DoorLock", "DoorOpen", "VIN" };

public void start( BundleContext context ) {
   Dictionary    properties = new Hashtable();
   properties.put(
      WireConstants.WIREADMIN_CONSUMER_SCOPE,
```

```
        scope );
    properties.put( WireConstants.WIREADMIN_CONSUMER_PID,
        "com.acme.composite.consumer" );
    properties.put(
        WireConstants.WIREADMIN_CONSUMER_COMPOSITE,
        new String[] { "OSGiSP-R3" } );
    context.registerService( Consumer.class.getName(),
        new AcmeConsumer(),
        properties );
}
```

Both a composite Consumer and Producer service must register a scope to receive scope support from the Wire object. These two scopes must be converted into a single Wire object's scope and scope names in this list must be checked for the appropriate permissions. This resulting scope is available from the Wire.getScope() method.

If no scope is set by either the Producer or the Consumer service the result must be null. In that case, the Producer or Consumer service must assume that no security checking is in place. A secure Consumer or Producer service should then refuse to operate with that Wire object.

Otherwise, the resulting scope is the intersection of the Consumer and Producer service scope where each name in the scope, called m, must be implied by a WirePermission[m,CONSUME] of the Consumer service, and WirePermission[m,PRODUCE] of the Producer service.

If either the Producer or Consumer service has registered a wildcard scope then it must not restrict the list of the other service, except for the permission check. If both the Producer and Consumer service registered a wild-card, the resulting list must be WIREADMIN_SCOPE_ALL (String[]{"*"}).

For example, the Consumer service has registered a scope of {A,B,C} and has WirePermission[*, CONSUME]. The Producer service has registered a scope of {B,C,E} and has WirePermission[C|E, PRODUCE,]. The resulting scope is then {C}. Table 108.2 shows this and more examples.

Table 108.2   *Examples of scope calculation. C=Consumer, P=Producer, p=WirePermission, s=scope*

Cs	Cp	Ps	Pp	Wire Scope
null		null		null
{A,B,C}	*	null		null
null		{C,D,E}		null
{A,B,C}	B|C	{A,B,C}	A|B	{B}
*	*	{A,B,C}	A|B|C	{A,B,C}
*	*	*	*	{*}
{A,B,C}	A|B|C	{A,B,C}	X	{}
{A,B,C}	*	{B,C,E}	C|E	{C}

The Wire object's scope must be calculated only once, when both the Producer and Consumer service become connected. When a Producer or Consumer service subsequently modifies its scope, the Wire object must *not* modify the original scope. A Consumer and a Produce service can thus assume that the scope does not change after the producersConnected method or consumersConnected method has been called.

108.6.3   Access Control

When an Envelope object is used as argument in Wire.update(Object) then the Wire object must verify that the Envelope object's scope name is included in the Wire object's scope. If this is not the case, the update must be ignored (the updated method on the Consumer service must not be called).

A composite Producer represents a number of values, which is different from a normal Producer that can always return a single object from the poll method. A composite Producer must therefore return an array of Envelope objects (Envelope[]). This array must contain Envelope objects for all the values that are in the Wire object's scope. It is permitted to return all possible values for the Producer because the Wire object must remove all Envelope objects that have a scope name not listed in the Wire object's scope.

108.6.4 Composites and Flavors

Composite Producer and Consumer services must always use a flavor of the Envelope class. The data types of the values must be associated with the scope name or identification and mutually agreed between the Consumer and Producer services.

Flavors and Envelope objects both represent categories of different values. Flavors, however, are different Java classes that represent the same kind of value. For example, the tire pressure of the left front wheel could be passed as a Float, an Integer, or a Measurement object. Whatever data type is chosen, it is still the tire pressure of the left front wheel. The Envelope object represents the kind of object, for example the right front wheel tire pressure, or the left rear wheel.

108.6.5 Scope name syntax

Scope names are normal String objects and can, in principle, contain any Unicode character. In use, scope names can be a full wildcard ('*') but they cannot be partially wildcarded for matching scopes.

Scope names are used with the WirePermission class that extends java.security.BasicPermission. The BasicPermission class implements the implies method and performs the name matching. The wildcard matching of this class is based on the concept of names where the constituents of the name are separated with a period ('.'): for example, org.osgi.service.http.port.

Scope names must therefore follow the rules for fully qualified Java class names. For example, door.lock is a correct scope name while door-lock is not.

108.7 Wire Flow Control

The WIREADMIN_FILTER property contains a filter expression (as defined in the OSGi Framework Filter class) that is used to limit the number of updates to the Consumer service. This is necessary because information can arrive at a much greater rate than can be processed by a Consumer service. For example, a single CAN bus (the electronic control bus used in current cars) in a car can easily deliver hundreds of measurements per second to an OSGi based controller. Most of these measurements are not relevant to the OSGi bundles, at least not all the time. For example, a bundle that maintains an indicator for the presence of frost is only interested in measurements when the outside temperature passes the 4 degrees Celsius mark.

Limiting the number of updates from a Producer service can make a significant difference in performance (meaning that less hardware is needed). For example, a vendor can implement the filter in native code and remove unnecessary updates prior to processing in the Java Virtual Machine (JVM). This is depicted in Figure 108.5 on page 174.

Figure 108.5   *Filtering of Updates*

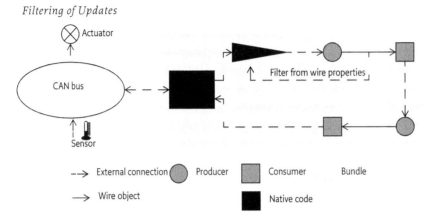

The filter can use any combination of the following attributes in a filter to implement many common filtering schemes:

Table 108.3   *Filter Attribute Names*

Constant	Description
WIREVALUE_CURRENT	Current value of the data from the Producer service.
WIREVALUE_PREVIOUS	Previous data value that was reported to the Consumer service.
WIREVALUE_DELTA_ABSOLUTE	The actual positive difference between the previous data value and the current data value. For example, if the previous data value was 3 and the current data value is -0.5, then the absolute delta is 3.5. This filter attribute is not set when the current or previous value is not a number.
WIREVALUE_DELTA_RELATIVE	The absolute (meaning always positive) relative change between the current and the previous data values, calculated with the following formula: |previous-current|/|current|. For example, if the previous value was 3 and the new value is 5, then the relative delta is |3-5|/|5| = 0.4. This filter attribute is not set when the current or previous value is not a number.
WIREVALUE_ELAPSED	The time in milliseconds between the last time the Consumer.updated(Wire,Object) returned and the time the filter is evaluated.

Filter attributes can be used to implement many common filtering schemes that limit the number of updates that are sent to a Consumer service. The Wire Admin service specification requires that updates to a Consumer service are always filtered if the WIREADMIN_FILTER Wire property is present. Producer services that wish to perform the filtering themselves should register with a service property WIREADMIN_PRODUCER_FILTERS. Filtering must be performed by the Wire object for all other Producer services.

Filtering for composite Producer services is not supported. When a filter is set on a Wire object, the Wire must still perform the filtering (which is limited to time filtering because an Envelope object is not a magnitude), but this approach may lose relevant information because the objects are of a different kind. For example, an update of every 500 ms could miss all speed updates because there is a wheel pressure update that resets the elapsed time. Producer services should, however, still implement a filtering scheme that could use proprietary attributes to filter on different kind of objects.

108.7.1 Filtering by Time

The simplest filter mechanism is based on time. The wirevalue.elapsed attribute contains the amount of milliseconds that have passed since the last update to the associated Consumer service. The following example filter expression illustrates how the updates can be limited to approximately 40 times per minute (once every 1500 ms).

    (wirevalue.elapsed>=1500)

Figure 108.6 depicts this example graphically.

Figure 108.6   *Elapsed Time Change*

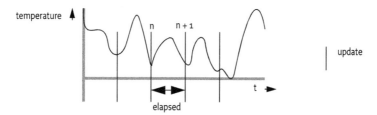

108.7.2 Filtering by Change

A Consumer service is often not interested in an update if the data value has not changed. The following filter expression shows how a Consumer service can limit the updates from a temperature sensor to be sent only when the temperature has changed at least 1 °K.

    (wirevalue.delta.absolute>=1)

Figure 108.7 depicts a band that is created by the absolute delta between the previous data value and the current data value. The Consumer is only notified with the updated(Wire,Object) method when a data value is outside of this band.

Figure 108.7   *Absolute Delta*

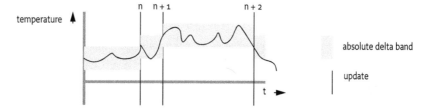

The delta may also be relative. For example, if a car is moving slowly, then updates for the speed of the car are interesting even for small variations. When a car is moving at a high rate of speed, updates are only interesting for larger variations in speed. The following example shows how the updates can be limited to data value changes of at least 10%.

    (wirevalue.delta.relative>=0.1)

Figure 108.8 on page 176 depicts a relative band. Notice that the size of the band is directly proportional to the size of the sample value.

Figure 108.8   *Relative Delta (not on scale)*

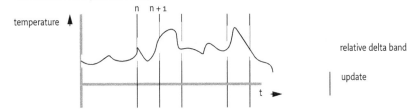

108.7.3   Hysteresis

A thermostat is a control device that usually has a hysteresis, which means that a heater should be switched on below a certain specified low temperature and should be switched off at a specified high temperature, where *high* > *low*. This is graphically depicted in Figure 108.9 on page 176. The specified acceptable temperatures reduce the amount of start/stops of the heater.

Figure 108.9   *Hysteresis*

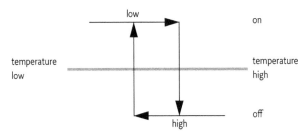

A Consumer service that controls the heater is only interested in events at the top and bottom of the hysteresis. If the specified high value is 250 °K and the specified low value is 249 °K, the following filter illustrates this concept:

```
(|(&(wirevalue.previous<=250)(wirevalue.current>250))
  (&(wirevalue.previous>=249)(wirevalue.current<249))
)
```

108.8   Flavors

Both Consumer and Producer services should register with a property describing the classes of the data types they can consume or produce respectively. The classes are the *flavors* that the service supports. The purpose of flavors is to allow an administrative user interface bundle to connect Consumer and Producer services. Bundles should only create a connection when there is at least one class shared between the flavors from a Consumer service and a Producer service. Producer services are responsible for selecting the preferred object type from the list of the object types preferred by the Consumer service. If the Producer service cannot convert its data to any of the flavors listed by the Consumer service, null should be used instead.

108.9   Converters

A converter is a bundle that registers a Consumer and a Producer service that are related and performs data conversions. Data values delivered to the Consumer service are processed and transferred via the related Producer service. The Producer service sends the converted data to other Consumer services. This is shown in Figure 108.10.

Figure 108.10   *Converter (for legend see Figure 108.2)*

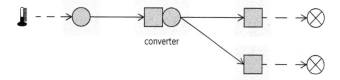

converter

108.10   Wire Admin Service Implementation

The Wire Admin service is the administrative service that is used to control the wiring topology in the OSGi Service Platform. It contains methods to create or update wires, delete wires, and list existing wires. It is intended to be used by user interfaces or management programs that control the wiring topology of the OSGi Service Platform.

The createWire(String,String,Dictionary) method is used to associate a Producer service with a Consumer service. The method always creates and returns a new object. It is therefore possible to create multiple, distinct wires between a Producer and a Consumer service. The properties can be used to create multiple associations between Producer and Consumer services in that act in different ways.

The properties of a Wire object can be updated with the update(Object) method. This method must update the properties in the Wire object and must notify the associated Consumer and Producer services if they are registered. Wire objects that are no longer needed can be removed with the deleteWire(Wire) method. All these methods are in the WireAdmin class and not in the Wire class for security reasons. See *Security* on page 180.

The getWires(String) method returns an array of Wire objects (or null). All objects are returned when the filter argument is null. Specifying a filter argument limits the returned objects. The filter uses the same syntax as the Framework Filter specification. This filter is applied to the properties of the Wire object and only Wire objects that match this filter are returned.

The following example shows how the getWires method can be used to print the PIDs of Producer services that are wired to a specific Consumer service.

```
String f = "(wireadmin.consumer.pid=com.acme.x)";
Wire [] wires = getWireAdmin().getWires( f );
for ( int i=0; wires != null && i < wires.length; i++ )
  System.out.println(
    wires[i].getProperties().get(
      "wireadmin.producer.pid")
  );
```

108.11 Wire Admin Listener Service Events

The Wire Admin service has an extensive list of events that it can deliver. The events allow other bundles to track changes in the topology as they happen. For example, a graphic user interface program can use the events to show when Wire objects become connected, when these objects are deleted, and when data flows over a Wire object.

A bundle that is interested in such events must register a WireAdminListener service object with a special Integer property WIREADMIN_EVENTS ("wireadmin.events"). This Integer object contains a bitmap of all the events in which this Wire Admin Listener service is interested (events have associated constants that can be OR'd together). A Wire Admin service must not deliver events to the Wire Admin Listener service when that event type is not in the bitmap. If no such property is registered, no events are delivered to the Wire Admin Listener service.

The WireAdminListener interface has only one method: wireAdminEvent(WireAdminEvent). The argument is a WireAdminEvent object that contains the event type and associated data.

A WireAdminEvent object can be sent asynchronously but must be ordered for each Wire Admin Listener service. The way events must be delivered is the same as described in *Delivering Events* on page 116 of the Core specification. Wire Admin Listener services must not assume that the state reflected by the event is still true when they receive the event.

The following types are defined for a WireEvent object:

Table 108.4   Events

Event type	Description
WIRE_CREATED	A new Wire object has been created.
WIRE_CONNECTED	Both the Producer service and the Consumer service are registered but may not have executed their respective connectedProducers/connectedConsumers methods.
WIRE_UPDATED	The Wire object's properties have been updated.
WIRE_TRACE	The Producer service has called the Wire.update(Object) method with a new value or the Producer service has returned from the Producer.polled(Wire) method.
WIRE_DISCONNECTED	The Producer service or Consumer service have become unregistered and the Wire object is no longer connected.
WIRE_DELETED	The Wire object is deleted from the repository and is no longer available from the getWires method.
CONSUMER_EXCEPTION	The Consumer service generated an exception and the exception is included in the event.
PRODUCER_EXCEPTION	The Producer service generated an exception in a callback and the exception is included in the event.

108.11.1 Event Admin Service Events

Wire admin events must be sent asynchronously to the Event Admin service by the Wire Admin implementation, if present. The topic of a Wire Admin Event is one of the following:

```
org/osgi/service/wireadmin/WireAdminEvent/<event type>
```

The following event types are supported:

```
WIRE_CREATED
WIRE_CONNECTED
WIRE_UPDATED
WIRE_TRACE
```

```
WIRE_DISCONNECTED
WIRE_DELETED
PRODUCER_EXCEPTION
CONSUMER_EXCEPTION
```

The properties of a wire admin event are the following.

- event – (WireAdminEvent) The WireAdminEvent object broadcast by the Wire Admin service.

If the getWire method returns a non null value:

- wire – (Wire) The Wire object returned by the getWire method.
- wire.flavors – (String[]) The names of the classes returned by the Wire getFlavors method.
- wire.scope – (String[]) The scope of the Wire object, as returned by its getScope method.
- wire.connected – (Boolean) The result of the Wire isConnected method.
- wire.valid – (Boolean) The result of the Wire isValid method.

If the getThrowable method does not return null:

- exception – (Throwable) The Exception returned by the getThrowable method.
- exception.class – (String) The fully-qualified class name of the related Exception.
- exception.message – (String) The message of the related Exception
- service – (ServiceReference) The Service Reference of the Wire Admin service.
- service.id – (Long) The service id of the WireAdmin service.
- service.objectClass – (String[]) The Wire Admin service's object class (which must include org.osgi.service.wireadmin.WireAdmin)
- service.pid – (String) The Wire Admin service's PID.

108.12   Connecting External Entities

The Wire Admin service can be used to control the topology of consumers and producers that are services, as well as external entities. For example, a video camera controlled over an IEEE 1394B bus can be registered as a Producer service in the Framework's service registry and a TV, also connected to this bus, can be registered as a Consumer service. It would be very inefficient to stream the video data through the OSGi environment. Therefore, the Wire Admin service can be used to supply the external addressing information to the camera and the monitor to make a direct connection *outside* the OSGi environment. The Wire Admin service provides a uniform mechanism to connect both external entities and internal entities.

Figure 108.11   *Connecting External Entities*

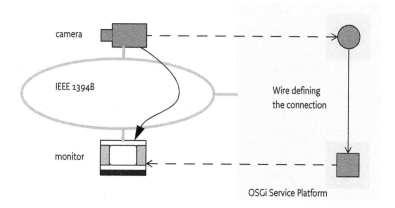

A Consumer service and a Producer service associated with a Wire object receive enough information to establish a direct link because the PIDs of both services are in the Wire object's properties. This situation, however, does not guarantee *compatibility* between Producer and the Consumer service. It is therefore recommended that flavors are used to ensure this compatibility. Producer services that participate in an external addressing scheme, like IEEE 1394B, should have a flavor that reflects this address. In this case, there should then for example be a IEEE 1394B address class. Consumer services that participate in this external addressing scheme should only accept data of this flavor.

The OSGi *Device Access Specification* on page 41, defines the concept of a device category. This is a description of what classes and properties are used in a specific device category: for example, a UPnP device category that defines the interface that must be used to register for a UPnP device, among other things.

Device category descriptions should include a section that addresses the external wiring issue. This section should include what objects are send over the wire to exchange addressing information.

108.13 Related Standards

108.13.1 Java Beans

The Wire Admin service leverages the component architecture that the Framework service registry offers. Java Beans attempt to achieve similar goals. Java Beans are classes that follow a number of recommendations that allow them to be configured at run time. The techniques that are used by Java Beans during configuration are serialization and the construction of adapter classes.

Creating adapter classes in a resource constrained OSGi Service Platform was considered too heavy weight. Also, the dynamic nature of the OSGi environment, where services are registered and unregistered continuously, creates a mismatch between the intended target area of Java Beans and the OSGi Service Platform.

Also, Java Beans can freely communicate once they have a reference to each other. This freedom makes it impossible to control the communication between Java Beans.

This Wire Admin service specification was developed because it is lightweight and leverages the unique characteristics of the OSGi Framework. The concept of a Wire object that acts as an intermediate between the Producer and Consumer service allows the implementation of a security policy because both parties cannot communicate directly.

108.14 Security

108.14.1 Separation of Consumer and Producer Services

The Consumer and Producer service never directly communicate with each other. All communication takes place through a Wire object. This allows a Wire Admin service implementation to control the security aspects of creating a connection, and implies that the Wire Admin service must be a trusted service in a secure environment. Only one bundle should have the ServicePermission[WireAdmin, REGISTER].

ServicePermission[Producer|Consumer, REGISTER] should not be restricted. ServicePermission[Producer|Consumer,GET] must be limited to trusted bundles (the Wire Admin service implementation) because a bundle with this permission can call such services and access information that it should not be able to access.

108.14.2   Using Wire Admin Service

This specification assumes that only a few applications require access to the Wire Admin service. The WireAdmin interface contains all the security sensitive methods that create, update, and remove Wire objects. (This is the reason that the update and delete methods are on the WireAdmin interface and not on the Wire interface). ServicePermission[WireAdmin,GET] should therefore only be given to trusted bundles that can manage the topology.

108.14.3   Wire Permission

Composite Producer and Consumer services can be restricted in their use of scope names. This restriction is managed with the WirePermission class. A WirePermission consists of a scope name and the action CONSUME or PRODUCE. The name used with the WirePermission may contain wild-cards as specified in the java.security.BasicPermission class.

108.15   org.osgi.service.wireadmin

Wire Admin Package Version 1.0.

Bundles wishing to use this package must list the package in the Import-Package header of the bundle's manifest. For example:

```
Import-Package: org.osgi.service.wireadmin; version="[1.0,2.0)"
```

108.15.1   Summary

- *BasicEnvelope* - BasicEnvelope is an implementation of the Envelope interface
- *Consumer* - Data Consumer, a service that can receive udpated values from Producer services.
- *Envelope* - Identifies a contained value.
- *Producer* - Data Producer, a service that can generate values to be used by Consumer services.
- *Wire* - A connection between a Producer service and a Consumer service.
- *WireAdmin* - Wire Administration service.
- *WireAdminEvent* - A Wire Admin Event.
- *WireAdminListener* - Listener for Wire Admin Events.
- *WireConstants* - Defines standard names for Wire properties, wire filter attributes, Consumer and Producer service properties.
- *WirePermission* - Permission for the scope of a Wire object.

108.15.2   public class BasicEnvelope
implements Envelope

BasicEnvelope is an implementation of the Envelope interface

108.15.2.1   public BasicEnvelope(Object value, Object identification, String scope)

value   Content of this envelope, may be null.

identification   Identifying object for this Envelope object, must not be null

scope   Scope name for this object, must not be null

     □   Constructor.

See Also   Envelope

108.15.2.2   public Object getIdentification( )

See Also   org.osgi.service.wireadmin.Envelope.getIdentification()

108.15.2.3   public String getScope( )

See Also   org.osgi.service.wireadmin.Envelope.getScope()

108.15.2.4   **public Object getValue( )**

See Also org.osgi.service.wireadmin.Envelope.getValue()

108.15.3   **public interface Consumer**

Data Consumer, a service that can receive udpated values from Producer services.

Service objects registered under the Consumer interface are expected to consume values from a Producer service via a Wire object. A Consumer service may poll the Producer service by calling the Wire.poll method. The Consumer service will also receive an updated value when called at it's updated method. The Producer service should have coerced the value to be an instance of one of the types specified by the Wire.getFlavors method, or one of their subclasses.

Consumer service objects must register with a service.pid and a WireConstants.WIREADMIN_CONSUMER_FLAVORS property. It is recommended that Consumer service objects also register with a service.description property.

If an Exception is thrown by any of the Consumer methods, a WireAdminEvent of type WireAdminEvent.CONSUMER_EXCEPTION is broadcast by the Wire Admin service.

Security Considerations - Data consuming bundles will require ServicePermission[Consumer, REGISTER]. In general, only the Wire Admin service bundle should have this permission. Thus only the Wire Admin service may directly call a Consumer service. Care must be taken in the sharing of Wire objects with other bundles.

Consumer services must be registered with their scope when they can receive different types of objects from the Producer service. The Consumer service should have WirePermission for each of these scope names.

108.15.3.1   **public void producersConnected(Wire[] wires)**

wires An array of the current and complete list of Wire objects to which this Consumer service is connected. May be null if the Consumer service is not currently connected to any Wire objects.

☐ Update the list of Wire objects to which this Consumer service is connected.

This method is called when the Consumer service is first registered and subsequently whenever a Wire associated with this Consumer service becomes connected, is modified or becomes disconnected.

The Wire Admin service must call this method asynchronously. This implies that implementors of Consumer can be assured that the callback will not take place during registration when they execute the registration in a synchronized method.

108.15.3.2   **public void updated(Wire wire, Object value)**

wire The Wire object which is delivering the updated value.

value The updated value. The value should be an instance of one of the types specified by the Wire.getFlavors method.

☐ Update the value. This Consumer service is called by the Wire object with an updated value from the Producer service.

Note: This method may be called by a Wire object prior to this object being notified that it is connected to that Wire object (via the producersConnected method).

When the Consumer service can receive Envelope objects, it must have registered all scope names together with the service object, and each of those names must be permitted by the bundle's WirePermission. If an Envelope object is delivered with the updated method, then the Consumer service should assume that the security check has been performed.

108.15.4   public interface Envelope

Identifies a contained value. An Envelope object combines a status value, an identification object and a scope name. The Envelope object allows the use of standard Java types when a Producer service can produce more than one kind of object. The Envelope object allows the Consumer service to recognize the kind of object that is received. For example, a door lock could be represented by a Boolean object. If the Producer service would send such a Boolean object, then the Consumer service would not know what door the Boolean object represented. The Envelope object contains an identification object so the Consumer service can discriminate between different kinds of values. The identification object may be a simple String object, but it can also be a domain specific object that is mutually agreed by the Producer and the Consumer service. This object can then contain relevant information that makes the identification easier.

The scope name of the envelope is used for security. The Wire object must verify that any Envelope object send through the update method or coming from the poll method has a scope name that matches the permissions of both the Producer service and the Consumer service involved. The wireadmin package also contains a class BasicEnvelope that implements the methods of this interface.

See Also   WirePermission, BasicEnvelope

108.15.4.1   public Object getIdentification( )

☐ Return the identification of this Envelope object. An identification may be of any Java type. The type must be mutually agreed between the Consumer and Producer services.

Returns   an object which identifies the status item in the address space of the composite producer, must not be null.

108.15.4.2   public String getScope( )

☐ Return the scope name of this Envelope object. Scope names are used to restrict the communication between the Producer and Consumer services. Only Envelopes objects with a scope name that is permitted for the Producer and the Consumer services must be passed through a Wire object.

Returns   the security scope for the status item, must not be null.

108.15.4.3   public Object getValue( )

☐ Return the value associated with this Envelope object.

Returns   the value of the status item, or null when no item is associated with this object.

108.15.5   public interface Producer

Data Producer, a service that can generate values to be used by Consumer services.

Service objects registered under the Producer interface are expected to produce values (internally generated or from external sensors). The value can be of different types. When delivering a value to a Wire object, the Producer service should coerce the value to be an instance of one of the types specified by Wire.getFlavors. The classes are specified in order of preference.

When the data represented by the Producer object changes, this object should send the updated value by calling the update method on each of Wire objects passed in the most recent call to this object's consumersConnected method. These Wire objects will pass the value on to the associated Consumer service object.

The Producer service may use the information in the Wire object's properties to schedule the delivery of values to the Wire object.

Producer service objects must register with a service.pid and a WireConstants.WIREADMIN_PRODUCER_FLAVORS property. It is recommended that a Producer service object also registers with a service.description property. Producer service objects must register with a WireConstants.WIREADMIN_PRODUCER_FILTERS property if the Producer service will be performing filtering instead of the Wire object.

If an exception is thrown by a Producer object method, a WireAdminEvent of type WireAdminEvent.PRODUCER_EXCEPTION is broadcast by the Wire Admin service.

Security Considerations. Data producing bundles will require ServicePermission[Producer, REGISTER] to register a Producer service. In general, only the Wire Admin service should have ServicePermission[Producer,GET]. Thus only the Wire Admin service may directly call a Producer service. Care must be taken in the sharing of Wire objects with other bundles.

Producer services must be registered with scope names when they can send different types of objects (composite) to the Consumer service. The Producer service should have WirePermission for each of these scope names.

108.15.5.1   public void consumersConnected(Wire[] wires)

wires An array of the current and complete list of Wire objects to which this Producer service is connected. May be null if the Producer is not currently connected to any Wire objects.

☐ Update the list of Wire objects to which this Producer object is connected.

This method is called when the Producer service is first registered and subsequently whenever a Wire associated with this Producer becomes connected, is modified or becomes disconnected.

The Wire Admin service must call this method asynchronously. This implies that implementors of a Producer service can be assured that the callback will not take place during registration when they execute the registration in a synchronized method.

108.15.5.2   public Object polled(Wire wire)

wire The Wire object which is polling this service.

☐ Return the current value of this Producer object.

This method is called by a Wire object in response to the Consumer service calling the Wire object's poll method. The Producer should coerce the value to be an instance of one of the types specified by Wire.getFlavors. The types are specified in order of of preference. The returned value should be as new or newer than the last value furnished by this object.

Note: This method may be called by a Wire object prior to this object being notified that it is connected to that Wire object (via the consumersConnected method).

If the Producer service returns an Envelope object that has an unpermitted scope name, then the Wire object must ignore (or remove) the transfer.

If the Wire object has a scope set, the return value must be an array of Envelope objects (Envelope[]). The Wire object must have removed any Envelope objects that have a scope name that is not in the Wire object's scope.

Returns The current value of the Producer service or null if the value cannot be coerced into a compatible type. Or an array of Envelope objects.

108.15.6   public interface Wire

A connection between a Producer service and a Consumer service.

A Wire object connects a Producer service to a Consumer service. Both the Producer and Consumer services are identified by their unique service.pid values. The Producer and Consumer services may communicate with each other via Wire objects that connect them. The Producer service may send updated values to the Consumer service by calling the update method. The Consumer service may request an updated value from the Producer service by calling the poll method.

A Producer service and a Consumer service may be connected through multiple Wire objects.

Security Considerations. Wire objects are available to Producer and Consumer services connected to a given Wire object and to bundles which can access the WireAdmin service. A bundle must have ServicePermission[WireAdmin,GET] to get the WireAdmin service to access all Wire objects. A bundle registering a Producer service or a Consumer service must have the appropriate ServicePermission[Consumer|Producer,REGISTER] to register the service and will be passed Wire objects when the service object's consumersConnected or producersConnected method is called.

Scope. Each Wire object can have a scope set with the setScope method. This method should be called by a Consumer service when it assumes a Producer service that is composite (supports multiple information items). The names in the scope must be verified by the Wire object before it is used in communication. The semantics of the names depend on the Producer service and must not be interpreted by the Wire Admin service.

108.15.6.1   public Class[] getFlavors( )

☐ Return the list of data types understood by the Consumer service connected to this Wire object. Note that subclasses of the classes in this list are acceptable data types as well.

The list is the value of the WireConstants.WIREADMIN_CONSUMER_FLAVORS service property of the Consumer service object connected to this object. If no such property was registered or the type of the property value is not Class[], this method must return null.

Returns An array containing the list of classes understood by the Consumer service or null if the Wire is not connected, or the consumer did not register a WireConstants.WIREADMIN_CONSUMER_FLAVORS property or the value of the property is not of type Class[].

108.15.6.2   public Object getLastValue( )

☐ Return the last value sent through this Wire object.

The returned value is the most recent, valid value passed to the update method or returned by the poll method of this object. If filtering is performed by this Wire object, this methods returns the last value provided by the Producer service. This value may be an Envelope[] when the Producer service uses scoping. If the return value is an Envelope object (or array), it must be verified that the Consumer service has the proper WirePermission to see it.

Returns The last value passed though this Wire object or null if no valid values have been passed or the Consumer service has no permission.

108.15.6.3   public Dictionary getProperties( )

☐ Return the wire properties for this Wire object.

Returns The properties for this Wire object. The returned Dictionary must be read only.

108.15.6.4   public String[] getScope( )

☐ Return the calculated scope of this Wire object. The purpose of the Wire object's scope is to allow a Producer and/or Consumer service to produce/consume different types over a single Wire object (this was deemed necessary for efficiency reasons). Both the Consumer service and the Producer service must set an array of scope names (their scope) with the service registration property WIREADMIN_PRODUCER_SCOPE, or WIREADMIN_CONSUMER_SCOPE when they can produce multiple types. If a Producer service can produce different types, it should set this property to the array of scope names it can produce, the Consumer service must set the array of scope names it can consume. The scope of a Wire object is defined as the intersection of permitted scope names of the Producer service and Consumer service.

If neither the Consumer, or the Producer service registers scope names with its service registration, then the Wire object's scope must be null.

The Wire object's scope must not change when a Producer or Consumer services modifies its scope.

A scope name is permitted for a Producer service when the registering bundle has WirePermission[name,PRODUCE], and for a Consumer service when the registering bundle has WirePermission[name,CONSUME].

If either Consumer service or Producer service has not set a WIREADMIN_*_SCOPE property, then the returned value must be null.

If the scope is set, the Wire object must enforce the scope names when Envelope objects are used as a parameter to update or returned from the poll method. The Wire object must then remove all Envelope objects with a scope name that is not permitted.

Returns A list of permitted scope names or null if the Produce or Consumer service has set no scope names.

108.15.6.5   public boolean hasScope(String name)

name The scope name

☐ Return true if the given name is in this Wire object's scope.

Returns true if the name is listed in the permitted scope names

108.15.6.6   public boolean isConnected( )

☐ Return the connection state of this Wire object.

A Wire is connected after the Wire Admin service receives notification that the Producer service and the Consumer service for this Wire object are both registered. This method will return true prior to notifying the Producer and Consumer services via calls to their respective consumersConnected and producersConnected methods.

A WireAdminEvent of type WireAdminEvent.WIRE_CONNECTED must be broadcast by the Wire Admin service when the Wire becomes connected.

A Wire object is disconnected when either the Consumer or Producer service is unregistered or the Wire object is deleted.

A WireAdminEvent of type WireAdminEvent.WIRE_DISCONNECTED must be broadcast by the Wire Admin service when the Wire becomes disconnected.

Returns true if both the Producer and Consumer for this Wire object are connected to the Wire object; false otherwise.

108.15.6.7   public boolean isValid( )

☐ Return the state of this Wire object.

A connected Wire must always be disconnected before becoming invalid.

Returns false if this Wire object is invalid because it has been deleted via WireAdmin.deleteWire; true otherwise.

108.15.6.8   public Object poll( )

☐ Poll for an updated value.

This methods is normally called by the Consumer service to request an updated value from the Producer service connected to this Wire object. This Wire object will call the Producer.polled method to obtain an updated value. If this Wire object is not connected, then the Producer service must not be called.

If this Wire object has a scope, then this method must return an array of Envelope objects. The objects returned must match the scope of this object. The Wire object must remove all Envelope objects with a scope name that is not in the Wire object's scope. Thus, the list of objects returned must only contain Envelope objects with a permitted scope name. If the array becomes empty, null must be returned.

A WireAdminEvent of type WireAdminEvent.WIRE_TRACE must be broadcast by the Wire Admin service after the Producer service has been successfully called.

Returns A value whose type should be one of the types returned by getFlavors, Envelope[], or null if the Wire object is not connected, the Producer service threw an exception, or the Producer service returned a value which is not an instance of one of the types returned by getFlavors.

108.15.6.9   public void update(Object value)

value The updated value. The value should be an instance of one of the types returned by getFlavors.

☐ Update the value.

This methods is called by the Producer service to notify the Consumer service connected to this Wire object of an updated value.

If the properties of this Wire object contain a WireConstants.WIREADMIN_FILTER property, then filtering is performed. If the Producer service connected to this Wire object was registered with the service property WireConstants.WIREADMIN_PRODUCER_FILTERS, the Producer service will perform the filtering according to the rules specified for the filter. Otherwise, this Wire object will perform the filtering of the value.

If no filtering is done, or the filter indicates the updated value should be delivered to the Consumer service, then this Wire object must call the Consumer.updated method with the updated value. If this Wire object is not connected, then the Consumer service must not be called and the value is ignored.

If the value is an Envelope object, and the scope name is not permitted, then the Wire object must ignore this call and not transfer the object to the Consumer service.

A WireAdminEvent of type WireAdminEvent.WIRE_TRACE must be broadcast by the Wire Admin service after the Consumer service has been successfully called.

See Also WireConstants.WIREADMIN_FILTER

108.15.7   public interface WireAdmin

Wire Administration service.

This service can be used to create Wire objects connecting a Producer service and a Consumer service. Wire objects also have wire properties that may be specified when a Wire object is created. The Producer and Consumer services may use the Wire object's properties to manage or control their interaction. The use of Wire object's properties by a Producer or Consumer services is optional.

Security Considerations. A bundle must have ServicePermission[WireAdmin,GET] to get the Wire Admin service to create, modify, find, and delete Wire objects.

108.15.7.1   public Wire createWire(String producerPID, String consumerPID, Dictionary properties)

producerPID The service.pid of the Producer service to be connected to the Wire object.

consumerPID The service.pid of the Consumer service to be connected to the Wire object.

properties The Wire object's properties. This argument may be null if the caller does not wish to define any Wire object's properties.

☐ Create a new Wire object that connects a Producer service to a Consumer service. The Producer service and Consumer service do not have to be registered when the Wire object is created.

The Wire configuration data must be persistently stored. All Wire connections are reestablished when the WireAdmin service is registered. A Wire can be permanently removed by using the deleteWire method.

The Wire object's properties must have case insensitive String objects as keys (like the Framework). However, the case of the key must be preserved.

The WireAdmin service must automatically add the following Wire properties:

- WireConstants.WIREADMIN_PID set to the value of the Wire object's persistent identity (PID). This value is generated by the Wire Admin service when a Wire object is created.
- WireConstants.WIREADMIN_PRODUCER_PID set to the value of Producer service's PID.
- WireConstants.WIREADMIN_CONSUMER_PID set to the value of Consumer service's PID.

If the properties argument already contains any of these keys, then the supplied values are replaced with the values assigned by the Wire Admin service.

The Wire Admin service must broadcast a WireAdminEvent of type WireAdmin-Event.WIRE_CREATED after the new Wire object becomes available from getWires.

Returns The Wire object for this connection.

Throws IllegalArgumentException – If properties contains invalid wire types or case variants of the same key name.

108.15.7.2   public void deleteWire(Wire wire)

wire The Wire object which is to be deleted.

☐ Delete a Wire object.

The Wire object representing a connection between a Producer service and a Consumer service must be removed. The persistently stored configuration data for the Wire object must destroyed. The Wire object's method Wire.isValid will return false after it is deleted.

The Wire Admin service must broadcast a WireAdminEvent of type WireAdmin-Event.WIRE_DELETED after the Wire object becomes invalid.

108.15.7.3   public Wire[] getWires(String filter) throws InvalidSyntaxException

filter Filter string to select Wire objects or null to select all Wire objects.

☐ Return the Wire objects that match the given filter.

The list of available Wire objects is matched against the specified filter.Wire objects which match the filter must be returned. These Wire objects are not necessarily connected. The Wire Admin service should not return invalid Wire objects, but it is possible that a Wire object is deleted after it was placed in the list.

The filter matches against the Wire object's properties including WireConstants.WIREADMIN_PRODUCER_PID, WireConstants.WIREADMIN_CONSUMER_PID and WireConstants.WIREADMIN_PID.

Returns An array of Wire objects which match the filter or null if no Wire objects match the filter.

Throws InvalidSyntaxException – If the specified filter has an invalid syntax.

See Also org.osgi.framework.Filter

108.15.7.4   **public void updateWire(Wire wire, Dictionary properties)**

wire   The Wire object which is to be updated.

properties   The new Wire object's properties or null if no properties are required.

□   Update the properties of a Wire object. The persistently stored configuration data for the Wire object is updated with the new properties and then the Consumer and Producer services will be called at the respective Consumer.producersConnected and Producer.consumersConnected methods.

The Wire Admin service must broadcast a WireAdminEvent of type WireAdmin-Event.WIRE_UPDATED after the updated properties are available from the Wire object.

Throws   IllegalArgumentException – If properties contains invalid wire types or case variants of the same key name.

108.15.8   public class WireAdminEvent

A Wire Admin Event.

WireAdminEvent objects are delivered to all registered WireAdminListener service objects which specify an interest in the WireAdminEvent type. Events must be delivered in chronological order with respect to each listener. For example, a WireAdminEvent of type WIRE_CONNECTED must be delivered before a WireAdminEvent of type WIRE_DISCONNECTED for a particular Wire object.

A type code is used to identify the type of event. The following event types are defined:

- WIRE_CREATED
- WIRE_CONNECTED
- WIRE_UPDATED
- WIRE_TRACE
- WIRE_DISCONNECTED
- WIRE_DELETED
- PRODUCER_EXCEPTION
- CONSUMER_EXCEPTION

Event type values must be unique and disjoint bit values. Event types must be defined as a bit in a 32 bit integer and can thus be bitwise OR'ed together.

Security Considerations. WireAdminEvent objects contain Wire objects. Care must be taken in the sharing of Wire objects with other bundles.

See Also   WireAdminListener

108.15.8.1   **public static final int CONSUMER_EXCEPTION = 2**

A Consumer service method has thrown an exception.

This WireAdminEvent type indicates that a Consumer service method has thrown an exception. The WireAdminEvent.getThrowable method will return the exception that the Consumer service method raised.

The value of CONSUMER_EXCEPTION is 0x00000002.

108.15.8.2   **public static final int PRODUCER_EXCEPTION = 1**

A Producer service method has thrown an exception.

This WireAdminEvent type indicates that a Producer service method has thrown an exception. The WireAdminEvent.getThrowable method will return the exception that the Producer service method raised.

The value of PRODUCER_EXCEPTION is 0x00000001.

108.15.8.3   **public static final int WIRE_CONNECTED = 32**

The WireAdminEvent type that indicates that an existing Wire object has become connected. The Consumer object and the Producer object that are associated with the Wire object have both been registered and the Wire object is connected. See Wire.isConnected for a description of the connected state. This event may come before the producersConnected and consumersConnected method have returned or called to allow synchronous delivery of the events. Both methods can cause other WireAdminEvent s to take place and requiring this event to be send before these methods are returned would mandate asynchronous delivery.

The value of WIRE_CONNECTED is 0x00000020.

108.15.8.4   **public static final int WIRE_CREATED = 4**

A Wire has been created.

This WireAdminEvent type that indicates that a new Wire object has been created. An event is broadcast when WireAdmin.createWire is called. The WireAdminEvent.getWire method will return the Wire object that has just been created.

The value of WIRE_CREATED is 0x00000004.

108.15.8.5   **public static final int WIRE_DELETED = 16**

A Wire has been deleted.

This WireAdminEvent type that indicates that an existing wire has been deleted. An event is broadcast when WireAdmin.deleteWire is called with a valid wire. WireAdminEvent.getWire will return the Wire object that has just been deleted.

The value of WIRE_DELETED is 0x00000010.

108.15.8.6   **public static final int WIRE_DISCONNECTED = 64**

The WireAdminEvent type that indicates that an existing Wire object has become disconnected. The Consumer object or/and Producer object is/are unregistered breaking the connection between the two. See Wire.isConnected for a description of the connected state.

The value of WIRE_DISCONNECTED is 0x00000040.

108.15.8.7   **public static final int WIRE_TRACE = 128**

The WireAdminEvent type that indicates that a new value is transferred over the Wire object. This event is sent after the Consumer service has been notified by calling the Consumer.updated method or the Consumer service requested a new value with the Wire.poll method. This is an advisory event meaning that when this event is received, another update may already have occurred and this the Wire.getLastValue method returns a newer value then the value that was communicated for this event.

The value of WIRE_TRACE is 0x00000080.

108.15.8.8   **public static final int WIRE_UPDATED = 8**

A Wire has been updated.

This WireAdminEvent type that indicates that an existing Wire object has been updated with new properties. An event is broadcast when WireAdmin.updateWire is called with a valid wire. The WireAdminEvent.getWire method will return the Wire object that has just been updated.

The value of WIRE_UPDATED is 0x00000008.

108.15.8.9   **public WireAdminEvent(ServiceReference reference, int type, Wire wire, Throwable exception)**

reference   The ServiceReference object of the Wire Admin service that created this event.

type The event type. See getType.

wire The Wire object associated with this event.

exception An exception associated with this event. This may be null if no exception is associated with this event.

☐ Constructs a WireAdminEvent object from the given ServiceReference object, event type, Wire object and exception.

108.15.8.10   **public ServiceReference getServiceReference( )**

☐ Return the ServiceReference object of the Wire Admin service that created this event.

Returns The ServiceReference object for the Wire Admin service that created this event.

108.15.8.11   **public Throwable getThrowable( )**

☐ Returns the exception associated with the event, if any.

Returns An exception or null if no exception is associated with this event.

108.15.8.12   **public int getType( )**

☐ Return the type of this event.

The type values are:

- WIRE_CREATED
- WIRE_CONNECTED
- WIRE_UPDATED
- WIRE_TRACE
- WIRE_DISCONNECTED
- WIRE_DELETED
- PRODUCER_EXCEPTION
- CONSUMER_EXCEPTION

Returns The type of this event.

108.15.8.13   **public Wire getWire( )**

☐ Return the Wire object associated with this event.

Returns The Wire object associated with this event or null when no Wire object is associated with the event.

108.15.9   public interface WireAdminListener

Listener for Wire Admin Events.

WireAdminListener objects are registered with the Framework service registry and are notified with a WireAdminEvent object when an event is broadcast.

WireAdminListener objects can inspect the received WireAdminEvent object to determine its type, the Wire object with which it is associated, and the Wire Admin service that broadcasts the event.

WireAdminListener objects must be registered with a service property WireConstants.WIREADMIN_EVENTS whose value is a bitwise OR of all the event types the listener is interested in receiving.

For example:

```
Integer mask = new Integer(WIRE_TRACE | WIRE_CONNECTED | WIRE_DISCONNECTED);
Hashtable ht = new Hashtable();
ht.put(WIREADMIN_EVENTS, mask);
context.registerService(WireAdminListener.class.getName(), this, ht);
```

If a WireAdminListener object is registered without a service property WireConstants.WIREADMIN_EVENTS, then the WireAdminListener will receive no events.

Security Considerations. Bundles wishing to monitor WireAdminEvent objects will require ServicePermission[WireAdminListener,REGISTER] to register a WireAdminListener service. Since WireAdminEvent objects contain Wire objects, care must be taken in assigning permission to register a WireAdminListener service.

See Also WireAdminEvent

108.15.9.1		**public void wireAdminEvent(WireAdminEvent event)**

event The WireAdminEvent object.

☐ Receives notification of a broadcast WireAdminEvent object. The event object will be of an event type specified in this WireAdminListener service's WireConstants.WIREADMIN_EVENTS service property.

## 108.15.10		public interface WireConstants

Defines standard names for Wire properties, wire filter attributes, Consumer and Producer service properties.

108.15.10.1		**public static final String WIREADMIN_CONSUMER_COMPOSITE = "wireadmin.consumer.composite"**

A service registration property for a Consumer service that is composite. It contains the names of the composite Producer services it can cooperate with. Inter-operability exists when any name in this array matches any name in the array set by the Producer service. The type of this property must be String[].

108.15.10.2		**public static final String WIREADMIN_CONSUMER_FLAVORS = "wireadmin.consumer.flavors"**

Service Registration property (named wireadmin.consumer.flavors) specifying the list of data types understood by this Consumer service.

The Consumer service object must be registered with this service property. The list must be in the order of preference with the first type being the most preferred. The value of the property must be of type Class[].

108.15.10.3		**public static final String WIREADMIN_CONSUMER_PID = "wireadmin.consumer.pid"**

Wire property key (named wireadmin.consumer.pid) specifying the service.pid of the associated Consumer service.

This wire property is automatically set by the Wire Admin service. The value of the property must be of type String.

108.15.10.4		**public static final String WIREADMIN_CONSUMER_SCOPE = "wireadmin.consumer.scope"**

Service registration property key (named wireadmin.consumer.scope) specifying a list of names that may be used to define the scope of this Wire object. A Consumer service should set this service property when it can produce more than one kind of value. This property is only used during registration, modifying the property must not have any effect of the Wire object's scope. Each name in the given list mist have WirePermission[name,CONSUME] or else is ignored. The type of this service registration property must be String[].

See Also Wire.getScope, WIREADMIN_PRODUCER_SCOPE

108.15.10.5   **public static final String WIREADMIN_EVENTS = "wireadmin.events"**

Service Registration property (named wireadmin.events) specifying the WireAdminEvent type of interest to a Wire Admin Listener service. The value of the property is a bitwise OR of all the WireAdminEvent types the Wire Admin Listener service wishes to receive and must be of type Integer.

See Also WireAdminEvent

108.15.10.6   **public static final String WIREADMIN_FILTER = "wireadmin.filter"**

Wire property key (named wireadmin.filter) specifying a filter used to control the delivery rate of data between the Producer and the Consumer service.

This property should contain a filter as described in the Filter class. The filter can be used to specify when an updated value from the Producer service should be delivered to the Consumer service. In many cases the Consumer service does not need to receive the data with the same rate that the Producer service can generate data. This property can be used to control the delivery rate.

The filter can use a number of pre-defined attributes that can be used to control the delivery of new data values. If the filter produces a match upon the wire filter attributes, the Consumer service should be notifed of the updated data value.

If the Producer service was registered with the WIREADMIN_PRODUCER_FILTERS service property indicating that the Producer service will perform the data filtering then the Wire object will not perform data filtering. Otherwise, the Wire object must perform basic filtering. Basic filtering includes supporting the following standard wire filter attributes:

- WIREVALUE_CURRENT - Current value
- WIREVALUE_PREVIOUS - Previous value
- WIREVALUE_DELTA_ABSOLUTE - Absolute delta
- WIREVALUE_DELTA_RELATIVE - Relative delta
- WIREVALUE_ELAPSED - Elapsed time

See Also org.osgi.framework.Filter

108.15.10.7   **public static final String WIREADMIN_PID = "wireadmin.pid"**

Wire property key (named wireadmin.pid) specifying the persistent identity (PID) of this Wire object.

Each Wire object has a PID to allow unique and persistent identification of a specific Wire object. The PID must be generated by the WireAdmin service when the Wire object is created.

This wire property is automatically set by the Wire Admin service. The value of the property must be of type String.

108.15.10.8   **public static final String WIREADMIN_PRODUCER_COMPOSITE =**
"wireadmin.producer.composite"

A service registration property for a Producer service that is composite. It contains the names of the composite Consumer services it can inter-operate with. Inter-operability exists when any name in this array matches any name in the array set by the Consumer service. The type of this property must be String[].

108.15.10.9   **public static final String WIREADMIN_PRODUCER_FILTERS = "wireadmin.producer.filters"**

Service Registration property (named wireadmin.producer.filters). A Producer service registered with this property indicates to the Wire Admin service that the Producer service implements at least the filtering as described for the WIREADMIN_FILTER property. If the Producer service is not registered with this property, the Wire object must perform the basic filtering as described in WIREADMIN_FILTER.

The type of the property value is not relevant. Only its presence is relevant.

108.15.10.10   **public static final String WIREADMIN_PRODUCER_FLAVORS = "wireadmin.producer.flavors"**

Service Registration property (named wireadmin.producer.flavors) specifying the list of data types available from this Producer service.

The Producer service object should be registered with this service property.

The value of the property must be of type Class[].

108.15.10.11   **public static final String WIREADMIN_PRODUCER_PID = "wireadmin.producer.pid"**

Wire property key (named wireadmin.producer.pid) specifying the service.pid of the associated Producer service.

This wire property is automatically set by the WireAdmin service. The value of the property must be of type String.

108.15.10.12   **public static final String WIREADMIN_PRODUCER_SCOPE = "wireadmin.producer.scope"**

Service registration property key (named wireadmin.producer.scope) specifying a list of names that may be used to define the scope of this Wire object. A Producer service should set this service property when it can produce more than one kind of value. This property is only used during registration, modifying the property must not have any effect of the Wire object's scope. Each name in the given list mist have WirePermission[name,PRODUCE] or else is ignored. The type of this service registration property must be String[].

See Also   Wire.getScope, WIREADMIN_CONSUMER_SCOPE

108.15.10.13   **public static final String WIREADMIN_SCOPE_ALL**

Matches all scope names.

108.15.10.14   **public static final String WIREVALUE_CURRENT = "wirevalue.current"**

Wire object's filter attribute (named wirevalue.current) representing the current value.

108.15.10.15   **public static final String WIREVALUE_DELTA_ABSOLUTE = "wirevalue.delta.absolute"**

Wire object's filter attribute (named wirevalue.delta.absolute) representing the absolute delta. The absolute (always positive) difference between the last update and the current value (only when numeric). This attribute must not be used when the values are not numeric.

108.15.10.16   **public static final String WIREVALUE_DELTA_RELATIVE = "wirevalue.delta.relative"**

Wire object's filter attribute (named wirevalue.delta.relative) representing the relative delta. The relative difference is |previous-current |/| current| (only when numeric). This attribute must not be used when the values are not numeric.

108.15.10.17   **public static final String WIREVALUE_ELAPSED = "wirevalue.elapsed"**

Wire object's filter attribute (named wirevalue.elapsed) representing the elapsed time, in ms, between this filter evaluation and the last update of the Consumer service.

108.15.10.18   **public static final String WIREVALUE_PREVIOUS = "wirevalue.previous"**

Wire object's filter attribute (named wirevalue.previous) representing the previous value.

108.15.11   public final class WirePermission extends BasicPermission

Permission for the scope of a Wire object. When a Envelope object is used for communication with the poll or update method, and the scope is set, then the Wire object must verify that the Consumer service has WirePermission[name,CONSUME] and the Producer service has WirePermission[name, PRODUCE] for all names in the scope.

The names are compared with the normal rules for permission names. This means that they may end with a "*" to indicate wildcards. E.g. Door.* indicates all scope names starting with the string "Door". The last period is required due to the implementations of the BasicPermission class.

Concurrency   Thread-safe

108.15.11.1   public static final String CONSUME = "consume"

The action string for the consume action.

108.15.11.2   public static final String PRODUCE = "produce"

The action string for the produce action.

108.15.11.3   public WirePermission(String name, String actions)

name   Wire name.

actions   produce, consume (canonical order).

□ Create a new WirePermission with the given name (may be wildcard) and actions.

108.15.11.4   public boolean equals(Object obj)

obj   The object to test for equality.

□ Determines the equalty of two WirePermission objects. Checks that specified object has the same name and actions as this WirePermission object.

Returns   true if obj is a WirePermission, and has the same name and actions as this WirePermission object; false otherwise.

108.15.11.5   public String getActions( )

□ Returns the canonical string representation of the actions. Always returns present actions in the following order: produce, consume.

Returns   The canonical string representation of the actions.

108.15.11.6   public int hashCode( )

□ Returns the hash code value for this object.

Returns   Hash code value for this object.

108.15.11.7   public boolean implies(Permission p)

p   The permission to check against.

□ Checks if this WirePermission object implies the specified permission.

More specifically, this method returns true if:

- *p* is an instanceof the WirePermission class,
- *p*'s actions are a proper subset of this object's actions, and
- *p*'s name is implied by this object's name. For example, java.* implies java.home.

Returns   true if the specified permission is implied by this object; false otherwise.

108.15.11.8   **public PermissionCollection newPermissionCollection( )**

☐ Returns a new PermissionCollection object for storing WirePermission objects.

Returns A new PermissionCollection object suitable for storing WirePermission objects.

108.15.11.9   **public String toString( )**

☐ Returns a string describing this WirePermission. The convention is to specify the class name, the permission name, and the actions in the following format: '(org.osgi.service.wireadmin.WirePermission "name" "actions")'.

Returns information about this Permission object.

108.16   References

[1]   *Design Patterns*
Erich Gamma, Richard Helm, Ralph Johnson, and John Vlissides. Addison Wesley, ISBN 0-201-63361

109   IO Connector Service Specification

Version 1.0

109.1   Introduction

Communication is at the heart of OSGi Service Platform functionality. Therefore, a flexible and extendable communication API is needed: one that can handle all the complications that arise out of the Reference Architecture. These obstacles could include different communication protocols based on different networks, firewalls, intermittent connectivity, and others.

Therefore, this IO Connector Service specification adopts the [1] *Java 2 Micro Edition* (J2ME) javax.microedition.io packages as a basic communications infrastructure. In J2ME, this API is also called the Connector framework. A key aspect of this framework is that the connection is configured by a single string, the URI.

In J2ME, the Connector framework can be extended by the vendor of the Virtual Machine, but cannot be extended at run-time by other code. Therefore, this specification defines a service that adopts the flexible model of the Connector framework, but allows bundles to extend the Connector Services into different communication domains.

109.1.1   Essentials

- *Abstract* – Provide an intermediate layer that abstracts the actual protocol and devices from the bundle using it.
- *Extendable* – Allow third-party bundles to extend the system with new protocols and devices.
- *Layered* – Allow a protocol to be layered on top of lower layer protocols or devices.
- *Configurable* – Allow the selection of an actual protocol/device by means of configuration data.
- *Compatibility* – Be compatible with existing standards.

109.1.2   Entities

- *Connector Service* – The service that performs the same function—creating connections from different providers—as the static methods in the Connector framework of javax.microediton.io.
- *Connection Factory* – A service that extends the Connector service with more schemes.
- *Scheme* – A protocol or device that is supported in the Connector framework.

Figure 109.1   *Class Diagram, org.osgi.service.io (jmi is javax.microedition.io)*

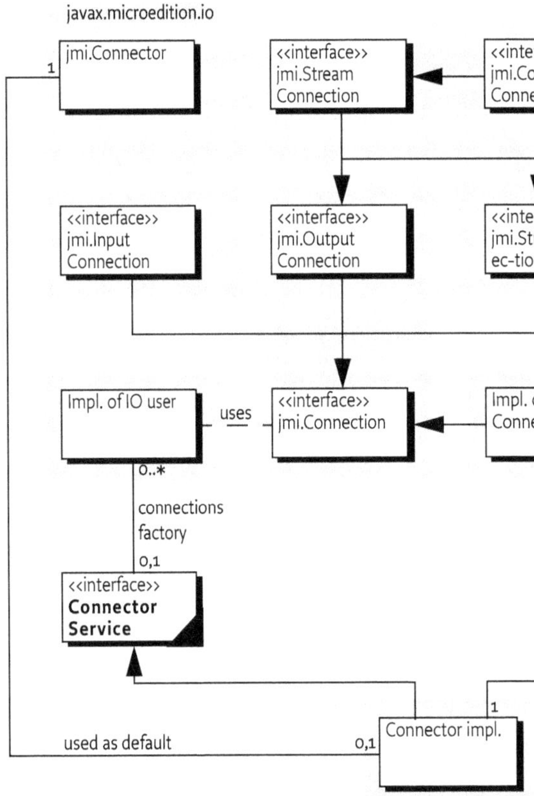

109.2   **The Connector Framework**

The [1] *Java 2 Micro Edition* specification introduces a package for communicating with back-end systems. The requirements for this package are very similar to the following OSGi requirements:

- Small footprint
- Allows many different implementations simultaneously
- Simple to use
- Simple configuration

The key design goal of the Connector framework is to allow an application to use a communication mechanism/protocol without understanding implementation details.

An application passes a Uniform Resource Identifier (URI) to the java.microedition.io.Connector class, and receives an object implementing one or more Connection interfaces. The java.microedition.io.Connector class uses the scheme in the URI to locate the appropriate Connection Factory service. The remainder of the URI may contain parameters that are used by the Connection Factory service to establish the connection; for example, they may contain the baud rate for a serial connection. Some examples:

- sms://+46705950899;expiry=24h;reply=yes;type=9
- datagram://:53
- socket://www.acme.com:5302
- comm://COM1;baudrate=9600;databits=9
- file:c:/autoexec.bat

The javax.microedition.io API itself does not prescribe any schemes. It is up to the implementer of this package to include a number of extensions that provide the schemes. The javax.microedition.io.Connector class dispatches a request to a class which provides an implementation of a Connection interface. J2ME does not specify how this dispatching takes place, but implementations usually offer a proprietary mechanism to connect user defined classes that can provide new schemes.

The Connector framework defines a taxonomy of communication mechanisms with a number of interfaces. For example, a javax.microedition.io.InputConnection interface indicates that the connection supports the input stream semantics, such as an I/O port. A javax.microedition.io.DatagramConnection interface indicates that communication should take place with messages.

When a javax.microedition.io.Connector.open method is called, it returns a javax.microedition.io.Connection object. The interfaces implemented by this object define the type of the communication session. The following interfaces may be implemented:

- *HttpConnection* – A javax.microedition.io.ContentConnection with specific HTTP support.
- *DatagramConnection* – A connection that can be used to send and receive datagrams.
- *OutputConnection* – A connection that can be used for streaming output.
- *InputConnection* – A connection that can be used for streaming input.
- *StreamConnection* – A connection that is both input and output.
- *StreamConnectionNotifier* – Can be used to wait for incoming stream connection requests.
- *ContentConnection* – A javax.microedition.io.StreamConnection that provides information about the type, encoding, and length of the information.

Bundles using this approach must indicate to the Operator what kind of interfaces they expect to receive. The operator must then configure the bundle with a URI that contains the scheme and appropriate options that match the bundle's expectations. Well-written bundles are flexible enough to communicate with any of the types of javax.microedition.io.Connection interfaces they have specified. For example, a bundle should support javax.microedition.io.StreamConnection as well as javax.microedition.io.DatagramConnection objects in the appropriate direction (input or output).

The following code example shows a bundle that sends an alarm message with the help of the javax.microedition.io.Connector framework:

```
public class Alarm {
    String    uri;
    public Alarm(String uri) { this.uri = uri; }
    private void send(byte[] msg) {
        while ( true ) try {
            Connection  connection = Connector.open( uri );
            DataOutputStream    dout = null;
            if ( connection instanceof OutputConnection ) {
                dout = ((OutputConnection)
                    connection).openDataOutputStream();
                dout.write( msg );
            }
            else if (connection instanceof DatagramConnection) {
                DatagramConnection dgc =
                    (DatagramConnection) connection;
                Datagram datagram = dgc.newDatagram(
                    msg, msg.length );
                dgc.send( datagram );
            } else {
                error( "No configuration for alarm" );
                return;
```

```
            }
            connection.close();
        } catch( Exception e ) { ... }
    }
}
```

109.3 Connector Service

The javax.microedition.io.Connector framework matches the requirements for OSGi applications very well. The actual creation of connections, however, is handled through static methods in the javax.microedition.io.Connector class. This approach does not mesh well with the OSGi service registry and dynamic life-cycle management.

This specification therefore introduces the Connector Service. The methods of the ConnectorService interface have the same signatures as the static methods of the javax.microedition.io.Connector class.

Each javax.microedition.io.Connection object returned by a Connector Service must implement interfaces from the javax.microedition.io package. Implementations must strictly follow the semantics that are associated with these interfaces.

The Connector Service must provide all the schemes provided by the exporter of the javax.microedition.io package. The Connection Factory services must have priority over schemes implemented in the Java run-time environment. For example, if a Connection Factory provides the http scheme and a built-in implementation exists, then the Connector Service must use the Connection Factory service with the http scheme.

Bundles that want to use the Connector Service should first obtain a ConnectorService service object. This object contains open methods that should be called to get a new javax.microedition.io.Connection object.

109.4 Providing New Schemes

The Connector Service must be able to be extended with the Connection Factory service. Bundles that can provide new schemes must register a ConnectionFactory service object.

The Connector Service must listen for registrations of new ConnectionFactory service objects and make the supplied schemes available to bundles that create connections.

Implementing a Connection Factory service requires implementing the following method:

*   createConnection(String,int,boolean) – Creates a new connection object from the given URI.

The Connection Factory service must be registered with the IO_SCHEME property to indicate the provided scheme to the Connector Service. The value of this property must be a String[].

If multiple Connection Factory services register with the same scheme, the Connector Service should select the Connection Factory service with the highest value for the service.ranking service registration property, or if more than one Connection Factory service has the highest value, the Connection Factory service with the lowest service.id is selected.

The following example shows how a Connection Factory service may be implemented. The example will return a javax.microedition.io.InputConnection object that returns the value of the URI after removing the scheme identifier.

```
public class ConnectionFactoryImpl
    implements BundleActivator, ConnectionFactory {
        public void start( BundleContext context ) {
            Hashtable  properties = new Hashtable();
```

```
                           properties.put( IO_SCHEME, new String[]{"data"} );
                           context.registerService(
                              ConnectorService.class.getName(),
                              this, properties );
                       }
                       public void stop( BundleContext context ) {}

                       public Connection createConnection(
                           String uri, int mode, boolean timeouts  ) {
                           return new DataConnection(uri);
                       }
                   }

                   class DataConnection
                      implements javax.microedition.io.InputConnection {
                      String    uri;
                      DataConnection( String uri ) {this.uri = uri;}
                      public DataInputStream openDataInputStream()
                         throws IOException {
                         return new DataInputStream( openInputStream() );
                      }

                      public InputStream openInputStream() throws IOException {
                         byte [] buf = uri.getBytes();
                         return new ByteArrayInputStream(buf,5,buf.length-5);
                      }
                      public void close() {}
                   }
```

109.4.1   Orphaned Connection Objects

When a Connection Factory service is unregistered, it must close all Connection objects that are still open. Closing these Connection objects should make these objects unusable, and they should subsequently throw an IOException when used.

Bundles should not unnecessarily hang onto objects they retrieved from services. Implementations of Connection Factory services should program defensively and ensure that resource allocation is minimized when a Connection object is closed.

109.5   Execution Environment

The javax.microedition.io package is available in J2ME configurations/profiles, but is not present in J2SE, J2EE, and the OSGi minimum execution requirements.

Implementations of the Connector Service that are targeted for all environments should carry their own implementation of the javax.microedition.io package and export it.

109.6   Security

The OSGi Connector Service is a key service available in the Service Platform. A malicious bundle which provides this service can spoof any communication. Therefore, it is paramount that the ServicePermission[ConnectorService, REGISTER] is given only to a trusted bundle. ServicePermission[ConnectorService,GET] may be handed to bundles that are allowed to communicate to the external world.

ServicePermission[ConnectionFactory, REGISTER] should also be restricted to trusted bundles because they can implement specific protocols or access devices. ServicePermission[ConnectionFactory,GET] should be limited to trusted bundles that implement the Connector Service.

Implementations of Connection Factory services must perform all I/O operations within a privileged region. For example, an implementation of the sms: scheme must have permission to access the mobile phone, and should not require the bundle that opened the connection to have this permission. Normally, the operations need to be implemented in a doPrivileged method or in a separate thread.

If a specific Connection Factory service needs more detailed permissions than provided by the OSGi or Java 2, it may create a new specific Permission sub-class for its purpose.

109.7 org.osgi.service.io

IO Connector Package Version 1.0.

Bundles wishing to use this package must list the package in the Import-Package header of the bundle's manifest. For example:

```
Import-Package: org.osgi.service.io; version="[1.0,2.0)", javax.microedition.io
```

109.7.1 Summary

- *ConnectionFactory* - A Connection Factory service is called by the implementation of the Connector Service to create javax.microedition.io.Connection objects which implement the scheme named by IO_SCHEME.
- *ConnectorService* - The Connector Service should be called to create and open javax.microedition.io.Connection objects.

109.7.2 public interface ConnectionFactory

A Connection Factory service is called by the implementation of the Connector Service to create javax.microedition.io.Connection objects which implement the scheme named by IO_SCHEME. When a ConnectorService.open method is called, the implementation of the Connector Service will examine the specified name for a scheme. The Connector Service will then look for a Connection Factory service which is registered with the service property IO_SCHEME which matches the scheme. The createConnection method of the selected Connection Factory will then be called to create the actual Connection object.

109.7.2.1 public static final String IO_SCHEME = "io.scheme"

Service property containing the scheme(s) for which this Connection Factory can create Connection objects. This property is of type String[].

109.7.2.2 public Connection createConnection(String name, int mode, boolean timeouts) throws IOException

name The full URI passed to the ConnectorService.open method

mode The mode parameter passed to the ConnectorService.open method

timeouts The timeouts parameter passed to the ConnectorService.open method

☐ Create a new Connection object for the specified URI.

Returns A new javax.microedition.io.Connection object.

Throws IOException – If a javax.microedition.io.Connection object can not not be created.

109.7.3   public interface ConnectorService

The Connector Service should be called to create and open javax.microedition.io.Connection objects. When an open* method is called, the implementation of the Connector Service will examine the specified name for a scheme. The Connector Service will then look for a Connection Factory service which is registered with the service property IO_SCHEME which matches the scheme. The createConnection method of the selected Connection Factory will then be called to create the actual Connection object.

If more than one Connection Factory service is registered for a particular scheme, the service with the highest ranking (as specified in its service.ranking property) is called. If there is a tie in ranking, the service with the lowest service ID (as specified in its service.id property), that is the service that was registered first, is called. This is the same algorithm used by BundleContext.getServiceReference.

109.7.3.1   public static final int READ = 1

Read access mode.

See Also   javax.microedition.io.Connector.READ

109.7.3.2   public static final int READ_WRITE = 3

Read/Write access mode.

See Also   javax.microedition.io.Connector.READ_WRITE

109.7.3.3   public static final int WRITE = 2

Write access mode.

See Also   javax.microedition.io.Connector.WRITE

109.7.3.4   public Connection open(String name) throws IOException

name   The URI for the connection.

    □   Create and open a Connection object for the specified name.

Returns   A new javax.microedition.io.Connection object.

Throws   IllegalArgumentException – If a parameter is invalid.

    javax.microedition.io.ConnectionNotFoundException – If the connection cannot be found.

    IOException – If some other kind of I/O error occurs.

See Also   javax.microedition.io.Connector.open(String name)

109.7.3.5   public Connection open(String name, int mode) throws IOException

name   The URI for the connection.

mode   The access mode.

    □   Create and open a Connection object for the specified name and access mode.

Returns   A new javax.microedition.io.Connection object.

Throws   IllegalArgumentException – If a parameter is invalid.

    javax.microedition.io.ConnectionNotFoundException – If the connection cannot be found.

    IOException – If some other kind of I/O error occurs.

See Also   javax.microedition.io.Connector.open(String name, int mode)

109.7.3.6   public Connection open(String name, int mode, boolean timeouts) throws IOException

name   The URI for the connection.

mode   The access mode.

timeouts A flag to indicate that the caller wants timeout exceptions.

☐ Create and open a Connection object for the specified name, access mode and timeouts.

Returns A new javax.microedition.io.Connection object.

Throws IllegalArgumentException – If a parameter is invalid.

javax.microedition.io.ConnectionNotFoundException – If the connection cannot be found.

IOException – If some other kind of I/O error occurs.

See Also javax.microedition.io.Connector.open

109.7.3.7 **public DataInputStream openDataInputStream(String name) throws IOException**

name The URI for the connection.

☐ Create and open a DataInputStream object for the specified name.

Returns A DataInputStream object.

Throws IllegalArgumentException – If a parameter is invalid.

javax.microedition.io.ConnectionNotFoundException – If the connection cannot be found.

IOException – If some other kind of I/O error occurs.

See Also javax.microedition.io.Connector.openDataInputStream(String name)

109.7.3.8 **public DataOutputStream openDataOutputStream(String name) throws IOException**

name The URI for the connection.

☐ Create and open a DataOutputStream object for the specified name.

Returns A DataOutputStream object.

Throws IllegalArgumentException – If a parameter is invalid.

javax.microedition.io.ConnectionNotFoundException – If the connection cannot be found.

IOException – If some other kind of I/O error occurs.

See Also javax.microedition.io.Connector.openDataOutputStream(String name)

109.7.3.9 **public InputStream openInputStream(String name) throws IOException**

name The URI for the connection.

☐ Create and open an InputStream object for the specified name.

Returns An InputStream object.

Throws IllegalArgumentException – If a parameter is invalid.

javax.microedition.io.ConnectionNotFoundException – If the connection cannot be found.

IOException – If some other kind of I/O error occurs.

See Also javax.microedition.io.Connector.openInputStream(String name)

109.7.3.10 **public OutputStream openOutputStream(String name) throws IOException**

name The URI for the connection.

☐ Create and open an OutputStream object for the specified name.

Returns An OutputStream object.

Throws IllegalArgumentException – If a parameter is invalid.

javax.microedition.io.ConnectionNotFoundException – If the connection cannot be found.

IOException – If some other kind of I/O error occurs.

See Also `javax.microedition.io.Connector.openOutputStream(String name)`

109.8   References

[1]   *Java 2 Micro Edition*
       http://java.sun.com/j2me/

[2]   *J2ME Foundation Profile*
       http://www.jcp.org/en/jsr/detail?id=46

110   Initial Provisioning

Version 1.2

110.1   Introduction

To allow freedom regarding the choice of management protocol, the OSGi Specifications assumes an architecture to remotely manage a Service Platform with a Management Agent. The Management Agent is implemented with a Management Bundle that can communicate with an unspecified management protocol.

This specification defines how the Management Agent can make its way to the Service Platform, and gives a structured view of the problems and their corresponding resolution methods.

The purpose of this specification is to enable the management of a Service Platform by an Operator, and (optionally) to hand over the management of the Service Platform later to another Operator. This approach is in accordance with the OSGi remote management reference architecture.

This bootstrapping process requires the installation of a Management Agent, with appropriate configuration data, in the Service Platform.

This specification consists of a prologue, in which the principles of the Initial Provisioning are outlined, and a number of mappings to different mechanisms.

110.1.1   Essentials

- *Policy Free* – The proposed solution must be business model agnostic; none of the affected parties (Operators, SPS Manufacturers, etc.) should be forced into any particular business model.
- *Inter-operability* – The Initial Provisioning must permit arbitrary inter-operability between management systems and Service Platforms. Any compliant Remote Manager should be able to manage any compliant Service Platform, even in the absence of a prior business relationship. Adhering to this requirement allows a particular Operator to manage a variety of makes and models of Service Platform Servers using a single management system of the Operator's choice. This rule also gives the consumer the greatest choice when selecting an Operator.
- *Flexible* – The management process should be as open as possible, to allow innovation and specialization while still achieving interoperability.

110.1.2   Entities

- *Provisioning Service* – A service registered with the Framework that provides information about the initial provisioning to the Management Agent.
- *Provisioning Dictionary* – A Dictionary object that is filled with information from the ZIP files that are loaded during initial setup.
- *RSH Protocol* – An OSGi specific secure protocol based on HTTP.
- *Management Agent* – A bundle that is responsible for managing a Service Platform under control of a Remote Manager.

Figure 110.1   *Initial Provisioning*

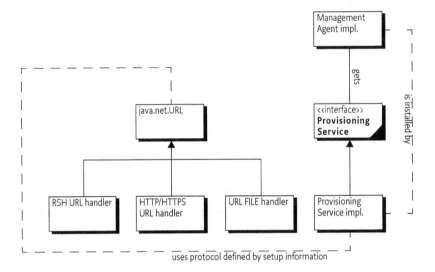

110.2   Procedure

The following procedure should be executed by an OSGi Framework implementation that supports this Initial Provisioning specification.

When the Service Platform is first brought under management control, it must be provided with an initial request URL in order to be provisioned. Either the end user or the manufacturer may provide the initial request URL. How the initial request URL is transferred to the Framework is not specified, but a mechanism might, for example, be a command line parameter when the framework is started.

When asked to start the Initial Provisioning, the Service Platform will send a request to the management system. This request is encoded in a URL, for example:

```
http://osgi.acme.com/remote-manager
```

This URL may use any protocol that is available on the Service Platform Server. Many standard protocols exist, but it is also possible to use a proprietary protocol. For example, software could be present which can communicate with a smart card and could handle, for example, this URL:

```
smart-card://com1:0/7F20/6F38
```

Before the request URL is executed, the Service Platform information is appended to the URL. This information includes at least the Service Platform Identifier, but may also contain proprietary information, as long as the keys for this information do not conflict. Different URL schemes may use different methods of appending parameters; these details are specified in the mappings of this specification to concrete protocols.

The result of the request must be a ZIP file (The content type should be application/zip). It is the responsibility of the underlying protocol to guarantee the integrity and authenticity of this ZIP file.

This ZIP file is unpacked and its entries (except bundle and bundle-url entries, described in Table 110.2) are placed in a Dictionary object. This Dictionary object is called the *Provisioning Dictionary*. It must be made available from the Provisioning Service in the service registry. The names of the entries in the ZIP file must not start with a slash ('/').

The ZIP file may contain only four types of dictionary entries: text, binary, bundle, or bundle-url. The type of an entry can be specified in different ways. An Initial Provisioning service must look in the following places to find the information about an entry's (MIME) type (in the given order):

1 The manifest header InitialProvisioning-Entries of the given ZIP file. This header is defined in *InitialProvisioning-Entries Manifest Header* on page 211. If this header is present, but a given entry's path is not named then try the next step.

2 The ZIP entry's extra field. If this ZIP entry field is present, the Initial Provisioning service should not look further, even if the extra field contains an erroneous value.

3 The extension of the entry path name if one of .txt, .jar, .url extensions. See *Content types of provisioning ZIP file* on page 209 for the mapping of types, MIME types, and extensions.

4 The entry is assumed to be a binary type

The types can optionally be specified as a MIME type as defined in [7] *MIME Types*. The text and bundle-url entries are translated into a String object from an UTF-8 encoded byte array. All other entries must be stored as a byte[].

Table 110.1   *Content types of provisioning ZIP file*

Type	MIME Type	Ext	Description
text	MIME_STRING text/ plain;charset=utf-8	.txt	Must be represented as a String object
binary	MIME_BYTE_ARRAY application/octet-stream	not .txt, .url, or .jar	Must be represented as a byte array (byte[]).
bundle	MIME_BUNDLE application/ vnd.osgi.bundle MIME_BUNDLE_ALT application/ x-osgi-bundle	.jar	Entries must be installed using BundleContext.installBundle(String,InputStream), with the InputStream object constructed from the contents of the ZIP entry. The location must be the name of the ZIP entry without leading slash. This entry must not be stored in the Provisioning Dictionary. If a bundle with this location name is already installed in this system, then this bundle must be updated instead of installed. The MIME_BUNDLE_ALT version is intended for backward compatibility, it specifies the original MIME type for bundles before there was an official IANA MIME type.
bundle-url	MIME_BUNDLE_URL text/ x-osgi-bundle-url; charset=utf-8	.url	The content of this entry is a string coded in utf-8. Entries must be installed using BundleContext.installBundle(String, InputStream), with the InputStream object created from the given URL. The location must be the name of the ZIP entry without leading slash. This entry must not be stored in the Provisioning Dictionary. If a bundle with this location url is already installed in this system, then this bundle must be updated instead of installed.

The Provisioning Service must install (but not start) all entries in the ZIP file that are typed with bundle or bundle-url.

If an entry named PROVISIONING_START_BUNDLE is present in the Provisioning Dictionary, then its content type must be text as defined in Table 110.1. The content of this entry must match the bundle location of a previously loaded bundle. This designated bundle must be given AllPermission and started.

If no PROVISIONING_START_BUNDLE entry is present in the Provisioning Dictionary, the Provisioning Dictionary should contain a reference to another ZIP file under the PROVISIONING_REFERENCE key. If both keys are absent, no further action must take place.

If this PROVISIONING_REFERENCE key is present and holds a String object that can be mapped to a valid URL, then a new ZIP file must be retrieved from this URL. The PROVISIONING_REFERENCE link may be repeated multiple times in successively loaded ZIP files.

Referring to a new ZIP file with such a URL allows a manufacturer to place a fixed reference inside the Service Platform Server (in a file or smart card) that will provide some platform identifying information and then also immediately load the information from the management system. The PROVISIONING_REFERENCE link may be repeated multiple times in successively loaded ZIP files. The entry PROVISIONING_UPDATE_COUNT must be an Integer object that must be incremented on every iteration.

Information retrieved while loading subsequent PROVISIONING_REFERENCE URLs may replace previous key/values in the Provisioning Dictionary, but must not erase unrecognized key/values. For example, if an assignment has assigned the key proprietary-x, with a value '3', then later assignments must not override this value, unless the later loaded ZIP file contains an entry with that name. All these updates to the Provisioning Dictionary must be stored persistently. At the same time, each entry of type bundle or bundle-url (see Table 110.1) must be installed and not started.

Once the Management Agent has been started, the Initial Provisioning service has become operational. In this state, the Initial Provisioning service must react when the Provisioning Dictionary is updated with a new PROVISIONING_REFERENCE property. If this key is set, it should start the cycle again. For example, if the control of a Service Platform needs to be transferred to another Remote Manager, the Management Agent should set the PROVISIONING_REFERENCE to the location of this new Remote Manager's Initial Provisioning ZIP file.This process is called *re-provisioning*.

If errors occur during this process, the Initial Provisioning service should try to notify the Service User of the problem.

The previous description is depicted in Figure 110.2 as a flow chart.

Figure 110.2   *Flow chart installation Management Agent bundle*

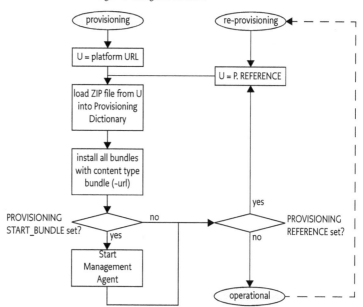

The Management Agent may require configuration data that is specific to the Service Platform instance. If this data is available outside the Management Agent bundle, the merging of this data with the Management Agent may take place in the Service Platform. Transferring the data separately will make it possible to simplify the implementation on the server side, as it is not necessary to create *personalized* Service Platform bundles. The PROVISIONING_AGENT_CONFIG key is reserved for this purpose, but the Management Agent may use another key or mechanisms if so desired.

The PROVISIONING_SPID key must contain the Service Platform Identifier.

110.2.1   InitialProvisioning-Entries Manifest Header

The InitialProvisioning-Entries manifest header optionally specifies the type of the entries in the ZIP file. This header, when present, overrides the extra field for the given entry. The syntax for this header is:

```
InitialProvisioning-Entries ::= ip-entry ( ',' ip-entry ) *
ip-entry                    ::= path ( ';' parameter ) *
```

The entry is the path name of a resource in the ZIP file. This InitialProvisioning-Entries header recognizes the following attribute:

- type – Gives the type of the dictionary entry. The type can have one of the following values: text, binary, bundle, or bundle-url

If the type parameter entry is not specified for an entry, then the type will be inferred from the extension of the entry, as defined in table *Content types of provisioning ZIP file* on page 209.

110.3   Special Configurations

The next section shows some examples of specially configured types of Service Platform Servers and how they are treated with the respect to the specifications in this document.

110.3.1 Branded Service Platform Server

If a Service Platform Operator is selling Service Platform Servers branded exclusively for use with their service, the provisioning will most likely be performed prior to shipping the Service Platform Server to the User. Typically the Service Platform is configured with the Dictionary entry PROVISIONING_REFERENCE pointing at a location controlled by the Operator.

Up-to-date bundles and additional configuration data must be loaded from that location at activation time. The Service Platform is probably equipped with necessary security entities, like certificates, to enable secure downloads from the Operator's URL over open networks, if necessary.

110.3.2 Non-connected Service Platform

Circumstances might exist in which the Service Platform Server has no WAN connectivity, or prefers not to depend on it for the purposes not covered by this specification.

The non-connected case can be implemented by specifying a file:// URL for the initial ZIP file (PROVISIONING_REFERENCE). That file:// URL would name a local file containing the response that would otherwise be received from a remote server.

The value for the Management Agent PROVISIONING_REFERENCE found in that file will be used as input to the load process. The PROVISIONING_REFERENCE may point to a bundle file stored either locally or remotely. No code changes are necessary for the non-connected scenario. The file:// URLs must be specified, and the appropriate files must be created on the Service Platform.

110.4 The Provisioning Service

Provisioning information is conveyed between bundles using the Provisioning Service, as defined in the ProvisioningService interface. The Provisioning Dictionary is retrieved from the ProvisioningService object using the getInformation() method. This is a read-only Dictionary object, any changes to this Dictionary object must throw an UnsupportedOperationException.

The Provisioning Service provides a number of methods to update the Provisioning Dictionary.

- addInformation(Dictionary) – Add all key/value pairs in the given Dictionary object to the Provisioning Dictionary.
- addInformation(ZipInputStream) – It is also possible to add a ZIP file to the Provisioning Service immediately. This will unpack the ZIP file and add the entries to the Provisioning Dictionary. This method must install the bundles contained in the ZIP file as described in *Procedure* on page 208.
- setInformation(Dictionary) – Set a new Provisioning Dictionary. This will remove all existing entries.

Each of these method will increment the PROVISIONING_UPDATE_COUNT entry.

110.5 Management Agent Environment

The Management Agent should be written with great care to minimize dependencies on other packages and services, as *all* services in OSGi are optional. Some Service Platforms may have other bundles pre-installed, so it is possible that there may be exported packages and services available. Mechanisms outside the current specification, however, must be used to discover these packages and services before the Management Agent is installed.

The Provisioning Service must ensure that the Management Agent is running with AllPermission. The Management Agent should check to see if the Permission Admin service is available, and establish the initial permissions as soon as possible to insure the security of the device when later bundles are installed. As the PermissionAdmin interfaces may not be present (it is an optional service), the Management Agent should export the PermissionAdmin interfaces to ensure they can be resolved.

Once started, the Management Agent may retrieve its configuration data from the Provisioning Service by getting the byte[] object that corresponds to the PROVISIONING_AGENT_CONFIG key in the Provisioning Dictionary. The structure of the configuration data is implementation specific.

The scope of this specification is to provide a mechanism to transmit the raw configuration data to the Management Agent. The Management Agent bundle may alternatively be packaged with its configuration data in the bundle, so it may not be necessary for the Management Agent bundle to use the Provisioning Service at all.

Most likely, the Management Agent bundle will install other bundles to provision the Service Platform. Installing other bundles might even involve downloading a more full featured Management Agent to replace the initial Management Agent.

110.6   Mapping To File Scheme

The file: scheme is the simplest and most completely supported scheme which can be used by the Initial Provisioning specification. It can be used to store the configuration data and Management Agent bundle on the Service Platform Server, and avoids any outside communication.

If the initial request URL has a file scheme, no parameters should be appended, because the file: scheme does not accept parameters.

110.6.1   Example With File Scheme

The manufacturer should prepare a ZIP file containing only one entry named PROVISIONING_START_BUNDLE that contains a location string of an entry of type bundle or bundle-url. For example, the following ZIP file demonstrates this:

```
provisioning.start.bundle  text    agent
agent                      bundle  C0AF0E9B2AB..
```

The bundle may also be specified with a URL:

```
provisioning.start.bundle  text      http://acme.com/a.jar
agent                      bundle-url http://acme.com/a.jar
```

Upon startup, the framework is provided with the URL with the file: scheme that points to this ZIP file:

```
file:/opt/osgi/ma.zip
```

110.7   Mapping To HTTP(S) Scheme

This section defines how HTTP and HTTPS URLs must be used with the Initial Provisioning specification.

- HTTP – May be used when the data exchange takes place over networks that are secured by other means, such as a Virtual Private Network (VPN) or a physically isolated network. Otherwise, HTTP is not a valid scheme because no authentication takes place.
- HTTPS – May be used if the Service Platform is equipped with appropriate certificates.

HTTP and HTTPS share the following qualities:

- Both are well known and widely used
- Numerous implementations of the protocols exist
- Caching of the Management Agent will be desired in many implementations where limited bandwidth is an issue. Both HTTP and HTTPS already contain an accepted protocol for caching.

Both HTTP and HTTPS must be used with the GET method. The response is a ZIP file, implying that the response header Content-Type header must contain application/zip.

110.7.1   HTTPS Certificates

In order to use HTTPS, certificates must be in place. These certificates, that are used to establish trust towards the Operator, may be made available to the Service Platform using the Provisioning Service. The root certificate should be assigned to the Provisioning Dictionary before the HTTPS provider is used. Additionally, the Service Platform should be equipped with a Service Platform certificate that allows the Service Platform to properly authenticate itself towards the Operator. This specification does not state how this certificate gets installed into the Service Platform.

The root certificate is stored in the Provisioning Dictionary under the key:

```
PROVISIONING_ROOTX509
```

The Root X.509 Certificate holds certificates used to represent a handle to a common base for establishing trust. The certificates are typically used when authenticating a Remote Manager to the Service Platform. In this case, a Root X.509 certificate must be part of a certificate chain for the Operator's certificate. The format of the certificate is defined in *Certificate Encoding* on page 214.

110.7.2   Certificate Encoding

Root certificates are X.509 certificates. Each individual certificate is stored as a byte[] object. This byte[] object is encoded in the default Java manner, as follows:

- The original, binary certificate data is DER encoded
- The DER encoded data is encoded into base64 to make it text.
- The base64 encoded data is prefixed with
  ```
  -----BEGIN CERTIFICATE-----
  ```
  and suffixed with:
  ```
  -----END CERTIFICATE-----
  ```
- If a record contains more than one certificate, they are simply appended one after the other, each with a delimiting prefix and suffix.

The decoding of such a certificate may be done with the java.security.cert.CertificateFactory class:

```
InputStream bis = new ByteArrayInputStream(x509); // byte[]
CertificateFactory cf =
    CertificateFactory.getInstance("X.509");
Collection c = cf.generateCertificates(bis);
Iterator i = c.iterator();
while (i.hasNext()) {
    Certificate cert = (Certificate)i.next();
    System.out.println(cert);
}
```

110.7.3   URL Encoding

The URL must contain the Service Platform Identity, and may contain more parameters. These parameters are encoded in the URL according to the HTTP(S) URL scheme. A base URL may be set by an end user but the Provisioning Service must add the Service Platform Identifier.

If the request URL already contains HTTP parameters (if there is a '?' in the request), the service_platform_id is appended to this URL as an additional parameter. If, on the other hand, the request URL does not contain any HTTP parameters, the service_platform_id will be appended to the URL after a '?', becoming the first HTTP parameter. The following two examples show these two variants:

```
http://server.operator.com/service-x? «
    foo=bar&service_platform_id=VIN:123456789

http://server.operator.com/service-x? «
```

service_platform_id=VIN:123456789

Proper URL encoding must be applied when the URL contains characters that are not allowed. See [6] *RFC 2396 - Uniform Resource Identifier (URI).*

110.8 Mapping To RSH Scheme

The RSH protocol is an OSGi-specific protocol, and is included in this specification because it is optimized for Initial Provisioning. It requires a shared secret between the management system and the Service Platform that is small enough to be entered by the Service User.

RSH bases authentication and encryption on Message Authentication Codes (MACs) that have been derived from a secret that is shared between the Service Platform and the Operator prior to the start of the protocol execution.

The protocol is based on an ordinary HTTP GET request/response, in which the request must be *signed* and the response must be *encrypted* and *authenticated.* Both the *signature* and *encryption key* are derived from the shared secret using Hashed Message Access Codes (HMAC) functions.

As additional input to the HMAC calculations, one client-generated nonce and one server-generated nonce are used to prevent replay attacks. The nonces are fairly large random numbers that must be generated in relation to each invocation of the protocol, in order to guarantee freshness. These nonces are called clientfg (client-generated freshness guarantee) and serverfg (server-generated freshness guarantee).

In order to separate the HMAC calculations for authentication and encryption, each is based on a different constant value. These constants are called the *authentication constant* and the *encryption constant.*

From an abstract perspective, the protocol may be described as follows.

- δ – Shared secret, 160 bits or more
- s – Server nonce, called servercfg, 128 bits
- c – Client nonce, called clientfg, 128 bits
- K_a – Authentication key, 160 bits
- K_e – Encryption key, 192 bits
- r – Response data
- e – Encrypted data
- E – Encryption constant, a byte[] of 05, 36, 54, 70, 00 (hex)
- A – Authentication constant, a byte[] of 00, 4f, 53, 47, 49 (hex)
- M – Message material, used for K_e calculation.
- m – The calculated message authentication code.
- *3DES* – Triple DES, encryption function, see [8] *3DES.* The bytes of the key must be set to odd parity. CBC mode must be used where the padding method is defined in [9] *RFC 1423 Part III: Algorithms, Modes, and Identifiers.* In [11] *Java Cryptography API (part of Java 1.4)* this is addressed as PKCS5Padding.
- *IV* – Initialization vector for 3DES.
- *SHA1* – Secure Hash Algorithm to generate the Hashed Message Authentication Code, see [12] *SHA-1.* The function takes a single parameter, the block to be worked upon.
- *HMAC* – The function that calculates a message authentication code, which must HMAC-SHA1. HMAC-SHA1 is defined in [1] *HMAC: Keyed-Hashing for Message Authentication.* The HMAC function takes a key and a block to be worked upon as arguments. Note that the lower 16 bytes of the result must be used.
- *{}* – Concatenates its arguments
- *[]* – Indicates access to a sub-part of a variable, in bytes. Index starts at one, not zero.

In each step, the emphasized server or client indicates the context of the calculation. If both are used at the same time, each variable will have server or client as a subscript.

1. The *client* generates a random nonce, stores it and denotes it clientfg

   $c = nonce$

2. The client sends the request with the clientfg to the server.

   $c_{server} \Leftarrow c_{client}$

3. The *server* generates a nonce and denotes it serverfg.

   $s = nonce$

4. The *server* calculates an authentication key based on the SHA1 function, the shared secret, the received clientfg, the serverfg and the authentication constant.

   $K_a \leftarrow SHA1(\{\delta, c, s, A\})$

5. The *server* calculates an encryption key using an SHA-1 function, the shared secret, the received clientfg, the serverfg and the encryption constant. It must first calculate the *key material* M.

   $M[1, 20] \leftarrow SHA1(\{\delta, c, s, E\})$

   $M[21, 40] \leftarrow SHA1(\{\delta, M[1, 20], c, s, E\})$

6. The key for DES consists K_e and IV.

   $K_e \leftarrow M[1, 24]$

   $IV \leftarrow M[25, 32]$

   The *server* encrypts the response data using the encryption key derived in 5. The encryption algorithm that must be used to encrypt/decrypt the response data is 3DES. 24 bytes (192 bits) from M are used to generate K_e, but the low order bit of each byte must be used as an odd parity bit. This means that before using K_e, each byte must be processed to set the low order bit so that the byte has odd parity.

   The encryption/decryption key used is specified by the following:

   $e \leftarrow 3DES(K_e, IV, r)$

7. The *server* calculates a MAC *m* using the HMAC function, the encrypted response data and the authentication key derived in 4.

   $m \leftarrow HMAC(K_a, e)$

8. The *server* sends a response to the *client* containing the serverfg, the MAC *m* and the encrypted response data

   $s_{client} \Leftarrow s_{server}$

   $m_{client} \Leftarrow m_{server}$

   $e_{client} \Leftarrow e_{server}$

   The *client* calculates the encryption key K_e the same way the server did in step 5 and 6, and uses this to decrypt the encrypted response data. The serverfg value received in the response is used in the calculation.

   $r \leftarrow 3DES(K_e, IV, e)$

9. The *client* performs the calculation of the MAC *m'* in the same way the server did, and checks that the results match the received MAC *m*. If they do not match, further processing is discarded. The serverfg value received in the response is used in the calculation.

   $K_a \leftarrow SHA1(\{\delta, c, s, A\})$

   $m' \leftarrow HMAC(K_a, e)$

   $m' = m$

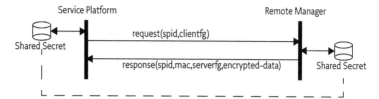

110.8.1   Shared Secret

The *shared secret* should be a key of length 160 bits (20 bytes) or more. The length is selected to match the output of the selected hash algorithm [2] *NIST, FIPS PUB 180-1: Secure Hash Standard, April 1995.*.

In some scenarios, the shared secret is generated by the Operator and communicated to the User, who inserts the secret into the Service Platform through some unspecified means.

The opposite is also possible: the shared secret can be stored within the Service Platform, extracted from it, and then communicated to the Operator. In this scenario, the source of the shared secret could be either the Service Platform or the Operator.

In order for the server to calculate the authentication and encryption keys, it requires the proper shared secret. The server must have access to many different shared secrets, one for each Service Platform it is to support. To be able to resolve this issue, the server must typically also have access to the Service Platform Identifier of the Service Platform. The normal way for the server to know the Service Platform Identifier is through the application protocol, as this value is part of the URL encoded parameters of the HTTP, HTTPS, or RSH mapping of the Initial Provisioning.

In order to be able to switch Operators, a new shared secret must be used. The new secret may be generated by the new Operator and then inserted into the Service Platform device using a mechanism not covered by this specification. Or the device itself may generate the new secret and convey it to the owner of the device using a display device or read-out, which is then communicated to the new operator out-of-band. Additionally, the generation of the new secret may be triggered by some external event, like holding down a button for a specified amount of time.

110.8.2   Request Coding

RSH is mapped to HTTP or HTTPS. Thus, the request parameters are URL encoded as discussed in 110.7.3 *URL Encoding*. RSH requires an additional parameter in the URL: the clientfg parameter. This parameter is a nonce that is used to counter replay attacks. See also *RSH Transport* on page 218.

110.8.3   Response Coding

The server's response to the client is composed of three parts:

- A header containing the protocol version and the serverfg
- The MAC
- The encrypted response

These three items are packaged into a binary container according to Table 110.2.

Table 110.2   *RSH Header description*

Bytes	Description	Value hex
4	Number of bytes in header	2E
1	Major version number	01
1	Minor version number	00
16	serverfg	...

Table 110.2   *RSH Header description*

Bytes	Description	Value hex
4	Number of bytes in MAC	10
16	Message Authentication Code	MAC
4	Number of bytes of encrypted ZIP file	N
N	Encrypted ZIP file	...

The response content type is an RSH-specific encrypted ZIP file, implying that the response header Content-Type must be application/x-rsh for the HTTP request. When the content file is decrypted, the content must be a ZIP file.

110.8.4   RSH URL

The RSH URL must be used internally within the Service Platform to indicate the usage of RSH for initial provisioning. The RSH URL format is identical to the HTTP URL format, except that the scheme is rsh: instead of http:. For example (« means line continues on next line):

```
rsh://server.operator.com/service-x
```

110.8.5   Extensions to the Provisioning Service Dictionary

RSH specifies one additional entry for the Provisioning Dictionary:

```
PROVISIONING_RSH_SECRET
```

The value of this entry is a byte[] containing the shared secret used by the RSH protocol.

110.8.6   RSH Transport

RSH is mapped to HTTP or HTTPS and follows the same URL encoding rules, except that the clientfg is additionally appended to the URL. The key in the URL must be clientfg and the value must be encoded in base 64 format:

The clientfg parameter is transported as an HTTP parameter that is appended after the service_platform_id parameter. The second example above would then be:

```
rsh://server.operator.com/service-x
```

Which, when mapped to HTTP, must become:

```
http://server.operator.com/service-x? «
    service_platform_id=VIN:123456789& «
    clientfg=AHPmWcw%2FsiWYC37xZNdKvQ%3D%3D
```

110.9   Exception Handling

The Initial Provisioning process is a a sensitive process that must run without user supervision. There is therefore a need to handle exceptional cases in a well defined way to simplify trouble shooting.

There are only 2 types of problems that halt the provisioning process. They are:

- IOException when reading or writing provisioning information.
- IOException when retrieving or processing a provisioning zip file.

Other exceptions can occur and the Provisioning Service must do any attempt to log these events.

In the cases that the provisioning process stops, it is important that the clients of the provisioning service have a way to find out that the process is stopped. The mechanism that is used for this is a special entry in the provisioning dictionary. The name of the entry must be provisioning.error. The value is a String object with the following format:

- Numeric error code
- Space
- A human readable string describing the error.

Permitted error codes are:

- 0 – Unknown error
- 1 – Couldn't load or save provisioning information
- 2 – MalformedURLException
- 3 – IOException when retrieving document of a URL
- 4 – Corrupted ZipInputStream

The provisioning.update.count will be incremented as normal when a provisioning.error entry is added to the provisioning information. After, the provisioning service will take no further action.

Some examples:

```
0 SIM card removed
2 "http://www.acme.com/secure/blib/ifa.zip"
```

110.10 Security

The security model for the Service Platform is based on the integrity of the Management Agent deployment. If any of the mechanisms used during the deployment of management agents are weak, or can be compromised, the whole security model becomes weak.

From a security perspective, one attractive means of information exchange would be a smart card. This approach enables all relevant information to be stored in a single place. The Operator could then provide the information to the Service Platform by inserting the smart card into the Service Platform.

110.10.1 Concerns

The major security concerns related to the deployment of the Management Agent are:

- The Service Platform is controlled by the intended Operator
- The Operator controls the intended Service Platform(s)
- The integrity and confidentiality of the information exchange that takes place during these processes must be considered

In order to address these concerns, an implementation of the OSGi Remote Management Architecture must assure that:

- The Operator authenticates itself to the Service Platform
- The Service Platform authenticates itself to the Operator
- The integrity and confidentiality of the Management Agent, certificates, and configuration data are fully protected if they are transported over public transports.

Each mapping of the Initial Provisioning specification to a concrete implementation must describe how these goals are met.

110.10.2 Service Platform Long-Term Security

Secrets for long-term use may be exchanged during the Initial Provisioning procedures. This way, one or more secrets may be shared securely, assuming that the Provisioning Dictionary assignments used are implemented with the proper security characteristics.

110.10.3   **Permissions**

The provisioning information may contain sensitive information. Also, the ability to modify provisioning information can have drastic consequences. Thus, only trusted bundles should be allowed to register, or get the Provisioning Service. This restriction can be enforced using ServicePermission[ProvisioningService, GET].

No Permission classes guard reading or modification of the Provisioning Dictionary, so care must be taken not to leak the Dictionary object received from the Provisioning Service to bundles that are not trusted.

Whether message-based or connection-based, the communications used for Initial Provisioning must support mutual authentication and message integrity checking, at a minimum.

By using both server and client authentication in HTTPS, the problem of establishing identity is solved. In addition, HTTPS will encrypt the transmitted data. HTTPS requires a Public Key Infrastructure implementation in order to retrieve the required certificates.

When RSH is used, it is vital that the shared secret is shared only between the Operator and the Service Platform, and no one else.

110.11   Changes

- Added an InitialProvisioning-Entries header
- Added support for the OSGi type header for a bundle

110.12   org.osgi.service.provisioning

Provisioning Package Version 1.2.

Bundles wishing to use this package must list the package in the Import-Package header of the bundle's manifest. For example:

```
Import-Package: org.osgi.service.provisioning; version="[1.2,2.0)"
```

110.12.1   **public interface ProvisioningService**

Service for managing the initial provisioning information.

Initial provisioning of an OSGi device is a multi step process that culminates with the installation and execution of the initial management agent. At each step of the process, information is collected for the next step. Multiple bundles may be involved and this service provides a means for these bundles to exchange information. It also provides a means for the initial Management Bundle to get its initial configuration information.

The provisioning information is collected in a Dictionary object, called the Provisioning Dictionary. Any bundle that can access the service can get a reference to this object and read and update provisioning information. The key of the dictionary is a String object and the value is a String or byte[] object. The single exception is the PROVISIONING_UPDATE_COUNT value which is an Integer. The provisioning prefix is reserved for keys defined by OSGi, other key names may be used for implementation dependent provisioning systems.

Any changes to the provisioning information will be reflected immediately in all the dictionary objects obtained from the Provisioning Service.

Because of the specific application of the Provisioning Service, there should be only one Provisioning Service registered. This restriction will not be enforced by the Framework. Gateway operators or manufactures should ensure that a Provisioning Service bundle is not installed on a device that already has a bundle providing the Provisioning Service.

The provisioning information has the potential to contain sensitive information. Also, the ability to modify provisioning information can have drastic consequences. Thus, only trusted bundles should be allowed to register and get the Provisioning Service. The ServicePermission is used to limit the bundles that can gain access to the Provisioning Service. There is no check of Permission objects to read or modify the provisioning information, so care must be taken not to leak the Provisioning Dictionary received from getInformation method.

110.12.1.1   **public static final String INITIALPROVISIONING_ENTRIES = "InitialProvisioning-Entries"**

Name of the header that specifies the type information for the ZIP file entries.

Since 1.2

110.12.1.2   **public static final String MIME_BUNDLE = "application/vnd.osgi.bundle"**

MIME type to be stored in the extra field of a ZipEntry object for an installable bundle file. Zip entries of this type will be installed in the framework, but not started. The entry will also not be put into the information dictionary.

110.12.1.3   **public static final String MIME_BUNDLE_ALT = "application/x-osgi-bundle"**

Alternative MIME type to be stored in the extra field of a ZipEntry object for an installable bundle file. Zip entries of this type will be installed in the framework, but not started. The entry will also not be put into the information dictionary. This alternative entry is only for backward compatibility, new applications are recommended to use MIME_BUNDLE, which is an official IANA MIME type.

Since 1.2

110.12.1.4   **public static final String MIME_BUNDLE_URL = "text/x-osgi-bundle-url"**

MIME type to be stored in the extra field of a ZipEntry for a String that represents a URL for a bundle. Zip entries of this type will be used to install (but not start) a bundle from the URL. The entry will not be put into the information dictionary.

110.12.1.5   **public static final String MIME_BYTE_ARRAY = "application/octet-stream"**

MIME type to be stored stored in the extra field of a ZipEntry object for byte[] data.

110.12.1.6   **public static final String MIME_STRING = "text/plain;charset=utf-8"**

MIME type to be stored in the extra field of a ZipEntry object for String data.

110.12.1.7   **public static final String PROVISIONING_AGENT_CONFIG = "provisioning.agent.config"**

The key to the provisioning information that contains the initial configuration information of the initial Management Agent. The value will be of type byte[].

110.12.1.8   **public static final String PROVISIONING_REFERENCE = "provisioning.reference"**

The key to the provisioning information that contains the location of the provision data provider. The value must be of type String.

110.12.1.9   **public static final String PROVISIONING_ROOTX509 = "provisioning.rootx509"**

The key to the provisioning information that contains the root X509 certificate used to establish trust with operator when using HTTPS.

110.12.1.10   **public static final String PROVISIONING_RSH_SECRET = "provisioning.rsh.secret"**

The key to the provisioning information that contains the shared secret used in conjunction with the RSH protocol.

110.12.1.11   **public static final String PROVISIONING_SPID = "provisioning.spid"**

The key to the provisioning information that uniquely identifies the Service Platform. The value must be of type String.

110.12.1.12   **public static final String PROVISIONING_START_BUNDLE = "provisioning.start.bundle"**

The key to the provisioning information that contains the location of the bundle to start with AllPermission. The bundle must have be previously installed for this entry to have any effect.

110.12.1.13   **public static final String PROVISIONING_UPDATE_COUNT = "provisioning.update.count"**

The key to the provisioning information that contains the update count of the info data. Each set of changes to the provisioning information must end with this value being incremented. The value must be of type Integer. This key/value pair is also reflected in the properties of the ProvisioningService in the service registry.

110.12.1.14   **public void addInformation(Dictionary info)**

info   the set of Provisioning Information key/value pairs to add to the Provisioning Information dictionary. Any keys are values that are of an invalid type will be silently ignored.

☐   Adds the key/value pairs contained in info to the Provisioning Information dictionary. This method causes the PROVISIONING_UPDATE_COUNT to be incremented.

110.12.1.15   **public void addInformation(ZipInputStream zis) throws IOException**

zis   the ZipInputStream that will be used to add key/value pairs to the Provisioning Information dictionary and install and start bundles. If a ZipEntry does not have an Extra field that corresponds to one of the four defined MIME types (MIME_STRING, MIME_BYTE_ARRAY,MIME_BUNDLE, and MIME_BUNDLE_URL) in will be silently ignored.

☐   Processes the ZipInputStream and extracts information to add to the Provisioning Information dictionary, as well as, install/update and start bundles. This method causes the PROVISIONING_UPDATE_COUNT to be incremented.

Throws   IOException – if an error occurs while processing the ZipInputStream. No additions will be made to the Provisioning Information dictionary and no bundles must be started or installed.

110.12.1.16   **public Dictionary getInformation( )**

☐   Returns a reference to the Provisioning Dictionary. Any change operations (put and remove) to the dictionary will cause an UnsupportedOperationException to be thrown. Changes must be done using the setInformation and addInformation methods of this service.

Returns   A reference to the Provisioning Dictionary.

110.12.1.17   **public void setInformation(Dictionary info)**

info   the new set of Provisioning Information key/value pairs. Any keys are values that are of an invalid type will be silently ignored.

☐   Replaces the Provisioning Information dictionary with the key/value pairs contained in info. Any key/value pairs not in info will be removed from the Provisioning Information dictionary. This method causes the PROVISIONING_UPDATE_COUNT to be incremented.

110.13   References

[1]   *HMAC:* Keyed-Hashing for Message Authentication
http://www.ietf.org/rfc/rfc2104.txt Krawczyk ,et. al. 1997.

[2]   *NIST, FIPS PUB 180-1: Secure Hash Standard, April 1995.*

[3]   *Hypertext Transfer Protocol - HTTP/1.1*
       http://www.ietf.org/rfc/rfc2616.txt *Fielding, R., et. al.*

[4]   *Rescorla, E., HTTP over TLS, IETF RFC 2818, May 2000*
       http://www.ietf.org/rfc/rfc2818.txt.

[5]   *ZIP Archive format*
       ftp://ftp.uu.net/pub/archiving/zip/doc/appnote-970311-iz.zip

[6]   *RFC 2396 - Uniform Resource Identifier (URI)*
       http://www.ietf.org/rfc/rfc2396.txt

[7]   *MIME Types*
       http://www.ietf.org/rfc/rfc2046.txt and http://www.iana.org/assignments/media-types

[8]   *3DES*
       W/ Tuchman, "Hellman Presents No Shortcut Solution to DES," IEEE Spectrum, v. 16, n. 7 July 1979, pp40-41.

[9]   *RFC 1423 Part III: Algorithms, Modes, and Identifiers*
       http://www.ietf.org/rfc/rfc1423.txt

[10]   *PKCS 5*
       ftp://ftp.rsasecurity.com/pub/pkcs/pkcs-5v2

[11]   *Java Cryptography API (part of Java 1.4)*
       http://java.sun.com/javase/technologies/security/

[12]   *SHA-1*
       U.S. Government, Proposed Federal Information Processing Standard for Secure Hash Standard, January 1992

[13]   *Transport Layer Security*
       http://www.ietf.org/rfc/rfc2246.txt, January 1999, The TLS Protocol Version 1.0, T. Dierks & C. Allen.

111   UPnP™ Device Service Specification

Version 1.1

111.1   Introduction

The UPnP Device Architecture specification provides the protocols for a peer-to-peer network. It specifies how to join a network and how devices can be controlled using XML messages sent over HTTP. The OSGi specifications address how code can be download and managed in a remote system. Both standards are therefore fully complimentary. Using an OSGi Service Platform to work with UPnP enabled devices is therefore a very successful combination.

This specification specifies how OSGi bundles can be developed that interoperate with UPnP™ (Universal Plug and Play) devices and UPnP control points. The specification is based on [1] *UPnP Device Architecture* and does not further explain the UPnP specifications. The UPnP specifications are maintained by [2] *UPnP Forum*.

UPnP™ is a trademark of the UPnP Implementers Corporation.

111.1.1   Essentials

- *Scope* – This specification is limited to device control aspects of the UPnP specifications. Aspects concerning the TCP/IP layer, like DHCP and limited TTL, are not addressed.
- *Transparency* – OSGi services should be made available to networks with UPnP enabled devices in a transparent way.
- *Network Selection* – It must be possible to restrict the use of the UPnP protocols to a selection of the connected networks. For example, in certain cases OSGi services that are UPnP enabled should not be published to the Wide Area Network side of a gateway, nor should UPnP devices be detected on this WAN.
- *Event handling* – Bundles must be able to listen to UPnP events.
- *Export OSGi services as UPnP devices* – Enable bundles that make a service available to UPnP control points.
- *Implement UPnP Control Points* – Enable bundles that control UPnP devices.

111.1.2   Entities

- *UPnP Base Driver* – The bundle that implements the bridge between OSGi and UPnP networks. This entity is not represented as a service.
- *UPnP RootDevice* – A physical device can contain one or more root devices. Root devices contain one ore more devices. A root device is modelled with a UPnPDevice object, there is no separate interface defined for root devices.
- *UPnP Device* – The representation of a UPnP device. A UPnP device may contain other UPnP devices and UPnP services. This entity is represented by a UPnPDevice object. A device can be local (implemented in the Framework) or external (implemented by another device on the net).
- *UPnP Service* – A UPnP device consists of a number of services. A UPnP service has a number of UPnP state variables that can be queried and modified with actions. This concept is represented by a UPnPService object.

- *UPnP Action* – A UPnP service is associated with a number of actions that can be performed on that service and that may modify the UPnP state variables. This entity is represented by a UPnPAction object.
- *UPnP State Variable* – A variable associated with a UPnP service, represented by a UPnPStateVariable object.
- *UPnPLocalStateVariable* – Extends the UPnPStateVariable interface when the state variable is implemented locally. This interface provides access to the actual value.
- *UPnP Event Listener Service* – A listener to events coming from UPnP devices.
- *UPnP Host* – The machine that hosts the code to run a UPnP device or control point.
- *UPnP Control Point* – A UPnP device that is intended to control UPnP devices over a network. For example, a UPnP remote controller.
- *UPnP Icon* – A representation class for an icon associated with a UPnP device.
- *UPnPException* – An exception that delivers errors that were discovered in the UPnP layer.
- *UDN* – Unique Device Name, a name that uniquely identifies the a specific device.

Figure 111.1   UPnP Service Specification class Diagram org.osgi.service.upnp package

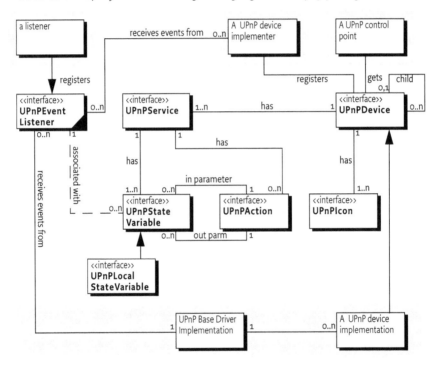

111.1.3   Operation Summary

To make a UPnP service available to UPnP control points on a network, an OSGi service object must be registered under the UPnPDevice interface with the Framework. The UPnP driver bundle must detect these UPnP Device services and must make them available to the network as UPnP devices using the UPnP protocol.

UPnP devices detected on the local network must be detected and automatically registered under the UPnPDevice interface with the Framework by the UPnP driver implementation bundle.

A bundle that wants to control UPnP devices, for example to implement a UPnP control point, should track UPnP Device services in the OSGi service registry and control them appropriately. Such bundles should not distinguish between resident or remote UPnP Device services.

111.2   UPnP Specifications

The UPnP DA is intended to be used in a broad range of device from the computing (PCs printers), consumer electronics (DVD, TV, radio), communication (phones) to home automation (lighting control, security) and home appliances (refrigerators, coffee makers) domains.

For example, a UPnP TV might announce its existence on a network by broadcasting a message. A UPnP control point on that network can then discover this TV by listening to those announce messages. The UPnP specifications allow the control point to retrieve information about the user interface of the TV. This information can then be used to allow the end user to control the remote TV from the control point, for example turn it on or change the channels.

The UPnP specification supports the following features:

- *Detect and control a UPnP standardized device.* In this case the control point and the remote device share a priori knowledge about how the device should be controlled. The UPnP Forum intends to define a large number of these standardized devices.
- *Use a user interface description.* A UPnP control point receives enough information about a device and its services to automatically build a user interface for it.
- *Programmatic Control.* A program can directly control a UPnP device without a user interface. This control can be based on detected information about the device or through a priori knowledge of the device type.
- *Allows the user to browse a web page supplied by the device.* This web page contains a user interface for the device that be directly manipulated by the user. However, this option is not well defined in the UPnP Device Architecture specification and is not tested for compliance.

The UPnP Device Architecture specification and the OSGi Service Platform provide *complementary* functionality. The UPnP Device Architecture specification is a data communication protocol that does not specify where and how programs execute. That choice is made by the implementations. In contrast, the OSGi Service Platform specifies a (managed) execution point and does not define what protocols or media are supported. The UPnP specification and the OSGi specifications are fully complementary and do not overlap.

From the OSGi perspective, the UPnP specification is a communication protocol that can be implemented by one or more bundles. This specification therefore defines the following:

- How an OSGi bundle can implement a service that is exported to the network via the UPnP protocols.
- How to find and control services that are available on the local network.

The UPnP specifications related to the assignment of IP addresses to new devices on the network or auto-IP self configuration should be handled at the operating system level. Such functions are outside the scope of this specification.

111.2.1   UPnP Base Driver

The functionality of the UPnP service is implemented in a UPnP *base driver*. This is a bundle that implements the UPnP protocols and handles the interaction with bundles that use the UPnP devices. A UPnP base driver bundle must provide the following functions:

- Discover UPnP devices on the network and map each discovered device into an OSGi registered UPnP Device service.
- Present UPnP marked services that are registered with the OSGi Framework on one or more networks to be used by other computers.

111.3   UPnP Device

The principle entity of the UPnP specification is the UPnP device. There is a UPnP *root device* that represents a physical appliance, such as a complete TV. The root device contains a number of sub-devices. These might be the tuner, the monitor, and the sound system. Each sub-device is further composed of a number of UPnP services. A UPnP service represents some functional unit in a device. For example, in a TV tuner it can represent the TV channel selector. Figure 111.2 on page 228 illustrates this hierarchy.

Figure 111.2   *UPnP device hierarchy*

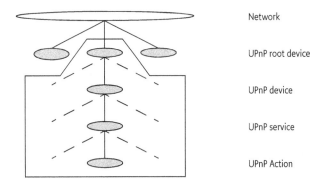

Network

UPnP root device

UPnP device

UPnP service

UPnP Action

Each UPnP service can be manipulated with a number of UPnP actions. UPnP actions can modify the state of a UPnP state variable that is associated with a service. For example, in a TV there might be a state variable *volume*. There are then actions to set the volume, to increase the volume, and to decrease the volume.

111.3.1   Root Device

The UPnP root device is registered as a UPnP Device service with the Framework, as well as all its sub-devices. Most applications will work with sub-devices, and, as a result, the children of the root device are registered under the UPnPDevice interface.

UPnP device properties are defined per sub-device in the UPnP specification. These properties must be registered with the OSGi Framework service registry so they are searchable.

Bundles that want to handle the UPnP device hierarchy can use the registered service properties to find the parent of a device (which is another registered UPnPDevice).

The following service registration properties can be used to discover this hierarchy:

- PARENT_UDN – The Universal Device Name (UDN) of the parent device. A root device most not have this property registered. Type is a String object.
- CHILDREN_UDN – An array of UDNs of this device's children. Type is a String[] object.

111.3.2   Exported Versus Imported Devices

Both imported (from the network to the OSGi service registry) and exported (from the service registry to the network) UPnPDevice services must have the same representation in the OSGi Service Platform for identical devices. For example, if an OSGi UPnP Device service is exported as a UPnP device from an OSGi Service Platform to the network, and it is imported into another OSGi Service Platform, the object representation should be equal. Application bundles should therefore be able to interact with imported and exported forms of the UPnP device in the same manner.

Imported and exported UPnP devices differ only by two marker properties that can be added to the service registration. One marker, DEVICE_CATEGORY, should typically be set only on imported devices. By not setting DEVICE_CATEGORY on internal UPnP devices, the Device Manager does not try to refine these devices (See the *Device Access Specification* on page 41 for more information about the Device Manager). If the device service does not implement the Device interface and does not have the DEVICE_CATEGORY property set, it is not considered a *device* according to the Device Access Specification.

The other marker, UPNP_EXPORT, should only be set on internally created devices that the bundle developer wants to export. By not setting UPNP_EXPORT on registered UPnP Device services, the UPnP Device service can be used by internally created devices that should not be exported to the network. This allows UPnP devices to be simulated within an OSGi Service Platform without announcing all of these devices to any networks.

111.3.3   Icons

A UPnP device can optionally support an icon. The purpose of this icon is to identify the device on a UPnP control point. UPnP control points can be implemented in large computers like PC's or simple devices like a remote control. However, the graphic requirements for these UPnP devices differ tremendously. The device can, therefore, export a number of icons of different size and depth.

In the UPnP specifications, an icon is represented by a URL that typically refers to the device itself. In this specification, a list of icons is available from the UPnP Device service.

In order to obtain localized icons, the method getIcons(String) can be used to obtain different versions. If the locale specified is a null argument, then the call returns the icons of the default locale of the called device (not the default locale of the UPnP control point). When a bundle wants to access the icon of an imported UPnP device, the UPnP driver gets the data and presents it to the application through an input stream.

A bundle that needs to export a UPnP Device service with one ore more icons must provide an implementation of the UPnPIcon interface. This implementation must provide an InputStream object to the actual icon data. The UPnP driver bundle must then register this icon with an HTTP server and include the URL to the icon with the UPnP device data at the appropriate place.

111.4   Device Category

UPnP Device services are devices in the context of the Device Manager. This means that these services need to register with a number of properties to participate in driver refinement. The value for UPnP devices is defined in the UPnPDevice constant DEVICE_CATEGORY. The value is UPnP. The UPnPDevice interface contains a number of constants for matching values. Refer to *MATCH_GENERIC* on page 236 for further information.

111.5   UPnPService

A UPnP Device contains a number of UPnPService objects. UPnPService objects combine zero or more actions and one or more state variables.

111.5.1   State Variables

The UPnPStateVariable interface encapsulates the properties of a UPnP state variable. In addition to the properties defined by the UPnP specification, a state variable is also mapped to a Java data type. The Java data type is used when an event is generated for this state variable and when an action is performed containing arguments related to this state variable. There must be a strict correspondence between the UPnP data type and the Java data type so that bundles using a particular UPnP device profile can predict the precise Java data type.

The function QueryStateVariable defined in the UPnP specification has been deprecated and is therefore not implemented. It is recommended to use the UPnP event mechanism to track UPnP state variables.

Additionally, a UPnPStateVariableobject can also implement the UPnPLocalStateVariable interface if the device is implemented locally. That is, the device is not imported from the network. The UPnPLocalStateVariable interface provides a getCurrentValue() method that provides direct access to the actual value of the state variable.

111.6 Working With a UPnP Device

The UPnP driver must register all discovered UPnP devices in the local networks. These devices are registered under a UPnPDevice interface with the OSGi Framework.

Using a remote UPnP device thus involves tracking UPnP Device services in the OSGi service registry. The following code illustrates how this can be done. The sample Controller class extends the ServiceTracker class so that it can track all UPnP Device services and add them to a user interface, such as a remote controller application.

```
class Controller extends ServiceTracker {
    UI      ui;

    Controller( BundleContext context ) {
        super( context, UPnPDevice.class.getName(), null );
    }
    public Object addingService( ServiceReference ref ) {
        UPnPDevice dev = (UPnPDevice)super.addingService(ref);
        ui.addDevice( dev );
        return dev;
    }
    public void removedService( ServiceReference ref,
        Object dev ) {
        ui.removeDevice( (UPnPDevice) dev );
    }
    ...
}
```

111.7 Implementing a UPnP Device

OSGi services can also be exported as UPnP devices to the local networks, in a way that is transparent to typical UPnP devices. This allows developers to bridge legacy devices to UPnP networks. A bundle should perform the following to export an OSGi service as a UPnP device:

- Register an UPnP Device service with the registration property UPNP_EXPORT.
- Use the registration property PRESENTATION_URL to provide the presentation page. The service implementer must register its own servlet with the Http Service to serve out this interface. This URL must point to that servlet.

There can be multiple UPnP root devices hosted by one OSGi platform. The relationship between the UPnP devices and the OSGi platform is defined by the PARENT_UDN and CHILDREN_UDN service properties. The bundle registering those device services must make sure these properties are set accordingly.

Devices that are implemented on the OSGi Service Platform (in contrast with devices that are imported from the network) should use the UPnPLocalStateVariable interface for their state variables instead of the UPnPStateVariable interface. This interface provides programmatic access to the actual value of the state variable as maintained by the device specific code.

111.8   Event API

There are two distinct event directions for the UPnP Service specification.

- External events from the network must be dispatched to listeners inside the OSGi Service Platforms. The UPnP Base driver is responsible for mapping the network events to internal listener events.
- Implementations of UPnP devices must send out events to local listeners as well as cause the transmission of the UPnP network events.

UPnP events are sent using the whiteboard model, in which a bundle interested in receiving the UPnP events registers an object implementing the UPnPEventListener interface. A filter can be set to limit the events for which a bundle is notified. The UPnP Base driver must register a UPnP Event Lister without filter that receives all events.

Figure 111.3   *Event Dispatching for Local and External Devices*

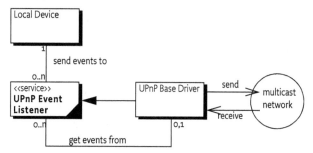

If a service is registered with a property named upnp.filter with the value of an instance of an Filter object, the listener is only notified for matching events (This is a Filter object and not a String object because it allows the InvalidSyntaxException to be thrown in the client and not the UPnP driver bundle).

The filter might refer to any valid combination of the following pseudo properties for event filtering:

- UPnPDevice.UDN – (UPnP.device.UDN) Only events generated by services contained in the specific device are delivered. For example: (UPnP.device.UDN=uuid:Upnp-TVEmulator-1_0-1234567890001)
- UPnPDevice.TYPE– (UPnP.device.type) Only events generated by services contained in a device of the given type are delivered. For example: (UPnP.device.type=urn:schemas-upnp-org:device:tvdevice:1)
- UPnPService.ID – (UPnP.service.id) Service identity. Only events generated by services matching the given service ID are delivered.
- UPnPService.TYPE – (UPnP.service.type) Only events generated by services of of the given type are delivered.

If an event is generated by either a local device or via the base driver for an external device, the notifyUPnPEvent(String,String,Dictionary) method is called on all registered UPnPEventListener services for which the optional filter matches for that event. If no filter is specified, all events must be delivered. If the filter does not match, the UPnP Driver must not call the UPnP Event Listener service. The way events must be delivered is the same as described in *Delivering Events* on page 116 of the Core specification.

One or multiple events are passed as parameters to the notifyUPnPEvent(String,String,Dictionary) method. The Dictionary object holds a pair of UpnPStateVariable objects that triggered the event and an Object for the new value of the state variable.

111.8.1 Initial Event Delivery

Special care must be taken with the initial subscription to events. According to the UPnP specification, when a client subscribes for notification of events for the first time, the device sends out a number of events for each state variable, indicating the current value of each state variable. This behavior simplifies the synchronization of a device and an event-driven client.

The UPnP Base Driver must mimic this event distribution on behalf of external devices. It must therefore remember the values of the state variables of external devices. A UPnP Device implementation must send out these initial events for each state variable they have a value for.

The UPnP Base Driver must have stored the last event from the device and retransmit the value over the multicast network. The UPnP Driver must register an event listener without any filter for this purpose.

The call to the listener's notification method must be done asynchronously.

111.9 UPnP Events and Event Admin service

UPnP events must be delivered asynchronously to the Event Admin service by the UPnP implementation, if present. UPnP events have the following topic:

    org/osgi/service/upnp/UPnPEvent

The properties of a UPnP event are the following:

- upnp.deviceId – (String) The identity as defined by UPnPDevice.UDN of the device sending the event.
- upnp.serviceId – (String) The identity of the service sending the events.
- upnp.events – (Dictionary) A Dictionary object containing the new values for the state variables that have changed.

111.10 Localization

All values of the UPnP properties are obtained from the device using the device's default locale. If an application wants to query a set of localized property values, it has to use the method getDescriptions(String). For localized versions of the icons, the method getIcons(String) is to be used.

111.11 Dates and Times

The UPnP specification uses different types for date and time concepts. An overview of these types is given in Table 111.1 on page 233.

Table 111.1　　　　*Mapping UPnP Date/Time types to Java*

UPnP Type	Class	Example	Value (TZ=CEST= +0200)
date	Date	1985-04-12	Sun April 12 00:00:00 CEST 1985
dateTime	Date	1985-04-12T10:15:30	Sun April 12 10:15:30 CEST 1985
dateTime.tz	Date	1985-04-12T10:15:30+0400	Sun April 12 08:15:30 CEST 1985
time	Long	23:20:50	84.050.000 (ms)
time.tz	Long	23:20:50+0300	1.250.000 (ms)

The UPnP specification points to [6] *XML Schema*. In this standard, [7] *ISo 8601 Date And Time formats* are referenced. The mapping is not completely defined which means that the this OSGi UPnP specification defines a complete mapping to Java classes. The UPnP types date, dateTime and dateTime.tz are represented as a Date object. For the date type, the hours, minutes and seconds must all be zero.

The UPnP types time and time.tz are represented as a Long object that represents the number of ms since midnight. If the time wraps to the next day due to a time zone value, then the final value must be truncated to modulo 86.400.000.

See also *TYPE_DATE* on page 243 and further.

111.12   UPnP Exception

The UPnP Exception can be thrown when a UPnPAction is invoked. This exception contains information about the different UPnP layers. The following errors are defined:

INVALID_ACTION – (401) No such action could be found.

INVALID_ARGS – (402) Invalid argument.

INVALID_SEQUENCE_NUMBER – (403) Out of synchronization.

INVALID_VARIABLE – (404) State variable not found.

DEVICE_INTERNAL_ERROR – (501) Internal error.

Further errors are categorized as follows:

- *Common Action Errors* – In the range of 600-69, defined by the UPnP Forum Technical Committee.
- *Action Specific Errors* – In the range of 700-799, defined by the UPnP Forum Working Committee.
- *Non-Standard Action Specific Errors* – In the range of 800-899. Defined by vendors.

111.13   Configuration

In order to provide a standardized way to configure a UPnP driver bundle, the Configuration Admin property upnp.ssdp.address is defined.

The value is a String[] with a list of IP addresses, optionally followed with a colon (':', \u003A) and a port number. For example:

239.255.255.250:1900

Those addresses define the interfaces which the UPnP driver is operating on. If no SSDP address is specified, the default assumed will be 239.255.255.250:1900. If no port is specified, port 1900 is assumed as default.

111.14   Networking considerations

111.14.1   The UPnP Multicasts

The operating system must support multicasting on the selected network device. In certain cases, a multicasting route has to be set in the operating system routing table.

These configurations are highly dependent on the underlying operating system and beyond the scope of this specification.

111.15   Security

The UPnP specification is based on HTTP and uses plain text SOAP (XML) messages to control devices. For this reason, it does not provide any inherent security mechanisms. However, the UPnP specification is based on the exchange of XML files and not code. This means that at least worms and viruses cannot be implemented using the UPnP protocols.

However, a bundle registering a UPnP Device service is represented on the outside network and has the ability to communicate. The same is true for getting a UPnP Device service. It is therefore recommended that ServicePermission[UPnPDevice|UPnPEventListener, REGISTER|GET] be used sparingly and only for bundles that are trusted.

111.16   org.osgi.service.upnp

UPnP Package Version 1.1.

Bundles wishing to use this package must list the package in the Import-Package header of the bundle's manifest. For example:

```
Import-Package: org.osgi.service.upnp; version="[1.1,2.0)"
```

111.16.1   Summary

- *UPnPAction* - A UPnP action.
- *UPnPDevice* - Represents a UPnP device.
- *UPnPEventListener* - UPnP Events are mapped and delivered to applications according to the OSGi whiteboard model.
- *UPnPException* - There are several defined error situations describing UPnP problems while a control point invokes actions to UPnPDevices.
- *UPnPIcon* - A UPnP icon representation.
- *UPnPLocalStateVariable* - A local UPnP state variable which allows the value of the state variable to be queried.
- *UPnPService* - A representation of a UPnP Service.
- *UPnPStateVariable* - The meta-information of a UPnP state variable as declared in the device's service state table (SST).

111.16.2   public interface UPnPAction

A UPnP action. Each UPnP service contains zero or more actions. Each action may have zero or more UPnP state variables as arguments.

111.16.2.1   public String[] getInputArgumentNames( )

☐ Lists all input arguments for this action.

Each action may have zero or more input arguments.

Returns   Array of input argument names or null if no input arguments.

See Also   UPnPStateVariable

111.16.2.2   public String getName( )

☐ Returns the action name. The action name corresponds to the name field in the actionList of the service description.

- For standard actions defined by a UPnP Forum working committee, action names must not begin with X_ nor A_.

- For non-standard actions specified by a UPnP vendor and added to a standard service, action names must begin with X_.

Returns Name of action, must not contain a hyphen character or a hash character

111.16.2.3 public String[] getOutputArgumentNames( )

    □ List all output arguments for this action.

Returns Array of output argument names or null if there are no output arguments.

See Also UPnPStateVariable

111.16.2.4 public String getReturnArgumentName( )

    □ Returns the name of the designated return argument.

      One of the output arguments can be flagged as a designated return argument.

Returns The name of the designated return argument or null if none is marked.

111.16.2.5 public UPnPStateVariable getStateVariable(String argumentName)

argumentName The name of the UPnP action argument.

    □ Finds the state variable associated with an argument name. Helps to resolve the association of state variables with argument names in UPnP actions.

Returns State variable associated with the named argument or null if there is no such argument.

See Also UPnPStateVariable

111.16.2.6 public Dictionary invoke(Dictionary args) throws Exception

args A Dictionary of arguments. Must contain the correct set and type of arguments for this action. May be null if no input arguments exist.

    □ Invokes the action. The input and output arguments are both passed as Dictionary objects. Each entry in the Dictionary object has a String object as key representing the argument name and the value is the argument itself. The class of an argument value must be assignable from the class of the associated UPnP state variable. The input argument Dictionary object must contain exactly those arguments listed by getInputArguments method. The output argument Dictionary object will contain exactly those arguments listed by getOutputArguments method.

Returns A Dictionary with the output arguments. null if the action has no output arguments.

Throws UPnPException – A UPnP error has occured.

      Exception – The execution fails for some reason.

See Also UPnPStateVariable

111.16.3 public interface UPnPDevice

Represents a UPnP device. For each UPnP root and embedded device, an object is registered with the framework under the UPnPDevice interface.

The relationship between a root device and its embedded devices can be deduced using the UPnPDevice.CHILDREN_UDN and UPnPDevice.PARENT_UDN service registration properties.

The values of the UPnP property names are defined by the UPnP Forum.

All values of the UPnP properties are obtained from the device using the device's default locale.

If an application wants to query for a set of localized property values, it has to use the method UPnPDevice.getDescriptions(String locale).

111.16.3.1 public static final String CHILDREN_UDN = "UPnP.device.childrenUDN"

The property key that must be set for all devices containing other embedded devices.

The value is an array of UDNs for each of the device's children (String[]). The array contains UDNs for the immediate descendants only.

If an embedded device in turn contains embedded devices, the latter are not included in the array.

The UPnP Specification does not encourage more than two levels of nesting.

The property is not set if the device does not contain embedded devices.

The property is of type String[]. Value is "UPnP.device.childrenUDN"

111.16.3.2   public static final String DEVICE_CATEGORY = "UPnP"

Constant for the value of the service property DEVICE_CATEGORY used for all UPnP devices. Value is "UPnP".

See Also   org.osgi.service.device.Constants.DEVICE_CATEGORY

111.16.3.3   public static final String FRIENDLY_NAME = "UPnP.device.friendlyName"

Mandatory property key for a short user friendly version of the device name. The property value holds a String object with the user friendly name of the device. Value is "UPnP.device.friendlyName".

111.16.3.4   public static final String ID = "UPnP.device.UDN"

Property key for the Unique Device ID property. This property is an alias to UPnPDevice.UDN. It is merely provided for reasons of symmetry with the UPnPService.ID property. The value of the property is a String object of the Device UDN. The value of the key is "UPnP.device.UDN".

111.16.3.5   public static final String MANUFACTURER = "UPnP.device.manufacturer"

Mandatory property key for the device manufacturer's property. The property value holds a String representation of the device manufacturer's name. Value is "UPnP.device.manufacturer".

111.16.3.6   public static final String MANUFACTURER_URL = "UPnP.device.manufacturerURL"

Optional property key for a URL to the device manufacturers Web site. The value of the property is a String object representing the URL. Value is "UPnP.device.manufacturerURL".

111.16.3.7   public static final int MATCH_GENERIC = 1

Constant for the UPnP device match scale, indicating a generic match for the device. Value is 1.

111.16.3.8   public static final int MATCH_MANUFACTURER_MODEL = 7

Constant for the UPnP device match scale, indicating a match with the device model. Value is 7.

111.16.3.9   public static final int MATCH_MANUFACTURER_MODEL_REVISION = 15

Constant for the UPnP device match scale, indicating a match with the device revision. Value is 15.

111.16.3.10   public static final int MATCH_MANUFACTURER_MODEL_REVISION_SERIAL = 31

Constant for the UPnP device match scale, indicating a match with the device revision and the serial number. Value is 31.

111.16.3.11   public static final int MATCH_TYPE = 3

Constant for the UPnP device match scale, indicating a match with the device type. Value is 3.

111.16.3.12   public static final String MODEL_DESCRIPTION = "UPnP.device.modelDescription"

Optional (but recommended) property key for a String object with a long description of the device for the end user. The value is "UPnP.device.modelDescription".

111.16.3.13   **public static final String MODEL_NAME = "UPnP.device.modelName"**

Mandatory property key for the device model name. The property value holds a String object giving more information about the device model. Value is "UPnP.device.modelName".

111.16.3.14   **public static final String MODEL_NUMBER = "UPnP.device.modelNumber"**

Optional (but recommended) property key for a String class typed property holding the model number of the device. Value is "UPnP.device.modelNumber".

111.16.3.15   **public static final String MODEL_URL = "UPnP.device.modelURL"**

Optional property key for a String typed property holding a string representing the URL to the Web site for this model. Value is "UPnP.device.modelURL".

111.16.3.16   **public static final String PARENT_UDN = "UPnP.device.parentUDN"**

The property key that must be set for all embedded devices. It contains the UDN of the parent device. The property is not set for root devices. The value is "UPnP.device.parentUDN".

111.16.3.17   **public static final String PRESENTATION_URL = "UPnP.presentationURL"**

Optional (but recommended) property key for a String typed property holding a string representing the URL to a device representation Web page. Value is "UPnP.presentationURL".

111.16.3.18   **public static final String SERIAL_NUMBER = "UPnP.device.serialNumber"**

Optional (but recommended) property key for a String typed property holding the serial number of the device. Value is "UPnP.device.serialNumber".

111.16.3.19   **public static final String TYPE = "UPnP.device.type"**

Property key for the UPnP Device Type property. Some standard property values are defined by the Universal Plug and Play Forum. The type string also includes a version number as defined in the UPnP specification. This property must be set.

For standard devices defined by a UPnP Forum working committee, this must consist of the following components in the given order separated by colons:

- urn
- schemas-upnp-org
- device
- a device type suffix
- an integer device version

For non-standard devices specified by UPnP vendors following components must be specified in the given order separated by colons:

- urn
- an ICANN domain name owned by the vendor
- device
- a device type suffix
- an integer device version

To allow for backward compatibility the UPnP driver must automatically generate additional Device Type property entries for smaller versions than the current one. If for example a device announces its type as version 3, then properties for versions 2 and 1 must be automatically generated.

In the case of exporting a UPnPDevice, the highest available version must be announced on the network.

Syntax Example: urn:schemas-upnp-org:device:deviceType:v

The value is "UPnP.device.type".

111.16.3.20   **public static final String UDN = "UPnP.device.UDN"**

Property key for the Unique Device Name (UDN) property. It is the unique identifier of an instance of a UPnPDevice. The value of the property is a String object of the Device UDN. Value of the key is "UPnP.device.UDN". This property must be set.

111.16.3.21   **public static final String UPC = "UPnP.device.UPC"**

Optional property key for a String typed property holding the Universal Product Code (UPC) of the device. Value is "UPnP.device.UPC".

111.16.3.22   **public static final String UPNP_EXPORT = "UPnP.export"**

The UPnP.export service property is a hint that marks a device to be picked up and exported by the UPnP Service. Imported devices do not have this property set. The registered property requires no value.

The UPNP_EXPORT string is "UPnP.export".

111.16.3.23   **public Dictionary getDescriptions(String locale)**

locale A language tag as defined by RFC 1766 and maintained by ISO 639. Examples include "de", "en" or " en-US". The default locale of the device is specified by passing a null argument.

☐ Get a set of localized UPnP properties. The UPnP specification allows a device to present different device properties based on the client's locale. The properties used to register the UPnPDevice service in the OSGi registry are based on the device's default locale. To obtain a localized set of the properties, an application can use this method.

Not all properties might be available in all locales. This method does **not** substitute missing properties with their default locale versions.

Returns Dictionary mapping property name Strings to property value Strings

111.16.3.24   **public UPnPIcon[] getIcons(String locale)**

locale A language tag as defined by RFC 1766 and maintained by ISO 639. Examples include "de", "en" or " en-US". The default locale of the device is specified by passing a null argument.

☐ Lists all icons for this device in a given locale. The UPnP specification allows a device to present different icons based on the client's locale.

Returns Array of icons or null if no icons are available.

111.16.3.25   **public UPnPService getService(String serviceId)**

serviceId The service id

☐ Locates a specific service by its service id.

Returns The requested service or null if not found.

111.16.3.26   **public UPnPService[] getServices( )**

☐ Lists all services provided by this device.

Returns Array of services or null if no services are available.

111.16.4   **public interface UPnPEventListener**

UPnP Events are mapped and delivered to applications according to the OSGi whiteboard model. An application that wishes to be notified of events generated by a particular UPnP Device registers a service extending this interface.

The notification call from the UPnP Service to any UPnPEventListener object must be done asynchronous with respect to the originator (in a separate thread).

Upon registration of the UPnP Event Listener service with the Framework, the service is notified for each variable which it listens for with an initial event containing the current value of the variable. Subsequent notifications only happen on changes of the value of the variable.

A UPnP Event Listener service filter the events it receives. This event set is limited using a standard framework filter expression which is specified when the listener service is registered.

The filter is specified in a property named "upnp.filter" and has as a value an object of type org.osgi.framework.Filter.

When the Filter is evaluated, the folowing keywords are recognized as defined as literal constants in the UPnPDevice class.

The valid subset of properties for the registration of UPnP Event Listener services are:

- UPnPDevice.TYPE-- Which type of device to listen for events.
- UPnPDevice.ID-- The ID of a specific device to listen for events.
- UPnPService.TYPE-- The type of a specific service to listen for events.
- UPnPService.ID-- The ID of a specific service to listen for events.

111.16.4.1   **public static final String UPNP_FILTER = "upnp.filter"**

Key for a service property having a value that is an object of type org.osgi.framework.Filter and that is used to limit received events.

111.16.4.2   **public void notifyUPnPEvent(String deviceId, String serviceId, Dictionary events)**

deviceId ID of the device sending the events

serviceId ID of the service sending the events

events Dictionary object containing the new values for the state variables that have changed.

☐ Callback method that is invoked for received events. The events are collected in a Dictionary object. Each entry has a String key representing the event name (= state variable name) and the new value of the state variable. The class of the value object must match the class specified by the UPnP State Variable associated with the event. This method must be called asynchronously

111.16.5   public class UPnPException
extends   Exception

There are several defined error situations describing UPnP problems while a control point invokes actions to UPnPDevices.

Since 1.1

111.16.5.1   **public static final int DEVICE_INTERNAL_ERROR = 501**

The invoked action failed during execution.

111.16.5.2   **public static final int INVALID_ACTION = 401**

No Action found by that name at this service.

111.16.5.3   **public static final int INVALID_ARGS = 402**

Not enough arguments, too many arguments with a specific name, or one of more of the arguments are of the wrong type.

111.16.5.4   **public static final int INVALID_SEQUENCE_NUMBER = 403**

The different end-points are no longer in synchronization.

111.16.5.5   **public static final int INVALID_VARIABLE = 404**

Refers to a non existing variable.

111.16.5.6   **public UPnPException(int errorCode, String errordesc)**

errorCode errorCode which defined UPnP Device Architecture V1.0.

errordesc errorDescription which explain the type of propblem.

☐ This constructor creates a UPnPException on the specified error code and error description.

111.16.5.7   **public int getUPnPError_Code( )**

☐ Returns the UPnPError Code occured by UPnPDevices during invocation.

Returns The UPnPErrorCode defined by a UPnP Forum working committee or specified by a UPnP vendor.

111.16.6   public interface UPnPIcon

A UPnP icon representation. Each UPnP device can contain zero or more icons.

111.16.6.1   **public int getDepth( )**

☐ Returns the color depth of the icon in bits.

Returns The color depth in bits. If the actual color depth of the icon is unknown, -1 is returned.

111.16.6.2   **public int getHeight( )**

☐ Returns the height of the icon in pixels. If the actual height of the icon is unknown, -1 is returned.

Returns The height in pixels, or -1 if unknown.

111.16.6.3   **public InputStream getInputStream( ) throws IOException**

☐ Returns an InputStream object for the icon data. The InputStream object provides a way for a client to read the actual icon graphics data. The number of bytes available from this InputStream object can be determined via the getSize() method. The format of the data encoded can be determined by the MIME type availble via the getMimeType() method.

Returns An InputStream to read the icon graphics data from.

Throws IOException – If the InputStream cannot be returned.

See Also UPnPIcon. getMimeType ()

111.16.6.4   **public String getMimeType( )**

☐ Returns the MIME type of the icon. This method returns the format in which the icon graphics, read from the InputStream object obtained by the getInputStream() method, is encoded.

The format of the returned string is in accordance to RFC2046. A list of valid MIME types is maintained by the IANA (http://www.iana.org/assignments/media-types/) .

Typical values returned include: "image/jpeg" or "image/gif"

Returns The MIME type of the encoded icon.

111.16.6.5   **public int getSize( )**

☐ Returns the size of the icon in bytes. This method returns the number of bytes of the icon available to read from the InputStream object obtained by the getInputStream() method. If the actual size can not be determined, -1 is returned.

Returns The icon size in bytes, or -1 if the size is unknown.

111.16.6.6   **public int getWidth( )**

☐ Returns the width of the icon in pixels. If the actual width of the icon is unknown, -1 is returned.

Returns The width in pixels, or -1 if unknown.

111.16.7   public interface UPnPLocalStateVariable extends UPnPStateVariable

A local UPnP state variable which allows the value of the state variable to be queried.

Since 1.1

111.16.7.1   **public Object getCurrentValue( )**

☐ This method will keep the current values of UPnPStateVariables of a UPnPDevice whenever UPnP-StateVariable's value is changed , this method must be called.

Returns Object current value of UPnPStateVariable. if the current value is initialized with the default value defined UPnP service description.

111.16.8   public interface UPnPService

A representation of a UPnP Service. Each UPnP device contains zero or more services. The UPnP description for a service defines actions, their arguments, and event characteristics.

111.16.8.1   **public static final String ID = "UPnP.service.id"**

Property key for the optional service id. The service id property is used when registering UPnP Device services or UPnP Event Listener services. The value of the property contains a String array (String[]) of service ids. A UPnP Device service can thus announce what service ids it contains. A UPnP Event Listener service can announce for what UPnP service ids it wants notifications. A service id does **not** have to be universally unique. It must be unique only within a device. A null value is a wildcard, matching **all** services. The value is "UPnP.service.id".

111.16.8.2   **public static final String TYPE = "UPnP.service.type"**

Property key for the optional service type uri. The service type property is used when registering UPnP Device services and UPnP Event Listener services. The property contains a String array (String[]) of service types. A UPnP Device service can thus announce what types of services it contains. A UPnP Event Listener service can announce for what type of UPnP services it wants notifications. The service version is encoded in the type string as specified in the UPnP specification. A null value is a wildcard, matching **all** service types. Value is "UPnP.service.type".

See Also UPnPService. getType ()

111.16.8.3   **public UPnPAction getAction(String name)**

name Name of action. Must not contain hyphen or hash characters. Should be < 32 characters.

☐ Locates a specific action by name. Looks up an action by its name.

Returns The requested action or null if no action is found.

111.16.8.4   **public UPnPAction[] getActions( )**

☐ Lists all actions provided by this service.

Returns Array of actions (UPnPAction[])or null if no actions are defined for this service.

111.16.8.5   **public String getId( )**

☐ Returns the serviceId field in the UPnP service description.

For standard services defined by a UPnP Forum working committee, the serviceId must contain the following components in the indicated order:

- urn:upnp-org:serviceId:
- service ID suffix

Example: urn:upnp-org:serviceId:serviceID.

Note that upnp-org is used instead of schemas-upnp-org in this example because an XML schema is not defined for each serviceId.

For non-standard services specified by UPnP vendors, the serviceId must contain the following components in the indicated order:

- urn:
- ICANN domain name owned by the vendor
- :serviceId:
- service ID suffix

Example: urn:domain-name:serviceId:serviceID.

Returns The service ID suffix defined by a UPnP Forum working committee or specified by a UPnP vendor. Must be <= 64 characters. Single URI.

111.16.8.6 **public UPnPStateVariable getStateVariable(String name)**

name Name of the State Variable

□ Gets a UPnPStateVariable objects provided by this service by name

Returns State variable or null if no such state variable exists for this service.

111.16.8.7 **public UPnPStateVariable[] getStateVariables( )**

□ Lists all UPnPStateVariable objects provided by this service.

Returns Array of state variables or null if none are defined for this service.

111.16.8.8 **public String getType( )**

□ Returns the serviceType field in the UPnP service description.

For standard services defined by a UPnP Forum working committee, the serviceType must contain the following components in the indicated order:

- urn:schemas-upnp-org:service:
- service type suffix:
- integer service version

Example: urn:schemas-upnp-org:service:serviceType:v.

For non-standard services specified by UPnP vendors, the serviceType must contain the following components in the indicated order:

- urn:
- ICANN domain name owned by the vendor
- :service:
- service type suffix:
- integer service version

Example: urn:domain-name:service:serviceType:v.

Returns The service type suffix defined by a UPnP Forum working committee or specified by a UPnP vendor. Must be <= 64 characters, not including the version suffix and separating colon. Single URI.

111.16.8.9 **public String getVersion( )**

□ Returns the version suffix encoded in the serviceType field in the UPnP service description.

Returns The integer service version defined by a UPnP Forum working committee or specified by a UPnP vendor.

111.16.9   public interface UPnPStateVariable

The meta-information of a UPnP state variable as declared in the device's service state table (SST).

Method calls to interact with a device (e.g. UPnPAction.invoke(…);) use this class to encapsulate meta information about the input and output arguments.

The actual values of the arguments are passed as Java objects. The mapping of types from UPnP data types to Java data types is described with the field definitions.

111.16.9.1   public static final String TYPE_BIN_BASE64 = "bin.base64"

MIME-style Base64 encoded binary BLOB.

Takes 3 Bytes, splits them into 4 parts, and maps each 6 bit piece to an octet. (3 octets are encoded as 4.) No limit on size.

Mapped to byte[] object. The Java byte array will hold the decoded content of the BLOB.

111.16.9.2   public static final String TYPE_BIN_HEX = "bin.hex"

Hexadecimal digits representing octets.

Treats each nibble as a hex digit and encodes as a separate Byte. (1 octet is encoded as 2.) No limit on size.

Mapped to byte[] object. The Java byte array will hold the decoded content of the BLOB.

111.16.9.3   public static final String TYPE_BOOLEAN = "boolean"

True or false.

Mapped to Boolean object.

111.16.9.4   public static final String TYPE_CHAR = "char"

Unicode string.

One character long.

Mapped to Character object.

111.16.9.5   public static final String TYPE_DATE = "date"

A calendar date.

Date in a subset of ISO 8601 format without time data.

See http://www.w3.org/TR/xmlschema-2/#date (http://www.w3.org/TR/xmlschema-2/#date) .

Mapped to java.util.Date object. Always 00:00 hours.

111.16.9.6   public static final String TYPE_DATETIME = "dateTime"

A specific instant of time.

Date in ISO 8601 format with optional time but no time zone.

See http://www.w3.org/TR/xmlschema-2/#dateTime (http://www.w3.org/TR/xmlschema-2/#dateTime) .

Mapped to java.util.Date object using default time zone.

111.16.9.7   public static final String TYPE_DATETIME_TZ = "dateTime.tz"

A specific instant of time.

Date in ISO 8601 format with optional time and optional time zone.

See http://www.w3.org/TR/xmlschema-2/#dateTime (http://www.w3.org/TR/xmlschema-2/ #dateTime).

Mapped to java.util.Date object adjusted to default time zone.

111.16.9.8 **public static final String TYPE_FIXED_14_4 = "fixed.14.4"**

Same as r8 but no more than 14 digits to the left of the decimal point and no more than 4 to the right.

Mapped to Double object.

111.16.9.9 **public static final String TYPE_FLOAT = "float"**

Floating-point number.

Mantissa (left of the decimal) and/or exponent may have a leading sign. Mantissa and/or exponent may have leading zeros. Decimal character in mantissa is a period, i.e., whole digits in mantissa separated from fractional digits by period. Mantissa separated from exponent by E. (No currency symbol.) (No grouping of digits in the mantissa, e.g., no commas.)

Mapped to Float object.

111.16.9.10 **public static final String TYPE_I1 = "i1"**

1 Byte int.

Mapped to Integer object.

111.16.9.11 **public static final String TYPE_I2 = "i2"**

2 Byte int.

Mapped to Integer object.

111.16.9.12 **public static final String TYPE_I4 = "i4"**

4 Byte int.

Must be between -2147483648 and 2147483647

Mapped to Integer object.

111.16.9.13 **public static final String TYPE_INT = "int"**

Integer number.

Mapped to Integer object.

111.16.9.14 **public static final String TYPE_NUMBER = "number"**

Same as r8.

Mapped to Double object.

111.16.9.15 **public static final String TYPE_R4 = "r4"**

4 Byte float.

Same format as float. Must be between 3.40282347E+38 to 1.17549435E-38.

Mapped to Float object.

111.16.9.16 **public static final String TYPE_R8 = "r8"**

8 Byte float.

Same format as float. Must be between -1.79769313486232E308 and -4.94065645841247E-324 for negative values, and between 4.94065645841247E-324 and 1.79769313486232E308 for positive values, i.e., IEEE 64-bit (8-Byte) double.

Mapped to Double object.

111.16.9.17 **public static final String TYPE_STRING = "string"**

Unicode string.

No limit on length.

Mapped to String object.

111.16.9.18 **public static final String TYPE_TIME = "time"**

An instant of time that recurs every day.

Time in a subset of ISO 8601 format with no date and no time zone.

See http://www.w3.org/TR/xmlschema-2/#time (http://www.w3.org/TR/xmlschema-2/#dateTime) .

Mapped to Long. Converted to milliseconds since midnight.

111.16.9.19 **public static final String TYPE_TIME_TZ = "time.tz"**

An instant of time that recurs every day.

Time in a subset of ISO 8601 format with optional time zone but no date.

See http://www.w3.org/TR/xmlschema-2/#time (http://www.w3.org/TR/xmlschema-2/#dateTime) .

Mapped to Long object. Converted to milliseconds since midnight and adjusted to default time zone, wrapping at 0 and 24*60*60*1000.

111.16.9.20 **public static final String TYPE_UI1 = "ui1"**

Unsigned 1 Byte int.

Mapped to an Integer object.

111.16.9.21 **public static final String TYPE_UI2 = "ui2"**

Unsigned 2 Byte int.

Mapped to Integer object.

111.16.9.22 **public static final String TYPE_UI4 = "ui4"**

Unsigned 4 Byte int.

Mapped to Long object.

111.16.9.23 **public static final String TYPE_URI = "uri"**

Universal Resource Identifier.

Mapped to String object.

111.16.9.24 **public static final String TYPE_UUID = "uuid"**

Universally Unique ID.

Hexadecimal digits representing octets. Optional embedded hyphens are ignored.

Mapped to String object.

111.16.9.25   **public String[] getAllowedValues( )**

☐ Returns the allowed values, if defined. Allowed values can be defined only for String types.

Returns The allowed values or null if not defined. Should be less than 32 characters.

111.16.9.26   **public Object getDefaultValue( )**

☐ Returns the default value, if defined.

Returns The default value or null if not defined. The type of the returned object can be determined by getJavaDataType.

111.16.9.27   **public Class getJavaDataType( )**

☐ Returns the Java class associated with the UPnP data type of this state variable.

Mapping between the UPnP data types and Java classes is performed according to the schema mentioned above.

```
Integer        ui1, ui2, i1, i2, i4, int
Long           ui4, time, time.tz
Float          r4, float
Double         r8, number, fixed.14.4
Character      char
String         string, uri, uuid
Date           date, dateTime, dateTime.tz
Boolean        boolean
byte[]         bin.base64, bin.hex
```

Returns A class object corresponding to the Java type of this argument.

111.16.9.28   **public Number getMaximum( )**

☐ Returns the maximum value, if defined. Maximum values can only be defined for numeric types.

Returns The maximum value or null if not defined.

111.16.9.29   **public Number getMinimum( )**

☐ Returns the minimum value, if defined. Minimum values can only be defined for numeric types.

Returns The minimum value or null if not defined.

111.16.9.30   **public String getName( )**

☐ Returns the variable name.

· All standard variables defined by a UPnP Forum working committee must not begin with X_ nor A_.
· All non-standard variables specified by a UPnP vendor and added to a standard service must begin with X_.

Returns Name of state variable. Must not contain a hyphen character nor a hash character. Should be < 32 characters.

111.16.9.31   **public Number getStep( )**

☐ Returns the size of an increment operation, if defined. Step sizes can be defined only for numeric types.

Returns The increment size or null if not defined.

111.16.9.32   **public String getUPnPDataType( )**

☐ Returns the UPnP type of this state variable. Valid types are defined as constants.

Returns The UPnP data type of this state variable, as defined in above constants.

111.16.9.33   **public boolean sendsEvents( )**

☐ Tells if this StateVariable can be used as an event source. If the StateVariable is eventable, an event listener service can be registered to be notified when changes to the variable appear.

Returns true if the StateVariable generates events, false otherwise.

111.17   References

[1] *UPnP Device Architecture*
     http://www.upnp.org/specs/arch/upnpda10_20000613.htm

[2] *UPnP Forum*
     http://www.upnp.org

[3] *Simple Object Access Protocol, SOAP*
     http://www.w3.org/TR/SOAP

[4] *General Event Notification Architecture, GENA*
     http://quimby.gnus.org/internet-drafts/draft-cohen-gena-p-base-01.txt

[5] *Simple Service Discovery Protocol, SSDP*
     http://en.wikipedia.org/wiki/Simple_Service_Discovery_Protocol

[6] *XML Schema*
     http://www.w3.org/TR/xmlschema-2

[7] *ISo 8601 Date And Time formats*
     www.iso.ch

112 Declarative Services Specification

Version 1.1

112.1 Introduction

The OSGi Framework contains a procedural service model which provides a publish/find/bind model for using *services*. This model is elegant and powerful, it enables the building of applications out of bundles that communicate and collaborate using these services.

This specification addresses some of the complications that arise when the OSGi service model is used for larger systems and wider deployments, such as:

- *Startup Time* – The procedural service model requires a bundle to actively register and acquire its services. This is normally done at startup time, requiring all present bundles to be initialized with a Bundle Activator. In larger systems, this quickly results in unacceptably long startup times.
- *Memory Footprint* – A service registered with the Framework implies that the implementation, and related classes and objects, are loaded in memory. If the service is never used, this memory is unnecessarily occupied. The creation of a class loader may therefore cause significant overhead.
- *Complexity* – Service can come and go at any time. This dynamic behavior makes the service programming model more complex than more traditional models. This complexity negatively influences the adoption of the OSGi service model as well as the robustness and reliability of applications because these applications do not always handle the dynamicity correctly.

The *service component* model uses a declarative model for publishing, finding and binding to OSGi services. This model simplifies the task of authoring OSGi services by performing the work of registering the service and handling service dependencies. This minimizes the amount of code a programmer has to write; it also allows service components to be loaded only when they are needed. As a result, bundles need not provide a BundleActivator class to collaborate with others through the service registry.

From a system perspective, the service component model means reduced startup time and potentially a reduction of the memory footprint. From a programmer's point of view the service component model provides a simplified programming model.

The Service Component model makes use of concepts described in [1] *Automating Service Dependency Management in a Service-Oriented Component Model.*

112.1.1 Essentials

- *Backward Compatibility* – The service component model must operate seamlessly with the existing service model.
- *Size Constraints* – The service component model must not require memory and performance intensive subsystems. The model must also be applicable on resource constrained devices.
- *Delayed Activation* – The service component model must allow delayed activation of a service component. Delayed activation allows for delayed class loading and object creation until needed, thereby reducing the overall memory footprint.
- *Simplicity* – The programming model for using declarative services must be very simple and not require the programmer to learn a complicated API or XML sub-language.

112.1.2   ## Entities

- *Service Component* – A service component contains a description that is interpreted at run time to create and dispose objects depending on the availability of other services, the need for such an object, and available configuration data. Such objects can optionally provide a service. This specification also uses the generic term *component* to refer to a service component.
- *Component Description* – The declaration of a service component. It is contained within an XML document in a bundle.
- *Component Properties* – A set of properties which can be specified by the component description, Configuration Admin service and from the component factory.
- *Component Configuration* – A component configuration represents a component description parameterized by component properties. It is the entity that tracks the component dependencies and manages a component instance. An activated component configuration has a component context.
- *Component Instance* – An instance of the component implementation class. A component instance is created when a component configuration is activated and discarded when the component configuration is deactivated. A component instance is associated with exactly one component configuration.
- *Delayed Component* – A component whose component configurations are activated when their service is requested.
- *Immediate Component* – A component whose component configurations are activated immediately upon becoming satisfied.
- *Factory Component* – A component whose component configurations are created and activated through the component's component factory.
- *Reference* – A specified dependency of a component on a set of target services.
- *Service Component Runtime (SCR)* – The actor that manages the components and their life cycle.
- *Target Services* – The set of services that is defined by the reference interface and target property filter.
- *Bound Services* – The set of target services that are bound to a component configuration.

Figure 112.1   *Service Component Runtime, org.osgi.service.component package*

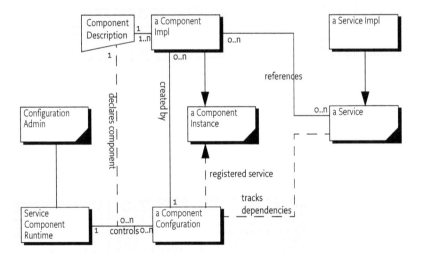

112.1.3   Synopsis

The Service Component Runtime reads component descriptions from started bundles. These descriptions are in the form of XML documents which define a set of components for a bundle. A component can refer to a number of services that must be available before a component configuration becomes satisfied. These dependencies are defined in the descriptions and the specific target services can be influenced by configuration information in the Configuration Admin service. After a component configuration becomes satisfied, a number of different scenarios can take place depending on the component type:

- *Immediate Component* – The component configuration of an immediate component must be activated immediately after becoming satisfied. Immediate components may provide a service.
- *Delayed Component* – When a component configuration of a delayed component becomes satisfied, SCR will register the service specified by the service element without activating the component configuration. If this service is requested, SCR must activate the component configuration creating an instance of the component implementation class that will be returned as the service object. If the servicefactory attribute of the service element is true, then, for each distinct bundle that requests the service, a different component configuration is created and activated and a new instance of the component implementation class is returned as the service object.
- *Factory Component* – If a component's description specifies the factory attribute of the component element, SCR will register a Component Factory service. This service allows client bundles to create and activate multiple component configurations and dispose of them. If the component's description also specifies a service element, then as each component configuration is activated, SCR will register it as a service.

112.1.4   Readers

- *Architects* – The chapter, *Components* on page 251, gives a comprehensive introduction to the capabilities of the component model. It explains the model with a number of examples. The section about *Component Life Cycle* on page 264 provides some deeper insight in the life cycle of components.
- *Service Programmers* – Service programmers should read *Components* on page 251. This chapter should suffice for the most common cases. For the more advanced possibilities, they should consult *Component Description* on page 259 for the details of the XML grammar for component descriptions.
- *Deployers* – Deployers should consult *Deployment* on page 273.

112.2   Components

A component is a normal Java class contained within a bundle. The distinguishing aspect of a component is that it is *declared* in an XML document. Component configurations are activated and deactivated under the full control of SCR. SCR bases its decisions on the information in the component's description. This information consists of basic component information like the name and type, optional services that are implemented by the component, and *references*. References are dependencies that the component has on other services.

SCR must *activate* a component configuration when the component is enabled and the component configuration is satisfied and a component configuration is needed. During the life time of a component configuration, SCR can notify the component of changes in its bound references.

SCR will *deactivate* a previously activated component configuration when the component becomes disabled, the component configuration becomes unsatisfied, or the component configuration is no longer needed.

If an activated component configuration's configuration properties change, SCR must deactivate the component configuration and then attempt to reactivate the component configuration using the new configuration information.

112.2.1   ## Declaring a Component

A component requires the following artifacts in the bundle:

- An XML document that contains the component description.
- The Service-Component manifest header which names the XML documents that contain the component descriptions.
- An implementation class that is specified in the component description.

The elements in the component's description are defined in *Component Description* on page 259. The XML grammar for the component declaration is defined by the XML Schema, see *Component Description Schema* on page 276.

112.2.2   ## Immediate Component

An *immediate component* is activated as soon as its dependencies are satisfied. If an immediate component has no dependencies, it is activated immediately. A component is an immediate component if it is not a factory component and either does not specify a service or specifies a service and the immediate attribute of the component element set to true. If an immediate component configuration is satisfied and specifies a service, SCR must register the component configuration as a service in the service registry and then activate the component configuration.

For example, the bundle entry /OSGI-INF/activator.xml contains:

```
<?xml version="1.0" encoding="UTF-8"?>
<scr:component name="example.activator"
   xmlns:scr="http://www.osgi.org/xmlns/scr/v1.1.0">
   <implementation class="com.acme.Activator"/>
</scr:component>
```

The manifest header Service-Component must also be specified in the bundle manifest. For example:

```
Service-Component: OSGI-INF/activator.xml
```

An example class for this component could look like:

```
public class Activator {
   public Activator() {...}
   private void activate(BundleContext context) {...}
   private void deactivate() {...}
}
```

This example component is virtually identical to a Bundle Activator. It has no references to other services so it will be satisfied immediately. It publishes no service so SCR will activate a component configuration immediately.

The activate method is called when SCR activates the component configuration and the deactivate method is called when SCR deactivates the component configuration. If the activate method throws an Exception, then the component configuration is not activated and will be discarded.

112.2.3   ## Delayed Component

A *delayed component* specifies a service, is not specified to be a factory component and does not have the immediate attribute of the component element set to true. If a delayed component configuration is satisfied, SCR must register the component configuration as a service in the service registry but the activation of the component configuration is delayed until the registered service is requested. The registered service of a delayed component look like on normal registered service but does not incur the overhead of an ordinarily registered service that require a service's bundle to be initialized to register the service.

For example, a bundle needs to see events of a specific topic. The Event Admin uses the white board pattern, receiving the events is therefore as simple as registering a Event Handler service. The example XML for the delayed component looks like:

```
<?xml version="1.0" encoding="UTF-8"?>
<scr:component name="example.handler"
   xmlns:scr="http://www.osgi.org/xmlns/scr/v1.1.0">
   <implementation class="com.acme.HandlerImpl"/>
   <property name="event.topics">some/topic</property>
   <service>
     <provide interface=
         "org.osgi.service.event.EventHandler"/>
   </service>
<scr:component>
```

The associated component class looks like:

```
public class HandlerImpl implements EventHandler {
   public void handleEvent(Event evt ) {
      ...
   }
}
```

The component configuration will only be activated once the Event Admin service requires the service because it has an event to deliver on the topic to which the component subscribed.

112.2.4   Factory Component

Certain software patterns require the creation of component configurations on demand. For example, a component could represent an application that can be launched multiple times and each application instance can then quit independently. Such a pattern requires a factory that creates the instances. This pattern is supported with a *factory component*. A factory component is used if the factory attribute of the component element is set to a *factory identifier*. This identifier can be used by a bundle to associate the factory with externally defined information.

SCR must register a Component Factory service on behalf of the component as soon as the component factory is satisfied. The service properties must be:

- component.name – The name of the component.
- component.factory – The factory identifier.

The service properties of the Component Factory service must not include the component properties.

New configurations of the component can be created and activated by calling the newInstance method on this Component Factory service. The newInstance(Dictionary) method has a Dictionary object as argument. This Dictionary object is merged with the component properties as described in *Component Properties* on page 272. If the component specifies a service, then the service is registered after the created component configuration is satisfied with the component properties. Then the component configuration is activated.

For example, a component can provide a connection to a USB device. Such a connection should normally not be shared and should be created each time such a service is needed. The component description to implement this pattern looks like:

```
<?xml version="1.0" encoding="UTF-8"?>
<scr:component name="example.factory"
   factory="usb.connection"
   xmlns:scr="http://www.osgi.org/xmlns/scr/v1.1.0">
   <implementation class="com.acme.USBConnectionImpl"/>
</scr:component>
```

The component class looks like:

```
public class USBConnectionImpl implements USBConnection {
  private void activate(Map properties) {
    ...
  }
}
```

A factory component can be associated with a service. In that case, such a service is registered for each component configuration. For example, the previous example could provide a USB Connection service.

```
<?xml version="1.0" encoding="UTF-8"?>
<scr:component name="example.factory"
  factory="usb.connection"
  xmlns:scr="http://www.osgi.org/xmlns/scr/v1.1.0">
  <implementation class="com.acme.USBConnectionImpl"/>
  <service>
    <provide interface="com.acme.USBConnection"/>
  </service>
</scr:component>
```

The associated component class looks like:

```
public class USBConnectionImpl implements USBConnection {
  private void activate(Map properties) {...}
  public void connect() { ... }
  ...
  public void close() { ... }
}
```

A new service will be registered each time a new component configuration is created and activated with the newInstance method. This allows a bundle other than the one creating the component configuration to utilize the service. If the component configuration is deactivated, the service must be unregistered.

112.3   References to Services

Most bundles will require access to other services from the service registry. The dynamics of the service registry require care and attention of the programmer because referenced services, once acquired, could be unregistered at any moment. The component model simplifies the handling of these service dependencies significantly.

The services that are selected by a reference are called the *target services*. These are the services selected by the BundleContext.getServiceReferences method where the first argument is the reference's interface and the second argument is the reference's target property, which must be a valid filter.

A component configuration becomes *satisfied* when each specified reference is satisfied. A reference is *satisfied* if it specifies optional cardinality or when the target services contains at least one member. An activated component configuration that becomes *unsatisfied* must be deactivated.

During the activation of a component configuration, SCR must bind some or all of the target services of a reference to the component configuration. Any target service that is bound to the component configuration is called a *bound* service. See *Binding Services* on page 268.

112.3.1   Accessing Services

A component instance must be able to use the services that are referenced by the component configuration, that is, the bound services of the references. There are two strategies for a component instance to acquire these bound services:

- *Event strategy* – SCR calls a method on the component instance when a service becomes bound and another method when a service becomes unbound. These methods are the bind and unbind methods specified by the reference. The event strategy is useful if the component needs to be notified of changes to the bound services for a dynamic reference.
- *Lookup strategy* – A component instance can use one of the locateService methods of Component-Context to locate a bound service. These methods take the name of the reference as a parameter. If the reference has a dynamic policy, it is important to not store the returned service object(s) but look it up every time it is needed.

A component may use either or both strategies to access bound services.

When using the event strategy, the bind and unbind methods must have one of the following prototypes:

```
1   void <method-name>(ServiceReference);
2   void <method-name>(<parameter-type>);
3   void <method-name>(<parameter-type>, Map);
```

If the bind or unbind method has the first prototype, then a Service Reference to the bound service will be passed to the method. This Service Reference may later be passed to the locateService(String, ServiceReference) method to obtain the actual service object. This approach is useful when the service properties need to be examined before accessing the service object. It also allows for the delayed activation of bound services when using the event strategy.

If the bind or unbind method has the second prototype, then the service object of the bound service is passed to the method. The method's parameter type must be assignable from the type specified by the reference's interface attribute. That is, the service object of the bound service must be castable to the method's parameter type.

If the bind or unbind method has the third prototype, then the service object of the bound service is passed to the method as the first argument and an unmodifiable Map containing the service properties of the bound service is passed as the second argument. The method's first parameter type must be assignable from the type specified by the reference's interface attribute. That is, the service object of the bound service must be castable to the method's first parameter type.

The methods must be called once for each bound service. This implies that if the reference has multiple cardinality, then the methods may be called multiple times.

A suitable method is selected using the following priority:

1   The method takes a single argument and the type of the argument is org.osgi.framework.ServiceReference.
2   The method takes a single argument and the type of the argument is the type specified by the reference's interface attribute.
3   The method takes a single argument and the type of the argument is assignable from the type specified by the reference's interface attribute. If multiple methods match this rule, this implies the method name is overloaded and SCR may choose any of the methods to call.
4   The method takes two argument and the type of the first argument is the type specified by the reference's interface attribute and the type of the second argument is java.util.Map.
5   The method takes two argument and the type of the first argument is assignable from the type specified by the reference's interface attribute and the type of the second argument is java.util.Map. If multiple methods match this rule, this implies the method name is overloaded and SCR may choose any of the methods to call.

When searching for the bind or unbind method to call, SCR must locate a suitable method as specified in *Locating Component Methods* on page 275. If no suitable method is located, SCR must log an error message with the Log Service, if present, and there will be no bind or unbind notification.

When the service object for a bound service is first provided to a component instance, that is passed to a bind or unbind method or returned by a locate service method, SCR must get the service object from the OSGi Framework's service registry using the getService method on the component's Bundle Context. If the service object for a bound service has been obtained and the service becomes unbound, SCR must unget the service object using the ungetService method on the component's Bundle Context and discard all references to the service object.

For example, a component requires the Log Service and uses the lookup strategy. The reference is declared without any bind and unbind methods:

```
<?xml version="1.0" encoding="UTF-8"?>
<scr:component name="example.listen"
  xmlns:scr="http://www.osgi.org/xmlns/scr/v1.1.0">
  <implementation class="com.acme.LogLookupImpl"/>
  <reference name="LOG"
    interface="org.osgi.service.log.LogService"/>
</scr:component>
```

The component implementation class must now lookup the service. This looks like:

```
public class LogLookupImpl {
    private void activate(ComponentContext ctxt) {
        LogService log = (LogService)
          ctxt.locateService("LOG");
        log.log(LogService.LOG_INFO, "Hello Components!"));
    }
}
```

Alternatively, the component could use the event strategy and ask to be notified with the Log Service by declaring bind and unbind methods.

```
<?xml version="1.0" encoding="UTF-8"?>
<scr:component name="example.listen"
  xmlns:scr="http://www.osgi.org/xmlns/scr/v1.1.0">
  <implementation class="com.acme.LogEventImpl"/>
  <reference name="LOG"
    interface="org.osgi.service.log.LogService"
    bind="setLog"
    unbind="unsetLog"
  />
</scr:component>
```

The component implementation class looks like:

```
public class LogEventImpl {
    private LogService log;
    private void setLog( LogService l ) { log = l; }
    private void unsetLog( LogService l ) { log = null; }
    private void activate() {
        log.log(LogService.LOG_INFO, "Hello Components!"));
    }
}
```

112.3.2   Reference Cardinality

A component implementation is always written with a certain *cardinality* in mind. The cardinality represents two important concepts:

- *Multiplicity* – Does the component implementation assume a single service or does it explicitly handle multiple occurrences? For example, when a component uses the Log Service, it only needs to bind to one Log Service to function correctly. Alternatively, when the Configuration Admin uses the Configuration Listener services it needs to bind to all target services present in the service registry to dispatch its events correctly.
- *Optionality* – Can the component function without any bound service present? Some components can still perform useful tasks even when no target service is available, other components must bind to at least one target service before they can be useful. For example, the Configuration Admin in the previous example must still provide its functionality even if there are no Configuration Listener services present. Alternatively, an application that solely presents a Servlet page has little to do when the Http Service is not present, it should therefore use a reference with a mandatory cardinality.

The cardinality is expressed with the following syntax:

```
cardinality   ::= optionality '..' multiplicity
optionality   ::= '0' | '1'
multiplicity ::= '1' | 'n'
```

A reference is *satisfied* if the number of target services is equal to or more than the optionality. The multiplicity is irrelevant for the satisfaction of the reference. The multiplicity only specifies if the component implementation is written to handle being bound to multiple services (n) or requires SCR to select and bind to a single service (1).

The cardinality for a reference can be specified as one of four choices:

- 0..1 – Optional and unary.
- 1..1 – Mandatory and unary (Default).
- 0..n – Optional and multiple.
- 1..n – Mandatory and multiple.

When a satisfied component configuration is activated, there must be at most one bound service for each reference with a unary cardinality and at least one bound service for each reference with a mandatory cardinality. If the cardinality constraints cannot be maintained after a component configuration is activated, that is the reference becomes unsatisfied, the component configuration must be deactivated. If the reference has a unary cardinality and there is more than one target service for the reference, then the bound service must be the target service with the highest service ranking as specified by the service.ranking property. If there are multiple target services with the same service ranking, then the bound service must be the target service with the highest service ranking and the lowest service ID as specified by the service.id property.

For example, a component wants to register a resource with all Http Services that are available. Such a scenario has the cardinality of 0..n. The code must be prepared to handle multiple calls to the bind method for each Http Service in such a case. In this example, the code uses the registerResources method to register a directory for external access.

```
<?xml version="1.0" encoding="UTF-8"?>
<scr:component name="example.listen"
   xmlns:scr="http://www.osgi.org/xmlns/scr/v1.1.0">
   <implementation class="com.acme.HttpResourceImpl"/>
   <reference name="HTTP"
      interface="org.osgi.service.http.HttpService"
      cardinality="0..n"
      bind="setPage"
      unbind="unsetPage"
```

```
        / >
   </scr:component>

   public class HttpResourceImpl {
      private void setPage(HttpService http) {
         http.registerResources("/scr", "scr", null );
      }
      private void unsetPage(HttpService http) {
         http.unregister("/scr");
      }
   }
```

112.3.3 Reference Policy

Once all the references of a component are satisfied, a component configuration can be activated and therefore bound to target services. However, the dynamic nature of the OSGi service registry makes it likely that services are registered, modified and unregistered after target services are bound. These changes in the service registry could make one or more bound services no longer a target service thereby making obsolete any object references that the component has to these service objects. Components therefore must specify a *policy* how to handle these changes in the set of bound services.

The *static policy* is the most simple policy and is the default policy. A component instance never sees any of the dynamics. Component configurations are deactivated before any bound service for a reference having a static policy becomes unavailable. If a target service is available to replace the bound service which became unavailable, the component configuration must be reactivated and bound to the replacement service. A reference with a static policy is called a *static reference*.

The static policy can be very expensive if it depends on services that frequently unregister and re-register or if the cost of activating and deactivating a component configuration is high. Static policy is usually also not applicable if the cardinality specifies multiple bound services.

The *dynamic policy* is slightly more complex since the component implementation must properly handle changes in the set of bound services. With the dynamic policy, SCR can change the set of bound services without deactivating a component configuration. If the component uses the event strategy to access services, then the component instance will be notified of changes in the set of bound services by calls to the bind and unbind methods. A reference with a dynamic policy is called a *dynamic reference*.

The previous example with the registering of a resource directory used a static policy. This implied that the component configurations are deactivated when there is a change in the bound set of Http Services. The code in the example can be seen to easily handle the dynamics of Http Services that come and go. The component description can therefore be updated to:

```
   <?xml version="1.0" encoding="UTF-8"?>
   <scr:component name="example.listen"
      xmlns:scr="http://www.osgi.org/xmlns/scr/v1.1.0">
      <implementation class="com.acme.HttpResourceImpl"/>
      <reference name="HTTP"
         interface="org.osgi.service.http.HttpService"
         cardinality="0..n"
         policy="dynamic"
         bind="setPage"
         unbind="unsetPage"
      />
   </scr:component>
```

The code is identical to the previous example.

112.3.4 Selecting Target Services

The target services for a reference are constrained by the reference's interface name and target property. By specifying a filter in the target property, the programmer and deployer can constrain the set of services that should be part of the target services.

For example, a component wants to track all Component Factory services that have a factory identification of acme.application. The following component description shows how this can be done.

```xml
<?xml version="1.0" encoding="UTF-8"?>
<scr:component name="example.listen"
  xmlns:scr="http://www.osgi.org/xmlns/scr/v1.1.0">
  <implementation class="com.acme.FactoryTracker"/>
  <reference name="FACTORY"
    interface=
      "org.osgi.service.component.ComponentFactory"
    target="(component.factory=acme.application)"
  />
</scr:component>
```

The filter is manifested as a component property called the *target property*. The target property can also be set by property and properties elements, see *Properties and Property Elements* on page 262. The deployer can also set the target property by establishing a configuration for the component which sets the value of the target property. This allows the deployer to override the target property in the component description. See *Component Properties* on page 272 for more information.

112.3.5 Circular References

It is possible for a set of component descriptions to create a circular dependency. For example, if component A references a service provided by component B and component B references a service provided by component A then a component configuration of one component cannot be satisfied without accessing a partially activated component instance of the other component. SCR must ensure that a component instance is never accessible to another component instance or as a service until it has been fully activated, that is it has returned from its activate method if it has one.

Circular references must be detected by SCR when it attempts to satisfy component configurations and SCR must fail to satisfy the references involved in the cycle and log an error message with the Log Service, if present. However, if one of the references in the cycle has optional cardinality SCR must break the cycle. The reference with the optional cardinality can be satisfied and bound to zero target services. Therefore the cycle is broken and the other references may be satisfied.

112.4 Component Description

Component descriptions are defined in XML documents contained in a bundle and any attached fragments.

If SCR detects an error when processing a component description, it must log an error message with the Log Service, if present, and ignore the component description. Errors can include XML parsing errors and ill-formed component descriptions.

112.4.1 Service Component Header

XML documents containing component descriptions must be specified by the Service-Component header in the manifest. The value of the header is a comma separated list of paths to XML entries within the bundle.

```
Service-Component ::= header // 3.2.4
```

The Service-Component header has no architected directives or properties.

The last component of each path in the Service-Component header may use wildcards so that Bundle.findEntries can be used to locate the XML document within the bundle and its fragments. For example:

```
Service-Component: OSGI-INF/*.xml
```

A Service-Component manifest header specified in a fragment is ignored by SCR. However, XML documents referenced by a bundle's Service-Component manifest header may be contained in attached fragments.

SCR must process each XML document specified in this header. If an XML document specified by the header cannot be located in the bundle and its attached fragments, SCR must log an error message with the Log Service, if present, and continue.

112.4.2   XML Document

A component description must be in a well-formed XML document [4] stored in a UTF-8 encoded bundle entry. The namespace for component descriptions is:

```
http://www.osgi.org/xmlns/scr/v1.1.0
```

The recommended prefix for this namespace is scr. This prefix is used by examples in this specification. XML documents containing component descriptions may contain a single, root component element or one or more component elements embedded in a larger document. Use of the namespace for component descriptions is mandatory. The attributes and sub-elements of a component element are always unqualified.

If an XML document contains a single, root component element which does not specify a namespace, then the http://www.osgi.org/xmlns/scr/v1.0.0 namespace is assumed. Component descriptions using the http://www.osgi.org/xmlns/scr/v1.0.0 namespace must be treated according to version 1.0 of this specification.

SCR must parse all component elements in the namespace. Elements not in this namespace must be ignored. Ignoring elements that are not recognized allows component descriptions to be embedded in any XML document. For example, an entry can provide additional information about components. These additional elements are parsed by another sub-system.

See *Component Description Schema* on page 276 for component description schema.

112.4.3   Component Element

The component element specifies the component description. The following text defines the structure of the XML grammar using a form that is similar to the normal grammar used in OSGi specifications. In this case the grammar should be mapped to XML elements:

```
<component>         ::= <implementation>
                        <properties> *
                        <service> ?
                        <reference> *
```

SCR must not require component descriptions to specify the elements in the order listed above and as required by the XML schema. SCR must allow other orderings since arbitrary orderings of these elements do not affect the meaning of the component description. Only the relative ordering of property and properties element have meaning.

The component element has the following attributes:

- name – The *name* of a component must be unique within a bundle. The component name is used as a PID to retrieve component properties from the OSGi Configuration Admin service if present. See *Deployment* on page 273 for more information. Since the component name is used as a PID, it should be unique within the framework. The XML schema allows the use of component names which are not valid PIDs. Care must be taken to use a valid PID for a component name if the component should be configured by the Configuration Admin service. This attribute is optional. The default value of this attribute is the value of the class attribute of the nested implementation element. If multiple component elements in a bundle use the same value for the class attribute of their nested implementation element, then using the default value for this attribute will result in duplicate component names. In this case, this attribute must be specified with a unique value.

- enabled – Controls whether the component is *enabled* when the bundle is started. The default value is true. If enabled is set to false, the component is disabled until the method enableComponent is called on the ComponentContext object. This allows some initialization to be performed by some other component in the bundle before this component can become satisfied. See *Enabled* on page 264.

- factory – If set to a non-empty string, it indicates that this component is a *factory component*. SCR must register a Component Factory service for each factory component. See *Factory Component* on page 253.

- immediate – Controls whether component configurations must be immediately activated after becoming satisfied or whether activation should be delayed. The default value is false if the factory attribute or if the service element is specified and true otherwise. If this attribute is specified, its value must be false if the factory attribute is also specified or must be true unless the service element is also specified.

- configuration-policy – Controls whether component configurations must be satisfied depending on the presence of a corresponding Configuration object in the OSGi Configuration Admin service. A corresponding configuration is a Configuration object where the PID is the name of the component.
  - optional – (default) Use the corresponding Configuration object if present but allow the component to be satisfied even if the corresponding Configuration object is not present.
  - require – There must be a corresponding Configuration object for the component configuration to become satisfied.
  - ignore – Always allow the component configuration to be satisfied and do not use the corresponding Configuration object even if it is present.

- activate – Specifies the name of the method to call when a component configuration is activated. The default value of this attribute is activate. See *Activate Method* on page 268 for more information.

- deactivate – Specifies the name of the method to call when a component configuration is deactivated. The default value of this attribute is deactivate. See *Deactivate Method* on page 270 for more information.

- modified – Specifies the name of the method to call when the configuration properties for a component configuration is using a Configuration object from the Configuration Admin service and that Configuration object is modified without causing the component configuration to become unsatisfied. If this attribute is not specified, then the component configuration will become unsatisfied if its configuration properties use a Configuration object that is modified in any way. See *Modified Method* on page 269 for more information.

112.4.4   Implementation Element

The implementation element is required and defines the name of the component implementation class. It has therefore only a single attribute:

- class – The Java fully qualified name of the implementation class.

The class is retrieved with the loadClass method of the component's bundle. The class must be public and have a public constructor without arguments (this is normally the default constructor) so component instances may be created by SCR with the newInstance method on Class.

If the component description specifies a service, the class must implement all interfaces that are provided by the service.

112.4.5   **Properties and Property Elements**

A component description can define a number of properties. There are two different elements for this:

- property – Defines a single property.
- properties – Reads a set of properties from a bundle entry.

The property and properties elements can occur multiple times and they can be interleaved. This interleaving is relevant because the properties are processed from top to bottom. Later properties override earlier properties that have the same name.

Properties can also be overridden by a Configuration Admin service's Configuration object before they are exposed to the component or used as service properties. This is described in *Component Properties* on page 272 and *Deployment* on page 273.

The property element has the following attributes:

- name – The name of the property.
- value – The value of the property. This value is parsed according to the property type. If the value attribute is specified, the body of the element is ignored. If the type of the property is not String, parsing of the value is done by the valueOf(String) method. If this method is not available for the given type, the conversion must be done according to the corresponding method in Java 2 SE. For Character types, the conversion is handled by Integer.valueOf method.
- type – The type of the property. Defines how to interpret the value. The type must be one of the following Java types:
    - String (default)
    - Long
    - Double
    - Float
    - Integer
    - Byte
    - Character
    - Boolean
    - Short
- element body – If the value attribute is not specified, the body of the property element must contain one or more values. The value of the property is then an array of the specified type. Except for String objects, the result will be translated to an array of primitive types. For example, if the type attribute specifies Integer, then the resulting array must be int[].
    Values must be placed one per line and blank lines are ignored. Parsing of the value is done by the parse methods in the class identified by the type, after trimming the line of any beginning and ending white space. String values are also trimmed of beginning and ending white space before being placed in the array.

For example, a component that needs an array of hosts can use the following property definition:

```
<property name="hosts">
    www. acme. com
    backup. acme. com
</property>
```

This property declaration results in the property hosts, with a value of String[] { "www.acme.com", "backup.acme.com" }.

The properties element references an entry in the bundle whose contents conform to a standard [3] *Java Properties File.*

The entry is read and processed to obtain the properties and their values. The properties element has the following attributes:

- entry – The entry path relative to the root of the bundle

For example, to include vendor identification properties that are stored in the OSGI-INF directory, the following definition could be used:

```
<properties entry="OSGI-INF/vendor.properties" />
```

112.4.6   Service Element

The service element is optional. It describes the service information to be used when a component configuration is to be registered as a service.

A service element has the following attribute:

- servicefactory – Controls whether the service uses the ServiceFactory concept of the OSGi Framework. The default value is false. If servicefactory is set to true, a different component configuration is created, activated and its component instance returned as the service object for each distinct bundle that requests the service. Each of these component configurations has the same component properties. Otherwise, the same component instance from the single component configuration is returned as the service object for all bundles that request the service.

The servicefactory attribute must not be true if the component is a factory component or an immediate component. This is because SCR is not free to create component configurations as necessary to support servicefactory. A component description is ill-formed if it specifies that the component is a factory component or an immediate component and servicefactory is set to true.

The service element must have one or more provide elements that define the service interfaces. The provide element has a single attribute:

- interface – The name of the interface that this service is registered under. This name must be the fully qualified name of a Java class. For example, org.osgi.service.log.LogService. The specified Java class should be an interface rather than a class, however specifying a class is supported.

The component implementation class must implement all the specified service interfaces.

For example, a component implements an Event Handler service.

```
<service>
  <provide interface=
    "org.osgi.service.eventadmin.EventHandler"/>
</service>
```

112.4.7   Reference Element

A *reference* declares a dependency that a component has on a set of target services. A component configuration is not satisfied, unless all its references are satisfied. A reference specifies target services by specifying their interface and an optional target filter.

A reference element has the following attributes:

- name – The name of the reference. This name is local to the component and can be used to locate a bound service of this reference with one of the locateService methods of ComponentContext. Each reference element within the component must have a unique name. This name attribute is optional. The default value of this attribute is the value of the interface attribute of this element. If multiple reference elements in the component use the same interface name, then using the default value for this attribute will result in duplicate reference names. In this case, this attribute must be specified with a unique name for the reference to avoid an error.
- interface – Fully qualified name of the class that is used by the component to access the service. The service provided to the component must be type compatible with this class. That is, the component must be able to cast the service object to this class. A service must be registered under this name to be considered for the set of target services.
- cardinality – Specifies if the reference is optional and if the component implementation support a single bound service or multiple bound services. See *Reference Cardinality* on page 257.

- policy – The policy declares the assumption of the component about dynamicity. See *Reference Policy* on page 258.
- target – An optional OSGi Framework filter expression that further constrains the set of target services. The default is no filter, limiting the set of matched services to all service registered under the given reference interface. The value of this attribute is used to set a target property. See *Selecting Target Services* on page 259.
- bind – The name of a method in the component implementation class that is used to notify that a service is bound to the component configuration. For static references, this method is only called before the activate method. For dynamic references, this method can also be called while the component configuration is active. See *Accessing Services* on page 255.
- unbind – Same as bind, but is used to notify the component configuration that the service is unbound. For static references, the method is only called after the deactivate method. For dynamic references, this method can also be called while the component configuration is active. See *Accessing Services* on page 255.

112.5 Component Life Cycle

112.5.1 Enabled

A component must first be *enabled* before it can be used. A component cannot be enabled unless the component's bundle is started. See *Starting Bundles* on page 98 of the Core specification. All components in a bundle become disabled when the bundle is stopped. So the life cycle of a component is contained within the life cycle of its bundle.

Every component can be enabled or disabled. The initial enabled state of a component is specified in the component description via the enabled attribute of the component element. See *Component Element* on page 260. Component configurations can be created, satisfied and activated only when the component is enabled.

The enabled state of a component can be controlled with the Component Context enableComponent(String) and disableComponent(String) methods. The purpose of later enabling a component is to be able to decide programmatically when a component can become enabled. For example, an immediate component can perform some initialization work before other components in the bundle are enabled. The component descriptions of all other components in the bundle can be disabled by having enabled set to false in their component descriptions. After any necessary initialization work is complete, the immediate component can call enableComponent to enable the remaining components.

The enableComponent and disableComponent methods must return after changing the enabled state of the named component. Any actions that result from this, such as activating or deactivating a component configuration, must occur asynchronously to the method call. Therefore a component can disable itself.

All components in a bundle can be enabled by passing a null as the argument to enableComponent.

112.5.2 Satisfied

Component configurations can only be activated when the component configuration is *satisfied*. A component configuration becomes satisfied when the following conditions are all satisfied:

- The component is *enabled.*
- If the component description specifies configuration-policy=required, then a Configuration object for the component is present in the Configuration Admin service.
- Using the component properties of the component configuration, all the component's references are satisfied. A reference is satisfied when the reference specifies optional cardinality or there is at least one target service for the reference.

Once any of the listed conditions are no longer true, the component configuration becomes *unsatisfied*. An activated component configuration that becomes unsatisfied must be deactivated.

112.5.3   Immediate Component

A component is an immediate component when it must be activated as soon as its dependencies are satisfied. Once the component configuration becomes unsatisfied, the component configuration must be deactivated. If an immediate component configuration is satisfied and specifies a service, SCR must register the component configuration as a service in the service registry and then activate the component configuration. The service properties for this registration consist of the component properties as defined in *Service Properties* on page 273.

The state diagram is shown in Figure 112.2.

Figure 112.2   *Immediate Component Configuration*

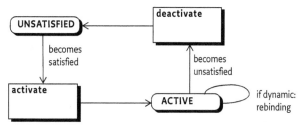

112.5.4   Delayed Component

A key attribute of a delayed component is the delaying of class loading and object creation. Therefore, the activation of a delayed component configuration does not occur until there is an actual request for a service object. A component is a delayed component when it specifies a service but it is not a factory component and does not have the immediate attribute of the component element set to true.

SCR must register a service after the component configuration becomes satisfied. The registration of this service must look to observers of the service registry as if the component's bundle actually registered this service. This strategy makes it possible to register services without creating a class loader for the bundle and loading classes, thereby allowing reduction in initialization time and a delay in memory footprint.

When SCR registers the service on behalf of a component configuration, it must avoid causing a class load to occur from the component's bundle. SCR can ensure this by registering a ServiceFactory object with the Framework for that service. By registering a ServiceFactory object, the actual service object is not needed until the ServiceFactory is called to provide the service object. The service properties for this registration consist of the component properties as defined in *Service Properties* on page 273.

The activation of a component configuration must be delayed until its service is requested. When the service is requested, if the service has the servicefactory attribute set to true, SCR must create and activate a unique component configuration for each bundle requesting the service. Otherwise, SCR must activate a single component configuration which is used by all bundles requesting the service. A component instance can determine the bundle it was activated for by calling the getUsingBundle() method on the Component Context.

The activation of delayed components is depicted in a state diagram in Figure 112.3. Notice that multiple component configurations can be created from the REGISTERED state if a delayed component specifies servicefactory set to true.

If the service registered by a component configuration becomes unused because there are no more bundles using it, then SCR should deactivate that component configuration. This allows SCR implementations to eagerly reclaim activated component configurations.

Figure 112.3   *Delayed Component Configuration*

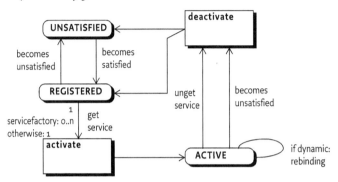

112.5.5   Factory Component

SCR must register a Component Factory service as soon as the *component factory* becomes satisfied. The component factory is satisfied when the following conditions are all satisfied:

*   The component is enabled.
*   Using the component properties specified by the component description, all the component's references are satisfied. A reference is satisfied when the reference specifies optional cardinality or there is at least one target service for the reference

The component factory, however, does not use any of the target services and does not bind to them.

Once any of the listed conditions are no longer true, the component factory becomes unsatisfied and the Component Factory service must be unregistered. Any component configurations activated via the component factory are unaffected by the unregistration of the Component Factory service, but may themselves become unsatisfied for the same reason.

The Component Factory service must be registered under the name org.osgi.service.component.ComponentFactory with the following service properties:

*   component.name – The name of the component.
*   component.factory – The value of the factory attribute.

The service properties of the Component Factory service must not include the component properties.

New component configurations are created and activated when the newInstance method of the Component Factory service is called. If the component description specifies a service, the component configuration is registered as a service under the provided interfaces. The service properties for this registration consist of the component properties as defined in *Service Properties* on page 273. The service registration must take place before the component configuration is activated. Service unregistration must take place before the component configuration is deactivated.

Figure 112.4   *Factory Component*

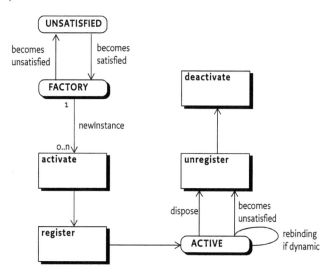

A Component Factory service has a single method: newInstance(Dictionary). This method must create, satisfy and activate a new component configuration and register its component instance as a service if the component description specifies a service. It must then return a ComponentInstance object. This ComponentInstance object can be used to get the component instance with the getInstance() method.

SCR must attempt to satisfy the component configuration created by newInstance before activating it. If SCR is unable to satisfy the component configuration given the component properties and the Dictionary argument to newInstance, the newInstance method must throw a ComponentException.

The client of the Component Factory service can also deactivate a component configuration with the dispose() method on the ComponentInstance object. If the component configuration is already deactivated, or is being deactivated, then this method is ignored. Also, if the component configuration becomes unsatisfied for any reason, it must be deactivated by SCR.

Once a component configuration created by the Component Factory has been deactivated, that component configuration will not be reactivated or used again.

112.5.6   Activation

Activating a component configuration consists of the following steps:

1   Load the component implementation class.
2   Create the component instance and component context.
3   Bind the target services. See *Binding Services* on page 268.
4   Call the activate method, if present. See *Activate Method* on page 268.

Component instances must never be reused. Each time a component configuration is activated, SCR must create a new component instance to use with the activated component configuration. A component instance must complete activation before it can be deactivated. Once the component configuration is deactivated or fails to activate due to an exception, SCR must unbind all the component's bound services and discard all references to the component instance associated with the activation.

112.5.7   Binding Services

When a component configuration's reference is satisfied, there is a set of zero or more target services for that reference. When the component configuration is activated, a subset of the target services for each reference are bound to the component configuration. The subset is chosen by the cardinality of the reference. See *Reference Cardinality* on page 257.

When binding services, the references are processed in the order in which they are specified in the component description. That is, target services from the first specified reference are bound before services from the next specified reference.

For each reference using the event strategy, the bind method must be called for each bound service of that reference. This may result in activating a component configuration of the bound service which could result in an exception. If the loss of the bound service due to the exception causes the reference's cardinality constraint to be violated, then activation of this component configuration will fail. Otherwise the bound service which failed to activate will be considered unbound. If a bind method throws an exception, SCR must log an error message containing the exception with the Log Service, if present, but the activation of the component configuration does not fail.

112.5.8   Activate Method

A component instance can have an activate method. The name of the activate method can be specified by the activate attribute. See *Component Element* on page 260. If the activate attribute is not specified, the default method name of activate is used. The prototype of the activate method is:

```
void <method-name>(<arguments>);
```

The activate method can take zero or more arguments. Each argument must be of one of the following types:

- ComponentContext – The component instance will be passed the Component Context for the component configuration.
- BundleContext – The component instance will be passed the Bundle Context of the component's bundle.
- Map – The component instance will be passed an unmodifiable Map containing the component properties.

A suitable method is selected using the following priority:

1 The method takes a single argument and the type of the argument is org.osgi.service.component.ComponentContext.
2 The method takes a single argument and the type of the argument is org.osgi.framework.BundleContext.
3 The method takes a single argument and the type of the argument is the java.util.Map.
4 The method takes two or more arguments and the type of each argument must be org.osgi.service.component.ComponentContext, org.osgi.framework.BundleContext or java.util.Map. If multiple methods match this rule, this implies the method name is overloaded and SCR may choose any of the methods to call.
5 The method takes zero arguments.

When searching for the activate method to call, SCR must locate a suitable method as specified in *Locating Component Methods* on page 275. If the activate attribute is specified and no suitable method is located, SCR must log an error message with the Log Service, if present, and the component configuration is not activated.

If an activate method is located, SCR must call this method to complete the activation of the component configuration. If the activate method throws an exception, SCR must log an error message containing the exception with the Log Service, if present, and the component configuration is not activated.

112.5.9   **Component Context**

The Component Context is made available to a component instance via the activate and deactivate methods. It provides the interface to the execution context of the component, much like the Bundle Context provides a bundle the interface to the Framework. A Component Context should therefore be regarded as a capability and not shared with other components or bundles.

Each distinct component instance receives a unique Component Context. Component Contexts are not reused and must be discarded when the component configuration is deactivated.

112.5.10   **Bound Service Replacement**

If an active component configuration has a dynamic reference with unary cardinality and the bound service is modified or unregistered and ceases to be a target service, SCR must attempt to replace the bound service with a new target service. SCR must first bind a replacement target service and then unbind the outgoing service. If the dynamic reference has a mandatory cardinality and no replacement target service is available, the component configuration must be deactivated because the cardinality constraints will be violated.

If a component configuration has a static reference and a bound service is modified or unregistered and ceases to be a target service, SCR must deactivate the component configuration. Afterwards, SCR must attempt to activate the component configuration again if another target service can be used as a replacement for the outgoing service.

112.5.11   **Modification**

Modifying a component configuration can occur if the component description specifies the modified attribute and the component properties of the component configuration use a Configuration object from the Configuration Admin service and that Configuration object is modified without causing the component configuration to become unsatisfied. If this occurs, the component instance will be notified of the change in the component properties.

If the modified attribute is not specified, then the component configuration will become unsatisfied if its component properties use a Configuration object and that Configuration object is modified in any way.

Modifying a component configuration consists of the following steps:

1   Update the component context for the component configuration with the modified configuration properties.
2   Call the modified method. See *Modified Method* on page 269.
3   Modify the bound services for the dynamic references if the set of target services changed due to changes in the target properties. See *Bound Service Replacement* on page 269.
4   If the component configuration is registered as a service, modify the service properties.

A component instance must complete activation, or a previous modification, before it can be modified.

See *Modified Configurations* on page 274 for more information.

112.5.12   **Modified Method**

The name of the modified method is specified by the modified attribute. See *Component Element* on page 260. The prototype and selection priority of the modified method is identical to that of the activate method. See *Activate Method* on page 268.

SCR must locate a suitable method as specified in *Locating Component Methods* on page 275. If the modified attribute is specified and no suitable method is located, SCR must log an error message with the Log Service, if present, and the component configuration becomes unsatisfied and is deactivated as if the modified attribute was not specified.

If a modified method is located, SCR must call this method to notify the component configuration of changes to the component properties. If the modified method throws an exception, SCR must log an error message containing the exception with the Log Service, if present and continue processing the modification.

112.5.13 Deactivation

Deactivating a component configuration consists of the following steps:

1 Call the deactivate method, if present. See *Deactivate Method* on page 270.
2 Unbind any bound services. See *Unbinding* on page 271.
3 Release all references to the component instance and component context.

A component instance must complete activation or modification before it can be deactivated. A component configuration can be deactivated for a variety of reasons. The deactivation reason can be received by the deactivate method. The following reason values are defined:

- 0 – Unspecified.
- 1 – The component was disabled.
- 2 – A reference became unsatisfied.
- 3 – A configuration was changed.
- 4 – A configuration was deleted.
- 5 – The component was disposed.
- 6 – The bundle was stopped.

Once the component configuration is deactivated, SCR must discard all references to the component instance and component context associated with the activation.

112.5.14 Deactivate Method

A component instance can have a deactivate method. The name of the deactivate method can be specified by the deactivate attribute. See *Component Element* on page 260. If the deactivate attribute is not specified, the default method name of deactivate is used. The prototype of the deactivate method is:

```
void <method-name>(<arguments>);
```

The deactivate method can take zero or more arguments. Each argument must be assignable from one of the following types:

- ComponentContext – The component instance will be passed the Component Context for the component.
- BundleContext – The component instance will be passed the Bundle Context of the component's bundle.
- Map – The component instance will be passed an unmodifiable Map containing the component properties.
- int or Integer – The component instance will be passed the reason the component configuration is being deactivated. See *Deactivation* on page 270.

A suitable method is selected using the following priority:

1 The method takes a single argument and the type of the argument is org.osgi.service.component.ComponentContext.
2 The method takes a single argument and the type of the argument is org.osgi.framework.BundleContext.
3 The method takes a single argument and the type of the argument is the java.util.Map.
4 The method takes a single argument and the type of the argument is the int.
5 The method takes a single argument and the type of the argument is the java.lang.Integer.
6 The method takes two or more arguments and the type of each argument must be org.osgi.service.component.ComponentContext, org.osgi.framework.BundleContext, java.util.Map, int or java.lang.Integer. If multiple methods match this rule, this implies the

method name is overloaded and SCR may choose any of the methods to call.

7   The method takes zero arguments.

When searching for the deactivate method to call, SCR must locate a suitable method as specified in *Locating Component Methods* on page 275. If the deactivate attribute is specified and no suitable method is located, SCR must log an error message with the Log Service, if present, and the deactivation of the component configuration will continue.

If a deactivate method is located, SCR must call this method to commence the deactivation of the component configuration. If the deactivate method throws an exception, SCR must log an error message containing the exception with the Log Service, if present, and the deactivation of the component configuration will continue.

112.5.15   Unbinding

When a component configuration is deactivated, the bound services are unbound from the component configuration.

When unbinding services, the references are processed in the reverse order in which they are specified in the component description. That is, target services from the last specified reference are unbound before services from the previous specified reference.

For each reference using the event strategy, the unbind method must be called for each bound service of that reference. If an unbind method throws an exception, SCR must log an error message containing the exception with the Log Service, if present, and the deactivation of the component configuration will continue.

112.5.16   Life Cycle Example

A component could declare a dependency on the Http Service to register some resources.

```xml
<?xml version="1.0" encoding="UTF-8"?>
<scr:component name="example.binding"
  xmlns:scr="http://www.osgi.org/xmlns/scr/v1.1.0">
  <implementation class="example.Binding"/>
  <reference name="LOG"
    interface="org.osgi.service.log.LogService"
    cardinality="1..1"
    policy="static"
  />
  <reference name="HTTP"
    interface="org.osgi.service.http.HttpService"
    cardinality="0..1"
    policy="dynamic"
    bind="setHttp"
    unbind="unsetHttp"
  />
</scr:component>
```

The component implementation code looks like:

```java
public class Binding {
    LogService  log;
    HttpService http;

    private void setHttp(HttpService h) {
        this.http = h;
        // register servlet
    }
```

```
        private void unsetHttp(HttpService h){
           this.h = null;
           // unregister servlet
        }
        private void activate(ComponentContext context ) {.
           log = (LogService) context.locateService("LOG");
        }
        private void deactivate(ComponentContext context ){...}
     }
```

This example is depicted in a sequence diagram in Figure 112.5. with the following scenario:

1 A bundle with the example.Binding component is started. At that time there is a Log Service l1
   and a Http Service h1 registered.
2 The Http Service h1 is unregistered
3 A new Http Service h2 is registered
4 The Log Service h1 is unregistered.

Figure 112.5   Sequence Diagram for binding

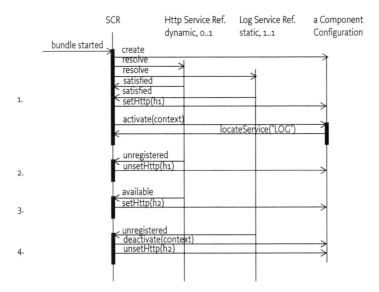

112.6   Component Properties

Each component configuration is associated with a set of component properties. The component
properties are specified in the following places (in order of precedence):

1 Properties specified in the argument of ComponentFactory.newInstance method. This is only
   applicable for factory components.
2 Properties retrieved from the OSGi Configuration Admin service with a Configuration object that
   has a PID equal to the name of the component.
3 Properties specified in the component description. Properties specified later in the component
   description override properties that have the same name specified earlier. Properties can be specified in the component description in the following ways:
   • target attribute of reference elements – Sets a component property called the *target property* of
      the reference. The key of a target property is the name of the reference appended with .target.

The value of a target property is the value of the target attribute. For example, a reference with the name http whose target attribute has the value "(http.port=80)" results in the component property having the name http.target and value "(http.port=80)". See *Selecting Target Services* on page 259. The target property can also be set wherever component properties can be set.

- property and properties elements – See *Properties and Property Elements* on page 262.

The precedence behavior allows certain default values to be specified in the component description while allowing properties to be replaced and extended by:

- A configuration in Configuration Admin
- The argument to ComponentFactory.newInstance method

SCR always adds the following component properties, which cannot be overridden:

- component.name – The component name.
- component.id – A unique value (Long) that is larger than all previously assigned values. These values are not persistent across restarts of SCR.

112.6.1 Service Properties

When SCR registers a service on behalf of a component configuration, SCR must follow the recommendations in *Property Propagation* on page 73 and must not propagate private configuration properties. That is, the service properties of the registered service must be all the component properties of the component configuration whose property names do not start with dot ('.' \u002E).

Component properties whose names start with dot are available to the component instance but are not available as service properties of the registered service.

112.7 Deployment

A component description contains default information to select target services for each reference. However, when a component is deployed, it is often necessary to influence the target service selection in a way that suits the needs of the deployer. Therefore, SCR uses Configuration objects from Configuration Admin to replace and extend the component properties for a component configuration. That is, through Configuration Admin, a deployer can configure component properties.

The name of the component is used as the key for obtaining additional component properties from Configuration Admin. The following situations can arise:

- *No Configuration* – If the component's configuration-policy is set to ignore or there is no Configuration with a PID or factory PID equal to the component name, then component configurations will not obtain component properties from Configuration Admin. Only component properties specified in the component description or via the ComponentFactory.newInstance method will be used.
- *Not Satisfied* – If the component's configuration-policy is set to require and there is no Configuration with a PID or factory PID equal to the component name, then the component configuration is not satisfied and will not be activated.
- *Single Configuration* – If there exists a Configuration with a PID equal to the component name, then component configurations will obtain additional component properties from Configuration Admin.
- *Factory Configuration* – If a factory PID exists, with zero or more Configurations, that is equal to the component name, then for each Configuration, a component configuration must be created that will obtain additional component properties from Configuration Admin.

A factory configuration must not be used if the component is a factory component. This is because SCR is not free to create component configurations as necessary to support multiple Configurations. When SCR detects this condition, it must log an error message with the Log Service, if present, and ignore the component description.

SCR must obtain the Configuration objects from the Configuration Admin service using the Bundle Context of the bundle containing the component.

For example, there is a component named com.acme.client with a reference named HTTP that requires an Http Service which must be bound to a component com.acme.httpserver which provides an Http Service. A deployer can establish the following configuration:

```
[PID=com.acme.client, factoryPID=null]
HTTP.target = (component.name=com.acme.httpserver)
```

112.7.1 Modified Configurations

SCR must track changes in the Configuration objects used in the component properties of a component configuration. If a Configuration object that is used by a component configuration is deleted, then the component configuration will become unsatisfied and SCR must deactivate that component configuration.

If a Configuration object that is used by a component configuration changes, then SCR must take action based upon whether the component configuration has been activated and whether the component description specifies the modified attribute.

If a component configuration has not been activated and it has a service registered, then a Configuration object change that leaves the component configuration satisfied will only cause the service properties of the service to be modified.

If a component description specifies the modified attribute and the changes to the target properties for the component configuration do not cause any references of the component configuration to become unsatisfied, SCR must modify the component properties for the component configuration. See *Modification* on page 269. A reference can become unsatisfied by a target property change if either:

- A bound service of a static reference is no longer a target service, or
- There are no target services for a mandatory dynamic reference.

Otherwise, the component configuration will become unsatisfied and SCR must deactivate that component configuration. SCR must attempt to satisfy the component configuration with the updated component properties.

112.8 Service Component Runtime

112.8.1 Relationship to OSGi Framework

The SCR must have access to the Bundle Context of any bundle that contains a component. The SCR needs access to the Bundle Context for the following reasons:

- To be able to register and get services on behalf of a bundle with components.
- To interact with the Configuration Admin on behalf of a bundle with components.
- To provide a component its Bundle Context when the Component Context getBundleContext method is called.

The SCR should use the Bundle.getBundleContext() method to obtain the Bundle Context reference.

112.8.2 Starting and Stopping SCR

When SCR is implemented as a bundle, any component configurations activated by SCR must be deactivated when the SCR bundle is stopped. When the SCR bundle is started, it must process any components that are declared in bundles that are started. This includes bundles which are started and are awaiting lazy activation.

112.8.3 Logging Error Messages

When SCR must log an error message to the Log Service, it must use a Log Service obtained using the component's Bundle Context so that the resulting Log Entry is associated with the component's bundle.

If SCR is unable to obtain, or use, a Log Service using the component's Bundle Context, then SCR must log the error message to a Log Service obtained using SCR's bundle context to ensure the error message is logged.

112.8.4 Locating Component Methods

SCR will need to locate activate, deactivate, modified, bind and unbind methods for a component instance. These methods will be located, and called, using reflection. The declared methods of each class in the component implementation class' hierarchy are examined for a suitable method. If a suitable method is found in a class, and it is accessible to the component implementation class, then that method must be used. If suitable methods are found in a class but none of the suitable methods are accessible by the component implementation class, then the search for suitable methods terminates with no suitable method having been located. If no suitable methods are found in a class, the search continues in the superclass.

Only methods that are accessible, [5] *Access Control Java Language Specification*, to the component implementation class will be used. If the method has the public or protected access modifier, then access is permitted. Otherwise, if the method has the private access modifier, then access is permitted only if the method is declared in the component implementation class. Otherwise, if the method has default access, also known as package private access, then access is permitted only if the method is declared in the component implementation class or if the method is declared in a superclass and all classes in the hierarchy from the component implementation class to the superclass, inclusive, are in the same package and loaded by the same class loader.

It is recommended that these methods should not be declared with the public access modifier so that they do not appear as public methods on the component instance when it is used as a service object. Having these methods declared public allows any code to call the methods with reflection, even if a Security Manager is installed. These methods are generally intended to only be called by SCR.

112.9 Security

112.9.1 Service Permissions

Declarative services are built upon the existing OSGi service infrastructure. This means that Service Permission applies regarding the ability to publish, find or bind services.

If a component specifies a service, then component configurations for the component cannot be satisfied unless the component's bundle has ServicePermission[<provides>, REGISTER] for each provided interface specified for the service.

If a component's reference does not specify optional cardinality, the reference cannot be satisfied unless the component's bundle has ServicePermission[<interface>, GET] for the specified interface in the reference. If the reference specifies optional cardinality but the component's bundle does not have ServicePermission[<interface>, GET] for the specified interface in the reference, no service must be bound for this reference.

If a component is a factory component, then the above Service Permission checks still apply. But the component's bundle is not required to have ServicePermission[ComponentFactory, REGISTER] as the Component Factory service is registered by SCR.

112.9.2 Required Admin Permission

The SCR requires AdminPermission[∗,CONTEXT] because it needs access to the bundle's Bundle Context object with the Bundle.getBundleContext() method.

112.9.3 Using hasPermission

SCR does all publishing, finding and binding of services on behalf of the component using the Bundle Context of the component's bundle. This means that normal stack-based permission checks will check SCR and not the component's bundle. Since SCR is registering and getting services on behalf of a component's bundle, SCR must call the Bundle.hasPermission method to validate that a component's bundle has the necessary permission to register or get a service.

112.10 Component Description Schema

This XML Schema defines the component description grammar.

```
<?xml version="1.0" encoding="UTF-8"?>
<schema xmlns="http://www.w3.org/2001/XMLSchema"
    xmlns:scr="http://www.osgi.org/xmlns/scr/v1.1.0"
    targetNamespace="http://www.osgi.org/xmlns/scr/v1.1.0"
    elementFormDefault="unqualified"
    attributeFormDefault="unqualified"
    version="1.1.0">

    <annotation>
        <documentation xml:lang="en">
            This is the XML Schema for component descriptions used by
            the Service Component Runtime (SCR). Component description
            documents may be embedded in other XML documents. SCR will
            process all XML documents listed in the Service-Component
            manifest header of a bundle. XML documents containing
            component descriptions may contain a single, root component
            element or one or more component elements embedded in a
            larger document. Use of the namespace for component
            descriptions is mandatory. The attributes and subelements
            of a component element are always unqualified.
        </documentation>
    </annotation>
    <element name="component" type="scr:Tcomponent" />
    <complexType name="Tcomponent">
        <sequence>
            <annotation>
                <documentation xml:lang="en">
                    Implementations of SCR must not require component
                    descriptions to specify the subelements of the component
                    element in the order as required by the schema. SCR
                    implementations must allow other orderings since
                    arbitrary orderings do not affect the meaning of the
                    component description. Only the relative ordering of
                    property and properties element have meaning.
                </documentation>
            </annotation>
            <choice minOccurs="0" maxOccurs="unbounded">
                <element name="property" type="scr:Tproperty" />
                <element name="properties" type="scr:Tproperties" />
            </choice>
            <element name="service" type="scr:Tservice" minOccurs="0"
                maxOccurs="1" />
            <element name="reference" type="scr:Treference"
                minOccurs="0" maxOccurs="unbounded" />
            <element name="implementation" type="scr:Timplementation"
                minOccurs="1" maxOccurs="1" />
            <any namespace="##any" processContents="lax" minOccurs="0"
                maxOccurs="unbounded" />
        </sequence>
        <attribute name="enabled" type="boolean" default="true"
            use="optional" />
        <attribute name="name" type="token" use="optional">
```

```
            <annotation>
                <documentation xml:lang="en">
                    The default value of this attribute is the value of
                    the class attribute of the nested implementation
                    element. If multiple component elements use the same
                    value for the class attribute of their nested
                    implementation element, then using the default value
                    for this attribute will result in duplicate names.
                    In this case, this attribute must be specified with
                    a unique value.
                </documentation>
            </annotation>
        </attribute>
        <attribute name="factory" type="string" use="optional" />
        <attribute name="immediate" type="boolean" use="optional" />
        <attribute name="configuration-policy"
            type="scr:Tconfiguration-policy" default="optional" use="optional" />
        <attribute name="activate" type="token" use="optional"
            default="activate" />
        <attribute name="deactivate" type="token" use="optional"
            default="deactivate" />
        <attribute name="modified" type="token" use="optional" />
        <anyAttribute />
    </complexType>
    <complexType name="Timplementation">
        <sequence>
            <any namespace="##any" processContents="lax" minOccurs="0"
                maxOccurs="unbounded" />
        </sequence>
        <attribute name="class" type="token" use="required" />
        <anyAttribute />
    </complexType>
    <complexType name="Tproperty">
        <simpleContent>
            <extension base="string">
                <attribute name="name" type="string" use="required" />
                <attribute name="value" type="string" use="optional" />
                <attribute name="type" type="scr:Tjava-types"
                    default="String" use="optional" />
                <anyAttribute />
            </extension>
        </simpleContent>
    </complexType>
    <complexType name="Tproperties">
        <sequence>
            <any namespace="##any" processContents="lax" minOccurs="0"
                maxOccurs="unbounded" />
        </sequence>
        <attribute name="entry" type="string" use="required" />
        <anyAttribute />
    </complexType>
    <complexType name="Tservice">
        <sequence>
            <element name="provide" type="scr:Tprovide" minOccurs="1"
                maxOccurs="unbounded" />
            <!-- It is non-deterministic, per W3C XML Schema 1.0:
            http://www.w3.org/TR/xmlschema-1/#cos-nonambig
            to use namespace="##any" below. -->
            <any namespace="##other" processContents="lax" minOccurs="0"
                maxOccurs="unbounded" />
        </sequence>
        <attribute name="servicefactory" type="boolean" default="false"
            use="optional" />
        <anyAttribute />
    </complexType>
    <complexType name="Tprovide">
        <sequence>
            <any namespace="##any" processContents="lax" minOccurs="0"
                maxOccurs="unbounded" />
        </sequence>
        <attribute name="interface" type="token" use="required" />
        <anyAttribute />
    </complexType>
    <complexType name="Treference">
        <sequence>
```

```
            <any namespace="##any" processContents="lax" minOccurs="0"
                maxOccurs="unbounded" />
        </sequence>
        <attribute name="name" type="token" use="optional">
            <annotation>
                <documentation xml:lang="en">
                    The default value of this attribute is the value of
                    the interface attribute of this element. If multiple
                    instances of this element within a component element
                    use the same value for the interface attribute, then
                    using the default value for this attribute will result
                    in duplicate names. In this case, this attribute
                    must be specified with a unique value.
                </documentation>
            </annotation>
        </attribute>
        <attribute name="interface" type="token" use="required" />
        <attribute name="cardinality" type="scr:Tcardinality"
            default="1..1" use="optional" />
        <attribute name="policy" type="scr:Tpolicy" default="static"
            use="optional" />
        <attribute name="target" type="string" use="optional" />
        <attribute name="bind" type="token" use="optional" />
        <attribute name="unbind" type="token" use="optional" />
        <anyAttribute />
    </complexType>
    <simpleType name="Tjava-types">
        <restriction base="string">
            <enumeration value="String" />
            <enumeration value="Long" />
            <enumeration value="Double" />
            <enumeration value="Float" />
            <enumeration value="Integer" />
            <enumeration value="Byte" />
            <enumeration value="Character" />
            <enumeration value="Boolean" />
            <enumeration value="Short" />
        </restriction>
    </simpleType>
    <simpleType name="Tcardinality">
        <restriction base="string">
            <enumeration value="0..1" />
            <enumeration value="0..n" />
            <enumeration value="1..1" />
            <enumeration value="1..n" />
        </restriction>
    </simpleType>
    <simpleType name="Tpolicy">
        <restriction base="string">
            <enumeration value="static" />
            <enumeration value="dynamic" />
        </restriction>
    </simpleType>
    <simpleType name="Tconfiguration-policy">
        <restriction base="string">
            <enumeration value="optional" />
            <enumeration value="require" />
            <enumeration value="ignore" />
        </restriction>
    </simpleType>
    <attribute name="must-understand" type="boolean">
        <annotation>
            <documentation xml:lang="en">
                This attribute should be used by extensions to documents
                to require that the document consumer understand the
                extension. This attribute must be qualified when used.
            </documentation>
        </annotation>
    </attribute>
</schema>
```

SCR must not require component descriptions to specify the elements in the order required by the schema. SCR must allow other orderings since arbitrary orderings of these elements do not affect the meaning of the component description. Only the relative ordering of property, properties and reference elements have meaning for overriding previously set property values.

The schema is also available in digital form from [6] *OSGi XML Schemas.*

112.11   Changes

- Definition of the Service-Component header now uses the definition of a header from the module layer. It also allows a wildcards to be used in the last component of the path of a header entry.
- SCR must follow the recommendations of *Property Propagation* on page 73 and not propagate properties whose names start with '.' to service properties.
- The component description now allows for a configuration policy to control whether component configurations are activated when Configuration object are present or not.
- The component description now allows the names of the activate and deactivate methods to be specified. The signatures of the activate and deactivate methods are also modified.
- The signatures of the bind and unbind methods are modified.
- The definition of accessible methods for activate, deactivate, bind and unbind methods is expanded to include any method accessible from the component implementation class. This allows private and package private method declared in the component implementation class to be used.
- The additional signatures and additional accessibility for the activate, deactivate, bind and unbind methods can cause problems for components written to version 1.0 of this specification. The behavior in this specification only applies to component descriptions using the v1.1.0 namespace.
- The XML schema and namespace have been updated to v1.1.0. It now supports extensibility for new attributes and elements. The name attribute of the component element is now optional and the default value of this attribute is the value of the class attribute of the nested implementation element. The name attribute of the reference element is now optional and the default value of this attribute is the value of the interface attribute of the reference element. The Char type for the property element has been renamed Character to match the Java type name. The attributes configuration-policy, activate, deactivate and modified have been added to the component element.
- When logging error messages, SCR must use a Log Service obtained using the component's bundle context so that the resulting Log Entry is associated with the component's bundle.
- Clarified that target properties are component properties that can be set wherever component properties can be set, including configurations.
- A component configuration can now avoid being deactivated when a Configuration changes by specifying the modified attribute.

112.12   org.osgi.service.component

Service Component Package Version 1.1.

Bundles wishing to use this package must list the package in the Import-Package header of the bundle's manifest. For example:

```
Import-Package: org.osgi.service.component; version="[1.1,2.0)"
```

112.12.1   Summary

- *ComponentConstants* - Defines standard names for Service Component constants.
- *ComponentContext* - A Component Context object is used by a component instance to interact with its execution context including locating services by reference name.
- *ComponentException* - Unchecked exception which may be thrown by the Service Component Runtime.

- *ComponentFactory* - When a component is declared with the factory attribute on its component element, the Service Component Runtime will register a Component Factory service to allow new component configurations to be created and activated rather than automatically creating and activating component configuration as necessary.
- *ComponentInstance* - A ComponentInstance encapsulates a component instance of an activated component configuration.

112.12.2　public interface ComponentConstants

Defines standard names for Service Component constants.

112.12.2.1　public static final String COMPONENT_FACTORY = "component.factory"

A service registration property for a Component Factory that contains the value of the factory attribute. The value of this property must be of type String.

112.12.2.2　public static final String COMPONENT_ID = "component.id"

A component property that contains the generated id for a component configuration. The value of this property must be of type Long.

The value of this property is assigned by the Service Component Runtime when a component configuration is created. The Service Component Runtime assigns a unique value that is larger than all previously assigned values since the Service Component Runtime was started. These values are NOT persistent across restarts of the Service Component Runtime.

112.12.2.3　public static final String COMPONENT_NAME = "component.name"

A component property for a component configuration that contains the name of the component as specified in the name attribute of the component element. The value of this property must be of type String.

112.12.2.4　public static final int DEACTIVATION_REASON_BUNDLE_STOPPED = 6

The component configuration was deactivated because the bundle was stopped.

Since 1.1

112.12.2.5　public static final int DEACTIVATION_REASON_CONFIGURATION_DELETED = 4

The component configuration was deactivated because its configuration was deleted.

Since 1.1

112.12.2.6　public static final int DEACTIVATION_REASON_CONFIGURATION_MODIFIED = 3

The component configuration was deactivated because its configuration was changed.

Since 1.1

112.12.2.7　public static final int DEACTIVATION_REASON_DISABLED = 1

The component configuration was deactivated because the component was disabled.

Since 1.1

112.12.2.8　public static final int DEACTIVATION_REASON_DISPOSED = 5

The component configuration was deactivated because the component was disposed.

Since 1.1

112.12.2.9　public static final int DEACTIVATION_REASON_REFERENCE = 2

The component configuration was deactivated because a reference became unsatisfied.

Since 1.1

112.12.2.10   **public static final int DEACTIVATION_REASON_UNSPECIFIED = 0**

The reason the component configuration was deactivated is unspecified.

Since 1.1

112.12.2.11   **public static final String REFERENCE_TARGET_SUFFIX = ".target"**

The suffix for reference target properties. These properties contain the filter to select the target services for a reference. The value of this property must be of type String.

112.12.2.12   **public static final String SERVICE_COMPONENT = "Service-Component"**

Manifest header specifying the XML documents within a bundle that contain the bundle's Service Component descriptions.

The attribute value may be retrieved from the Dictionary object returned by the Bundle.getHeaders method.

112.12.3   public interface ComponentContext

A Component Context object is used by a component instance to interact with its execution context including locating services by reference name. Each component instance has a unique Component Context.

A component instance may have an activate method. If a component instance has a suitable and accessible activate method, this method will be called when a component configuration is activated. If the activate method takes a ComponentContext argument, it will be passed the component instance's Component Context object. If the activate method takes a BundleContext argument, it will be passed the component instance's Bundle Context object. If the activate method takes a Map argument, it will be passed an unmodifiable Map containing the component properties.

A component instance may have a deactivate method. If a component instance has a suitable and accessible deactivate method, this method will be called when the component configuration is deactivated. If the deactivate method takes a ComponentContext argument, it will be passed the component instance's Component Context object. If the deactivate method takes a BundleContext argument, it will be passed the component instance's Bundle Context object. If the deactivate method takes a Map argument, it will be passed an unmodifiable Map containing the component properties. If the deactivate method takes an int or Integer argument, it will be passed the reason code for the component instance's deactivation.

Concurrency Thread-safe

112.12.3.1   **public void disableComponent(String name)**

name The name of a component.

□ Disables the specified component name. The specified component name must be in the same bundle as this component.

112.12.3.2   **public void enableComponent(String name)**

name The name of a component or null to indicate all components in the bundle.

□ Enables the specified component name. The specified component name must be in the same bundle as this component.

112.12.3.3   **public BundleContext getBundleContext( )**

□ Returns the BundleContext of the bundle which contains this component.

Returns The BundleContext of the bundle containing this component.

112.12.3.4   **public ComponentInstance getComponentInstance( )**

    ☐ Returns the Component Instance object for the component instance associated with this Component Context.

Returns The Component Instance object for the component instance.

112.12.3.5   **public Dictionary getProperties( )**

    ☐ Returns the component properties for this Component Context.

Returns The properties for this Component Context. The Dictionary is read only and cannot be modified.

112.12.3.6   **public ServiceReference getServiceReference( )**

    ☐ If the component instance is registered as a service using the service element, then this method returns the service reference of the service provided by this component instance.

      This method will return null if the component instance is not registered as a service.

Returns The ServiceReference object for the component instance or null if the component instance is not registered as a service.

112.12.3.7   **public Bundle getUsingBundle( )**

    ☐ If the component instance is registered as a service using the servicefactory="true" attribute, then this method returns the bundle using the service provided by the component instance.

      This method will return null if:

- The component instance is not a service, then no bundle can be using it as a service.
- The component instance is a service but did not specify the servicefactory="true" attribute, then all bundles using the service provided by the component instance will share the same component instance.
- The service provided by the component instance is not currently being used by any bundle.

Returns The bundle using the component instance as a service or null.

112.12.3.8   **public Object locateService(String name)**

    name The name of a reference as specified in a reference element in this component's description.

    ☐ Returns the service object for the specified reference name.

      If the cardinality of the reference is 0..n or 1..n and multiple services are bound to the reference, the service with the highest ranking (as specified in its Constants.SERVICE_RANKING property) is returned. If there is a tie in ranking, the service with the lowest service ID (as specified in its Constants.SERVICE_ID property); that is, the service that was registered first is returned.

Returns A service object for the referenced service or null if the reference cardinality is 0..1 or 0..n and no bound service is available.

Throws ComponentException – If the Service Component Runtime catches an exception while activating the bound service.

112.12.3.9   **public Object locateService(String name, ServiceReference reference)**

    name The name of a reference as specified in a reference element in this component's description.

  reference The ServiceReference to a bound service. This must be a ServiceReference provided to the component via the bind or unbind method for the specified reference name.

    ☐ Returns the service object for the specified reference name and ServiceReference.

Returns A service object for the referenced service or null if the specified ServiceReference is not a bound service for the specified reference name.

Throws ComponentException – If the Service Component Runtime catches an exception while activating the bound service.

112.12.3.10   **public Object[] locateServices(String name)**

name The name of a reference as specified in a reference element in this component's description.

□ Returns the service objects for the specified reference name.

Returns An array of service objects for the referenced service or null if the reference cardinality is 0..1 or 0..n and no bound service is available. If the reference cardinality is 0..1 or 1..1 and a bound service is available, the array will have exactly one element.

Throws ComponentException – If the Service Component Runtime catches an exception while activating a bound service.

112.12.4   public class ComponentException extends RuntimeException

Unchecked exception which may be thrown by the Service Component Runtime.

112.12.4.1   **public ComponentException(String message, Throwable cause)**

message The message for the exception.

cause The cause of the exception. May be null.

□ Construct a new ComponentException with the specified message and cause.

112.12.4.2   **public ComponentException(String message)**

message The message for the exception.

□ Construct a new ComponentException with the specified message.

112.12.4.3   **public ComponentException(Throwable cause)**

cause The cause of the exception. May be null.

□ Construct a new ComponentException with the specified cause.

112.12.4.4   **public Throwable getCause( )**

□ Returns the cause of this exception or null if no cause was set.

Returns The cause of this exception or null if no cause was set.

112.12.4.5   **public Throwable initCause(Throwable cause)**

cause The cause of this exception.

□ Initializes the cause of this exception to the specified value.

Returns This exception.

Throws IllegalArgumentException – If the specified cause is this exception.

IllegalStateException – If the cause of this exception has already been set.

112.12.5   public interface ComponentFactory

When a component is declared with the factory attribute on its component element, the Service Component Runtime will register a Component Factory service to allow new component configurations to be created and activated rather than automatically creating and activating component configuration as necessary.

Concurrency Thread-safe

112.12.5.1   **public ComponentInstance newInstance(Dictionary properties)**

properties Additional properties for the component configuration or null if there are no additional properties.

    ❑ Create and activate a new component configuration. Additional properties may be provided for the component configuration.

Returns   A ComponentInstance object encapsulating the component instance of the component configuration. The component configuration has been activated and, if the component specifies a service element, the component instance has been registered as a service.

Throws   ComponentException – If the Service Component Runtime is unable to activate the component configuration.

112.12.6   public interface ComponentInstance

A ComponentInstance encapsulates a component instance of an activated component configuration. ComponentInstances are created whenever a component configuration is activated.

ComponentInstances are never reused. A new ComponentInstance object will be created when the component configuration is activated again.

Concurrency   Thread-safe

112.12.6.1   public void dispose( )

    ❑ Dispose of the component configuration for this component instance. The component configuration will be deactivated. If the component configuration has already been deactivated, this method does nothing.

112.12.6.2   public Object getInstance( )

    ❑ Returns the component instance of the activated component configuration.

Returns   The component instance or null if the component configuration has been deactivated.

112.13   References

[1]   *Automating Service Dependency Management in a Service-Oriented Component Model*
Humberto Cervantes, Richard S. Hall, Proceedings of the Sixth Component-Based Software Engineering Workshop, May 2003, pp. 91-96.
http://www.adele.imag.fr/Les.Publications/intConferences/CBSE2003Cer.pdf

[2]   *Service Binder*
Humberto Cervantes, Richard S. Hall, http://gravity.sourceforge.net/servicebinder

[3]   *Java Properties File*
http://java.sun.com/j2se/1.4.1/docs/api/java/util/Properties.html#load(java.io.InputStream)

[4]   *Extensible Markup Language (XML) 1.0*
http://www.w3.org/TR/REC-xml/

[5]   *Access Control Java Language Specification*
http://java.sun.com/docs/books/jls/second_edition/html/names.doc.html#104285

[6]   *OSGi XML Schemas*
http://www.osgi.org/Release4/XMLSchemas

113 Event Admin Service Specification

Version 1.2

113.1 Introduction

Nearly all the bundles in an OSGi framework must deal with events, either as an event publisher or as an event handler. So far, the preferred mechanism to disperse those events have been the service interface mechanism.

Dispatching events for a design related to X, usually involves a service of type XListener. However, this model does not scale well for fine grained events that must be dispatched to many different handlers. Additionally, the dynamic nature of the OSGi environment introduces several complexities because both event publishers and event handlers can appear and disappear at any time.

The Event Admin service provides an inter-bundle communication mechanism. It is based on a event *publish* and *subscribe* model, popular in many message based systems.

This specification defines the details for the participants in this event model.

113.1.1 Essentials

- *Simplifications* – The model must significantly simplify the process of programming an event source and an event handler.
- *Dependencies* – Handle the myriad of dependencies between event sources and event handlers for proper cleanup.
- *Synchronicity* – It must be possible to deliver events asynchronously or synchronously with the caller.
- *Event Window* – Only event handlers that are active when an event is published must receive this event, handlers that register later must not see the event.
- *Performance* – The event mechanism must impose minimal overhead in delivering events.
- *Selectivity* – Event listeners must only receive notifications for the event types for which they are interested
- *Reliability* – The Event Admin must ensure that events continue to be delivered regardless the quality of the event handlers.
- *Security* – Publishing and receiving events are sensitive operations that must be protected per event type.
- *Extensibility* – It must be possible to define new event types with their own data types.
- *Native Code* – Events must be able to be passed to native code or come from native code.
- *OSGi Events* – The OSGi Framework, as well as a number of OSGi services, already have number of its own events defined. For uniformity of processing, these have to be mapped into generic event types.

113.1.2 Entities

- *Event* – An Event object has a topic and a Dictionary object that contains the event properties. It is an immutable object.
- *Event Admin* – The service that provides the publish and subscribe model to Event Handlers and Event Publishers.

- *Event Handler* – A service that receives and handles Event objects.
- *Event Publisher* – A bundle that sends event through the Event Admin service.
- *Event Subscriber* – Another name for an Event Handler.
- *Topic* – The name of an Event type.
- *Event Properties* – The set of properties that is associated with an Event.

Figure 113.1   *The Event Admin service org.osgi.service.event package*

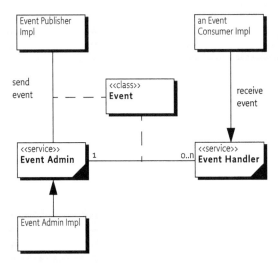

113.1.3   Synopsis

The Event Admin service provides a place for bundles to publish events, regardless of their destination. It is also used by Event Handlers to subscribe to specific types of events.

Events are published under a topic, together with a number of event properties. Event Handlers can specify a filter to control the Events they receive on a very fine grained basis.

113.1.4   What To Read

- *Architects* – The *Event Admin Architecture* on page 286 provides an overview of the Event Admin service.
- *Event Publishers* – The *Event Publisher* on page 289 provides an introduction of how to write an Event Publisher. The *Event Admin Architecture* on page 286 provides a good overview of the design.
- *Event Subscribers/Handlers* – The *Event Handler* on page 288 provides the rules on how to subscribe and handle events.

113.2   Event Admin Architecture

The Event Admin is based on the *Publish-Subscribe* pattern. This pattern decouples sources from their handlers by interposing an *event channel* between them. The publisher posts events to the channel, which identifies which handlers need to be notified and then takes care of the notification process. This model is depicted in Figure 113.2.

Figure 113.2   *Channel Pattern*

In this model, the event source and event handler are completely decoupled because neither has any direct knowledge of the other. The complicated logic of monitoring changes in the event publishers and event handlers is completely contained within the event channel. This is highly advantageous in an OSGi environment because it simplifies the process of both sending and receiving events.

113.3   The Event

Events have the following attributes:

- *Topic* – A topic that defines what happened. For example, when a bundle is started an event is published that has a topic of org/osgi/framework/BundleEvent/STARTED.
- *Properties* – Zero or more properties that contain additional information about the event. For example, the previous example event has a property of bundle.id which is set to a Long object, among other properties.

113.3.1   Topics

The topic of an event defines the *type* of the event. It is fairly granular in order to give handlers the opportunity to register for just the events they are interested in. When a topic is designed, its name should not include any other information, such as the publisher of the event or the data associated with the event, those parts are intended to be stored in the event properties.

The topic is intended to serve as a first-level filter for determining which handlers should receive the event. Event Admin service implementations use the structure of the topic to optimize the dispatching of the events to the handlers.

Topics are arranged in a hierarchical namespace. Each level is defined by a token and levels are separated by slashes. More precisely, the topic must conform to the following grammar:

```
topic ::= token ( '/' token ) *      // See 1.3.2 Core book
```

Topics should be designed to become more specific when going from left to right. Handlers can provide a prefix that matches a topic, using the preferred order allows a handler to minimize the number of prefixes it needs to register.

Topics are case-sensitive. As a convention, topics should follow the reverse domain name scheme used by Java packages to guarantee uniqueness. The separator must be slashes ('/' \u002F) instead of the dot ('.' \u002E).

This specification uses the convention fully/qualified/package/ClassName/ACTION. If necessary, a pseudo-class-name is used.

113.3.2   Properties

Information about the actual event is provided as properties. The property name is a case-sensitive string and the value can be any object. Although any Java object can be used as a property value, only String objects and the eight primitive types (plus their wrappers) should be used. Other types cannot be passed to handlers that reside external from the Java VM.

Another reason that arbitrary classes should not be used is the mutability of objects. If the values are not immutable, then any handler that receives the event could change the value. Any handlers that received the event subsequently would see the altered value and not the value as it was when the event was sent.

The topic of the event is available as a property with the key EVENT_TOPIC. This allows filters to include the topic as a condition if necessary.

113.4 Event Handler

Event handlers must be registered as services with the OSGi framework under the object class org.osgi.service.event.EventHandler.

Event handlers should be registered with a property (constant from the EventConstants class) EVENT_TOPIC. The value being a String or String[] object that describes which *topics* the handler is interested in. A wildcard ('*' \u002A) may be used as the last token of a topic name, for example com/action/*. This matches any topic that shares the same first tokens. For example, com/action/* matches com/action/listen.

Event Handlers which have not specified the EVENT_TOPIC service property must not receive events.

The value of each entry in the EVENT_TOPIC service registration property must conform to the following grammar:

```
topic-scope ::= '*' | ( topic '/*' ? )
```

Event handlers can also be registered with a service property named EVENT_FILTER. The value of this property must be a string containing a Framework filter specification. Any of the event's properties can be used in the filter expression.

```
event-filter ::= filter          // 3.2.7 Core book
```

Each Event Handler is notified for any event which belongs to the topics the handler has expressed an interest in. If the handler has defined a EVENT_FILTER service property then the event properties must also match the filter expression. If the filter is an error, then the Event Admin service should log a warning and further ignore the Event Handler.

For example, a bundle wants to see all Log Service events with a level of WARNING or ERROR, but it must ignore the INFO and DEBUG events. Additionally, the only events of interest are when the bundle symbolic name starts with com.acme.

```
public AcmeWatchDog implements BundleActivator,
     EventHandler {
  final static String [] topics = new String[] {
     "org/osgi/service/log/LogEntry/LOG_WARNING",
     "org/osgi/service/log/LogEntry/LOG_ERROR" };

  public void start(BundleContext context) {
     Dictionary d = new Hashtable();
     d.put(EventConstants.EVENT_TOPIC, topics );
     d.put(EventConstants.EVENT_FILTER,
       "(bundle.symbolicName=com.acme.*)" );
     context.registerService( EventHandler.class.getName(),
       this, d );
  }
  public void stop( BundleContext context) {}

  public void handleEvent(Event event ) {
     //...
```

```
    }
  }
```

If there are multiple Event Admin services registered with the Framework then all Event Admin services must send their published events to all registered Event Handlers.

113.5   Event Publisher

To fire an event, the event source must retrieve the Event Admin service from the OSGi service registry. Then it creates the event object and calls one of the Event Admin service's methods to fire the event either synchronously or asynchronously.

The following example is a class that publishes a time event every 60 seconds.

```
public class TimerEvent extends Thread
  implements BundleActivator {
  Hashtable          time = new Hashtable();
  ServiceTracker     tracker;

  public TimerEvent() { super("TimerEvent"); }

  public void start(BundleContext context ) {
    tracker = new ServiceTracker(context,
      EventAdmin.class.getName(), null );
    tracker.open();
    start();
  }

  public void stop( BundleContext context ) {
    interrupt();
    tracker.close();
  }

  public void run() {
      while ( ! Thread.interrupted() ) try {
        Calendar   c = Calendar.getInstance();
        set(c,Calendar.MINUTE,"minutes");
        set(c,Calendar.HOUR,"hours");
        set(c,Calendar.DAY_OF_MONTH,"day");
        set(c,Calendar.MONTH,"month");
        set(c,Calendar.YEAR,"year");

        EventAdmin ea =
          (EventAdmin) tracker.getService();
        if ( ea != null )
          ea.sendEvent(new Event("com/acme/timer",
            time ));
        Thread.sleep(60000-c.get(Calendar.SECOND)*1000);
      } catch( InterruptedException e ) {
        // ignore, treated by while loop
      }
  }

  void set( Calendar c, int field, String key ) {
    time.put( key, new Integer(c.get(field)) );
  }
```

}

113.6   Specific Events

113.6.1   General Conventions

Some handlers are more interested in the contents of an event rather than what actually happened. For example, a handler wants to be notified whenever an Exception is thrown anywhere in the system. Both Framework Events and Log Entry events may contain an exception that would be of interest to this hypothetical handler. If both Framework Events and Log Entries use the same property names then the handler can access the Exception in exactly the same way. If some future event type follows the same conventions then the handler can receive and process the new event type even though it had no knowledge of it when it was compiled.

The following properties are suggested as conventions. When new event types are defined they should use these names with the corresponding types and values where appropriate. These values should be set only if they are not null

A list of these property names can be found in Table 113.1..

Table 113.1   General property names for events

Name	Type	Notes
BUNDLE_SIGNER	String | Collection \<String\>	A bundle's signers DN
BUNDLE_VERSION	Version	A bundle's version
BUNDLE_SYMBOLICNAME	String	A bundle's symbolic name
EVENT	Object	The actual event object. Used when rebroadcasting an event that was sent via some other event mechanism
EXCEPTION	Throwable	An exception or error
EXCEPTION_MESSAGE	String	Must be equal to exception.getMessage().
EXCEPTION_CLASS	String	Must be equal to the name of the Exception class.
MESSAGE	String	A human-readable message that is usually not localized.
SERVICE	Service Reference	A Service Reference
SERVICE_ID	Long	A service's id
SERVICE_OBJECTCLASS	String[]	A service's objectClass
SERVICE_PID	String	A service's persistent identity
TIMESTAMP	Long	The time when the event occurred, as reported by System.currentTimeMillis()

The topic of an OSGi event is constructed by taking the fully qualified name of the event class, substituting a slash for every period, and appending a slash followed by the name of the constant that defines the event type. For example, the topic of

    BundleEvent.STARTED

Event becomes

    org/osgi/framework/BundleEvent/STARTED

If a type code for the event is unknown then the event must be ignored.

113.6.2 OSGi Events

In order to present a consistent view of all the events occurring in the system, the existing Framework-level events are mapped to the Event Admin's publish-subscribe model. This allows event subscribers to treat framework events exactly the same as other events.

It is the responsibility of the Event Admin service implementation to map these Framework events to its queue.

The properties associated with the event depends on its class as outlined in the following sections.

113.6.3 Framework Event

Framework Events must be delivered asynchronously with a topic of:

```
org/osgi/framework/FrameworkEvent/<event type>
```

The following event types are supported:

```
STARTED
ERROR
PACKAGES_REFRESHED
STARTLEVEL_CHANGED
WARNING
INFO
```

Other events are ignored, no event will be send by the Event Admin. The following event properties must be set for a Framework Event.

- event – (FrameworkEvent) The original event object.

If the FrameworkEvent getBundle method returns a non-null value, the following fields must be set:

- bundle.id – (Long) The source's bundle id.
- bundle.symbolicName – (String) The source bundle's symbolic name. Only set if the bundle's symbolic name is not null.
- bundle – (Bundle) The source bundle.

If the FrameworkEvent getThrowable method returns a non-null value:

- exception.class – (String) The fully-qualified class name of the attached Exception.
- exception.message –(String) The message of the attached exception. Only set if the Exception message is not null.
- exception – (Throwable) The Exception returned by the getThrowable method.

113.6.4 Bundle Event

Framework Events must be delivered asynchronously with a topic of:

```
org/osgi/framework/BundleEvent/<event type>
```

The following event types are supported:

```
INSTALLED
STARTED
STOPPED
UPDATED
UNINSTALLED
RESOLVED
UNRESOLVED
```

Unknown events must be ignored.

The following event properties must be set for a Bundle Event. If listeners require synchronous delivery then they should register a Synchronous Bundle Listener with the Framework.

- event – (BundleEvent) The original event object.
- bundle.id – (Long) The source's bundle id.
- bundle.symbolicName – (String) The source bundle's symbolic name. Only set if the bundle's symbolic name is not null.
- bundle – (Bundle) The source bundle.

113.6.5   Service Event

Service Events must be delivered asynchronously with the topic:

    org/osgi/framework/ServiceEvent/<event type>

The following event types are supported:

    REGISTERED
    MODIFIED
    UNREGISTERING

Unknown events must be ignored.

- event – (ServiceEvent) The original Service Event object.
- service – (ServiceReference) The result of the getServiceReference method
- service.id – (Long) The service's ID.
- service.pid – (String) The service's persistent identity. Only set if not null.
- service.objectClass – (String[]) The service's object class.

113.6.6   Other Event Sources

Several OSGi service specifications define their own event model. It is the responsibility of these services to map their events to Event Admin events. Event Admin is seen as a core service that will be present in most devices. However, if there is no Event Admin service present, applications are not mandated to buffer events.

113.7   Event Admin Service

The Event Admin service must be registered as a service with the object class org.osgi.service.event.EventAdmin. Multiple Event Admin services can be registered. Publishers should publish their event on the Event Admin service with the highest value for the SERVICE_RANKING service property. This is the service selected by the getServiceReference method.

The Event Admin service is responsible for tracking the registered handlers, handling event notifications and providing at least one thread for asynchronous event delivery.

113.7.1   Synchronous Event Delivery

Synchronous event delivery is initiated by the sendEvent method. When this method is invoked, the Event Admin service determines which handlers must be notified of the event and then notifies each one in turn. The handlers can be notified in the caller's thread or in an event-delivery thread, depending on the implementation. In either case, all notifications must be completely handled before the sendEvent method returns to the caller.

Synchronous event delivery is significantly more expensive than asynchronous delivery. All things considered equal, the asynchronous delivery should be preferred over the synchronous delivery.

Callers of this method will need to be coded defensively and assume that synchronous event notifications could be handled in a separate thread. That entails that they must not be holding any monitors when they invoke the sendEvent method. Otherwise they significantly increase the likelihood of deadlocks because Java monitors are not reentrant from another thread by definition. Not holding monitors is good practice even when the event is dispatched in the same thread.

113.7.2   Asynchronous Event Delivery

Asynchronous event delivery is initiated by the postEvent method. When this method is invoked, the Event Admin service must determine which handlers are interested in the event. By collecting this list of handlers during the method invocation, the Event Admin service ensures that only handlers that were registered at the time the event was posted will receive the event notification. This is the same as described in *Delivering Events* on page 116 of the Core specification.

The Event Admin service can use more than one thread to deliver events. If it does then it must guarantee that each handler receives the events in the same order as the events were posted. This ensures that handlers see events in the expected order. For example, it would be an error to see a destroyed event before the corresponding created event.

Before notifying each handler, the event delivery thread must ensure that the handler is still registered in the service registry. If it has been unregistered then the handler must not be notified.

The Event Admin service ensures that events are delivered in a well-defined order. For example, if a thread posts events A and B in the same thread then the handlers should not receive them in the order B, A. if A and B are posted by different threads at about the same time then no guarantees about the order of delivery are made.

113.7.3   Order of Event Delivery

Asynchronous events are delivered in the order in which they arrive in the event queue. Thus if two events are posted by the same thread then they will be delivered in the same order (though other events may come between them). However, if two or more events are posted by different threads then the order in which they arrive in the queue (and therefore the order in which they are delivered) will depend very much on subtle timing issues. The event delivery system cannot make any guarantees in this case.

Synchronous events are delivered as soon as they are sent. If two events are sent by the same thread, one after the other, then they must be guaranteed to be processed serially and in the same order. However, if two events are sent by different threads then no guarantees can be made. The events can be processed in parallel or serially, depending on whether or not the Event Admin service dispatches synchronous events in the caller's thread or in a separate thread.

Note that if the actions of a handler trigger a synchronous event, then the delivery of the first event will be paused and delivery of the second event will begin. Once delivery of the second event has completed, delivery of the first event will resume. Thus some handlers may observe the second event before they observe the first one.

113.8   Reliability

113.8.1   Exceptions in callbacks

If a handler throws an Exception during delivery of an event, it must be caught by the Event Admin service and handled in some implementation specific way. If a Log Service is available the exception should be logged. Once the exception has been caught and dealt with, the event delivery must continue with the next handlers to be notified, if any.

113.8.2   Dealing with Stalled Handlers

Event handlers should not spend too long in the handleEvent method. Doing so will prevent other handlers in the system from being notified. If a handler needs to do something that can take a while, it should do it in a different thread.

An event admin implementation can attempt to detect stalled or deadlocked handlers and deal with them appropriately. Exactly how it deals with this situation is left as implementation specific. One allowed implementation is to mark the current event delivery thread as invalid and spawn a new event delivery thread. Event delivery must resume with the next handler to be notified.

Implementations can choose to blacklist any handlers that they determine are misbehaving. Blacklisted handlers must not be notified of any events. If a handler is blacklisted, the event admin should log a message that explains the reason for it.

113.9   Inter-operability with Native Applications

Implementations of the Event Admin service can support passing events to, and/or receiving events from native applications.

If the implementation supports native inter-operability, it must be able to pass the topic of the event and its properties to/from native code. Implementations must be able to support property values of the following types:

- String objects, including full Unicode support
- Integer, Long, Byte, Short, Float, Double, Boolean, Character objects
- Single-dimension arrays of the above types (including String)
- Single-dimension arrays of Java's eight primitive types (int, long, byte, short, float, double, boolean, char)

Implementations can support additional types. Property values of unsupported types must be silently discarded.

113.10   Security

113.10.1   Topic Permission

The TopicPermission class allows fine-grained control over which bundles may post events to a given topic and which bundles may receive those events.

The target parameter for the permission is the topic name. TopicPermission classes uses a wildcard matching algorithm similar to the BasicPermission class, except that slashes are used as separators instead of periods. For example, a name of a/b/* implies a/b/c but not x/y/z or a/b.

There are two available actions: PUBLISH and SUBSCRIBE. These control a bundle's ability to either publish or receive events, respectively. Neither one implies the other.

113.10.2   Required Permissions

Bundles that need to register an event handler must be granted ServicePermission[org.osgi.service.event.EventHandler, REGISTER]. In addition, handlers require TopicPermission[<topic>, SUBSCRIBE] for each topic they want to be notified about.

Bundles that need to publish an event must be granted ServicePermission[org.osgi.service.event.EventAdmin, GET] so that they may retrieve the Event Admin service and use it. In addition, event sources require TopicPermission[<topic>, PUBLISH] for each topic they want to send events to.

Bundles that need to iterate the handlers registered with the system must be granted ServicePermission[org.osgi.service.event.EventHandler, GET] to retrieve the event handlers from the service registry.

Only a bundle that contains an Event Admin service implementation should be granted ServicePermission[org.osgi.service.event.EventAdmin, REGISTER] to register the event channel admin service.

113.10.3 Security Context During Event Callbacks

During an event notification, the Event Admin service's Protection Domain will be on the stack above the handler's Protection Domain. In the case of a synchronous event, the event publisher's protection domain can also be on the stack.

Therefore, if a handler needs to perform a secure operation using its own privileges, it must invoke the doPrivileged method to isolate its security context from that of its caller.

The event delivery mechanism must not wrap event notifications in a doPrivileged call.

113.11 Changes

- Made it more clear that the Event Admin service is not responsible for mapping other service's events to the queue.
- Added a new constant BUNDLE_VERSION
- The Bundle signers event property is returned as a collection of String.
- Event topics can now be String or String[]

113.12 org.osgi.service.event

Event Admin Package Version 1.2.

Bundles wishing to use this package must list the package in the Import-Package header of the bundle's manifest. For example:

Import-Package: org.osgi.service.event; version="[1.2,2.0)"

113.12.1 Summary

- *Event* - An event.
- *EventAdmin* - The Event Admin service.
- *EventConstants* - Defines standard names for EventHandler properties.
- *EventHandler* - Listener for Events.
- *TopicPermission* - A bundle's authority to publish or subscribe to event on a topic.

113.12.2 public class Event

An event. Event objects are delivered to EventHandler services which subscribe to the topic of the event.

Concurrency Immutable

113.12.2.1 public Event(String topic, Map properties)

topic The topic of the event.

properties The event's properties (may be null). A property whose key is not of type String will be ignored.

□ Constructs an event.

Throws IllegalArgumentException – If topic is not a valid topic name.

Since 1.2

113.12.2.2   **public Event(String topic, Dictionary properties)**

topic The topic of the event.

properties The event's properties (may be null). A property whose key is not of type String will be ignored.

☐ Constructs an event.

Throws IllegalArgumentException – If topic is not a valid topic name.

113.12.2.3   **public boolean equals(Object object)**

object The Event object to be compared.

☐ Compares this Event object to another object.

An event is considered to be **equal to** another event if the topic is equal and the properties are equal.

Returns true if object is a Event and is equal to this object; false otherwise.

113.12.2.4   **public final Object getProperty(String name)**

name the name of the property to retrieve

☐ Retrieves a property.

Returns The value of the property, or null if not found.

113.12.2.5   **public final String[] getPropertyNames( )**

☐ Returns a list of this event's property names.

Returns A non-empty array with one element per property.

113.12.2.6   **public final String getTopic( )**

☐ Returns the topic of this event.

Returns The topic of this event.

113.12.2.7   **public int hashCode( )**

☐ Returns a hash code value for the object.

Returns An integer which is a hash code value for this object.

113.12.2.8   **public final boolean matches(Filter filter)**

filter The filter to test.

☐ Tests this event's properties against the given filter using a case sensitive match.

Returns true If this event's properties match the filter, false otherwise.

113.12.2.9   **public String toString( )**

☐ Returns the string representation of this event.

Returns The string representation of this event.

113.12.3   public interface EventAdmin

The Event Admin service. Bundles wishing to publish events must obtain the Event Admin service and call one of the event delivery methods.

Concurrency Thread-safe

113.12.3.1   **public void postEvent(Event event)**

event The event to send to all listeners which subscribe to the topic of the event.

☐ Initiate asynchronous delivery of an event. This method returns to the caller before delivery of the event is completed.

Throws SecurityException – If the caller does not have TopicPermission[topic,PUBLISH] for the topic specified in the event.

113.12.3.2   public void sendEvent(Event event)

event The event to send to all listeners which subscribe to the topic of the event.

□ Initiate synchronous delivery of an event. This method does not return to the caller until delivery of the event is completed.

Throws SecurityException – If the caller does not have TopicPermission[topic,PUBLISH] for the topic specified in the event.

113.12.4   public interface EventConstants

Defines standard names for EventHandler properties.

113.12.4.1   public static final String BUNDLE = "bundle"

The Bundle object of the bundle relevant to the event. The type of the value for this event property is Bundle.

Since 1.1

113.12.4.2   public static final String BUNDLE_ID = "bundle.id"

The Bundle id of the bundle relevant to the event. The type of the value for this event property is Long.

Since 1.1

113.12.4.3   public static final String BUNDLE_SIGNER = "bundle.signer"

The Distinguished Names of the signers of the bundle relevant to the event. The type of the value for this event property is String or Collection of String.

113.12.4.4   public static final String BUNDLE_SYMBOLICNAME = "bundle.symbolicName"

The Bundle Symbolic Name of the bundle relevant to the event. The type of the value for this event property is String.

113.12.4.5   public static final String BUNDLE_VERSION = "bundle.version"

The version of the bundle relevant to the event. The type of the value for this event property is Version.

Since 1.2

113.12.4.6   public static final String EVENT = "event"

The forwarded event object. Used when rebroadcasting an event that was sent via some other event mechanism. The type of the value for this event property is Object.

113.12.4.7   public static final String EVENT_FILTER = "event.filter"

Service Registration property (named event.filter) specifying a filter to further select Event s of interest to a Event Handler service.

Event handlers MAY be registered with this property. The value of this property is a string containing an LDAP-style filter specification. Any of the event's properties may be used in the filter expression. Each event handler is notified for any event which belongs to the topics in which the handler has expressed an interest. If the event handler is also registered with this service property, then the properties of the event must also match the filter for the event to be delivered to the event handler.

If the filter syntax is invalid, then the Event Handler must be ignored and a warning should be logged.

See Also Event, Filter

113.12.4.8   **public static final String EVENT_TOPIC = "event.topics"**

Service registration property (named event.topics) specifying the Event topics of interest to a Event Handler service.

Event handlers SHOULD be registered with this property. The value of the property is a string or an array of strings that describe the topics in which the handler is interested. An asterisk ('*') may be used as a trailing wildcard. Event Handlers which do not have a value for this property must not receive events. More precisely, the value of each string must conform to the following grammar:

```
topic-description := '*' | topic ( '/*' )?
topic := token ( '/' token )*
```

See Also Event

113.12.4.9   **public static final String EXCEPTION = "exception"**

An exception or error. The type of the value for this event property is Throwable.

113.12.4.10   **public static final String EXCEPTION_CLASS = "exception.class"**

The name of the exception type. Must be equal to the name of the class of the exception in the event property EXCEPTION. The type of the value for this event property is String.

Since 1.1

113.12.4.11   **public static final String EXCEPTION_MESSAGE = "exception.message"**

The exception message. Must be equal to the result of calling getMessage() on the exception in the event property EXCEPTION. The type of the value for this event property is String.

113.12.4.12   **public static final String EXECPTION_CLASS = "exception.class"**

This constant was released with an incorrectly spelled name. It has been replaced by EXCEPTION_CLASS

Deprecated As of 1.1, replaced by EXCEPTION_CLASS

113.12.4.13   **public static final String MESSAGE = "message"**

A human-readable message that is usually not localized. The type of the value for this event property is String.

113.12.4.14   **public static final String SERVICE = "service"**

A service reference. The type of the value for this event property is ServiceReference.

113.12.4.15   **public static final String SERVICE_ID = "service.id"**

A service's id. The type of the value for this event property is Long.

113.12.4.16   **public static final String SERVICE_OBJECTCLASS = "service.objectClass"**

A service's objectClass. The type of the value for this event property is String[].

113.12.4.17   **public static final String SERVICE_PID = "service.pid"**

A service's persistent identity. The type of the value for this event property is String.

113.12.4.18   **public static final String TIMESTAMP = "timestamp"**

The time when the event occurred, as reported by System.currentTimeMillis(). The type of the value for this event property is Long.

113.12.5   public interface EventHandler

Listener for Events.

EventHandler objects are registered with the Framework service registry and are notified with an Event object when an event is sent or posted.

EventHandler objects can inspect the received Event object to determine its topic and properties.

EventHandler objects must be registered with a service property EventConstants.EVENT_TOPIC whose value is the list of topics in which the event handler is interested.

For example:

```
String[] topics = new String[] {"com/isv/*"};
Hashtable ht = new Hashtable();
ht.put(EventConstants.EVENT_TOPIC, topics);
context.registerService(EventHandler.class.getName(), this, ht);
```

Event Handler services can also be registered with an EventConstants.EVENT_FILTER service property to further filter the events. If the syntax of this filter is invalid, then the Event Handler must be ignored by the Event Admin service. The Event Admin service should log a warning.

Security Considerations. Bundles wishing to monitor Event objects will require ServicePermission[EventHandler,REGISTER] to register an EventHandler service. The bundle must also have TopicPermission[topic,SUBSCRIBE] for the topic specified in the event in order to receive the event.

See Also Event

Concurrency Thread-safe

113.12.5.1   public void handleEvent(Event event)

event The event that occurred.

□ Called by the EventAdmin service to notify the listener of an event.

113.12.6   public final class TopicPermission
extends Permission

A bundle's authority to publish or subscribe to event on a topic.

A topic is a slash-separated string that defines a topic.

For example:

```
org / osgi / service / foo / FooEvent / ACTION
```

TopicPermission has two actions: publish and subscribe.

Concurrency Thread-safe

113.12.6.1   public static final String PUBLISH = "publish"

The action string publish.

113.12.6.2   public static final String SUBSCRIBE = "subscribe"

The action string subscribe.

113.12.6.3   public TopicPermission(String name, String actions)

name Topic name.

actions publish,subscribe (canonical order).

□ Defines the authority to publich and/or subscribe to a topic within the EventAdmin service.

The name is specified as a slash-separated string. Wildcards may be used. For example:

```
org/osgi/service/fooFooEvent/ACTION
com/isv/*
*
```

A bundle that needs to publish events on a topic must have the appropriate TopicPermission for that topic; similarly, a bundle that needs to subscribe to events on a topic must have the appropriate TopicPermssion for that topic.

113.12.6.4   public boolean equals(Object obj)

obj   The object to test for equality with this TopicPermission object.

☐   Determines the equality of two TopicPermission objects. This method checks that specified TopicPermission has the same topic name and actions as this TopicPermission object.

Returns   true if obj is a TopicPermission, and has the same topic name and actions as this TopicPermission object; false otherwise.

113.12.6.5   public String getActions( )

☐   Returns the canonical string representation of the TopicPermission actions.

Always returns present TopicPermission actions in the following order: publish,subscribe.

Returns   Canonical string representation of the TopicPermission actions.

113.12.6.6   public int hashCode( )

☐   Returns the hash code value for this object.

Returns   A hash code value for this object.

113.12.6.7   public boolean implies(Permission p)

p   The target permission to interrogate.

☐   Determines if the specified permission is implied by this object.

This method checks that the topic name of the target is implied by the topic name of this object. The list of TopicPermission actions must either match or allow for the list of the target object to imply the target TopicPermission action.

```
x/y/*,"publish" -> x/y/z,"publish" is true
*,"subscribe" -> x/y,"subscribe"   is true
*,"publish" -> x/y,"subscribe"     is false
x/y,"publish" -> x/y/z,"publish"   is false
```

Returns   true if the specified TopicPermission action is implied by this object; false otherwise.

113.12.6.8   public PermissionCollection newPermissionCollection( )

☐   Returns a new PermissionCollection object suitable for storing TopicPermission objects.

Returns   A new PermissionCollection object.

114 Deployment Admin Specification

Version 1.1

114.1 Introduction

The ability to install new software components after the time of manufacture is of increasing interest to manufacturers, operators, and end users. End users already are, or soon will be, accustomed to installing applications or services on their devices from remote servers.

The OSGi Service Platform provides mechanisms to manage the lifecycle of bundles, configuration objects, and permission objects, but the overall consistency of the runtime configuration is the responsibility of the *management agent*. In other words, the management agent decides to install, update, or uninstall bundles, create or delete configuration or permission objects, and manage other resource types.

The task of the management agent is extensive because it must track the sometimes fine-grained dependencies and constraints between the different resource types. This model, though extremely flexible, leaves many details up to the implementation—significantly hindering the inter-operability of devices because it does not unify the management aspects from the management systems point of view. This specification, therefore, introduces the *Deployment Admin service* that standardizes the access to some of the responsibilities of the management agent: that is, the life-cycle management of interlinked resources on an OSGi Service Platform.The role of the Deployment Admin service is depicted in Figure 114.1.

Figure 114.1 *Deployment Admin role*

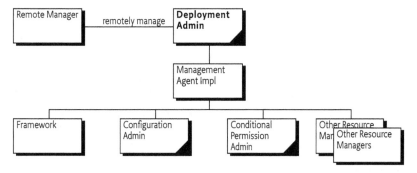

114.1.1 Essentials

- *Installing/Uninstalling* – Provide a Deployment Package concept to install and uninstall bundles and related resources on an OSGi Service Platform as an atomic unit.
- *Tamper Detection* – Provide detection of changes to a Deployment Package.
- *Securing* – Provide a security model that allows Operators to control the Deployment Packages that are installed on an OSGi Service Platform.
- *Media Independence* – Deployment Packages must have the capacity to load from different media such as CD-ROM, over the air, wireless, etc.

- *Management* – Management of a repository of Deployment Packages must be possible locally on the device as well as remotely.
- *Customizing* – The author of a Deployment Package must be permitted to customize the environment during the installation and uninstallation operations.
- *Extending* – The resource types that are used in a Deployment Package must be easy to extend.

114.1.2 Entities

- *Resource* – A file in a Deployment Package that is processed to create artifacts in the Service Platform. For example, bundles, configurations, and permissions are different resources.
- *Deployment Admin Service* – The service that is used to install and uninstall Deployment Packages, as well as to provide information about the repository of Deployment Packages.
- *Resource Processor* – A service that can handle the lifecycle of a specific resource type. It processes a resource to create a number of artifacts that are removed when the resource is dropped.
- *Deployment Package* – A group of resources that must be treated as a unit. Unbreakable dependencies exist among these resources.
- *Artifact* – A construct that is created from a Resource in a Deployment Package. A resource can have zero or more artifacts related to it. Artifacts do not have a common interface because their nature differs and their existence is abstracted by the Resource Processor services. Artifacts must be removed when their related resources are dropped. An example of an artifact is a Configuration object that is created from an configuration file in a Deployment Package.
- *Customizer* – A bundle carried in a Deployment Package that can perform initialization during an install operation and cleanup during an uninstall operation.
- *Fix Package* – A Deployment Package that is an update to an resident Deployment Package, which does not carry some resources because they are unchanged.

Figure 114.2   *Deployment Admin Service, org.osgi.service.deploymentadmin package*

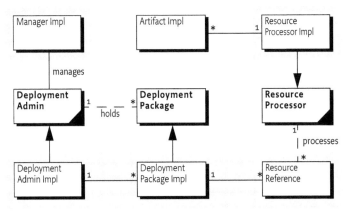

114.1.3 Synopsis

A developer can package a number of resources in a Deployment Package. A Deployment Package is stored in a JAR file, with a format that is similar to bundles. A Deployment Package JAR can be installed via the Deployment Admin service via an input stream. The Deployment Admin service manages the bundle resources itself, but processes every other resource in the Deployment Package by handing them off to a Resource Processor service that is designated for that resource. The Resource Processor service will then process the resource to create a number of artifacts.

The uninstallation and update of a Deployment Package works in a similar manner. All Resource Processor services are notified about any resources that are dropped or changed.

If all resources have been processed, the changes are committed. If an operation on the Deployment Admin service fails, all changes are rolled back. The Deployment Admin service is not, however, guaranteed to support all features of transactions.

114.2   Deployment Package

A Deployment Package is a set of related *resources* that need to be managed as a *unit* rather than individual pieces. For example, a Deployment Package can contain both a bundle and its configuration data. The resources of a Deployment Package are tightly coupled to the Deployment Package and cannot be shared with other Deployment Packages.

A Deployment Package is not a script that brings the system from one consistent state to another; several deployment packages may be needed to achieve a new consistent state. Like a bundle, a Deployment Package does not have to be self-contained. Its bundle resources can have dependencies on Java packages and services provided by other Deployment Packages.

For example, a suite of games shares some parts that are common to both games. The suite contains two games: Chess (com.acme.chess) and Backgammon (com.acme.backg). Both share a top-score database as well as a 3D graphic library.

- com.third.3d – The 3D graphic library comes from a third-party provider. It is a Deployment Package of its own, composed of several bundles and possible configuration objects.
- com.acme.score – The top-score database would also be its own Deployment Package, and would in fact be optional. It offers a service for storing top scores, but games can function without this service.

Each game is a Deployment Package, allowing them to be installed independently. Alternatively, the two games can be packaged into the same Deployment Package, but in this case they must be installed and removed together and can no longer be deployed independently.

These two different packaging strategies cannot be used simultaneously. Once the games are deployed separately, they can no longer be grouped later in an update, because that action would move ownership of the bundle resource to another Deployment Package—which is specifically not allowed. A bundle resource can belong to only one Deployment Package.

These two packaging scenarios are depicted in Figure 114.3.

Figure 114.3   *Packaged game*

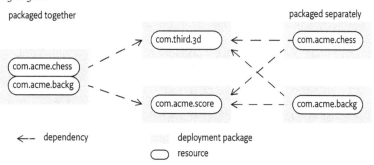

Deployment Packages are managed as *first-class citizens* during runtime, similar to bundles. The DeploymentPackage object represents this concept in runtime.

114.2.1   Resources

A Deployment Package consists of installable *resources*. Resources are described in the *Name sections* of the Manifest. They are stored in the JAR file under a path. This path is called the *resource id*.

Subsets of these resources are the bundles. Bundles are treated differently from the other resources by the Deployment Admin service. Non-bundle resources are called *processed resources*.

Bundles are managed by the Deployment Admin service directly. When installing a new bundle, the Deployment Admin service must set the bundle location to the following URL:

```
location    ::= 'osgi-dp:' bsn
bsn         ::= unique-name     // See 1.3.2 Core
```

The bsn stands for the bundle's Bundle Symbolic Name, without any parameters, which implies that only a single version of a bundle can be installed at any moment in time. The osgi-dp: scheme is not required to have a valid URL handler.

Processed resources are not managed directly by the Deployment Admin service; their management must be handed off to a Resource Processor service that is selected in the Name section. The logical structure and processing of resources is depicted in Figure 114.4.

Figure 114.4   *Structure of a Deployment Package*

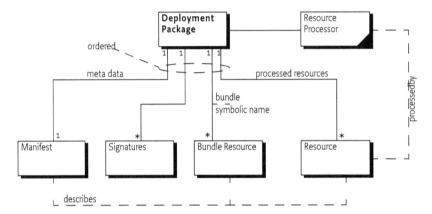

114.2.2   Atomicity and Sharing

A Deployment Package is a reified concept, like a bundle, in an OSGi Service Platform. It is created and managed by the Deployment Admin service. As a unit, a Deployment Package should be installed or uninstalled atomically.

Deployment packages provide an ownership model for resources installed in an OSGi Service Platform. A Deployment Package contains resources, which once processed, will result in the creation of a number of artifacts in the OSGi Platform such as:

- Installed bundles
- Configuration objects
- System properties
- Certificates
- Wiring schemes

A Deployment Package will *own* its resources. If a Deployment Package is uninstalled, all its resources, and thus its artifacts, must be removed as well. The ownership model follows a *no-sharing* principle: equal resources are not shared between deployment packages.

The meaning of "equal" is dependent on the resource type. For example, two bundles are considered equal if their bundle symbolic name is equal, regardless of the version.

A sharing violation must be considered an error. The install or update of the offending Deployment Package must fail if a resource would be affected by another Deployment Package. The verification of this rule is delegated to the Resource Processor services, or the Deployment Admin service in case of bundles.

For example, a Deployment Package could be used to install bundles and configuration objects for Managed Services (singleton configurations). Because of the no-sharing principle, an installed bundle must belong to one—and only one—Deployment Package (as defined by its Bundle Symbolic Name). A singleton configuration can be set only when the associated bundle is in the same Deployment Package. Trying to install a Deployment Package when one of the bundles or one of the configuration objects is already present and associated with another Deployment Package is an error, and the install must fail in such a case.

This strong no-sharing rule ensures a clean and robust lifecycle. It allows the simple cleanup rule: the Deployment Package that installs a resource is the one that must uninstall it.

114.2.3 Naming

Every Deployment Package must have a name and a version. Package authors should use unique reverse domain naming, like the naming used for Java packages. The version syntax must follow the rules defined in *Version* on page 32 in [2] *OSGi Service Platform Core Specification*; the version must be specified.

The name is set with a Manifest header. This name is used to detect whether an install is an update (an Deployment Package has the given name) or an install (no such Deployment Package exists). The name must be compared in a case-sensitive manner.

Together, the name and version specify a unique Deployment Package; a device will consider any Deployment Package with the same name and version pairs to be identical. Installing a Deployment Package with a name version identical to the existing Deployment Package must not result in any actions.

Deployment packages with the same name but different versions are considered to be *versions* of the *same* deployment package. The Deployment Admin service maintains a repository of installed Deployment Packages. This set must not contain multiple versions of the same Deployment Package. Installing a deployment package when a prior or later version was already present must cause replacement of the existing deployment package. In terms of version, this action can be either an upgrade or downgrade.

114.3 File Format

A Deployment Package is a standard JAR file as specified in [1] *JAR File Specification*. The extension of a Deployment Package JAR file name should be .dp. The MIME type of a Deployment Package JAR should be:

```
application/vnd.osgi.dp
```

For example, valid Deployment Package JAR names are:

```
com.acme.chess.dp
chess.dp
```

A Deployment Package must be formed in such a way that it can be read with a JarInputStream object. Therefore, the order of the files in the JAR file is important. The order must be:

1 META-INF/MANIFEST.MF – A Deployment Package must begin with a standard Java Manifest file. This rule is not explicitly defined in the Java JAR file specification; it is implied, however, by the known JarInputStream class implementations.
2 META-INF/*.SF, META-INF/*.DSA, META-INF/*.RS – If the Deployment Package is signed, subsequent files in the JAR must be the signature files as defined in the manifest specification. The sig-

nature files are not considered resources. Signing is discussed in *Signing* on page 306.

3   *Localization files* – Any manifest localization files are normally stored in the OSGI-INF directory. Localization files must precede the other files because the resource processors can require localized information.

4   *Bundles* must come before any other resource types so that they can be installed before any processed resources.

5   *Resources* – Any processed resources needed for this package. Resources are processed in the order in which they appear in the JAR file, and dropped in reverse order.

The order of all the resources in the JAR file is significant, and is called the *resource order*. The purpose of the resource order is to allow the JAR to be processed as a stream. It is not necessary to buffer the input stream in memory or to hard disk, or to allow random access to its contents. The specification allows access to the stream sequentially. To increase the determinism, the resource order must also determine the processing order of the bundles and the resources.

The format is shown graphically in Figure 114.5.

Figure 114.5   *Deployment Package JAR format*

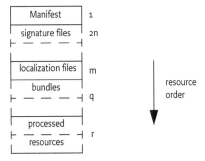

114.3.1   Signing

Deployment packages are optionally signed by JAR signing, compatible with the operation of the standard java.util.jar.JarInputStream class, i.e. as defined in *JAR Structure and Manifest* on page 13 of [2] *OSGi Service Platform Core Specification*. This compatibility requires that the manifest must be the first file in the input stream, and the signature files must follow directly thereafter.

A Deployment Package must follow the same rules for signing as bundles, described in the Framework specification, *Digitally Signed JAR Files* on page 12 in [2] *OSGi Service Platform Core Specification*.

The Deployment Admin service must reject a Deployment Package that has an invalid signature.

114.3.2   Path Names

Path names must be limited to remove some of the unnecessary complexities that are caused by path names that can contain any Unicode character. Therefore, a path name must not contain any character except:

    [A-Za-z0-9_.-]

Directories are separated by a forward slash character ('/' \u002F).

114.3.3   Deployment Package Manifest

The Manifest of a Deployment Package consists of a *global section* and separate sections for each resource contained within it, called the *Name sections*. The global section of a Deployment Package Manifest can contain the following headers that have a defined meaning in this specification:

- DeploymentPackage-SymbolicName – The name of the deployment package as a reverse domain name. For example, com.acme.chess. See further *DeploymentPackage-SymbolicName* on page 308.
- DeploymentPackage-Version – The version of the deployment package as defined in [2] *OSGi Service Platform Core Specification.* See further *DeploymentPackage-Version* on page 309.
- DeploymentPackage-FixPack – Marks this deployment package as a partial update to a resident deployment package. See *Fix Package* on page 312.

The following headers provide information about the Deployment Package, but are not interpreted by the Deployment Admin service.

- *DeploymentPackage-Name* – A human readable of this deployment package. This name can be localized.
- *DeploymentPackage-Copyright* – Specifies the copyright statement for this Deployment Package.
- *DeploymentPackage-ContactAddress* – How to contact the vendor/developer of this Deployment Package.
- *DeploymentPackage-Description* – A short description of this Deployment Package.
- *DeploymentPackage-DocURL* – A URL to any documentation that is available for this Deployment Package. The URL can be relative to the JAR file.
- *DeploymentPackage-Icon* – A URL to an image file that is an icon for this deployment package. The URL can be relative to the JAR file.
- *DeploymentPackage-Vendor* – The vendor of the Deployment Package.
- *DeploymentPackage-License* – A URL to a license file. The URL can be relative to the Deployment Package JAR file.
- *DeploymentPackage-RequiredStorage* – The minimum amount of persistent storage required by the deployment package after successful install or update.

As with any JAR file Manifest, additional headers can be added and must be ignored by the Deployment Admin service. If any fields have human readable content, localization can be provided through property files as described in *Localization* on page 68 in [2] *OSGi Service Platform Core Specification.* The Deployment Admin service must always use the raw, untranslated version of the header values.

For example, the global section of a Deployment Package Manifest could look like:

```
Manifest-Version: 1.0
DeploymentPackage-SymbolicName: com.third._3d
DeploymentPacakge-Version: 1.2.3.build22032005
DeploymentPackage-Copyright: ACME Inc. (c) 2003
↵
```

Additionally, the Deployment Package Manifest must carry a *Name section* for each resource in the JAR file (except the resources in the META-INF directory). Each name section must start with an empty line (carriage return and line feed, shown as ↵ when its usage could be ambiguous).

The Name section must start with a Name header that contains the path name of the resource. This path name is also used as resource id. The path name must be constructed with the characters as defined in *Path Names* on page 306. For example:

```
Name: bundles/3dlib.jar
```

The name section can include any additional relevant meta data for the named resource. For bundles, only the specification of the Bundle-SymbolicName and Bundle-Version headers are required, but other headers can be added. Unrecognized headers are allowed and must be ignored by the Deployment Admin service. The Name section is also used by the JAR signing to include digests of the actual resources.

The following headers are architected for the Name section in the manifest of a deployment package:

- *Bundle-SymbolicName* – Only for bundle resources. This header must be identical to the Bundle Symbolic Name of the named bundle. If there is a discrepancy, the install of the Deployment Package must fail. If the bundle resource has no Bundle-SymbolicName in its manifest, however, the Deployment Admin must use the given symbolic name for the calculation of the location of this bundle.

· *Bundle-Version* – Only for bundle resources. This header must be identical to the bundle version of the named bundle. Its syntax must follow the version syntax as defined in the Framework specification. The installation must fail if incorrect.

· *DeploymentPackage-Missing* – (true|false) Indicates that the resource is logically part of the Deployment Package but that a previous version of the Deployment Package already contained this resource—there is no data for this resource. See *Fix Package* on page 312 for a further explanation.

· *Resource-Processor* – The PID of the Resource Processor service that must install the given resource.

· *DeploymentPackage-Customizer* – (true|false) Indicates whether this bundle is a customizer bundle by listing a PID for the customizer service. See a further discussion in *Customizer* on page 313.

An example Manifest of a Deployment Package that deploys the 3D package, consisting of two bundles and no resources, could look like:

```
Manifest-Version: 1.0
DeploymentPackage-Icon: %icon
DeploymentPackage-SymbolicName: com.third._3d
DeploymentPacakge-Version: 1.2.3.build22032005
↵
Name: bundles/3dlib.jar
SHA1-Digest: MOez1l4gXHBo8ycYdAxstK3UvEg=
Bundle-SymbolicName: com.third._3d
Bundle-Version: 2.3.1
↵
Name: bundles/3dnative.jar
SHA1-Digest: N8Ow2UY4yjnHZv5zeq2I1Uv/+uE=
Bundle-SymbolicName: com.third._3d.native
Bundle-Version: 1.5.3
↵
Name: OSGI-INF/autoconf.xml
SHA1-Digest: M78w24912HgiZv5zeq2X1Uv-+uF=
Resource-Processor:
  org.osgi.deployment.rp.autoconf
↵
```

114.3.4   Deployment Package Headers

This section contains a detailed description of the different headers for a Deployment Package with their value syntax.

114.3.4.1   DeploymentPackage-SymbolicName

The name of the deployment package. A name must follow the same rules as Java packages. The grammar is as follows:

```
DeploymentPackage-SymbolicName ::= unique-name
                               // See 1.3.2 Core
```

This header is mandatory and must not be localized.

An example is:

```
DeploymentPackage-SymbolicName: com.acme.chess
```

114.3.4.2   DeploymentPackage-Version

This header defines the version of the deployment package. The syntax follows the standard OSGi Framework rules for versions.

```
DeploymentPackage-Version ::= version    // See 3.2.5 Core
```

This header is mandatory and must follow the syntax of the version. It must not be localized.

An example:

```
DeploymentPackage-Version: 1.2.3.build200501041230
```

114.3.4.3   DeploymentPackage-FixPack

A fix package can be distinguished from the full format Deployment Package through the presence of the DeploymentPackage-FixPack header, contained within the global section of the Manifest. The format of this header is:

```
DeploymentPackage-FixPack ::= version-range
                          // See 3.2.6 Core
```

The version range syntax is identical to the Framework module's layer version range as defined in [2] *OSGi Service Platform Core Specification*. For example, a Manifest header that denotes a fix package which is only applicable to versions 1.3 through 3.4 of a given deployment package looks like:

```
DeploymentPackage-FixPack: [1.3,3.4]
```

See *Fix Package* on page 312 for more information about Fix Packages.

114.3.4.4   DeploymentPackage-Icon

This header contains a URL (absolute or relative to the JAR file) to an image resource that represents this deployment package. Implementations should support at least the HTTP protocol as well as the PNG image file. This URL can be localized. The Deployment Admin service must maintain a local copy of the image resource. A URL to this local resource can be obtained with the getIcon() method.

```
DeploymentPackage-Icon ::= url
url ::= <absolute or relative URL or localization name>
```

For example:

```
DeploymentPackage-Icon: %icon
```

114.3.4.5   DeploymentPackage-Name

This header is available as the DeploymentPackage getDisplayName method. It provides a human readable name that can be localized. It is available through the getDisplayName() method. This name can be localized.

```
DeploymentPackage ::= name
name              ::= <any value or a localization name>
```

Example:

```
DeploymentPackage: 3D-Library
```

114.3.4.6   DeploymentPackage-RequiredStorage

This header specifies the minimum amount of persistent storage required by the deployment package after successful install or update. The value is an integer that represent kilo-bytes. The value includes the size of the bundles and any persistent storage needs and storage needed to run the resource processors and customizers. An installation agent can verify the availability of sufficient memory before installing the package. A fix-pack must specify the minimum memory requirements of the complete deployment package after the it is applied.

```
DeploymentPackage-RequiredStorage ::= number
```

Example

```
DeploymentPackage-RequiredStorage: 15
```

114.3.4.7   **Bundle-SymbolicName (Name Section)**

The Bundle-SymbolicName header must be a copy of the Bundle-SymbolicName header in the named bundle, including any parameters. This header must match the Bundle-SymbolicName of the actual bundle; if it does not, the install or update must fail. The parameters, however, can differ between updates. The header has the following format:

```
Bundle-SymbolicName: unique-name (';' parameter ) *
```

If the bundle resource has no Bundle-SymbolicName header, the given symbolic name must be used to calculate the location of the bundle.

For example:

```
Name: bundles/http.jar
Bundle-SymbolicName: com.acme.http; singleton=true
```

114.3.4.8   **Bundle-Version (Name Section)**

The Bundle-Version header must be equal to the Bundle-Version header in the named bundle. It must follow the format as defined for the version clause in [2] *OSGi Service Platform Core Specification.*

```
Bundle-Version ::= version        // See 3.2.5 Core
```

A mismatch between the version indicated in the Manifest of the Deployment Package and the actual value in the Bundle's Manifest must cause an installation or update to fail.

For example

```
Bundle-Version: 1.2
```

114.3.4.9   **Resource-Processor (Name Section)**

The Resource-Processor header selects an OSGi Resource Processor service for this resource by selecting the Resource-Processor service with the given PID as service.id service property. This header is optional, so that the Deployment Package can carry resources that are not processed: for example, license and documentation files. The format of the header is:

```
Resource-Processor ::= pid      // See 1.3.2 Core
```

For example:

```
Name: certificate/certificates.xml
SHA1-Digest: M78w249126182Ak5zeq2X1Uv-+uF=
Resource-Processor: com.securitas.keystore
```

In the example, the certificates.xml in the certificate directory will be processed by the Resource Processor service registered with the service property service.pid set to com.securitas.keystore. The service.pid is a standard Framework property to uniquely identify a service instance called a Persistent IDentity a.k.a. PID.

114.3.4.10   **DeploymentPackage-Missing (Name Section)**

Fix packs (see *Fix Package* on page 312) are Deployment Packages that do not contain all the resources for a full install. This header indicates the Bundle Symbolic Name of a bundle that is not present in the enclosing JAR file but should be part of a prior version of this Deployment Package. The format is:

```
DeploymentPackage-Missing ::= 'true' | 'false'
```

The default value for this header is false. An error results if this header is true and the resource is not present in the existing Deployment Package.

For example:

```
Name: bundles/3dlib.jar
DeploymentPackage-Missing: true
Bundle-SymbolicName: com.acme.http
```

```
Bundle-Version: 3.0
```

DeploymentPackage-Customizer (Name Section)

This header is used to indicated that a resource is a customizer bundle, as described in *Customizer* on page 313. The syntax of this optional header is:

```
DeploymentPackage-Customizer ::= 'true' | 'false'
```

The default for this header is false.

For example:

```
Name: bundles/3dlibcustomizer.jar
DeploymentPackage-Customizer: true
Bundle-SymbolicName: com.acme.customizer
Bundle-Version: 3.6
```

114.3.5   Localization

All human readable headers can be localized using the same mechanism as is used to localize the manifest of a bundle. This mechanism is described in *Localization* on page 68 of the [2] *OSGi Service Platform Core Specification.*

For example, a Manifest could look like:

```
Manifest-Version: 1.0
DeploymentPackage-ManifestVersion: 1
DeploymentPackage-SymbolicName: com.third._3d
DeploymentPacakge-Version: 1.2.3.build22032005
DeploymentPackage-Copyright: %copyright
DeploymentPackage-Vendor: %vendor
DeploymentPackage-License: %licenseurl
DeploymentPackage-Description: %3dlib
DeploymentPackage-Icon: %iconurl
DeploymentPackage-Name: %name
Bundle-Localization: OSGI-INF/l10n/dp
↵
Name: bundles/3dlib.jar
SHA1-Digest: MOez1l4gXHBo8ycYdAxstK3UvEg=
Bundle-SymbolicName: com.third._3d
Bundle-Version: 2.3.1
↵
Name: OSGI-INF/autoconf.xml
SHA1-Digest: M78w24912HgiZv5zeq2X1Uv-+uF=
Resource-Processor:
   org.osgi.deployment.rp.autoconf
↵
Name: icon_nl.gif
SHA1-Digest: n72w21124hGiZV5zQeAXxUvaaUf=
↵
Name: OSGI-INF/l10n/dp.properties
SHA1-Digest: V5zQeAXxUvaaUfn72w21124hGiZ=
↵
Name: OSGI-INF/l10n/dp_nl.properties
SHA1-Digest: xUvaaUfn72w21124hGiZV5zQeAXx
↵
```

Different language translations can be provided, such as:

```
OSGI-INF/l10n/dp.properties:
```

```
copyright=ACME Inc. (c) 2005
vendor=ACME Inc.
license=OSGI-INF/license.en.txt
3dlib=High performance graphic library
name=3D-Lib
icon=htpp:/www.acm.com/3dlib/icon.gif

OSGI-INF/l1on/dp_nl.properties:
copyright=ACME Holland BV (c) 2005
vendor=ACME Holland BV.
license=OSGI-INF/licentie.txt
3dlib=Zeer snelle 3D grafische routine bibliotheek
icon = icon_nl.gif
name = 3D-Bibliotheek
```

The language translation resources should appear in the Name section of the manifest so they can be signed.

114.4 Fix Package

A Fix Package is a Deployment Package that minimizes download time by excluding resources that are not required to upgrade or downgrade a Deployment Package. It can only be installed on a Service Platform if a previous version of that Deployment Package is already installed. The Fix Package contains only the changed and new resources. A Fix Package (called the *source*) therefore must specify the range of versions that the existing Deployment Package (called the *target*) must have installed. This range is specified with the DeploymentPackage-FixPack header in the manifest of the source.

The Manifest format for a Fix Package is, except for the Fix Package header, the same as for a Deployment Package manifest: each resource must be named in the Name section of the Manifest. Resources that are absent, however, must be marked in the named section with the DeploymentPackage-Missing header set to true.

Thus, the name sections of the manifest of a Fix Package must list *all* resources, absent or present, in order to distinguish between resources that must be removed or resources that are absent. Name sections that specify the DeploymentPackage-Missing header, however, indicate that the actual content of the resource is not carried in the Deployment Package—that is, the resource content is absent. Only a Fix Package is permitted to contain the DeploymentPackage-Missing headers.

For example, the following headers define a valid Fix Package that can update an existing Deployment Package, only if the version is between 1 and 2.

```
Manifest-Version: 1.0
DeploymentPackage-SymbolicName: com.acme.package.chess
DeploymentPackage-Version: 2.1
DeploymentPackage-FixPack: [1,2)
↵
Name: chess.jar
Bundle-SymbolicName: com.acme.bundle.chess
DeploymentPackage-Missing: true
Bundle-Version: 5.7
↵
Name: score.jar
Bundle-SymbolicName: com.acme.bundle.chessscore
Bundle-Version: 5.7
↵
```

In this example, the Fix Package requires that version 1.x.y of the deployment package is already installed. The presence of the com.acme.bundle. chess bundle on the Service Platform is assumed, and it must be part of the existing Deployment Package com.acme.package.chess. After installation, this Deployment Package must contain the two listed bundles.

114.5 Customizer

The standardized Deployment Admin service installation and uninstallation functions do not always cover the needs of a developer. In certain cases, running custom code at install and uninstall time is required. This need is supported with the Deployment Package *Customizer*. Typical Customizer bundles are:

- Database initialization
- Data conversion
- Wiring

A Customizer bundle is indicated by a DeploymentPackage-Customizer header in a Name section for a bundle resource. A Deployment Package can a number of customizers, or none. A Customizer bundle must be installed and started by the Deployment Admin service *before* any of the resources are processed.

As a Customizer bundle is started, it should register one or more Resource Processor services. These Resource Processor services must only be used by resources originating from the same Deployment Package. Customizer bundles must never process a resource from another Deployment Package, which must be ensured by the Deployment Admin service.

Customizers are installed and started in the order that they appear in the Deployment Package.

114.5.1 Bundle's Data File Area

Each bundle in the OSGi Framework has its own persistent private storage area. This private area is accessed by a bundle with the getDataFile method on the Bundle Context. The location in the file system where these files are stored is not defined, and thus is implementation-dependent. A Customizer bundle, however, typically needs access to this private storage area.

The Deployment Admin service provides access to the Bundle private storage area with the getData-File(Bundle) method on the DeploymentSession object. This method returns a File object to the root of the data directory.

The location of a bundle's private storage area is impossible to determine because it depends on the implementation of the OSGi Framework. It is therefore impossible to give a Customizer bundle an appropriate File Permission for customization of a bundle's data area.

Therefore, if a Customizer bundle calls the getDataFile method for a specific bundle, the Deployment Admin must add to the Customizer bundle the required File Permission to access this area. This File Permission must be removed after the session ends.

114.5.2 Customizers and Update

The lifecycle of a customizer bundle is intertwined with the lifecycle of the resources it processes. Care should be taken to ensure that updates and uninstallations are handled correctly. A Customizer bundle is updated *before* a resource is processed—implying that a deployment session n is always dropped or processed by the customizer from session n+1. In this case, a session is an install or uninstall of a Deployment or Fix Package.

Figure 114.6   *Time line for customizer versus resource versions*

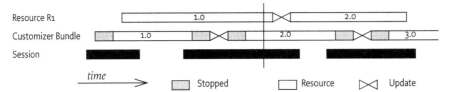

In Figure 114.6, Customizer bundle 2.0 must update the resource from version 1.0, and customizer 3.0 must drop the resource from version 2.0. As a consequence, the Customizer bundle that processes a resource will be a different version than the one that processes or drops it.

The same ordering issue is also relevant with respect to the Autoconf resources (see *Auto Configuration Specification* on page 349). Autoconf resources will not be available until the commit method is called. This condition implies that a customizer cannot receive fresh configuration information from the Deployment Package.

114.6   Deployment Admin Service

The Deployment Admin service provides the following services:

- *Introspecting* – Provide information about the Deployment Package repository. Introspecting is further discussed on *Introspection* on page 314.
- *Install* – The installation of a Deployment Package is described in *Installing a Deployment Package* on page 318.
- *Uninstall* – The uninstallation of a Deployment Package is described in *Uninstalling a Deployment Package* on page 322.
- *Canceling* – An ongoing session can be canceled with the cancel method described in *Canceling* on page 315.

An important concept of the Deployment Admin service is the *session*. Installations and uninstallations of Deployment Packages take place inside a session. This session is represented by a DeploymentSession object. The session provides access to the Deployment Package that is being (un)installed, as well as access to the data area of bundles. The transactional aspects of this sessions are discussed in *Sessions* on page 316.

114.6.1   Introspection

The Deployment Admin service can provide the list of currently installed Deployment Packages with the listDeploymentPackages() method. Given a name, it is also possible to get a Deployment Package with getDeploymentPackage(String) using the name, or getDeploymentPackage(Bundle) for the Deployment Package of a specific bundle.

The listDeploymentPackages() method returns an array of DeploymentPackage objects. This list of Deployment Packages must contain only valid installed packages. During an installation or upgrade of an existing package, the target must remain in this list until the installation process is complete, after which the source replaces the target. If the installation fails, the source must never become visible, even transiently.

DeploymentPackage objects provide access to the following identity information:

- getName() – The name of the Deployment Package.
- getVersion() – The version of the Deployment Package.

The Deployment Package also provides access to the bundles that are associated with a Deployment Package.

- getBundleInfos() – Returns an array of information about all bundles that are *owned* by this Deployment Package. The return type is a BundleInfo object that has a getVersion() and getSymbolicName() method.
- getBundle(String) – Returns the bundle with the given Bundle Symbolic Name that is associated with this Deployment Package. As this instance is transient—for example, a bundle can be removed at any time because of the dynamic nature of the OSGi platform—this method may also return null, if the bundle is part of this deployment package but is temporarily not defined in the Framework.

The Deployment Package also provides access to the headers in its Manifest. The global section and the Name sections are both supported. This information can be used to provide human-readable information to the end user. If the Manifest is using localization, this information must be returned in the default locale. It is not possible to specify a specific locale. See *Localization* on page 311 for more information.

- getHeader(String) – Provides access to the Deployment Package's Manifest header global section. Header names must be matched in a case-insensitive manner.
- getResourceHeader(String,String) – Provides access to a header in the Name section. The first argument specifies the resource id (JAR path); the second argument is the (case insensitive) header name.

The Deployment Package contains a number of resources. Each resource can be queried for its associated Resource Processor service.

- getResourceProcessor(String) – Return the Service Reference of the Resource Processor service that is associated with the given resource. For a Bundle resource, the returned Resource Processor must be null.
- getResources() – Return an array of resource names. This array must include the Bundle resources.

The isStale() method returns true when DeploymentPackage object is no longer available.

114.6.2 Canceling

An ongoing session can be canceled with the Deployment Admin service's cancel() method. This method must find the currently executing Resource Processor service and call its cancel method. The remainder of the session must be immediately rolled back after the Resource Processor returns from the active method.

114.7 Sessions

The (un)installation or upgrade of a deployment package requires the cooperation and interaction of a large number of services. This operation, therefore, takes place in a *session*. A session must be created by the Deployment Admin service before any activity on behalf of the Deployment Package takes place, including any bundle installations. Sessions are not visible to the clients of Deployment Admin service.

Before using a resource processor in a session, the Deployment Admin service must *join* the Resource Processor service to the session. The begin(DeploymentSession) method must be called before a Resource Processor service calls the process, drop, or dropAllResources method. For brevity, this joining is not shown in the following sections, but must be assumed to have taken place before any of the methods is called.

A Resource Processor has *joined the session* when it has returned from its begin(DeploymentSession) method without an Exception being thrown. A Resource Processor service must not be joined to more than a single session at any moment in time—implying that a Resource Processor can assume that only one install takes place at a time.

A roll back can take place at any moment during a session. It can be caused by a Resource Processor service that throws an Exception during a method call, or it can be caused by canceling the session (see *Canceling* on page 315).

If all methods in a session are executed without throwing Exceptions, then the session must be committed. Commitment first requires a vote about the outcome of the session in the so-called *prepare* phase. The Deployment Admin service must therefore call the prepare method on all Resource Processor services that have joined the session. The Resource Processor services must be called in the reverse order of joining.

Any Resource Processor that wants to roll back the session in the prepare phase can, at that moment, still throw an Exception. The prepare method can also be used to persist some of the changes, although the possibility remains that the session will be rolled back and that those changes must then be undone.

If all joined Resource Processors have successfully executed the prepare method, the Deployment Admin service must call the commit method on all Resource Processor services that have joined the session. The Resource Processor services must be called in the reverse order of joining. Resource Processor services must not throw an Exception in this method; they should only finalize the commit. Any Exceptions thrown should be logged, but must be ignored by the Deployment Admin service.

114.7.1   Roll Back

At the moment of the roll back, a number of Resource Processor services can have joined the session and bundles could have been installed. For each of these joined Resource Processor services, the Deployment Admin service must call the rollback() method. A roll back can be caused by a thrown Exception during an operation, or can be initiated by the caller. The roll back can even happen after the prepare() method has been called if another Resource Processor throws an Exception in its prepare method. The Resource Processor services must be called in the reverse order of joining for the rollback method.

The system should make every attempt to roll back the situation to its pre-session state:

- Changed artifacts must be restored to their prior state
- New artifacts must be removed
- Stale artifacts must be created again
- Any installed or updated bundles must be removed
- The state of the target bundles must be restored

If the target bundles were started before, and the state can be restored successfully, the target bundles must be refreshed (the PackageAdmin refreshPackages method) and started again before the method returns.

If the roll back cannot completely restore the state of the target bundles, the target bundles that were restored must not be restarted, in order to prevent running bundles with incompatible versions. An appropriate warning should be logged in this case.

After the commit or rollback method, the DeploymentAdminSession object is no longer usable.

The transactional aspects of the session are depicted in Figure 114.7.

Figure 114.7   *Transactional Sessions*

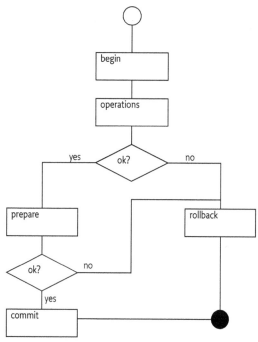

The Deployment Admin service must uninstall any new bundles and install *stale* bundles (bundles that were uninstalled during the session), and should roll back updated bundles. Rolling back a bundle update, as well as reinstalling a stale bundle, requires an implementation-dependent back door into the OSGi Framework, because the Framework specification is not transactional over multiple lifecycle operations. Therefore, this specification does not mandate full transactional behavior.

After a roll back, however, a Deployment Package must still be removable with all its resources and bundles dropped. A roll back must not bring the Deployment Package to a state where it can no longer be removed, or where resources become orphaned.

114.7.2   Bundle Events During Deployment

Deployment operations usually result in bundles being installed or uninstalled. These deployment operations can fail in mid-operation, and cause a roll back by Deployment Admin—meaning that the platform can go through some transient states in which bundles are installed, then uninstalled due to roll back.

Therefore, the order of Bundle events produced by a transactional implementation must be compatible with the Bundle events produced by a non-transactional implementation. A transactional implementation, however, can choose to postpone all events while maintaining ordering until the end of the session and thereby canceling any events that cancel each other (e.g. install and uninstall). A non-transactional Deployment Admin service must send out the events as they occur.

In the following example, a simple Deployment Package consists of bundles A, B, and C. If this Deployment Package is successfully installed, an implementation must produce the following Bundle events (in order):

1   BundleEvent(INSTALLED) for bundle A
2   BundleEvent(INSTALLED) for bundle B
3   BundleEvent(INSTALLED) for bundle C

If an operation of this Deployment Package was unsuccessful because, for example, Bundle C could not be installed due to an error, then the Deployment Admin service must roll back the deployment operation to return the platform to its original state. If the Deployment Admin service is transactional, then it must not expose the events because no persistent bundle changes were made to the platform.

On the other hand, a non-transactional implementation must expose the transient bundle states that occur during the deployment operation. In this case, the following bundle events could have been generated (in order):

1 BundleEvent(INSTALLED) for bundle A
2 BundleEvent(INSTALLED) for bundle B
3 BundleEvent(UNINSTALLED) for bundle A
4 BundleEvent(UNINSTALLED) for bundle B

114.8 Installing a Deployment Package

Installation starts with the installDeploymentPackage(InputStream). No separate function exists for an update; if the given Deployment Package already exists, it must be replaced with this new version. The purpose of the installDeploymentPackage method is to replace the *target* Deployment Package (existing) with the *source* Deployment Package (contained in the Input Stream).

The InputStream object must stream the bytes of a valid Deployment Package JAR; it is called the *source* deployment package. The InputStream object must be a general InputStream object and not an instance of the JarInputStream class, because these objects do not read the JAR file as bytes.

If an installed Deployment Package has the same name as the source, it is called the *target* Deployment Package. If no target exists, an invisible empty target with a version of 0.0.0. must be assumed without any bundles and resources.

The installation of a deployment package can result in these qualifications for any resource r:

- $r \in source, r \notin target$ – New resource
- $r \notin source, r \in target$ – Stale resource
- $r \in source, r \in target$ – Updated resource

The short scenario for an install is depicted in Figure 114.8.

Figure 114.8   *Overview of install process*

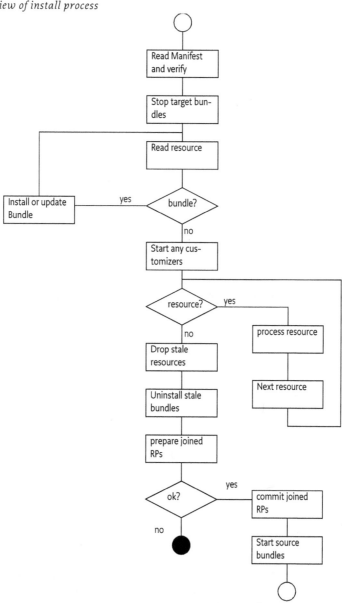

In more detail, to install a Deployment Package, a Deployment Admin service must:

1 Create a Deployment Session
2 Assert that the Manifest file is the first resource in the Deployment Package JAR file.
3 Assert the following:
   • The source must not contain any bundle that exists in other deployment packages, except for the target. The source bundles, as defined by the symbolic name, must belong to the target or be absent.
   If the source is a Fix Package, assert that:
   • The version of the target matches the required source version range.
   • All the missing source bundles are present in the target.
   Otherwise:

- Assert that are no missing resources or bundles declared.

4   All target bundles must be stopped in reverse target resource order. Exceptions thrown during stopping must be ignored, but should be logged as warnings.

The target is now stopped; none of its bundles are running any longer. The next step requires the sequential processing of the resources from the source JAR file in source resource order. The bundles must be processed first (if present), and can be followed by any number of resources, or none.

For each bundle read from the source JAR stream:

5   If the bundle symbolic name already exists in the system with a different version number, update that bundle with the resource stream. If the version is identical, the resource stream must be ignored. The update method must follow the semantics of the OSGi Framework update method. An exception thrown during the update must roll back the session.
Otherwise, install the bundle according to the semantics of the OSGi Framework installBundle method. The location of the bundle must be set to the Bundle Symbolic Name without any parameters and be prefixed with the osgi-dp: scheme. An exception thrown during the install must roll back the session.
Framework events are discussed in *Bundle Events During Deployment* on page 317.

6   Assert that the installed bundle has the Bundle Symbolic Name and version as defined by the source manifest. If not, the session must be rolled back.

All the source's bundles are now installed or updated successfully. Next, any customizers must be started so that they can participate in the resource processing:

7   If Customizer bundles or stale customizers are defined, start them. If any Customizer bundle's start method throws an exception, the session must be rolled back.

For each resource read from the JAR stream:

8   Find the Resource Processor service that processes the resource by using the PID in the Resource-Processor header. If it cannot be found, the session must be rolled back.

9   Assert that the matched Resource Processor service is not from a Customizer bundle in another Deployment Package.

10 Call the matched Resource Processor service process(String,InputStream) method. The argument is the JAR path of the resource. Any Exceptions thrown during this method must abort the installation.

All resource updates and installs have now occurred. The next steps must remove any stale resources. First the stale resources are dropped, and then the bundles are uninstalled. Exceptions are ignored in this phase to allow repairs to always succeed, even if the existing package is corrupted.

11 In reverse target order, drop all the resources that are in the target but not in the source by calling the matching Resource Processor service dropped(String) method. Any exceptions thrown during this method should be logged as warnings, but must be ignored.

12 Uninstall all stale bundles in reverse target order, using the OSGi Framework uninstall method semantics. Any exceptions thrown should be logged as warnings, but must be ignored.

The deployment package is now cleaned up, and can be activated and committed.

13 All the Resource Processor services that have joined the session must now prepare to commit, which is achieved by calling the prepare() method. If any Resource Processor throws an Exception, the session must roll back. The Resource Processors must be called in the reverse order of joining.

14 If all the Resource Processors have successfully prepared their changes, then all the Resource Processor services that have joined the session must now be committed, which is achieved by calling the commit() method. The Resource Processors must be called in the reverse order of joining. Any exceptions should be logged as warnings, but must be ignored.

15 Call the Package Admin service refreshPackages method so that any new packages are resolved.

16 Wait until the refresh is finished.

17 Start the bundles in the source resource order. Exceptions thrown during the start must be logged, but must not abort the deployment operation.

The session is closed and the source replaces the target in the Deployment Admin service's repository.

The installDeploymentPackage method returns the source Deployment Package object.

114.8.1   Example Installation

The target Deployment Package has the following manifest:

```
Manifest-Version: 1.0 ↵
DeploymentPackage-SymbolicName: com.acme.daffy ↵
DeploymentPackage-Version: 1 ↵
↵
Name: bundle-1.jar
Bundle-SymbolicName: com.acme.1
Bundle-Version: 5.7↵
↵
Name: r0.x↵
Resource-Processor: RP-x↵
↵
Name: r1.x↵
Resource-Processor: RP-x ↵
↵
Name: r1.y↵
Resource-Processor: RP-y↵
↵
```

This deployment package is updated with a new version, with the following manifest:

```
Manifest-Version: 1.0
DeploymentPackage-SymbolicName: com.acme.daffy
DeploymentPackage-Version: 2
↵
Name: bundle-2.jar
Bundle-SymbolicName: com.acme.2
Bundle-Version: 5.7↵
↵
Name: r1.x↵
Resource-Processor: RP-x↵
↵
Name: r2.x↵
Resource-Processor: RP-x↵
↵
Name: r1.y↵
Resource-Processor: RP-y↵
↵
```

The delta between version 1 and version 2 of the com.acme.daffy Deployment Package is depicted in Figure 114.9. Bundle-1 must be uninstalled because it is no longer present in the Deployment Package com.acme.daffy version 2. Bundle-2 is a new bundle and thus must be installed. The resource r0.x must be dropped and r1.x must be updated (this must be detected and treated accordingly by Resource Processor RP-x). r2.x is a new resource. The resource r1.y is updated by Resource Processor RP-y).

Figure 114.9   *Delta*

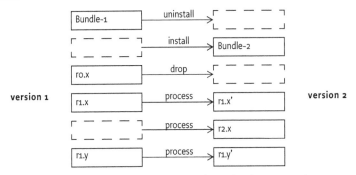

The sequence diagram for the installation is shown in Figure 114.10.

Figure 114.10   *Sequence Diagram for a Resource Processor*

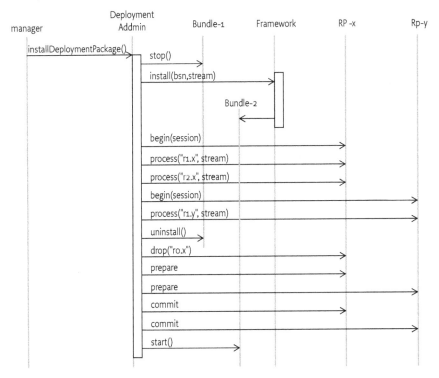

114.9   Uninstalling a Deployment Package

Uninstalling a Deployment Package must remove all the effects of its installation(s). The uninstall is started by calling uninstall() or uninstallForced() method on a *target* DeploymentPackage object.

The Deployment Packages are uninstalled explicitly, which may break the overall runtime configuration. No attempt is made to ensure that the uninstalled Deployment Package is required as a provider of Java packages or services, or fulfills other dependencies.

The Deployment Admin service must take the following actions to remove the target Deployment Package when uninstall() is called. This procedure must run inside a Deployment Admin session. A Resource Processor that is called must first join the session as described in *Sessions* on page 316.

Uninstalling is composed of the following steps:

1 Start a new Deployment Admin session.
2 Stop all the bundles owned by the Deployment Package. If this step throws a Bundle Exception, this error should be logged but must be ignored.
3 Call the dropAllResources() method on all the Resource Processor services that are owned by this Deployment Package. Absent Resource Processor services or Exceptions that are thrown must immediately roll back this session.
4 Call the prepare method on the Resource Processor services that joined the session. If any Resource Processor service throws an Exception, the session must be rolled back.
5 Call the commit method on the Resource Processors that joined the session.
6 Uninstall all owned bundles.

Uninstalling a Deployment Package can break the overall runtime configuration. No attempt is made to ensure that a Deployment Package being uninstalled is not necessary as a provider of Java packages or services, or fulfills other dependencies.

An error condition results if the Resource Processor services are no longer present when uninstalling or updating a deployment package. A request to carry out an uninstall operation on such a Deployment Package must be refused until the Resource Processor services are all available. A means must be provided, however, to handle permanent unavailability of these services.

To address this issue, the DeploymentPackage interface provides a method, uninstallForced(), which forces removal of the Deployment Package from the repository maintained by the Deployment Admin service. This method follows the same steps described earlier. Any errors, or the absence of Resource Processor services, should be logged but ignored; they must not cause a roll back.

If errors occur or Resource Processor services are absent, it is likely that the uninstallation will be incomplete, and that some residual artifacts will remain on the platform. Whether this residue is eventually cleaned up, and how, is left up to the implementation.

114.10   Resource Processors

The Resource Processor service interprets the byte stream of a resource. Typically, the stream is parsed and its information is stored as *artifacts*. Examples of resource processors are:

- *Configuration Management* – This processor is standardized by the OSGi and more information can be found in *Auto Configuration Specification* on page 349.
- *Certificate Keystore* – A Certificate Keystore processor could extract certificates from a bundle and install them in a keystore.
- *SyncML Script* – Execute a series of SyncML commands.

The Deployment Admin service maintains the list of *resource ids* (the path name in the JAR) that are contained in a Deployment Package. Each resource is uniquely identified within a Deployment Package by its path name—hence the term "resource id." The Deployment Package's getResources() method provides a list of the resources ids.

The Resource Processor service is responsible for actually creating and deleting the resource related artifacts. The Resource Processor service must be able to remove the artifacts related to a resource that is being dropped using only the resource id.

The ResourceProcessor interface is based on a session (see *Sessions* on page 316). The transactionality is limited to the bracketing of any processing or dropping of resources.The bracketing begins when a Resource Processor joins an install session. A Resource Processor service can assume that it is never in two sessions at the same time (see *Threading* on page 328). It can, however, be called multiple times during the session to process different resources.

Before the Resource Processor service is used in an install or uninstall session, the Deployment Admin service must call the begin(DeploymentSession) method; this action makes the Resource Processor service join the session. This method must be used by the Resource Processor service to mark any changes for potential roll back, from this time until the prepare()/ commit() or rollback() method is called.

When the session is opened, the Deployment Admin service can call the following methods on the Resource Processor service:

- process(String,InputStream) – The Resource processor must parse the Input Stream and persistently associate the resulting artifacts with the given resource id. It must be possible to remove those artifacts in a future time, potentially after a complete system restart. Keep in mind that a resource can be processed many times. A Deployment Package that updates to a newer version is likely to contain the same resources again. Care should be taken to ensure that these updates are real updates and do not add new, unwanted artifacts.
- dropped(String) – The artifacts that were associated with the given resource id must be removed. If the named resource does not exist, a warning should be logged but no Exception should be thrown.
- dropAllResources() – Remove all artifacts that are related to the current target Deployment Package. This method is called when a Deployment Package is uninstalled.
- cancel() – This method is called when the Resource Processor is in the process(String,InputStream), dropped(String) or dropAllResources() method, allowing the caller to cancel a long-running session. In that case, the Deployment Admin must call the cancel() method for the active Resource Processor service. The Resource Processor service should terminate its action as quickly as possible. The Resource Processor service must still handle a roll back of the session after it has returned.

All methods must perform any integrity checks immediately and throw an Exception with an appropriate code if the verification fails. These checks must not be delayed until the prepare or commit method. As stated earlier, changes must be recorded, but it should be possible to roll back the changes when the rollback method is called.

Deployment Packages can be upgraded or downgraded. Resource Processor services must therefore be capable of processing resources that have a lower, equal, or higher version.

114.10.1   Example Resource Processor

An example is a Resource Processor service that wires services with the Wire Admin service. The Wire Admin service creates wires between a *producer* and a *consumer* service, each identified by a PID. Wires are the artifacts that are installed and removed. Each wire contains a Dictionary object that is a convenient place to tag wires with the Deployment Package name and resource id. The Wire Admin stores this information persistently, which makes it very suitable for use in a transactional model. This small example supports full transactionality, although without crash recovery.

For simplicity, the wire definitions are stored in a format compatible with the java.util.Properties format (because it can simply be loaded from an Input Stream object). The key is the producer and the value is the consumer. A sample wiring could look like:

```
com.acme.gps = com.acme.navigation
com.acme.asn = com.acme.navigation
com.acme.navigation = com.acme.poi
```

This wiring is depicted in Figure 114.11.

Figure 114.11   *Sample Wiring*

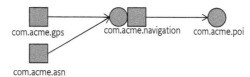

This resource is stored in a Deployment Package JAR file. In this example there are no bundles, so the Deployment Package's manifest would look like:

```
Manifest-Version: 1.0
DeploymentPackage-SymbolicName: com.acme.model.E45.wiring
DeploymentPackage-Version: 1.2832
↵
Name: sample.wiring
Resource-Processor: wire.admin.processor
↵
```

To reduce the size of the code in this example, the Wire Admin service is received as a parameter. The constructor registers the object as a Resource Processor service with the required wire.admin.processor PID.

The transaction strategy of this code is to create wires when new wires have to be created, but to delay the deletion of wires until the end of the session. Any created wires are kept in the createdWires field, and the wires that are to be deleted are kept in the toBeDeletedWires field.

The current DeploymentPackage object is saved in the current field when the begin method is called.

```
public class WireAdminProcessor implements ResourceProcessor {
    WireAdmin            admin;
    DeploymentPackage    current;
    List                 createdWires= new Vector();
    List                 toBeDeletedWires= new Vector();

    public WireAdminProcessor(
        WireAdmin admin, BundleContext context)
        throws Exception {
      this.admin = admin;
      Dictionary properties = new Hashtable();
      properties.put(Constants.SERVICE_PID,
          "wire.admin.processor");
        context.registerService(
          ResourceProcessor.class.getName(), this,
          properties);
    }
```

When the Deployment Admin service is installing a Deployment Package JAR, it must call the Resource Processor service's begin method before the first time it calls a Resource Processor service to join it to the current session. In this case, only the source DeploymentPackage object is saved in the current field.

```
    public void begin(DeploymentSession session) {
      current = session.getSourceDeploymentPackage();
    }
```

The most complicated method that must be implemented is the process method. This method receives the resource id and an input stream with the contents. In this case, the stream is easily converted to a java.util.Properties object that contains the definitions of the wires.

The key and value of the Properties object are the producer and consumer respectively, which are used to create new wires. Each wire has a Dictionary object in the Wire Admin service. This Dictionary object is used to store the following properties:

- deployment.package – The symbolic name of the current (target) deployment package. This property associates the wire with a specific deployment package.
- resource.id – The resource id, or JAR path name. This id associates the specific resource with the wire.

Associating these fields with the wire simplifies finding all wires related to a Deployment Package or all wires related to a specific resource id and Deployment Package. The Wire Admin service supports a search method for wires that takes a filter as argument, further simplifying this process.

After a wire is created, it is stored in the createdWires list so that the wires can be deleted if the session is rolled back.

The process method looks as follows:

```
public void process(String resourceId, InputStream in)
        throws Exception {
    Properties properties = new Properties();
    properties.load(in);
    Dictionary dict = new Hashtable();
    dict.put("deployment.package", current.getName());
    for (Iterator i = properties.values().iterator();
        i.hasNext();) {
        dict.put("resource.id", resourceId );
        String producer = (String) i.next();
        String consumer = properties.getProperty(producer);
        Wire wire = admin.createWire(producer,
            consumer, dict);
        createdWires.add(wire);
    }
}
```

If a resource is not in the source but is in the target Deployment Package, it must be dropped from the Resource Processor service. The Deployment Admin will call the dropped(String) method for those resources. Therefore, the wires that are tagged with the given resource id and Deployment Package name must be deleted.

The Wire Admin service has a convenient function to get all the wires that match a filter. This method is used to list all the wires that belong to the current Deployment Package as well as those that have the matching resource id. This array is added to the toBeDeletedWires field so that it can be deleted when the session is successfully completed—that is, wires are not deleted until the commit phase. When the session is rolled back, the list of wires to be deleted can be discarded, because they were never really deleted.

```
public void dropped(String name) throws Exception {
    List list = getWires(
        "(&(resource.id=" + name + ")(deployment.package="
            + current.getName() + "))");
    toBeDeletedWires.addAll(list);
}
```

If the session concludes without errors, the Deployment Admin service must call the prepare() method. In this example, it is possible to roll back the persistent changes made so far. The method can therefore just return.

```
public void prepare(){}
```

The commit() method must now actually delete the wires that were removed during the session. After these wires are deleted, the method can throw away the list of wires that were created. This list was only kept to remove the wires in case of a roll back.

```
public void commit() {
    delete(toBeDeletedWires);
    toBeDeletedWires.clear();
    createdWires.clear();
}
```

The rollback() method is the reverse of the commit. Any created wires must now be deleted to undo their creations in this session. The wires that are to be deleted can now be discarded, because they have not been deleted yet and therefore do not have to be rolled back.

```
public void rollback() {
    delete(createdWires);
    toBeDeletedWires.clear();
    createdWires.clear();
}
```

The dropAllResources() method must drop all the wires that were created on behalf of the current Deployment Package. The filter on the getWires method makes this process very straightforward. Just delete all the wires that were tagged with the Deployment Package name.

```
public void dropAllResources() {
    List list = getWires("(deployment.package="
    + current.getName() + ")");
    toBeDeletedWires.addAll(list);
}
```

The cancel() method must cancel ongoing operations. This example does not have any long-running operations. The cancel method can therefore just return.

```
public void cancel() {}
```

And finally, some helper methods should be self-explanatory.

```
void delete(List wires) {
    while ( ! wires.isEmpty() )
        admin.deleteWire((Wire) wires.remove(0));
}

List getWires(String filter) {
    try {
        Wire[] wires = admin.getWires(filter);
        return Arrays.asList(wires);
    }
    catch (InvalidSyntaxException ise) {
        ise.printStackTrace();
    }
    return new Vector();
}
}
```

This example is obviously not an "industrial-strength" implementation; its only purpose is to high-light the different problems that must be addressed. Implementers should therefore consider the following additional issues when implementing a Resource Processor service.

- Changes could have been made to the Deployment Package objects when a Resource Processor's bundle was updated or has been offline for some time, which can happen when the uninstallForceful method has been used. The Deployment Admin service can provide sufficient information to verify its repository to the information maintained in the Resource Processor service.

- A Resource Processor service should have a strategy for transactions that can handle crash recovery. For example, in the previous code the list of createdWires and toBeDeletedWires should have been logged. Logging these lists would have allowed full crash recovery.
- Better file formats should be considered. The Properties class is too restrictive because it can only have a single wire per Producer object. The Properties class was only chosen for its convenience.
- Multi-threading issues may exist with the cancel method.

114.11 Events

The Deployment Admin service must publish several generic events to the Event Admin service in the course of a deployment operation. The purpose of these events is to allow, for example, a user interface to display the progress of a deployment operation to the user.

The topics to which Deployment Admin publishes events are:

- org/osgi/service/deployment/INSTALL – The installDeploymentPackage(InputStream) method has been called.
- org/osgi/service/deployment/UNINSTALL – The uninstall() or uninstallForced() method has been called..
- org/osgi/service/deployment/COMPLETE – The deployment operation has completed.

The INSTALL, UNINSTALL and COMPLETE events have the following property:

- EVENT_DEPLOYMENTPACKAGE_NAME – (String) The name of the Deployment Package. This name is the same name as that specified in the DeploymentPackage-SymbolicName Manifest header.
- EVENT_DEPLOYMENTPACKAGE_READABLENAME – (String)
- EVENT_DEPLOYMENTPACKAGE_CURRENTVERSION – (Version) The currently installed version of the Deployment Packages. This attribute is only present when there is a version of the Deployment Package installed before the method that generated the event.
- EVENT_DEPLOYMENTPACKAGE_NEXTVERSION – (Version) The version of Deployment Package after the successful completion of the install operation.

The COMPLETE event additionally has the following property:

- *successful* – (Boolean) Whether the deployment operation was successful or not.

114.12 Threading

The Deployment Admin service must be a singleton and must only process a single session at a time. When a client requests a new session with an install or uninstall operation, it must block that call until the earlier session is completed. The Deployment Admin service must throw a Deployment Exception when the session cannot be created after an appropriate time-out period. Resource Processor services can thus assume that all calls from begin to commit or rollback methods are called from the same thread.

Special care should be taken with the cancel method that is usually called from another thread.

114.13 Security

114.13.1 Deployment Admin Permission

The Deployment Admin Permission is needed to access the methods of the Deployment Admin service. The target for a Deployment Admin Permission is the same Filter string as for an Admin Permission, see *Admin Permission* on page 117 of [2] *OSGi Service Platform Core Specification.*

The actions are:

- LIST – The permission to call the listDeploymentPackages() method and getDeployment-Package(String).
- INSTALL – Allowed to call the installDeploymentPackage(InputStream) method.
- UNINSTALL – Allowed to call the uninstall() method.
- UNINSTALL_FORCED – Allowed to call the uninstallForced() method.
- CANCEL – Allowed to cancel an ongoing session.
- METADATA – Provide access to the Deployment Package meta data.

114.13.2 Deployment Customizer Permission

The DeploymentCustomizerPermission is used by customizer bundles. The target is the same as the target of Admin Permission: a filter that selects bundles. It has the following action:

- PRIVATEAREA – Permits the use of the private area of the target bundles.

114.13.3 Permissions During an Install Session

Unprotected, Resource Processor services can unwittingly disrupt the device by processing incorrect or malicious resources in a Deployment Package. In order to protect the device, Resource Processor service's capabilities must be limited by the permissions granted to the union of the permissions of the Deployment Package's *signers*. This union is called the *security scope*. Given a signer, its security scope can be obtained from the *Conditional Permission Admin Specification* on page 247.

The Deployment Admin service must execute all Resource Processor service calls inside a doPrivileged block. This privileged block must use an AccessControlContext object that limits the permissions to the security scope. Therefore, a Resource Processor service must assume that it is always running inside the correct security scope. A Resource Processor can, of course, use its own security scope by doing a local doPrivileged block.

Bundle life cycle operations (install, uninstall, update) must be performed with the permissions granted to the Deployment Admin service implementation, they should not be further scoped because this could make it impossible to install unsigned Deployment Packages.

114.13.4 Contained Bundle Permissions

Bundles can be signed independently from the vehicle that deployed them. As a consequence, a bundle can be granted more permissions than its parent Deployment Package.

114.13.5 Service Registry Security

114.13.5.1 Deployment Admin Service

The Deployment Admin service is likely to require All Permission. This requirement is caused by the plugin model. Any permission required by any of the Resource Processor services must be granted to the Deployment Admin service as well. This set is large and difficult to define. The following list, however, shows the minimum permissions required if the permissions for the Resource Processor service permissions are ignored.

```
ServicePermission    ..DeploymentAdmin        REGISTER
ServicePermission    ..ResourceProcessor      GET
```

PackagePermission	..deployment	EXPORTONLY

114.13.5.2   **Resource Processor**

ServicePermission	..DeploymentAdmin	GET
ServicePermission	..ResourceProcessor	REGISTER
PackagePermission	..deployment	IMPORT

114.13.5.3   **Client**

ServicePermission	..DeploymentAdmin	GET
PackagePermission	..deployment	IMPORT

114.14   Changes

- Clarified that though Resource Processors are security scoped by the security scope of the Deployment Package, bundle operations are not.
- Added new headers: DeploymentPackage-Name and DeploymentPackage-Icon. See *Deployment-Package-Icon* on page 309 and *DeploymentPackage-Icon* on page 309.
- Added a two new methods: getIcon() and getDisplayName().
- Added a new header DeploymentPackage-RequiredStorage to specify the number of kilobytes needed. See *DeploymentPackage-RequiredStorage* on page 310.
- Added new event attributes as well as constants all event attributes.

114.15   org.osgi.service.deploymentadmin

Deployment Admin Package Version 1.1.

Bundles wishing to use this package must list the package in the Import-Package header of the bundle's manifest. For example:

```
Import-Package: org.osgi.service.deploymentadmin; version="[1.1,2.0)"
```

114.15.1   Summary

- *BundleInfo* - Represents a bundle in the array given back by the DeploymentPackage.get-BundleInfos() method.
- *DeploymentAdmin* - This is the interface of the Deployment Admin service.
- *DeploymentAdminPermission* - DeploymentAdminPermission controls access to the Deployment Admin service.
- *DeploymentException* - Checked exception received when something fails during any deployment processes.
- *DeploymentPackage* - The DeploymentPackage object represents a deployment package (already installed or being currently processed).

114.15.2   public interface BundleInfo

Represents a bundle in the array given back by the DeploymentPackage.getBundleInfos() method.

114.15.2.1   **public String getSymbolicName( )**

☐ Returns the Bundle Symbolic Name of the represented bundle.

Returns   the Bundle Symbolic Name

114.15.2.2   **public Version getVersion( )**

☐ Returns the version of the represented bundle.

Returns   the version of the represented bundle

114.15.3　　public interface DeploymentAdmin

This is the interface of the Deployment Admin service.

The OSGi Service Platform provides mechanisms to manage the life cycle of bundles, configuration objects, permission objects, etc. but the overall consistency of the runtime configuration is the responsibility of the management agent. In other words, the management agent decides to install, update, or uninstall bundles, create or delete configuration or permission objects, as well as manage other resource types, etc.

The Deployment Admin service standardizes the access to some of the responsibilities of the management agent. The service provides functionality to manage Deployment Packages (see Deployment-Package). A Deployment Package groups resources as a unit of management. A Deployment Package is something that can be installed, updated, and uninstalled as a unit.

The Deployment Admin functionality is exposed as a standard OSGi service with no mandatory service parameters.

114.15.3.1　　public boolean cancel( )

□ This method cancels the currently active deployment session. This method addresses the need to cancel the processing of excessively long running, or resource consuming install, update or uninstall operations.

Returns　true if there was an active session and it was successfully cancelled.

Throws　SecurityException – if the caller doesn't have the appropriate DeploymentAdminPermission("<filter>", "cancel") permission.

See Also　DeploymentAdminPermission

114.15.3.2　　public DeploymentPackage getDeploymentPackage(String symbName)

symbName　the symbolic name of the Deployment Package to be retrieved. It mustn't be null.

□ Gets the currenlty installed DeploymentPackage instance which has the given symbolic name.

During an installation of an existing package (update) or during an uninstallation, the target Deployment Package must remain the return value until the installation (uninstallation) process is completed, after which the source (or null in case of uninstall) is the return value.

Returns　The DeploymentPackage for the given symbolic name. If there is no Deployment Package with that symbolic name currently installed, null is returned.

Throws　IllegalArgumentException – if the given symbName is null

SecurityException – if the caller doesn't have the appropriate DeploymentAdminPermission("<filter>", "list") permission.

See Also　DeploymentPackage, DeploymentAdminPermission

114.15.3.3　　public DeploymentPackage getDeploymentPackage(Bundle bundle)

bundle　the bundle whose owner is queried

□ Gives back the installed DeploymentPackage that owns the bundle. Deployment Packages own their bundles by their Bundle Symbolic Name. It means that if a bundle belongs to an installed Deployment Packages (and at most to one) the Deployment Admin assigns the bundle to its owner Deployment Package by the Symbolic Name of the bundle.

Returns　the Deployment Package Object that owns the bundle or null if the bundle doesn't belong to any Deployment Packages (standalone bundles)

Throws　IllegalArgumentException – if the given bundle is null

SecurityException – if the caller doesn't have the appropriate DeploymentAdminPermission("<filter>", "list") permission.

See Also   DeploymentPackage, DeploymentAdminPermission

114.15.3.4   **public DeploymentPackage installDeploymentPackage(InputStream in) throws DeploymentException**

in the input stream the Deployment Package can be read from. It mustn't be null.

☐ Installs a Deployment Package from an input stream. If a version of that Deployment Package is already installed and the versions are different, the installed version is updated with this new version even if it is older (downgrade). If the two versions are the same, then this method simply returns with the old (target) Deployment Package without any action.

Returns A DeploymentPackage object representing the newly installed/updated Deployment Package. It is never null.

Throws IllegalArgumentException – if the got InputStream parameter is null

DeploymentException – if the installation was not successful. For detailed error code description see DeploymentException.

SecurityException – if the caller doesn't have the appropriate DeploymentAdminPermission("<filter>", "install") permission.

See Also   DeploymentAdminPermission, DeploymentPackage, DeploymentPackage

114.15.3.5   **public DeploymentPackage[] listDeploymentPackages( )**

☐ Lists the Deployment Packages currently installed on the platform.

DeploymentAdminPermission("<filter>", "list") is needed for this operation to the effect that only those packages are listed in the array to which the caller has appropriate DeploymentAdminPermission. It has the consequence that the method never throws SecurityException only doesn't put certain Deployment Packages into the array.

During an installation of an existing package (update) or during an uninstallation, the target must remain in this list until the installation (uninstallation) process is completed, after which the source (or null in case of uninstall) replaces the target.

Returns the array of DeploymentPackage objects representing all the installed Deployment Packages. The return value cannot be null. In case of missing permissions it may give back an empty array.

See Also   DeploymentPackage, DeploymentAdminPermission

114.15.4   **public final class DeploymentAdminPermission**
extends Permission

DeploymentAdminPermission controls access to the Deployment Admin service.

The permission uses a filter string formatted similarly to the org.osgi.framework.Filter. The filter determines the target of the permission. The DeploymentAdminPermission uses the name and the signer filter attributes only. The value of the signer attribute is matched against the signer chain (represented with its semicolon separated Distinguished Name chain) of the Deployment Package, and the value of the name attribute is matched against the value of the "DeploymentPackage-Name" manifest header of the Deployment Package. Example:

- (signer=cn = Bugs Bunny, o = ACME, c = US)
- (name=org.osgi.ExampleApp)

Wildcards also can be used:

  (signer=cn=*, o=ACME, c=*)

"cn" and "c" may have an arbitrary value

(signer=*, o=ACME, c=US)

Only the value of "o" and "c" are significant

(signer=* ; ou=S & V, o=Tweety Inc., c=US)

The first element of the certificate chain is not important, only the second (the Distingushed Name of the root certificate)

(signer=- ; *, o=Tweety Inc., c=US)

The same as the previous but '-' represents zero or more certificates, whereas the asterisk only represents a single certificate

(name=*)

The name of the Deployment Package doesn't matter

(name=org.osgi.*)

The name has to begin with "org.osgi."

The following actions are allowed:

list

A holder of this permission can access the inventory information of the deployment packages selected by the ⟨filter⟩ string. The filter selects the deployment packages on which the holder of the permission can acquire detailed inventory information. See DeploymentAdmin.getDeployment-Package(Bundle), DeploymentAdmin.getDeploymentPackage(String) and DeploymentAdmin.list-DeploymentPackages.

install

A holder of this permission can install/update deployment packages if the deployment package satisfies the ⟨filter⟩ string. See DeploymentAdmin.installDeploymentPackage.

uninstall

A holder of this permission can uninstall deployment packages if the deployment package satisfies the ⟨filter⟩ string. See DeploymentPackage.uninstall.

uninstall_forced

A holder of this permission can forcefully uninstall deployment packages if the deployment package satisfies the ⟨filter⟩ string. See DeploymentPackage.uninstallForced.

cancel

A holder of this permission can cancel an active deployment action. This action being cancelled could correspond to the install, update or uninstall of a deployment package that satisfies the ⟨filter⟩ string. See DeploymentAdmin.cancel

metadata

A holder of this permission is able to retrieve metadata information about a Deployment Package (e.g. is able to ask its manifest hedares). See org.osgi.service.deploymentadmin.DeploymentPack-age.getBundle(String), org.osgi.service.deploymentadmin.DeploymentPackage.getBundleInfos(), org.osgi.service.deploymentadmin.DeploymentPackage.getHeader(String), org.osgi.ser-vice.deploymentadmin.DeploymentPackage.getResourceHeader(String, String), org.osgi.ser-vice.deploymentadmin.DeploymentPackage.getResourceProcessor(String), org.osgi.service.deploymentadmin.DeploymentPackage.getResources()

The actions string is converted to lowercase before processing.

114.15.4.1   **public static final String CANCEL = "cancel"**

Constant String to the "cancel" action.

See Also `DeploymentAdmin.cancel`

114.15.4.2   **public static final String INSTALL = "install"**

Constant String to the "install" action.

See Also `DeploymentAdmin.installDeploymentPackage(InputStream)`

114.15.4.3   **public static final String LIST = "list"**

Constant String to the "list" action.

See Also `DeploymentAdmin.listDeploymentPackages()`,
`DeploymentAdmin.getDeploymentPackage(String)`,
`DeploymentAdmin.getDeploymentPackage(Bundle)`

114.15.4.4   **public static final String METADATA = "metadata"**

Constant String to the "metadata" action.

See Also `org.osgi.service.deploymentadmin.DeploymentPackage.getBundle(String)`,
`org.osgi.service.deploymentadmin.DeploymentPackage.getBundleInfos()`,
`org.osgi.service.deploymentadmin.DeploymentPackage.getHeader(String)`,
`org.osgi.service.deploymentadmin.DeploymentPackage.getResourceHeader(String,`
`String)`,
`org.osgi.service.deploymentadmin.DeploymentPackage.getResourceProcessor(String)`,
`org.osgi.service.deploymentadmin.DeploymentPackage.getResources()`

114.15.4.5   **public static final String UNINSTALL = "uninstall"**

Constant String to the "uninstall" action.

See Also `DeploymentPackage.uninstall()`

114.15.4.6   **public static final String UNINSTALL_FORCED = "uninstall_forced"**

Constant String to the "uninstall_forced" action.

See Also `DeploymentPackage.uninstallForced()`

114.15.4.7   **public DeploymentAdminPermission(String name, String actions)**

name   filter string, must not be null.

actions   action string, must not be null. "∗" means all the possible actions.

☐ Creates a new DeploymentAdminPermission object for the given name and action.

The name parameter identifies the target deployment package the permission relates to. The actions parameter contains the comma separated list of allowed actions.

Throws `IllegalArgumentException` – if the filter is invalid, the list of actions contains unknown operations or one of the parameters is null

114.15.4.8   **public boolean equals(Object obj)**

obj   The reference object with which to compare.

☐ Checks two DeploymentAdminPermission objects for equality. Two permission objects are equal if:

- their target filters are semantically equal and
- their actions are the same

Returns   true if the two objects are equal.

See Also `java.lang.Object.equals(java.lang.Object)`

114.15.4.9   **public String getActions( )**

☐ Returns the String representation of the action list.

The method always gives back the actions in the following (alphabetical) order: cancel, install, list, metadata, uninstall, uninstall_forced

Returns Action list of this permission instance. This is a comma-separated list that reflects the action parameter of the constructor.

See Also java.security.Permission.getActions()

114.15.4.10   **public int hashCode( )**

☐ Returns hash code for this permission object.

Returns Hash code for this permission object.

See Also java.lang.Object.hashCode()

114.15.4.11   **public boolean implies(Permission permission)**

permission Permission to check.

☐ Checks if this DeploymentAdminPermission would imply the parameter permission.

Precondition of the implication is that the action set of this permission is the superset of the action set of the other permission. Further rules of implication are determined by the org.osgi.framework.Filter rules and the "OSGi Service Platform, Core Specification Release 4, Chapter Certificate Matching".

The allowed attributes are: name (the symbolic name of the deployment package) and signer (the signer of the deployment package). In both cases wildcards can be used.

Examples:

```
1. DeploymentAdminPermission("(name=org.osgi.ExampleApp)", "list")
2. DeploymentAdminPermission("(name=org.osgi.ExampleApp)", "list, install")
3. DeploymentAdminPermission("(name=org.osgi.*)", "list")
4. DeploymentAdminPermission("(signer=*, o=ACME, c=US)", "list")
5. DeploymentAdminPermission("(signer=cn = Bugs Bunny, o = ACME, c = US)", "list")
```

```
1. implies 1.
2. implies 1.
1. doesn't implies 2.
3. implies 1.
4. implies 5.
```

Returns true if this DeploymentAdminPermission object implies the specified permission.

See Also java.security.Permission.implies(java.security.Permission),
org.osgi.framework.Filter

114.15.4.12   **public PermissionCollection newPermissionCollection( )**

☐ Returns a new PermissionCollection object for storing DeploymentAdminPermission objects.

Returns The new PermissionCollection.

See Also java.security.Permission.newPermissionCollection()

114.15.5   public class DeploymentException
extends Exception

Checked exception received when something fails during any deployment processes. A DeploymentException always contains an error code (one of the constants specified in this class), and may optionally contain the textual description of the error condition and a nested cause exception.

114.15.5.1   **public static final int CODE_BAD_HEADER = 452**

Syntax error in any manifest header.

DeploymentAdmin.installDeploymentPackage(InputStream) throws exception with this error code.

114.15.5.2   **public static final int CODE_BUNDLE_NAME_ERROR = 457**

Bundle symbolic name is not the same as defined by the deployment package manifest.

DeploymentAdmin.installDeploymentPackage(InputStream) throws exception with this error code.

114.15.5.3   **public static final int CODE_BUNDLE_SHARING_VIOLATION = 460**

Bundle with the same symbolic name alerady exists.

DeploymentAdmin.installDeploymentPackage(InputStream) throws exception with this error code.

114.15.5.4   **public static final int CODE_CANCELLED = 401**

DeploymentAdmin.installDeploymentPackage(InputStream), DeploymentPackage.uninstall() and DeploymentPackage.uninstallForced() methods can throw DeploymentException with this error code if the DeploymentAdmin.cancel() method is called from another thread.

114.15.5.5   **public static final int CODE_COMMIT_ERROR = 462**

Exception with this error code is thrown when one of the Resource Processors involved in the deployment session threw a ResourceProcessorException with the org.osgi.service.deploymentadmin.spi.ResourceProcessorException.CODE_PREPARE error code.

DeploymentAdmin.installDeploymentPackage(InputStream) and DeploymentPackage.uninstall() methods throw exception with this error code.

114.15.5.6   **public static final int CODE_FOREIGN_CUSTOMIZER = 458**

Matched resource processor service is a customizer from another deployment package.

DeploymentAdmin.installDeploymentPackage(InputStream) throws exception with this error code.

114.15.5.7   **public static final int CODE_MISSING_BUNDLE = 454**

A bundle in the deployment package is marked as DeploymentPackage-Missing but there is no such bundle in the target deployment package.

DeploymentAdmin.installDeploymentPackage(InputStream) throws exception with this error code.

114.15.5.8   **public static final int CODE_MISSING_FIXPACK_TARGET = 453**

Fix pack version range doesn't fit to the version of the target deployment package or the target deployment package of the fix pack doesn't exist.

DeploymentAdmin.installDeploymentPackage(InputStream) throws exception with this error code.

114.15.5.9   **public static final int CODE_MISSING_HEADER = 451**

Missing mandatory manifest header.

DeploymentAdmin.installDeploymentPackage(InputStream) can throw exception with this error code.

114.15.5.10   **public static final int CODE_MISSING_RESOURCE = 455**

A resource in the source deployment package is marked as DeploymentPackage-Missing but there is no such resource in the target deployment package.

DeploymentAdmin.installDeploymentPackage(InputStream) throws exception with this error code.

114.15.5.11   **public static final int CODE_NOT_A_JAR = 404**

DeploymentAdmin.installDeploymentPackage(InputStream) methods can throw DeploymentException with this error code if the got InputStream is not a jar.

114.15.5.12   **public static final int CODE_ORDER_ERROR = 450**

Order of files in the deployment package is bad. The right order is the following:

1   META-INF/MANIFEST.MF
2   META-INF/*.SF, META-INF/*.DSA, META-INF/*.RS
3   Localization files
4   Bundles
5   Resources

DeploymentAdmin.installDeploymentPackage(InputStream) throws exception with this error code.

114.15.5.13   **public static final int CODE_OTHER_ERROR = 463**

Other error condition.

All Deployment Admin methods which throw DeploymentException can throw an exception with this error code if the error condition cannot be categorized.

114.15.5.14   **public static final int CODE_PROCESSOR_NOT_FOUND = 464**

The Resource Processor service with the given PID (see Resource-Processor manifest header) is not found.

DeploymentAdmin.installDeploymentPackage(InputStream), DeploymentPackage.uninstall() and DeploymentPackage.uninstallForced() throws exception with this error code.

114.15.5.15   **public static final int CODE_RESOURCE_SHARING_VIOLATION = 461**

An artifact of any resource already exists.

This exception is thrown when the called resource processor throws a ResourceProcessorException with the org.osgi.service.deploymentadmin.spi.ResourceProcessorException.CODE_RESOURCE_SHARING_VIOLATION error code.

DeploymentAdmin.installDeploymentPackage(InputStream) throws exception with this error code.

114.15.5.16   **public static final int CODE_SIGNING_ERROR = 456**

Bad deployment package signing.

DeploymentAdmin.installDeploymentPackage(InputStream) throws exception with this error code.

114.15.5.17   **public static final int CODE_TIMEOUT = 465**

When a client requests a new session with an install or uninstall operation, it must block that call until the earlier session is completed. The Deployment Admin service must throw a Deployment Exception with this error code when the session can not be created after an appropriate time out period.

DeploymentAdmin.installDeploymentPackage(InputStream), DeploymentPackage.uninstall() and DeploymentPackage.uninstallForced() throws exception with this error code.

114.15.5.18   **public DeploymentException(int code, String message, Throwable cause)**

code   The error code of the failure. Code should be one of the predefined integer values (CODE_X).

message   Message associated with the exception

cause   the originating exception

    ☐ Create an instance of the exception.

114.15.5.19   **public DeploymentException(int code, String message)**

    code The error code of the failure. Code should be one of the predefined integer values (CODE_X).

  message Message associated with the exception

    ☐ Create an instance of the exception. Cause exception is implicitly set to null.

114.15.5.20   **public DeploymentException(int code)**

    code The error code of the failure. Code should be one of the predefined integer values (CODE_X).

    ☐ Create an instance of the exception. Cause exception and message are implicitly set to null.

114.15.5.21   **public Throwable getCause( )**

    ☐ Returns the cause of this exception or null if no cause was set.

  Returns The cause of this exception or null if no cause was set.

114.15.5.22   **public int getCode( )**

  Returns Returns the code.

114.15.5.23   **public Throwable initCause(Throwable cause)**

  cause The cause of this exception.

    ☐ Initializes the cause of this exception to the specified value.

  Returns This exception.

  Throws IllegalArgumentException – If the specified cause is this exception.

          IllegalStateException – If the cause of this exception has already been set.

  Since 1.1

114.15.6   public interface DeploymentPackage

The DeploymentPackage object represents a deployment package (already installed or being currently processed). A Deployment Package groups resources as a unit of management. A deployment package is something that can be installed, updated, and uninstalled as a unit. A deployment package is a reified concept, like a bundle, in an OSGi Service Platform. It is not known by the OSGi Framework, but it is managed by the Deployment Admin service. A deployment package is a stream of resources (including bundles) which, once processed, will result in new artifacts (effects on the system) being added to the OSGi platform. These new artifacts can include installed Bundles, new configuration objects added to the Configuration Admin service, new Wire objects added to the Wire Admin service, or changed system properties, etc. All the changes caused by the processing of a deployment package are persistently associated with the deployment package, so that they can be appropriately cleaned up when the deployment package is uninstalled. There is a strict no overlap rule imposed on deployment packages. Two deployment packages are not allowed to create or manipulate the same artifact. Obviously, this means that a bundle cannot be in two different deployment packages. Any violation of this no overlap rule is considered an error and the install or update of the offending deployment package must be aborted.

The Deployment Admin service should do as much as possible to ensure transactionality. It means that if a deployment package installation, update or removal (uninstall) fails all the side effects caused by the process should be disappeared and the system should be in the state in which it was before the process.

If a deployment package is being updated the old version is visible through the DeploymentPackage interface until the update process ends. After the package is updated the updated version is visible and the old one is not accessible any more.

114.15.6.1　**public static final String EVENT_DEPLOYMENTPACKAGE_CURRENTVERSION = "deploymentpackage.currentversion"**

The currently installed version of the Deployment Package. The attribute is not present, if no version is installed:

- in the INSTALL event, when an installDeploymentPackage was called and no earlier version is present
- in the COMPLETE event after the _successfully_ completing an uninstallDeploymentPackage call

Since 1.1

114.15.6.2　**public static final String EVENT_DEPLOYMENTPACKAGE_NAME = "deploymentpackage.name"**

The name of the Deployment Package. This name is the same name as that specified in the DeploymentPackage-SymbolicName Manifest header.

Since 1.1

114.15.6.3　**public static final String EVENT_DEPLOYMENTPACKAGE_NEXTVERSION = "deploymentpackage.nextversion"**

The version of DP after the successful completion of the install operation (used in INSTALL event only). The value for this event must be a Version object.

Since 1.1

114.15.6.4　**public static final String EVENT_DEPLOYMENTPACKAGE_READABLENAME = "deploymentpackage.readablename"**

The human readable name of the DP localized to the default locale.

Since 1.1

114.15.6.5　**public boolean equals(Object other)**

other　the reference object with which to compare.

□ Indicates whether some other object is "equal to" this one. Two deployment packages are equal if they have the same deployment package symbolicname and version.

Returns　true if this object is the same as the obj argument; false otherwise.

114.15.6.6　**public Bundle getBundle(String symbolicName)**

symbolicName　the symbolic name of the requested bundle

□ Returns the bundle instance, which is part of this deployment package, that corresponds to the bundle's symbolic name passed in the symbolicName parameter. This method will return null for request for bundles that are not part of this deployment package.

As this instance is transient (i.e. a bundle can be removed at any time because of the dynamic nature of the OSGi platform), this method may also return null if the bundle is part of this deployment package, but is not currently defined to the framework.

Returns　The Bundle instance for a given bundle symbolic name.

Throws　SecurityException – if the caller doesn't have the appropriate DeploymentAdminPermission with "metadata" action

IllegalStateException – if the package is stale

114.15.6.7　　**public BundleInfo[] getBundleInfos( )**

　　　　□ Returns an array of BundleInfo objects representing the bundles specified in the manifest of this deployment package. Its size is equal to the number of the bundles in the deployment package.

Returns　array of BundleInfo objects

Throws　SecurityException – if the caller doesn't have the appropriate DeploymentAdminPermission with "metadata" action

114.15.6.8　　**public String getDisplayName( )**

　　　　□ Returns the Deployment Package human readable name. This method returns the localized human readable name as set with the DeploymentPackage-Name manifest header using the default locale. If no header is set, this method will return null.

Returns　The human readable name of the deployment package or null if header is not set.

Since　1.1

114.15.6.9　　**public String getHeader(String header)**

header　the requested header

　　　　□ Returns the requested deployment package manifest header from the main section. Header names are case insensitive. If the header doesn't exist it returns null.

　　　　If the header is localized then the localized value is returned (see OSGi Service Platform, Mobile Specification Release 4 - Localization related chapters).

Returns　the value of the header or null if the header does not exist

Throws　SecurityException – if the caller doesn't have the appropriate DeploymentAdminPermission with "metadata" action

114.15.6.10　　**public URL getIcon( )**

　　　　□ Returns a URL pointing to an image that represents the icon for this Deployment Package. The DeploymentPackage-Icon header can set an icon for the the deployment package. This method returns an absolute URL that is defined by this header. The Deployment Admin service must provide this icon as a local resource. That is, the Deployment Admin must make a local copy of the specified icon. The returned URL's must point to a local resource.

Returns　An absolute URL to a local (device resident) image resource or null if not found

Since　1.1

114.15.6.11　　**public String getName( )**

　　　　□ Returns the Deployment Package Symbolic Name of the package.

Returns　The name of the deployment package. It cannot be null.

114.15.6.12　　**public String getResourceHeader(String resource, String header)**

resource　the name of the resource (it is the same as the value of the "Name" attribute in the deployment package's manifest)

header　the requested header

　　　　□ Returns the requested deployment package manifest header from the name section determined by the resource parameter. Header names are case insensitive. If the resource or the header doesn't exist it returns null.

　　　　If the header is localized then the localized value is returned (see OSGi Service Platform, Mobile Specification Release 4 - Localization related chapters).

Returns　the value of the header or null if the resource or the header doesn't exist

Throws SecurityException – if the caller doesn't have the appropriate DeploymentAdminPermission with "metadata" action

114.15.6.13　　**public ServiceReference getResourceProcessor(String resource)**

resource　the name of the resource (it is the same as the value of the "Name" attribute in the deployment package's manifest)

☐ At the time of deployment, resource processor service instances are located to resources contained in a deployment package.

This call returns a service reference to the corresponding service instance. If the resource is not part of the deployment package or this call is made during deployment, prior to the locating of the service to process a given resource, null will be returned. Services can be updated after a deployment package has been deployed. In this event, this call will return a reference to the updated service, not to the instance that was used at deployment time.

Returns　resource processor for the resource or null.

Throws　SecurityException – if the caller doesn't have the appropriate DeploymentAdminPermission with "metadata" action

IllegalStateException – if the package is stale

114.15.6.14　　**public String[] getResources( )**

☐ Returns an array of strings representing the resources (including bundles) that are specified in the manifest of this deployment package. A string element of the array is the same as the value of the "Name" attribute in the manifest. The array contains the bundles as well.

E.g. if the "Name" section of the resource (or individual-section as the Manifest Specification (http://java.sun.com/j2se/1.4.2/docs/guide/jar/jar.html#Manifest%20Specification) calls it) in the manifest is the following

```
Name: foo/readme.txt
Resource-Processor: foo.rp
```

then the corresponding array element is the "foo/readme.txt" string.

Returns　The string array corresponding to resources. It cannot be null but its length can be zero.

Throws　SecurityException – if the caller doesn't have the appropriate DeploymentAdminPermission with "metadata" action

114.15.6.15　　**public Version getVersion( )**

☐ Returns the version of the deployment package.

Returns　version of the deployment package. It cannot be null.

114.15.6.16　　**public int hashCode( )**

☐ Returns a hash code value for the object.

Returns　a hash code value for this object

114.15.6.17　　**public boolean isStale( )**

☐ Gives back the state of the deployment package whether it is stale or not). After uninstall of a deployment package it becomes stale. Any active method calls to a stale deployment package raise IllegalStateException. Active methods are the following:

- getBundle(String)
- getResourceProcessor(String)
- uninstall()
- uninstallForced()

Returns　true if the deployment package is stale. false otherwise

See Also   uninstall, uninstallForced

114.15.6.18   **public void uninstall( ) throws DeploymentException**

❑ Uninstalls the deployment package. After uninstallation, the deployment package object becomes stale. This can be checked by using isStale(), which will return true when stale.

Throws DeploymentException – if the deployment package could not be successfully uninstalled. For detailed error code description see DeploymentException.

SecurityException – if the caller doesn't have the appropriate DeploymentAdminPermission("<filter>", "uninstall") permission.

IllegalStateException – if the package is stale

114.15.6.19   **public boolean uninstallForced( ) throws DeploymentException**

❑ This method is called to completely uninstall a deployment package, which couldn't be uninstalled using traditional means (uninstall()) due to exceptions. After uninstallation, the deployment package object becomes stale. This can be checked by using isStale(), which will return true when stale.

The method forces removal of the Deployment Package from the repository maintained by the Deployment Admin service. This method follows the same steps as uninstall. However, any errors or the absence of Resource Processor services are ignored, they must not cause a roll back. These errors should be logged.

Returns   true if the operation was successful

Throws DeploymentException – only DeploymentException.CODE_TIMEOUT and DeploymentException.CODE_CANCELLED can be thrown. For detailed error code description see DeploymentException.

SecurityException – if the caller doesn't have the appropriate DeploymentAdminPermission("<filter>", "uninstall_forced") permission.

IllegalStateException – if the package is stale

114.16   **org.osgi.service.deploymentadmin.spi**

Deployment Admin SPI Package Version 1.0. The SPI is used by Resource Processors.

Bundles wishing to use this package must list the package in the Import-Package header of the bundle's manifest. For example:

```
Import-Package: org.osgi.service.deploymentadmin.spi; version="[1.0,2.0)"
```

114.16.1   ## Summary

- *DeploymentCustomizerPermission* - The DeploymentCustomizerPermission permission gives the right to Resource Processors to access a bundle's (residing in a Deployment Package) private area.
- *DeploymentSession* - The session interface represents a currently running deployment session (install/update/uninstall).
- *ResourceProcessor* - ResourceProcessor interface is implemented by processors handling resource files in deployment packages.
- *ResourceProcessorException* - Checked exception received when something fails during a call to a Resource Processor.

114.16.2   **public class DeploymentCustomizerPermission**
extends Permission

The DeploymentCustomizerPermission permission gives the right to Resource Processors to access a bundle's (residing in a Deployment Package) private area. The bundle and the Resource Processor (customizer) have to be in the same Deployment Package.

The Resource Processor that has this permission is allowed to access the bundle's private area by calling the DeploymentSession.getDataFile method during the session (see DeploymentSession). After the session ends the FilePermissions are withdrawn. The Resource Processor will have FilePermission with "read", "write" and "delete" actions for the returned java.io.File that represents the the base directory of the persistent storage area and for its subdirectories.

The actions string is converted to lowercase before processing.

114.16.2.1   **public static final String PRIVATEAREA = "privatearea"**

Constant String to the "privatearea" action.

114.16.2.2   **public DeploymentCustomizerPermission(String name, String actions)**

name   Bundle Symbolic Name of the target bundle, must not be null.

actions   action string (only the "privatearea" or "*" action is valid; "*" means all the possible actions), must not be null.

☐ Creates a new DeploymentCustomizerPermission object for the given name and action.

The name parameter is a filter string. This filter has the same syntax as an OSGi filter but only the "name" attribute is allowed. The value of the attribute is a Bundle Symbolic Name that represents a bundle. The only allowed action is the "privatearea" action. E.g.

```
Permission perm = new DeploymentCustomizerPermission("(name=com.acme.bundle)",
"privatearea");
```

The Resource Processor that has this permission is allowed to access the bundle's private area by calling the DeploymentSession.getDataFile method. The Resource Processor will have FilePermission with "read", "write" and "delete" actions for the returned java.io.File and its subdirectories during the deployment session.

Throws   IllegalArgumentException – if the filter is invalid, the list of actions contains unknown operations or one of the parameters is null

114.16.2.3   **public boolean equals(Object obj)**

obj   the reference object with which to compare.

☐ Checks two DeploymentCustomizerPermission objects for equality. Two permission objects are equal if:

- their target filters are equal (semantically and not character by character) and
- their actions are the same

Returns   true if the two objects are equal.

See Also   java.lang.Object.equals(java.lang.Object)

114.16.2.4   **public String getActions( )**

☐ Returns the String representation of the action list.

Returns   Action list of this permission instance. It is always "privatearea".

See Also   java.security.Permission.getActions()

114.16.2.5   **public int hashCode( )**

☐ Returns hash code for this permission object.

Returns Hash code for this permission object.

See Also java.lang.Object.hashCode()

114.16.2.6   **public boolean implies(Permission permission)**

permission Permission to check.

☐ Checks if this DeploymentCustomizerPermission would imply the parameter permission. This permission implies another DeploymentCustomizerPermission permission if:

- both of them has the "privatearea" action (other actions are not allowed) and
- their filters (only name attribute is allowed in the filters) match similarly to DeploymentAdmin-Permission.

The value of the name attribute means Bundle Symbolic Name and not Deployment Package Symbolic Name here!

Returns true if this DeploymentCustomizerPermission object implies the specified permission.

See Also java.security.Permission.implies(java.security.Permission)

114.16.2.7   **public PermissionCollection newPermissionCollection( )**

☐ Returns a new PermissionCollection object for storing DeploymentCustomizerPermission objects.

Returns The new PermissionCollection.

See Also java.security.Permission.newPermissionCollection()

114.16.3   public interface DeploymentSession

The session interface represents a currently running deployment session (install/update/uninstall).

When a deployment package is installed the target package, when uninstalled the source package is an empty deployment package. The empty deployment package is a virtual entity it doesn't appear for the outside world. It is only visible on the DeploymentSession interface used by Resource Processors. Although the empty package is only visible for Resource Processors it has the following characteristics:

- has version 0.0.0
- its name is an empty string
- it is stale
- it has no bundles (see DeploymentPackage.getBundle(String))
- it has no resources (see DeploymentPackage.getResources())
- it has no headers except
  DeploymentPackage-SymbolicName and
  DeploymentPackage-Version
    (see DeploymentPackage.getHeader(String))
- it has no resource headers (see DeploymentPackage.getResourceHeader(String, String))
- DeploymentPackage.uninstall() throws java.lang.IllegalStateException
- DeploymentPackage.uninstallForced() throws java.lang.IllegalStateException

114.16.3.1   **public File getDataFile(Bundle bundle)**

bundle the bundle the private area belongs to

☐ Returns the private data area of the specified bundle. The bundle must be part of either the source or the target deployment packages. The permission set the caller resource processor needs to manipulate the private area of the bundle is set by the Deployment Admin on the fly when this method is called. The permissions remain available during the deployment action only.

The bundle and the caller Resource Processor have to be in the same Deployment Package.

Returns   file representing the private area of the bundle. It cannot be null.

Throws   SecurityException – if the caller doesn't have the appropriate DeploymentCustomizerPermission("<filter>", "privatearea") permission.

See Also   DeploymentPackage, DeploymentCustomizerPermission

114.16.3.2   public DeploymentPackage getSourceDeploymentPackage( )

□   If the deployment action is an install or an update, this call returns the DeploymentPackage instance that corresponds to the deployment package being streamed in for this session. If the deployment action is an uninstall, this call returns the empty deploymet package (see DeploymentPackage).

Returns   the source deployment package

See Also   DeploymentPackage

114.16.3.3   public DeploymentPackage getTargetDeploymentPackage( )

□   If the deployment action is an update or an uninstall, this call returns the DeploymentPackage instance for the installed deployment package. If the deployment action is an install, this call returns the empty deploymet package (see DeploymentPackage).

Returns   the target deployment package

See Also   DeploymentPackage

114.16.4   public interface ResourceProcessor

ResourceProcessor interface is implemented by processors handling resource files in deployment packages. Resource Processors expose their services as standard OSGi services. Bundles exporting the service may arrive in the deployment package (customizers) or may be preregistered (they are installed prevoiusly). Resource processors has to define the service.pid standard OSGi service property which should be a unique string.

The order of the method calls on a particular Resource Processor in case of install/update session is the following:

1   begin(DeploymentSession)
2   process(String, InputStream) calls till there are resources to process or rollback() and the further steps are ignored
3   dropped(String) calls till there are resources to drop
4   prepare()
5   commit() or rollback()

The order of the method calls on a particular Resource Processor in case of uninstall session is the following:

1   begin(DeploymentSession)
2   dropAllResources() or rollback() and the further steps are ignored
3   prepare()
4   commit() or rollback()

114.16.4.1   public void begin(DeploymentSession session)

session   object that represents the current session to the resource processor

□   Called when the Deployment Admin starts a new operation on the given deployment package, and the resource processor is associated a resource within the package. Only one deployment package can be processed at a time.

See Also   DeploymentSession

114.16.4.2   **public void cancel( )**

☐ Processing of a resource passed to the resource processor may take long. The cancel() method notifies the resource processor that it should interrupt the processing of the current resource. This
method is called by the DeploymentAdmin implementation after the DeploymentAdmin.cancel()
method is called.

114.16.4.3   **public void commit( )**

☐ Called when the processing of the current deployment package is finished. This method is called if
the processing of the current deployment package was successful, and the changes must be made
permanent.

114.16.4.4   **public void dropAllResources( ) throws ResourceProcessorException**

☐ This method is called during an "uninstall" deployment session. This method will be called on all
resource processors that are associated with resources in the deployment package being uninstalled.
This provides an opportunity for the processor to cleanup any memory and persistent data being
maintained for the deployment package.

Throws ResourceProcessorException – if all resources could not be dropped. Only the ResourceProcessor-
Exception.CODE_OTHER_ERROR is allowed.

114.16.4.5   **public void dropped(String resource) throws ResourceProcessorException**

resource the name of the resource to drop (it is the same as the value of the "Name" attribute in the deployment
package's manifest)

☐ Called when a resource, associated with a particular resource processor, had belonged to an earlier
version of a deployment package but is not present in the current version of the deployment package. This provides an opportunity for the processor to cleanup any memory and persistent data being
maintained for the particular resource. This method will only be called during "update" deployment
sessions.

Throws ResourceProcessorException – if the resource is not allowed to be dropped. Only the ResourcePro-
cessorException.CODE_OTHER_ERROR error code is allowed

114.16.4.6   **public void prepare( ) throws ResourceProcessorException**

☐ This method is called on the Resource Processor immediately before calling the commit method. The
Resource Processor has to check whether it is able to commit the operations since the last begin
method call. If it determines that it is not able to commit the changes, it has to raise a
ResourceProcessorException with the ResourceProcessorException.CODE_PREPARE error code.

Throws ResourceProcessorException – if the resource processor is able to determine it is not able to commit. Only the ResourceProcessorException.CODE_PREPARE error code is allowed.

114.16.4.7   **public void process(String name, InputStream stream) throws ResourceProcessorException**

name The name of the resource relative to the deployment package root directory.

stream The stream for the resource.

☐ Called when a resource is encountered in the deployment package for which this resource processor
has been selected to handle the processing of that resource.

Throws ResourceProcessorException – if the resource cannot be processed. Only ResourceProcessorEx-
ception.CODE_RESOURCE_SHARING_VIOLATION and ResourceProcessorExcep-
tion.CODE_OTHER_ERROR error codes are allowed.

114.16.4.8   **public void rollback( )**

□ Called when the processing of the current deployment package is finished. This method is called if the processing of the current deployment package was unsuccessful, and the changes made during the processing of the deployment package should be removed.

114.16.5   public class ResourceProcessorException extends Exception

Checked exception received when something fails during a call to a Resource Processor. A ResourceProcessorException always contains an error code (one of the constants specified in this class), and may optionally contain the textual description of the error condition and a nested cause exception.

114.16.5.1   **public static final int CODE_OTHER_ERROR = 463**

Other error condition.

All Resource Processor methods which throw ResourceProcessorException is allowed throw an exception with this erro code if the error condition cannot be categorized.

114.16.5.2   **public static final int CODE_PREPARE = 1**

Resource Processors are allowed to raise an exception with this error code to indicate that the processor is not able to commit the operations it made since the last call of ResourceProcessor.begin(DeploymentSession) method.

Only the ResourceProcessor.prepare() method is allowed to throw exception with this error code.

114.16.5.3   **public static final int CODE_RESOURCE_SHARING_VIOLATION = 461**

An artifact of any resource already exists.

Only the ResourceProcessor.process(String, InputStream) method is allowed to throw exception with this error code.

114.16.5.4   **public ResourceProcessorException(int code, String message, Throwable cause)**

code The error code of the failure. Code should be one of the predefined integer values (CODE_X).

message Message associated with the exception

cause the originating exception

□ Create an instance of the exception.

114.16.5.5   **public ResourceProcessorException(int code, String message)**

code The error code of the failure. Code should be one of the predefined integer values (CODE_X).

message Message associated with the exception

□ Create an instance of the exception. Cause exception is implicitly set to null.

114.16.5.6   **public ResourceProcessorException(int code)**

code The error code of the failure. Code should be one of the predefined integer values (CODE_X).

□ Create an instance of the exception. Cause exception and message are implicitly set to null.

114.16.5.7   **public Throwable getCause( )**

□ Returns the cause of this exception or null if no cause was set.

Returns The cause of this exception or null if no cause was set.

114.16.5.8   **public int getCode( )**

Returns Returns the code.

114.16.5.9   **public Throwable initCause(Throwable cause)**

cause The cause of this exception.

☐ Initializes the cause of this exception to the specified value.

Returns This exception.

Throws IllegalArgumentException – If the specified cause is this exception.

IllegalStateException – If the cause of this exception has already been set.

Since 1.0.1

114.17 References

[1] *JAR File Specification*
http://java.sun.com/j2se/1.5.0/docs/guide/jar/jar.html

[2] *OSGi Service Platform Core Specification*
http://www.osgi.org

115   Auto Configuration Specification

Version 1.0

115.1   Introduction

The purpose of the Auto Configuration specification is to allow the configuration of bundles. These bundles can be embedded in Deployment Packages or bundles that are already present on the OSGi Service Platform. This specification defines the format and processing rules of a Autoconf Resource Processor. Resource processors are defined in *Deployment Admin Specification* on page 301.

An Auto Configuration Resource contains information to define Configuration objects for the *Configuration Admin Service Specification* on page 67.

115.1.1   Entities

- *Autoconf Resource* – One or more resources in a Deployment Package that are processed by the Autoconf Processor.
- *Deployment Package* – A named and versioned file that groups resources into a single management unit. Deployment packages are the unit of deployment and uninstallation. Deployment packages can contain bundles and associated deployment-time resources that are processed by Resource Processors.
- *Resource Processor* – A deployment-time customizer that accepts a resource in a Deployment Package and turns it into a number of artifacts. A resource processor is a service that implements the ResourceProcessor interface.
- *Autoconf Resource Processor* – The Resource Processor that processes the autoconf resources in a Deployment Package.

Figure 115.1   *Autoconf Context Diagram*

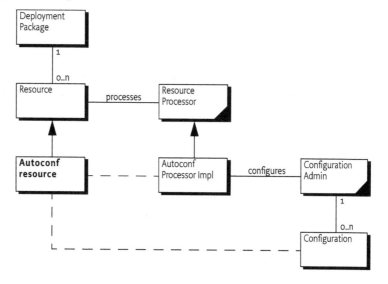

115.1.2   ### Synopsis

A Deployment Package can contain one or more Autoconf resources. The Manifest of the Deployment Package connects this resource to the Autoconf Resource Processor. When the Deployment Package is deployed, the Autoconf Resource Processor reads the information from the Autoconf resources and creates Configuration objects: both Managed Service as well as Managed Service Factory Configuration objects.

When the Deployment Package is updated or uninstalled, the Autoconf Resource Processor must delete the appropriate Configuration objects.

115.2   Configuration Data

Bundles usually require configuration data when they are deployed. For example, a bundle that has to contact a central server needs one or more server URLs. In practice, a complete application can consist of:

- A number of bundles
- Their configuration data
- Other required resources

The Deployment Package allows such an application to be installed, updated, and uninstalled in a single operation. This specification extends the Deployment Package with a facility to create Configuration objects. The extension uses the Resource Processor mechanism to read one or more resources from the Deployment Package and create Configuration objects based on these resources.

For example, a Deployment Package contains a single bundle Chat. This bundle, when started, registers a Managed Service with a PID of com.acme.pid.Chat. The expected Configuration Dictionary contains a single property: serverurl.

The schema explanation for an Autoconf resource can be found in *Metatype Service Specification* on page 105. An Autoconf resource could look like:

```
<?xml version="1.0" encoding="UTF-8"?>
<metatype:MetaData
  xmlns:metatype=
     "http://www.osgi.org/xmlns/metatype/v1.1.0">

  <OCD id="ChatConfiguration">
    <AD id="server" type="String">
  </OCD>

  <Designate pid="com.acme.pid.Chat"
     bundle="http://www.acme.com/chat.jar>
  <Object ocdref="ChatConfiguration">
    <Attribute adref="server" name="serverurl"
       content="http://chat.acme.com"/>
  </Object>
  </Designate>

</metatype:MetaData>
```

The OCD element (an abbreviation of Object Class Definition) defines the type of the Configuration Dictionary. This typing is based on the *Metatype Service Specification* on page 105. The Designate element links the configuration data to a PID. This PID is the PID for the configuration object. The content is defined in an Object element. An Object element links to an OCD element and defines the values of the attributes in Attribute elements.

The Autoconf Resource Processor in the example is instructed by this resource to create a Managed Service Configuration object with a Dictionary object that contains serverurl="http://chat.acme.com".

An Autoconf resource can configure Managed Service configurations, as long as the bundle is contained in the same Deployment Package. For bundles that are not contained in the Deployment Package, a.k.a. *foreign bundles*, only Managed Service Factory configurations can be created. Configuring foreign bundles with a Managed Service configuration could create ownership conflicts and is therefore explicitly not allowed.

The Autoconf Resource Processor must be able to handle installations, updates, and uninstallations of Deployment Packages.

115.3   Processing

The Autoconf Resource Processor must register itself with the following PID to become available to the Deployment Admin service:

```
org.osgi.deployment.rp.autoconf
```

The Autoconf Resource Processor must process each Designate element in order of appearance. This element has the following information:

- *pid* – The PID of the Configuration object. If the Configuration object is a factory configuration, the PID is actually an alias of the actual PID because a factory configuration PID is generated.
- *factoryPid* – (String) Defines a factory PID when this Designate is a *factory configuration*; otherwise it is for a *singleton configuration*.
- *bundle* – The location of the bundle. It must be used to set the location of the Configuration object. This attribute is mandatory for autoconf though it is not mandatory for the schema because other applications might not need a bundle location.
- *merge* – (true|false) Indicates that the value of the contained Object definition replaces (merge=false) the configuration data, or only replaces properties (merge=true) that do not exist in the configuration data.
- *optional* – (true|false) If true, then this Designate element is optional, and errors during processing must be ignored. Otherwise, errors during processing must abort the installation of the Deployment Package. This requires the undoing of any work done so far.

The content of a Designate element is an Object element. This element contains the value for the configuration Dictionary.

If the Designate element was marked optional, then any errors during these steps can be ignored and the next Designate element must be processed.

A factory configuration is processed differently from a singleton configuration. These two different processing methods are discussed in the following sections.

115.3.1   Factory Configurations

Factory configurations can be created and deleted any number of times. This concept of multiplicity makes it straightforward to associate factory configurations with a Deployment Package. Each Deployment Package can create its unique configurations that are independent of any other Deployment Packages. When the Deployment Package is uninstalled, the created configurations can be deleted without any concern for sharing.

A factory configuration is defined in a Designate element. The factoryPid must be set to the PID of the related Managed Service Factory service. For example:

```
<Designate pid="a" factoryPid="com.acme.a"
        bundle="osgi-dp:com.acme.A">
  <Object ocdref="a">
```

```
        <Attribute adref="foo" content="Zaphod Beeblebrox"/>
    </Object>
</Designate>
```

The Autoconf resource cannot use the actual PID of the Configuration object because the Configuration Admin service automatically generates the PID of factory configurations. This created PID is called the *actual* PID.

The Autoconf resource author cannot know the actual PID ahead of time. The Autoconf resource must therefore specify a *alias*. The alias does not have to be globally unique; it must only be unique for a specific Autoconf resource. The Autoconf Processor must maintain the following association (per Autoconf resource):

```
alias → actual PID
```

The alias can be viewed as an Autoconf resource local name for the factory configuration PID. The actual PID is generated when the Autoconf processor creates a new factory configuration. This mapping is identical to the mapping defined for the Configuration Admin Plugin; see *Factory and Singleton Configurations* on page 15.

The alias → actual PID association must be used by the Autoconf Processor to decide what life cycle operation to execute.

- *Alias → ∅* – This installation is a first-time installation of the factory configuration. The Autoconf resource specifies a factory configuration that was not part of a previous installation. The Autoconf Processor must therefore create a new factory configuration, set the configuration dictionary to the values in the Object element (see *Assigning a Value* on page 354), and create the Alias → Actual association.
- *Alias → Actual* – The factory configuration already exists from a previous Autoconf resource installation. The Autoconf Processor must merge or override (depending on the merge attribute) the Configuration object designated by the actual PID with the values in the Object element (see *Assigning a Value* on page 354).
- *∅ → Actual* – The Autoconf resource no longer contains an alias that it previously contained. The configuration identified by the actual PID must be deleted.

Uninstalling an Autoconf resource requires that the Autoconf Resource Processor deletes all Configuration objects associated with the resource.

115.3.2 Singleton Configuration

A singleton configuration is associated with a Managed Service. The Autoconf Resource Processor must only use singleton configurations for bundles that are contained in the same Deployment Package as the Autoconf resource. The target Deployment Package can provide a list of these bundles.

This ownership policy is required to prevent sharing conflicts. For this reason, the bundle attribute in the Designate element must be set to the location of the bundle so that this ownership is enforced by the Configuration Admin service. The location of the bundle is defined by the Bundle Symbolic Name of the given bundle prefixed with osgi-dp:.

The processing must abort with a fatal error if the bundle attribute is not set. The Autoconf Resource processor must bind the singleton configuration to the given bundle.

If a singleton configuration with a given PID already exists, it must be unbound or bound to the same location contained by the bundle attribute. Otherwise the processing must abort.

The singleton configuration must be merged with or replaced by the information in the Object element, depending on the merge attribute as described in *Assigning a Value* on page 354.

115.3.3   Example

For example, bundle A uses a factory configuration with the factory PID com.acme.a and bundle B uses a singleton configuration with PID com.acme.b. They define the following configuration properties:

```
com.acme.a:
gear                Integer
ratio               Vector of Float

com.acme.b:
foo                 String
bar                 Short[]
```

For proper operation, a Deployment Package P needs a configuration for com.acme.a and com.acme.b with the following values:

```
gear    = 3
ratio   = {3.14159,  1.41421356, 6.022E23}
foo     = "Zaphod Beeblebrox"
bar     = {1,2,3,4,5}
```

The corresponding autoconf.xml resource associated with Deployment Package P would look like:

```xml
<?xml version="1.0" encoding="UTF-8"?>
<metatype:MetaData
  xmlns:metatype=
    "http://www.osgi.org/xmlns/metatype/v1.1.0">

<OCD id="a">
  <AD id="gear"  type="Integer" cardinality="0" />
  <AD id="ratio" type="Float" cardinality="-3" />
</OCD>

<OCD id="b">
  <AD id="foo"   type="String" cardinality="0"/>
  <AD id="bar"   type="Short" cardinality="5"/>
</OCD>

<Designate pid="x" factoryPid="com.acme.a"
    bundle="osgi-dp:com.acme.a">
  <Object ocdref="a">
    <Attribute adref="gear" content="3" />
    <Attribute adref="ratio">
      <Value>3.14159</Value>
      <Value>1.41421356"</Value>
      <Value>6.022E23"</Value>
    </Attribute>
  </Object>
</Designate>

<Designate pid="com.acme.b"
    bundle="osgi-dp:com.acme.B">
  <Object ocdref="b">
    <Attribute adref="foo" content="Zaphod Beeblebrox"/>
    <Attribute adref="bar">
      <Value>1</Value>
      <Value>2</Value>
```

```
            <Value>3</Value>
            <Value>4</Value>
            <Value>5</Value>
          </Attribute>
        </Object>
      </Designate>
    </metatype:MetaData>
```

115.3.4   Assigning a Value

The Autoconf resources share a scheme and can cooperate with the *Metatype Service Specification* on page 105. An Autoconf resource primarily contains a number of values for configuration objects in the Designate elements. Designate elements:

- Are for a factory or singleton configuration (factoryPid attribute)
- Are bound to a bundle location (bundle attribute)
- Are meant to be merged with an existing value or replace an existing value (merge attribute). Merging means only setting the values for which the existing Configuration object has no value.
- Provide a value for the Configuration object with the Object element.

Designate elements contain an Object element that contains the actual value. Object elements refer to an OCD element by name. The OCD elements act as a descriptor of the properties.

The OCD elements that are referred from an Object element can be contained in the Autoconf resource, or they can come from the Meta Type service. The reference takes place through the ocdref attribute of the Object element. The Autoconf Resource Processor must first match this name to any OCD elements in the Autoconf resources. If the reference cannot be found in this file, it must consult the Meta Type service (if present) for the bundle that is associated with the PID that is configured.

115.3.5   Process Ordering

The Autoconf Processor must create any factory and singleton configurations when it is called with an Autoconf resource. This phase should perform as much validation as possible. The configurations must be created in the order of appearance in the Autoconf resource.

In the commit method, the Autoconf Resource Processor must first delete all Configuration objects that were uninstalled. Thereafter, it must set or update the appropriate Configuration objects.

This ordering implies that a customizer bundle cannot receive configuration parameters from an Autoconf resource.

115.4   Security Considerations

Allowing a deployment package's Autoconf resources to (re)configure arbitrary configurations creates security threats. The possible threats are discussed in the following sections.

115.4.1   Location Binding

As described in *Configuration Admin Service Specification* on page 67, it is possible for a malicious bundle to register a Managed Service under a PID used by another (legitimate) bundle. This activity essentially *hijacks* the Managed Service PID, and constitutes a denial of service attack on the legitimate bundle (as it never receives the configuration information it needs). The Configuration Admin specification describes a location binding technique that can be used to prevent this attack. The Autoconf Resource Processor must bind Configuration objects to locations specified in the Autoconf resources using the mandatory bundle attribute.

115.4.2   Autoconf Resource Permissions

The capabilities of an Autoconf Resource Processor must be limited to the permissions that are granted to the signer of a Deployment Package. This is the specified way for the Deployment Admin service to act. The Autoconf Resource Processor does not have to take any special actions; all its actions are automatically scoped by the signer of the Deployment Package.

This restriction implies, however, that the Autoconf Resource Processor must do a doPrivileged method for any actions that should not be scoped: for example, when it persists the associations of the alias → actual PID.

A Deployment Package that requires any activity from the Autoconf Resource processor must at least provide ConfigurationPermission[*,CONFIGURE].

116 **Application Admin Specification**

Version 1.1

116.1 Introduction

The OSGi Application Admin specification is intended to simplify the management of an environment with many different *types* of applications that are simultaneously available. A diverse set of application types are a fact of life because backward compatibility and normal evolution require modern devices to be able to support novel as well as legacy applications. End users do not care if an application is an Applet, a Midlet, a bundle, a Symbian, or a BREW application. This specification enables applications that manage other applications, regardless of application type. These applications are called *application managers*. This specification supports enumerating, launching, stopping and locking applications. This specification does not specify a user interface or end-user interactions.

The OSGi Service Platform is an excellent platform on which to host different Application Containers. The class loading and code sharing mechanisms available in the OSGi Service Platform can be used to implement powerful and extendable containers for Java based application models with relative ease. Native code based application models like Symbian and BREW can be supported with proxies.

116.1.1 Essentials

- *Generic Model* - The Application Admin specification defines how all applications, regardless of type, can be launched and destroyed. This application-type neutral model allows a screen or desktop manager access to all executable content in a uniform manner.
- *Schedule* - A mechanism that allows the launching of applications at a pre-defined time, interval, or event.
- *Dynamic* - Detects installations and un-installations of applications in real time.
- *Locking* - Allows applications to be persistently locked so that they cannot be launched.
- *Exit Value* – Provide a return value for an application that has exited.

116.1.2 Entities

- *Application* - A software component, which has well-defined entry and exit criteria. Applications can be started and destroyed, and usually are designed for user interaction. Applications may be of various types, each having their own specification. Applications and application instances are visible through the their Application Descriptor services and Application Handle services.
- *Application Container* - An implementation of a runtime environment for one or more application types. It provides specialized Application Descriptor and Application Handle services that correspond to the supported application type and their instances. The design of a particular Application Container is defined by other specifications. For example, an Application Container which implements MIDlets must follow the appropriate JSR specifications for MIDP.
- *Application Handle* - A service that represents an *instance* of an application. This service is available in the OSGi service registry as long as the application instance exists.
- *Application Instance* – The actual application that has been launched. Registered in the service registry as long as the application is running.
- *Application Descriptor* - A service that represents an installed Application and provides information about the application as well as launching, scheduling and locking features. An Application Descriptor must be registered for each application as long as the Application is installed
- *Application Manager* – A bundle that manages a number of applications.

- *Scheduled Application* – An information record for a scheduled application.

Figure 116.1   *Application Management Diagram org.osgi.service.application package*

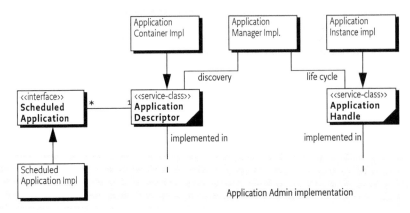

116.1.3   Synopsis

Different types of applications can be accommodated in the Application Admin specification using a model of Application Containers. An Application Container typically follows an external specification, for example, the MIDP specification. In an OSGi environment, the implementer of such a specification can allow its applications (MIDlets in the previous example) to participate in the OSGi Application Model by registering an Application Descriptor service for each of its installed applications, and an Application Handle service for each of its running instances.

This model leverages the capabilities of the OSGi service registry. Installed applications and running applications can be found by enumerating the appropriate services, possibly using a filter if a specific application is sought.The service registry provides necessary isolation of the clients of the applications and their implementers. Typical clients of this specification are desktop/screen managers that provide the end user access to the installed applications.

116.2   Application Managers

An application manager (a bundle or application that manages other applications) must be able to discover the available applications, present them to an end user and launch applications on demand. A bundle that maintains the display of a mobile phone is a typical client of this specification.

116.2.1   Discovery

The primary means of discovery is the Application Descriptor service. An Application Container must register an Application Descriptor service for each of its applications. An application manager can detect the installation and uninstallation of applications by listening to service events.

Service properties on the Application Descriptor carry most of the information that an application manager requires to present the application to the end user. The properties as defined in Table 116.1.

Specialized application descriptors can offer further service properties and method. For example, a MIDP container can register a property that describes that the MIDLet comes from a specific JAD file, thereby allowing a MIDLet aware Application Manager to group these MIDLets.

Application Descriptor services must not be declarative. That is. they can be obtained from the service registry at any time without accidentally initializing a class loader.

Table 116.1   *Service Properties for an Application Descriptor*

Key Name	Type	Default	Description
service.pid	String	*must be set*	Unique identifier of the application. It is recommended to set a value generated from the vendor's reverse domain name, e.g. com.acme.application.chess. The service.pid service property is a standard Framework property.
application.version	String	*empty string*	Specifies the version of the application. The default value is an empty string
service.vendor	String	*empty string*	Specifies the vendor of the application.
application.container	String	*must be set*	A unique identifier (like a PID) of the container implementation that registered this application descriptor.
application.location	String	*must be set*	The identifier of package that contains the application corresponding to this descriptor. It represents the installation unit that contains the corresponding application. It should be a URL. For applications installed as bundles, it should be the location of the bundle. For others, it is defined by the container implementation.
application.visible	Boolean	true	Specifies whether the application should be visible for the user. For example, some applications may provide features to other applications but nothing directly to the user. In this case the application should not be revealed to the user to start it individually.
application.launchable	Boolean	false	Specifies whether the application is ready to be launched. If the value is true, it means that all the requirements of the application are fulfilled.
application.locked	Boolean	false	Specifies whether the represented application is locked to prevent launching it.

The following example shows how to track all visible, launchable, and unlocked applications. These tracked applications are the ones that can be started.

```
public class TrackLaunchables {
    final static String filter=
       "(&(objectclass="
    + ApplicationDescriptor.class.getName()
    + ")(application.launchable=true)"
    + "(application.visible=true)"
    + "(application.locked=false))";
    static ApplicationDescriptor[] EMPTY =
        new ApplicationDescriptor[0];
    ServiceTracker tracker;

    public void init(BundleContext cntxt) throws Exception {
        tracker = new ServiceTracker(cntxt,
```

```
                cntxt.createFilter(filter), null);
            tracker.open();
        }

        public ApplicationDescriptor[] getActive() {
            Object [] result = tracker.getServices();
            List list = Arrays.asList(result);
            return (ApplicationDescriptor[]) list.toArray(EMPTY);
        }
    }
```

The code is quite simple because the Service Tracker does the actual tracking. The most important part is therefore the filter. The filter selects all the Application Descriptor services that are visible, launchable, and not locked. The getActive method converts the Object[] that the Service Tracker maintains into an array of Application Descriptors.

116.2.2   Application Descriptor Properties

The Application Descriptor object has an additional number of properties that are not available as service properties. These descriptor properties can be localized. The getProperties(String) method therefore takes a *locale* String object. This is a standard locale string as defined by the java.util.Locale class. The order for the locale constituents is:

- language
- country
- variant

For example, the following files provide manifest translations for English, Dutch (Belgium and the Netherlands) and Swedish.

```
    en          nl_BE
    nl_NL       sv
```

It returns a Map object containing localized versions of the properties. This is a copy of the original objects so changes to this Map object are not reflected in the Application Descriptor properties.

If the locale string is null, the localization will be based on the default locale, as specified by the java.util.Locale.getDefault method. If the locale is the empty String object (""), no localization must be used. This will contain the raw values that are usually used as keys. If a specific locale has no appropriate translations, a less specific locale must be used, as described in the Locale class. As last resort, the raw values must be returned.

The key names in the Map object are case-sensitive. Application Containers can add additional properties to this Map object, however, they must avoid key names starting with application. They should use key names that have a prefix that does not collide with other Application Containers.

If no locale specific value of an application property is available then the default one must be returned. The following case-sensitive key names are treated as standard for locale specific values in the Map object. Additional elements may also be stored in the Map object. The specified properties are explained in Table 116.2.

Table 116.2   *Descriptor localized properties*

Key Name	Type	Default	Description
application.name	String	*must be set*	The name of the application.
application.icon	URL	*No Icon*	A URL an icon's image resource. A compliant implementation of this specification must support the [1] *PNG Image Format.*

Table 116.2   Descriptor localized properties

Key Name	Type	Default	Description
application.version	String	0.0.0	The version of the application
service.vendor	String		The vendor of the application
application.visible	Boolean	true	
application.launchable	Boolean	true	If the application can be launched
application.locked	Boolean	true	If the application is locked
application.description	String		A description of the application
application.documentation	String		Document
application.copyright	String		A Copyright statement
application.license	String		A URL to the license related to the application
application.container	String	must be set	The PID of the associated container
application.location	String		The URL of the location of the corresponding JAR file of the application, if exists.

116.2.3   Launching

The Application Descriptor provides the launch(Map) methods for application managers to launch an application. Launching consists of creating the specific application object, starting it, registering an Application Handle service that represents that instance and return the Application Handle service.

The Map object parameter is application specific. Applications should use unique names for the keys in this map, for example com.acme.ringsignal. This specification does not specify any keys for this map except for:

- org.osgi.triggeringevent – This property is set to the Event object that cause the application to be launched (if any).

When an application is started successfully the corresponding Application Handle service will be registered with the service registry.

116.2.4   Application States

An Application Handle service represents an instance of an application. The application handle is registered by the Application Container after successfully launching a new application instance.

An Application Handle service can be used to query the state and manipulate the application instance. It is the responsibility of the Application Handle service to maintain the application instance life cycle state by interacting with the implementation object of the application.

A running instance can have the following state according to this specification:

- RUNNING – This is the state of the Application Handle when it gets registered. It indicates that the application instance is active.
- STOPPING – The application is stopping. This is a transient state.

Application Containers can extend the number of states.

The Application Handle service maintains the service properties as listed in Table 116.2. Specialized application handles may offer further service properties, but the key names specified in the table below must not be used for other purposes.

Table 116.3   *Application Handle service properties*

Key Name	Type	Default	Description
service.pid	String	*must be set*	The Application Instance ID as returned by the getInstanceId method.
application.state	String	*must be set*	Contains the current state of the application instance represented by this application handle. These states can be application model specific.
application.descriptor	String	*must be set*	The PID of the associated Application Descriptor service

Specialized application handles may offer further application states. The name of additional states must be qualified names (dotted); non-qualified names are reserved for future specifications.

116.2.5   Destroying an Application Instance

An application instance can be stopped with its associated Application Handle using the destroy() method. This first turns the state of the Application to STOPPING. The application instance may save its persistent data before termination and it must release all the used resources. The application instance's artifacts should not be reused any more. The Application Admin implementation and the application container should ensure (even forcefully) that all allocated resources are cleaned up.

If the application instance has completely stopped, then its Application Handle must be unregistered.

116.2.6   Getting the Exit Value of an Application

Many application containers allow an application to specify a value when the application is stopped. This value is called the *exit value*. The Application Handle can therefore return the exit value when this is supported by the underlying application model. It is possible to find out if the underlying container support exit values because not all application containers support exit values.

The Application Descriptor has a special service property that it must set when it supports exit values. This service property name is defined on the ApplicationHandle class as APPLICATION_SUPPORTS_EXITVALUE. Setting this property to any value signals that the application instance supports an exit value return.

The getExitValue(long) method on the ApplicationHandle class returns the exit value object from the underlying application container. If the application container does not support exit values, then this method must always throw an Unsupported Operation Exception.

The method takes a time out value which allows it to wait for the application instance to finish. This time-out can take the following values:

- *negative* – When the time-out is negative, there is no waiting. If the application instance has finished, the exit value will be returned. Otherwise an Application Exception must be thrown with the error code set to APPLICATION_EXITVALUE_NOT_AVAILABLE.
- *zero* – The method will wait indefinitely until the application is finished.
- *positive* – The method will wait for the application to finish the given number of milliseconds. If after that time the application instance is still not finished, an Application Exception must be thrown with the error code set to APPLICATION_EXITVALUE_NOT_AVAILABLE.

The type of the exit value is undefined, it is a generic Java object. It is up to the application container to define the actual type for this Object.

116.2.7   Locking an Application

Applications represented by the application descriptors can be locked. If an application is locked then no new instance of the represented application can be started until it is unlocked. The locking state of the application has no effect on the already launched instance(s). The Application Descriptor provides the methods lock and unlock to set, unset the locking state. Locking and unlocking an application represented by an Application Descriptor requires the proper Application Admin Permission. The methods to lock, unlock, and query the locked status of an application are implemented as final methods of the abstract application descriptor class to ensure that an application container implementation will not be able to circumvent this security policy.

116.2.8   Scheduling

Scheduling can be used to launch an a new application instance in the future when a specific event occurs, if needed on a recurring basis.

The Application Descriptor service provides the schedule(String,Map,String,String,boolean) method to schedule an application to be launched when an specific event occurs. The parameters to this method are:

- *Schedule Id* – (String) An id for this application that identifies the schedule, even over system restarts. Ids must be unique for one application. This id will be registered as service property on the Scheduled Application service under the name of SCHEDULE_ID. The name must match the following format:

```
scheduleId ::= symbolic-name
            // Core 1.3.2 General Syntax Definitions
```

- *Arguments* – (Map) These arguments will be passed to the application in the launch method. The keys in this map must not be null or the empty string.
- *Topic* – (String) The topic of the event that must trigger the launch of the application.
- *Filter* – (String) A filter that is passed to the Event Admin for subscribing to specific events, can be null. The syntax of the string is the same as an OSGi Framework filter.
- *Recurring* – (boolean) Repeatedly launch the application when the specified events occur until the schedule is canceled.

The schedule method must register a Scheduled Application service with the service registry and return the Schedule Application service object.

For example, the invocation

```
appDesc.schedule(
    null,      // System generates schedule id
    null,      // No arguments
    "org/osgi/application/timer",
    "(&(hour_of_day=0)(minute=0))",
    true)
```

Schedules the application to be launched when a timer event is received and the hour_of_day and minute properties are zero.

The Scheduled Application service must have the following properties:

- APPLICATION_PID - (String) The PID of the Application Descriptor service.
- SCHEDULE_ID - (String) a unique id (within the schedules for one application).

The list of active Scheduled Application services can be obtained from the service registry. A non-recurrent Scheduled Application service is unregistered once the application is successfully launched.

The timer used to start an application from a schedule has a resolution of one minute. It is therefore possible that an application is delayed up to a minute before it is started.

116.2.9 Application Exceptions

Exceptional conditions that arise during processing of application requests. The Exception identifies the actual error with an integer code. The following codes are supported:

- APPLICATION_INTERNAL_ERROR – An internal error occurred.
- APPLICATION_LOCKED – The application is locked and can therefore not be launched.
- APPLICATION_NOT_LAUNCHABLE – The application could not be launched.
- APPLICATION_SCHEDULING_FAILED – The application scheduling could not be created due to some internal error. This entails that the scheduling information is not persisted.
- APPLICATION_DUPLICATE_SCHEDULE_ID – The application scheduling failed because the specified identifier is already in use.

116.2.10 Application Events

The event mechanism of the Application Admin specification is based on the OSGi service registry event model. Both Application Descriptor and Application Handle are services. Bundles can listen to these events registering a ServiceListener object with a Bundle Context or they can listen to events from the Event Admin, see for more information *Service Event* on page 292.

- Application Descriptor service
  - REGISTERED – A new application has become available. Depending on its properties, this application could be launched.
  - MODIFIED – The visibility, launchable or locked status is changed.
  - UNREGISTERING – The application is no longer available. All running instances of this application must be destroyed before this event is delivered.
- Application Handle service
  - REGISTERED – A new instance is created and started running.
  - MODIFIED – The application instance is changed its state. This specification only specifies the STOPPING state but application containers are free to add additional states. Transitions between all these states must be signalled with the MODIFIED service event.
  - UNREGISTERING – The application instance is no longer running.

116.3 Application Containers

Application Containers provide the implementation of a specific application model like MIDP, BREW,.NET, or Symbian. Application Containers can be implemented inside the OSGi environment or run externally, in another VM or as native code. When the container runs externally, it is necessary to run a proxy inside the OSGi environment that communicates with the external container. This is shown in Figure 116.2.

Figure 116.2   *Application Container Model with Proxy*

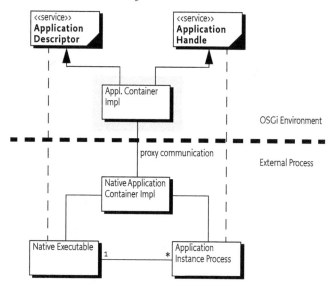

116.3.1   The Application Descriptor

The first responsibility of the Application Container is to register an Application Descriptor for each available application. The Application Container must therefore extend the ApplicationDescriptor base class that is provided by the Application Admin implementer and provided in the org.osgi.service.application package. The base class is defined as an abstract class in this specification with only minimal implementation code. Implementers of the Application Admin implementation can replace this class with an implementation that enforces their desired policies.

The Application Container must override the methods that have a Specific suffix. These methods are:

- ApplicationDescriptor(String) – The Base class Application Descriptor takes the PID of the Application Descriptor as argument.
- getPropertiesSpecific(String) – Return the properties (including service properties) based on a specific locale. See the locale rules at *Application Descriptor Properties* on page 360. The Application Container must fill the returned Map object with the properties listed in Table 116.2 on page 361 as well as other service properties. Non-localized data is returned if the corresponding application container doesn't support the localization of application properties. Changes in the Map object must not be reflected in Application Descriptor properties.
- launchSpecific(Map) – Launch a new instance and return its handle. The container must ensure that the application is started in a doPrivileged block I.e. the permissions of the caller must not influence the capabilities of the started application.
- lockSpecific() – Do the specific locking of the Application Descriptor.
- unlockSpecific() – Do the specific unlocking of the Application Descriptor.
- isLaunchableSpecific() – This method must return true when the application can be launched. This method can be called by the Application Descriptor implementation to find out if an application can be launched according to the container.

The specific methods must be made protected because the specific Application Descriptor is registered as a service and is intended to be used by a wide array of clients. These clients can call public methods so care should be taken to ensure that no intrusion can take place this way. The Application Admin implementer must provide the implementation for the public methods and perform the appropriate security checks.

The specific Application Descriptor must be registered for each possible application with the set of service properties listed in Table 116.1 on page 359.

An application is launched with the launchSpecific method. This method is called by the Application Admin implementation, as implemented in the ApplicationDescriptor base class. The implementation of the launchSpecific method must return expediently. The Application Descriptor must perform the following steps (in the given order):

1   Create a new instance of the associated application
2   Start the application in another process or thread.
3   If the application cannot be started, an appropriate Exception must be thrown.
4   Register an Application Handle for this running application. The registration of the Application Handle must be accompanied by the service properties from Table 116.3 on page 362.
5   Return the new Application Handle.

116.3.2   The Application Handle

The Application Handle represents the running instance. The Application Container must extend the provided base class and implement the following methods:

• ApplicationHandle(String,ApplicationDescriptor) – The constructor of the base class takes the executable id and the Application Descriptor as parameter.
• destroySpecific() – Clients of the Application Admin specification use the destroy method on the Application Handle service to make an application instance quit. The Application Admin implementer must at an appropriate time call the destroySpecific method. The Application Container must destroy the application instance (if it had not destroyed already) and clean up.
• getApplicationDescriptor() – Return the Application Descriptor that belongs to this Application Handle.
• getInstanceId() – A unique id for this instance.
• getState() – Returns the state for the instance. The Application Admin specification only specifies two states: RUNNING and STOPPING. Application Containers can add new states to represent for example PAUSED. States are strings and must be qualified to prevent conflicts. For example, the Midlet state for paused could be MIDLET.PAUSED.

The most important method is destroySpecific. This method must perform the following actions in the given order:

1   Set the state to STOPPING
2   Modify the service properties of the Service Handle to reflect the new state. This sends out a service event.
3   If the application instance is active, use any proprietary mechanism to stop it. Any errors and problems should be logged.
4   Using proprietary means, clean up any resources on the system that were used by the application: locks, open files, etc.
5   Unregister the Application Handle service.

The Application container should monitor the progress of its instances. If an instance stops, for example due an exception or it quits voluntarily, the Application Container must call the destroy method on the Application Handle itself and handle the fact correctly that the instance is already stopped in the destroySpecific method.

116.3.3   Certificates

The following method on the Application Descriptor provides access to the certificate chain that was used to sign the application. This method is used by the Application Permission.

• matchDNChain(String) – Verifies that the given pattern matches one or more of the certificates that were used to sign the application. This method is primarily used by the Application Admin

Permission to verify permissions. Matching certificates is described in *Certificate Matching* on page 21 of the OSGi Release 4 Core Specification.

116.3.4   Application Descriptor Example

This is an Application Container that scans a directory for executables. Each executable is registered as an Application Descriptor. The example assumes that there is a bundle activator that creates the Application Descriptor services. This activator must also ensure that when it is stopped no handles remain.

The example is not an robust implementation, its only intention is to show the concepts of the Application Admin specification in practice.

The (simple) Application Descriptor could look like:

```
public class SimpleDescriptor extends ApplicationDescriptor{
    ServiceRegistration   registration;
    File                  executable;
    SimpleModel           model;
    boolean               locked;
    static URLgenericIcon= SimpleDescriptor.class
                            .getResource("icon.png");

    SimpleDescriptor(SimpleModel model, File executable) {
        super("com.acme." + executable.getName());
        this.model = model;
        this.executable = executable;
    }

    public Map getPropertiesSpecific(String locale) {
        Map map = new Hashtable();
        map.put(APPLICATION_ICON, genericIcon);
        map.put(APPLICATION_NAME, executable.getName());
        return map;
    }

    protected ApplicationHandle launchSpecific(
        final Map args) throws Exception {
        final SimpleDescriptor descriptor = this;

        return (ApplicationHandle) AccessController
            .doPrivileged(new PrivilegedExceptionAction() {
                public Object run() throws Exception {
                    SimpleHandle handle =
                        new SimpleHandle(descriptor, args);
                    handle.registration =
                        model.register(handle);
                    return handle;
                }
            });
    }

    Dictionary getServiceProperties() {
        Hashtable p = new Hashtable();
        p.put(APPLICATION_LAUNCHABLE, Boolean.TRUE);
        p.put(APPLICATION_LOCKED, Boolean.valueOf(locked));
```

```
                p.put(Constants.SERVICE_PID, getApplicationId());
                return p;
        }

        protected void lockSpecific() {locked = true; }
        protected void unlockSpecific() { locked = false; }
        public boolean matchDNChain(String arg) { return false; }
        protected boolean isLaunchableSpecific() { return true; }
    }
```

The associated Application Handle must launch the external executable and track its process. If the process dies autonomously or is stopped via the destroy method, it must unregister the Application Handle service. The class could be implemented like:

```
    public class SimpleHandle extends
        ApplicationHandle implements Runnable {

        ServiceRegistration   registration;
        Process               process;
        int                   instance;
        String                state = RUNNING;
        static int            INSTANCE= 0;
        Thread                thread;

        public SimpleHandle(SimpleDescriptor descriptor,
            Map arguments) throws IOException {
            super(descriptor.getApplicationId()
                + ":" + (INSTANCE++), descriptor);
            String path = descriptor.executable.getAbsolutePath();
            process = Runtime.getRuntime().exec(path);
            thread = new Thread(this, getInstanceId());
            thread.start();
        }

        public String getState() {return state; }

        protected void destroySpecific() throws Exception {
            state = STOPPING;
            registration.setProperties(getServiceProperties());
            thread.interrupt();
        }

        // Wait until process finishes or when
        // interrupted
        public void run() {
            try {
                process.waitFor();
                destroy();
            }
            catch (InterruptedException ie) {
                process.destroy();
                try {
                    process.waitFor();
                }
                catch (InterruptedException iee) {
                    // Ignore
```

```
            }
        }
        catch( Exception e ) {
            .. logging
        }
        registration.unregister();
    }

    Dictionary getServiceProperties() {
        Hashtable p = new Hashtable();
        p.put(APPLICATION_PID, getInstanceId());
        p.put(APPLICATION_STATE, state);
        p.put(APPLICATION_DESCRIPTOR,
            getApplicationDescriptor().getApplicationId());
        return p;
    }
}
```

The Application Container must create the Application Descriptor services from some source. Care should be taken to optimize this scanning so that the initialization time is not significantly increased. Running application instances should be stopped if the Application Container is stopped. The following code shows a possible implementation:

```
public class SimpleModel implements BundleActivator {
    BundleContext       context;
    Set                 handles= new HashSet();

    public ServiceRegistration register(SimpleHandle handle){
        handles.add(handle);
        return context.registerService(
            ApplicationHandle.class.getName(),
            handle, handle.getServiceProperties());
    }

    public void start(BundleContext context) throws Exception
    {
        this.context = context;

        File file = new File("c:/windows");
        final SimpleModel me = this;

        file.list(new FilenameFilter() {
            public boolean accept(File dir, String name) {
                if (name.endsWith(".exe")) {
                    SimpleDescriptor sd = new SimpleDescriptor(me,
                        new File(dir, name));
                    sd.registration = me.context.registerService(
                        ApplicationDescriptor.class.getName(),
                        sd, sd.getServiceProperties());
                }
                // We ignore the return anyway
                return false;
            }});;}

    public void stop(BundleContext context) throws Exception{
```

```
              for (Iterator handle = handles.iterator();
                handle.hasNext();) {
                SimpleHandle sh = (SimpleHandle) handle.next();
                try {
                   sh.destroy();
                }
                catch (Exception e) {
                   // We are cleaning up ...
                }
        }}}
```

116.4 Application Admin Implementations

116.4.1 Implementing the Base Classes

The OSGi specified org.osgi.service.application package that is delivered with the specification in a JAR file is a dummy implementation. The intention of this package is to be replaced by an Application Admin implementation. This implementation can then enforce policies by intercepting the calls from any Application Managers to the Application Containers.

The Application Admin implementer must re-implement the following methods in the ApplicationDescriptor class:

- launch(Map) – The method can perform any checks before it must call the launchSpecific(Map) method. This must be a protected method. The implementation must perform any security checks. If these succeed, the launchSpecific method must not be called in a doPrivileged block.
- lock() – Must call the lockSpecific method.
- unlock() – Must call the unlockSpecific method.
- schedule(String,Map,String,String,boolean) – Register a new Scheduled Application service with the given arguments, thereby scheduling the application for launching when the topic and filter match an event. A virtual event is defined for timer based scheduling, see *Virtual Timer Event* on page 371.

The Application Admin implementer must also implement the following method in the ApplicationHandle class:

- destroy() – The Application Admin implementer should call the protected destroySpecific() method after which it should perform any possible cleanup operations.

Implementers must not change the signature of the public and protected parts of the ApplicationDescriptor and ApplicationHandle classes. Adding fields or methods, either public or protected is explicitly forbidden.

116.4.2 Exception Handling

The implementation of the container must ensure that Security Exceptions are only thrown during the invocation of any of the Application Descriptor methods when the required permissions are lacking. If the Application Descriptor is not valid, an Illegal State Exception must be thrown and never a Security Exception.

116.4.3 Launching

The launch method of the Application Descriptor must be implemented by the Application Admin implementer. Launching must be performed in the following steps:

1 Verify that the caller has the appropriate permissions, see *Security* on page 373.
2 Verify that the Application Descriptor is not locked and launchable
3 Perform any policy actions that are deemed necessary before the application is really launched.

4 Call the protected launchSpecific method. If the method throws an Exception, then this exception should be logged, and must be re-thrown.

5 Otherwise, return the received Application Handle

116.4.4   Destroying

The implementation of the ApplicationHandle destroy method must follow the following steps:

1 Verify that the caller has the appropriate permissions, see *Security* on page 373.
2 Call the destroySpecific method. If an Exception is thrown, then this should be logged but must be further ignored.
3 Perform any cleanup deemed necessary.

116.4.5   Scheduling

Application Descriptor services can be scheduled by calling the schedule method, as described in *Scheduling* on page 363. This method must be implemented by the Application Admin implementer.

Application Admin implementations must make a reasonable effort to launch scheduled applications in a timely manner. However, launching is not guaranteed, implementations can drop and forget events if it is necessary in order to preserve the stability and integrity of the device. The granularity of the timer should also be taken into account, this granularity is one minute so the actual time an application will be launched can be shifted up to 60 seconds.

If an event would launch multiple applications then the order of launching is not defined, it is implementation specific.

Launching a scheduled application is constrained by the same rules as application launching. Thus, attempting to launch a locked application on the specified event must fail to launch. Launching can only succeed when the application is unlocked.

If the scheduling is non-recurring and launching a new instance fails then when the specified event occurs again launching the application must be attempted again until it succeeds. Non recurring schedules must be removed once the launch succeeds.

The triggering event will be delivered to the starting application instance as an additional item identified by the org.osgi.triggeringevent argument in its startup parameters. This property must not be used for other purposes in the startup parameters. To ensure that no events are leaked to applications without the appropriate permission, the event is delivered in a java.security.GuardedObject, where the guarding permission is the Topic Permission for the topic to which the event was posted.

Scheduling and unscheduling an application, or retrieving information about scheduled applications requires the Application Admin Permission for the target application to be scheduled. If the target is the unique identifier of the scheduling application itself then it can schedule itself. In addition, the scheduling entity must have Topic Permission for the specified topic.

116.4.6   Virtual Timer Event

The application scheduler can use a virtual timer event for time scheduled applications. This event is not actually sent out by the Event Admin; this virtual event is only used for the syntax to specify a recurring launch.

The topic name of this virtual timer event is:

    org/osgi/application/timer

The properties of the virtual timer event are:

- year – (Integer) The year of the specified date. The value is defined by Calendar.YEAR field.
- month - (Integer) The month of the year. The value is defined by Calendar.MONTH field.
- day_of_month – (Integer) The day of the month. The value is defined by the Calendar.DAY_OF_MONTH field.

- day_of_week – (Integer) The day of the week. The value is defined by the Calendar.DAY_OF_WEEK field.
- hour_of_day – (Integer) The hour of the day. The value is defined by the Calendar.HOUR_OF_DAY field.
- minute – (Integer) The minute of the hour. The value is defined by the Calendar.MINUTE field.

The timer has a resolution of a minute. That is, it is not possible to schedule per second.

A property that is not included into the filter matches any value. Not including a field implies that it always matches. For example, if the minute=0 clause from the filter is missing, the timer event will be fired every minute.

The following examples are filters for the timer event to specify certain time in the device local time. The topic is always org/osgi/application/timer.

Noon every day:

    (&(hour_of_day=12)(minute=0))

Every whole hour, on every sunday:

    (&(day_of_week=0)(minute=0))

Every whole hour:

    (minute=0)

116.5 Interaction

116.5.1 Application Installation

Figure 116.3 shows how an application manager can be notified about the installation of a new application. The actual installation may be done prior to the notification or may be done by the application container. At the end of the successful installation the application container must register a specialized Application Descriptor service which properly represents the installed application. If the installed application's dependencies are fulfilled (which are container specific) then the application descriptor's application.visible and application.launchable properties should be set to true.

Figure 116.3   *Installing a bundle that is managed by an Application Container*

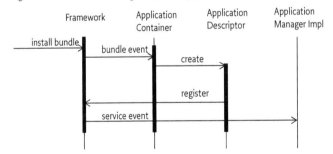

116.5.2 Launching an Application

Firstly the appropriate Application Descriptor service on which the operation will be made is fetched from the service registry. This Application Descriptor is a container specific sub-class of the Application Descriptor class. Its launch method is called which is in the base class.

The application instance may not receive the startup arguments if its application container does not support startup arguments. The launch method checks if the a new application instance can be launched, for example, that the necessary rights are granted, the application is not locked and the application is not a singleton that already has an instance.

If the application can be launched then the launchSpecific method, which is in the subclass, will create and start a new application instance according to its application container. It will create a specific application handle and associate the newly created application instance to it. The launchSpecific method will register the application handle with proper service properties. The value of application.state service property must be RUNNING. The call chain returns the application handle.

Figure 116.4　　*Launching an application*

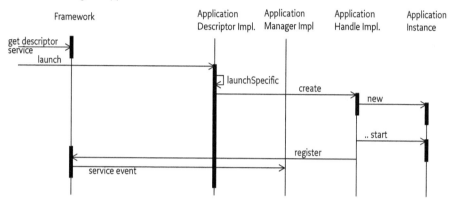

116.5.3　Destroying an Application Instance

To destroy an application, the proper application handle has to be fetched from the service registry to call its destroy() method. It checks if the instance can be destroyed, for example that the necessary permissions are granted, it then calls the destroySpecific method to let its implementation destroy the instance in an application container specific way. First, it sets the application.state service property to STOPPING then stops the application instance. Finally it unregisters the application handle.

116.6　Security

The Application Admin specification is an interaction of the:

- *Application Container implementers*
- *Applications*
- *Application Managers*

There are two permissions used in the security model of the Application Admin specification. The first is the Service Permission that grants access to getting or registering the Application Descriptor and Application Handle services. The second security is specific for the Application Admin specification and is the Application Permission.

The Application Container must be very powerful because it starts the application code, which should be able to perform almost any function.

The security checks are performed in the ApplicationDescriptor and ApplicationHandle base classes.

116.6.1   Application Admin Permissions

This ApplicationAdminPermission class implements permissions for manipulating applications and their instances. The permission must be held by any bundle that manipulates application descriptors or application handles.

The target of the Application Admin Permission is an OSGi filter that matches a number of properties. This is similar to the Admin Permission in the Framework. Alternatively, instead of the filter the pseudo target <<SELF>> can be used.

The following properties can be tested in the filter:

* *signer* – A Distinguished Name chain that is used to sign the application. The matching of this property must be done according to the rules described for DN matching in the OSGi Core Service Platform specification. The Application Admin Permission must use the ApplicationDescrptor class' matchDNChain method. Matching DN's is described in *Certificate Matching* on page 21 of the OSGi Service Platform Core specification.
* *pid* – The PID of the target application.

The pseudo target <<SELF>> indicates that the calling application is allowed to manipulate its own descriptors and handlers.

The following actions can be granted:

* SCHEDULE_ACTION – The caller is allowed to schedule an application., i.e. call the ApplicationDescriptor schedule method. This action implies LIFECYCLE_ACTION.
* LIFECYCLE_ACTION – The caller is allowed to manipulate the life cycle state of an application instance: launch and destroy.
* LOCK_ACTION – The caller is allowed to the lock and unlock methods.

116.6.2   Service and Package Permissions

116.6.2.1   Application Admin Implementation

The Application Admin implementation must have the following permissions:

```
ServicePermission    ..ScheduledApplication        REGISTER
ServicePermission    ..ApplicationDescriptor       GET
ServicePermission    ..ApplicationHandle           GET
PackagePermission    org.osgi.service.application   EXPORTONLY
ServicePermission    ..ApplicationDescriptor       GET
ServicePermission    ..ApplicationHandle           GET
ApplicationAdminPermission *                        *
```

116.6.2.2   Application Container
```
ServicePermission    ..ApplicationDescriptor       REGISTER
ServicePermission    ..ApplicationHandle           REGISTER
PackagePermission    org.osgi.service.application   IMPORT
```

Additionally, an Application Container requires all the permissions that are needed to run the applications. This is likely to be All Permission.

116.7   Changes

* Added an exit value for applications
* Minor updates

116.8 org.osgi.service.application

Application Package Version 1.1.

Bundles wishing to use this package must list the package in the Import-Package header of the bundle's manifest. For example:

```
Import-Package: org.osgi.service.application; version="[1.1,2.0)"
```

116.8.1 Summary

- *ApplicationAdminPermission* - This class implements permissions for manipulating applications and their instances.
- *ApplicationDescriptor* - An OSGi service that represents an installed application and stores information about it.
- *ApplicationException* - This exception is used to indicate problems related to application lifecycle management.
- *ApplicationHandle* - ApplicationHandle is an OSGi service interface which represents an instance of an application.
- *ScheduledApplication* - It is allowed to schedule an application based on a specific event.

116.8.2 public class ApplicationAdminPermission
extends Permission

This class implements permissions for manipulating applications and their instances.

ApplicationAdminPermission can be targeted to applications that matches the specified filter.

ApplicationAdminPermission may be granted for different actions: lifecycle, schedule and lock. The permission schedule implies the permission lifecycle.

116.8.2.1 public static final String LIFECYCLE_ACTION = "lifecycle"

Allows the lifecycle management of the target applications.

116.8.2.2 public static final String LOCK_ACTION = "lock"

Allows setting/unsetting the locking state of the target applications.

116.8.2.3 public static final String SCHEDULE_ACTION = "schedule"

Allows scheduling of the target applications. The permission to schedule an application implies that the scheduler can also manage the lifecycle of that application i.e. schedule implies lifecycle

116.8.2.4 public ApplicationAdminPermission(String filter, String actions) throws InvalidSyntaxException

filter filter to identify application. The value null is equivalent to "*" and it indicates "all application".

actions comma-separated list of the desired actions granted on the applications or "*" means all the actions. It must not be null. The order of the actions in the list is not significant.

□ Constructs an ApplicationAdminPermission. The filter specifies the target application. The filter is an LDAP-style filter, the recognized properties are signer and pid. The pattern specified in the signer is matched with the Distinguished Name chain used to sign the application. Wildcards in a DN are not matched according to the filter string rules, but according to the rules defined for a DN chain. The attribute pid is matched with the PID of the application according to the filter string rules.

If the filter is null then it matches "*". If actions is "*" then it identifies all the possible actions.

Throws InvalidSyntaxException – is thrown if the specified filter is not syntactically correct.

NullPointerException – is thrown if the actions parameter is null

See Also `ApplicationDescriptor`, `org.osgi.framework.AdminPermission`

116.8.2.5   **public ApplicationAdminPermission(ApplicationDescriptor application, String actions)**

application the tareget of the operation, it must not be null

actions the required operation. it must not be null

☐ This contructor should be used when creating ApplicationAdminPermission instance for checkPermission call.

Throws `NullPointerException` – if any of the arguments is null.

116.8.2.6   **public boolean equals(Object with)**

116.8.2.7   **public String getActions( )**

☐ Returns the actions of this permission.

Returns the actions specified when this permission was created

116.8.2.8   **public int hashCode( )**

116.8.2.9   **public boolean implies(Permission otherPermission)**

otherPermission the implied permission

☐ Checks if the specified permission is implied by this permission. The method returns true under the following conditions:

- This permission was created by specifying a filter (see ApplicationAdminPermission(String, String))
- The implied otherPermission was created for a particular ApplicationDescriptor (see ApplicationAdminPermission(ApplicationDescriptor, String))
- The filter of this permission mathes the ApplicationDescriptor specified in the otherPermission. If the filter in this permission is the <<SELF>> pseudo target, then the currentApplicationId set in the otherPermission is compared to the application Id of the target ApplicationDescriptor.
- The list of permitted actions in this permission contains all actions required in the otherPermission

Returns true if this permission implies the otherPermission, false otherwise.

116.8.2.10   **public ApplicationAdminPermission setCurrentApplicationId(String applicationId)**

applicationId the ID of the current application.

☐ This method can be used in the java.security.ProtectionDomain implementation in the implies method to insert the application ID of the current application into the permission being checked. This enables the evaluation of the <<SELF>> pseudo targets.

Returns the permission updated with the ID of the current application

116.8.3   public abstract class ApplicationDescriptor

An OSGi service that represents an installed application and stores information about it. The application descriptor can be used for instance creation.

116.8.3.1   **public static final String APPLICATION_CONTAINER = "application.container"**

The property key for the application container of the application.

116.8.3.2   **public static final String APPLICATION_COPYRIGHT = "application.copyright"**

The property key for the localized copyright notice of the application.

116.8.3.3   **public static final String APPLICATION_DESCRIPTION = "application.description"**

The property key for the localized description of the application.

116.8.3.4   **public static final String APPLICATION_DOCUMENTATION = "application.documentation"**

The property key for the localized documentation of the application.

116.8.3.5   **public static final String APPLICATION_ICON = "application.icon"**

The property key for the localized icon of the application.

116.8.3.6   **public static final String APPLICATION_LAUNCHABLE = "application.launchable"**

The property key for the launchable property of the application.

116.8.3.7   **public static final String APPLICATION_LICENSE = "application.license"**

The property key for the localized license of the application.

116.8.3.8   **public static final String APPLICATION_LOCATION = "application.location"**

The property key for the location of the application.

116.8.3.9   **public static final String APPLICATION_LOCKED = "application.locked"**

The property key for the locked property of the application.

116.8.3.10   **public static final String APPLICATION_NAME = "application.name"**

The property key for the localized name of the application.

116.8.3.11   **public static final String APPLICATION_PID = "service.pid"**

The property key for the unique identifier (PID) of the application.

116.8.3.12   **public static final String APPLICATION_VENDOR = "service.vendor"**

The property key for the name of the application vendor.

116.8.3.13   **public static final String APPLICATION_VERSION = "application.version"**

The property key for the version of the application.

116.8.3.14   **public static final String APPLICATION_VISIBLE = "application.visible"**

The property key for the visibility property of the application.

116.8.3.15   **protected ApplicationDescriptor(String applicationId)**

applicationId The identifier of the application. Its value is also available as the service.pid service property of this ApplicationDescriptor service. This parameter must not be null.

☐ Constructs the ApplicationDescriptor.

Throws NullPointerException – if the specified applicationId is null.

116.8.3.16   **public final String getApplicationId( )**

☐ Returns the identifier of the represented application.

Returns the identifier of the represented application

116.8.3.17   **public final Map getProperties(String locale)**

locale the locale string, it may be null, the value null means the default locale. If the provided locale is the empty String ("")then raw (non-localized) values are returned.

      ☐ Returns the properties of the application descriptor as key-value pairs. The return value contains the locale aware and unaware properties as well. The returned Map will include the service properties of this ApplicationDescriptor as well.

This method will call the getPropertiesSpecific method to enable the container implementation to insert application model and/or container implementation specific properties.

The returned java.util.Map will contain the standard OSGi service properties as well (e.g. service.id, service.vendor etc.) and specialized application descriptors may offer further service properties. The returned Map contains a snapshot of the properties. It will not reflect further changes in the property values nor will the update of the Map change the corresponding service property.

Returns copy of the service properties of this application descriptor service, according to the specified locale. If locale is null then the default locale's properties will be returned. (Since service properties are always exist it cannot return null.)

Throws IllegalStateException – if the application descriptor is unregistered

116.8.3.18   **protected abstract Map getPropertiesSpecific(String locale)**

locale the locale to be used for localizing the properties. If null the default locale should be used. If it is the empty String ("") then raw (non-localized) values should be returned.

      ☐ Container implementations can provide application model specific and/or container implementation specific properties via this method. Localizable properties must be returned localized if the provided locale argument is not the empty String. The value null indicates to use the default locale, for other values the specified locale should be used. The returned java.util.Map must contain the standard OSGi service properties as well (e.g. service.id, service.vendor etc.) and specialized application descriptors may offer further service properties. The returned Map contains a snapshot of the properties. It will not reflect further changes in the property values nor will the update of the Map change the corresponding service property.

Returns the application model specific and/or container implementation specific properties of this application descriptor.

Throws IllegalStateException – if the application descriptor is unregistered

116.8.3.19   **protected abstract boolean isLaunchableSpecific( )**

      ☐ This method is called by launch() to verify that according to the container, the application is launchable.

Returns true, if the application is launchable according to the container, false otherwise.

Throws IllegalStateException – if the application descriptor is unregistered

116.8.3.20   **public final ApplicationHandle launch(Map arguments) throws ApplicationException**

arguments Arguments for the newly launched application, may be null

      ☐ Launches a new instance of an application. The args parameter specifies the startup parameters for the instance to be launched, it may be null.

The following steps are made:

- Check for the appropriate permission.
- Check the locking state of the application. If locked then throw an ApplicationException with the reason code ApplicationException.APPLICATION_LOCKED.
- Calls the launchSpecific() method to create and start an application instance.
- Returns the ApplicationHandle returned by the launchSpecific()

The Map argument of the launch method contains startup arguments for the application. The keys used in the Map must be non-null, non-empty String objects. They can be standard or application specific. OSGi defines the org.osgi.triggeringevent key to be used to pass the triggering event to a scheduled application, however in the future it is possible that other well-known keys will be defined. To avoid unwanted clashes of keys, the following rules should be applied:

- The keys starting with the dash (-) character are application specific, no well-known meaning should be associated with them.
- Well-known keys should follow the reverse domain name based naming. In particular, the keys standardized in OSGi should start with org.osgi..

The method is synchronous, it return only when the application instance was successfully started or the attempt to start it failed.

This method never returns null. If launching an application fails, the appropriate exception is thrown.

Returns the registered ApplicationHandle, which represents the newly launched application instance. Never returns null.

Throws SecurityException – if the caller doesn't have "lifecycle" ApplicationAdminPermission for the application.

ApplicationException – if starting the application failed

IllegalStateException – if the application descriptor is unregistered

IllegalArgumentException – if the specified Map contains invalid keys (null objects, empty String or a key that is not String)

116.8.3.21   **protected abstract ApplicationHandle launchSpecific(Map arguments) throws Exception**

arguments the startup parameters of the new application instance, may be null

☐ Called by launch() to create and start a new instance in an application model specific way. It also creates and registeres the application handle to represent the newly created and started instance and registeres it. The method is synchonous, it return only when the application instance was successfully started or the attempt to start it failed.

This method must not return null. If launching the application failed, and exception must be thrown.

Returns the registered application model specific application handle for the newly created and started instance.

Throws IllegalStateException – if the application descriptor is unregistered

Exception – if any problem occures.

116.8.3.22   **public final void lock( )**

☐ Sets the lock state of the application. If an application is locked then launching a new instance is not possible. It does not affect the already launched instances.

Throws SecurityException – if the caller doesn't have "lock" ApplicationAdminPermission for the application.

IllegalStateException – if the application descriptor is unregistered

116.8.3.23   **protected abstract void lockSpecific( )**

☐ This method is used to notify the container implementation that the corresponding application has been locked and it should update the application.locked service property accordingly.

Throws IllegalStateException – if the application descriptor is unregistered

116.8.3.24   **public abstract boolean matchDNChain(String pattern)**

pattern a pattern for a chain of Distinguished Names. It must not be null.

☐ This method verifies whether the specified pattern matches the Distinguished Names of any of the certificate chains used to authenticate this application.

The pattern must adhere to the syntax defined in org.osgi.service.application.ApplicationAdmin-Permission for signer attributes.

This method is used by ApplicationAdminPermission.implies(java.security.Permission) method to match target ApplicationDescriptor and filter.

Returns true if the specified pattern matches at least one of the certificate chains used to authenticate this application

Throws NullPointerException – if the specified pattern is null.

IllegalStateException – if the application descriptor was unregistered

116.8.3.25   **public final ScheduledApplication schedule(String scheduleId, Map arguments, String topic, String eventFilter, boolean recurring) throws InvalidSyntaxException, ApplicationException**

scheduleId the identifier of the created schedule. It can be null, in this case the identifier is automatically generated.

arguments the startup arguments for the scheduled application, may be null

topic specifies the topic of the triggering event, it may contain a trailing asterisk as wildcard, the empty string is treated as "*", must not be null

eventFilter specifies and LDAP filter to filter on the properties of the triggering event, may be null

recurring if the recurring parameter is false then the application will be launched only once, when the event firstly occurs. If the parameter is true then scheduling will take place for every event occurrence; i.e. it is a recurring schedule

☐ Schedules the application at a specified event. Schedule information should not get lost even if the framework or the device restarts so it should be stored in a persistent storage. The method registers a ScheduledApplication service in Service Registry, representing the created schedule.

The Map argument of the method contains startup arguments for the application. The keys used in the Map must be non-null, non-empty String objects. The argument values must be of primitive types, wrapper classes of primitive types, String or arrays or collections of these.

The created schedules have a unique identifier within the scope of this ApplicationDescriptor. This identifier can be specified in the scheduleId argument. If this argument is null, the identifier is automatically generated.

Returns the registered scheduled application service

Throws NullPointerException – if the topic is null

InvalidSyntaxException – if the specified eventFilter is not syntactically correct

ApplicationException – if the schedule couldn't be created. The possible error codes are ApplicationException.APPLICATION_DUPLICATE_SCHEDULE_ID if the specified scheduleId is already used for this ApplicationDescriptor
ApplicationException.APPLICATION_SCHEDULING_FAILED if the scheduling failed due to some internal reason (e.g. persistent storage error).
ApplicationException.APPLICATION_INVALID_STARTUP_ARGUMENT if the specified startup argument doesn't satisfy the type or value constraints of startup arguments.

SecurityException – if the caller doesn't have "schedule" ApplicationAdminPermission for the application.

IllegalStateException – if the application descriptor is unregistered

IllegalArgumentException – if the specified Map contains invalid keys (null objects, empty String or a key that is not String)

116.8.3.26   **public final void unlock( )**

　　　□ Unsets the lock state of the application.

Throws SecurityException – if the caller doesn't have "lock" ApplicationAdminPermission for the application.

　　　IllegalStateException – if the application descriptor is unregistered

116.8.3.27   **protected abstract void unlockSpecific( )**

　　　□ This method is used to notify the container implementation that the corresponding application has been unlocked and it should update the application.locked service property accordingly.

Throws IllegalStateException – if the application descriptor is unregistered

116.8.4   public class ApplicationException
extends Exception

This exception is used to indicate problems related to application lifecycle management. ApplicationException object is created by the Application Admin to denote an exception condition in the lifecycle of an application. ApplicationExceptions should not be created by developers. ApplicationExceptions are associated with an error code. This code describes the type of problem reported in this exception. The possible codes are:

- APPLICATION_LOCKED - The application couldn't be launched because it is locked.
- APPLICATION_NOT_LAUNCHABLE - The application is not in launchable state.
- APPLICATION_INTERNAL_ERROR - An exception was thrown by the application or its container during launch.
- APPLICATION_SCHEDULING_FAILED - The scheduling of an application failed.
- APPLICATION_DUPLICATE_SCHEDULE_ID - The application scheduling failed because the specified identifier is already in use.
- APPLICATION_EXITVALUE_NOT_AVAILABLE - The exit value is not available for an application instance because the instance has not terminated.
- APPLICATION_INVALID_STARTUP_ARGUMENT - One of the specified startup arguments is invalid, for example its type is not permitted.

116.8.4.1   **public static final int APPLICATION_DUPLICATE_SCHEDULE_ID = 5**

The application scheduling failed because the specified identifier is already in use.

116.8.4.2   **public static final int APPLICATION_EXITVALUE_NOT_AVAILABLE = 6**

The exit value is not available for an application instance because the instance has not terminated.

Since 1.1

116.8.4.3   **public static final int APPLICATION_INTERNAL_ERROR = 3**

An exception was thrown by the application or the corresponding container during launch. The exception is available from getCause().

116.8.4.4   **public static final int APPLICATION_INVALID_STARTUP_ARGUMENT = 7**

One of the specified startup arguments is invalid, for example its type is not permitted.

Since 1.1

116.8.4.5   **public static final int APPLICATION_LOCKED = 1**

The application couldn't be launched because it is locked.

116.8.4.6   **public static final int APPLICATION_NOT_LAUNCHABLE = 2**

The application is not in launchable state, it's ApplicationDescriptor.APPLICATION_LAUNCHABLE
attribute is false.

116.8.4.7   **public static final int APPLICATION_SCHEDULING_FAILED = 4**

The application schedule could not be created due to some internal error (for example, the schedule
information couldn't be saved due to some storage error).

116.8.4.8   **public ApplicationException(int errorCode)**

errorCode The code of the error

□ Creates an ApplicationException with the specified error code.

116.8.4.9   **public ApplicationException(int errorCode, Throwable cause)**

errorCode The code of the error

cause The cause of this exception.

□ Creates a ApplicationException that wraps another exception.

116.8.4.10   **public ApplicationException(int errorCode, String message)**

errorCode The code of the error

message The associated message

□ Creates an ApplicationException with the specified error code.

116.8.4.11   **public ApplicationException(int errorCode, String message, Throwable cause)**

errorCode The code of the error

message The associated message.

cause The cause of this exception.

□ Creates a ApplicationException that wraps another exception.

116.8.4.12   **public Throwable getCause( )**

□ Returns the cause of this exception or null if no cause was set.

Returns The cause of this exception or null if no cause was set.

116.8.4.13   **public int getErrorCode( )**

□ Returns the error code associated with this exception.

Returns The error code of this exception.

116.8.5   **public abstract class ApplicationHandle**

ApplicationHandle is an OSGi service interface which represents an instance of an application. It
provides the functionality to query and manipulate the lifecycle state of the represented application
instance. It defines constants for the lifecycle states.

116.8.5.1   **public static final String APPLICATION_DESCRIPTOR = "application.descriptor"**

The property key for the pid of the corresponding application descriptor.

116.8.5.2   **public static final String APPLICATION_PID = "service.pid"**

The property key for the unique identifier (PID) of the application instance.

116.8.5.3 **public static final String APPLICATION_STATE = "application.state"**

The property key for the state of this application instance.

116.8.5.4 **public static final String APPLICATION_SUPPORTS_EXITVALUE = "application.supports.exitvalue"**

The property key for the supports exit value property of this application instance.

Since 1.1

116.8.5.5 **public static final String RUNNING = "RUNNING"**

The application instance is running. This is the initial state of a newly created application instance.

116.8.5.6 **public static final String STOPPING = "STOPPING"**

The application instance is being stopped. This is the state of the application instance during the execution of the destroy() method.

116.8.5.7 **protected ApplicationHandle(String instanceId, ApplicationDescriptor descriptor)**

instanceId the instance identifier of the represented application instance. It must not be null.

descriptor the ApplicationDescriptor of the represented application instance. It must not be null.

□ Application instance identifier is specified by the container when the instance is created. The instance identifier must remain static for the lifetime of the instance, it must remain the same even across framework restarts for the same application instance. This value must be the same as the service.pid service property of this application handle.

The instance identifier should follow the following scheme: *‹application descriptor PID›.‹index›* where *‹application descriptor PID›* is the PID of the corresponding ApplicationDescriptor and *‹index›* is a unique integer index assigned by the application container. Even after destroying the application index the same index value should not be reused in a reasonably long timeframe.

Throws NullPointerException – if any of the arguments is null.

116.8.5.8 **public final void destroy( )**

□ The application instance's lifecycle state can be influenced by this method. It lets the application instance perform operations to stop the application safely, e.g. saving its state to a permanent storage.

The method must check if the lifecycle transition is valid; a STOPPING application cannot be stopped. If it is invalid then the method must exit. Otherwise the lifecycle state of the application instance must be set to STOPPING. Then the destroySpecific() method must be called to perform any application model specific steps for safe stopping of the represented application instance.

At the end the ApplicationHandle must be unregistered. This method should free all the resources related to this ApplicationHandle.

When this method is completed the application instance has already made its operations for safe stopping, the ApplicationHandle has been unregistered and its related resources has been freed. Further calls on this application should not be made because they may have unexpected results.

Throws SecurityException – if the caller doesn't have "lifecycle" ApplicationAdminPermission for the corresponding application.

IllegalStateException – if the application handle is unregistered

116.8.5.9 **protected abstract void destroySpecific( )**

□ Called by the destroy() method to perform application model specific steps to stop and destroy an application instance safely.

Throws IllegalStateException – if the application handle is unregistered

---

116.8.5.10   **public final ApplicationDescriptor getApplicationDescriptor( )**

☐ Retrieves the ApplicationDescriptor to which this ApplicationHandle belongs.

Returns The corresponding ApplicationDescriptor

116.8.5.11   **public Object getExitValue(long timeout) throws ApplicationException, InterruptedException**

timeout The maximum time in milliseconds to wait for the application to timeout.

☐ Returns the exit value for the application instance. The timeout specifies how the method behaves when the application has not yet terminated. A negative, zero or positive value may be used.

- negative - The method does not wait for termination. If the application has not terminated then an ApplicationException is thrown.
- zero - The method waits until the application terminates.
- positive - The method waits until the application terminates or the timeout expires. If the timeout expires and the application has not terminated then an ApplicationException is thrown.

The default implementation throws an UnsupportedOperationException. The application model should override this method if exit values are supported.

Returns The exit value for the application instance. The value is application specific.

Throws UnsupportedOperationException – If the application model does not support exit values.

InterruptedException – If the thread is interrupted while waiting for the timeout.

ApplicationException – If the application has not terminated. The error code will be Application-Exception.APPLICATION_EXITVALUE_NOT_AVAILABLE.

Since 1.1

116.8.5.12   **public final String getInstanceId( )**

☐ Returns the unique identifier of this instance. This value is also available as a service property of this application handle's service.pid.

Returns the unique identifier of the instance

116.8.5.13   **public abstract String getState( )**

☐ Get the state of the application instance.

Returns the state of the application.

Throws IllegalStateException – if the application handle is unregistered

116.8.6   public interface ScheduledApplication

It is allowed to schedule an application based on a specific event. ScheduledApplication service keeps the schedule information. When the specified event is fired a new instance must be launched. Note that launching operation may fail because e.g. the application is locked.

Each ScheduledApplication instance has an identifier which is unique within the scope of the application being scheduled.

ScheduledApplication instances are registered as services. The APPLICATION_PID service property contains the PID of the application being scheduled, the SCHEDULE_ID service property contains the schedule identifier.

116.8.6.1   **public static final String APPLICATION_PID = "service.pid"**

The property key for the identifier of the application being scheduled.

116.8.6.2   **public static final String DAY_OF_MONTH = "day_of_month"**

The name of the *day of month* attribute of a virtual timer event. The value is defined by java.util.Calendar.DAY_OF_MONTH.

116.8.6.3   **public static final String DAY_OF_WEEK = "day_of_week"**

The name of the *day of week* attribute of a virtual timer event. The value is defined by java.util.Calendar.DAY_OF_WEEK.

116.8.6.4   **public static final String HOUR_OF_DAY = "hour_of_day"**

The name of the *hour of day* attribute of a virtual timer event. The value is defined by java.util.Calendar.HOUR_OF_DAY.

116.8.6.5   **public static final String MINUTE = "minute"**

The name of the *minute* attribute of a virtual timer event. The value is defined by java.util.Calendar.MINUTE.

116.8.6.6   **public static final String MONTH = "month"**

The name of the *month* attribute of a virtual timer event. The value is defined by java.util.Calendar.MONTH.

116.8.6.7   **public static final String SCHEDULE_ID = "schedule.id"**

The property key for the schedule identifier. The identifier is unique within the scope of the application being scheduled.

116.8.6.8   **public static final String TIMER_TOPIC = "org/osgi/application/timer"**

The topic name for the virtual timer topic. Time based schedules should be created using this topic.

116.8.6.9   **public static final String TRIGGERING_EVENT = "org.osgi.triggeringevent"**

The key for the startup argument used to pass the event object that triggered the schedule to launch the application instance. The event is passed in a java.security.GuardedObject protected by the corresponding org.osgi.service.event.TopicPermission.

116.8.6.10   **public static final String YEAR = "year"**

The name of the *year* attribute of a virtual timer event. The value is defined by java.util.Calendar.YEAR.

116.8.6.11   **public ApplicationDescriptor getApplicationDescriptor( )**

☐ Retrieves the ApplicationDescriptor which represents the application and necessary for launching.

Returns   the application descriptor that represents the scheduled application

Throws   IllegalStateException – if the scheduled application service is unregistered

116.8.6.12   **public Map getArguments( )**

☐ Queries the startup arguments specified when the application was scheduled. The method returns a copy of the arguments, it is not possible to modify the arguments after scheduling.

Returns   the startup arguments of the scheduled application. It may be null if null argument was specified.

Throws   IllegalStateException – if the scheduled application service is unregistered

116.8.6.13   **public String getEventFilter( )**

☐ Queries the event filter for the triggering event.

Returns the event filter for triggering event

Throws IllegalStateException – if the scheduled application service is unregistered

116.8.6.14   **public String getScheduleId( )**

□ Returns the identifier of this schedule. The identifier is unique within the scope of the application that the schedule is related to.

Returns the identifier of this schedule

116.8.6.15   **public String getTopic( )**

□ Queries the topic of the triggering event. The topic may contain a trailing asterisk as wildcard.

Returns the topic of the triggering event

Throws IllegalStateException – if the scheduled application service is unregistered

116.8.6.16   **public boolean isRecurring( )**

□ Queries if the schedule is recurring.

Returns true if the schedule is recurring, otherwise returns false

Throws IllegalStateException – if the scheduled application service is unregistered

116.8.6.17   **public void remove( )**

□ Cancels this schedule of the application.

Throws SecurityException – if the caller doesn't have "schedule" ApplicationAdminPermission for the scheduled application.

IllegalStateException – if the scheduled application service is unregistered

116.9   References

[1]   *PNG Image Format*
http://www.libpng.org/pub/png/

117 DMT Admin Service Specification

Version 1.0

117.1 Introduction

This specification defines an API for managing a device using concepts from the OMA DM specifications. This API is has been designed to be useful with or without an OSGi service platform. The API is decomposed in the following packages/functionality:

- info.dmtree – Main package that provides access to the local Device Management Tree. Access is session based.
- info.dmtree.notification – The notification package provides the capability to send alerts to the management server.
- info.dmtree.registry – This package provides access to the services defined in this specification when there is no service registry available.
- info.dmtree.spi – Provides the capability to register subtree handlers in the Device Management Tree.
- info.dmtree.notification.spi – The API to provide the possibilitity to send alerts and notifications to management servers.
- info.dmtree.security – Security classes.

This specification defines a number of services. Normally in an OSGi specification a service is a well defined entity. However, this specification is also applicable to environments where no OSGi service registry is present. In this case, the specified services are available from the DmtServiceFactory class.

117.1.1 Entities

- *Device Management Tree* – The Device Management Tree (DMT) is the logical view of manageable aspects of an OSGi Environment, structured in a tree with named nodes.
- *Dmt Admin* – A service through which the DMT can be manipulated. It is used by *local managers* or by *protocol adapters* that initiate DMT operations. The Dmt Admin service forwards selected DMT operations to Data Plugins and execute operations to Exec Plugins; in certain cases the Dmt Admin service handles the operations itself. The Dmt Admin service is a singleton.
- *Dmt Session* – A session groups a set of operations with optional transactionality and locking. Dmt Session objects are created by the Dmt Admin service and are given to a plugin when they first join the session.
- *Local Manager* – A bundle which uses the Dmt Admin service directly to read or manipulate the DMT. Local Managers usually do not have a principal associated with the session.
- *Protocol Adapter* – A bundle that communicates with a management server external to the device and uses the Dmt Admin service to operate on the DMT.
- *Meta Node* – Information provided by the node implementation about a node for the purpose of performing validation and providing assistance to users when these values are edited.
- *Multi nodes* – Interior nodes that have a homogeneous set of children. All these children share the same meta node.
- *Plugin* – Services which take the responsibility over a given sub-tree of the DMT: Data Plugin services and Exec Plugin services. Plugins exclusively manage a particular sub-tree, though Exec and Data Plugins can overlap.

- *Data Plugin* – A Plugin that can create a Readable Data Session, Read Write Data Session, or Transactional Data Session that handle data operations on a sub-tree for a Dmt Session.
- *Exec Plugin* – A Plugin that can handle execute operations.
- *Readable Data Session* – A plugin session that can only read.
- *Read Write Data Session* – A plugin session that can read and write.
- *Transactional Data Session* – A plugin session that is transactional.
- *Principal* – Represents the identity of the optional initiator of a Dmt Session. When a session has a principal, the Dmt Admin must enforce ACLs and must ignore Dmt Permissions.
- *ACL* – An Access Control List is a set of principals that is associated with permitted operations.
- *Dmt Event* – Provides information about an event inside Dmt Admin.
- *Dmt Event Listener* – Listeners to Dmt Events. These listeners can be registered with a Dmt Admin service.
- *Dmt Service Factory* – Provide access to the Dmt Admin service and Notification Service.

Figure 117.1   *Using Dmt Admin service, info.dmtree package*

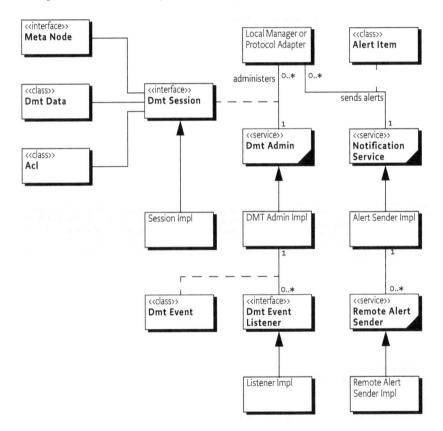

Figure 117.2   *Extending the Dmt Admin service, info.dmtree.spi package*

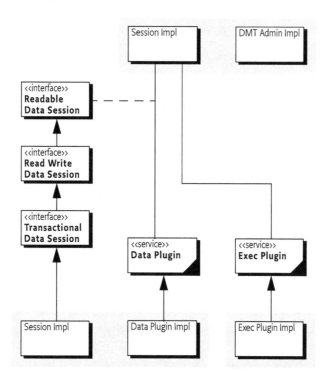

The bundle and service boundaries are not present when there is no Service Platform. In that case, the DmtServiceFactory class provides access to the Dmt Admin and Notification Service instances with a static method.

Figure 117.3   *Dmt Admin service without Service Platform*

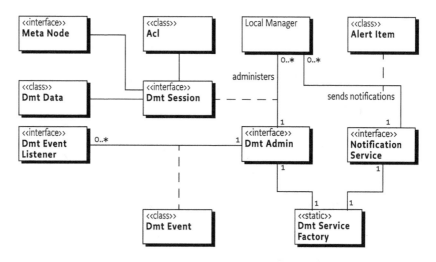

117.2 The Device Management Model

The most important decision in determining any fundamentally new architecture is choosing a single meta-data model that expresses a common conceptual and semantic view for all consumers of that architecture. In the case of networked systems management, a number of meta-data models exist to choose from:

- *SNMP* – The best-established and most ubiquitous model for network management. See [7] *SNMP* for more information.
- JMX, a generic systems management model for Java, a de-facto standard in J2EE management. See [4] *Java™ Management Extensions Instrumentation and Agent Specification* for more information.
- *JSR 9 FMA* – Federated Management Architecture (FMA) [5], another Java standard originating in storage management. See [5] *JSR 9 - Federated Management Architecture (FMA) Specification.*
- *CIM/WBEM* – Common Information Model (CIM) and Web-Based Enterprise Management, a rich and extensible management meta-model developed by the DMTF. See [6] *WBEM Profile Template, DSP1000.*

For various reasons, none of these models enjoy any significant mind share within the mobile device community. Some, like SNMP, are primitive and very limited in functionality. Some, such as JMX and FMA, are too Java-centric and not well-suited for mobile devices.

One model that appears to have gained an almost universal acceptance is the Device Management Tree (DMT), introduced in support of the OMA DM protocol (formerly known as SyncML DM); see [1] *OMA DM-TND v1.2 draft.*

OMA DM provides a hierarchical model, like SNMP, but it is more sophisticated in the kinds of operations and data structures it can support.

117.2.1 The Device Management Tree

The standard-based features of the DMT model are:

- The Device Management Tree consists of interior nodes and leaf nodes. Interior nodes can have children and leaf nodes have primitive values.
- All nodes have a set of properties: Name, Title, Format, ACL, Version, Size, Type, Value, and TimeStamp.
- The storage of the nodes is undefined. Nodes typically map to peripheral registers, settings, configuration, databases, etc.
- A node's name must be unique within its parent.
- Nodes can have Access Control Lists (ACLs), associating operations allowed on those nodes with a particular principal.
- Nodes can have Meta nodes that describe nodes and their siblings.
- Base value types (called *formats* in the standard) are
  - Integer
  - Unicode string
  - Boolean
  - Binary data
  - Date
  - Time
  - Float
  - XML fragments
- Leaf nodes in the tree can have default values specified in the meta node.
- Meta nodes have allowed access operations defined (Get, Add, Replace, Delete and Exec)

Figure 117.4   *Device Management Tree example*

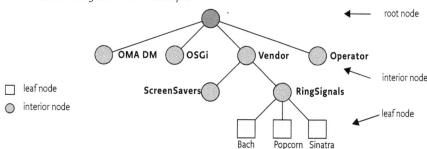

Based on its industry acceptance and technical features, the *DMT model* was chosen as the uniform meta-data and operational model. In this capacity it is considered separately and independently from OMA DM or any other provisioning protocol. The DMT *model*, not the protocol, underlies all local and remote device management operations on the OSGi Environment.

Users of this specification should be familiar with the concept of the Device Management Tree and its properties and operations as defined by OMA DM; see [1] *OMA DM-TND v1.2 draft.*

117.2.2   Extensions

This specification introduces attributes in the meta nodes, refining semantics of both interior and leaf nodes. The following constraint information has been added to the meta data:

- *Range* – Max/min. values for numbers.
- *Enumeration* – Valid values for the node value as well as the node name.
- *Validation* – Provides a basis for determining whether a node name or value is valid.
- *Raw Format* – Support for future and non-standardized data formats.

117.2.3   Tree Terminology

In the following sections, the DMT is discussed frequently. Thus, well-defined terms for all the concepts that the DMT introduces are needed. The different terms are shown in Figure 117.5.

Figure 117.5   *DMT naming, relative to node F*

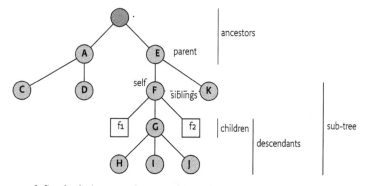

All terms are defined relative to node F. For this node, the terminology is as follows:

- *ancestors* – All nodes that are above the given node ordered in proximity. The closest node must be first in the list. In the example, this list is [./E, .]
- *parent* – The first ancestor, in this example this is ./E.
- *children* – A list of nodes that are directly beneath the given node without any preferred ordering. For node F this list is { ./E/F/f1, ./E/F/f2, ./E/F/G }.
- *siblings* – An unordered list of nodes that have the same parent. All siblings must have different names. For F, this is { ./E/K}

- *descendants* – A list of all nodes below the given node. For F this is { ./E/F/f1, ./E/F/G, ./E/F/f2, ./E/F/G/H, ./E/F/G/I, ./E/F/G/| }
- *sub-tree* – The given node plus the list of all descendants. For node F this is { ./E/F, ./E/F/f1, ./E/F/G, ./E/F/f2, ./E/F/G/H, ./E/F/G/I, ./E/F/G/| }
- *overlap* – Two given URIs overlap if they share any node in their sub-trees. In the example, the sub-tree ./E/F and ./E/F/G overlap.
- *Context Tree* – The context tree consists of the nodes that belong to the same logical unit as a given node. For example, the f1 node could describe an aspect of the | node. In that case, they both belong to the same context tree.

117.2.4   Actors

There are two typical users of the Dmt Admin service:

- *Remote manager* – The typical client of the Dmt Admin service is a *Protocol Adapter*. A management server external to the device can issue DMT operations over some management protocol. The protocol to be used is not specified by this specification; for example, OMA DM, OMA CP, and IOTA could be used. The protocol operations reach the service platform through the protocol adapter, which forwards the calls to the Dmt Admin service in a session. Protocol Adapters should authenticate the remote manager and set the principal in the session. This association will make the Dmt Admin enforce the ACLs. This requires that the principal is equal to the server name.
  The Dmt Admin provides a facility to send notifications to the remote manager with the Notification Service.
- *Local Manager* – A bundle which uses the Dmt Admin service to operate on the DMT: for example, a GUI application that allows the end user to change settings through the DMT.
  Although it is possible to manage some aspects of the system through the DMT, it can be easier for such applications to directly use the services that underlie the DMT; many of the management features available through the DMT are also available as services. These services shield the callers from the underlying details of the abstract, and sometimes hard to use DMT structure. As an example, it is more straightforward to use the Monitor Admin service than to operate upon the monitoring sub-tree. The local management application might listen to Dmt Events if it is interested in updates in the tree made by other entities, however, these events do not necessarily reflect the state of the underlying services.

Figure 117.6   Actors

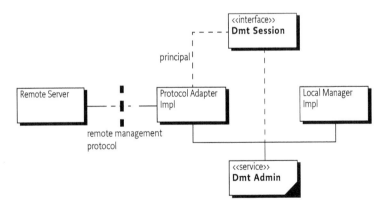

117.3   The DMT Admin Service

The Dmt Admin service operates on the Device Management Tree of an OSGi-based device. The Dmt Admin API is closely modelled after the OMA DM protocol: the operations for Get, Replace, Add, Delete and Exec are directly available. The Dmt Admin is a singleton service.

Access to the DMT is session-based to allow for locking and transactionality. The sessions are, in principle, concurrent, but implementations that queue sessions can be compliant. The client indicates to the Dmt Admin service what kind of session is needed:

- *Exclusive Update Session*– Two or more updating sessions cannot access the same part of the tree simultaneously. An updating session must acquire an exclusive lock on the sub-tree which blocks the creation of other sessions that want to operate on an overlapping sub-tree.
- *Multiple Readers Session* – Any number of read-only sessions can run concurrently, but ongoing read-only sessions must block the creation of an updating session on an overlapping sub-tree.
- *Atomic Session* – An atomic session is the same as an exclusive update session, except that the session can be rolled back at any moment, undoing all changes made so far in the session. The participants must accept the outcome: rollback or commit. There is no prepare phase. This specification does not mandate the support of atomic sessions. The lack of real transaction support can lead to error situations which are described later in this document; see *Plugins and Transactions* on page 406.

Although the DMT represents a persistent data store with transactional access and without size limitations, the notion of the DMT should not be confused with a general purpose database.

The intended purpose of the DMT is to provide a *dynamic view* of the management state of the device; the DMT model and the Dmt Admin service are designed for this purpose. Other kinds of usage, like storing and sharing generic application-specific data, are strictly discouraged because they can have severe performance implications.

117.4   Manipulating the DMT

117.4.1   The DMT Addressing URI

The OMA DM limits URIs to the definition of a URI in [8] *RFC 2396 Uniform Resource Identifiers (URI): Generic Syntax.* The Uri utility classes handles nearly all escaping issues with a number of static methods. All URIs in any of the API methods can use the full Unicode character set. For example, the following URIs as used in Java code are valid URIs for the Dmt Admin service.

```
"./ACME © 2000/A/x"
"./ACME/Address/Street/9C, Avenue St. Drézéry"
```

This strategy has a number of consequences.

- A slash ('/' \u002F) collides with the use of the slash as separator of the node names. Slashes must therefore be escaped using a backslash slash ('\/'). The backslash must be escaped with a double backslash sequence. Dmt Admin service must ignore a backslash when it is not followed by a slash or backslash. The slash and backslash must not be escaped using the %00 escaping. For example, a node that has the name of a MIME type could look like:

```
./OSGi/mime/application\/png
```

In Java, a backslash must be escaped as well, therefore requiring double backslashes:

```
String a = "./OSGi/mime/application\\/png";
```

- The length of a node name is defined to be the length of the byte array that results from UTF-8 encoding a string. This definition assumes that implementations store each character in the encoded URI as a single byte.
- Using the full Unicode character set for node names is discouraged because the encoding in the underlying storage—as well as the encoding needed in communications—can create significant performance and memory usage overhead. Names that are restricted to the URI set [-a-zA-Zo-9_.!-*'()] are most efficient.

Dmt Admin service implementations usually have a limit on node length. This length can be found out with the getMaxSegmentNameLength() method. If a node name (not a URI, but only the name part of a node) is too long, the Dmt Admin service must throw an Exception. Clients of the Dmt Admin service can use the mangle(String) method; this method is described in *Node Name Mangling* on page 400. This method also handles any necessary escaping. Names are not automatically mangled, because a mangled name cannot be distinguished from a non-mangled name.

Nodes are addressed by presenting a *relative* or *absolute URI* for the requested node. Absolute URIs start with dot ('.' \u002E), if a URI starts with something else it is a relative URI. The Uri isAbsoluteUri(String) method makes it simple to find out if a URI is relative or absolute. Relative URIs require a base URI that is for example provided by the session, see *Locking and Sessions* on page 394.

Each node name is appended to the previous ones using a slash ('/' \u002F) as the separating character. The first node of an absolute URI must be the dot ('.'\u002E).

For example, to access the Bach leaf node in the RingTones interior node from Figure 117.4 on page 391, the URI must be:

    ./Vendor/RingSignals/Bach

The URI must be given with the root of the management tree as the starting point. URIs used in the DMT must be treated and interpreted as *case-sensitive*. I.e. ./Vendor and ./vendor designate two different nodes. The following mandatory restrictions on URI syntax are intended to simplify the parsing of URIs.

- *No End Slash* – A URI must not end with the delimiter slash ('/' \u002F). The root node must be denoted as . and not ./.
- *Parents* – A URI must not be constructed using the character sequence ../ to traverse the tree upwards.
- *Single Root* – The character sequence ./ must not be used anywhere other than in the beginning of a URI.
- *Max number of segments* – A URI can have a maximum number of segments. This maximum can be found out with the getMaxUriSegments() method.
- *Maximum length* – A URI is restricted in its total length. The maximum length can be discovered with the getMaxUriLength() method.

The isValidUri(String) method verifies that a URI fulfills all its obligations and is valid.

117.4.2   Locking and Sessions

The Dmt Admin service is the main entry point into the Device Management API, its usage is to create sessions.

A simple example is getting a session on a specific sub-tree. Such a session can be created with the getSession(String) method. This method creates an updating session with an exclusive lock on the given sub-tree. The given sub-tree can be a single leaf node if so desired.

Each session has an ID associated with it which is unique to the machine and is never reused. The URI argument addresses the sub-tree root. If null, it addresses the root of the DMT. All nodes can be reached from the root, so specifying a session root node is not strictly necessary but it permits certain optimizations in the implementation.

If the default exclusive locking mode of a session is not adequate, it is possible to specify the locking mode with the getSession(String,int) and getSession(String,String,int) method. These methods supports the following locking modes:

- LOCK_TYPE_SHARED – Creates a *shared session*. It is limited to read-only access to the given sub-tree, which means that multiple sessions are allowed to read the given sub-tree at the same time.
- LOCK_TYPE_EXCLUSIVE – Creates an *exclusive session*. The lock guarantees full read-write access to the tree. Such sessions, however, cannot share their sub-tree with any other session. This type of lock requires that the underlying implementation supports Read Write Data Sessions.
- LOCK_TYPE_ATOMIC – Creates an *atomic session* with an exclusive lock on the sub-tree, but with added transactionality. Operations on such a session must either succeed together or fail together. This type of lock requires that the underlying implementation supports Transactional Data Sessions. If the Dmt Admin service does not support transactions, then it must throw a Dmt Exception with the FEATURE_NOT_SUPPORTED code. If the session accesses data plugins that are not transactional in write mode, then the Dmt Admin service must throw a Dmt Exception with the TRANSACTION_ERROR code. That is, data plugins can participate in a atomic sessions as long as they only perform read operations.

The Dmt Admin service must lock the sub-tree in the requested mode before any operations are performed. If the requested sub-tree is not accessible, the getSession(String,int), getSession(String,int), or getSession(String) method must block until the sub-tree becomes available. The implementation can decide after an implementation-dependent period to throw a Dmt Exception with the SESSION_CREATION_TIMEOUT code.

As a simplification, the Dmt Admin service is allowed to lock the entire tree irrespective of the given sub-tree. For performance reasons, implementations should provide more fine-grained locking when possible.

Persisting the changes of a session works differently for exclusive and atomic sessions. Changes to the sub-tree in an atomic session are not persisted until the commit or close method of the session is called. Changes since the last transaction point can be rolled back with the rollback method.

The commit and rollback methods can be called multiple times in a session; they do not close the session. The open, commit, and rollback methods all establish a *transaction point*. The rollback operation cannot roll back further than the last transaction point.

Once a fatal error is encountered (as defined by the DmtException isFatal() method), all successful changes must be rolled back automatically. Non-fatal errors do not rollback the session. Any error/exception in the commit or rollback methods invalidates the session.

Changes in an exclusive session are persisted immediately after each operation. Errors do not roll back any changes made in such a session.

Due to locking and transactional behavior, a session of any type must be closed once it is no longer used. Locks must always be released, even if the close method throws an exception.

Once a session is closed no further operations are allowed and manipulation methods must throw an Illegal State Exception when called. Certain information methods like for example getState() and getRootUri() can still be called for logging or diagnostic purposes. This is documented with the Dmt Session methods.

The close or commit method can be expected to fail even if all or some of the individual operations were successful. This failure can occur due to multi-node constraints defined by a specific implementation. The details of how an implementation specifies such constraints is outside the scope of this specification.

Events in an atomic session must only be sent at commit time.

117.4.3   Associating a Principal

Protocol adapters must use the getSession(String,String,int) method which features the principal as the first parameter. The principal identifies the external entity on whose behalf the session is created. This server identification string is determined during the authentication process in a way specific to the management protocol.

For example, the identity of the OMA DM server can be established during the handshake between the OMA DM agent and the server. In the simpler case of OMA CP protocol, which is a one-way protocol based on WAP Push, the identity of the agent can be a fixed value.

117.4.4   Relative Addressing

All tree operation methods are found on the session object. Most of these methods accept a relative or absolute URI as their first parameter: for example, the method isLeafNode(String).

This URI is absolute or relative to the sub-tree with which the session is associated. For example, if the session is opened on:

    ./Vendor

then the following URIs address the Bach ring tone:

    RingTones/Bach
    ./Vendor/RingTones/Bach

Opening the session with a null URI is identical to opening the session at the root. But the absolute URI can be used to address the Bach ring tone as well as a relative URI.

    ./Vendor/RingTones/Bach
    Vendor/RingTones/Bach

If the URI specified does not correspond to a legitimate node in the tree, a Dmt Exception must be thrown. The only exception to this rule is the isNodeUri(String) method that can verify if a node is actually valid. The getMetaNode(String) method must accept URIs to non-existing nodes if an applicable meta node is available; otherwise it must also throw a Dmt Exception.

117.4.5   Creating Nodes

The methods that create interior nodes are:

- createInteriorNode(String) – Create a new interior node using the default meta data. If the principal does not have Replace access rights on the parent of the new node then the session must automatically set the ACL of the new node so that the creating server has Add, Delete and Replace rights on the new node.
- createInteriorNode(String,String) – Create a new interior node. The meta data for this new node is identified by the second argument, which is a URI *identifying* an OMA DM Device Description Framework (DDF) file, this does not have to be a valid location. It uses a format like org.osgi/1.0/LogManagementObject. This meta node must be consistent with any meta information from the parent node.
- createLeafNode(String) – Create a new leaf node with a default value.
- createLeafNode(String,DmtData) – Create a leaf node and assign a value to the leaf-node.
- createLeafNode(String,DmtData,String) – Create a leaf node and assign a value for the node. The last argument is the MIME type, which can be null.

For a node to be created, the following conditions must be fulfilled:

- The URI of the new node has to be a valid URI.
- The principal of the Dmt Session, if present, must have ACL Add permission to add the node to the parent. Otherwise, the caller must have the necessary permission.

- All constraints of the meta node must be verified, including value constraints, name constraints, type constraints, and MIME type constraints. If any of the constraints fail, a Dmt Exception must be thrown with an appropriate code.

117.4.6   Node Properties

A DMT node has a number of runtime properties that can be set through the session object. These properties are:

- *Title* – (String) A human readable title for the object. The title is distinct from the node name. The title can be set with setNodeTitle(String,String) and read with getNodeTitle(String). This specification does not define how this information is localized. This property is optional depending on the implementation that handles the node.
- *Type* –(String) The MIME type, as defined in [9] *MIME Media Types*, of the node's value.The type of an interior node is an URL identifying an OMA DM Device Description Framework file (DDF). The type can be set with setNodeType(String,String) and read with getNodeType(String).
- *Version* – (int) Version number, which must start at 0, incremented after every modification (for both a leaf and an interior node) modulo 0x10000. Changes to the value or any of the properties (including ACLs), or adding/deleting nodes, are considered changes. The getNodeVersion(String) method returns this version; the value is read-only. In certain cases, the underlying data structure does not support change notifications or makes it difficult to support versions. This property is optional depending on the node's implementation.
- *Size* – (int) The size is read-only and can be read with getNodeSize(String).
- *Time Stamp* –(Date) Time of the last change in version. The getNodeTimestamp(String) returns the time stamp. The value is read only. This property is optional depending on the node's implementation.
- *ACL* – The Access Control List for this and descendant nodes. The property can be set with set-NodeAcl(String,Acl) and obtained with getNodeAcl(String).

If a plugin that does not implement an optional property is accessed, a Dmt Exception with the code FEATURE_NOT_SUPPORTED must be thrown.

117.4.7   Setting and Getting Data

Values are represented as DmtData objects, which are immutable. The are acquired with the get-NodeValue(String) method and set with the setNodeValue(String[],info.dmtree.DmtData) method.

DmtData objectcs are dynamically typed by an integer enumeration. In OMA DM, this integer is called the *format* of the data value. The format of the DmtData class is similar to the type of a variable in a programming language, but the word *format* is used here to align it with the OMA DM specification.

Formats are defined with an integer enumeration:

- FORMAT_NULL–No valid data is available. DmtData objects with this format cannot be constructed; the only instance is the DmtData NULL_VALUE constant.
- FORMAT_BINARY– A byte array. The DmtData object is created with the DmtData(byte[]) constructor. The byte array can only be acquired with the getBinary() method.
- FORMAT_BOOLEAN– A boolean, it can only be acquired with the getBoolean() method. It can be created with the DmtData(boolean) constructor.
- FORMAT_INTEGER–An int. Only the getInt() method returns this value. It can be created with the DmtData(int) constructor.
- FORMAT_FLOAT– A float. Only the getFloat() method returns this value. It can be created with the DmtData(float) constructor.
- FORMAT_STRING– A String, can only be obtained with getString() and is constructed with the DmtData(String) method.
- FORMAT_TIME – A String object that is interpreted as an OMA time type. It can be set with the DmtData(String,int) method that takes the FORMAT_TIME as the second parameter.

- FORMAT_DATE – A String object that is interpreted as an OMA date type. It can be set with the DmtData(String,int) method that takes the FORMAT_DATE as the second parameter.
- FORMAT_XML – A string containing an XML fragment. It can be obtained with getXml(). The constructor is DmtData(String,int) with the int argument set to FORMAT_XML. The validity of the XML must not be verified by the Dmt Admin service.
- FORMAT_BASE64 – A byte[] that is formatted base 64. This format is created with the DmtData(byte[],boolean) method, where the boolean must be true. It can be obtained with getBase64().
- FORMAT_RAW_BINARY – A raw binary format is always created with a format name. This format name allows the creator to define a proprietary format. The constructor is DmtData(String, byte[]) and the value can be obtained with getRawBinary(). The format name is available from the getFormatName() method, which has predefined values for the standard formats.
- FORMAT_RAW_STRING – A raw string format is always created with a format name. This format name allows the creator to define a proprietary format. The constructor is DmtData(String, String) and the value can be obtained with getRawString(). The format name is available from the getFormatName() method, which has predefined values for the standard formats.
- FORMAT_NODE – A DmtData object can have a format of FORMAT_NODE. This value is returned from a MetaNode getFormat() method if the node is an interior node or for a data value when the Plugin supports complex values. This format is created with the DmtData(Object) constructor and can be obtained with the getNode() method.

The format of a DmtData object can be retrieved with the getFormat() and getFormatName(). The names for the standard formats are the OMA DM names. For example, the name for FORMAT_TIME must be time.

117.4.8 Complex Values

The OMA DM model prescribes that only leaf nodes have primitive values. This model maps very well to remote managers. However, when a manager is written in Java and uses the Dmt Admin API to access the tree, there are often unnecessary conversions from a complex object, to leaf nodes, and back to a complex object. For example, an interior node could hold the current GPS position as an OSGi Position object, which consists of a longitude, latitude, altitude, speed, and direction. All these objects are Measurement objects which consist of value, error, and unit. Reading such a Position object through its leaves only to make a new Position object is wasting resources. It is therefore that the Dmt Admin service also supports *complex values* as a supplementary facility.

If a complex value is used then the leaves must also be accessible and represent the same semantics as the complex value. A manager unaware of complex values must work correctly by only using the leaf nodes. Setting or getting the complex value of an interior node must be identical to setting or getting the leaf nodes.

Setting a complex value to an interior node must not change the structure of the tree. No new subnodes must be added, nor is it allowed to remove sub-nodes.

Accessing a complex value requires Get access to the node and all its decendants. Setting a complex value requires Replace access to the interior node.

Trying to set or get a complex value on an interior node that does not support complex values must throw a Dmt Exception with the code COMMAND_NOT_ALLOWED.

117.4.9 Nodes and MIME Types

The Dmt Admin service recognizes a MIME type for a node. This MIME type reflects how the data of the node should be *interpreted*. For example, it is possible to store a GIF and a JPEG image in a DmtData object with a FORMAT_BINARY format. Both the GIF and the JPEG object share the same *format*, but will have MIME types of image/jpg and image/gif respectively.

The node's MIME type can be set with the setNodeType(String,String) method and acquired with getNodeType(String).

117.4.10   Deleting Nodes

The deleteNode(String) method on the session represents the Delete operation. It deletes the sub-tree of that node. This method is applicable to both leaf and interior nodes. Nodes can be deleted by the Dmt Admin service in any order. The root node of the session can not be deleted.

For example, given Figure 117.7, deleting node P must delete the nodes ./P,./P/ M, ./P/M/X, ./P/M/n2 and ./P/M/n3 in any order.

Figure 117.7   *DMT node and deletion*

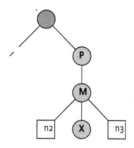

117.4.11   Copying Nodes

The copy(String,String,boolean) method on the DmtSession object represents the Copy operation. A node is completely copied to a new URI. It can be specified with a boolean if the whole sub-tree (true) or just the indicated node is copied.

The ACLs must not be copied; the new access rights must be the same as if the caller had created the new nodes individually. This restriction means that the copied nodes inherit the access rights from the parent of the destination node, unless the calling principal does not have Replace rights for the parent. See *Creating Nodes* on page 396 for details.

117.4.12   Renaming Nodes

The renameNode(String,String) method on the DmtSession object represents the Rename operation, which replaces the node name. It requires permission for the Replace operation. The root node for the current session can not be renamed.

117.4.13   Execute

The execute(String,String) and execute(String,String,String) methods can *execute* a node. Executing a node is intended to be used when a problem is hard to model as a set of leaf nodes. This can be related to synchronization issues or data manipulation. The execute methods can provide a correlator for a notification and an opaque string that is forwarded to the implementer of the node.

Execute operations can not take place in a read only session because simultaneous execution could make conflicting changes to the tree.

117.4.14   Closing

When all the changes have been made, the session must be closed by calling the close() method on the session. The Dmt Admin service must then finalize, clean up, and release any locks.

For atomic sessions, the Dmt Admin service must automatically commit any changes that were made since the last transaction point.

A session times out and is invalidated after an extended period of inactivity. The exact length of this period is not specified, but is recommended to be at least 1 minute and at most 24 hours. All methods of an invalidated session must throw an Invalid State Exception after the session is invalidated.

A session's state is one of the following: STATE_CLOSED, STATE_INVALID or STATE_OPEN, as can be queried by the getState() call. The invalid state is reached either after a fatal error case is encountered or after the session is timed out. When an atomic session is invalidated, it is automatically rolled back to the last transaction point of the session, at which the session had not yet been committed.

117.4.15 Node Name Mangling

Implementations of a Dmt Admin service can set a limit on the node name length. The node name length is defined as the length of the byte array of a UTF-8 encoded string. The node name length is a system-wide defined limit. For OMA DM, this limit can be found at the node ./DevDetail/URI/MaxSegLen. In this text this limit is called the *segment length*. As a convenience, these values are also available via static methods in the Uri class.

The Dmt Admin service must not accept long node names, and must throw a Dmt Exception with the code URI_TOO_LONG.

The user can prevent long names (and escaping issues) by mangling the name first with the mangle method on the Dmt Admin service. For example:

```
String uri = "./OSGi/Configuration/"
   + Uri.mangle( pid );
```

This method works as follows.

- A name with a node name length that is less or equal than the system defined limit only has to be escaped. Escaping is prefixing the slash ('/' \u002F) and back slash ('\' \u005C) characters with a backslash. Escaping does not influence the node name length, because this length is defined as the length of the unescaped UTF-8 encoded byte array.
- A longer name must be turned into a SHA 1 digest; see [11] *Secure Hash Algorithm 1.*
- This digest is then encoded with the base 64 algorithm; see [10] *RFC 3548 The Base16, Base32, and Base64 Data Encodings.*
- The encoded digest can now contain the slash ('/' \u002F). This character must be changed to an underscore ('_' \u005F).
- Any trailing equal signs ('=' \u003D) must be removed.

117.5 Meta Data

The getMetaNode(String) method returns a MetaNode object for a given URI. This node is called the *meta node*. A meta node provides information about nodes.

Any node can optionally have a meta node associated with it. The one or more nodes that are described by the meta nodes are called the meta node's *related instances*. A meta node can describe a singleton-related instance, or it can describe all the children of a given parent. That is to say, meta nodes can exist without an actual instance being present. For example, if a new ring tone, Grieg, was created in Figure 117.8 it would be possible to get the Meta Node for ./Vendor/RingSignals/Grieg before the node was created. This is usually the case for multi nodes. The model is depicted in Figure 117.8.

Figure 117.8   *Nodes and meta nodes*

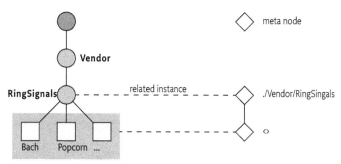

A URI must always be associated with the same Meta Node. The getMetaNode(String) always returns the same meta node for the same URI.

The actual meta data can come from two sources:

- *Dmt Admin* – Each Dmt Admin likely has a private meta data repository. This meta data is placed in the device in a proprietary way.
- *Plugins* – Plugins can carry meta nodes and provide these to Dmt Admin by implementing the getMetaNode(String[]) method. If a plugin returns a non-null value, the Dmt Admin must use that value—possibly complemented by its own metadata for elements not provided by the plugin.

The MetaNode interface supports methods to retrieve read-only meta data: both standard OMA DM as well as defined OSGi extensions and user extensions. The extensions were added to provide for better DMT data quality in an environment where many software components manipulate this data. These extensions do not break compatibility with OMA DM. Compatibility with OMA DM is further discussed in *Differences with OMA DM* on page 403.

117.5.1   Operations

The can(int) methods provide information as to whether the associated node can perform the given operation. This information is only about the capability; it can still be restricted in runtime by ACLs and permissions.

For example, if the can(MetaNode.CMD_EXECUTE) method returns true, the target object supports the Execute operation. That is, calling the execute(String,String) method with the target URI is possible.

The can(int) method can take the following constants as parameters:

- CMD_ADD
- CMD_DELETE
- CMD_EXECUTE
- CMD_GET
- CMD_REPLACE

For example:

```
void foo( DmtSession session, String nodeUri ) {
    MetaNode meta = session.getMetaNode(nodeUri);
    if ( meta !=null && meta.can(MetaNode.CMD_EXECUTE) )
        session.execute(nodeUri,"foo" );
}
```

117.5.2   Miscellaneous Meta Data

- getScope() – (int) Certain nodes represent structures in the devices that can never just be deleted or created; they represent an aspect of the device that cannot be controlled remotely. The scope defines whether the nodes can be created and deleted, or are permanent. Permanent nodes can, however, still appear and disappear. For example, an accessory that is plugged into the phone can create a new node. The return value of the getScope method describes this scope:

- DYNAMIC – Nodes can be dynamically created and deleted.
- PERMANENT – Nodes are permanent and cannot be created or deleted.
- AUTOMATIC – A dynamic node that is created automatically, either when its parent node is created, or triggered by some other condition.

For example, a node representing the battery level can never be deleted because it is an intrinsic part of the device; it will therefore be PERMANENT.

- getDescription() – (String) A description of the node. Descriptions can be used in dialogs with end users: for example, a GUI application that allows the user to set the value of a node. Localization of these values is not defined.
- getDefault() – (DmtData) A default data value.

117.5.3 Validation

The validation information allows the runtime system to verify constraints on the values; it also, however, allows user interfaces to provide guidance.

A node does not have to exist in the DMT in order to have meta data associated with it. Nodes may exist that have only partial meta data, or no metadata, associated with them. For each type of metadata, the default value to assume when it is omitted is described in *MetaNode* on page 458.

117.5.3.1 Data Types

A leaf node can be constrained to a certain format and one of a set of MIME types.

- getFormat() – (int) The required type. This type is a logical OR of the supported formats.
- getRawFormatNames() – Return an array of possible raw format names. This is only applicable when the getFormat() returns the FORMAT_RAW_BINARY or FORMAT_RAW_STRING formats. The method must return null otherwise.
- getMimeTypes() – (String[]) A list of MIME types. If this list is null, the DmtData value object can hold an arbitrary MIME type. Otherwise, the MIME type of the given DmtData object must be a member of the list returned from the getMimeTypes() method. The default value is the first entry.

117.5.3.2 Cardinality

A meta node can constrain the number of *siblings* (i.e., not the number of children) of an interior or leaf node. This constraint can be used to verify that a node must not be deleted, because there should be at least one node left on that level (isZeroOccurrenceAllowed()), or to verify that a node cannot be created, because there are already too many siblings (getMaxOccurrence()).

If the cardinality of a meta node is more than one, all siblings must share the same meta node to prevent an invalid situation. For example, if a node has two children that are described by different meta nodes, and any of the meta nodes has a cardinality > 1, that situation is invalid.

For example, the ./Vendor/RingSignals/<> meta node (where <> stands for any name) could specify that there should be between 0 and 12 ring signals.

- getMaxOccurrence() – (int) A value greater than 0 that specifies the maximum number of instances for this node.
- isZeroOccurrenceAllowed() – (boolean) Returns true if zero instances are allowed. If not, the last instance must not be deleted.

117.5.3.3 Matching

The following methods provide validation capabilities for leaf nodes.

- isValidValue(DmtData) – (DmtData) Verify that the given value is valid for this meta node.
- getValidValues() – (DmtData[]) A set of possible values for a node, or null otherwise. This can for example be used to give a user a set of options to choose from.

117.5.3.4   **Numeric Ranges**

Numeric leaf nodes (format must be FORMAT_INTEGER or FORMAT_FLOAT) can be checked for a minimum and maximum value.

Minimum and maximum values are inclusive. That is, the range is [getMin(),getMax()]. For example, if the maximum value is 5 and the minimum value is -5, then the range is [-5,5]. This means that valid values are -5,-4,-3,-2... 4, 5.

- getMax() – (double) The value of the node must be less than or equal to this maximum value.
- getMin() – (double) The value of the node must be greater than or equal to this minimum value.

If no meta data is provided for the minimum and maximum values, the meta node must return the Double.MIN_VALUE, and Double.MAX_VALUE respectively.

117.5.3.5   **Name Validation**

The meta node provides the following name validation facilities for both leaf and interior nodes:

- isValidName(String) – (String) Verifies that the given name matches the rules for this meta node.
- getValidNames() – (String[]) An array of possible names. A valid name for this node must appear in this list.

117.5.4   **User Extensions**

The Meta Node provides an extension mechanism; each meta node can be associated with a number of properties. These properties are then interpreted in a proprietary way. The following methods are used for user extensions:

- getExtensionPropertyKeys() – Returns an array of key names that can be provided by this meta node.
- getExtensionProperty(String) – Returns the value of an extension property.

For example, a manufacturer could use a regular expression to validate the node names with the isValidName(String) method. In a web based user interface it is interesting to provide validity checking in the browser, however, in such a case the regular expression string is required. This string could then be provided as a user extension under the key x-acme-regex-javascript.

117.5.5   **Differences with OMA DM**

As the meta data of a node in OSGi provides more features than are mandated by OMA DM, the Dmt Admin nodes cannot be fully described by OMA DM's DDF (Device Description Framework). How the management server learns the OSGi management object structure is out of the scope of this specification.

The following table shows the differences between the OSGi meta data and the Data Description Framework of the OMA. The DTD description of DDF can be found at [1] *OMA DM-TND v1.2 draft.*

Table 117.1   Comparison of OMA DM DDF versus OSGi meta data

	DDF Fragment	Comment
can	AccessType: Add, Delete, Exec, Get, Replace	
	AccessType: Copy	Missing in OSGi
getScope	Scope: Permanent | Dynamic | Automatic	
getDefault	DefaultValue:	
getFormat	Single format allowed for leaf nodes	OSGi allows multiple formats
isLeaf		

Table 117.1   *Comparison of OMA DM DDF versus OSGi meta data*

	DDF Fragment	Comment
getDescription	Description:	
getMaxOccurrences, isZeroOccurrencesAllowed	Occurrence: One | ZeroOrOne | ZeroOrMore | OneOrMore | ZeroOrN | OneOrN	
getMax, getMin		Missing in OMA
getMimeTypes	Type: MIME List or DDF document URI	OSGi does not allow specifying the DDF document URI; only MIME types are supported
getValidValues		Missing in OMA
getValidNames		Missing in OMA

117.6 Plugins

The Plugins take the responsibility of handling DMT operations within certain sub-trees of the DMT. It is the responsibility of the Dmt Admin service to forward the operation requests to the appropriate plugin. The only exceptions are the ACL manipulation commands. ACLs must be enforced by the Dmt Admin service: never by the plugin.

Figure 117.9   *Device Management Tree example*

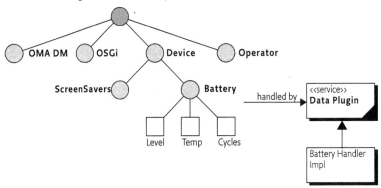

Plugins are OSGi services. The Dmt Admin must dynamically add and remove the plugins, acting as node handler, as they are registered and unregistered. Service properties are used to specify the sub-tree that the plugin can manage. Overlapping plugins are explicitly not allowed. Therefore, it is not possible for a plugin to control the same, or part of the same, sub-tree that another plugins controls.

It is the responsibility of the Dmt Admin service to guard against the registration of plugins that attempt to manage an overlapping sub-tree. If more than one plugin of the same type (Data or Exec) is registered for a particular node, the Dmt Admin service must log an error and ignore the second registration. In other words, the plugin which registered itself first will get priority over other plugins that register later. Exec Plugins are allowed to overlap Data Plugins.

For example, a plugin related to Configuration Admin handles the sub-tree which stores configuration data. This sub-tree could start at ./OSGi/Configuration. When the client wants to add a new configuration object to the DMT, it must issue an Add operation to the ./OSGi/Configuration node. The Dmt Admin then forwards this operation to the configuration plugin. The plugin maps the request to one or more method calls on the Configuration Admin service. Such a plugin can be a simple proxy to the Configuration Admin service, so it can provide a DMT view of the configuration data store.

In other cases, plugin implementations may need a proprietary backdoor to the service they make available in the DMT. For instance, the Monitor Admin service provides only methods to start local monitoring jobs; there is no public method for creating a remotely initiated job.

There are two types of Dmt plugins: *data plugins* and *exec plugins*. A data plugin is responsible for handling the sub-tree retrieval, addition and deletion operations, and handling of meta data, while an exec plugin handles the node execution operation.

117.6.1 Data Sessions

Data Plugins must participate in the Dmt Admin sessions. A Data Plugin provider must therefore register a Data Plugin service. Such a service can create a session for the Dmt Admin service when the given sub-tree is accessed by a Dmt Session. If the associated Dmt Session is later closed, the Data Session will also be closed. Three types of sessions provide different capabilities. Data Plugins do not have to implement all session types; if they do not, they can return null.

- *Readable Data Session* – Must always be supported. It provides the basic read-only access to the nodes and the close method. The Dmt Admin service uses this session type when the lock mode is LOCK_TYPE_SHARED for the Dmt Session. Such a session is created with the plugin's openReadOnlySession(String[],info.dmtree.DmtSession), method which returns a Readable-DataSession object.
- *Read Write Data Session* – Extends the Readable Data Session with capabilities to modify the DMT. This is used for Dmt Sessions that are opened with LOCK_TYPE_EXCLUSIVE. Such a session is created with the plugin's openReadWriteSession(String[],info.dmtree.DmtSession) method, which returns a ReadWriteDataSession object.
- *Transactional Data Session* – Extends the Read Write Data Session with commit and rollback methods so that this session can be used with transactions. It is used when the Dmt Session is opened with lock mode LOCK_TYPE_ATOMIC. Such a session is created with the plugin's openAtomicSession(String[],info.dmtree.DmtSession) method, which returns a Transactional-DataSession object.

117.6.2 URIs and Plugins

The plugin Data Sessions do not use a simple string to identify a node, like the Dmt Session does. Instead the URI parameter is a String[]. The members of this String[] are the different segments. The first node after the root is the second segment and the node name is the last segment. The different segments require escaping of the slash and backslash ('/' and'\').

The reason to use String[] objects instead of the original string is to reduce the number times that the URI is parsed. The entry String objects, however, are still escaped (and potentially mangled). For example, the URI ./A/B/image\/jpg gives the following String[]:

```
{ ".", "A", "B", "image\/jpg" }
```

A plugin can assume that the path is validated and can be used directly.

117.6.3 Associating a sub-tree

Each plugin is associated with one ore more DMT sub-trees. The top node of a sub-tree is called the *plugin root*. The plugin root is defined by a service registration property. This property is different for exec plugins and data plugins:

- dataRootURIs – (String[], String) Must be used by data plugins.

- execRootURIs – (String[], String) Must be used by exec plugins.

The reason for the different properties is to allow a single service to register both as a Data Plugin service as well as an Exec Plugin service.

Only nodes having occurrence=1 in their meta data can be plugin roots. If a given type of node can occur in multiple instances with different names on the same level, a plugin cannot be rooted at any of these nodes.

For example, a data plugin can register itself in its activator to handle the sub-tree ./Dev/Battery:

```
public void start(BundleContext context) {
    Hashtable ht = new Hashtable();
    ht.put(Constants.SERVICE_PID, "com.acme.data.plugin");
    ht.put( "dataRootURIs", "./Dev/Battery");
    context.registerService(
        DataPlugin.class.getName(),
        new BatteryHandler(context);
        ht );
}
```

If this activator was executed, an access to ./Dev/Battery must be forwarded by the Dmt Admin service to this plugin via a data session.

117.6.4 Synchronization with Dmt Admin Service

The Dmt Admin service can, in certain cases, detect that a node was changed without the plugin knowing about this change. For example, if the ACL is changed, the version and timestamp must be updated; these properties are maintained by the plugin. In these cases, the Dmt Admin service must open a ReadableDataSession and call nodeChanged(String[]) method with the changed URI.

117.6.5 Plugin Meta Data

Plugins can provide meta data; meta data from the Plugin must take precedence over the meta data of the Dmt Admin service.

If a plugin provides meta information, the Dmt Admin service must verify that an operation is compatible with the meta data of the given node.

For example if the plugin reports in its meta data that the ./A leaf node can only have the text/plain MIME type, the createLeafNode(String[],info.dmtree.DmtData,String) call must not be forwarded to the Plugin if the third argument specifies any other MIME type. If this contract between the Admin and the plugin is violated, the plugin should throw an Illegal State Exception.

117.6.6 Plugins and Transactions

For the Dmt Admin service to be transactional, transactions must be supported by the data plugins. This support is not mandatory in this specification, and therefore the Dmt Admin service has no transactional guarantees for atomicity, consistency, isolation or durability. The DmtAdmin interface and the DataPlugin (or more specifically the data session) interfaces, however, are designed to support Data Plugin services that are transactional. Exec plugins need not be transaction-aware because the execute method does not provide transactional semantics, although it can be executed in an atomic transaction.

Data Plugins do not have to support atomic sessions. When the Dmt Admin service creates a Transactional Data Session by calling openAtomicSession(String[],info.dmtree.DmtSession) the Data Plugin is allowed to return null. In that case, the plugin does not support atomic sessions. The caller receives a Dmt Exception with a TRANSACTION_ERROR code.

Plugins must persist any changes immediately for Read Write Data Sessions. Transactional Data Sessions must delay changes until the commit method is called, which can happen multiple times during a session. The open, commit, and rollback methods all establish a *transaction point*. Rollback can never go further back than the last transaction point.

- commit() – Commit any changes that were made to the DMT but not yet persisted. This method should not throw an Exception because other Plugins already could have persisted their data and can no longer roll it back. The commit method can be called multiple times in an open session, and if so, the commit must make persistent the changes since the last transaction point.
- rollback() – Undo any changes made to the sub-tree since the last transaction point.
- close() – Clean up and release any locks. The Dmt Admin service must call the commit methods before the close method is called. A Plugin must not perform any persistency operations in the close method.

The commit(), rollback(), and close() plugin data session methods must all be called in reverse order of that in which Plugins joined the session.

If a Plugin throws a fatal exception during an operation, the Dmt Session must be rolled back immediately, automatically rolling back all data plugins, as well as the plugins that threw the fatal Dmt Exception. The fatality of an Exception can be checked with the Dmt Exception isFatal() method.

If a plugin throws a non-fatal exception in any method accessing the DMT, the current operation fails, but the session remains open for further commands. All errors due to invalid parameters (e.g. non-existing nodes, unrecognized values), all temporary errors, etc. should fall into this category.

A rollback of the transaction can take place due to any irregularity during the session. For example:

- A necessary Plugin is unregistered
- A fatal exception is thrown while calling a plugin
- Critical data is not available
- An attempt is made to breach the security

Any Exception thrown during the course of a commit or rollback method call is considered fatal, because the session can be in a half-committed state and is not safe for further use. The operation in progress should be continued with the remaining Plugins to achieve a *best-effort* solution in this limited transactional model. Once all plugins have been committed or rolled back, the Dmt Admin service must throw an exception, specifying the cause exception(s) thrown by the plugin(s), and should log an error.

117.6.7 Side Effects

Changing a node's value will have a side effect of changing the system. A plugin can also, however, cause state changes with a get operation. Sometimes the pattern to use a get operation to perform a state changing action can be quite convenient. The get operation, however, is defined to have no side effects. This definition is reflected in the session model, which allows the DMT to be shared among readers. Therefore, plugins should refrain from causing side effects for read-only operations.

117.6.8 Copying

Plugins do not have to support the copy operation. They can throw a Dmt Exception with a code FEATURE_NOT_SUPPORTED. In this case, the Dmt Admin service must do the copying node by node. For the clients of the Dmt Admin service, it therefore appears that the copy method is always supported.

117.7 Access Control Lists

Each node in the DMT can be protected with an *access control list*, or *ACL*. An ACL is a list of associations between *Principal* and *Operation*:

- *Principal* – The identity that is authorized to use the associated operations. Special principal is the wildcard ('*' \u002A); the operations granted to this principal are called the *global permissions*. The global permissions are available to all principals.
- *Operation* – A list of operations: ADD, DELETE, GET, REPLACE, EXECUTE.

DMT ACLs are defined as strings with an internal syntax in [1] *OMA DM-TND v1.2 draft*. Instances of the ACL class can be created by supplying a valid OMA DM ACL string as its parameter. The syntax of the ACL is presented here in shortened form for convenience:

```
acl        ::= ( acl-entry ( '&' acl-entry )* )?
acl-entry ::= command '=' ( principals | '*' )
principals ::=  principal ( '+' principal )*
principal  ::= [^=&*+ \t\n\r]+
```

The principal name should only use printable characters according to the OMA DM specification.

```
command    ::= 'Add' | 'Delete' | 'Exec' | 'Get' | 'Replace'
```

White space between tokens is not allowed.

Examples:

```
Add=*&Replace=*&Get=*
```

```
Add=www. sonera. fi-8765&Delete=www. sonera. fi-8765&Replace=www. sonera. fi-
8765+321_ibm. com&Get=*
```

The Acl(String) constructor can be used to construct an ACL from an ACL string. The toString() method returns a String object that is formatted in the specified form, also called the canonical form. In this form, the principals must be sorted alphabetically and the order of the commands is:

```
ADD,    DELETE,    EXEC,    GET,    REPLACE
```

The Acl class is immutable, meaning that a Acl object can be treated like a string, and that the object cannot be changed after it has been created.

ACLs must only be verified by the Dmt Admin service when the session has an associated principal.

ACLs are properties of nodes. If an ACL is *not set* (i.e. contains no commands nor principals), the *effective* ACL of that node must be the ACL of its first ancestor that has a non-empty ACL. This effective ACL can be acquired with the getEffectiveNodeAcl(String) method. The root node of DMT must always have an ACL associated with it. If this ACL is not explicitly set, it should be set to Add=*&Get=*&Replace=*.

This effect is shown in Figure 117.10. This diagram shows the ACLs set on a node and their effect (which is shown by the shaded rectangles). Any principal can get the value of p, q and r, but they cannot replace, add or delete the node. Node t can only be read and replaced by principal S1.

Node X is fully accessible to any authenticated principal because the root node specifies that all principals have Get, Add and Replace access (*->G,A,R).

Figure 117.10   *ACL inheritance*

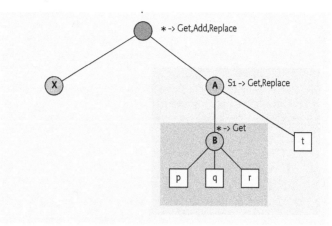

The definition and example demonstrate the access rights to the properties of a node, which includes the value.

Changing the ACL property itself has different rules. If a principal has Replace access to an interior node, the principal is permitted to change its own ACL property *and* the ACL properties of all its child nodes. Replace access on a leaf node does not allow changing the ACL property itself.

In the previous example, only principal S1 is authorized to change the ACL of node B because it has Replace permission on node B's parent node A.

Figure 117.11   *ACLs for the ACL property*

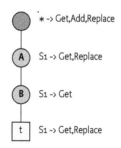

Figure 117.11 demonstrates the effect of this rule with an example. Server S1 can change the ACL properties of all interior nodes. A more detailed analysis:

- *Root* – The root allows all authenticated principals to access it. The root is an interior node so the Replace permission permits the change of the ACL property.
- *Node A* – Server S1 has Replace permission and node A is an interior node so principal S1 can modify the ACL.
- *Node B* – Server S1 has no Replace permission for node B, but the parent node A of node B grants principal S1 Replace permission, and S1 is therefore permitted to change the ACL.
- *Node t* – Server S1 must not be allowed to change the ACL of node t, despite the fact that it has Replace permission on node t. For leaf nodes, permission to change an ACL is defined by the Replace permission in the parent node's ACL. This parent, node B, has no such permission set and thus, access is denied.

The following methods provide access to the ACL property of the node.

- getNodeAcl(String) – Return the ACL for the given node, this method must not take any ACL inheritance into account. The ACL may be null if no ACL is set.

- getEffectiveNodeAcl(String) – Return the effective ACL for the given node, taking any inheritance into account.
- setNodeAcl(String,Acl) – Set the node's ACL. The ACL can be null, in which case the effective permission must be derived from an ancestor. The Dmt Admin service must call nodeChanged(String[]) on the data session with the given plugin to let the plugin update any timestamps and versions.

The Acl class maintains the permissions for a given principal in a bit mask. The following permission masks are defined as constants in the Acl class:

- ADD
- DELETE
- EXEC
- GET
- REPLACE

The class features methods for getting permissions for given principals. A number of methods allow an existing ACL to be modified while creating a new ACL.

- addPermission(String,int) – Return a new Acl object where the given permissions have been added to permissions of the given principal.
- deletePermission(String,int) – Return a new Acl object where the given permissions have been removed from the permissions of the given principal.
- setPermission(String,int) – Return a new Acl object where the permissions of the given principal are overwritten with the given permissions.

Information from a given ACL can be retrieved with:

- getPermissions(String) – (int) Return the combined permission mask for this principal.
- getPrincipals() – (String[]) Return a list of principals (String objects) that have been granted permissions for this node.

Additionally, the isPermitted(String,int) method verifies if the given ACL authorizes the given permission mask. The method returns true if all commands in the mask are allowed by the ACL.

For example:

```
Acl   acl = new Acl("Get=S1&Replace=S1");

if ( acl.isPermitted("S1", Acl.GET+Acl.REPLACE ))
    ... // will execute

if ( acl.isPermitted(
    "S1", Acl.GET+Acl.REPLACE+Acl.ADD ))
    ... // will NOT execute
```

117.7.1   Global Permissions

Global permissions are indicated with the '*' and the given permissions apply to all principals. Processing the global permissions, however, has a number of non-obvious side effects:

- Global permissions can be retrieved and manipulated using the special'*' principal: all methods of the Acl class that have a principal parameter also accept this principal.
- Global permissions are automatically granted to all specific principals. That is, the result of the getPermissions or isPermitted methods will be based on the OR of the global permissions and the principal-specific permissions.
- If a global permission is revoked, it is revoked from all specific principals, even if the specific principals already had that permission before it was made global.

- None of the global permissions can be revoked from a specific principal. The OMA DM ACL format does not handle exceptions, which must be enforced by the deletePermission and setPermission methods.

117.7.2   Ghost ACLs

The ACLs are fully maintained by the Dmt Admin service and enforced when the session has an associated principal. A plugin must be completely unaware of any ACLs. The Dmt Admin service must synchronize the ACLs with any change in the DMT that is made through its service interface. For example, if a node is deleted through the Dmt Admin service, it must also delete an associated ACL.

The DMT nodes, however, are mapped to plugins, and plugins can delete nodes outside the scope of the Dmt Admin service.

As an example, consider a configuration record which is mapped to a DMT node that has an ACL. If the configuration record is deleted using the Configuration Admin service, the data disappears, but the ACL entry in the Dmt Admin remains. If the configuration dictionary is recreated with the same PID, it will get the old ACL, which is likely not the intended behavior.

This specification does not specify a solution to solve this problem. Suggestions to solve this problem are:

- Use a proprietary callback mechanism from the underlying representation to notify the Dmt Admin service to clean up the related ACLs.
- Implement the services on top of the DMT. For example, the Configuration Admin service could use a plugin that provides general data storage service.

117.8   Notifications

In certain cases it is necessary for some code on the device to alert a remote management server or to initiate a session; this process is called sending a notification or an *alert.* Some examples:

- A Plugin that must send the result of an asynchronous EXEC operation.
- Sending a request to the server to start a management session.
- Notifying the server of completion of a software update operation.

Notifications can be sent to a management server using the sendNotification(String,int,String,AlertItem[]) method on the Notification Service, which is available from the service registry or from the DmtServiceFactory getNotificationService(). This method is on the Notification Service and not on the session, because the session can already be closed when the need for an alert arises. If an alert is related to a session, the session can provide the required principal, even after it is closed.

The remote server is alerted with one or more AlertItem objects. The AlertItem class describes details of the alert. In OMA DM, sending an alert requires an *alert code.* Alert codes are defined by OMA DM and others. An alert code is a type identifier, usually requiring specifically formatted AlertItem objects.

The data syntax and semantics varies widely between various alerts, and so does the optionality of particular parameters of an alert item. If an item, such as source or type, is not defined, the corresponding getter method must return null.

The AlertItem class contains the following items. The value of these items must be defined in an alert definition:

- source – (String) The URI of a node that is related to this request. This parameter can be null.

- type – (String) The type of the item. For example, x-oma-application:syncml.samplealert in the Generic Alert example.

- mark – (String) Mark field of an alert. Contents depend on the alert type.

- data – (DmtData) The payload of the alert with its type.

An AlertItem object can be constructed with two different constructors:

- AlertItem(String,String,String,info.dmtree.DmtData) – This method takes all the previously defined fields.

- AlertItem(String[],String,String,info.dmtree.DmtData) – Same as previous but with a convenience parameter for a segmented URI.

The Notification Service provides the following method to send AlertItem objects to the management server:

- sendNotification(String,int,String,AlertItem[]) – Send the alert to the server that is associated with the session. The first argument is the name of the principal (identifying the remote management system) or null for implementation defined routing. The int argument is the *alert type*. The alert types are defined by *managed object types*. The third argument (String) can be used for the correlation id of a previous execute operation that triggered the alert. The AlertItem objects contain the data of the alert. The method will run asynchronously from the caller. The Notification Service must provide a reliable delivery method for these alerts. Alerts must therefore not be re-transmitted.
  When this method is called with null and 0 as values, it should send a protocol specific notification that must initiate a new management session.

Implementers should base the routing on the session or server information provided as a parameter in the sendNotification(String,int,String,AlertItem[]) method. Routing might even be possible without any routing information if there is a well known remote server for the device.

If the request cannot be routed, the Alert Sender service must immediately throw a Dmt Exception with a code of ALERT_NOT_ROUTED. The caller should not attempt to retry the sending of the notification. It is the responsibility of the Notification Service to deliver the notification to the remote management system.

117.8.1   Routing Alerts

The Notification Service allows external parties to route alerts to their destination. This mechanism enables protocol adapters to receive any alerts for systems with which they can communicate.

Such a protocol adapter should register a Remote Alert Sender service. It should provide the following service property:

- *principals* – (String[]) The array of principals to which this Remote Alert Sender service can route alerts. If this property is not registered, the Remote Alert Sender service will be treated as the default sender. The default alert sender is only used when a more specific alert sender cannot be found.

If multiple Remote Alert Sender services register for the same principals, then the service with the highest value for the service.ranking property must be used.

117.9   Exceptions

Most of the methods of this Dmt Admin service API throw Dmt Exceptions whenever an operation fails. The DmtException class contains numeric error codes which describe the cause of the error. Some of the error codes correspond to the codes described by the OMA DM spec, while some are introduced by the OSGi Alliance. The documentation of each method describes what codes could potentially be used for that method.

The fatality of the exception decides if a thrown Exception rolls back an atomic session or not. If the isFatal() method returns true, the Exception is fatal and the session must be rolled back.

All possible error codes are constants in the DmtException class.

117.10 Events

There are two mechanisms to work with events when using the Dmt Admin service. The first mechanism is based on the Event Admin service, the second uses a traditional event listener model.

117.10.1 Event Admin based Events

The Dmt Admin service uses the Event Admin service for event delivery. For atomic sessions, events are only sent at the time the session is committed (which can happen multiple times during a session). Otherwise they are sent immediately.

Each event must carry the information of all nodes that underwent the related operation.

- info/dmtree/DmtEvent/ADDED – New nodes were added.
- info/dmtree/DmtEvent/DELETED – Existing nodes were removed.
- info/dmtree/DmtEvent/REPLACED – Existing node values or other properties were changed.
- info/dmtree/DmtEvent/RENAMED – Existing nodes were renamed.
- info/dmtree/DmtEvent/COPIED – Existing nodes were copied. A copy operation does not trigger an ADDED event (in addition to the COPIED event), even though new node(s) are created.
- info/dmtree/DmtEvent/SESSION_OPENED – A new sessions was opened.
- info/dmtree/DmtEvent/SESSION_CLOSED – A session was closed (by means of the close operation or an error).

For an atomic session, a maximum of five events can be sent: one for each operation type. In this case, the ordering for the events must follow the order of the previous list.

For efficiency reasons, recursive copy and delete operations must only generate a single COPIED and DELETED event for the root of the affected sub-tree. An event must only be sent when that type of event actually occurred.

DMT events have the following properties:

- session.id – (Integer) A unique identifier for the session that triggered the event. This property has the same value as getSessionId() of the associated DMT session.
- nodes – (String[]) The absolute URIs of each affected node. This is the nodeUri parameter of the Dmt API methods. The order of the URIs in the array corresponds to the chronological order of the operations. In case of a recursive delete, only the root URI is present in the array. Session events do not have this property.
- newnodes – (String[]) – The absolute URIs of new renamed or copied nodes. Only the RENAMED and COPIED events have this property.
  The newnodes array runs parallel to the nodes array. In case of a rename, newnodes[i] must contains the new name of nodes[i], and in case of a copy, newnodes[i] is the URI to which nodes[i] was copied.

The Dmt Event contains information about activities of the tree, which could be confidential. Topic Permission should be used to control access to the events. However, this permission only supports blank access, it can not restrict access for specific URIs.

Figure 117.12   *Example DMT before*

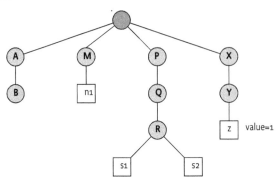

For example, in a given session, when the DMT in Figure 117.12 is modified with the following operations:

- Add node ./A/B/C
- Add node ./A/B/C/D
- Rename ./M/n1 to ./M/n2
- Copy ./M/n2 to ./M/n3
- Delete node ./P/Q
- Replace ./X/Y/z with 3

Figure 117.13   *Example DMT after*

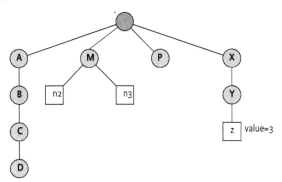

When the Dmt Session is closed (assuming it is atomic), the following events are published by the Dmt Admin in the defined order:

```
info/dmtree/DmtEvent/ADDED {
        nodes       = [. /A/B/C,  ./A/B/C/D ]
        session. id  = 42
}
info/dmtree/DmtEvent/DELETED {
        nodes       = [ ./P/Q ]
        session. id  = 42
}
info/dmtree/dmt/DmtEvent/REPLACED {
        nodes       = [ ./X/Y/z ]
        session. id  = 42
}
info/dmtree/DmtEvent/RENAMED {
        nodes       = [ ./M/n1 ]
```

```
                    newnodes     = [ ./M/n2 ]
                    session.id   = 42
            }
            info/dmtree/DmtEvent/COPIED {
                    nodes        = [ ./M/n2 ]
                    newnodes     = [ ./M/n3 ]
                    session.id   = 42
            }
```

117.10.2 Event Listeners

The traditional event listener model is provided to allow compatibility with solutions that do not support an OSGi service platform.

A Dmt Event Listener is registered and unregistered with a Dmt Admin service using the following methods:

- addEventListener(int,String,DmtEventListener) – Registers an event listener on behalf of a local application. The given listener will receive notification on all changes affecting the specified subtree. An event is delivered to the registered listener if at least one affected node is within this subtree. The events can also be filtered by specifying a bit mask of relevant event types. If the listener object was already registered, it is removed first. The listener must only see the nodes for which it has Get permission.
- addEventListener(String,int,String,DmtEventListener) – This method is the same as the previous but provides a principal on who's behalf the listening takes place. The principal must only see nodes for which it has the Get access right.
- removeEventListener(DmtEventListener) – Remove the event listener.

A Dmt Event Listener must implement the changeOccurred(DmtEvent) method. This method is called asynchronously from the actual event occurrence.

The DmtEvent object is used for the following events:

- ADDED – New nodes were added.
- DELETED – Existing nodes were removed.
- REPLACED – Existing node values or other properties were changed.
- RENAMED – Existing nodes were renamed.
- COPIED – Existing nodes were copied. A copy operation does not trigger an ADDED event (in addition to the COPIED event), even though new node(s) are created.
- SESSION_OPENED – A new session is opened. Both the nodes and the new nodes must be null for this event.
- SESSION_CLOSED – A session is closed. Both the nodes and the new nodes must be null for this event.

For efficiency reasons, recursive copy and delete operations must only generate a single COPIED and DELETED event for the root of the affected sub-tree. An event must only be sent when that type of event actually occurred.

The DmtEvent object can provide the following information:

- getType() – Returns the type of the event.
- getNodes() – The absolute URIs of each affected node. This is the nodeUri parameter of the Dmt API methods. The order of the URIs in the array corresponds to the chronological order of the operations. In case of a recursive delete, only the root URI is present in the array.
- getNewNodes() – The absolute URIs of new renamed or copied nodes. Only the RENAMED and COPIED events have this property.
- The newnodes array runs parallel to the nodes array. In case of a rename, newnodes[i] must contains the new name of nodes[i], and in case of a copy, newnodes[i] is the URI to which nodes[i] was copied.
- getSessionId() – The id of the session in which the event was generated.

117.11   Access Without Service Registry

The Dmt Admin can be used without access to an OSGi Service Registry. The DmtServiceFactory class provides a number of methods to access the Dmt Admin service and the Notification Service.

* getDmtAdmin() – Returns the Dmt Admin service for the calling application.
* getNotificationService() – Returns the Notification Service for the calling application.

117.12   Security

The Dmt Admin service specification can run on both OSGi based Service Platform (which normally requires CDC or J2SE) and CLDC based solutions. A crucial difference between these environments is the handling of security. The OSGi Service Platform uses Java 2 security with an open ended set of class based permissions while the security handling of CLDC based solutions is dependent on the profile. For example, MIDP uses a solution that uses a fixed set of permissions that are name based.

A key aspect of the Dmt Admin service model is the separation from DMT clients and plugins. The Dmt Admin service receives all the operation requests and, after verification of authority, forwards the requests to the plugins.

Figure 117.14   *Separation of clients and plugins*

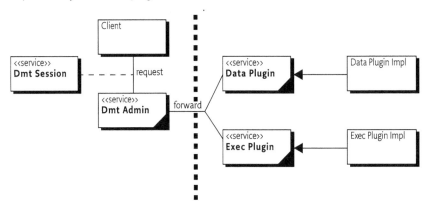

This architecture makes it straightforward to use the OSGi security architecture to protect the different actors.

117.12.1   Principals

The caller of the getSession(String,String,int) method must have the Dmt Principal Permission with a target that matches the given principal. This Dmt Principal Permission is used to enforce that only trusted entities can act on behalf of remote managers.

The Dmt Admin service must verify that all operations from a session with a principal can be executed on the given nodes using the available ACLs.

The other two forms of the getSession method are meant for local management applications where no principal is available. No special permission is defined to restrict the usage of these methods. The callers that want to execute device management commands, however, need to have the appropriate Dmt Permissions.

117.12.2   Operational Permissions

The operational security of a local manager and a remote manager is distinctly different. The distinction is made on the principal. Protocol adapters should use the getSession method that takes an authenticated principal. Local managers should not specify a principal.

Figure 117.15   *Access control context, for local manager and protocol adapter operation*

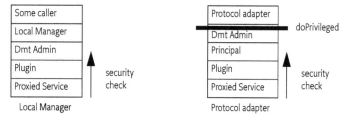

117.12.3   Protocol Adapters

A protocol adapter must provide a principal to the Dmt Admin service when it gets a session. It must use the getSession(String,String,int) method. The protocol adapter must have Dmt Principal Permission for the given principal. The Dmt Admin must then use this principal to determine the *security scope* of the given principal. This security scope is a set of permissions. How these permissions are found is not defined in this specification; they are usually in the management tree of a device. For example, the Mobile Specification stores these under the $/Policy/Java/DmtPrincipalPermission subtree.

Additionally, a Dmt Session with a principal implies that the Dmt Admin service must verify the ACLs on the node for all operations.

Any operation that is requested by a protocol adapter must be executed in a doPrivileged block that takes the principal's security scope. The doPrivileged block effectively hides the permissions of the protocol adapter; all operations must be performed under the security scope of the principal.

The security check for a protocol adapter is therefore as follows:

- The operation method calls doPrivileged with the security scope of the principal.
- The operation is forwarded to the appropriate plugin. The underlying service must perform its normal security checks. For example, the Configuration Admin service must check for the appropriate Configuration Permission.

The Access Control context is shown in Figure 117.15 within the protocol adapter column.

This principal-based security model allows for minimal permissions on the protocol adapter, because the Dmt Admin service performs a doPrivileged on behalf of the principal, inserting the permissions for the principal on the call stack. This model does not guard against malicious protocol adapters, though the protocol adapter must have the appropriate Dmt Principal Permission.

The protocol adapter is responsible for the authentication of the principal. The Dmt Admin must trust that the Protocol Adapter has correctly verified the identity of the other party. This specification does not address the type of authentication mechanisms that can be used. Once it has permission to use that principal, it can use any DMT command that is permitted for that principal at any time.

117.12.4   Local Manager

A local manager does not specify a principal. Security checks are therefore performed against the security scope of the local manager bundle, as shown in Figure 117.15 with the local manager stack. An operation is checked only with a Dmt Permission for the given node URI and operation. A thrown Security Exception must be passed unmodified to the caller of the operation method. The Dmt Admin service must not check the ACLs when no principal is set.

A local manager, and all its callers, must therefore have sufficient permission to handle the DMT operations as well as the permissions required by the plugins when they proxy other services (which is likely an extensive set of Permissions).

117.12.5 Plugin Security

Plugins are required to hold the maximum security scope for any services they proxy. For example, the plugin that manages the Configuration Admin service must have ConfigurationPermission("*", "*") to be effective.

Plugins should not make doPrivileged calls, but should use the caller's context on the stack for permission checks.

117.12.6 Events and Permissions

The addEventListener(String,int,String,DmtEventListener) method requires Dmt Principal Permission for the given principal. In this case, the principal must have Get access to see the nodes for the event. Any nodes that the listener does not have access to must be removed from the event.

The listener registered with the addEventListener(int,String,DmtEventListener) method requires to have the appropriate Dmt Permission to receive the event.

117.12.7 Dmt Principal Permission

Execution of the getSession methods of the Dmt Admin service featuring an explicit principal name is guarded by the Dmt Principal Permission. This permission must be granted only to protocol adapters that open Dmt Sessions on behalf of remote management servers.

The DmtPrincipalPermission class does not have defined actions; it must always be created with a * to allow future extensions. The target is the principal name. A wildcard character is allowed at the end of the string to match a prefix.

Example:

```
new DmtPrincipalPermission("com.acme.dep*", "*" )
```

117.12.8 Dmt Permission

The Dmt Permission controls access to management objects in the DMT. It is intended to control only the *local* access to the DMT. The Dmt Permission target string identifies the target node's URI (absolute path is required, starting with the './' prefix) and the action field lists the management commands that are permitted on the node.

The URI can end in a wildcard character * to indicate it is a prefix that must be matched. This comparison is string based so that node boundaries can be ignored.

The following actions are defined:

- ADD
- DELETE
- EXEC
- GET
- REPLACE

For example, the following code creates a Dmt Permission for a bundle to add and replace nodes in any URI that starts with ./D.

```
new DmtPermission("./D*", "Add,Replace")
```

This permission must imply the following permission:

```
new DmtPermission("./Dev/Operator/Name", "Replace")
```

117.12.9   Alert Permission

The Alert Permission permits the holder of this permission to send a notification to a specific *target principal*. The target is identical to *Dmt Principal Permission* on page 418. No actions are defined for Alert Permission.

117.12.10   Security Summary

117.12.10.1   Dmt Admin Service and Notification Service

The Dmt Admin service is likely to require All Permission. This requirement is caused by the plugin model. Any permission required by any of the plugins must be granted to the Dmt Admin service. This set of permissions is large and hard to define. The following list shows the minimum permissions required if the plugin permissions are left out.

```
ServicePermission       ..DmtAdmin                      REGISTER
ServicePermission       ..NotificationService           REGISTER
ServicePermission       ..DataPlugin                    GET
ServicePermission       ..ExecPlugin                    GET
ServicePermission       ..EventAdmin                    GET
ServicePermission       ..RemoteAlertSender             GET
DmtPermission           *                               *
DmtPrincipal
   Permission           *                               *
PackagePermission       info.dmtree                     EXPORTONLY
PackagePermission       info.dmtree.spi                 EXPORTONLY
PackagePermission       info.dmtree.notification        EXPORTONLY
PackagePermission       info.dmtree.notification.spi    EXPORTONLY
PackagePermission       info.dmtree.registry            EXPORTONLY
PackagePermission       info.dmtree.security            EXPORTONLY
```

117.12.10.2   Data and Exec Plugin

```
ServicePermission       ..NotificationService           GET
ServicePermission       ..DataPlugin                    REGISTER
ServicePermission       ..ExecPlugin                    REGISTER
PackagePermission       info.dmtree                     IMPORT
PackagePermission       info.dmtree.notification        IMPORT
PackagePermission       info.dmtree.spi                 IMPORT
PackagePermission       info.dmtree.security            IMPORT
```

The plugin is also required to have any permissions to call its underlying services.

117.12.10.3   Local Manager

```
ServicePermission       ..DmtAdmin                      GET
PackagePermission       info.dmtree                     IMPORT
PackagePermission       info.dmtree.security            IMPORT
DmtPermission           <scope>                         ...
```

Additionally, the local manager requires all permissions that are needed by the plugins it addresses.

117.12.10.4   Protocol Adapter

The Protocol adapter only requires Dmt Principal Permission for the instances that it is permitted to manage. The other permissions are taken from the security scope of the principal.

```
ServicePermission       ..DmtAdmin                      GET
ServicePermission       ..RemoteAlertSender             REGISTER
PackagePermission       info.dmtree                     IMPORT
PackagePermission       info.dmtree.notification.spi    IMPORT
PackagePermission       info.dmtree.notification        IMPORT
```

DmtPrincipalPermission<scope>

117.13 info.dmtree

Device Management Tree Package Version 1.0. This package contains the public API for the Device Management Tree manipulations. Permission classes are provided by the info.dmtree.security package, and DMT plugin interfaces can be found in the info.dmtree.spi package. Asynchronous notifications to remote management servers can be sent using the interfaces in the info.dmtree.notification package.

Bundles wishing to use this package must list the package in the Import-Package header of the bundle's manifest. For example:

Import-Package: info.dmtree;version="[1.0,2.0)"

117.13.1 Summary

- *Acl* - Acl is an immutable class representing structured access to DMT ACLs.
- *DmtAdmin* - An interface providing methods to open sessions and register listeners.
- *DmtData* - An immutable data structure representing the contents of a leaf or interior node.
- *DmtEvent* - Event class storing the details of a change in the tree.
- *DmtEventListener* - Registered implementations of this class are notified via DmtEvent objects about important changes in the tree.
- *DmtException* - Checked exception received when a DMT operation fails.
- *DmtIllegalStateException* - Unchecked illegal state exception.
- *DmtSession* - DmtSession provides concurrent access to the DMT.
- *MetaNode* - The MetaNode contains meta data as standardized by OMA DM but extends it (without breaking the compatibility) to provide for better DMT data quality in an environment where many software components manipulate this data.
- *Uri* - This class contains static utility methods to manipulate DMT URIs.

117.13.2 public final class Acl

Acl is an immutable class representing structured access to DMT ACLs. Under OMA DM the ACLs are defined as strings with an internal syntax.

The methods of this class taking a principal as parameter accept remote server IDs (as passed to DmtAdmin.getSession), as well as "*"indicating any principal.

The syntax for valid remote server IDs:
⟨*server-identifier*⟩ ::= All printable characters except '=', '&', '*', '+' or white-space characters.

117.13.2.1 public static final int ADD = 2

Principals holding this permission can issue ADD commands on the node having this ACL.

117.13.2.2 public static final int ALL_PERMISSION = 31

Principals holding this permission can issue any command on the node having this ACL. This permission is the logical OR of ADD, DELETE, EXEC, GET and REPLACE permissions.

117.13.2.3 public static final int DELETE = 8

Principals holding this permission can issue DELETE commands on the node having this ACL.

117.13.2.4 public static final int EXEC = 16

Principals holding this permission can issue EXEC commands on the node having this ACL.

117.13.2.5   **public static final int GET = 1**

Principals holding this permission can issue GET command on the node having this ACL.

117.13.2.6   **public static final int REPLACE = 4**

Principals holding this permission can issue REPLACE commands on the node having this ACL.

117.13.2.7   **public Acl(String acl)**

acl The string representation of the ACL as defined in OMA DM. If null or empty then it represents an empty list of principals with no permissions.

☐ Create an instance of the ACL from its canonic string representation.

Throws IllegalArgumentException – if acl is not a valid OMA DM ACL string

117.13.2.8   **public Acl(String[] principals, int[] permissions)**

principals The array of principals

permissions The array of permissions

☐ Creates an instance with a specified list of principals and the permissions they hold. The two arrays run in parallel, that is principals[i] will hold permissions[i] in the ACL.

A principal name may not appear multiple times in the 'principals' argument. If the "*" principal appears in the array, the corresponding permissions will be granted to all principals (regardless of whether they appear in the array or not).

Throws IllegalArgumentException – if the length of the two arrays are not the same, if any array element is invalid, or if a principal appears multiple times in the principals array

117.13.2.9   **public synchronized Acl addPermission(String principal, int permissions)**

principal The entity to which permissions should be granted, or "*" to grant permissions to all principals.

permissions The permissions to be given. The parameter can be a logical or of more permission constants defined in this class.

☐ Create a new Acl instance from this Acl with the given permission added for the given principal. The already existing permissions of the principal are not affected.

Returns a new Acl instance

Throws IllegalArgumentException – if principal is not a valid principal name or if permissions is not a valid combination of the permission constants defined in this class

117.13.2.10   **public synchronized Acl deletePermission(String principal, int permissions)**

principal The entity from which permissions should be revoked, or "*" to revoke permissions from all principals.

permissions The permissions to be revoked. The parameter can be a logical or of more permission constants defined in this class.

☐ Create a new Acl instance from this Acl with the given permission revoked from the given principal. Other permissions of the principal are not affected.

Note, that it is not valid to revoke a permission from a specific principal if that permission is granted globally to all principals.

Returns a new Acl instance

Throws IllegalArgumentException – if principal is not a valid principal name, if permissions is not a valid combination of the permission constants defined in this class, or if a globally granted permission would have been revoked from a specific principal

117.13.2.11   **public boolean equals(Object obj)**

obj   the object to compare with this Acl instance

☐   Checks whether the given object is equal to this Acl instance. Two Acl instances are equal if they allow the same set of permissions for the same set of principals.

Returns   true if the parameter represents the same ACL as this instance

117.13.2.12   **public synchronized int getPermissions(String principal)**

principal   The entity whose permissions to query, or "*" to query the permissions that are granted globally, to all principals

☐   Get the permissions associated to a given principal.

Returns   The permissions of the given principal. The returned int is a bitmask of the permission constants defined in this class

Throws   IllegalArgumentException – if principal is not a valid principal name

117.13.2.13   **public String[] getPrincipals( )**

☐   Get the list of principals who have any kind of permissions on this node. The list only includes those principals that have been explicitly assigned permissions (so "*" is never returned), globally set permissions naturally apply to all other principals as well.

Returns   The array of principals having permissions on this node.

117.13.2.14   **public int hashcode( )**

☐   Returns the hash code for this ACL instance. If two Acl instances are equal according to the equals method, then calling this method on each of them must produce the same integer result.

Returns   hash code for this ACL

117.13.2.15   **public synchronized boolean isPermitted(String principal, int permissions)**

principal   The entity to check, or "*" to check whether the given permissions are granted to all principals globally

permissions   The permissions to check

☐   Check whether the given permissions are granted to a certain principal. The requested permissions are specified as a bitfield, for example (Acl.ADD | Acl.DELETE | Acl.GET).

Returns   true if the principal holds all the given permissions

Throws   IllegalArgumentException – if principal is not a valid principal name or if permissions is not a valid combination of the permission constants defined in this class

117.13.2.16   **public synchronized Acl setPermission(String principal, int permissions)**

principal   The entity to which permissions should be granted, or "*" to globally grant permissions to all principals.

permissions   The set of permissions to be given. The parameter is a bitmask of the permission constants defined in this class.

☐   Create a new Acl instance from this Acl where all permissions for the given principal are overwritten with the given permissions.

Note, that when changing the permissions of a specific principal, it is not allowed to specify a set of permissions stricter than the global set of permissions (that apply to all principals).

Returns   a new Acl instance

Throws   IllegalArgumentException – if principal is not a valid principal name, if permissions is not a valid combination of the permission constants defined in this class, or if a globally granted permission would have been revoked from a specific principal

117.13.2.17   **public synchronized String toString( )**

☐ Give the canonic string representation of this ACL. The operations are in the following order: {Add, Delete, Exec, Get, Replace}, principal names are sorted alphabetically.

Returns The string representation as defined in OMA DM.

117.13.3   public interface DmtAdmin

An interface providing methods to open sessions and register listeners. The implementation of DmtAdmin should register itself in the OSGi service registry as a service. DmtAdmin is the entry point for applications to use the DMT API.

The getSession methods are used to open a session on a specified subtree of the DMT. A typical way of usage:

```
serviceRef = context.getServiceReference(DmtAdmin.class.getName());
DmtAdmin admin = (DmtAdmin) context.getService(serviceRef);
DmtSession session = admin.getSession("./OSGi/Configuration");
session.createInteriorNode("./OSGi/Configuration/my.table");
```

The methods for opening a session take a node URI (the session root) as a parameter. All segments of the given URI must be within the segment length limit of the implementation, and the special characters '/' and '\' must be escaped (preceded by a '\'). Any string can be converted to a valid URI segment using the Uri.mangle(String) method.

It is possible to specify a lock mode when opening the session (see lock type constants in DmtSession). This determines whether the session can run in parallel with other sessions, and the kinds of operations that can be performed in the session. All Management Objects constituting the device management tree must support read operations on their nodes, while support for write operations depends on the Management Object. Management Objects supporting write access may support transactional write, non-transactional write or both. Users of DmtAdmin should consult the Management Object specification and implementation for the supported update modes. If Management Object definition permits, implementations are encouraged to support both update modes.

This interface also contains methods for manipulating the set of DmtEventListener objects that are called when the structure or content of the tree is changed. These methods are not needed in an OSGi environment, clients should register listeners through the Event Admin service.

117.13.3.1   **public void addEventListener(int type, String uri, DmtEventListener listener)**

type a bitmask of event types the caller is interested in

uri the URI of the root node of a subtree, must not be null

listener the listener to be registered, must not be null

☐ Registers an event listener on behalf of a local application. The given listener will receive notification on all changes affecting the specified subtree. The subtree is specified by its root node URI. An event is delivered to the registered listener if at least one affected node is within this subtree. The events can also be filtered by specifying a bitmask of relevant event types (e.g. DmtEvent.ADDED | DmtEvent.REPLACED | DmtEvent.SESSION_CLOSED). Only event types included in the bitmask will be delivered to the listener.

The listener will only receive the change notifications of nodes for which the registering application has the appropriate GET info.dmtree.security.DmtPermission.

If the specified listener was already registered, calling this method will update the registration.

Throws SecurityException – if the caller doesn't have the necessary GET DmtPermission for the given URI

NullPointerException – if the uri or listener parameter is null

IllegalArgumentException – if the type parameter contains invalid bits (not corresponding to any event type defined in DmtEvent), or if the uri parameter is invalid (is not an absolute URI or is syntactically incorrect)

117.13.3.2   public void addEventListener(String principal, int type, String uri, DmtEventListener listener)

principal the management server identity the caller is acting on behalf of, must not be null

type a bitmask of event types the caller is interested in

uri the URI of the root node of a subtree, must not be null

listener the listener to be registered, must not be null

☐ Registers an event listener on behalf of a remote principal. The given listener will receive notification on all changes affecting the specified subtree. The subtree is specified by its root node URI. An event is delivered to the registered listener if at least one affected node is within this subtree. The events can also be filtered by specifying a bitmask of relevant event types (e.g. DmtEvent.ADDED | DmtEvent.REPLACED | DmtEvent.SESSION_CLOSED). Only event types included in the bitmask will be delivered to the listener.

The listener will only receive the change notifications of nodes for which the node ACL grants GET access to the specified principal.

If the specified listener was already registered, calling this method will update the registration.

Throws SecurityException – if the caller doesn't have the necessary DmtPrincipalPermission to use the specified principal

NullPointerException – if the principal, uri or listener parameter is null

IllegalArgumentException – if the type parameter contains invalid bits (not corresponding to any event type defined in DmtEvent), or if the uri parameter is invalid (is not an absolute URI or is syntactically incorrect)

117.13.3.3   public DmtSession getSession(String subtreeUri) throws DmtException

subtreeUri the subtree on which DMT manipulations can be performed within the returned session

☐ Opens a DmtSession for local usage on a given subtree of the DMT with non transactional write lock. This call is equivalent to the following: getSession(null, subtreeUri, DmtSession.LOCK_TYPE_EXCLUSIVE)

The subtreeUri parameter must contain an absolute URI. It can also be null, in this case the session is opened with the default session root, ".", that gives access to the whole tree.

To perform this operation the caller must have DmtPermission for the subtreeUri node with the Get action present.

Returns a DmtSession object for the requested subtree

Throws DmtException – with the following possible error codes:
URI_TOO_LONG if subtreeUri or a segment of it is too long, or if it has too many segments
INVALID_URI if subtreeUri is syntactically invalid
NODE_NOT_FOUND if subtreeUri specifies a non-existing node
SESSION_CREATION_TIMEOUT if the operation timed out because of another ongoing session
COMMAND_FAILED if subtreeUri specifies a relative URI, or some unspecified error is encountered while attempting to complete the command

SecurityException – if the caller does not have DmtPermission for the given root node with the Get action present

117.13.3.4　　**public DmtSession getSession(String subtreeUri, int lockMode) throws DmtException**

subtreeUri the subtree on which DMT manipulations can be performed within the returned session

lockMode one of the lock modes specified in DmtSession

☐ Opens a DmtSession for local usage on a specific DMT subtree with a given lock mode. This call is equivalent to the following: getSession(null, subtreeUri, lockMode)

The subtreeUri parameter must contain an absolute URI. It can also be null, in this case the session is opened with the default session root, ".", that gives access to the whole tree.

To perform this operation the caller must have DmtPermission for the subtreeUri node with the Get action present.

Returns a DmtSession object for the requested subtree

Throws DmtException – with the following possible error codes:
URI_TOO_LONG if subtreeUri or a segment of it is too long, or if it has too many segments
INVALID_URI if subtreeUri is syntactically invalid
NODE_NOT_FOUND if subtreeUri specifies a non-existing node
FEATURE_NOT_SUPPORTED if atomic sessions are not supported by the implementation and lockMode requests an atomic session
SESSION_CREATION_TIMEOUT if the operation timed out because of another ongoing session
COMMAND_FAILED if subtreeUri specifies a relative URI, if lockMode is unknown, or some unspecified error is encountered while attempting to complete the command

SecurityException – if the caller does not have DmtPermission for the given root node with the Get action present

117.13.3.5　　**public DmtSession getSession(String principal, String subtreeUri, int lockMode) throws DmtException**

principal the identifier of the remote server on whose behalf the data manipulation is performed, or null for local sessions

subtreeUri the subtree on which DMT manipulations can be performed within the returned session

lockMode one of the lock modes specified in DmtSession

☐ Opens a DmtSession on a specific DMT subtree using a specific lock mode on behalf of a remote principal. If local management applications are using this method then they should provide null as the first parameter. Alternatively they can use other forms of this method without providing a principal string.

The subtreeUri parameter must contain an absolute URI. It can also be null, in this case the session is opened with the default session root, ".", that gives access to the whole tree.

This method is guarded by DmtPrincipalPermission in case of remote sessions. In addition, the caller must have Get access rights (ACL in case of remote sessions, DmtPermission in case of local sessions) on the subtreeUri node to perform this operation.

Returns a DmtSession object for the requested subtree

Throws DmtException – with the following possible error codes:
URI_TOO_LONG if subtreeUri or a segment of it is too long, or if it has too many segments
INVALID_URI if subtreeUri is syntactically invalid
NODE_NOT_FOUND if subtreeUri specifies a non-existing node
PERMISSION_DENIED if principal is not null and the ACL of the node does not allow the Get operation for the principal on the given root node
FEATURE_NOT_SUPPORTED if atomic sessions are not supported by the implementation and lockMode requests an atomic session
SESSION_CREATION_TIMEOUT if the operation timed out because of another ongoing session
COMMAND_FAILED if subtreeUri specifies a relative URI, if lockMode is unknown, or some unspec-

ified error is encountered while attempting to complete the command

SecurityException – in case of remote sessions, if the caller does not have the required DmtPrincipalPermission with a target matching the principal parameter, or in case of local sessions, if the caller does not have DmtPermission for the given root node with the Get action present

117.13.3.6 public void removeEventListener(DmtEventListener listener)

listener the listener to be unregistered, must not be null

☐ Remove a previously registered listener. After this call, the listener will not receive change notifications.

Throws NullPointerException – if the listener parameter is null

117.13.4 public final class DmtData

An immutable data structure representing the contents of a leaf or interior node. This structure represents only the value and the format property of the node, all other properties (like MIME type) can be set and read using the DmtSession interface.

Different constructors are available to create nodes with different formats. Nodes of null format can be created using the static NULL_VALUE constant instance of this class.

FORMAT_RAW_BINARY and FORMAT_RAW_STRING enable the support of future data formats. When using these formats, the actual format name is specified as a String. The application is responsible for the proper encoding of the data according to the specified format.

117.13.4.1 public static final int FORMAT_BASE64 = 128

The node holds an OMA DM b64 value. Like FORMAT_BINARY, this format is also represented by the Java byte[] type, the difference is only in the corresponding OMA DM format.

117.13.4.2 public static final int FORMAT_BINARY = 64

The node holds an OMA DM bin value. The value of the node corresponds to the Java byte[] type.

117.13.4.3 public static final int FORMAT_BOOLEAN = 8

The node holds an OMA DM bool value.

117.13.4.4 public static final int FORMAT_DATE = 16

The node holds an OMA DM date value.

117.13.4.5 public static final int FORMAT_FLOAT = 2

The node holds an OMA DM float value.

117.13.4.6 public static final int FORMAT_INTEGER = 1

The node holds an OMA DM int value.

117.13.4.7 public static final int FORMAT_NODE = 1024

Format specifier of an internal node. An interior node can hold a Java object as value (see DmtData.DmtData(Object) and DmtData.getNode()). This value can be used by Java programs that know a specific URI understands the associated Java type. This type is further used as a return value of the MetaNode.getFormat method for interior nodes.

117.13.4.8 public static final int FORMAT_NULL = 512

The node holds an OMA DM null value. This corresponds to the Java null type.

117.13.4.9 **public static final int FORMAT_RAW_BINARY = 4096**

The node holds raw protocol data encoded in binary format. The getFormatName() method can be used to get the actual format name.

117.13.4.10 **public static final int FORMAT_RAW_STRING = 2048**

The node holds raw protocol data encoded as String. The getFormatName() method can be used to get the actual format name.

117.13.4.11 **public static final int FORMAT_STRING = 4**

The node holds an OMA DM chr value.

117.13.4.12 **public static final int FORMAT_TIME = 32**

The node holds an OMA DM time value.

117.13.4.13 **public static final int FORMAT_XML = 256**

The node holds an OMA DM xml value.

117.13.4.14 **public static final DmtData NULL_VALUE**

Constant instance representing a leaf node of null format.

117.13.4.15 **public DmtData(String str)**

str the string value to set

☐ Create a DmtData instance of chr format with the given string value. The null string argument is valid.

117.13.4.16 **public DmtData(Object complex)**

complex the complex data object to set

☐ Create a DmtData instance of node format with the given object value. The value represents complex data associated with an interior node.

Certain interior nodes can support access to their subtrees through such complex values, making it simpler to retrieve or update all leaf nodes in a subtree.

The given value must be a non-null immutable object.

117.13.4.17 **public DmtData(String value, int format)**

value the string, XML, date or time value to set

format the format of the DmtData instance to be created, must be one of the formats specified above

☐ Create a DmtData instance of the specified format and set its value based on the given string. Only the following string-based formats can be created using this constructor:

- FORMAT_STRING - value can be any string
- FORMAT_XML - value must contain an XML fragment (the validity is not checked by this constructor)
- FORMAT_DATE - value must be parseable to an ISO 8601 calendar date in complete representation, basic format (pattern CCYYMMDD)
- FORMAT_TIME - value must be parseable to an ISO 8601 time of day in either local time, complete representation, basic format (pattern hhmmss) or Coordinated Universal Time, basic format (pattern hhmmssZ)

null string argument is only valid if the format is string or XML.

Throws IllegalArgumentException – if format is not one of the allowed formats, or value is not a valid string for the given format

NullPointerException – if a date or time is constructed and value is null

117.13.4.18   **public DmtData(int integer)**

integer   the integer value to set

> ☐ Create a DmtData instance of int format and set its value.

117.13.4.19   **public DmtData(float flt)**

flt   the float value to set

> ☐ Create a DmtData instance of float format and set its value.

117.13.4.20   **public DmtData(boolean bool)**

bool   the boolean value to set

> ☐ Create a DmtData instance of bool format and set its value.

117.13.4.21   **public DmtData(byte[] bytes)**

bytes   the byte array to set, must not be null

> ☐ Create a DmtData instance of bin format and set its value.

Throws   NullPointerException – if bytes is null

117.13.4.22   **public DmtData(byte[] bytes, boolean base64)**

bytes   the byte array to set, must not be null

base64   if true, the new instance will have b64 format, if false, it will have bin format

> ☐ Create a DmtData instance of bin or b64 format and set its value. The chosen format is specified by the base64 parameter.

Throws   NullPointerException – if bytes is null

117.13.4.23   **public DmtData(String formatName, String data)**

formatName   the name of the format, must not be null

data   the data encoded according to the specified format, must not be null

> ☐ Create a DmtData instance in FORMAT_RAW_STRING format. The data is provided encoded as a String. The actual data format is specified in formatName. The encoding used in data must conform to this format.

Throws   NullPointerException – if formatName or data is null

117.13.4.24   **public DmtData(String formatName, byte[] data)**

formatName   the name of the format, must not be null

data   the data encoded according to the specified format, must not be null

> ☐ Create a DmtData instance in FORMAT_RAW_BINARY format. The data is provided encoded as binary. The actual data format is specified in formatName. The encoding used in data must conform to this format.

Throws   NullPointerException – if formatName or data is null

117.13.4.25   **public boolean equals(Object obj)**

obj   the object to compare with this DmtData

         ☐ Compares the specified object with this DmtData instance. Two DmtData objects are considered equal if their format is the same, and their data (selected by the format) is equal.

           In case of FORMAT_RAW_BINARY and FORMAT_RAW_STRING the textual name of the data format - as returned by getFormatName() - must be equal as well.

Returns   true if the argument represents the same DmtData as this object

117.13.4.26   public byte[] getBase64( )

         ☐ Gets the value of a node with base 64 (b64) format.

Returns   the binary value

Throws   DmtIllegalStateException – if the format of the node is not base 64.

117.13.4.27   public byte[] getBinary( )

         ☐ Gets the value of a node with binary (bin) format.

Returns   the binary value

Throws   DmtIllegalStateException – if the format of the node is not binary

117.13.4.28   public boolean getBoolean( )

         ☐ Gets the value of a node with boolean (bool) format.

Returns   the boolean value

Throws   DmtIllegalStateException – if the format of the node is not boolean

117.13.4.29   public String getDate( )

         ☐ Gets the value of a node with date format. The returned date string is formatted according to the ISO 8601 definition of a calendar date in complete representation, basic format (pattern CCYYMMDD).

Returns   the date value

Throws   DmtIllegalStateException – if the format of the node is not date

117.13.4.30   public float getFloat( )

         ☐ Gets the value of a node with float format.

Returns   the float value

Throws   DmtIllegalStateException – if the format of the node is not float

117.13.4.31   public int getFormat( )

         ☐ Get the node's format, expressed in terms of type constants defined in this class. Note that the 'format' term is a legacy from OMA DM, it is more customary to think of this as 'type'.

Returns   the format of the node

117.13.4.32   public String getFormatName( )

         ☐ Returns the format of this DmtData as String. For the predefined data formats this is the OMA DM defined name of the format. For FORMAT_RAW_STRING and FORMAT_RAW_BINARY this is the format specified when the object was created.

Returns   the format name as String

117.13.4.33   public int getInt( )

         ☐ Gets the value of a node with integer (int) format.

Returns   the integer value

Throws   DmtIllegalStateException – if the format of the node is not integer

117.13.4.34   **public Object getNode( )**

☐ Gets the complex data associated with an interior node (node format).

Certain interior nodes can support access to their subtrees through complex values, making it simpler to retrieve or update all leaf nodes in the subtree.

Returns the data object associated with an interior node

Throws DmtIllegalStateException – if the format of the data is not node

117.13.4.35   **public byte[] getRawBinary( )**

☐ Gets the value of a node in raw binary (FORMAT_RAW_BINARY) format.

Returns the data value in raw binary format

Throws DmtIllegalStateException – if the format of the node is not raw binary

117.13.4.36   **public String getRawString( )**

☐ Gets the value of a node in raw String (FORMAT_RAW_STRING) format.

Returns the data value in raw String format

Throws DmtIllegalStateException – if the format of the node is not raw String

117.13.4.37   **public int getSize( )**

☐ Get the size of the data. The returned value depends on the format of data in the node:

- FORMAT_STRING, FORMAT_XML, FORMAT_BINARY, FORMAT_BASE64, FORMAT_RAW_STRING, and FORMAT_RAW_BINARY: the length of the stored data, or 0 if the data is null
- FORMAT_INTEGER and FORMAT_FLOAT: 4
- FORMAT_DATE and FORMAT_TIME: the length of the date or time in its string representation
- FORMAT_BOOLEAN: 1
- FORMAT_NODE: -1 (unknown)
- FORMAT_NULL: 0

Returns the size of the data stored by this object

117.13.4.38   **public String getString( )**

☐ Gets the value of a node with string (chr) format.

Returns the string value

Throws DmtIllegalStateException – if the format of the node is not string

117.13.4.39   **public String getTime( )**

☐ Gets the value of a node with time format. The returned time string is formatted according to the ISO 8601 definition of the time of day. The exact format depends on the value the object was initialized with: either local time, complete representation, basic format (pattern hhmmss) or Coordinated Universal Time, basic format (pattern hhmmssZ).

Returns the time value

Throws DmtIllegalStateException – if the format of the node is not time

117.13.4.40   **public String getXml( )**

☐ Gets the value of a node with xml format.

Returns the XML value

Throws DmtIllegalStateException – if the format of the node is not xml

117.13.4.41   **public int hashCode( )**

☐ Returns the hash code value for this DmtData instance. The hash code is calculated based on the data (selected by the format) of this object.

Returns the hash code value for this object

117.13.4.42   **public String toString( )**

☐ Gets the string representation of the DmtData. This method works for all formats.

For string format data - including FORMAT_RAW_STRING - the string value itself is returned, while for XML, date, time, integer, float, boolean and node formats the string form of the value is returned. Binary - including FORMAT_RAW_BINARY - and base64 data is represented by two-digit hexadecimal numbers for each byte separated by spaces. The NULL_VALUE data has the string form of "null". Data of string or XML format containing the Java null value is represented by an empty string.

Returns the string representation of this DmtData instance

117.13.5   public interface DmtEvent

Event class storing the details of a change in the tree. DmtEvent is used by DmtAdmin to notify registered EventListeners about important changes. Events are generated after every successful DMT change, and also when sessions are opened or closed. If a DmtSession is opened in atomic mode, DMT events are only sent when the session is committed, when the changes are actually performed.

An event is generated for each group of nodes added, deleted, replaced, renamed or copied, in this order. Events are also generated when sessions are opened and closed.

The type of the event describes the change that triggered the event delivery. Each event carries the unique identifier of the session in which the described change happened. The events describing changes in the DMT carry the list of affected nodes. In case of COPIED or RENAMED events, the event carries the list of new nodes as well.

When a DmtEvent is delivered to a listener, the event contains only those node URIs that the listener has access to. This access control decision is based on the principal specified when the listener was registered:

- If the listener was registered specifying an explicit principal, using the DmtAdmin.addEventListener(String, int, String, DmtEventListener) method, then the target node ACLs should be checked for providing GET access to the specified principal;
- When the listener was registered without an explicit principal then the listener needs GET info.dmtree.security.DmtPermission for the corresponding node.

117.13.5.1   **public static final int ADDED = 1**

Event type indicating nodes that were added.

117.13.5.2   **public static final int COPIED = 2**

Event type indicating nodes that were copied.

117.13.5.3   **public static final int DELETED = 4**

Event type indicating nodes that were deleted.

117.13.5.4   **public static final int RENAMED = 8**

Event type indicating nodes that were renamed.

117.13.5.5   **public static final int REPLACED = 16**

Event type indicating nodes that were replaced.

117.13.5.6   **public static final int SESSION_CLOSED = 64**

Event type indicating that a session was closed. This type of event is sent when the session is closed by the client or becomes inactive for any other reason (session timeout, fatal errors in business methods, etc.).

117.13.5.7   **public static final int SESSION_OPENED = 32**

Event type indicating that a new session was opened.

117.13.5.8   **public String[] getNewNodes( )**

☐ This method can be used to query the new nodes, when the type of the event is COPIED or RENAMED. For all other event types this method returns null.

The array returned by this method runs parallel to the array returned by getNodes, the elements in the two arrays contain the source and destination URIs for the renamed or copied nodes in the same order. All returned URIs are absolute.

This method returns only those nodes where the caller has the GET permission for the source or destination node of the operation. Therefore, it is possible that the method returns an empty array.

Returns   the array of newly created nodes

117.13.5.9   **public String[] getNodes( )**

☐ This method can be used to query the subject nodes of this event. The method returns null for SESSION_OPENED and SESSION_CLOSED.

The method returns only those affected nodes that the caller has the GET permission for (or in case of COPIED or RENAMED events, where the caller has GET permissions for either the source or the destination nodes). Therefore, it is possible that the method returns an empty array. All returned URIs are absolute.

Returns   the array of affected nodes

See Also   getNewNodes

117.13.5.10   **public int getSessionId( )**

☐ This method returns the identifier of the session in which this event took place. The ID is guaranteed to be unique on a machine.

Returns   the unique indetifier of the session that triggered the event

117.13.5.11   **public int getType( )**

☐ This method returns the type of this event.

Returns   the type of this event.

117.13.6   public interface DmtEventListener

Registered implementations of this class are notified via DmtEvent objects about important changes in the tree. Events are generated after every successful DMT change, and also when sessions are opened or closed. If a DmtSession is opened in atomic mode, DMT events are only sent when the session is committed, when the changes are actually performed.

117.13.6.1   **public void changeOccurred(DmtEvent event)**

event   the DmtEvent describing the change in detail

☐ DmtAdmin uses this method to notify the registered listeners about the change. This method is called asynchronously from the actual event occurrence.

117.13.7   public class DmtException
extends Exception

Checked exception received when a DMT operation fails. Beside the exception message, a DmtException always contains an error code (one of the constants specified in this class), and may optionally contain the URI of the related node, and information about the cause of the exception.

Some of the error codes defined in this class have a corresponding error code defined in OMA DM, in these cases the name and numerical value from OMA DM is used. Error codes without counterparts in OMA DM were given numbers from a different range, starting from 1.

The cause of the exception (if specified) can either be a single Throwable instance, or a list of such instances if several problems occurred during the execution of a method. An example for the latter is the close method of DmtSession that tries to close multiple plugins, and has to report the exceptions of all failures.

Each constructor has two variants, one accepts a String node URI, the other accepts a String[] node path. The former is used by the DmtAdmin implementation, the latter by the plugins, who receive the node URI as an array of segment names. The constructors are otherwise identical.

Getter methods are provided to retrieve the values of the additional parameters, and the printStackTrace(PrintWriter) method is extended to print the stack trace of all causing throwables as well.

117.13.7.1   public static final int ALERT_NOT_ROUTED = 5

An alert can not be sent from the device to the given principal. This can happen if there is no Remote Alert Sender willing to forward the alert to the given principal, or if no principal was given and the DmtAdmin did not find an appropriate default destination.

This error code does not correspond to any OMA DM response status code. It should be translated to the code 500 "Command Failed" when transferring over OMA DM.

117.13.7.2   public static final int COMMAND_FAILED = 500

The recipient encountered an error which prevented it from fulfilling the request.

This error code is only used in situations not covered by any of the other error codes that a method may use. Some methods specify more specific error situations for this code, but it can generally be used for any unexpected condition that causes the command to fail.

This error code corresponds to the OMA DM response status code 500 "Command Failed".

117.13.7.3   public static final int COMMAND_NOT_ALLOWED = 405

The requested command is not allowed on the target node. This includes the following situations:

- an interior node operation is requested for a leaf node, or vice versa (e.g. trying to retrieve the children of a leaf node)
- an attempt is made to create a node where the parent is a leaf node
- an attempt is made to rename or delete the root node of the tree
- an attempt is made to rename or delete the root node of the session
- a write operation (other than setting the ACL) is performed in a non-atomic write session on a node provided by a plugin that is read-only or does not support non-atomic writing
- a node is copied to its descendant
- the ACL of the root node is changed not to include Add rights for all principals

This error code corresponds to the OMA DM response status code 405 "Command not allowed".

117.13.7.4   **public static final int CONCURRENT_ACCESS = 4**

An error occurred related to concurrent access of nodes. This can happen for example if a configuration node was deleted directly through the Configuration Admin service, while the node was manipulated via the tree.

This error code does not correspond to any OMA DM response status code. It should be translated to the code 500 "Command Failed" when transferring over OMA DM.

117.13.7.5   **public static final int DATA_STORE_FAILURE = 510**

An error related to the recipient data store occurred while processing the request. This error code may be thrown by any of the methods accessing the tree, but whether it is really used depends on the implementation, and the data store it uses.

This error code corresponds to the OMA DM response status code 510 "Data store failure".

117.13.7.6   **public static final int FEATURE_NOT_SUPPORTED = 406**

The requested command failed because an optional feature required by the command is not supported. For example, opening an atomic session might return this error code if the DmtAdmin implementation does not support transactions. Similarly, accessing the optional node properties (Title, Timestamp, Version, Size) might not succeed if either the DmtAdmin implementation or the underlying plugin does not support the property.

When getting or setting values for interior nodes (an optional optimization feature), a plugin can use this error code to indicate that the given interior node does not support values.

This error code corresponds to the OMA DM response status code 406 "Optional feature not supported".

117.13.7.7   **public static final int INVALID_URI = 3**

The requested command failed because the target URI or node name is null or syntactically invalid. This covers the following cases:

- the URI or node name ends with the '\'or '/' character
- the URI is an empty string (only invalid if the method does not accept relative URIs)
- the URI contains the segment "." at a position other than the beginning of the URI
- the node name is ".." or the URI contains such a segment
- the node name is an empty string or the URI contains an empty segment
- the node name contains an unescaped '/' character

See the Uri.mangle(String) method for support on escaping invalid characters in a URI.

This code is only used if the URI or node name does not match any of the criteria for URI_TOO_LONG. This error code does not correspond to any OMA DM response status code. It should be translated to the code 404 "Not Found" when transferring over OMA DM.

117.13.7.8   **public static final int METADATA_MISMATCH = 2**

Operation failed because of meta data restrictions. This covers any attempted deviation from the parameters defined by the MetaNode objects of the affected nodes, for example in the following situations:

- creating, deleting or renaming a permanent node, or modifying its type or value
- creating an interior node where the meta-node defines it as a leaf, or vice versa
- any operation on a node which does not have the required access type (e.g. executing a node that lacks the MetaNode.CMD_EXECUTE access type)
- any node creation or deletion that would violate the cardinality constraints
- any leaf node value setting that would violate the allowed formats, values, mime types, etc.
- any node creation that would violate the allowed node names

This error code can also be used to indicate any other meta data violation, even if it cannot be described by the MetaNode class. For example, detecting a multi-node constraint violation while committing an atomic session should result in this error.

This error code does not correspond to any OMA DM response status code. It should be translated to the code 405 "Command not allowed" when transferring over OMA DM.

117.13.7.9   public static final int NODE_ALREADY_EXISTS = 418

The requested node creation operation failed because the target already exists. This can occur if the node is created directly (with one of the create... methods), or indirectly (during a copy operation).

This error code corresponds to the OMA DM response status code 418 "Already exists".

117.13.7.10   public static final int NODE_NOT_FOUND = 404

The requested target node was not found. No indication is given as to whether this is a temporary or permanent condition, unless otherwise noted.

This is only used when the requested node name is valid, otherwise the more specific error codes URI_TOO_LONG or INVALID_URI are used. This error code corresponds to the OMA DM response status code 404 "Not Found".

117.13.7.11   public static final int PERMISSION_DENIED = 425

The requested command failed because the principal associated with the session does not have adequate access control permissions (ACL) on the target. This can only appear in case of remote sessions, i.e. if the session is associated with an authenticated principal.

This error code corresponds to the OMA DM response status code 425 "Permission denied".

117.13.7.12   public static final int REMOTE_ERROR = 1

A device initiated remote operation failed. This is used when the protocol adapter fails to send an alert for any reason.

Alert routing errors (that occur while looking for the proper protocol adapter to use) are indicated by ALERT_NOT_ROUTED, this code is only for errors encountered while sending the routed alert. This error code does not correspond to any OMA DM response status code. It should be translated to the code 500 "Command Failed" when transferring over OMA DM.

117.13.7.13   public static final int ROLLBACK_FAILED = 516

The rollback command was not completed successfully. The tree might be in an inconsistent state after this error.

This error code corresponds to the OMA DM response status code 516 "Atomic roll back failed".

117.13.7.14   public static final int SESSION_CREATION_TIMEOUT = 7

Creation of a session timed out because of another ongoing session. The length of time while the DmtAdmin waits for the blocking session(s) to finish is implementation dependant.

This error code does not correspond to any OMA DM response status code. OMA has several status codes related to timeout, but these are meant to be used when a request times out, not if a session can not be established. This error code should be translated to the code 500 "Command Failed" when transferring over OMA DM.

117.13.7.15   public static final int TRANSACTION_ERROR = 6

A transaction-related error occurred in an atomic session. This error is caused by one of the following situations:

- an updating method within an atomic session can not be executed because the underlying plugin is read-only or does not support atomic writing
- a commit operation at the end of an atomic session failed because one of the underlying plugins failed to close

The latter case may leave the tree in an inconsistent state due to the lack of a two-phase commit system, see DmtSession.commit for details.

This error code does not correspond to any OMA DM response status code. It should be translated to the code 500 "Command Failed" when transferring over OMA DM.

117.13.7.16   public static final int UNAUTHORIZED = 401

The originator's authentication credentials specify a principal with insufficient rights to complete the command.

This status code is used as response to device originated sessions if the remote management server cannot authorize the device to perform the requested operation.

This error code corresponds to the OMA DM response status code 401 "Unauthorized".

117.13.7.17   public static final int URI_TOO_LONG = 414

The requested command failed because the target URI or one of its segments is too long for what the recipient is able or willing to process, or the target URI contains too many segments. The length and segment number limits are implementation dependent, their minimum values can be found in the Non Functional Requirements section of the OSGi specification.

The Uri.mangle(String) method provides support for ensuring that a URI segment conforms to the length limits set by the implementation.

This error code corresponds to the OMA DM response status code 414 "URI too long".

See Also   OSGi Service Platform, Mobile Specification Release 4

117.13.7.18   public DmtException(String uri, int code, String message)

uri   the node on which the failed DMT operation was issued, or null if the operation is not associated with a node

code   the error code of the failure

message   the message associated with the exception, or null if there is no error message

□ Create an instance of the exception. The uri and message parameters are optional. No originating exception is specified.

117.13.7.19   public DmtException(String uri, int code, String message, Throwable cause)

uri   the node on which the failed DMT operation was issued, or null if the operation is not associated with a node

code   the error code of the failure

message   the message associated with the exception, or null if there is no error message

cause   the originating exception, or null if there is no originating exception

□ Create an instance of the exception, specifying the cause exception. The uri, message and cause parameters are optional.

117.13.7.20   public DmtException(String uri, int code, String message, Vector causes, boolean fatal)

uri   the node on which the failed DMT operation was issued, or null if the operation is not associated with a node *code* the error code of the failure

    message the message associated with the exception, or null if there is no error message

    causes the list of originating exceptions, or empty list or null if there are no originating exceptions

    fatal whether the exception is fatal

□ Create an instance of the exception, specifying the list of cause exceptions and whether the exception is a fatal one. This constructor is meant to be used by plugins wishing to indicate that a serious error occurred which should invalidate the ongoing atomic session. The uri, message and causes parameters are optional.

If a fatal exception is thrown, no further business methods will be called on the originator plugin. In case of atomic sessions, all other open plugins will be rolled back automatically, except if the fatal exception was thrown during commit.

117.13.7.21   **public DmtException(String[] path, int code, String message)**

    path the path of the node on which the failed DMT operation was issued, or null if the operation is not associated with a node

    code the error code of the failure

    message the message associated with the exception, or null if there is no error message

□ Create an instance of the exception, specifying the target node as an array of path segments. This method behaves in exactly the same way as if the path was given as a URI string.

    See Also DmtException(String, int, String)

117.13.7.22   **public DmtException(String[] path, int code, String message, Throwable cause)**

    path the path of the node on which the failed DMT operation was issued, or null if the operation is not associated with a node

    code the error code of the failure

    message the message associated with the exception, or null if there is no error message

    cause the originating exception, or null if there is no originating exception

□ Create an instance of the exception, specifying the target node as an array of path segments, and specifying the cause exception. This method behaves in exactly the same way as if the path was given as a URI string.

    See Also DmtException(String, int, String, Throwable)

117.13.7.23   **public DmtException(String[] path, int code, String message, Vector causes, boolean fatal)**

    path the path of the node on which the failed DMT operation was issued, or null if the operation is not associated with a node

    code the error code of the failure

    message the message associated with the exception, or null if there is no error message

    causes the list of originating exceptions, or empty list or null if there are no originating exceptions

    fatal whether the exception is fatal

□ Create an instance of the exception, specifying the target node as an array of path segments, the list of cause exceptions, and whether the exception is a fatal one. This method behaves in exactly the same way as if the path was given as a URI string.

    See Also DmtException(String, int, String, Vector, boolean)

117.13.7.24   **public Throwable getCause( )**

☐ Get the cause of this exception. Returns non-null, if this exception is caused by one or more other exceptions (like a NullPointerException in a DmtPlugin). If there are more than one cause exceptions, the first one is returned.

Returns the cause of this exception, or null if no cause was given

117.13.7.25   **public Throwable[] getCauses( )**

☐ Get all causes of this exception. Returns the causing exceptions in an array. If no cause was specified, an empty array is returned.

Returns the list of causes of this exception

117.13.7.26   **public int getCode( )**

☐ Get the error code associated with this exception. Most of the error codes within this exception correspond to OMA DM error codes.

Returns the error code

117.13.7.27   **public String getMessage( )**

☐ Get the message associated with this exception. The returned string also contains the associated URI (if any) and the exception code. The resulting message has the following format (parts in square brackets are only included if the field inside them is not null):

```
<exception_code>[: '<uri>'][: <error_message>]
```

Returns the error message in the format described above

117.13.7.28   **public String getURI( )**

☐ Get the node on which the failed DMT operation was issued. Some operations like DmtSession.close() don't require an URI, in this case this method returns null.

Returns the URI of the node, or null

117.13.7.29   **public boolean isFatal( )**

☐ Check whether this exception is marked as fatal in the session. Fatal exceptions trigger an automatic rollback of atomic sessions.

Returns whether the exception is marked as fatal

117.13.7.30   **public void printStackTrace(PrintStream s)**

s PrintStream to use for output

☐ Prints the exception and its backtrace to the specified print stream. Any causes that were specified for this exception are also printed, together with their backtraces.

117.13.8   public class DmtIllegalStateException extends RuntimeException

Unchecked illegal state exception. This class is used in DMT because java.lang.IllegalStateException does not exist in CLDC.

117.13.8.1   **public DmtIllegalStateException( )**

☐ Create an instance of the exception with no message.

117.13.8.2   **public DmtIllegalStateException(String message)**

message the reason for the exception

☐ Create an instance of the exception with the specified message.

117.13.8.3   **public DmtIllegalStateException(Throwable cause)**

cause the cause of the exception

    □ Create an instance of the exception with the specified cause exception and no message.

117.13.8.4   **public DmtIllegalStateException(String message, Throwable cause)**

message the reason for the exception

cause the cause of the exception

    □ Create an instance of the exception with the specified message and cause exception.

117.13.8.5   **public Throwable getCause( )**

    □ Returns the cause of this exception or null if no cause was set.

Returns The cause of this exception or null if no cause was set.

117.13.8.6   **public Throwable initCause(Throwable cause)**

cause The cause of this exception.

    □ Initializes the cause of this exception to the specified value.

Returns This exception.

Throws IllegalArgumentException – If the specified cause is this exception.

        IllegalStateException – If the cause of this exception has already been set.

Since 1.0.1

117.13.9   public interface DmtSession

DmtSession provides concurrent access to the DMT. All DMT manipulation commands for management applications are available on the DmtSession interface. The session is associated with a root node which limits the subtree in which the operations can be executed within this session.

Most of the operations take a node URI as parameter, which can be either an absolute URI (starting with "./") or a URI relative to the root node of the session. The empty string as relative URI means the root URI the session was opened with. All segments of a URI must be within the segment length limit of the implementation, and the special characters '/' and '\' must be escaped (preceded by a '\'). Any string can be converted to a valid URI segment using the Uri.mangle(String) method.

If the URI specified does not correspond to a legitimate node in the tree an exception is thrown. The only exception is the isNodeUri(String) method which returns false in case of an invalid URI.

Each method of DmtSession that accesses the tree in any way can throw DmtIllegalStateException if the session has been closed or invalidated (due to timeout, fatal exceptions, or unexpectedly unregistered plugins).

117.13.9.1   **public static final int LOCK_TYPE_ATOMIC = 2**

LOCK_TYPE_ATOMIC is an exclusive lock with transactional functionality. Commands of an atomic session will either fail or succeed together, if a single command fails then the whole session will be rolled back.

117.13.9.2   **public static final int LOCK_TYPE_EXCLUSIVE = 1**

LOCK_TYPE_EXCLUSIVE lock guarantees full access to the tree, but can not be shared with any other locks.

117.13.9.3   **public static final int LOCK_TYPE_SHARED = 0**

Sessions created with LOCK_TYPE_SHARED lock allows read-only access to the tree, but can be shared between multiple readers.

117.13.9.4   **public static final int STATE_CLOSED = 1**

The session is closed, DMT manipulation operations are not available, they throw DmtIllegalStateException if tried.

117.13.9.5   **public static final int STATE_INVALID = 2**

The session is invalid because a fatal error happened. Fatal errors include the timeout of the session, any DmtException with the 'fatal' flag set, or the case when a plugin service is unregistered while in use by the session. DMT manipulation operations are not available, they throw DmtIllegalStateException if tried.

117.13.9.6   **public static final int STATE_OPEN = 0**

The session is open, all session operations are available.

117.13.9.7   **public void close( ) throws DmtException**

☐ Closes a session. If the session was opened with atomic lock mode, the DmtSession must first persist the changes made to the DMT by calling commit() on all (transactional) plugins participating in the session. See the documentation of the commit method for details and possible errors during this operation.

The state of the session changes to DmtSession.STATE_CLOSED if the close operation completed successfully, otherwise it becomes DmtSession.STATE_INVALID.

Throws DmtException – with the following possible error codes:
METADATA_MISMATCH in case of atomic sessions, if the commit operation failed because of meta-data restrictions
CONCURRENT_ACCESS in case of atomic sessions, if the commit operation failed because of some modification outside the scope of the DMT to the nodes affected in the session
TRANSACTION_ERROR in case of atomic sessions, if an underlying plugin failed to commit
DATA_STORE_FAILURE if an error occurred while accessing the data store
COMMAND_FAILED if an underlying plugin failed to close, or if some unspecified error is encountered while attempting to complete the command

DmtIllegalStateException – if the session is already closed or invalidated

SecurityException – if the caller does not have the necessary permissions to execute the underlying management operation

117.13.9.8   **public void commit( ) throws DmtException**

☐ Commits a series of DMT operations issued in the current atomic session since the last transaction boundary. Transaction boundaries are the creation of this object that starts the session, and all subsequent commit and rollback calls.

This method can fail even if all operations were successful. This can happen due to some multi-node semantic constraints defined by a specific implementation. For example, node A can be required to always have children A/B, A/C and A/D. If this condition is broken when commit() is executed, the method will fail, and throw a METADATA_MISMATCH exception.

An error situation can arise due to the lack of a two phase commit mechanism in the underlying plugins. As an example, if plugin A has committed successfully but plugin B failed, the whole session must fail, but there is no way to undo the commit performed by A. To provide predictable behaviour, the commit operation should continue with the remaining plugins even after detecting a failure. All exceptions received from failed commits are aggregated into one TRANSACTION_ERROR exception thrown by this method.

In many cases the tree is not the only way to manage a given part of the system. It may happen that while modifying some nodes in an atomic session, the underlying settings are modified in parallel outside the scope of the DMT. If this is detected during commit, an exception with the code CONCURRENT_ACCESS is thrown.

Throws DmtException – with the following possible error codes:
METADATA_MISMATCH if the operation failed because of meta-data restrictions
CONCURRENT_ACCESS if it is detected that some modification has been made outside the scope of the DMT to the nodes affected in the session's operations
TRANSACTION_ERROR if an error occurred during the commit of any of the underlying plugins
DATA_STORE_FAILURE if an error occurred while accessing the data store
COMMAND_FAILED if some unspecified error is encountered while attempting to complete the command

DmtIllegalStateException – if the session was not opened using the LOCK_TYPE_ATOMIC lock type, or if the session is already closed or invalidated

SecurityException – if the caller does not have the necessary permissions to execute the underlying management operation

117.13.9.9   **public void copy(String nodeUri, String newNodeUri, boolean recursive) throws DmtException**

nodeUri the node or root of a subtree to be copied

newNodeUri the URI of the new node or root of a subtree

recursive false if only a single node is copied, true if the whole subtree is copied

□ Create a copy of a node or a whole subtree. Beside the structure and values of the nodes, most properties are also copied, with the exception of the ACL (Access Control List), Timestamp and Version properties.

The copy method is essentially a convenience method that could be substituted with a sequence of retrieval and update operations. This determines the permissions required for copying. However, some optimization can be possible if the source and target nodes are all handled by DmtAdmin or by the same plugin. In this case, the handler might be able to perform the underlying management operation more efficiently: for example, a configuration table can be copied at once instead of reading each node for each entry and creating it in the new tree.

This method may result in any of the errors possible for the contributing operations. Most of these are collected in the exception descriptions below, but for the full list also consult the documentation of getChildNodeNames(String), isLeafNode(String), getNodeValue(String), getNodeType(String), getNodeTitle(String), setNodeTitle(String, String), createLeafNode(String, DmtData, String) and createInteriorNode(String, String).

Throws DmtException – with the following possible error codes:
URI_TOO_LONG if nodeUri or newNodeUri or any segment of them is too long, or if they have too many segments
INVALID_URI if nodeUri or newNodeUri is null or syntactically invalid
NODE_NOT_FOUND if nodeUri points to a non-existing node, or if newNodeUri points to a node that cannot exist in the tree according to the meta-data (see getMetaNode(String))
NODE_ALREADY_EXISTS if newNodeUri points to a node that already exists
PERMISSION_DENIED if the session is associated with a principal and the ACL of the copied node(s) does not allow the Get operation, or the ACL of the parent of the target node does not allow the Add

operation for the associated principal

COMMAND_NOT_ALLOWED if nodeUri is an ancestor of newNodeUri, or if any of the implied retrieval or update operations are not allowed

METADATA_MISMATCH if any of the meta-data constraints of the implied retrieval or update operations are violated

TRANSACTION_ERROR in an atomic session if the underlying plugin is read-only or does not support atomic writing

DATA_STORE_FAILURE if an error occurred while accessing the data store

COMMAND_FAILED if either URI is not within the current session's subtree, or if some unspecified error is encountered while attempting to complete the command

DmtIllegalStateException – if the session was opened using the LOCK_TYPE_SHARED lock type, or if the session is already closed or invalidated

SecurityException – if the caller does not have the necessary permissions to execute the underlying management operation, or, in case of local sessions, if the caller does not have DmtPermission for the copied node(s) with the Get action present, or for the parent of the target node with the Add action

117.13.9.10   **public void createInteriorNode(String nodeUri) throws DmtException**

nodeUri   the URI of the node to create

☐   Create an interior node. If the parent node does not exist, it is created automatically, as if this method were called for the parent URI. This way all missing ancestor nodes leading to the specified node are created. Any exceptions encountered while creating the ancestors are propagated to the caller of this method, these are not explicitly listed in the error descriptions below.

If meta-data is available for the node, several checks are made before creating it. The node must have MetaNode.CMD_ADD access type, it must be defined as a non-permanent interior node, the node name must conform to the valid names, and the creation of the new node must not cause the maximum occurrence number to be exceeded.

If the meta-data cannot be retrieved because the given node cannot possibly exist in the tree (it is not defined in the specification), the NODE_NOT_FOUND error code is returned (see getMetaNode(String)).

Throws   DmtException – with the following possible error codes:
URI_TOO_LONG if nodeUri or a segment of it is too long, or if it has too many segments
INVALID_URI if nodeUri is null or syntactically invalid
NODE_NOT_FOUND if nodeUri points to a node that cannot exist in the tree (see above)
NODE_ALREADY_EXISTS if nodeUri points to a node that already exists
PERMISSION_DENIED if the session is associated with a principal and the ACL of the parent node does not allow the Add operation for the associated principal
COMMAND_NOT_ALLOWED if the parent node is not an interior node, or in non-atomic sessions if the underlying plugin is read-only or does not support non-atomic writing
METADATA_MISMATCH if the node could not be created because of meta-data restrictions (see above)
TRANSACTION_ERROR in an atomic session if the underlying plugin is read-only or does not support atomic writing
DATA_STORE_FAILURE if an error occurred while accessing the data store
COMMAND_FAILED if the URI is not within the current session's subtree, or if some unspecified error is encountered while attempting to complete the command

DmtIllegalStateException – if the session was opened using the LOCK_TYPE_SHARED lock type, or if the session is already closed or invalidated

SecurityException – if the caller does not have the necessary permissions to execute the underlying management operation, or, in case of local sessions, if the caller does not have DmtPermission for the parent node with the Add action present

117.13.9.11   **public void createInteriorNode(String nodeUri, String type) throws DmtException**

nodeUri the URI of the node to create

type the type URI of the interior node, can be null if no node type is defined

☐ Create an interior node with a given type. The type of interior node, if specified, is a URI identifying a DDF document. If the parent node does not exist, it is created automatically, as if createInteriorNode(String) were called for the parent URI. This way all missing ancestor nodes leading to the specified node are created. Any exceptions encountered while creating the ancestors are propagated to the caller of this method, these are not explicitly listed in the error descriptions below.

If meta-data is available for the node, several checks are made before creating it. The node must have MetaNode.CMD_ADD access type, it must be defined as a non-permanent interior node, the node name must conform to the valid names, and the creation of the new node must not cause the maximum occurrence number to be exceeded.

If the meta-data cannot be retrieved because the given node cannot possibly exist in the tree (it is not defined in the specification), the NODE_NOT_FOUND error code is returned (see getMetaNode(String)).

Interior node type identifiers must follow the format defined in section 7.7.7.2 of the OMA Device Management Tree and Description document. Checking the validity of the type string does not have to be done by the DmtAdmin, this can be left to the plugin handling the node (if any), to avoid unnecessary double-checks.

Throws DmtException – with the following possible error codes:
URI_TOO_LONG if nodeUri or a segment of it is too long, or if it has too many segments
INVALID_URI if nodeUri is null or syntactically invalid
NODE_NOT_FOUND if nodeUri points to a node that cannot exist in the tree (see above)
NODE_ALREADY_EXISTS if nodeUri points to a node that already exists
PERMISSION_DENIED if the session is associated with a principal and the ACL of the parent node does not allow the Add operation for the associated principal
COMMAND_NOT_ALLOWED if the parent node is not an interior node, or in non-atomic sessions if the underlying plugin is read-only or does not support non-atomic writing
METADATA_MISMATCH if the node could not be created because of meta-data restrictions (see above)
TRANSACTION_ERROR in an atomic session if the underlying plugin is read-only or does not support atomic writing
DATA_STORE_FAILURE if an error occurred while accessing the data store
COMMAND_FAILED if the URI is not within the current session's subtree, if the type string is invalid (see above), or if some unspecified error is encountered while attempting to complete the command

DmtIllegalStateException – if the session was opened using the LOCK_TYPE_SHARED lock type, or if the session is already closed or invalidated

SecurityException – if the caller does not have the necessary permissions to execute the underlying management operation, or, in case of local sessions, if the caller does not have DmtPermission for the parent node with the Add action present

See Also createInteriorNode(String), OMA Device Management Tree and Description v1.2 draft (http://member.openmobilealliance.org/ftp/public_documents/dm/Permanent_documents/OMA-TS-DM-TND-V1_2-20050615-C.zip)

117.13.9.12   **public void createLeafNode(String nodeUri) throws DmtException**

nodeUri the URI of the node to create

☐ Create a leaf node with default value and MIME type. If a node does not have a default value or MIME type, this method will throw a DmtException with error code METADATA_MISMATCH. Note that a node might have a default value or MIME type even if there is no meta-data for the node or its meta-data does not specify the default.

If the parent node does not exist, it is created automatically, as if createInteriorNode(String) were called for the parent URI. This way all missing ancestor nodes leading to the specified node are created. Any exceptions encountered while creating the ancestors are propagated to the caller of this method, these are not explicitly listed in the error descriptions below.

If meta-data is available for a node, several checks are made before creating it. The node must have MetaNode.CMD_ADD access type, it must be defined as a non-permanent leaf node, the node name must conform to the valid names, and the creation of the new node must not cause the maximum occurrence number to be exceeded.

If the meta-data cannot be retrieved because the given node cannot possibly exist in the tree (it is not defined in the specification), the NODE_NOT_FOUND error code is returned (see getMetaNode(String)).

Throws   DmtException – with the following possible error codes:
URI_TOO_LONG if nodeUri or a segment of it is too long, or if it has too many segments
INVALID_URI if nodeUri is null or syntactically invalid
NODE_NOT_FOUND if nodeUri points to a node that cannot exist in the tree (see above)
NODE_ALREADY_EXISTS if nodeUri points to a node that already exists
PERMISSION_DENIED if the session is associated with a principal and the ACL of the parent node does not allow the Add operation for the associated principal
COMMAND_NOT_ALLOWED if the parent node is not an interior node, or in non-atomic sessions if the underlying plugin is read-only or does not support non-atomic writing
METADATA_MISMATCH if the node could not be created because of meta-data restrictions (see above)
TRANSACTION_ERROR in an atomic session if the underlying plugin is read-only or does not support atomic writing
DATA_STORE_FAILURE if an error occurred while accessing the data store
COMMAND_FAILED if the URI is not within the current session's subtree, or if some unspecified error is encountered while attempting to complete the command

DmtIllegalStateException – if the session was opened using the LOCK_TYPE_SHARED lock type, or if the session is already closed or invalidated

SecurityException – if the caller does not have the necessary permissions to execute the underlying management operation, or, in case of local sessions, if the caller does not have DmtPermission for the parent node with the Add action present

See Also   createLeafNode(String, DmtData)

117.13.9.13   public void createLeafNode(String nodeUri, DmtData value) throws DmtException

nodeUri   the URI of the node to create

value   the value to be given to the new node, can be null

☐   Create a leaf node with a given value and the default MIME type. If the specified value is null, the default value is taken. If the node does not have a default MIME type or value (if needed), this method will throw a DmtException with error code METADATA_MISMATCH. Note that a node might have a default value or MIME type even if there is no meta-data for the node or its meta-data does not specify the default.

If the parent node does not exist, it is created automatically, as if createInteriorNode(String) were called for the parent URI. This way all missing ancestor nodes leading to the specified node are created. Any exceptions encountered while creating the ancestors are propagated to the caller of this method, these are not explicitly listed in the error descriptions below.

If meta-data is available for a node, several checks are made before creating it. The node must have MetaNode.CMD_ADD access type, it must be defined as a non-permanent leaf node, the node name must conform to the valid names, the node value must conform to the value constraints, and the creation of the new node must not cause the maximum occurrence number to be exceeded.

If the meta-data cannot be retrieved because the given node cannot possibly exist in the tree (it is not defined in the specification), the NODE_NOT_FOUND error code is returned (see getMetaNode(String)).

Nodes of null format can be created by using DmtData.NULL_VALUE as second argument.

Throws DmtException – with the following possible error codes:
URI_TOO_LONG if nodeUri or a segment of it is too long, or if it has too many segments
INVALID_URI if nodeUri is null or syntactically invalid
NODE_NOT_FOUND if nodeUri points to a node that cannot exist in the tree (see above)
NODE_ALREADY_EXISTS if nodeUri points to a node that already exists
PERMISSION_DENIED if the session is associated with a principal and the ACL of the parent node does not allow the Add operation for the associated principal
COMMAND_NOT_ALLOWED if the parent node is not an interior node, or in non-atomic sessions if the underlying plugin is read-only or does not support non-atomic writing
METADATA_MISMATCH if the node could not be created because of meta-data restrictions (see above)
TRANSACTION_ERROR in an atomic session if the underlying plugin is read-only or does not support atomic writing
DATA_STORE_FAILURE if an error occurred while accessing the data store
COMMAND_FAILED if the URI is not within the current session's subtree, or if some unspecified error is encountered while attempting to complete the command

DmtIllegalStateException – if the session was opened using the LOCK_TYPE_SHARED lock type, or if the session is already closed or invalidated

SecurityException – if the caller does not have the necessary permissions to execute the underlying management operation, or, in case of local sessions, if the caller does not have DmtPermission for the parent node with the Add action present

117.13.9.14   **public void createLeafNode(String nodeUri, DmtData value, String mimeType) throws DmtException**

nodeUri the URI of the node to create

value the value to be given to the new node, can be null

mimeType the MIME type to be given to the new node, can be null

☐ Create a leaf node with a given value and MIME type. If the specified value or MIME type is null, their default values are taken. If the node does not have the necessary defaults, this method will throw a DmtException with error code METADATA_MISMATCH. Note that a node might have a default value or MIME type even if there is no meta-data for the node or its meta-data does not specify the default.

If the parent node does not exist, it is created automatically, as if createInteriorNode(String) were called for the parent URI. This way all missing ancestor nodes leading to the specified node are created. Any exceptions encountered while creating the ancestors are propagated to the caller of this method, these are not explicitly listed in the error descriptions below.

If meta-data is available for a node, several checks are made before creating it. The node must have MetaNode.CMD_ADD access type, it must be defined as a non-permanent leaf node, the node name must conform to the valid names, the node value must conform to the value constraints, the MIME type must be among the listed types, and the creation of the new node must not cause the maximum occurrence number to be exceeded.

If the meta-data cannot be retrieved because the given node cannot possibly exist in the tree (it is not defined in the specification), the NODE_NOT_FOUND error code is returned (see getMetaNode(String)).

Nodes of null format can be created by using DmtData.NULL_VALUE as second argument.

The MIME type string must conform to the definition in RFC 2045. Checking its validity does not have to be done by the DmtAdmin, this can be left to the plugin handling the node (if any), to avoid unnecessary double-checks.

Throws DmtException – with the following possible error codes:

URI_TOO_LONG if nodeUri or a segment of it is too long, or if it has too many segments

INVALID_URI if nodeUri is null or syntactically invalid

NODE_NOT_FOUND if nodeUri points to a node that cannot exist in the tree (see above)

NODE_ALREADY_EXISTS if nodeUri points to a node that already exists

PERMISSION_DENIED if the session is associated with a principal and the ACL of the parent node does not allow the Add operation for the associated principal

COMMAND_NOT_ALLOWED if the parent node is not an interior node, or in non-atomic sessions if the underlying plugin is read-only or does not support non-atomic writing

METADATA_MISMATCH if the node could not be created because of meta-data restrictions (see above)

TRANSACTION_ERROR in an atomic session if the underlying plugin is read-only or does not support atomic writing

DATA_STORE_FAILURE if an error occurred while accessing the data store

COMMAND_FAILED if the URI is not within the current session's subtree, if mimeType is not a proper MIME type string (see above), or if some unspecified error is encountered while attempting to complete the command

DmtIllegalStateException – if the session was opened using the LOCK_TYPE_SHARED lock type, or if the session is already closed or invalidated

SecurityException – if the caller does not have the necessary permissions to execute the underlying management operation, or, in case of local sessions, if the caller does not have DmtPermission for the parent node with the Add action present

See Also createLeafNode(String, DmtData), RFC 2045 (http://www.ietf.org/rfc/rfc2045.txt)

117.13.9.15   public void deleteNode(String nodeUri) throws DmtException

nodeUri the URI of the node

☐   Delete the given node. Deleting interior nodes is recursive, the whole subtree under the given node is deleted. It is not allowed to delete the root node of the session.

If meta-data is available for a node, several checks are made before deleting it. The node must be non-permanent, it must have the MetaNode.CMD_DELETE access type, and if zero occurrences of the node are not allowed, it must not be the last one.

Throws DmtException – with the following possible error codes:

URI_TOO_LONG if nodeUri or a segment of it is too long, or if it has too many segments

INVALID_URI if nodeUri is null or syntactically invalid

NODE_NOT_FOUND if nodeUri points to a non-existing node

PERMISSION_DENIED if the session is associated with a principal and the ACL of the node does not allow the Delete operation for the associated principal

COMMAND_NOT_ALLOWED if the target node is the root of the session, or in non-atomic sessions if the underlying plugin is read-only or does not support non-atomic writing

METADATA_MISMATCH if the node could not be deleted because of meta-data restrictions (see above)

TRANSACTION_ERROR in an atomic session if the underlying plugin is read-only or does not support atomic writing

DATA_STORE_FAILURE if an error occurred while accessing the data store

COMMAND_FAILED if the URI is not within the current session's subtree, or if some unspecified error is encountered while attempting to complete the command

DmtIllegalStateException – if the session was opened using the LOCK_TYPE_SHARED lock type, or if the session is already closed or invalidated

SecurityException – if the caller does not have the necessary permissions to execute the underlying management operation, or, in case of local sessions, if the caller does not have DmtPermission for the node with the Delete action present

117.13.9.16   public void execute(String nodeUri, String data) throws DmtException

nodeUri the node on which the execute operation is issued

data the parameter of the execute operation, can be null

☐ Executes a node. This corresponds to the EXEC operation in OMA DM. This method cannot be called in a read-only session.

The semantics of an execute operation and the data parameter it takes depends on the definition of the managed object on which the command is issued.

Throws DmtException – with the following possible error codes:
URI_TOO_LONG if nodeUri or a segment of it is too long, or if it has too many segments
INVALID_URI if nodeUri is null or syntactically invalid
NODE_NOT_FOUND if the node does not exist and the plugin does not allow executing unexisting nodes
PERMISSION_DENIED if the session is associated with a principal and the ACL of the node does not allow the Execute operation for the associated principal
METADATA_MISMATCH if the node cannot be executed according to the meta-data (does not have MetaNode.CMD_EXECUTE access type)
DATA_STORE_FAILURE if an error occurred while accessing the data store
COMMAND_FAILED if the URI is not within the current session's subtree, if no DmtExecPlugin is associated with the node and the DmtAdmin can not execute the node, or if some unspecified error is encountered while attempting to complete the command

DmtIllegalStateException – if the session was opened using the LOCK_TYPE_SHARED lock type, or if the session is already closed or invalidated

SecurityException – if the caller does not have the necessary permissions to execute the underlying management operation, or, in case of local sessions, if the caller does not have DmtPermission for the node with the Exec action present

See Also execute(String, String, String)

117.13.9.17   public void execute(String nodeUri, String correlator, String data) throws DmtException

nodeUri the node on which the execute operation is issued

correlator an identifier to associate this operation with any notifications sent in response to it, can be null if not needed

data the parameter of the execute operation, can be null

☐ Executes a node, also specifying a correlation ID for use in response notifications. This operation corresponds to the EXEC command in OMA DM. This method cannot be called in a read-only session.

The semantics of an execute operation and the data parameter it takes depends on the definition of the managed object on which the command is issued. If a correlation ID is specified, it should be used as the correlator parameter for notifications sent in response to this execute operation.

Throws DmtException – with the following possible error codes:
URI_TOO_LONG if nodeUri or a segment of it is too long, or if it has too many segments
INVALID_URI if nodeUri is null or syntactically invalid
NODE_NOT_FOUND if the node does not exist and the plugin does not allow executing unexisting nodes
PERMISSION_DENIED if the session is associated with a principal and the ACL of the node does not allow the Execute operation for the associated principal
METADATA_MISMATCH if the node cannot be executed according to the meta-data (does not have MetaNode.CMD_EXECUTE access type)

DATA_STORE_FAILURE if an error occurred while accessing the data store
COMMAND_FAILED if the URI is not within the current session's subtree, if no DmtExecPlugin is associated with the node, or if some unspecified error is encountered while attempting to complete the command

DmtIllegalStateException – if the session was opened using the LOCK_TYPE_SHARED lock type, or if the session is already closed or invalidated

SecurityException – if the caller does not have the necessary permissions to execute the underlying management operation, or, in case of local sessions, if the caller does not have DmtPermission for the node with the Exec action present

See Also execute(String, String)

117.13.9.18   **public String[] getChildNodeNames(String nodeUri) throws DmtException**

nodeUri the URI of the node

☐ Get the list of children names of a node. The returned array contains the names - not the URIs - of the immediate children nodes of the given node. The returned child names are mangled (Uri.mangle(String)). The elements are in no particular order. The returned array must not contain null entries.

Returns the list of child node names as a string array or an empty string array if the node has no children

Throws DmtException – with the following possible error codes:
URI_TOO_LONG if nodeUri or a segment of it is too long, or if it has too many segments
INVALID_URI if nodeUri is null or syntactically invalid
NODE_NOT_FOUND if nodeUri points to a non-existing node
PERMISSION_DENIED if the session is associated with a principal and the ACL of the node does not allow the Get operation for the associated principal
COMMAND_NOT_ALLOWED if the specified node is not an interior node
METADATA_MISMATCH if node information cannot be retrieved according to the meta-data (it does not have MetaNode.CMD_GET access type)
DATA_STORE_FAILURE if an error occurred while accessing the data store
COMMAND_FAILED if the URI is not within the current session's subtree, or if some unspecified error is encountered while attempting to complete the command

DmtIllegalStateException – if the session is already closed or invalidated

SecurityException – if the caller does not have the necessary permissions to execute the underlying management operation, or, in case of local sessions, if the caller does not have DmtPermission for the node with the Get action present

117.13.9.19   **public Acl getEffectiveNodeAcl(String nodeUri) throws DmtException**

nodeUri the URI of the node

☐ Gives the Access Control List in effect for a given node. The returned Acl takes inheritance into account, that is if there is no ACL defined for the node, it will be derived from the closest ancestor having an ACL defined.

Returns the Access Control List belonging to the node

Throws DmtException – with the following possible error codes:
URI_TOO_LONG if nodeUri or a segment of it is too long, or if it has too many segments
INVALID_URI if nodeUri is null or syntactically invalid
NODE_NOT_FOUND if nodeUri points to a non-existing node
PERMISSION_DENIED if the session is associated with a principal and the ACL of the node does not allow the Get operation for the associated principal
METADATA_MISMATCH if node information cannot be retrieved according to the meta-data (the node does not have MetaNode.CMD_GET access type)
DATA_STORE_FAILURE if an error occurred while accessing the data store

COMMAND_FAILED if the URI is not within the current session's subtree, or if some unspecified error is encountered while attempting to complete the command

DmtIllegalStateException – if the session is already closed or invalidated

SecurityException – in case of local sessions, if the caller does not have DmtPermission for the node with the Get action present

See Also getNodeAcl

117.13.9.20   public int getLockType( )

□ Gives the type of lock the session has.

Returns the lock type of the session, one of LOCK_TYPE_SHARED, LOCK_TYPE_EXCLUSIVE and LOCK_TYPE_ATOMIC

117.13.9.21   public MetaNode getMetaNode(String nodeUri) throws DmtException

nodeUri the URI of the node

□ Get the meta data which describes a given node. Meta data can only be inspected, it can not be changed.

The MetaNode object returned to the client is the combination of the meta data returned by the data plugin (if any) plus the meta data returned by the DmtAdmin. If there are differences in the meta data elements known by the plugin and the DmtAdmin then the plugin specific elements take precedence.

Note, that a node does not have to exist for having meta-data associated with it. This method may provide meta-data for any node that can possibly exist in the tree (any node defined in the specification). For nodes that are not defined, it may throw DmtException with the error code NODE_NOT_FOUND. To allow easier implementation of plugins that do not provide meta-data, it is allowed to return null for any node, regardless of whether it is defined or not.

Returns a MetaNode which describes meta data information, can be null if there is no meta data available for the given node

Throws DmtException – with the following possible error codes:
URI_TOO_LONG if nodeUri or a segment of it is too long, or if it has too many segments
INVALID_URI if nodeUri is null or syntactically invalid
NODE_NOT_FOUND if nodeUri points to a node that is not defined in the tree (see above)
PERMISSION_DENIED if the session is associated with a principal and the ACL of the node does not allow the Get operation for the associated principal
DATA_STORE_FAILURE if an error occurred while accessing the data store
COMMAND_FAILED if the URI is not within the current session's subtree, or if some unspecified error is encountered while attempting to complete the command

DmtIllegalStateException – if the session is already closed or invalidated

SecurityException – if the caller does not have the necessary permissions to execute the underlying management operation, or, in case of local sessions, if the caller does not have DmtPermission for the node with the Get action present

117.13.9.22   public Acl getNodeAcl(String nodeUri) throws DmtException

nodeUri the URI of the node

□ Get the Access Control List associated with a given node. The returned Acl object does not take inheritance into account, it gives the ACL specifically given to the node.

Returns the Access Control List belonging to the node or null if none defined

Throws DmtException – with the following possible error codes:
URI_TOO_LONG if nodeUri or a segment of it is too long, or if it has too many segments
INVALID_URI if nodeUri is null or syntactically invalid

NODE_NOT_FOUND if nodeUri points to a non-existing node
PERMISSION_DENIED if the session is associated with a principal and the ACL of the node does not allow the Get operation for the associated principal
METADATA_MISMATCH if node information cannot be retrieved according to the meta-data (the node does not have MetaNode.CMD_GET access type)
DATA_STORE_FAILURE if an error occurred while accessing the data store
COMMAND_FAILED if the URI is not within the current session's subtree, or if some unspecified error is encountered while attempting to complete the command

DmtIllegalStateException – if the session is already closed or invalidated

SecurityException – in case of local sessions, if the caller does not have DmtPermission for the node with the Get action present

See Also getEffectiveNodeAcl

117.13.9.23   **public int getNodeSize(String nodeUri) throws DmtException**

nodeUri the URI of the leaf node

□ Get the size of the data in a leaf node. The returned value depends on the format of the data in the node, see the description of the DmtData.getSize() method for the definition of node size for each format.

Returns the size of the data in the node

Throws DmtException – with the following possible error codes:
URI_TOO_LONG if nodeUri or a segment of it is too long, or if it has too many segments
INVALID_URI if nodeUri is null or syntactically invalid
NODE_NOT_FOUND if nodeUri points to a non-existing node
PERMISSION_DENIED if the session is associated with a principal and the ACL of the node does not allow the Get operation for the associated principal
COMMAND_NOT_ALLOWED if the specified node is not a leaf node
METADATA_MISMATCH if node information cannot be retrieved according to the meta-data (it does not have MetaNode.CMD_GET access type)
FEATURE_NOT_SUPPORTED if the Size property is not supported by the DmtAdmin implementation or the underlying plugin
DATA_STORE_FAILURE if an error occurred while accessing the data store
COMMAND_FAILED if the URI is not within the current session's subtree, or if some unspecified error is encountered while attempting to complete the command

DmtIllegalStateException – if the session is already closed or invalidated

SecurityException – if the caller does not have the necessary permissions to execute the underlying management operation, or, in case of local sessions, if the caller does not have DmtPermission for the node with the Get action present

See Also DmtData.getSize

117.13.9.24   **public Date getNodeTimestamp(String nodeUri) throws DmtException**

nodeUri the URI of the node

□ Get the timestamp when the node was created or last modified.

Returns the timestamp of the last modification

Throws DmtException – with the following possible error codes:
URI_TOO_LONG if nodeUri or a segment of it is too long, or if it has too many segments
INVALID_URI if nodeUri is null or syntactically invalid
NODE_NOT_FOUND if nodeUri points to a non-existing node
PERMISSION_DENIED if the session is associated with a principal and the ACL of the node does not allow the Get operation for the associated principal

METADATA_MISMATCH if node information cannot be retrieved according to the meta-data (it does not have MetaNode.CMD_GET access type)

FEATURE_NOT_SUPPORTED if the Timestamp property is not supported by the DmtAdmin implementation or the underlying plugin

DATA_STORE_FAILURE if an error occurred while accessing the data store

COMMAND_FAILED if the URI is not within the current session's subtree, or if some unspecified error is encountered while attempting to complete the command

DmtIllegalStateException – if the session is already closed or invalidated

SecurityException – if the caller does not have the necessary permissions to execute the underlying management operation, or, in case of local sessions, if the caller does not have DmtPermission for the node with the Get action present

117.13.9.25   **public String getNodeTitle(String nodeUri) throws DmtException**

nodeUri the URI of the node

☐ Get the title of a node. There might be no title property set for a node.

Returns the title of the node, or null if the node has no title

Throws DmtException – with the following possible error codes:
URI_TOO_LONG if nodeUri or a segment of it is too long, or if it has too many segments
INVALID_URI if nodeUri is null or syntactically invalid
NODE_NOT_FOUND if nodeUri points to a non-existing node
PERMISSION_DENIED if the session is associated with a principal and the ACL of the node does not allow the Get operation for the associated principal
METADATA_MISMATCH if node information cannot be retrieved according to the meta-data (it does not have MetaNode.CMD_GET access type)
FEATURE_NOT_SUPPORTED if the Title property is not supported by the DmtAdmin implementation or the underlying plugin
DATA_STORE_FAILURE if an error occurred while accessing the data store
COMMAND_FAILED if the URI is not within the current session's subtree, or if some unspecified error is encountered while attempting to complete the command

DmtIllegalStateException – if the session is already closed or invalidated

SecurityException – if the caller does not have the necessary permissions to execute the underlying management operation, or, in case of local sessions, if the caller does not have DmtPermission for the node with the Get action present

117.13.9.26   **public String getNodeType(String nodeUri) throws DmtException**

nodeUri the URI of the node

☐ Get the type of a node. The type of leaf node is the MIME type of the data it contains. The type of an interior node is a URI identifying a DDF document; a null type means that there is no DDF document overriding the tree structure defined by the ancestors.

Returns the type of the node, can be null

Throws DmtException – with the following possible error codes:
URI_TOO_LONG if nodeUri or a segment of it is too long, or if it has too many segments
INVALID_URI if nodeUri is null or syntactically invalid
NODE_NOT_FOUND if nodeUri points to a non-existing node
PERMISSION_DENIED if the session is associated with a principal and the ACL of the node does not allow the Get operation for the associated principal
METADATA_MISMATCH if node information cannot be retrieved according to the meta-data (it does not have MetaNode.CMD_GET access type)
DATA_STORE_FAILURE if an error occurred while accessing the data store
COMMAND_FAILED if the URI is not within the current session's subtree, or if some unspecified er-

ror is encountered while attempting to complete the command

DmtIllegalStateException – if the session is already closed or invalidated

SecurityException – if the caller does not have the necessary permissions to execute the underlying management operation, or, in case of local sessions, if the caller does not have DmtPermission for the node with the Get action present

117.13.9.27   public DmtData getNodeValue(String nodeUri) throws DmtException

nodeUri the URI of the node to retrieve

☐ Get the data contained in a leaf or interior node. When retrieving the value associated with an interior node, the caller must have rights to read all nodes in the subtree under the given node.

Returns the data of the node, can not be null

Throws DmtException – with the following possible error codes:
URI_TOO_LONG if nodeUri or a segment of it is too long, or if it has too many segments
INVALID_URI if nodeUri is null or syntactically invalid
NODE_NOT_FOUND if nodeUri points to a non-existing node
PERMISSION_DENIED if the session is associated with a principal and the ACL of the node (and the ACLs of all its descendants in case of interior nodes) do not allow the Get operation for the associated principal
METADATA_MISMATCH if the node value cannot be retrieved according to the meta-data (it does not have MetaNode.CMD_GET access type)
FEATURE_NOT_SUPPORTED if the specified node is an interior node and does not support Java object values
DATA_STORE_FAILURE if an error occurred while accessing the data store
COMMAND_FAILED if the URI is not within the current session's subtree, or if some unspecified error is encountered while attempting to complete the command

DmtIllegalStateException – if the session is already closed or invalidated

SecurityException – if the caller does not have the necessary permissions to execute the underlying management operation, or, in case of local sessions, if the caller does not have DmtPermission for the node (and all its descendants in case of interior nodes) with the Get action present

117.13.9.28   public int getNodeVersion(String nodeUri) throws DmtException

nodeUri the URI of the node

☐ Get the version of a node. The version can not be set, it is calculated automatically by the device. It is incremented modulo 0x10000 at every modification of the value or any other property of the node, for both leaf and interior nodes. When a node is created the initial value is 0.

Returns the version of the node

Throws DmtException – with the following possible error codes:
URI_TOO_LONG if nodeUri or a segment of it is too long, or if it has too many segments
INVALID_URI if nodeUri is null or syntactically invalid
NODE_NOT_FOUND if nodeUri points to a non-existing node
PERMISSION_DENIED if the session is associated with a principal and the ACL of the node does not allow the Get operation for the associated principal
METADATA_MISMATCH if node information cannot be retrieved according to the meta-data (it does not have MetaNode.CMD_GET access type)
FEATURE_NOT_SUPPORTED if the Version property is not supported by the DmtAdmin implementation or the underlying plugin
DATA_STORE_FAILURE if an error occurred while accessing the data store
COMMAND_FAILED if the URI is not within the current session's subtree, or if some unspecified error is encountered while attempting to complete the command

DmtIllegalStateException – if the session is already closed or invalidated

SecurityException – if the caller does not have the necessary permissions to execute the underlying management operation, or, in case of local sessions, if the caller does not have DmtPermission for the node with the Get action present

117.13.9.29   public String getPrincipal( )

☐ Gives the name of the principal on whose behalf the session was created. Local sessions do not have an associated principal, in this case null is returned.

Returns the identifier of the remote server that initiated the session, or null for local sessions

117.13.9.30   public String getRootUri( )

☐ Get the root URI associated with this session. Gives "." if the session was created without specifying a root, which means that the target of this session is the whole DMT.

Returns the root URI

117.13.9.31   public int getSessionId( )

☐ The unique identifier of the session. The ID is generated automatically, and it is guaranteed to be unique on a machine.

Returns the session identification number

117.13.9.32   public int getState( )

☐ Get the current state of this session.

Returns the state of the session, one of STATE_OPEN, STATE_CLOSED and STATE_INVALID

117.13.9.33   public boolean isLeafNode(String nodeUri) throws DmtException

nodeUri the URI of the node

☐ Tells whether a node is a leaf or an interior node of the DMT.

Returns true if the given node is a leaf node

Throws DmtException – with the following possible error codes:
URI_TOO_LONG if nodeUri or a segment of it is too long, or if it has too many segments
INVALID_URI if nodeUri is null or syntactically invalid
NODE_NOT_FOUND if nodeUri points to a non-existing node
PERMISSION_DENIED if the session is associated with a principal and the ACL of the node does not allow the Get operation for the associated principal
METADATA_MISMATCH if node information cannot be retrieved according to the meta-data (it does not have MetaNode.CMD_GET access type)
DATA_STORE_FAILURE if an error occurred while accessing the data store
COMMAND_FAILED if the URI is not within the current session's subtree, or if some unspecified error is encountered while attempting to complete the command

DmtIllegalStateException – if the session is already closed or invalidated

SecurityException – if the caller does not have the necessary permissions to execute the underlying management operation, or, in case of local sessions, if the caller does not have DmtPermission for the node with the Get action present

117.13.9.34   public boolean isNodeUri(String nodeUri)

nodeUri the URI to check

☐ Check whether the specified URI corresponds to a valid node in the DMT.

Returns true if the given node exists in the DMT

Throws DmtIllegalStateException – if the session is already closed or invalidated

SecurityException – if the caller does not have the necessary permissions to execute the underlying management operation, or, in case of local sessions, if the caller does not have DmtPermission for the node with the Get action present

117.13.9.35   **public void renameNode(String nodeUri, String newName) throws DmtException**

nodeUri   the URI of the node to rename

newName   the new name property of the node

☐ Rename a node. This operation only changes the name of the node (updating the timestamp and version properties if they are supported), the value and the other properties are not changed. The new name of the node must be provided, the new URI is constructed from the base of the old URI and the given name. It is not allowed to rename the root node of the session.

If available, the meta-data of the original and the new nodes are checked before performing the rename operation. Neither node can be permanent, their leaf/interior property must match, and the name change must not violate any of the cardinality constraints. The original node must have the MetaNode.CMD_REPLACE access type, and the name of the new node must conform to the valid names.

Throws   DmtException – with the following possible error codes:
URI_TOO_LONG if nodeUri or a segment of it is too long, if nodeUri has too many segments, or if newName is too long
INVALID_URI if nodeUri or newName is null or syntactically invalid
NODE_NOT_FOUND if nodeUri points to a non-existing node, or if the new node is not defined in the tree according to the meta-data (see getMetaNode(String))
NODE_ALREADY_EXISTS if there already exists a sibling of nodeUri with the name newName
PERMISSION_DENIED if the session is associated with a principal and the ACL of the node does not allow the Replace operation for the associated principal
COMMAND_NOT_ALLOWED if the target node is the root of the session, or in non-atomic sessions if the underlying plugin is read-only or does not support non-atomic writing
METADATA_MISMATCH if the node could not be renamed because of meta-data restrictions (see above)
TRANSACTION_ERROR in an atomic session if the underlying plugin is read-only or does not support atomic writing
DATA_STORE_FAILURE if an error occurred while accessing the data store
COMMAND_FAILED if the URI is not within the current session's subtree, or if some unspecified error is encountered while attempting to complete the command

DmtIllegalStateException – if the session was opened using the LOCK_TYPE_SHARED lock type, or if the session is already closed or invalidated

SecurityException – if the caller does not have the necessary permissions to execute the underlying management operation, or, in case of local sessions, if the caller does not have DmtPermission for the node with the Replace action present

117.13.9.36   **public void rollback( ) throws DmtException**

☐ Rolls back a series of DMT operations issued in the current atomic session since the last transaction boundary. Transaction boundaries are the creation of this object that starts the session, and all subsequent commit and rollback calls.

Throws   DmtException – with the error code ROLLBACK_FAILED in case the rollback did not succeed

DmtIllegalStateException – if the session was not opened using the LOCK_TYPE_ATOMIC lock type, or if the session is already closed or invalidated

SecurityException – if the caller does not have the necessary permissions to execute the underlying management operation

117.13.9.37   public void setDefaultNodeValue(String nodeUri) throws DmtException

nodeUri the URI of the node

☐ Set the value of a leaf or interior node to its default. The default can be defined by the node's MetaNode. The method throws a METADATA_MISMATCH exception if the node does not have a default value.

Throws DmtException – with the following possible error codes:
URI_TOO_LONG if nodeUri or a segment of it is too long, or if it has too many segments
INVALID_URI if nodeUri is null or syntactically invalid
NODE_NOT_FOUND if nodeUri points to a non-existing node
PERMISSION_DENIED if the session is associated with a principal and the ACL of the node does not allow the Replace operation for the associated principal
COMMAND_NOT_ALLOWED in non-atomic sessions if the underlying plugin is read-only or does not support non-atomic writing
METADATA_MISMATCH if the node is permanent or cannot be modified according to the meta-data (does not have the MetaNode.CMD_REPLACE access type), or if there is no default value defined for this node
FEATURE_NOT_SUPPORTED if the specified node is an interior node and does not support Java object values
TRANSACTION_ERROR in an atomic session if the underlying plugin is read-only or does not support atomic writing
DATA_STORE_FAILURE if an error occurred while accessing the data store
COMMAND_FAILED if the URI is not within the current session's subtree, or if some unspecified error is encountered while attempting to complete the command

DmtIllegalStateException – if the session was opened using the LOCK_TYPE_SHARED lock type, or if the session is already closed or invalidated

SecurityException – if the caller does not have the necessary permissions to execute the underlying management operation, or, in case of local sessions, if the caller does not have DmtPermission for the node with the Replace action present

See Also setNodeValue

117.13.9.38   public void setNodeAcl(String nodeUri, Acl acl) throws DmtException

nodeUri the URI of the node

acl the Access Control List to be set on the node, can be null

☐ Set the Access Control List associated with a given node. To perform this operation, the caller needs to have replace rights (Acl.REPLACE or the corresponding Java permission depending on the session type) as described below:

- if nodeUri specifies a leaf node, replace rights are needed on the parent of the node
- if nodeUri specifies an interior node, replace rights on either the node or its parent are sufficient

If the given acl is null or an empty ACL (not specifying any permissions for any principals), then the ACL of the node is deleted, and the node will inherit the ACL from its parent node.

Throws DmtException – with the following possible error codes:
URI_TOO_LONG if nodeUri or a segment of it is too long, or if it has too many segments
INVALID_URI if nodeUri is null or syntactically invalid
NODE_NOT_FOUND if nodeUri points to a non-existing node
PERMISSION_DENIED if the session is associated with a principal and the ACL of the node or its parent (see above) does not allow the Replace operation for the associated principal
COMMAND_NOT_ALLOWED if the command attempts to set the ACL of the root node not to include Add rights for all principals
DATA_STORE_FAILURE if an error occurred while accessing the data store
COMMAND_FAILED if the URI is not within the current session's subtree, or if some unspecified er-

ror is encountered while attempting to complete the command

DmtIllegalStateException – if the session was opened using the LOCK_TYPE_SHARED lock type, or if the session is already closed or invalidated

SecurityException – in case of local sessions, if the caller does not have DmtPermission for the node or its parent (see above) with the Replace action present

117.13.9.39   **public void setNodeTitle(String nodeUri, String title) throws DmtException**

nodeUri the URI of the node

title the title text of the node, can be null

☐ Set the title property of a node. The length of the title string in UTF-8 encoding must not exceed 255 bytes.

Throws DmtException – with the following possible error codes:
URI_TOO_LONG if nodeUri or a segment of it is too long, or if it has too many segments
INVALID_URI if nodeUri is null or syntactically invalid
NODE_NOT_FOUND if nodeUri points to a non-existing node
PERMISSION_DENIED if the session is associated with a principal and the ACL of the node does not allow the Replace operation for the associated principal
COMMAND_NOT_ALLOWED in non-atomic sessions if the underlying plugin is read-only or does not support non-atomic writing
METADATA_MISMATCH if the node cannot be modified according to the meta-data (does not have the MetaNode.CMD_REPLACE access type)
FEATURE_NOT_SUPPORTED if the Title property is not supported by the DmtAdmin implementation or the underlying plugin
TRANSACTION_ERROR in an atomic session if the underlying plugin is read-only or does not support atomic writing
DATA_STORE_FAILURE if an error occurred while accessing the data store
COMMAND_FAILED if the title string is too long, if the URI is not within the current session's subtree, or if some unspecified error is encountered while attempting to complete the command

DmtIllegalStateException – if the session was opened using the LOCK_TYPE_SHARED lock type, or if the session is already closed or invalidated

SecurityException – if the caller does not have the necessary permissions to execute the underlying management operation, or, in case of local sessions, if the caller does not have DmtPermission for the node with the Replace action present

117.13.9.40   **public void setNodeType(String nodeUri, String type) throws DmtException**

nodeUri the URI of the node

type the type of the node, can be null

☐ Set the type of a node. The type of leaf node is the MIME type of the data it contains. The type of an interior node is a URI identifying a DDF document.

For interior nodes, a null type string means that there is no DDF document overriding the tree structure defined by the ancestors. For leaf nodes, it requests that the default MIME type is used for the given node. If the node does not have a default MIME type this method will throw a DmtException with error code METADATA_MISMATCH. Note that a node might have a default MIME type even if there is no meta-data for the node or its meta-data does not specify the default.

MIME types must conform to the definition in RFC 2045. Interior node type identifiers must follow the format defined in section 7.7.7.2 of the OMA Device Management Tree and Description document. Checking the validity of the type string does not have to be done by the DmtAdmin, this can be left to the plugin handling the node (if any), to avoid unnecessary double-checks.

Throws DmtException – with the following possible error codes:
URI_TOO_LONG if nodeUri or a segment of it is too long, or if it has too many segments
INVALID_URI if nodeUri is null or syntactically invalid
NODE_NOT_FOUND if nodeUri points to a non-existing node
PERMISSION_DENIED if the session is associated with a principal and the ACL of the node does not allow the Replace operation for the associated principal
COMMAND_NOT_ALLOWED in non-atomic sessions if the underlying plugin is read-only or does not support non-atomic writing
METADATA_MISMATCH if the node is permanent or cannot be modified according to the meta-data (does not have the MetaNode.CMD_REPLACE access type), and in case of leaf nodes, if null is given and there is no default MIME type, or the given MIME type is not allowed
TRANSACTION_ERROR in an atomic session if the underlying plugin is read-only or does not support atomic writing
DATA_STORE_FAILURE if an error occurred while accessing the data store
COMMAND_FAILED if the URI is not within the current session's subtree, if the type string is invalid (see above), or if some unspecified error is encountered while attempting to complete the command

DmtIllegalStateException – if the session was opened using the LOCK_TYPE_SHARED lock type, or if the session is already closed or invalidated

SecurityException – if the caller does not have the necessary permissions to execute the underlying management operation, or, in case of local sessions, if the caller does not have DmtPermission for the node with the Replace action present

See Also RFC 2045 (http://www.ietf.org/rfc/rfc2045.txt) , OMA Device Management Tree and Description v1.2 draft (http://member.openmobilealliance.org/ftp/public_documents/dm/Permanent_documents/ OMA-TS-DM-TND-V1_2-20050615-C.zip)

117.13.9.41   **public void setNodeValue(String nodeUri, DmtData data) throws DmtException**

nodeUri the URI of the node

data the data to be set, can be null

□ Set the value of a leaf or interior node. The format of the node is contained in the DmtData object. For interior nodes, the format must be FORMAT_NODE, while for leaf nodes this format must not be used.

If the specified value is null, the default value is taken. In this case, if the node does not have a default value, this method will throw a DmtException with error code METADATA_MISMATCH. Nodes of null format can be set by using DmtData.NULL_VALUE as second argument.

An Event of type REPLACE is sent out for a leaf node. A replaced interior node sends out events for each of its children in depth first order and node names sorted with Arrays.sort(String[]). When setting a value on an interior node, the values of the leaf nodes under it can change, but the structure of the subtree is not modified by the operation.

Throws DmtException – with the following possible error codes:
URI_TOO_LONG if nodeUri or a segment of it is too long, or if it has too many segments
INVALID_URI if nodeUri is null or syntactically invalid
NODE_NOT_FOUND if nodeUri points to a non-existing node
PERMISSION_DENIED if the session is associated with a principal and the ACL of the node does not allow the Replace operation for the associated principal
COMMAND_NOT_ALLOWED if the given data has FORMAT_NODE format but the node is a leaf node (or vice versa), or in non-atomic sessions if the underlying plugin is read-only or does not support non-atomic writing
METADATA_MISMATCH if the node is permanent or cannot be modified according to the meta-data (does not have the MetaNode.CMD_REPLACE access type), or if the given value does not conform to the meta-data value constraints
FEATURE_NOT_SUPPORTED if the specified node is an interior node and does not support Java ob-

ject values

TRANSACTION_ERROR in an atomic session if the underlying plugin is read-only or does not support atomic writing

DATA_STORE_FAILURE if an error occurred while accessing the data store

COMMAND_FAILED if the URI is not within the current session's subtree, or if some unspecified error is encountered while attempting to complete the command

DmtIllegalStateException – if the session was opened using the LOCK_TYPE_SHARED lock type, or if the session is already closed or invalidated

SecurityException – if the caller does not have the necessary permissions to execute the underlying management operation, or, in case of local sessions, if the caller does not have DmtPermission for the node with the Replace action present

117.13.10   public interface MetaNode

The MetaNode contains meta data as standardized by OMA DM but extends it (without breaking the compatibility) to provide for better DMT data quality in an environment where many software components manipulate this data.

The interface has several types of functions to describe the nodes in the DMT. Some methods can be used to retrieve standard OMA DM metadata such as access type, cardinality, default, etc., others are for data extensions such as valid names and values. In some cases the standard behaviour has been extended, for example it is possible to provide several valid MIME types, or to differentiate between normal and automatic dynamic nodes.

Most methods in this interface receive no input, just return information about some aspect of the node. However, there are two methods that behave differently, isValidName and isValidValue. These validation methods are given a potential node name or value (respectively), and can decide whether it is valid for the given node. Passing the validation methods is a necessary condition for a name or value to be used, but it is not necessarily sufficient: the plugin may carry out more thorough (more expensive) checks when the node is actually created or set.

If a MetaNode is available for a node, the DmtAdmin must use the information provided by it to filter out invalid requests on that node. However, not all methods on this interface are actually used for this purpose, as many of them (e.g. getFormat or getValidNames) can be substituted with the validating methods. For example, isValidValue can be expected to check the format, minimum, maximum, etc. of a given value, making it unnecessary for the DmtAdmin to call getFormat(), getMin(), getMax() etc. separately. It is indicated in the description of each method if the DmtAdmin does not enforce the constraints defined by it - such methods are only for external use, for example in user interfaces.

Most of the methods of this class return null if a certain piece of meta information is not defined for the node or providing this information is not supported. Methods of this class do not throw exceptions.

117.13.10.1   public static final int AUTOMATIC = 2

Constant for representing an automatic node in the tree. This must be returned by getScope() for all nodes that are created automatically by the management object. Automatic nodes represent a special case of dynamic nodes, so this scope should be mapped to DYNAMIC when used in an OMA DM context.

An automatic node is usually created instantly when its parent is created, but it is also valid if it only appears later, triggered by some other condition. The exact behaviour must be defined by the Management Object.

117.13.10.2   **public static final int CMD_ADD = 0**

Constant for the ADD access type. If can(int) returns true for this operation, this node can potentially be added to its parent. Nodes with PERMANENT or AUTOMATIC scope typically do not have this access type.

117.13.10.3   **public static final int CMD_DELETE = 1**

Constant for the DELETE access type. If can(int) returns true for this operation, the node can potentially be deleted.

117.13.10.4   **public static final int CMD_EXECUTE = 2**

Constant for the EXECUTE access type. If can(int) returns true for this operation, the node can potentially be executed.

117.13.10.5   **public static final int CMD_GET = 4**

Constant for the GET access type. If can(int) returns true for this operation, the value, the list of child nodes (in case of interior nodes) and the properties of the node can potentially be retrieved.

117.13.10.6   **public static final int CMD_REPLACE = 3**

Constant for the REPLACE access type. If can(int) returns true for this operation, the value and other properties of the node can potentially be modified.

117.13.10.7   **public static final int DYNAMIC = 1**

Constant for representing a dynamic node in the tree. This must be returned by getScope for all nodes that are not permanent and are not created automatically by the management object.

117.13.10.8   **public static final int PERMANENT = 0**

Constant for representing a permanent node in the tree. This must be returned by getScope if the node cannot be added, deleted or modified in any way through tree operations. Permanent nodes cannot have non-permanent nodes as parents.

117.13.10.9   **public boolean can(int operation)**

operation One of the MetaNode.CMD_... constants.

□ Check whether the given operation is valid for this node. If no meta-data is provided for a node, all operations are valid.

Returns false if the operation is not valid for this node or the operation code is not one of the allowed constants

117.13.10.10   **public DmtData getDefault( )**

□ Get the default value of this node if any.

Returns The default value or null if not defined

117.13.10.11   **public String getDescription( )**

□ Get the explanation string associated with this node. Can be null if no description is provided for this node.

Returns node description string or null for no description

117.13.10.12   **public Object getExtensionProperty(String key)**

key the key for the extension property

□ Returns the value for the specified extension property key. This method only works if the provider of this MetaNode provides proprietary extensions to node meta data.

Returns the value of the requested property, cannot be null

Throws IllegalArgumentException – if the specified key is not supported by this MetaNode

117.13.10.13   public String[] getExtensionPropertyKeys( )

☐ Returns the list of extension property keys, if the provider of this MetaNode provides proprietary extensions to node meta data. The method returns null if the node doesn't provide such extensions.

Returns the array of supported extension property keys

117.13.10.14   public int getFormat( )

☐ Get the node's format, expressed in terms of type constants defined in DmtData. If there are multiple formats allowed for the node then the format constants are OR-ed. Interior nodes must have Dmt-Data.FORMAT_NODE format, and this code must not be returned for leaf nodes. If no meta-data is provided for a node, all applicable formats are considered valid (with the above constraints regarding interior and leaf nodes).

Note that the 'format' term is a legacy from OMA DM, it is more customary to think of this as 'type'.

The formats returned by this method are not checked by DmtAdmin, they are only for external use, for example in user interfaces. DmtAdmin only calls isValidValue for checking the value, its behaviour should be consistent with this method.

Returns the allowed format(s) of the node

117.13.10.15   public double getMax( )

☐ Get the maximum allowed value associated with a node of numeric format. If no meta-data is provided for a node, there is no upper limit to its value. This method is only meaningful if the node has integer or float format. The returned limit has double type, as this can be used to denote both integer and float limits with full precision. The actual maximum should be the largest integer or float number that does not exceed the returned value.

The information returned by this method is not checked by DmtAdmin, it is only for external use, for example in user interfaces. DmtAdmin only calls isValidValue for checking the value, its behaviour should be consistent with this method.

Returns the allowed maximum, or Double.MAX_VALUE if there is no upper limit defined or the node's format is not integer or float

117.13.10.16   public int getMaxOccurrence( )

☐ Get the number of maximum occurrences of this type of nodes on the same level in the DMT. Returns Integer.MAX_VALUE if there is no upper limit. Note that if the occurrence is greater than 1 then this node can not have siblings with different metadata. In other words, if different types of nodes coexist on the same level, their occurrence can not be greater than 1. If no meta-data is provided for a node, there is no upper limit on the number of occurrences.

Returns The maximum allowed occurrence of this node type

117.13.10.17   public String[] getMimeTypes( )

☐ Get the list of MIME types this node can hold. The first element of the returned list must be the default MIME type.

All MIME types are considered valid if no meta-data is provided for a node or if null is returned by this method. In this case the default MIME type cannot be retrieved from the meta-data, but the node may still have a default. This hidden default (if it exists) can be utilized by passing null as the type parameter of DmtSession.setNodeType(String, String) or DmtSession.createLeafNode(String, DmtData, String).

Returns the list of allowed MIME types for this node, starting with the default MIME type, or null if all types are allowed

---

117.13.10.18   **public double getMin( )**

□ Get the minimum allowed value associated with a node of numeric format. If no meta-data is provided for a node, there is no lower limit to its value. This method is only meaningful if the node has integer or float format. The returned limit has double type, as this can be used to denote both integer and float limits with full precision. The actual minimum should be the smallest integer or float number that is larger than the returned value.

The information returned by this method is not checked by DmtAdmin, it is only for external use, for example in user interfaces. DmtAdmin only calls isValidValue for checking the value, its behaviour should be consistent with this method.

Returns the allowed minimum, or Double.MIN_VALUE if there is no lower limit defined or the node's format is not integer or float

117.13.10.19   **public String[] getRawFormatNames( )**

□ Get the format names for any raw formats supported by the node. This method is only meaningful if the list of supported formats returned by getFormat() contains DmtData.FORMAT_RAW_STRING or DmtData.FORMAT_RAW_BINARY: it specifies precisely which raw format(s) are actually supported. If the node cannot contain data in one of the raw types, this method must return null.

The format names returned by this method are not checked by DmtAdmin, they are only for external use, for example in user interfaces. DmtAdmin only calls isValidValue for checking the value, its behaviour should be consistent with this method.

Returns the allowed format name(s) of raw data stored by the node, or null if raw formats are not supported

117.13.10.20   **public int getScope( )**

□ Return the scope of the node. Valid values are MetaNode.PERMANENT, MetaNode.DYNAMIC and MetaNode.AUTOMATIC. Note that a permanent node is not the same as a node where the DELETE operation is not allowed. Permanent nodes never can be deleted, whereas a non-deletable node can disappear in a recursive DELETE operation issued on one of its parents. If no meta-data is provided for a node, it can be assumed to be a dynamic node.

Returns PERMANENT for permanent nodes, AUTOMATIC for nodes that are automatically created, and DYNAMIC otherwise

117.13.10.21   **public String[] getValidNames( )**

□ Return an array of Strings if valid names are defined for the node, or null if no valid name list is defined or if this piece of meta info is not supported. If no meta-data is provided for a node, all names are considered valid.

The information returned by this method is not checked by DmtAdmin, it is only for external use, for example in user interfaces. DmtAdmin only calls isValidName for checking the name, its behaviour should be consistent with this method.

Returns the valid values for this node name, or null if not defined

117.13.10.22   **public DmtData[] getValidValues( )**

□ Return an array of DmtData objects if valid values are defined for the node, or null otherwise. If no meta-data is provided for a node, all values are considered valid.

The information returned by this method is not checked by DmtAdmin, it is only for external use, for example in user interfaces. DmtAdmin only calls isValidValue for checking the value, its behaviour should be consistent with this method.

Returns the valid values for this node, or null if not defined

117.13.10.23   **public boolean isLeaf( )**

□ Check whether the node is a leaf node or an internal one.

Returns true if the node is a leaf node

117.13.10.24   public boolean isValidName(String name)

name   the node name to check for validity

☐   Checks whether the given name is a valid name for this node. This method can be used for example to ensure that the node name is always one of a predefined set of valid names, or that it matches a specific pattern. This method should be consistent with the values returned by getValidNames (if any), the DmtAdmin only calls this method for name validation.

This method may return true even if not all aspects of the name have been checked, expensive operations (for example those that require external resources) need not be performed here. The actual node creation may still indicate that the node name is invalid.

Returns   false if the specified name is found to be invalid for the node described by this meta-node, true otherwise

117.13.10.25   public boolean isValidValue(DmtData value)

value   the value to check for validity

☐   Checks whether the given value is valid for this node. This method can be used to ensure that the value has the correct format and range, that it is well formed, etc. This method should be consistent with the constraints defined by the getFormat, getValidValues, getMin and getMax methods (if applicable), as the Dmt Admin only calls this method for value validation.

This method may return true even if not all aspects of the value have been checked, expensive operations (for example those that require external resources) need not be performed here. The actual value setting method may still indicate that the value is invalid.

Returns   false if the specified value is found to be invalid for the node described by this meta-node, true otherwise

117.13.10.26   public boolean isZeroOccurrenceAllowed( )

☐   Check whether zero occurrence of this node is valid. If no meta-data is returned for a node, zero occurrences are allowed.

Returns   true if zero occurrence of this node is valid

117.13.11   public final class Uri

This class contains static utility methods to manipulate DMT URIs.

Syntax of valid DMT URIs:

- A slash ('/' \u002F) is the separator of the node names. Slashes used in node name must therefore be escaped using a backslash slash ("\/"). The backslash must be escaped with a double backslash sequence. A backslash found must be ignored when it is not followed by a slash or backslash.
- The node name can be constructed using full Unicode character set (except the Supplementary code, not being supported by CLDC/CDC). However, using the full Unicode character set for node names is discouraged because the encoding in the underlying storage as well as the encoding needed in communications can create significant performance and memory usage overhead. Names that are restricted to the URI set [-a-zA-Zo-9_.!-*'()] are most efficient.
- URIs used in the DMT must be treated and interpreted as case sensitive.
- No End Slash: URI must not end with the delimiter slash ('/' \u002F). This implies that the root node must be denoted as "." and not "./".
- No parent denotation: URI must not be constructed using the character sequence "../" to traverse the tree upwards.
- Single Root: The character sequence "./" must not be used anywhere else but in the beginning of a URI.

117.13.11.1   **public static int getMaxSegmentNameLength( )**

☐ Returns the maximum allowed length of a URI segment. The value is implementation specific. The length of the URI segment is defined as the number of bytes in the unescaped, UTF-8 encoded represenation of the segment.

The return value of Integer.MAX_VALUE indicates that there is no upper limit on the length of segment names.

Returns maximum URI segment length supported by the implementation

117.13.11.2   **public static int getMaxUriLength( )**

☐ Returns the maximum allowed length of a URI. The value is implementation specific. The length of the URI is defined as the number of bytes in the unescaped, UTF-8 encoded represenation of the URI.

The return value of Integer.MAX_VALUE indicates that there is no upper limit on the length of URIs.

Returns maximum URI length supported by the implementation

117.13.11.3   **public static int getMaxUriSegments( )**

☐ Returns the maximum allowed number of URI segments. The returned value is implementation specific.

The return value of Integer.MAX_VALUE indicates that there is no upper limit on the number of URI segments.

Returns maximum number of URI segments supported by the implementation

117.13.11.4   **public static boolean isAbsoluteUri(String uri)**

uri the URI to be checked, must not be null and must contain a valid URI

☐ Checks whether the specified URI is an absolute URI. An absolute URI contains the complete path to a node in the DMT starting from the DMT root (".").

Returns whether the specified URI is absolute

Throws NullPointerException – if the specified URI is null

IllegalArgumentException – if the specified URI is malformed

117.13.11.5   **public static boolean isValidUri(String uri)**

uri the URI to be validated

☐ Checks whether the specified URI is valid. A URI is considered valid if it meets the following constraints:

- the URI is not null;
- the URI follows the syntax defined for valid DMT URIs;
- the length of the URI is not more than getMaxUriLength();
- the URI doesn't contain more than getMaxUriSegments() segments;
- the length of each segment of the URI is less than or equal to getMaxSegmentNameLength().

getMaxUriLength() and getMaxSegmentNameLength() methods.

Returns whether the specified URI is valid

117.13.11.6   **public static String mangle(String nodeName)**

nodeName the node name to be mangled (if necessary), must not be null or empty

☐ Returns a node name that is valid for the tree operation methods, based on the given node name. This transformation is not idempotent, so it must not be called with a parameter that is the result of a previous mangle method call.

Node name mangling is needed in the following cases:

- if the name contains '/' or '\'characters
- if the length of the name exceeds the limit defined by the implementation

A node name that does not suffer from either of these problems is guaranteed to remain unchanged by this method. Therefore the client may skip the mangling if the node name is known to be valid (though it is always safe to call this method).

The method returns the normalized nodeName as described below. Invalid node names are normalized in different ways, depending on the cause. If the length of the name does not exceed the limit, but the name contains '/' or '\'characters, then these are simply escaped by inserting an additional '\'before each occurrence. If the length of the name does exceed the limit, the following mechanism is used to normalize it:

- the SHA 1 digest of the name is calculated
- the digest is encoded with the base 64 algorithm
- all '/' characters in the encoded digest are replaced with '_'
- trailing '=' signs are removed

Returns   the normalized node name that is valid for tree operations

Throws   NullPointerException – if nodeName is null

　　　 IllegalArgumentException – if nodeName is empty

117.13.11.7   **public static String[] toPath(String uri)**

uri   the URI to be split, must not be null

　 □   Split the specified URI along the path separator '/' charaters and return an array of URI segments. Special characters in the returned segments are escaped. The returned array may be empty if the specifed URI was empty.

Returns   an array of URI segments created by splitting the specified URI

Throws   NullPointerException – if the specified URI is null

　　　 IllegalArgumentException – if the specified URI is malformed

117.13.11.8   **public static String toUri(String[] path)**

path   a possibly empty array of URI segments, must not be null

　 □   Construct a URI from the specified URI segments. The segments must already be mangled.

　　If the specified path is an empty array then an empty URI ("") is returned.

Returns   the URI created from the specified segments

Throws   NullPointerException – if the specified path or any of its segments are null

　　　 IllegalArgumentException – if the specified path contains too many or malformed segments or the resulting URI is too long

117.14   **info.dmtree.spi**

Device Management Tree SPI Package Version 1.0. This package contains the interface classes that compose the Device Management SPI (Service Provider Interface). These interfaces are implemented by DMT plugins; users of the DmtAdmin interface do not interact directly with these.

Bundles wishing to use this package must list the package in the Import-Package header of the bundle's manifest. For example:

```
Import-Package: info.dmtree.spi;version="[1.0,2.0)"
```

117.14.1   **Summary**

- *DataPlugin* - An implementation of this interface takes the responsibility of handling data requests in a subtree of the DMT.
- *ExecPlugin* - An implementation of this interface takes the responsibility of handling node execute requests requests in a subtree of the DMT.
- *ReadableDataSession* - Provides read-only access to the part of the tree handled by the plugin that created this session.
- *ReadWriteDataSession* - Provides non-atomic read-write access to the part of the tree handled by the plugin that created this session.
- *TransactionalDataSession* - Provides atomic read-write access to the part of the tree handled by the plugin that created this session.

117.14.2   **public interface DataPlugin**

An implementation of this interface takes the responsibility of handling data requests in a subtree of the DMT.

In an OSGi environment such implementations should be registered at the OSGi service registry specifying the list of root node URIs in a String array in the dataRootURIs registration parameter.

When the first reference in a session is made to a node handled by this plugin, the DmtAdmin calls one of the open... methods to retrieve a plugin session object for processing the request. The called method depends on the lock type of the current session. In case of openReadWriteSession(String[], DmtSession) and openAtomicSession(String[], DmtSession), the plugin may return null to indicate that the specified lock type is not supported. In this case the DmtAdmin may call openReadOnlySession(String[], DmtSession) to start a read-only plugin session, which can be used as long as there are no write operations on the nodes handled by this plugin.

The sessionRoot parameter of each method is a String array containing the segments of the URI pointing to the root of the session. This is an absolute path, so the first segment is always ".". Special characters appear escaped in the segments.

117.14.2.1   **public TransactionalDataSession openAtomicSession(String[] sessionRoot, DmtSession session) throws DmtException**

sessionRoot   the path to the subtree which is locked in the current session, must not be null

session   the session from which this plugin instance is accessed, must not be null

☐ This method is called to signal the start of an atomic read-write session when the first reference is made within a DmtSession to a node which is handled by this plugin. Session information is given as it is needed for sending alerts back from the plugin.

The plugin can assume that there are no other sessions open on any subtree that has any overlap with the subtree of this session.

Returns   a plugin session capable of executing read-write operations in an atomic block, or null if the plugin does not support atomic read-write sessions

Throws   DmtException – with the following possible error codes:
NODE_NOT_FOUND if sessionRoot points to a non-existing node
COMMAND_FAILED if some unspecified error is encountered while attempting to complete the command

SecurityException – if some underlying operation failed because of lack of permissions

117.14.2.2   **public ReadableDataSession openReadOnlySession(String[] sessionRoot, DmtSession session) throws DmtException**

sessionRoot   the path to the subtree which is accessed in the current session, must not be null

session   the session from which this plugin instance is accessed, must not be null

☐ This method is called to signal the start of a read-only session when the first reference is made within a DmtSession to a node which is handled by this plugin. Session information is given as it is needed for sending alerts back from the plugin.

The plugin can assume that there are no writing sessions open on any subtree that has any overlap with the subtree of this session.

Returns a plugin session capable of executing read operations

Throws DmtException – with the following possible error codes:
NODE_NOT_FOUND if sessionRoot points to a non-existing node
COMMAND_FAILED if some unspecified error is encountered while attempting to complete the command

SecurityException – if some underlying operation failed because of lack of permissions

117.14.2.3 **public ReadWriteDataSession openReadWriteSession(String[] sessionRoot, DmtSession session) throws DmtException**

sessionRoot the path to the subtree which is locked in the current session, must not be null

session the session from which this plugin instance is accessed, must not be null

☐ This method is called to signal the start of a non-atomic read-write session when the first reference is made within a DmtSession to a node which is handled by this plugin. Session information is given as it is needed for sending alerts back from the plugin.

The plugin can assume that there are no other sessions open on any subtree that has any overlap with the subtree of this session.

Returns a plugin session capable of executing read-write operations, or null if the plugin does not support non-atomic read-write sessions

Throws DmtException – with the following possible error codes:
NODE_NOT_FOUND if sessionRoot points to a non-existing node
COMMAND_FAILED if some unspecified error is encountered while attempting to complete the command

SecurityException – if some underlying operation failed because of lack of permissions

117.14.3 **public interface ExecPlugin**

An implementation of this interface takes the responsibility of handling node execute requests requests in a subtree of the DMT.

In an OSGi environment such implementations should be registered at the OSGi service registry specifying the list of root node URIs in a String array in the execRootURIs registration parameter.

117.14.3.1 **public void execute(DmtSession session, String[] nodePath, String correlator, String data) throws DmtException**

session a reference to the session in which the operation was issued, must not be null

nodePath the absolute path of the node to be executed, must not be null

correlator an identifier to associate this operation with any alerts sent in response to it, can be null

data the parameter of the execute operation, can be null

☐ Execute the given node with the given data. This operation corresponds to the EXEC command in OMA DM.

The semantics of an execute operation and the data parameter it takes depends on the definition of the managed object on which the command is issued. Session information is given as it is needed for sending alerts back from the plugin. If a correlation ID is specified, it should be used as the correlator parameter for alerts sent in response to this execute operation.

The nodePath parameter contains an array of path segments identifying the node to be executed in the subtree of this plugin. This is an absolute path, so the first segment is always ".". Special characters appear escaped in the segments.

Throws   DmtException – with the following possible error codes:
NODE_NOT_FOUND if the node does not exist and the plugin does not allow executing unexisting nodes
METADATA_MISMATCH if the command failed because of meta-data restrictions
DATA_STORE_FAILURE if an error occurred while accessing the data store
COMMAND_FAILED if some unspecified error is encountered while attempting to complete the command

See Also   DmtSession.execute(String, String), DmtSession.execute(String, String, String)

117.14.4   public interface ReadableDataSession

Provides read-only access to the part of the tree handled by the plugin that created this session.

Since the ReadWriteDataSession and TransactionalDataSession interfaces inherit from this interface, some of the method descriptions do not apply for an instance that is only a ReadableDataSession. For example, the close method description also contains information about its behaviour when invoked as part of a transactional session.

The nodePath parameters appearing in this interface always contain an array of path segments identifying a node in the subtree of this plugin. This parameter contains an absolute path, so the first segment is always ".". Special characters appear escaped in the segments.

Error handling

When a tree access command is called on the DmtAdmin service, it must perform an extensive set of checks on the parameters and the authority of the caller before delegating the call to a plugin. Therefore plugins can take certain circumstances for granted: that the path is valid and is within the subtree of the plugin and the session, the command can be applied to the given node (e.g. the target of getChildNodeNames is an interior node), etc. All errors described by the error codes DmtException.INVALID_URI, DmtException.URI_TOO_LONG, DmtException.PERMISSION_DENIED, DmtException.COMMAND_NOT_ALLOWED and DmtException.TRANSACTION_ERROR are fully filtered out before control reaches the plugin.

If the plugin provides meta-data for a node, the DmtAdmin service must also check the constraints specified by it, as described in MetaNode. If the plugin does not provide meta-data, it must perform the necessary checks for itself and use the DmtException.METADATA_MISMATCH error code to indicate such discrepancies.

The DmtAdmin also ensures that the targeted nodes exist before calling the plugin (except, of course, before the isNodeUri call). However, some small amount of time elapses between the check and the call, so in case of plugins where the node structure can change independantly from the DMT, the target node might disappear in that time. For example, a whole subtree can disappear when a Monitorable application is unregistered, which might happen in the middle of a DMT session accessing it. Plugins managing such nodes always need to check whether they still exist and throw DmtException.NODE_NOT_FOUND as necessary, but for more static subtrees there is no need for the plugin to use this error code.

The plugin can use the remaining error codes as needed. If an error does not fit into any other category, the DmtException.COMMAND_FAILED code should be used.

117.14.4.1   **public void close( ) throws DmtException**

☐ Closes a session. This method is always called when the session ends for any reason: if the session is closed, if a fatal error occurs in any method, or if any error occurs during commit or rollback. In case the session was invalidated due to an exception during commit or rollback, it is guaranteed that no methods are called on the plugin until it is closed. In case the session was invalidated due to a fatal exception in one of the tree manipulation methods, only the rollback method is called before this (and only in atomic sessions).

This method should not perform any data manipulation, only cleanup operations. In non-atomic read-write sessions the data manipulation should be done instantly during each tree operation, while in atomic sessions the DmtAdmin always calls TransactionalDataSession.commit automatically before the session is actually closed.

Throws   DmtException – with the error code COMMAND_FAILED if the plugin failed to close for any reason

117.14.4.2   **public String[] getChildNodeNames(String[] nodePath) throws DmtException**

nodePath   the absolute path of the node

☐ Get the list of children names of a node. The returned array contains the names - not the URIs - of the immediate children nodes of the given node. The returned child names must be mangled (info.dmtree.Uri.mangle(String)). The returned array may contain null entries, but these are removed by the DmtAdmin before returning it to the client.

Returns   the list of child node names as a string array or an empty string array if the node has no children

Throws   DmtException – with the following possible error codes:
NODE_NOT_FOUND if nodePath points to a non-existing node
METADATA_MISMATCH if the information could not be retrieved because of meta-data restrictions
DATA_STORE_FAILURE if an error occurred while accessing the data store
COMMAND_FAILED if some unspecified error is encountered while attempting to complete the command

SecurityException – if the caller does not have the necessary permissions to execute the underlying management operation

117.14.4.3   **public MetaNode getMetaNode(String[] nodePath) throws DmtException**

nodePath   the absolute path of the node

☐ Get the meta data which describes a given node. Meta data can be only inspected, it can not be changed.

Meta data support by plugins is an optional feature. It can be used, for example, when a data plugin is implemented on top of a data store or another API that has their own metadata, such as a relational database, in order to avoid metadata duplication and inconsistency. The meta data specific to the plugin returned by this method is complemented by meta data from the DmtAdmin before returning it to the client. If there are differences in the meta data elements known by the plugin and the DmtAdmin then the plugin specific elements take precedence.

Note, that a node does not have to exist for having meta-data associated with it. This method may provide meta-data for any node that can possibly exist in the tree (any node defined by the Management Object provided by the plugin). For nodes that are not defined, a DmtException may be thrown with the NODE_NOT_FOUND error code. To allow easier implementation of plugins that do not provide meta-data, it is allowed to return null for any node, regardless of whether it is defined or not.

Returns   a MetaNode which describes meta data information, can be null if there is no meta data available for the given node

Throws   DmtException – with the following possible error codes:
NODE_NOT_FOUND if nodeUri points to a node that is not defined in the tree (see above)
DATA_STORE_FAILURE if an error occurred while accessing the data store

COMMAND_FAILED if some unspecified error is encountered while attempting to complete the command

SecurityException – if the caller does not have the necessary permissions to execute the underlying management operation

117.14.4.4   **public int getNodeSize(String[] nodePath) throws DmtException**

nodePath the absolute path of the leaf node

□ Get the size of the data in a leaf node. The value to return depends on the format of the data in the node, see the description of the DmtData.getSize() method for the definition of node size for each format.

Returns the size of the data in the node

Throws DmtException – with the following possible error codes:
NODE_NOT_FOUND if nodePath points to a non-existing node
METADATA_MISMATCH if the information could not be retrieved because of meta-data restrictions
FEATURE_NOT_SUPPORTED if the Size property is not supported by the plugin
DATA_STORE_FAILURE if an error occurred while accessing the data store
COMMAND_FAILED if some unspecified error is encountered while attempting to complete the command

SecurityException – if the caller does not have the necessary permissions to execute the underlying management operation

See Also DmtData.getSize

117.14.4.5   **public Date getNodeTimestamp(String[] nodePath) throws DmtException**

nodePath the absolute path of the node

□ Get the timestamp when the node was last modified.

Returns the timestamp of the last modification

Throws DmtException – with the following possible error codes:
NODE_NOT_FOUND if nodePath points to a non-existing node
METADATA_MISMATCH if the information could not be retrieved because of meta-data restrictions
FEATURE_NOT_SUPPORTED if the Timestamp property is not supported by the plugin
DATA_STORE_FAILURE if an error occurred while accessing the data store
COMMAND_FAILED if some unspecified error is encountered while attempting to complete the command

SecurityException – if the caller does not have the necessary permissions to execute the underlying management operation

117.14.4.6   **public String getNodeTitle(String[] nodePath) throws DmtException**

nodePath the absolute path of the node

□ Get the title of a node. There might be no title property set for a node.

Returns the title of the node, or null if the node has no title

Throws DmtException – with the following possible error codes:
NODE_NOT_FOUND if nodePath points to a non-existing node
METADATA_MISMATCH if the information could not be retrieved because of meta-data restrictions
FEATURE_NOT_SUPPORTED if the Title property is not supported by the plugin
DATA_STORE_FAILURE if an error occurred while accessing the data store
COMMAND_FAILED if some unspecified error is encountered while attempting to complete the command

SecurityException – if the caller does not have the necessary permissions to execute the underlying management operation

117.14.4.7   public String getNodeType(String[] nodePath) throws DmtException

nodePath   the absolute path of the node

☐   Get the type of a node. The type of leaf node is the MIME type of the data it contains. The type of an interior node is a URI identifying a DDF document; a null type means that there is no DDF document overriding the tree structure defined by the ancestors.

Returns   the type of the node, can be null

Throws   DmtException – with the following possible error codes:
NODE_NOT_FOUND if nodePath points to a non-existing node
METADATA_MISMATCH if the information could not be retrieved because of meta-data restrictions
DATA_STORE_FAILURE if an error occurred while accessing the data store
COMMAND_FAILED if some unspecified error is encountered while attempting to complete the command

SecurityException – if the caller does not have the necessary permissions to execute the underlying management operation

117.14.4.8   public DmtData getNodeValue(String[] nodePath) throws DmtException

nodePath   the absolute path of the node to retrieve

☐   Get the data contained in a leaf or interior node.

Returns   the data of the leaf node, must not be null

Throws   DmtException – with the following possible error codes:
NODE_NOT_FOUND if nodePath points to a non-existing node
METADATA_MISMATCH if the information could not be retrieved because of meta-data restrictions
FEATURE_NOT_SUPPORTED if the specified node is an interior node and does not support Java object values
DATA_STORE_FAILURE if an error occurred while accessing the data store
COMMAND_FAILED if some unspecified error is encountered while attempting to complete the command

SecurityException – if the caller does not have the necessary permissions to execute the underlying management operation

117.14.4.9   public int getNodeVersion(String[] nodePath) throws DmtException

nodePath   the absolute path of the node

☐   Get the version of a node. The version can not be set, it is calculated automatically by the device. It is incremented modulo 0x10000 at every modification of the value or any other property of the node, for both leaf and interior nodes. When a node is created the initial value is 0.

Returns   the version of the node

Throws   DmtException – with the following possible error codes:
NODE_NOT_FOUND if nodePath points to a non-existing node
METADATA_MISMATCH if the information could not be retrieved because of meta-data restrictions
FEATURE_NOT_SUPPORTED if the Version property is not supported by the plugin
DATA_STORE_FAILURE if an error occurred while accessing the data store
COMMAND_FAILED if some unspecified error is encountered while attempting to complete the command

SecurityException – if the caller does not have the necessary permissions to execute the underlying management operation

117.14.4.10   public boolean isLeafNode(String[] nodePath) throws DmtException

nodePath   the absolute path of the node

    □ Tells whether a node is a leaf or an interior node of the DMT.

Returns true if the given node is a leaf node

Throws DmtException – with the following possible error codes:
NODE_NOT_FOUND if nodePath points to a non-existing node
METADATA_MISMATCH if the information could not be retrieved because of meta-data restrictions
DATA_STORE_FAILURE if an error occurred while accessing the data store
COMMAND_FAILED if some unspecified error is encountered while attempting to complete the command

SecurityException – if the caller does not have the necessary permissions to execute the underlying management operation

117.14.4.11   public boolean isNodeUri(String[] nodePath)

nodePath the absolute path to check

    □ Check whether the specified path corresponds to a valid node in the DMT.

Returns true if the given node exists in the DMT

117.14.4.12   public void nodeChanged(String[] nodePath) throws DmtException

nodePath the absolute path of the node that has changed

    □ Notifies the plugin that the given node has changed outside the scope of the plugin, therefore the Version and Timestamp properties must be updated (if supported). This method is needed because the ACL property of a node is managed by the DmtAdmin instead of the plugin. The DmtAdmin must call this method whenever the ACL property of a node changes.

Throws DmtException – with the following possible error codes:
NODE_NOT_FOUND if nodePath points to a non-existing node
DATA_STORE_FAILURE if an error occurred while accessing the data store
COMMAND_FAILED if some unspecified error is encountered while attempting to complete the command

117.14.5   public interface ReadWriteDataSession
extends ReadableDataSession

Provides non-atomic read-write access to the part of the tree handled by the plugin that created this session.

The nodePath parameters appearing in this interface always contain an array of path segments identifying a node in the subtree of this plugin. This parameter contains an absolute path, so the first segment is always ".". Special characters appear escaped in the segments.

Error handling

When a tree manipulation command is called on the DmtAdmin service, it must perform an extensive set of checks on the parameters and the authority of the caller before delegating the call to a plugin. Therefore plugins can take certain circumstances for granted: that the path is valid and is within the subtree of the plugin and the session, the command can be applied to the given node (e.g. the target of setNodeValue is a leaf node), etc. All errors described by the error codes DmtException.INVALID_URI, DmtException.URI_TOO_LONG, DmtException.PERMISSION_DENIED, DmtException.COMMAND_NOT_ALLOWED and DmtException.TRANSACTION_ERROR are fully filtered out before control reaches the plugin.

If the plugin provides meta-data for a node, the DmtAdmin service must also check the constraints specified by it, as described in MetaNode. If the plugin does not provide meta-data, it must perform the necessary checks for itself and use the DmtException.METADATA_MISMATCH error code to indicate such discrepancies.

The DmtAdmin also ensures that the targeted nodes exist before calling the plugin (or that they do not exist, in case of node creation). However, some small amount of time elapses between the check and the call, so in case of plugins where the node structure can change independantly from the DMT, the target node might appear/disappear in that time. For example, a whole subtree can disappear when a Monitorable application is unregistered, which might happen in the middle of a DMT session accessing it. Plugins managing such nodes always need to check the existance or non-existance of nodes and throw DmtException.NODE_NOT_FOUND or DmtException.NODE_ALREADY_EXISTS as necessary, but for more static subtrees there is no need for the plugin to use these error codes.

The plugin can use the remaining error codes as needed. If an error does not fit into any other category, the DmtException.COMMAND_FAILED code should be used.

117.14.5.1   public void copy(String[] nodePath, String[] newNodePath, boolean recursive) throws DmtException

nodePath an absolute path specifying the node or the root of a subtree to be copied

newNodePath the absolute path of the new node or root of a subtree

recursive false if only a single node is copied, true if the whole subtree is copied

☐ Create a copy of a node or a whole subtree. Beside the structure and values of the nodes, most properties managed by the plugin must also be copied, with the exception of the Timestamp and Version properties.

Throws DmtException – with the following possible error codes:
NODE_NOT_FOUND if nodePath points to a non-existing node, or if newNodePath points to a node that cannot exist in the tree
NODE_ALREADY_EXISTS if newNodePath points to a node that already exists
METADATA_MISMATCH if the node could not be copied because of meta-data restrictions
FEATURE_NOT_SUPPORTED if the copy operation is not supported by the plugin
DATA_STORE_FAILURE if an error occurred while accessing the data store
COMMAND_FAILED if some unspecified error is encountered while attempting to complete the command

SecurityException – if the caller does not have the necessary permissions to execute the underlying management operation

See Also DmtSession.copy(String, String, boolean)

117.14.5.2   public void createInteriorNode(String[] nodePath, String type) throws DmtException

nodePath the absolute path of the node to create

type the type URI of the interior node, can be null if no node type is defined

☐ Create an interior node with a given type. The type of interior node, if specified, is a URI identifying a DDF document.

Throws DmtException – with the following possible error codes:
NODE_NOT_FOUND if nodePath points to a node that cannot exist in the tree
NODE_ALREADY_EXISTS if nodeUri points to a node that already exists
METADATA_MISMATCH if the node could not be created because of meta-data restrictions
DATA_STORE_FAILURE if an error occurred while accessing the data store
COMMAND_FAILED if some unspecified error is encountered while attempting to complete the command

SecurityException – if the caller does not have the necessary permissions to execute the underlying management operation

See Also DmtSession.createInteriorNode(String), DmtSession.createInteriorNode(String, String)

117.14.5.3   public void createLeafNode(String[] nodePath, DmtData value, String mimeType) throws

DmtException

nodePath the absolute path of the node to create

value the value to be given to the new node, can be null

mimeType the MIME type to be given to the new node, can be null

☐ Create a leaf node with a given value and MIME type. If the specified value or MIME type is null, their default values must be taken.

Throws DmtException – with the following possible error codes:
NODE_NOT_FOUND if nodePath points to a node that cannot exist in the tree
NODE_ALREADY_EXISTS if nodePath points to a node that already exists
METADATA_MISMATCH if the node could not be created because of meta-data restrictions
DATA_STORE_FAILURE if an error occurred while accessing the data store
COMMAND_FAILED if some unspecified error is encountered while attempting to complete the command

SecurityException – if the caller does not have the necessary permissions to execute the underlying management operation

See Also DmtSession.createLeafNode(String), DmtSession.createLeafNode(String, DmtData), DmtSession.createLeafNode(String, DmtData, String)

117.14.5.4   **public void deleteNode(String[] nodePath) throws DmtException**

nodePath the absolute path of the node to delete

☐ Delete the given node. Deleting interior nodes is recursive, the whole subtree under the given node is deleted.

Throws DmtException – with the following possible error codes:
NODE_NOT_FOUND if nodePath points to a non-existing node
METADATA_MISMATCH if the node could not be deleted because of meta-data restrictions
DATA_STORE_FAILURE if an error occurred while accessing the data store
COMMAND_FAILED if some unspecified error is encountered while attempting to complete the command

SecurityException – if the caller does not have the necessary permissions to execute the underlying management operation

See Also DmtSession.deleteNode(String)

117.14.5.5   **public void renameNode(String[] nodePath, String newName) throws DmtException**

nodePath the absolute path of the node to rename

newName the new name property of the node

☐ Rename a node. This operation only changes the name of the node (updating the timestamp and version properties if they are supported), the value and the other properties are not changed. The new name of the node must be provided, the new path is constructed from the base of the old path and the given name.

Throws DmtException – with the following possible error codes:
NODE_NOT_FOUND if nodePath points to a non-existing node, or if the new node is not defined in the tree
NODE_ALREADY_EXISTS if there already exists a sibling of nodePath with the name newName
METADATA_MISMATCH if the node could not be renamed because of meta-data restrictions
DATA_STORE_FAILURE if an error occurred while accessing the data store
COMMAND_FAILED if some unspecified error is encountered while attempting to complete the command

SecurityException – if the caller does not have the necessary permissions to execute the underlying management operation

See Also DmtSession.renameNode(String, String)

117.14.5.6   **public void setNodeTitle(String[] nodePath, String title) throws DmtException**

nodePath the absolute path of the node

title the title text of the node, can be null

☐ Set the title property of a node. The length of the title is guaranteed not to exceed the limit of 255 bytes in UTF-8 encoding.

Throws DmtException – with the following possible error codes:
NODE_NOT_FOUND if nodePath points to a non-existing node
METADATA_MISMATCH if the title could not be set because of meta-data restrictions
FEATURE_NOT_SUPPORTED if the Title property is not supported by the plugin
DATA_STORE_FAILURE if an error occurred while accessing the data store
COMMAND_FAILED if some unspecified error is encountered while attempting to complete the command

SecurityException – if the caller does not have the necessary permissions to execute the underlying management operation

See Also DmtSession.setNodeTitle(String, String)

117.14.5.7   **public void setNodeType(String[] nodePath, String type) throws DmtException**

nodePath the absolute path of the node

type the type of the node, can be null

☐ Set the type of a node. The type of leaf node is the MIME type of the data it contains. The type of an interior node is a URI identifying a DDF document.

For interior nodes, the null type should remove the reference (if any) to a DDF document overriding the tree structure defined by the ancestors. For leaf nodes, it requests that the default MIME type is used for the given node.

Throws DmtException – with the following possible error codes:
NODE_NOT_FOUND if nodePath points to a non-existing node
METADATA_MISMATCH if the type could not be set because of meta-data restrictions
DATA_STORE_FAILURE if an error occurred while accessing the data store
COMMAND_FAILED if some unspecified error is encountered while attempting to complete the command

SecurityException – if the caller does not have the necessary permissions to execute the underlying management operation

See Also DmtSession.setNodeType(String, String)

117.14.5.8   **public void setNodeValue(String[] nodePath, DmtData data) throws DmtException**

nodePath the absolute path of the node

data the data to be set, can be null

☐ Set the value of a leaf or interior node. The format of the node is contained in the DmtData object. For interior nodes, the format is FORMAT_NODE, while for leaf nodes this format is never used.

If the specified value is null, the default value must be taken; if there is no default value, a DmtException with error code METADATA_MISMATCH must be thrown.

Throws DmtException – with the following possible error codes:
NODE_NOT_FOUND if nodePath points to a non-existing node

METADATA_MISMATCH if the value could not be set because of meta-data restrictions
FEATURE_NOT_SUPPORTED if the specified node is an interior node and does not support Java object values
DATA_STORE_FAILURE if an error occurred while accessing the data store
COMMAND_FAILED if some unspecified error is encountered while attempting to complete the command

SecurityException – if the caller does not have the necessary permissions to execute the underlying management operation

See Also   DmtSession.setNodeValue(String, DmtData)

117.14.6   public interface TransactionalDataSession extends ReadWriteDataSession

Provides atomic read-write access to the part of the tree handled by the plugin that created this session.

117.14.6.1   public void commit( ) throws DmtException

☐ Commits a series of DMT operations issued in the current atomic session since the last transaction boundary. Transaction boundaries are the creation of this object that starts the session, and all subsequent commit and rollback calls.

This method can fail even if all operations were successful. This can happen due to some multi-node semantic constraints defined by a specific implementation. For example, node A can be required to always have children A/B, A/C and A/D. If this condition is broken when commit() is executed, the method will fail, and throw a METADATA_MISMATCH exception.

In many cases the tree is not the only way to manage a given part of the system. It may happen that while modifying some nodes in an atomic session, the underlying settings are modified parallelly outside the scope of the DMT. If this is detected during commit, an exception with the code CONCURRENT_ACCESS is thrown.

Throws   DmtException – with the following possible error codes
METADATA_MISMATCH if the operation failed because of meta-data restrictions
CONCURRENT_ACCESS if it is detected that some modification has been made outside the scope of the DMT to the nodes affected in the session's operations
DATA_STORE_FAILURE if an error occurred while accessing the data store
COMMAND_FAILED if some unspecified error is encountered while attempting to complete the command

SecurityException – if the caller does not have the necessary permissions to execute the underlying management operation

117.14.6.2   public void rollback( ) throws DmtException

☐ Rolls back a series of DMT operations issued in the current atomic session since the last transaction boundary. Transaction boundaries are the creation of this object that starts the session, and all subsequent commit and rollback calls.

Throws   DmtException – with the error code ROLLBACK_FAILED in case the rollback did not succeed

SecurityException – if the caller does not have the necessary permissions to execute the underlying management operation

117.15   info.dmtree.notification

Device Management Tree Notification Package Version 1.0. This package contains the public API of the Notification service. This service enables the sending of asynchronous notifications to management servers. Permission classes are provided by the info.dmtree.security package.

Bundles wishing to use this package must list the package in the Import-Package header of the bundle's manifest. For example:

```
Import-Package: info.dmtree.notification;version="[1.0,2.0)"
```

117.15.1   Summary

- *AlertItem* - Immutable data structure carried in an alert (client initiated notification).
- *NotificationService* - NotificationService enables sending aynchronous notifications to a management server.

117.15.2   public class AlertItem

Immutable data structure carried in an alert (client initiated notification). The AlertItem describes details of various notifications that can be sent by the client, for example as alerts in the OMA DM protocol. The use cases include the client sending a session request to the server (alert 1201), the client notifying the server of completion of a software update operation (alert 1226) or sending back results in response to an asynchronous EXEC command.

The data syntax and semantics varies widely between various alerts, so does the optionality of particular parameters of an alert item. If an item, such as source or type, is not defined, the corresponding getter method returns null. For example, for alert 1201 (client-initiated session) all elements will be null.

The syntax used in AlertItem class corresponds to the OMA DM alert format. NotificationService implementations on other management protocols should map these constructs to the underlying protocol.

117.15.2.1   public AlertItem(String source, String type, String mark, DmtData data)

source the URI of the node which is the source of the alert item

type a MIME type or a URN that identifies the type of the data in the alert item

data a DmtData object that contains the format and value of the data in the alert item

mark the mark parameter of the alert item

☐ Create an instance of the alert item. The constructor takes all possible data entries as parameters. Any of these parameters can be null. The semantics of the parameters may be refined by the definition of a specific alert, identified by its alert code (see NotificationService.sendNotification). In case of Generic Alerts for example (code 1226), the mark parameter contains a severity string.

117.15.2.2   public AlertItem(String[] source, String type, String mark, DmtData data)

source the path of the node which is the source of the alert item

type a MIME type or a URN that identifies the type of the data in the alert item

data a DmtData object that contains the format and value of the data in the alert item

mark the mark parameter of the alert item

□ Create an instance of the alert item, specifying the source node URI as an array of path segments. The constructor takes all possible data entries as parameters. Any of these parameters can be null. The semantics of the parameters may be refined by the definition of a specific alert, identified by its alert code (see NotificationService.sendNotification). In case of Generic Alerts for example (code 1226), the mark parameter contains a severity string.

117.15.2.3   public DmtData getData( )

□ Get the data associated with the alert item. The returned DmtData object contains the format and the value of the data in the alert item. There might be no data associated with the alert item.

Returns   the data associated with the alert item, or null if there is no data

117.15.2.4   public String getMark( )

□ Get the mark parameter associated with the alert item. The interpretation of the mark parameter depends on the alert being sent, as identified by the alert code in NotificationService.sendNotification. There might be no mark associated with the alert item.

Returns   the mark associated with the alert item, or null if there is no mark

117.15.2.5   public String getSource( )

□ Get the node which is the source of the alert. There might be no source associated with the alert item.

Returns   the URI of the node which is the source of this alert, or null if there is no source

117.15.2.6   public String getType( )

□ Get the type associated with the alert item. The type string is a MIME type or a URN that identifies the type of the data in the alert item (returned by getData). There might be no type associated with the alert item.

Returns   the type type associated with the alert item, or null if there is no type

117.15.2.7   public String toString( )

□ Returns the string representation of this alert item. The returned string includes all parameters of the alert item, and has the following format:

```
AlertItem(<source>, <type>, <mark>, <data>)
```

The last parameter is the string representation of the data value. The format of the data is not explicitly included.

Returns   the string representation of this alert item

117.15.3   public interface NotificationService

NotificationService enables sending aynchronous notifications to a management server. The implementation of NotificationService should register itself in the OSGi service registry as a service.

117.15.3.1   public void sendNotification(String principal, int code, String correlator, AlertItem[] items) throws DmtException

principal   the principal name which is the recipient of this notification, can be null

code   the alert code, can be 0 if not needed

correlator   optional field that contains the correlation identifier of an associated exec command, can be null if not needed

items   the data of the alert items carried in this alert, can be null or empty if not needed

□ Sends a notification to a named principal. It is the responsibility of the NotificationService to route the notification to the given principal using the registered info.dmtree.notification.spi.RemoteAlertSender services.

In remotely initiated sessions the principal name identifies the remote server that created the session, this can be obtained using the session's getPrincipal call.

The principal name may be omitted if the client does not know the principal name. Even in this case the routing might be possible if the Notification Service finds an appropriate default destination (for example if it is only connected to one protocol adapter, which is only connected to one management server).

Since sending the notification and receiving acknowledgment for it is potentially a very time-consuming operation, notifications are sent asynchronously. This method should attempt to ensure that the notification can be sent successfully, and should throw an exception if it detects any problems. If the method returns without error, the notification is accepted for sending and the implementation must make a best-effort attempt to deliver it.

In case the notification is an asynchronous response to a previous execute command, a correlation identifier can be specified to provide the association between the execute and the notification.

In order to send a notification using this method, the caller must have an AlertPermission with a target string matching the specified principal name. If the principal parameter is null (the principal name is not known), the target of the AlertPermission must be "*".

When this method is called with all its parameters null or 0 (except principal), it should send a protocol specific default notification to initiate a management session. For example, in case of OMA DM this is alert 1201 "Client Initiated Session". The principal parameter can be used to determine the recipient of the session initiation request.

Throws DmtException – with the following possible error codes:
UNAUTHORIZED when the remote server rejected the request due to insufficient authorization
ALERT_NOT_ROUTED when the alert can not be routed to the given principal
REMOTE_ERROR in case of communication problems between the device and the destination
COMMAND_FAILED for unspecified errors encountered while attempting to complete the command
FEATURE_NOT_SUPPORTED if the underlying management protocol doesn't support asynchronous notifications

SecurityException – if the caller does not have the required AlertPermission with a target matching the principal parameter, as described above

117.16   info.dmtree.notification.spi

Device Management Tree Notification SPI Package Version 1.0. This package contains the SPI (Service Provider Interface) of the Notification service. These interfaces are implemented by Protocol Adapters capable of delivering notifications to management servers on a specific protocol. Users of the NotificationService interface do not interact directly with this package.

Bundles wishing to use this package must list the package in the Import-Package header of the bundle's manifest. For example:

Import-Package: info.dmtree.notification.spi;version="[1.0,2.0)"

117.16.1   public interface RemoteAlertSender

The RemoteAlertSender can be used to send notifications to (remote) entities identified by principal names. This service is provided by Protocol Adapters, and is used by the info.dmtree.notification.NotificationService when sending alerts. Implementations of this interface have to be able to connect and send alerts to one or more management servers in a protocol specific way.

The properties of the service registration should specify a list of destinations (principals) where the service is capable of sending alerts. This can be done by providing a String array of principal names in the principals registration property. If this property is not registered, the service will be treated as the default sender. The default alert sender is only used when a more specific alert sender cannot be found.

The principals registration property is used when the info.dmtree.notification.NotificationService.sendNotification method is called, to find the proper RemoteAlertSender for the given destination. If the caller does not specify a principal, the alert is only sent if the Notification Sender finds a default alert sender, or if the choice is unambiguous for some other reason (for example if only one alert sender is registered).

117.16.1.1   **public void sendAlert(String principal, int code, String correlator, AlertItem[] items) throws Exception**

principal the name identifying the server where the alert should be sent, can be null

code the alert code, can be 0 if not needed

correlator the correlation identifier of an associated EXEC command, or null if there is no associated EXEC

items the data of the alert items carried in this alert, can be empty or null if no alert items are needed

☐ Sends an alert to a server identified by its principal name. In case the alert is sent in response to a previous execute command, a correlation identifier can be specified to provide the association between the execute and the alert.

The principal parameter specifies which server the alert should be sent to. This parameter can be null if the client does not know the name of the destination. The alert should still be delivered if possible; for example if the alert sender is only connected to one destination.

Any exception thrown on this method will be propagated to the original sender of the event, wrapped in a DmtException with the code REMOTE_ERROR.

Since sending the alert and receiving acknowledgment for it is potentially a very time-consuming operation, alerts are sent asynchronously. This method should attempt to ensure that the alert can be sent successfully, and should throw an exception if it detects any problems. If the method returns without error, the alert is accepted for sending and the implementation must make a best-effort attempt to deliver it.

Throws Exception – if the alert can not be sent to the server

117.17   info.dmtree.registry

Device Management Tree Registry Package Version 1.0. This package contains the factory class providing access to the different Device Management services for non-OSGi applications. The DmtServiceFactory class contained in this package provides methods for retrieving NotificationService and DmtAdmin service implementations.

Bundles wishing to use this package must list the package in the Import-Package header of the bundle's manifest. For example:

```
Import-Package: info.dmtree.registry;version="[1.0,2.0)"
```

117.17.1   **public final class DmtServiceFactory**

This class is the central access point for Device Management services. Applications can use the static factory methods provided in this class to obtain access to the different Device Management related services, such as the DmtAdmin for manipulating the tree, or the Notification Service for sending notifications to management servers.

These methods are not needed in an OSGi environment, clients should retrieve the required service objects from the OSGi Service Registry.

117.17.1.1   **public static DmtAdmin getDmtAdmin( )**

    ☐ This method is used to obtain access to DmtAdmin, which enables applications to manipulate the Device Management Tree.

Returns a DmtAdmin service object

117.17.1.2   **public static NotificationService getNotificationService( )**

    ☐ This method is used to obtain access to NotificationService, which enables applications to send asynchronous notifications to management servers.

Returns a NotificationService service object

117.18   info.dmtree.security

Device Management Tree Security Package Version 1.0. This package contains the permission classes used by the Device Management API in environments that support the Java 2 security model.

Bundles wishing to use this package must list the package in the Import-Package header of the bundle's manifest. For example:

```
Import-Package: info.dmtree.security;version="[1.0,2.0)"
```

117.18.1   Summary

- *AlertPermission* - Indicates the callers authority to send alerts to management servers, identified by their principal names.
- *DmtPermission* - Controls access to management objects in the Device Management Tree (DMT).
- *DmtPrincipalPermission* - Indicates the callers authority to create DMT sessions on behalf of a remote management server.

117.18.2   public class AlertPermission
extends Permission

Indicates the callers authority to send alerts to management servers, identified by their principal names.

AlertPermission has a target string which controls the principal names where alerts can be sent. A wildcard is allowed at the end of the target string, to allow sending alerts to any principal with a name matching the given prefix. The "∗" target means that alerts can be sent to any destination.

117.18.2.1   **public AlertPermission(String target)**

target the name of a principal, can end with ∗ to match any principal identifier with the given prefix

    ☐ Creates a new AlertPermission object with its name set to the target string. Name must be non-null and non-empty.

Throws NullPointerException – if name is null

       IllegalArgumentException – if name is empty

117.18.2.2   **public AlertPermission(String target, String actions)**

target the name of the server, can end with ∗ to match any server identifier with the given prefix

actions no actions defined, must be "∗" for forward compatibility

□ Creates a new AlertPermission object using the 'canonical' two argument constructor. In this version this class does not define any actions, the second argument of this constructor must be "*" so that this class can later be extended in a backward compatible way.

Throws NullPointerException – if name or actions is null

IllegalArgumentException – if name is empty or actions is not "*"

117.18.2.3   public boolean equals(Object obj)

obj the object to compare to this AlertPermission instance

□ Checks whether the given object is equal to this AlertPermission instance. Two AlertPermission instances are equal if they have the same target string.

Returns true if the parameter represents the same permissions as this instance

117.18.2.4   public String getActions( )

□ Returns the action list (always * in the current version).

Returns the action string "*"

117.18.2.5   public int hashCode( )

□ Returns the hash code for this permission object. If two AlertPermission objects are equal according to the equals method, then calling this method on each of the two AlertPermission objects must produce the same integer result.

Returns hash code for this permission object

117.18.2.6   public boolean implies(Permission p)

p the permission to check for implication

□ Checks if this AlertPermission object implies the specified permission. Another AlertPermission instance is implied by this permission either if the target strings are identical, or if this target can be made identical to the other target by replacing a trailing "*" with any string.

Returns true if this AlertPermission instance implies the specified permission

117.18.2.7   public PermissionCollection newPermissionCollection( )

□ Returns a new PermissionCollection object for storing AlertPermission objects.

Returns the new PermissionCollection

117.18.3   public class DmtPermission
extends Permission

Controls access to management objects in the Device Management Tree (DMT). It is intended to control local access to the DMT. DmtPermission target string identifies the management object URI and the action field lists the OMA DM commands that are permitted on the management object. Example:

```
DmtPermission("./OSGi/bundles", "Add,Replace,Get");
```

This means that owner of this permission can execute Add, Replace and Get commands on the ./OSGi/bundles management object. It is possible to use wildcards in both the target and the actions field. Wildcard in the target field means that the owner of the permission can access children nodes of the target node. Example:

```
DmtPermission("./OSGi/bundles/*", "Get");
```

This means that owner of this permission has Get access on every child node of ./OSGi/bundles. The asterix does not necessarily have to follow a '/' character. For example the "./OSGi/a*" target matches the ./OSGi/applications subtree.

If wildcard is present in the actions field, all legal OMA DM commands are allowed on the designated nodes(s) by the owner of the permission. Action names are interpreted case-insensitively, but the canonical action string returned by getActions uses the forms defined by the action constants.

117.18.3.1   **public static final String ADD = "Add"**

Holders of DmtPermission with the Add action present can create new nodes in the DMT, that is they are authorized to execute the createInteriorNode() and createLeafNode() methods of the DmtSession. This action is also required for the copy() command, which needs to perform node creation operations (among others).

117.18.3.2   **public static final String DELETE = "Delete"**

Holders of DmtPermission with the Delete action present can delete nodes from the DMT, that is they are authorized to execute the deleteNode() method of the DmtSession.

117.18.3.3   **public static final String EXEC = "Exec"**

Holders of DmtPermission with the Exec action present can execute nodes in the DMT, that is they are authorized to call the execute() method of the DmtSession.

117.18.3.4   **public static final String GET = "Get"**

Holders of DmtPermission with the Get action present can query DMT node value or properties, that is they are authorized to execute the isLeafNode(), getNodeAcl(), getEffectiveNodeAcl(), getMetaNode(), getNodeValue(), getChildNodeNames(), getNodeTitle(), getNodeVersion(), getNodeTimeStamp(), getNodeSize() and getNodeType() methods of the DmtSession. This action is also required for the copy() command, which needs to perform node query operations (among others).

117.18.3.5   **public static final String REPLACE = "Replace"**

Holders of DmtPermission with the Replace action present can update DMT node value or properties, that is they are authorized to execute the setNodeAcl(), setNodeTitle(), setNodeValue(), setNodeType() and renameNode() methods of the DmtSession. This action is also be required for the copy() command if the original node had a title property (which must be set in the new node).

117.18.3.6   **public DmtPermission(String dmtUri, String actions)**

dmtUri   URI of the management object (or subtree)

actions   OMA DM actions allowed

☐   Creates a new DmtPermission object for the specified DMT URI with the specified actions. The given URI can be:

- "*", which matches all valid (see Uri.isValidUri) absolute URIs;
- the prefix of an absolute URI followed by the * character (for example "./OSGi/L*"), which matches all valid absolute URIs beginning with the given prefix;
- a valid absolute URI, which matches itself.

Since the * character is itself a valid URI character, it can appear as the last character of a valid absolute URI. To distinguish this case from using * as a wildcard, the * character at the end of the URI must be escaped with the \ charater. For example the URI "./a*" matches "./a", "./aa", "./a/b" etc. while "./a*" matches "./a*" only.

The actions string must either be "*" to allow all actions, or it must contain a non-empty subset of the valid actions, defined as constants in this class.

Throws   NullPointerException – if any of the parameters are null

IllegalArgumentException – if any of the parameters are invalid

117.18.3.7   **public boolean equals(Object obj)**

> *obj* the object to compare to this DmtPermission instance

> ☐ Checks whether the given object is equal to this DmtPermission instance. Two DmtPermission instances are equal if they have the same target string and the same action mask. The "*" action mask is considered equal to a mask containing all actions.

> *Returns* true if the parameter represents the same permissions as this instance

117.18.3.8   **public String getActions( )**

> ☐ Returns the String representation of the action list. The allowed actions are listed in the following order: Add, Delete, Exec, Get, Replace. The wildcard character is not used in the returned string, even if the class was created using the "*" wildcard.

> *Returns* canonical action list for this permission object

117.18.3.9   **public int hashCode( )**

> ☐ Returns the hash code for this permission object. If two DmtPermission objects are equal according to the equals method, then calling this method on each of the two DmtPermission objects must produce the same integer result.

> *Returns* hash code for this permission object

117.18.3.10   **public boolean implies(Permission p)**

> *p* the permission to check for implication

> ☐ Checks if this DmtPermission object "implies" the specified permission. This method returns false if and only if at least one of the following conditions are fulfilled for the specified permission:

> - it is not a DmtPermission
> - its set of actions contains an action not allowed by this permission
> - the set of nodes defined by its path contains a node not defined by the path of this permission

> *Returns* true if this DmtPermission instance implies the specified permission

117.18.3.11   **public PermissionCollection newPermissionCollection( )**

> ☐ Returns a new PermissionCollection object for storing DmtPermission objects.

> *Returns* the new PermissionCollection

117.18.4   **public class DmtPrincipalPermission extends Permission**

Indicates the callers authority to create DMT sessions on behalf of a remote management server. Only protocol adapters communicating with management servers should be granted this permission.

DmtPrincipalPermission has a target string which controls the name of the principal on whose behalf the protocol adapter can act. A wildcard is allowed at the end of the target string, to allow using any principal name with the given prefix. The "*" target means the adapter can create a session in the name of any principal.

117.18.4.1   **public DmtPrincipalPermission(String target)**

> *target* the name of the principal, can end with * to match any principal with the given prefix

> ☐ Creates a new DmtPrincipalPermission object with its name set to the target string. Name must be non-null and non-empty.

> *Throws* NullPointerException – if name is null

>   IllegalArgumentException – if name is empty

117.18.4.2   **public DmtPrincipalPermission(String target, String actions)**

target   the name of the principal, can end with ∗ to match any principal with the given prefix

actions no actions defined, must be "∗" for forward compatibility

   ☐ Creates a new DmtPrincipalPermission object using the 'canonical' two argument constructor. In this version this class does not define any actions, the second argument of this constructor must be "∗" so that this class can later be extended in a backward compatible way.

Throws   NullPointerException – if name or actions is null

   IllegalArgumentException – if name is empty or actions is not "∗"

117.18.4.3   **public boolean equals(Object obj)**

obj   the object to compare to this DmtPrincipalPermission instance

   ☐ Checks whether the given object is equal to this DmtPrincipalPermission instance. Two DmtPrincipalPermission instances are equal if they have the same target string.

Returns true if the parameter represents the same permissions as this instance

117.18.4.4   **public String getActions( )**

   ☐ Returns the action list (always ∗ in the current version).

Returns the action string "∗"

117.18.4.5   **public int hashCode( )**

   ☐ Returns the hash code for this permission object. If two DmtPrincipalPermission objects are equal according to the equals method, then calling this method on each of the two DmtPrincipalPermission objects must produce the same integer result.

Returns hash code for this permission object

117.18.4.6   **public boolean implies(Permission p)**

p   the permission to check for implication

   ☐ Checks if this DmtPrincipalPermission object implies the specified permission. Another DmtPrincipalPermission instance is implied by this permission either if the target strings are identical, or if this target can be made identical to the other target by replacing a trailing "∗" with any string.

Returns true if this DmtPrincipalPermission instance implies the specified permission

117.18.4.7   **public PermissionCollection newPermissionCollection( )**

   ☐ Returns a new PermissionCollection object for storing DmtPrincipalPermission objects.

Returns the new PermissionCollection

117.19   References

[1]   *OMA DM-TND v1.2 draft*
      http://member.openmobilealliance.org/ftp/public_documents/dm/Permanent_documents/OMA-TS-DM-TND-V1_2-20050615-C.zip

[2]   *OMA DM-RepPro v1.2 draft:*
      http://member.openmobilealliance.org/ftp/public_documents/dm/Permanent_documents/OMA-DM-RepPro-V1_2_0-20050131-D.zip

[3]   *IETF RFC2578. Structure of Management Information*
      Version 2 (SMIv2), http://www.ietf.org/rfc/rfc2578.txt

[4]   *Java™ Management Extensions Instrumentation and Agent Specification*
      v1.2, October 2002, http://java.sun.com/javase/technologies/core/mntr-mgmt/javamanagement/

[5]   *JSR 9 - Federated Management Architecture (FMA) Specification*
      Version 1.0, January 2000, http://www.jcp.org/en/jsr/detail?id=9

[6]   *WBEM Profile Template, DSP1000*
      Status: Draft, Version 1.0 Preliminary, March 11, 2004
      http://www.dmtf.org/standards/wbem

[7]   *SNMP*
      http://www.wtcs.org/snmp4tpc/snmp_rfc.htm#rfc

[8]   *RFC 2396 Uniform Resource Identifiers (URI): Generic Syntax*
      http://www.ietf.org/rfc/rfc2396.txt

[9]   *MIME Media Types*
      http://www.iana.org/assignments/media-types/

[10] *RFC 3548 The Base16, Base32, and Base64 Data Encodings*
      http://www.ietf.org/rfc/rfc3548.txt

[11] *Secure Hash Algorithm 1*
      http://csrc.nist.gov/publications/fips/fips180-2/fips180-2withchangenotice.pdf

119 Monitor Admin Service Specification

Version 1.0

119.1 Introduction

Applications and services may publish status information that management systems can receive to monitor the status of the device. For example, a bundle could publish Status Variables for a number key VM variables like the amount of available memory, batter power, number of SMSs sent, etc.

Status Variables can be used in performance management, fault management as well as in customer relations management systems.

This specification outlines how a bundle can publish Status Variables and how administrative bundles can discover Status Variables as well as read and reset their values.

119.1.1 Entities

- *Status Variable* – Application specific variables that a *Status Variable Provider* publishes with a Monitorable service to the Monitor Admin service.Status Variable values can be long, double, boolean or String objects.
- *Status Variable Provider* – A bundle which has a number of Status Variables that it publishes with one or more Monitorable services.
- *Monitor Admin* – Provides unified and secure access to available Status Variables as well as providing a function to create monitoring jobs to monitor the Status Variables.
- *Monitorable* – A service that is registered by a Status Variable Provider to publish its Status Variables.
- *Monitor Job* – An event or time based query of a given set of Status Variables. When a monitored Status Variable is updated, or the timer expires, the Monitor Admin must generate an event via the Event Admin service.
- *Local Administrator* – A management application which uses the Monitor Admin service to query Status Variables and to initiate monitoring jobs.
- *Status Variable Name* – The unique name, within a Monitorable service, of a Status Variable.
- *Status Variable Path* – A string that uniquely identifies the Status Variable in an OSGi environment. It consists of the PID of the Monitorable service and the Status Variable name separated by a slash.

Figure 119.1   *Monitor Admin Diagram org.osgi.service.monitor package*

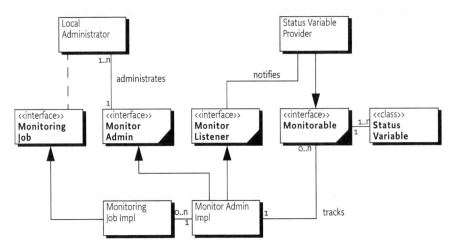

119.1.2   Synopsis

A bundle that provides a Status Variable must register a Monitorable service. This service is used by the Monitor Admin to get Status Variables and provide meta information to clients.

Clients can use the Monitor Admin to obtain Status Variables in a protected way. Clients can also create Monitoring Jobs. These Monitoring Jobs send out notifications to the clients when the value changes or periodically.

119.2   Monitorable

A Status Variable is a simple scalar that represents some key indicator of the environment, for example amount of available memory. Status Variables are further discussed in *Status Variable* on page 490.

A Status Variable Provider must therefore register a Monitorable service with the service property service.pid set to a PID. This PID must have the following format:

```
monitorable-pid ::= symbolic-name        // See 3.2.5 Core
```

The length of this PID must fit in 32 bytes when UTF-8 encoded.

Monitorable services are tracked by the Monitor Admin service. The Monitor Admin service can provide the local administrator unified access to all the Status Variables in the system. This is depicted in Figure 119.2.

Figure 119.2   *Access to Status Variables*

The main responsibility of a Monitorable service is therefore to provide access to its own Status Variables as well as providing information about those Status Variables.

The Monitorable interface contains the following methods:

- getStatusVariableNames() – Provides a list of the Status Variable names. The status variables can subsequently be acquired with the getStatusVariable(String) method.
- getStatusVariable(String) – Given the name of a Status Variable, return the StatusVariable object, if exists.
- resetStatusVariable(String) – Reset the given Status Variable if there is a reasonable reset value. If the Status Variable could not be reset, false is returned. Otherwise true is returned. Resetting a Status Variable triggers a Monitor Event, as described in *Monitoring events* on page 494.
- notifiesOnChange(String) – Tells whether the given Status Variable sends a notification when its value changes or when it is reset. This is further discussed in *Providing Notifications* on page 489.
- getDescription(String) – Provide a non-localized description of the given Status Variable.

119.2.1   Providing Notifications

If a Monitorable service returns true for the notifiesOnChange(String) method then it must notify all Monitor Listener services when the related Status Variable changes. These Status Variables are called *dynamic Status Variables*.

After the value of a dynamic Status Variable is changed, the Monitorable service must get *the singleton* Monitor Listener service and call the updated(String,StatusVariable) method. The Monitor Admin service must use this notification mechanism to send out a generic event via the Event Admin service, as described in *Monitoring events* on page 494. The Monitor Admin can also use this information to signal a remote server in a proprietary way. Figure 119.3 shows a sequence diagram for such an update. This indirection is required for security reasons.

Figure 119.3   *Notification on Update*

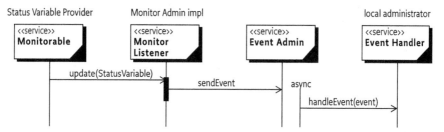

119.2.2   Example Monitorable Implementation

The following code shows how a bundle could provide a Status Variable that contains the current amount of memory.

```
public class MemoryMonitor
    implements BundleActivator, Monitorable {

    public void start(BundleContext context) {
        Hashtable ht = new Hashtable();
        ht.put("service.pid", "com.acme.foo");
        context.registerService(
            Monitorable.class.getName(), this, ht);
    }

    public void stop(BundleContext context) {}

    public String[] getStatusVariableNames() {
        return new String[] {"memory.free"};
    }
```

```
public StatusVariable getStatusVariable(String name)
   throws IllegalArgumentException {
   if ("memory.free".equals(name))
      return
         new StatusVariable(name,
         StatusVariable.CM_GAUGE,
         Runtime.getRuntime().freeMemory());
   else
      throw new IllegalArgumentException(
         "Invalid Status Variable name " + name);
}

public boolean notifiesOnChange(String name)
   throws IllegalArgumentException {
   return false;
}

public boolean resetStatusVariable(String name)
   throws IllegalArgumentException {
   return false;
}

public String getDescription(String name)
   throws IllegalArgumentException {
   if ("memory.free".equals(name))
      return "current amount of free memory in the JVM";
   else
      throw new IllegalArgumentException(
         "Invalid Status Variable name " + name);
   }
}
```

119.3   Status Variable

A Status Variable is a simple value that is published from a Monitorable service. A Status Variable has a name, a value, a timestamp, and a collection method. Additionally, the Monitorable service that publishes the Status Variable can be used to reset the Status Variable and provide a description of it.

The OSGi Specification provides an implementation class for a Status Variable. This class is final and immutable, it must be treated as a value.

119.3.1   Name

Each Status Variable must have a unique identity in the scope of a Monitorable service. This identity can be obtained with the getID() method. A Status Variable identity must have the following syntax:

```
status-variable-name ::= symbolic-name    // See 3.2.5 Core
```

The name should be descriptive and concise. Additionally, it has the following limitations:

- The length must be limited to 32 characters in UTF-8 encoded form.
- It must be unique in the scope of the Monitorable service.

119.3.2   Value

A Status Variable provides the type of its value with the getType() method. The return value of this method can take the following values:

- TYPE_BOOLEAN – A boolean value. The associated method to retrieve the value is getBoolean(). The corresponding constructor is StatusVariable(String,int,boolean).
- TYPE_INTEGER – A signed numeric value that fits in a Java int type. The associated method to retrieve the value is getInteger(). The corresponding constructor is StatusVariable(String,int, int).
- TYPE_FLOAT – A floating point value that fits in a Java float type. The associated method to retrieve the value is getFloat(). The corresponding constructor is StatusVariable(String,int,float).
- TYPE_STRING – A String object. The associated method to retrieve the value is getString().The corresponding constructor is StatusVariable(String,int,String)

If a method is called that does not match the return value of the getType() method, the Status Variable must throw an Illegal State Exception.

119.3.3 Time Stamp

The time stamp must reflect the time that the measurement was taken from the standard Java System.currentTimeMillis method. The time stamp can be obtained with the getTimeStamp() method.

119.3.4 Collection Method

This specification is compatible with terminology used in [2] *ETSI Performance Management [TS 132 403]*. An important concept of a Status Variable is the way it was collected, this is called the *collection method*. The collection method is independent of how (if and when) the reporting of the Status Variables happens. The collection method is part of the Status Variable's definition and cannot be changed. The collection method of a Status Variable can be obtained with the getCollection-Method() method.

The ETSI document defines the following collection methods:

- CM_CC – A numeric counter whose value can only increase, except when the Status Variable is reset. An example of a CC is a variable which stores the number of incoming SMSs handled by the protocol driver since it was started or reset.
- CM_GAUGE – A numeric counter whose value can vary up or down. An example of a GAUGE is a variable which stores the current battery level percentage. The value of the Status Variable must be the absolute value not a difference.
- CM_DER – (Discrete Event Registration) A status variable (numeric or string) which can change when a certain event happens in the system one or more times. The event which fires the change of the Status Variable is typically some event like the arrival of an SMS. The definition of a DER counter contains an integer N which means how many events it takes for the counter to change its value. The most usual value for N is 1, but if N is greater than 1 then it means that the variable changes after each Nth event.
- - CM_SI – (Status Inspect) The most general status variable which can be a string or numeric. An example of an SI is a string variable which contains the name of the currently logged in user.

119.4 Using Monitor Admin Service

The Monitor Admin service is a singleton service that provides unified access to the Status Variables in the system. It provides security checking, resolution of the Status Variable paths and scheduling of periodic or event based Monitoring Jobs.

119.4.1 Discovery

The Monitor Admin manages the status variables from any registered Monitorable services. The Monitorable services can be discovered using the getMonitorableNames() method. This returns a sorted list of PIDs, or null when no services are registered. This list can contain the PIDs of Monitorable services where the caller has no access to any of its Status Variables.

119.4.2   Status Variable Administration

The Monitor Admin provides the following methods for manipulating the Status Variables:

getStatusVariable(String) – Return a Status Variable given a Status Variable path. A path must have the following syntax:

```
status-variable-path ::= pid '/' status-variable-name
```

- getStatusVariableNames(String) – Returns the Status Variable names given the PID of a Monitorable service.
- getStatusVariables(String) – Returns an array of Status Variable objects given the PID of a Monitorable service.
- resetStatusVariable(String) – Reset the value of a Status Variable.

Figure 119.4 is the simple sequence diagram for getting a Status Variable from the Monitor Admin service. The caller requests a Status Variable from the Monitor Admin service with the getStatusVariable(String) method. Its sole argument specifies a path to the Status Variable. For example:

```
com.acme.foo/memory.free
```

The Monitor Admin service finds the associated Monitorable service by looking for a Monitorable service with the given PID (com.acme.foo). It will then query the Monitorable service for the Status Variable memory.free, which is then subsequently returned to the caller.

Figure 119.4   *Status Variable request through the Monitor Admin service*

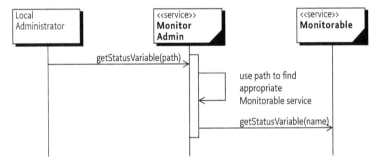

119.4.3   Notifications

The Monitor Admin service can receive events from Monitorable services as described in *Providing Notifications* on page 489. The Monitor Admin Service can control the sending of events with the switchEvents(String,boolean) method. The argument is a path to a Status Variable, with a possible wildcard character in place of the Status Variable or Monitorable PID. For example:

```
*/*
com.acme.sv.carots/*
*/received.packets
```

The use of wildcards is the same as described in *Monitor Permission* on page 495 The Monitor Admin service must expand this wildcard to the set of Status Variable names at the time the events are switched. If the boolean argument is set to false, no more events will be sent to the Event Admin service.

The default state is sending events. The state of sending events must not be persistent, switching the events off must not be remembered between system restarts.

119.4.4   Monitoring jobs

A local administrator can create a *monitoring job*. A monitoring job consists of a set of Status Variables and *reporting rules*. According to these rules, the Monitor Admin service will send events to the Event Admin service. The same Status Variable can participate in any number of monitoring jobs.

There are two types of monitoring jobs, each created with a different method. One is based on periodic measurements and one based on changes in the value of the Status Variable. The results of the measurements are sent to the Event Admin service, these events are described in *Monitoring events* on page 494.

- startScheduledJob(String,String[],int,int) – Start a job based on a periodic measurement. Both the period of measurements as well as the number of measurements can be given.
- startJob(String,String[],int) – Start a job based on notifications. The load on the Event Admin service can be minimized by specifying that only every n-th measurement must be reported. Status Variables used with this monitoring job must support notifications, otherwise an Illegal Argument Exception must be thrown.

Both monitoring jobs take an identification String object as first argument. This identification is placed in the properties of the Event object under the key: listener.id. The initiator of the monitoring job should set this id to a unique value and so that it can discriminate the monitoring events that are related to his monitoring job.

The second argument is a list of paths to Status Variables.

The difference between the Time based monitoring and event based monitoring is further elucidated in Figure 119.5.

Figure 119.5   Time and event based monitoring job

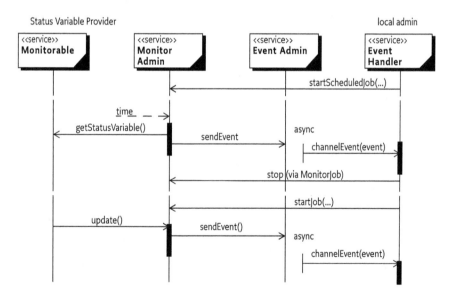

Monitoring jobs can be started also remotely by a management server through Device Management Tree operations. The monitoring job therefore has a boolean method which tells whether it was started locally or remotely: isLocal().

A monitoring job is transient, it must not survive a system restart. A monitoring job can be explicitly stopped with the stop() method.

119.4.4.1   **Example Monitoring Job**

For example, a bundle is interested in working with periodic samples of the com. acme. foo/memory. free Status Variable. It should therefore register an Event Handler with the correct topic and a filter on its Event Handler service. It then starts a monitoring job that is stopped in the BundleActivator stop method.

```
public class MemoryListener
    implements BundleActivator, EventHandler {
    MonitoringJob job;

    public void start(BundleContext context) throws Exception {
        Hashtable p = new Hashtable();
        p.put(EventConstants.EVENT_TOPIC,
            new String[] { "org/osgi/service/monitor" });
        p.put(EventConstants.EVENT_FILTER,
            "(mon.listener.id=foo.bar)");

        context.registerService(
            EventHandler.class.getName(),this,p );

        job = getMonitorAdmin().startScheduledJob(
            "foo.bar",    // listener.id
             new String[] {"com.acme.foo/memory.free"},
            15,            // seconds
            0              // Forever
        );
    }

    public void stop(BundleContext ctxt) throws Exception {
        job.stop();
    }

    public void handleEvent(Event event) {
        String value = (String) event.getProperty(
            "mon.statusvariable.value");
        String name = (String) event.getProperty(
            "mon.statusvariable.name");
        System.out.println("Mon: " name + "=" value );
    }
    ...
}
```

After starting the job, the Monitor Admin queries the com. acme. foo/memory. free Status Variable every 15 seconds. At each acquisition, the Monitor Admin sends a org/osgi/service/monitor event to the Event Admin service. The event properties contain the mon.listener.id set to foo.bar. The Event Admin service updates the Event Handler service that is registered by the example bundle. After receiving the event, the bundle can get the updated value of the Status Variable from the event properties.

The events are therefore repeated once every 15 seconds until the bundle stops.

119.5   Monitoring events

The Monitor Admin must send an asynchronous event to the Event Admin service when:

- A Monitorable reported the change on the Monitor Listener service
- The Status Variable was explicitly reset to its starting value with the resetStatusVariable(String) method.
- The Status Variable is queried from within a scheduled monitoring job by the Monitor Admin service.

Event sending in the first two cases can be switched on and off, but in the case of monitoring jobs, it cannot be disabled. Monitoring events must be sent asynchronously.

The topic of the event must be:

```
org/osgi/service/monitor
```

The properties of the event are:

- mon.monitorable.pid – (String) The unique identifier of the Monitorable service which the changed Status Variable.
- mon.statusvariable.name – (String) The name of the changed status variable.
- mon.listener.id – (String|String[ ]) Name or names representing the initiators of any monitoring jobs in which the Status Variable was included. Listeners can use this field for filtering, so that they receive only events related to their own jobs. If the event is fired because of a notification on the MonitorListener interface of the Monitor Admin service (and not because of an measurement taken within a monitoring job) then this property is absent.
- mon.statusvariable.value – (String) The value of the status variable in string format. The following methods must be used to format the String object.
  - long – Long.toString(long).
  - double – Double.toString(double).
  - boolean – Boolean.toString(boolean).
  - String – No conversion

119.6   Security

119.6.1   Monitor Permission

Registering Monitorable services, querying and resetting Status Variables and starting monitoring jobs requires a Monitor Permission. If the entity issuing the operation does not have this permission, a Security Exception must be thrown.

Unless noted otherwise, the target of the Monitor Permission identifies the Status Variable paths. It has the following format:

```
widldcard-path ::= wildcard-pid '/' wildcard-name
wildcard-pid   ::= pid '*' ? | '*'
wildcard-name  ::= unique-id '*' ? | '*'
```

Example:

```
*/*
com.acme.*/*
*/count
com.acme.foo/memory.free
```

The actions that can be used are:

- READ –Reading of the value of the given Status Variables.
- RESET – Resetting the given Status Variables.
- PUBLISH – Publishing a Status Variable. This does not forbid the Status Variable Provider to register the Monitorable. However, the Monitor Admin must not show a Status Variables to any caller when the Status Variable Provider has no permission to publish that specific Status Variable.

- STARTJOB – Initiating monitoring jobs involving the given Status Variables A minimal sampling interval can be optionally defined in the following form:

  startjob:n

  The n is the allowed minimal value of the schedule parameter of time based monitoring jobs. If n is not specified or zero then there is no lower limit for the minimum sampling interval specified. The purpose of the minimum sampling interval is to prevent the system from flooding. The target specifies the Status Variables that can be monitored.
- SWITCHEVENTS – Switch event sending on or off for the notification of value changes for the given Status Variables.

The permissions must all be checked by the Monitor Admin.

Further, the different actors must have the permissions as specified in Table 119.1 to operate correctly.

Table 119.1   *Permission for the different actors*

ServicePermission	Status Variable Provider	Local Admin	Monitor Admin
MonitorAdmin	-	GET	REGISTER
UpdateListener	GET	-	REGISTER
Monitorable	REGISTER	-	GET

119.7   org.osgi.service.monitor

Monitor Admin Package Version 1.0.

Bundles wishing to use this package must list the package in the Import-Package header of the bundle's manifest. For example:

Import-Package: org.osgi.service.monitor; version="[1.0,2.0)"

119.7.1   Summary

- *Monitorable* - A Monitorable can provide information about itself in the form of StatusVariables.
- *MonitorAdmin* - The MonitorAdmin service is a singleton service that handles StatusVariable query requests and measurement job control requests.
- *MonitoringJob* - A Monitoring Job is a request for scheduled or event based notifications on update of a set of StatusVariables.
- *MonitorListener* - The MonitorListener is used by Monitorable services to send notifications when a StatusVariable value is changed.
- *MonitorPermission* - Indicates the callers authority to publish, read or reset StatusVariables, to switch event sending on or off or to start monitoring jobs.
- *StatusVariable* - A StatusVariable object represents the value of a status variable taken with a certain collection method at a certain point of time.

119.7.2   public interface Monitorable

A Monitorable can provide information about itself in the form of StatusVariables. Instances of this interface should register themselves at the OSGi Service Registry. The MonitorAdmin listens to the registration of Monitorable services, and makes the information they provide available also through the Device Management Tree (DMT) for remote access.

The monitorable service is identified by its PID string which must be a non-null, non-empty string that conforms to the "symbolic-name" definition in the OSGi core specification. This means that only the characters [-_.a-zA-Z0-9] may be used. The length of the PID must not exceed 20 characters.

A Monitorable may optionally support sending notifications when the status of its StatusVariables change. Support for change notifications can be defined per StatusVariable.

Publishing StatusVariables requires the presence of the MonitorPermission with the publish action string. This permission, however, is not checked during registration of the Monitorable service. Instead, the MonitorAdmin implemenatation must make sure that when a StatusVariable is queried, it is shown only if the Monitorable is authorized to publish the given StatusVariable.

119.7.2.1   **public String getDescription(String id) throws IllegalArgumentException**

id   the identifier of the StatusVariable, cannot be null

☐ Returns a human readable description of a StatusVariable. This can be used by management systems on their GUI. The null return value is allowed if there is no description for the specified Status Variable.

The given identifier does not contain the Monitorable PID, i.e. it specifies the name and not the path of the Status Variable.

Returns   the human readable description of this StatusVariable or null if it is not set

Throws   IllegalArgumentException – if id points to a non-existing StatusVariable

119.7.2.2   **public StatusVariable getStatusVariable(String id) throws IllegalArgumentException**

id   the identifier of the StatusVariable, cannot be null

☐ Returns the StatusVariable object addressed by its identifier. The StatusVariable will hold the value taken at the time of this method call.

The given identifier does not contain the Monitorable PID, i.e. it specifies the name and not the path of the Status Variable.

Returns   the StatusVariable object

Throws   IllegalArgumentException – if id points to a non-existing StatusVariable

119.7.2.3   **public String[] getStatusVariableNames( )**

☐ Returns the list of StatusVariable identifiers published by this Monitorable. A StatusVariable name is unique within the scope of a Monitorable. The array contains the elements in no particular order. The returned value must not be null.

Returns   the StatusVariable identifiers published by this object, or an empty array if none are published

119.7.2.4   **public boolean notifiesOnChange(String id) throws IllegalArgumentException**

id   the identifier of the StatusVariable, cannot be null

☐ Tells whether the StatusVariable provider is able to send instant notifications when the given StatusVariable changes. If the Monitorable supports sending change updates it must notify the MonitorListener when the value of the StatusVariable changes. The Monitorable finds the MonitorListener service through the Service Registry.

The given identifier does not contain the Monitorable PID, i.e. it specifies the name and not the path of the Status Variable.

Returns   true if the Monitorable can send notification when the given StatusVariable changes, false otherwise

Throws   IllegalArgumentException – if id points to a non-existing StatusVariable

119.7.2.5   **public boolean resetStatusVariable(String id) throws IllegalArgumentException**

id   the identifier of the StatusVariable, cannot be null

   ☐ Issues a request to reset a given StatusVariable. Depending on the semantics of the actual Status Variable this call may or may not succeed: it makes sense to reset a counter to its starting value, but for example a StatusVariable of type String might not have a meaningful default value. Note that for numeric StatusVariables the starting value may not necessarily be 0. Resetting a StatusVariable must trigger a monitor event.

    The given identifier does not contain the Monitorable PID, i.e. it specifies the name and not the path of the Status Variable.

Returns true if the Monitorable could successfully reset the given StatusVariable, false otherwise

Throws IllegalArgumentException – if id points to a non-existing StatusVariable

119.7.3 public interface MonitorAdmin

The MonitorAdmin service is a singleton service that handles StatusVariable query requests and measurement job control requests.

Note that an alternative but not recommended way of obtaining StatusVariables is that applications having the required ServicePermissions can query the list of Monitorable services from the service registry and then query the list of StatusVariable names from the Monitorable services. This way all services which publish StatusVariables will be returned regardless of whether they do or do not hold the necessary MonitorPermission for publishing StatusVariables. By using the MonitorAdmin to obtain the StatusVariables it is guaranteed that only those Monitorable services will be accessed who are authorized to publish StatusVariables. It is the responsibility of the MonitorAdmin implementation to check the required permissions and show only those variables which pass this check.

The events posted by MonitorAdmin contain the following properties:

- mon.monitorable.pid: The identifier of the Monitorable
- mon.statusvariable.name: The identifier of the StatusVariable within the given Monitorable
- mon.statusvariable.value: The value of the StatusVariable, represented as a String
- mon.listener.id: The identifier of the initiator of the monitoring job (only present if the event was generated due to a monitoring job)

Most of the methods require either a Monitorable ID or a Status Variable path parameter, the latter in [Monitorable_ID]/[StatusVariable_ID] format. These parameters must not be null, and the IDs they contain must conform to their respective definitions in Monitorable and StatusVariable. If any of the restrictions are violated, the method must throw an IllegalArgumentException.

119.7.3.1 public String getDescription(String path) throws IllegalArgumentException, SecurityException

path the full path of the StatusVariable in [Monitorable_ID]/[StatusVariable_ID] format

   ☐ Returns a human readable description of the given StatusVariable. The null value may be returned if there is no description for the given StatusVariable.

    The entity that queries a StatusVariable needs to hold MonitorPermission for the given target with the read action present.

Returns the human readable description of this StatusVariable or null if it is not set

Throws IllegalArgumentException – if path is null or otherwise invalid, or points to a non-existing StatusVariable

    SecurityException – if the caller does not hold a MonitorPermission for the StatusVariable specified by path with the read action present

119.7.3.2   **public String[] getMonitorableNames( )**

> ☐ Returns the names of the Monitorable services that are currently registered. The Monitorable instances are not accessible through the MonitorAdmin, so that requests to individual status variables can be filtered with respect to the publishing rights of the Monitorable and the reading rights of the caller.
>
> The returned array contains the names in alphabetical order. It cannot be null, an empty array is returned if no Monitorable services are registered.

Returns the array of Monitorable names

119.7.3.3   **public MonitoringJob[] getRunningJobs( )**

> ☐ Returns the list of currently running MonitoringJobs. Jobs are only visible to callers that have the necessary permissions: to receive a Monitoring Job in the returned list, the caller must hold all permissions required for starting the job. This means that if the caller does not have MonitorPermission with the proper startjob action for all the Status Variables monitored by a job, then that job will be silently omitted from the results.
>
> The returned array cannot be null, an empty array is returned if there are no running jobs visible to the caller at the time of the call.

Returns the list of running jobs visible to the caller

119.7.3.4   **public StatusVariable getStatusVariable(String path) throws IllegalArgumentException, SecurityException**

> *path* the full path of the StatusVariable in [Monitorable_ID]/[StatusVariable_ID] format

> ☐ Returns a StatusVariable addressed by its full path. The entity which queries a StatusVariable needs to hold MonitorPermission for the given target with the read action present.

Returns the StatusVariable object

Throws IllegalArgumentException – if path is null or otherwise invalid, or points to a non-existing StatusVariable

> SecurityException – if the caller does not hold a MonitorPermission for the StatusVariable specified by path with the read action present

119.7.3.5   **public String[] getStatusVariableNames(String monitorableId) throws IllegalArgumentException**

> *monitorableId* the identifier of a Monitorable instance

> ☐ Returns the list of StatusVariable names published by a Monitorable instance. Only those status variables are listed where the following two conditions are met:
>
> • the specified Monitorable holds a MonitorPermission for the status variable with the publish action present
> • the caller holds a MonitorPermission for the status variable with the read action present
>
> The returned array does not contain duplicates, and the elements are in alphabetical order. It cannot be null, an empty array is returned if no (authorized and readable) Status Variables are provided by the given Monitorable.

Returns a list of StatusVariable objects names published by the specified Monitorable

Throws IllegalArgumentException – if monitorableId is null or otherwise invalid, or points to a non-existing Monitorable

119.7.3.6   **public StatusVariable[] getStatusVariables(String monitorableId) throws IllegalArgumentException**

> *monitorableId* the identifier of a Monitorable instance

□ Returns the StatusVariable objects published by a Monitorable instance. The StatusVariables will hold the values taken at the time of this method call. Only those status variables are returned where the following two conditions are met:

- the specified Monitorable holds a MonitorPermission for the status variable with the publish action present
- the caller holds a MonitorPermission for the status variable with the read action present

The elements in the returned array are in no particular order. The return value cannot be null, an empty array is returned if no (authorized and readable) Status Variables are provided by the given Monitorable.

Returns a list of StatusVariable objects published by the specified Monitorable

Throws IllegalArgumentException – if monitorableId is null or otherwise invalid, or points to a non-existing Monitorable

119.7.3.7   **public boolean resetStatusVariable(String path) throws IllegalArgumentException, SecurityException**

path the identifier of the StatusVariable in [Monitorable_id]/[StatusVariable_id] format

□ Issues a request to reset a given StatusVariable. Depending on the semantics of the StatusVariable this call may or may not succeed: it makes sense to reset a counter to its starting value, but e.g. a StatusVariable of type String might not have a meaningful default value. Note that for numeric StatusVariables the starting value may not necessarily be 0. Resetting a StatusVariable triggers a monitor event if the StatusVariable supports update notifications.

The entity that wants to reset the StatusVariable needs to hold MonitorPermission with the reset action present. The target field of the permission must match the StatusVariable name to be reset.

Returns true if the Monitorable could successfully reset the given StatusVariable, false otherwise

Throws IllegalArgumentException – if path is null or otherwise invalid, or points to a non-existing StatusVariable

SecurityException – if the caller does not hold MonitorPermission with the reset action or if the specified StatusVariable is not allowed to be reset as per the target field of the permission

119.7.3.8   **public MonitoringJob startJob(String initiator, String[] statusVariables, int count) throws IllegalArgumentException, SecurityException**

initiator the identifier of the entity that initiated the job

statusVariables the list of StatusVariables to be monitored, with each StatusVariable name given in [Monitorable_PID]/[StatusVariable_ID] format

count the number of changes that must happen to a StatusVariable before a new notification is sent

□ Starts a change based MonitoringJob with the parameters provided. Monitoring events will be sent when the StatusVariables of this job are updated. All specified StatusVariables must exist when the job is started, and all must support update notifications. The initiator string is used in the mon.listener.id field of all events triggered by the job, to allow filtering the events based on the initiator.

The count parameter specifies the number of changes that must happen to a StatusVariable before a new notification is sent, this must be a positive integer.

The entity which initiates a MonitoringJob needs to hold MonitorPermission for all the specified target StatusVariables with the startjob action present.

Returns the successfully started job object, cannot be null

Throws IllegalArgumentException – if the list of StatusVariable names contains an invalid or non-existing StatusVariable, or one that does not support notifications; if the initiator is null or empty; or if count is invalid

SecurityException – if the caller does not hold MonitorPermission for all the specified StatusVariables, with the startjob action present

119.7.3.9   **public MonitoringJob startScheduledJob(String initiator, String[] statusVariables, int schedule, int count) throws IllegalArgumentException, SecurityException**

initiator the identifier of the entity that initiated the job

statusVariables the list of StatusVariables to be monitored, with each StatusVariable name given in [Monitorable_PID]/[StatusVariable_ID] format

schedule the time in seconds between two measurements

count the number of measurements to be taken, or 0 for the measurement to run until explicitly stopped

☐ Starts a time based MonitoringJob with the parameters provided. Monitoring events will be sent according to the specified schedule. All specified StatusVariables must exist when the job is started. The initiator string is used in the mon.listener.id field of all events triggered by the job, to allow filtering the events based on the initiator.

The schedule parameter specifies the time in seconds between two measurements, it must be greater than 0. The first measurement will be taken when the timer expires for the first time, not when this method is called.

The count parameter defines the number of measurements to be taken, and must either be a positive integer, or 0 if the measurement is to run until explicitly stopped.

The entity which initiates a MonitoringJob needs to hold MonitorPermission for all the specified target StatusVariables with the startjob action present. If the permission's action string specifies a minimal sampling interval then the schedule parameter should be at least as great as the value in the action string.

Returns the successfully started job object, cannot be null

Throws IllegalArgumentException – if the list of StatusVariable names contains an invalid or non-existing StatusVariable; if initiator is null or empty; or if the schedule or count parameters are invalid

SecurityException – if the caller does not hold MonitorPermission for all the specified StatusVariables, with the startjob action present, or if the permission does not allow starting the job with the given frequency

119.7.3.10   **public void switchEvents(String path, boolean on) throws IllegalArgumentException, SecurityException**

path the identifier of the StatusVariable(s) in [Monitorable_id]/[StatusVariable_id] format, possibly with the "∗" wildcard at the end of either path fragment

on false if event sending should be switched off, true if it should be switched on for the given path

☐ Switches event sending on or off for the specified StatusVariables. When the MonitorAdmin is notified about a StatusVariable being updated it sends an event unless this feature is switched off. Note that events within a monitoring job can not be switched off. The event sending state of the StatusVariables must not be persistently stored. When a StatusVariable is registered for the first time in a framework session, its event sending state is set to ON by default.

Usage of the "∗" wildcard is allowed in the path argument of this method as a convenience feature. The wildcard can be used in either or both path fragments, but only at the end of the fragments. The semantics of the wildcard is that it stands for any matching StatusVariable at the time of the method call, it does not affect the event sending status of StatusVariables which are not yet registered. As an example, when the switchEvents("MyMonitorable/∗", false) method is executed, event sending from all StatusVariables of the MyMonitorable service are switched off. However, if the MyMonitorable service starts to publish a new StatusVariable later, it's event sending status is on by default.

Throws   SecurityException – if the caller does not hold MonitorPermission with the switchevents action or if there is any StatusVariable in the path field for which it is not allowed to switch event sending on or off as per the target field of the permission

IllegalArgumentException – if path is null or otherwise invalid, or points to a non-existing StatusVariable

119.7.4   public interface MonitoringJob

A Monitoring Job is a request for scheduled or event based notifications on update of a set of StatusVariables. The job is a data structure that holds a non-empty list of StatusVariable names, an identification of the initiator of the job, and the sampling parameters. There are two kinds of monitoring jobs: time based and change based. Time based jobs take samples of all StatusVariables with a specified frequency. The number of samples to be taken before the job finishes may be specified. Change based jobs are only interested in the changes of the monitored StatusVariables. In this case, the number of changes that must take place between two notifications can be specified.

The job can be started on the MonitorAdmin interface. Running the job (querying the StatusVariables, listening to changes, and sending out notifications on updates) is the task of the MonitorAdmin implementation.

Whether a monitoring job keeps track dynamically of the StatusVariables it monitors is not specified. This means that if we monitor a StatusVariable of a Monitorable service which disappears and later reappears then it is implementation specific whether we still receive updates of the StatusVariable changes or not.

119.7.4.1   public String getInitiator( )

□ Returns the identitifier of the principal who initiated the job. This is set at the time when MonitorAdmin.startJob() method is called. This string holds the ServerID if the operation was initiated from a remote manager, or an arbitrary ID of the initiator entity in the local case (used for addressing notification events).

Returns   the ID of the initiator, cannot be null

119.7.4.2   public int getReportCount( )

□ Returns the number of times MonitorAdmin will query the StatusVariables (for time based jobs), or the number of changes of a StatusVariable between notifications (for change based jobs). Time based jobs with non-zero report count will take getReportCount()*getSchedule() time to finish. Time based jobs with 0 report count and change based jobs do not stop automatically, but all jobs can be stopped with the stop method.

Returns   the number of measurements to be taken, or the number of changes between notifications

119.7.4.3   public int getSchedule( )

□ Returns the delay (in seconds) between two samples. If this call returns N (greater than 0) then the MonitorAdmin queries each StatusVariable that belongs to this job every N seconds. The value 0 means that the job is not scheduled but event based: in this case instant notification on changes is requested (at every nth change of the value, as specified by the report count parameter).

Returns   the delay (in seconds) between samples, or 0 for change based jobs

119.7.4.4   public String[] getStatusVariableNames( )

□ Returns the list of StatusVariable names that are the targets of this measurement job. For time based jobs, the MonitorAdmin will iterate through this list and query all StatusVariables when its timer set by the job's frequency rate expires.

Returns the target list of the measurement job in [Monitorable_ID]/[StatusVariable_ID] format, cannot be null

119.7.4.5 public boolean isLocal( )

☐ Returns whether the job was started locally or remotely. Jobs started by the clients of this API are always local, remote jobs can only be started using the Device Management Tree.

Returns true if the job was started from the local device, false if the job was initiated from a management server through the device management tree

119.7.4.6 public boolean isRunning( )

☐ Returns whether the job is running. A job is running until it is explicitely stopped, or, in case of time based jobs with a finite report count, until the given number of measurements have been made.

Returns true if the job is still running, false if it has finished

119.7.4.7 public void stop( )

☐ Stops a Monitoring Job. Note that a time based job can also stop automatically if the specified number of samples have been taken.

119.7.5 public interface MonitorListener

The MonitorListener is used by Monitorable services to send notifications when a StatusVariable value is changed. The MonitorListener should register itself as a service at the OSGi Service Registry. This interface must (only) be implemented by the Monitor Admin component.

119.7.5.1 public void updated(String monitorableId, StatusVariable statusVariable) throws IllegalArgumentException

monitorableId the identifier of the Monitorable instance reporting the change

statusVariable the StatusVariable that has changed

☐ Callback for notification of a StatusVariable change.

Throws IllegalArgumentException – if the specified monitorable ID is invalid (null, empty, or contains illegal characters) or points to a non-existing Monitorable, or if statusVariable is null

119.7.6 public class MonitorPermission
extends Permission

Indicates the callers authority to publish, read or reset StatusVariables, to switch event sending on or off or to start monitoring jobs. The target of the permission is the identifier of the StatusVariable, the action can be read, publish, reset, startjob, switchevents, or the combination of these separated by commas. Action names are interpreted case-insensitively, but the canonical action string returned by getActions uses the forms defined by the action constants.

If the wildcard * appears in the actions field, all legal monitoring commands are allowed on the designated target(s) by the owner of the permission.

119.7.6.1 public static final String PUBLISH = "publish"

Holders of MonitorPermission with the publish action present are Monitorable services that are allowed to publish the StatusVariables specified in the permission's target field. Note, that this permission cannot be enforced when a Monitorable registers to the framework, because the Service Registry does not know about this permission. Instead, any StatusVariables published by a Monitorable without the corresponding publish permission are silently ignored by MonitorAdmin, and are therefore invisible to the users of the monitoring service.

119.7.6.2   **public static final String READ = "read"**

Holders of MonitorPermission with the read action present are allowed to read the value of the StatusVariables specified in the permission's target field.

119.7.6.3   **public static final String RESET = "reset"**

Holders of MonitorPermission with the reset action present are allowed to reset the value of the StatusVariables specified in the permission's target field.

119.7.6.4   **public static final String STARTJOB = "startjob"**

Holders of MonitorPermission with the startjob action present are allowed to initiate monitoring jobs involving the StatusVariables specified in the permission's target field.

A minimal sampling interval can be optionally defined in the following form: startjob:n. This allows the holder of the permission to initiate time based jobs with a measurement interval of at least n seconds. If n is not specified or 0 then the holder of this permission is allowed to start monitoring jobs specifying any frequency.

119.7.6.5   **public static final String SWITCHEVENTS = "switchevents"**

Holders of MonitorPermission with the switchevents action present are allowed to switch event sending on or off for the value of the StatusVariables specified in the permission's target field.

119.7.6.6   **public MonitorPermission(String statusVariable, String actions) throws IllegalArgumentException**

statusVariable   the identifier of the StatusVariable in [Monitorable_id]/[StatusVariable_id] format

actions   the list of allowed actions separated by commas, or * for all actions

☐ Create a MonitorPermission object, specifying the target and actions.

The statusVariable parameter is the target of the permission, defining one or more status variable names to which the specified actions apply. Multiple status variable names can be selected by using the wildcard * in the target string. The wildcard is allowed in both fragments, but only at the end of the fragments.

For example, the following targets are valid: com.mycomp.myapp/queue_length, com.mycomp.myapp/*, com.mycomp.*/*, */*, */queue_length, */queue*.

The following targets are invalid: *.myapp/queue_length, com.*.myapp/*, *.

The actions parameter specifies the allowed action(s): read, publish, startjob, reset, switchevents, or the combination of these separated by commas. String constants are defined in this class for each valid action. Passing "*" as the action string is equivalent to listing all actions.

Throws   IllegalArgumentException – if either parameter is null, or invalid with regard to the constraints defined above and in the documentation of the used actions

119.7.6.7   **public boolean equals(Object o)**

o   the object being compared for equality with this object

☐ Determines the equality of two MonitorPermission objects. Two MonitorPermission objects are equal if their target strings are equal and the same set of actions are listed in their action strings.

Returns   true if the two permissions are equal

119.7.6.8   **public String getActions( )**

☐ Get the action string associated with this permission. The actions are returned in the following order: read, reset, publish, startjob, switchevents.

Returns   the allowed actions separated by commas, cannot be null

119.7.6.9   **public int hashCode( )**

☐ Create an integer hash of the object. The hash codes of MonitorPermissions p1 and p2 are the same if p1.equals(p2).

Returns the hash of the object

119.7.6.10   **public boolean implies(Permission p)**

p the permission to be checked

☐ Determines if the specified permission is implied by this permission.

This method returns false if and only if at least one of the following conditions are fulfilled for the specified permission:

- it is not a MonitorPermission
- it has a broader set of actions allowed than this one
- it allows initiating time based monitoring jobs with a lower minimal sampling interval
- the target set of Monitorables is not the same nor a subset of the target set of Monitorables of this permission
- the target set of StatusVariables is not the same nor a subset of the target set of StatusVariables of this permission

Returns true if the given permission is implied by this permission

119.7.7   public final class StatusVariable

A StatusVariable object represents the value of a status variable taken with a certain collection method at a certain point of time. The type of the StatusVariable can be int, float, boolean or String.

A StatusVariable is identified by an ID string that is unique within the scope of a Monitorable. The ID must be a non-null, non-empty string that conforms to the "symbolic-name" definition in the OSGi core specification. This means that only the characters [-_.a-zA-Z0-9] may be used. The length of the ID must not exceed 32 bytes when UTF-8 encoded.

119.7.7.1   **public static final int CM_CC = 0**

Constant for identifying 'Cumulative Counter' data collection method.

119.7.7.2   **public static final int CM_DER = 1**

Constant for identifying 'Discrete Event Registration' data collection method.

119.7.7.3   **public static final int CM_GAUGE = 2**

Constant for identifying 'Gauge' data collection method.

119.7.7.4   **public static final int CM_SI = 3**

Constant for identifying 'Status Inspection' data collection method.

119.7.7.5   **public static final int TYPE_BOOLEAN = 3**

Constant for identifying boolean data type.

119.7.7.6   **public static final int TYPE_FLOAT = 1**

Constant for identifying float data type.

119.7.7.7   **public static final int TYPE_INTEGER = 0**

Constant for identifying int data type.

119.7.7.8   **public static final int TYPE_STRING = 2**

Constant for identifying String data type.

119.7.7.9   **public StatusVariable(String id, int cm, int data)**

id the identifier of the StatusVariable

cm the collection method, one of the CM_ constants

data the int value of the StatusVariable

☐ Constructor for a StatusVariable of int type.

Throws IllegalArgumentException – if the given id is not a valid StatusVariable name, or if cm is not one of the collection method constants

NullPointerException – if the id parameter is null

119.7.7.10   **public StatusVariable(String id, int cm, float data)**

id the identifier of the StatusVariable

cm the collection method, one of the CM_ constants

data the float value of the StatusVariable

☐ Constructor for a StatusVariable of float type.

Throws IllegalArgumentException – if the given id is not a valid StatusVariable name, or if cm is not one of the collection method constants

NullPointerException – if the id parameter is null

119.7.7.11   **public StatusVariable(String id, int cm, boolean data)**

id the identifier of the StatusVariable

cm the collection method, one of the CM_ constants

data the boolean value of the StatusVariable

☐ Constructor for a StatusVariable of boolean type.

Throws IllegalArgumentException – if the given id is not a valid StatusVariable name, or if cm is not one of the collection method constants

NullPointerException – if the id parameter is null

119.7.7.12   **public StatusVariable(String id, int cm, String data)**

id the identifier of the StatusVariable

cm the collection method, one of the CM_ constants

data the String value of the StatusVariable, can be null

☐ Constructor for a StatusVariable of String type.

Throws IllegalArgumentException – if the given id is not a valid StatusVariable name, or if cm is not one of the collection method constants

NullPointerException – if the id parameter is null

119.7.7.13   **public boolean equals(Object obj)**

obj the object to compare with this StatusVariable

☐ Compares the specified object with this StatusVariable. Two StatusVariable objects are considered equal if their full path, collection method and type are identical, and the data (selected by their type) is equal.

Returns true if the argument represents the same StatusVariable as this object

119.7.7.14   **public boolean getBoolean( ) throws IllegalStateException**

☐ Returns the StatusVariable value if its type is boolean.

Returns the StatusVariable value as a boolean

Throws IllegalStateException – if the type of this StatusVariable is not boolean

119.7.7.15   **public int getCollectionMethod( )**

☐ Returns the collection method of this StatusVariable. See section 3.3 b) in [ETSI TS 132 403]

Returns one of the CM_ constants

119.7.7.16   **public float getFloat( ) throws IllegalStateException**

☐ Returns the StatusVariable value if its type is float.

Returns the StatusVariable value as a float

Throws IllegalStateException – if the type of this StatusVariable is not float

119.7.7.17   **public String getID( )**

☐ Returns the ID of this StatusVariable. The ID is unique within the scope of a Monitorable.

Returns the ID of this StatusVariable

119.7.7.18   **public int getInteger( ) throws IllegalStateException**

☐ Returns the StatusVariable value if its type is int.

Returns the StatusVariable value as an int

Throws IllegalStateException – if the type of this StatusVariable is not int

119.7.7.19   **public String getString( ) throws IllegalStateException**

☐ Returns the StatusVariable value if its type is String.

Returns the StatusVariable value as a String

Throws IllegalStateException – if the type of the StatusVariable is not String

119.7.7.20   **public Date getTimeStamp( )**

☐ Returns the timestamp associated with the StatusVariable. The timestamp is stored when the StatusVariable instance is created, generally during the Monitorable.getStatusVariable method call.

Returns the time when the StatusVariable value was queried, cannot be null

119.7.7.21   **public int getType( )**

☐ Returns information on the data type of this StatusVariable.

Returns one of the TYPE_ constants indicating the type of this StatusVariable

119.7.7.22   **public int hashCode( )**

☐ Returns the hash code value for this StatusVariable. The hash code is calculated based on the full path, collection method and value of the StatusVariable.

Returns the hash code of this object

119.7.7.23   **public String toString( )**

☐ Returns a String representation of this StatusVariable. The returned String contains the full path, collection method, timestamp, type and value parameters of the StatusVariable in the following format:

```
StatusVariable(<path>, <cm>, <timestamp>, <type>, <value>)
```

The collection method identifiers used in the string representation are "CC", "DER", "GAUGE" and "SI" (without the quotes). The format of the timestamp is defined by the Date.toString method, while the type is identified by one of the strings "INTEGER", "FLOAT", "STRING" and "BOOLEAN". The final field contains the string representation of the value of the status variable.

Returns the String representation of this StatusVariable

119.8   References

[1]   *SyncML Device Management Tree Description*

[2]   *ETSI Performance Management [TS 132 403]*
       http://webapp.etsi.org/action/PU/20040113/ts_132403v050500p.pdf

[3]   *RFC-2396 Uniform Resource Identifiers (URI): Generic Syntax*
       http://www.ietf.org/rfc/rfc2396.txt

120 Foreign Application Access Specification

Version 1.0

120.1 Introduction

The OSGi Framework contains an advanced collaboration model which provides a publish/find/bind model using *services*. This OSGi service architecture is not natively supported by foreign application models like MIDP, Xlets, Applets, other Java application models. The purpose of this specification is to enable these foreign applications to participate in the OSGi service oriented architecture.

120.1.1 Essentials

- *Inter-operatbility* – Full inter-operability between foreign application models and OSGi services is required. This requires both getting services, registering services, and listening to Framework events.
- *No Change* – The inter-working specification cannot modify the life cycle model of the foreign application models. The foreign application model specifications cannot be changed.
- *Familiarity* – Programmers familiar with a foreign application model should be able to leverage the services architecture without much effort.
- *Simplicity* – The programming model for using services must be very simple and not require the programmer to learn many new concepts.
- *Management* – Support managing the foreign applications; both through proper OSGi APIs and from a remote management server.

120.1.2 Entities

- *Foreign Application* – Java Applications, which must be delivered in JAR files, which are not OSGi bundles.
- *Application Container* – An Application Container is responsible for controlling a foreign application and providing the appropriate environment. It must interact with the OSGi Framework to give the foreign application instances access to the OSGi services and package sharing.
- *Application Activator* – A class in the foreign application JAR file that is used to notify the application of life cycle changes. One JAR file can contain multiple application activators.
- *Framework* – A class that provides access to the application container's *application context* for a given application activator.
- *Application Context* – The interface to the application container's functions to inter-work with the OSGi Framework.
- *Application Declaration* – An XML resource that must be placed in the application's JAR file at OSGI-INF/app/apps.xml. This is an optional declaration.
- *Application Instance* – A launched application. Most foreign application models permit an application to be launched multiple times.

Figure 120.1   *Foreign Applications, org.osgi.application package*

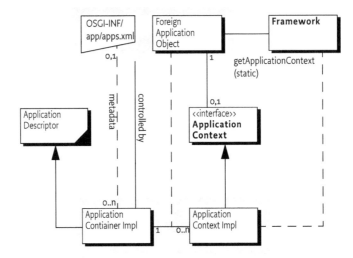

120.1.3   Synopsis

Foreign application JAR files can be installed in an OSGi Framework as if they were normal bundles. Application containers running on the OSGi Framework must detect the installation of recognized foreign applications and provide a bridge to the OSGi Environment. This bridge can include interaction with the *Application Admin Specification* on page 357, as well as provide access to the OSGi services and Framework events.

The Application container reads the application XML resource from the JAR file and treats the foreign application according to this information. When the foreign application is launched, the application container creates an application instance.

Foreign application instances can get an application context through a static method on the Framework class. The Application Context provides access to getting services, registering services and registering listeners.

The foreign application instance's life cycle can be influenced by the application declaration. If desired, an application can be prevented from launching or stopping when required services are, or become, unavailable.

120.2   Foreign Applications

Foreign applications are Java applications that can be installed and managed through the normal OSGi mechanisms. However, they use another application programming model than the bundle programming model. For example: MIDP, MHP, DOJA.

Foreign applications must fulfill the following requirements to be able to inter-work with the OSGi environment:

- The applications must be written in Java
- The applications must be delivered in JAR files. This is the common model for Java applications.
- They must have a clearly defined life cycle with a start and stop state.
- One or more classes in the application must be available to start and stop the application. For example the Midlet in MIDP or the Xlet in MHP. This object is called the *application's activator*. As the application container uses this object for life cycle control of the application, the lifetime of this object equals the lifetime of the application.

Foreign applications are managed by *application containers*. Application containers provide the environment and life cycle management as defined by foreign application model.

This specification does not require any changes in the foreign application model; existing applications must run unmodified. However, to allow the foreign applications to participate as a first class OSGi citizen, a number of additional artifacts in the JAR file are required. These artifacts use Manifest headers and an XML resource in the applications JAR file; these artifacts are permitted and ignored by the foreign application models that are currently known.

120.2.1 Foreign Metadata

There are different types of metadata associated with application models. Descriptive information, for example the name, icon, documentation etc. of the application, is usually provided in an application model specific way. Application models can also define behavioral metadata, that is, prescribe that the application needs to be started automatically at device startup (auto start) or whether multiple instances of an application can be executed concurrently (singleton). These kinds of metadata are supported by different application models to different extent and are not in the scope of this specification. The application container is responsible for interpreting this metadata and treating the foreign application in the appropriate way.

120.2.2 OSGi Manifest Headers

Foreign applications can import packages by specifying the appropriate OSGi module headers in the manifest. These headers are fully described in the OSGi Core Specification. Their semantics remain unchanged. The following headers must not be used in foreign applications:

- *Export-Package* – Exporting packages is forbidden in foreign applications.
- *Bundle-Activator* – Foreign applications have their own activator.
- *Service-Component* – Service components should be bundles.

Foreign applications that intend to use the OSGi Framework features should have Bundle-Symbolic-Name and Bundle-Version headers. If they do not have such a header, they can be deployed with Deployment Package, which can assign these headers in the Deployment Package manifest.

Any JAR that uses these headers must not be recognized as a foreign application, even if their manifest is conforming and valid with respect to the foreign application model. This entails that a JAR cannot both be a bundle with activator or exports and a foreign application.

For example, a MIDlet can be extended to import the org.osgi.application package from the OSGi environment. The Import-Package header is used to describe such an import:

```
Manifest-Version: 1.0
MIDlet-Name: Example
MIDlet-1: Example, , osgi.ExampleMidlet
MIDlet-Version: 1.1.0
MIDlet-Vendor: OSGi
MicroEdition-Configuration: CDC-1.0
MicroEdition-Profile: MIDP-1.0
Bundle-ManifestVersion: 2
Bundle-SymbolicName: osgi.example
Import-Package: org.osgi.application;version=1.0,
  org.osgi.framework;version=1.3
```

120.2.3 Interacting with the OSGi Framework

The application container must maintain an application context for each started application, that is, the application instance. This context is related to the application's activator. The Application Context can be acquired using a static getApplicationContext(Object) method on the Framework class. The parameter of this method is the application's activator itself. The getApplicationContext method cannot check if the caller is really the given application; the application activator is therefore a *capability*, any application that has this object can get the Application Context. The application activator should never be shared with other applications. The Application Context must therefore deny the application activator to be used as a service object.

The getApplicationContext method must not be called from the application activator's constructor; at that time it must not be available yet.

For example, a MIDlet could acquire the application context with the following code:

```
import org.osgi.framework.*;
import org.osgi.application.*;
import javax.microedition.midlet.*;

public class Example extends MIDlet {
    ApplicationContext    context;
    public void startApp() {
        context = Framework.getApplicationContext(this);
    }

    public void pauseApp() { ... }

    public void destroyApp(boolean unconditional) { ... }
}
```

The getApplicationContext method must throw an Illegal Argument Exception if it is called with an object that is not an application's activator.

The ApplicationContext object is singleton for the corresponding application's activator. Subsequent calls to the getApplicationContext method with the same application's activator must return the same ApplicationContext object; therefore, applications are free to forget and get the object any number of times during their lifetime. However, it is an error to get the ApplicationContext object for an application that is already stopped. Existing ApplicationContext objects must be invalidated once the application's activator is stopped.

120.2.4   Introspection

The Application Context provides the following methods about the application:

- getApplicationId() – Return the Application Descriptor id for this application.
- getInstanceId() – Return the instance id for this application.

120.2.5   Access to Services

Foreign applications do not have direct access to the OSGi service registry. However, the application context provides the mechanism to interact with this service registry.

Access to services is more protected and controlled than traditional OSGi access that uses the BundleContext object. The service model is conceptually based on the *Declarative Services Specification* on page 249. It uses the same concepts as that specification. Albeit there are a number of differences due the nature of foreign applications.

Applications can use the locateService or locateServices methods of their associated application context to obtain service objects from the OSGi service registry. Just like OSGi Declarative services, these service objects must be declared a priori in the reference element of the metadata, see *Application Descriptor Resource* on page 515. This metadata declares a number of *named references*; References contain the criteria which services are eligible for use by the application and how these dependencies should be handled. The foreign application can only use services defined in references; the application context only takes the name of a reference as parameter in the locateService and locateServices methods. That is, a foreign application cannot indiscriminately use the service registry, it is restricted by the application declaration.

A reference *selects* a subset of services in the service registry. The primary selector is its *interface*. However, this subset can be further narrowed down with a *target* filter. The target specifies an OSGi filter expression that is used to additionally qualify the subset of appropriate services.

There are two different methods to access the services selected by the reference:

- locateService(String) – Return one of the services that is selected by the reference with the given name. If multiple services are selected by the reference, then the service with the highest ranking must be returned. This is compatible with the getServiceReference method in the OSGi Framework's BundleContext class.
- locateServices(String) – Return all the services that are selected by the reference with the given name.

Once the application instance has obtained a service object, that service is said to be *bound* to the application instance. There is no method to unbind a service.

For example, a foreign application that wants to log via the Log Service, should declare the following metadata in OSGI-INF/app/apps.xml:

```
<?xml version="1.0" ?>
  <descriptor xmlns="http://www.osgi.org/xmlns/app/v1.1.0">
    <application class="com.acme.app.SampleMidlet">
    <reference name="log"
       interface="org.osgi.service.log.LogService"/>
  </application>
</descriptor>
```

The code to log could look like:

```
void log(String msg) {
  ApplicationContext ctxt=
     Framework.getApplicationContext(this);
  LogService log = (LogService) ctxt.locateService("log");
  log.log( LogService.LOG_INFO, msg );
}
```

120.2.6 Service Properties

The foreign applications receive the services objects they have access to directly. This means that they cannot access the service properties that are normally associated with the service registrations.

The getServiceProperties(Object) returns a Map object with a copy of these service properties.

120.2.7 Dependencies on Services

The availability of services can influence the life cycle of the foreign application. The life cycle is influenced by the *policy* and the *cardinality*.

The policy defines how the unregistration of a bound service must be handled. The following policies are supported:

- *static* – The application assumes that bound services will never go away. So if a bound service becomes unregistered, the Application Container must stop the application to prevent it from using a stale service.
- *dynamic* – The application must never store service objects and will always get them on demand. Once a service is bound, it can become unregistered without any effect on the application.

Additionally, the *cardinality* defines if a reference is optional. An optional reference does not influence the life cycle of an application, a mandatory reference does. The cardinality is expressed as one of the following values:

- 0..1 or 0..n – Optional reference
- 1..1 or 1..n – Mandatory reference

The multiplicity is only for compatibility with the Declarative Services. Both locateService and locateServices methods can be used regardless of the given multiplicity and return the selected subset for the given reference.

Mandatory references can influence the launching of an application. An application must only be started when a mandatory reference is *satisfied*. A reference is satisfied when there is at least one registered service selected by the reference.

If a mandatory reference of an application is about to become unsatisfied, due to unregistering a service, the application container must stop the application instance according to corresponding application model semantics.

120.2.8   Registering Services

A common pattern in the OSGi is registering a service to listen to certain events. For example, the Configuration Admin service requires their clients to register a callback Managed Service, so that the service can asynchronously update the client with new configurations. The ApplicationContext interface contains methods that allow the applications to register such services. These services must be automatically unregistered by the application container after the application has been stopped.

The available methods are:

- registerService(String[],Object,Dictionary) – Register a service under a single interface.
- registerService(String,Object,Dictionary) – Register a service under a number of interfaces.

Either method requires that the given object implements all the interfaces that are given. The Dictionary object provides the properties. See the OSGi registerService methods in the BundleContext class. These identical methods specifies the behavior in detail.

The use of the application activator as a service object is explicitly forbidden. Registering the application activator as a service allows other applications in the OSGi environment to access the Application Context using this object and the getApplicationContext method.

Both methods return a ServiceRegistration object that can be used to unregister the service. Services must be automatically unregistered when the application instance is stopped.

120.2.9   Listening to Service Events

The Application Context provides the following methods to listen to service events:

- addServiceListener(ApplicationServiceListener,String) – Add an Application Service Listener. The listener will receive the service events for the given reference name.
- addServiceListener(ApplicationServiceListener,String[]) – Add an Application Service Listener that will receive the events for all the services identified with the given reference name.

If a Application Service Listener is registered more than once, then the previous registration is removed. Listeners can be removed with removeServiceListener(ApplicationServiceListener). When the application instance is stopped, the listeners are automatically unregistered.

120.2.10   Access to Startup Parameters

Applications can use the getStartupArguments method on the application context to obtain their startup arguments. The startup arguments are represented as map with name and value pairs. The name is a non-null and non-empty ("") String object. The value can be any type of object.

The reason for providing the startup parameters through a special mechanism is that it allows foreign applications access to the parameters of a schedule application, see *Scheduling* on page 363.

This uniform access to the startup parameters provides a uniform way for applications of any foreign application model. This facility does not remove the need for any mechanisms required by the foreign application model for startup parameters access.

120.2.11 Sibling Instances

Most foreign application models allow an application to be launched multiple times, creating multiple instances. In OSGi, a bundle can only be started once, which creates certain assumptions. For example, the Service Factory concept creates a unique service object per bundle.

Each application instance must be seen as a unique bundle while it runs. That is, it should not share anything with other instances. The foreign application container is responsible for this isolation; implementing this isolation requires implementation dependent constructs.

120.3 Application Containers

Application containers:

- Provide management for the foreign applications
- Launches application instances in a defined environment
- Provide a specific a application model context to foreign application instances
- Interact with the Application Admin service to provide the foreign applications to application managers.

A single OSGi environment can host multiple application containers.

120.3.1 Installation

Applications are installed into the system using OSGi bundle installation mechanism (i.e. installBundle method of the BundleContext interface). This allows including application JARs to Deployment Packages without any changes to the Deployment Package format or Deployment Admin behavior. It also allows the OSGi framework to process the dependency information (the package dependencies) included in the application metadata.

The application container can listen to the BundleEvent.INSTALLED events and examine the installed JARs whether they contain applications supported by the particular container. After the installation, the application container is responsible for registering the corresponding Application Descriptor as defined in the *Application Admin Specification* on page 357. Similarly, the container can recognize the removal of the package by listening to BundleEvent.UNINSTALLED events and then it can unregister the corresponding descriptors. Additionally, application container must check the bundle registry for changes when they are started.

Receiving BundleEvent.INSTALLED events via a Synchronous Bundle Listener makes it possible for the application container to examine the package content during installation. A foreign application must not become available for execution unless it is started as a bundle. This mechanism allows foreign applications to be installed but not yet recognized as a foreign application.

120.4 Application Descriptor Resource

Applications' dependencies on services must be declared in the OSGI-INF/app/apps.xml resource. The XML file must use the http://www.osgi.org/xmlns/app/v1.1.0 namespace. The preferred abbreviation is app. The XML schema definition can be found at *Component Description Schema* on page 517. The apps.xml file is optional if a foreign application does not require any dependencies.

The structure of the XML must conform to the description below.

```
<descriptor>        ::= <application> +
<application>       ::= <reference> *
```

120.4.1 Descriptor Element

The descriptor is the top level element. The descriptor element has no attributes.

120.4.2 Application Element

A JAR file can contain multiple application activators. The application element can therefore be repeated one or more times in the descriptor element.

The application element has the following attribute:

- class – The class attribute of the application element must contain the fully qualified name of the application's activator.

120.4.3 Reference Element

A reference element represents the applications use of a particular service. All services that an application uses must be declared in a reference element.

A reference element has the following attributes:

- name – A reference element is identified by a name. This name can be used in the locateService or locateService, see *Access to Services* on page 512. This name must be unique within an application element.
- interface – The fully qualified name of the interface or class that defines the selected service.
- policy – The choice of action when a bound services becomes unregistered while an application instance is running. It can have the following values:
  - static – If a bound service becomes unregistered, the application instance must be stopped but the corresponding Application Descriptor is still launchable.
  - dynamic – If a bound service becomes unregistered, the application can continue to run if the mandatory reference can still be satisfied by another service.
- cardinality – Defines the optionality of the reference. If it starts with a 0, an application can handle that the reference selects no service. That is, locateService method can return a null. If it starts with 1, the reference is mandatory and at least one service must be available before an application instance can be launched. The cardinality can have one of the following values:
  - 0..1 or 0..n – Optional reference
  - 1..1 or 1..n – Mandatory reference
- target – The optional target attribute of the element can be used to further narrow which services are acceptable for the application by providing an OSGi filter on the properties of the services.

120.4.4 Example XML

The following example is an application declaration for a MIDlet application that depends on the OSGi Log Service and another service:

```
<?xml version="1.0" ?>
<descriptor xmlns="http://www.osgi.org/xmlns/app/v1.1.0">
  <application class="com.acme.apps.SampleMidlet">
    <reference name="log" interface="org.osgi.service.log"/>
    <reference name="foo"
      interface="com.acme.service.FooService"
      policy="dynamic"
      cardinality="0..n" />
  </application>
</descriptor>
```

A similar example for an imaginary Xlet, with different dependencies:

```
<?xml version="1.0" encoding="UTF-8" ?>
<descriptor xmlns="http://www.osgi.org/xmlns/app/v1.1.0">
  <application class="com.acme.apps.SampleXlet">
    <reference name="log" interface="org.osgi.service.log"/>
    <reference name="bar"
          interface="com.acme.service.BarService"
          policy="static" cardinality="1..n" />
  </application>
</descriptor>
```

120.5   Component Description Schema

This XML Schema defines the component description grammar.

```
<?xml version="1.0" encoding="UTF-8"?>
<schema xmlns="http://www.w3.org/2001/XMLSchema"
    xmlns:app="http://www.osgi.org/xmlns/app/v1.1.0"
    targetNamespace="http://www.osgi.org/xmlns/app/v1.1.0"
    version="1.1.0">

    <element name="descriptor" type="app:Tdescriptor">
        <annotation>
            <documentation xml:lang="en">
                descriptor element encloses the application descriptors
                provided in a document
            </documentation>
        </annotation>
    </element>

    <complexType name="Tdescriptor">
        <sequence>
            <element name="application" type="app:Tapplication"
                minOccurs="1" maxOccurs="unbounded" />
            <any namespace="##other" processContents="lax" minOccurs="0"
                maxOccurs="unbounded" />
        </sequence>
        <anyAttribute />
    </complexType>

    <complexType name="Tapplication">
        <annotation>
            <documentation xml:lang="en">
                describes the service dependencies of an application
            </documentation>
        </annotation>
        <sequence>
            <element name="reference" minOccurs="0"
                maxOccurs="unbounded" type="app:Treference" />
            <any namespace="##other" processContents="lax" minOccurs="0"
                maxOccurs="unbounded" />
        </sequence>
        <attribute name="class" type="string" />
        <anyAttribute />
    </complexType>

    <complexType name="Treference">
        <sequence>
            <any namespace="##any" processContents="lax" minOccurs="0"
                maxOccurs="unbounded" />
        </sequence>
        <attribute name="name" type="NMTOKEN" use="required" />
        <attribute name="interface" type="string" use="required" />
        <attribute name="cardinality" default="1..1" use="optional"
            type="app:Tcardinality" />
        <attribute name="policy" use="optional" default="static"
            type="app:Tpolicy" />
        <attribute name="target" type="string" use="optional" />
        <anyAttribute />
    </complexType>
```

```
<simpleType name="Tcardinality">
    <restriction base="string">
        <enumeration value="0..1" />
        <enumeration value="0..n" />
        <enumeration value="1..1" />
        <enumeration value="1..n" />
    </restriction>
</simpleType>

<simpleType name="Tpolicy">
    <restriction base="string">
        <enumeration value="static" />
        <enumeration value="dynamic" />
    </restriction>
</simpleType>

<attribute name="must-understand" type="boolean">
    <annotation>
        <documentation xml:lang="en">
            This attribute should be used by extensions to documents
            to require that the document consumer understand the
            extension.
        </documentation>
    </annotation>
</attribute>
</schema>
```

120.6 Security

120.6.1 Application Context Access

The getApplicationContext method provides access to the Application Context of a given application activator. The application activator is therefore a capability; any party that has access to this object can potentially get its related Application Context and use it in intended ways.

A common pattern in small applications is to (ab)use the application activator class for all tasks, among them as service object. However, registering the application activator as a service will allow any party that can use that service to use it as the parameter to the getApplicationContext method.

The Application Context must therefore be protected to not allow the registration of the application activator.

120.6.2 Signing

Application models can include the definition of a security model. For example, MIDP 2 defines a security model different from the standard Java 2 security model. If the foreign application model defines a security model different from Java 2 security, then it is the responsibility of the application container to implement this model and enforce it.

OSGi services are protected by Java 2 permissions. Applications wishing to use such services must have the appropriate permissions for those services.

Java 2 permissions are assigned during class loading based on the location of the code, the JAR signatures, and possibly based on other conditions, when using the Conditional Permission framework.

Signing is a very common technique to handle the granting of permissions. It requires that the JAR be signed according to the JAR Signing model. Therefore, OSGi-aware application packages should be signed by JAR signing. However, some foreign application models have alternative signing models in place. However, it is unlikely that this conflicts because JAR signing uses well defined separate files and manifest headers. If the foreign application model changes the JAR file outside the META-INF directory, then the signing according to the foreign application model must be performed before the standard JAR signing.

For example, in the case of MIDP signing and both models are used, the JAR signature should be put to the file first as it modifies the content of the file, and MIDP signing should be applied afterwards.

120.6.3 Permission Management

Applications that use OSGi services must have the corresponding Java 2 permissions granted. In order to simplify the policy management, and ensure that the overall device policy is consistent, application containers should not define separate policy management for each application model; rather they should use the existing OSGi policy management and express the complete security policy by the means of Java 2 permissions with the Conditional Permission Admin service. This way, policy administrator can define the boundaries of the sandbox available for a particular application based on its location, signer or other condition. The application container is responsible for enforcing both the foreign application specific security mechanisms as well as the OSGi granted permissions.

Applications can package permissions as described in the Conditional Permission Admin, section 9.10 in the OSGi R4 Core specification. These permissions will restrict the foreign's application permissions to maximally the permissions in this file scoped by the signer's permissions.

120.7 org.osgi.application

Foreign Application Package Version 1.0.

Bundles wishing to use this package must list the package in the Import-Package header of the bundle's manifest. For example:

```
Import-Package: org.osgi.application; version="[1.0,2.0)"
```

120.7.1 Summary

- *ApplicationContext* - ApplicationContext is the access point for an OSGi-aware application to the features of the OSGi Service Platform.
- *ApplicationServiceEvent* - An event from the Framework describing a service lifecycle change.
- *ApplicationServiceListener* - An ApplicationServiceEvent listener.
- *Framework* - Using this class, OSGi-aware applications can obtain their ApplicationContext.

120.7.2 public interface ApplicationContext

ApplicationContext is the access point for an OSGi-aware application to the features of the OSGi Service Platform. Each application instance will have its own ApplicationContext instance, which will not be reused after destorying the corresponding application instace.

Application instances can obtain their ApplicationContext using the Framework.getApplicationContext method.

The lifecycle of an ApplicationContext instance is bound to the lifecycle of the corresponding application instance. The ApplicationContext becomes available when the application is started and it is invalidated when the application instance is stopped (i.e. the "stop" method of the application activator object returned). All method calls (except getApplicationId() and getInstanceId()) to an invalidated context object result an IllegalStateException.

See Also org.osgi.application.Framework

120.7.2.1 public void addServiceListener(ApplicationServiceListener listener, String referenceName) throws IllegalArgumentException

listener The org.osgi.application.ApplicationServiceListener to be added. It must not be null

referenceName the reference name of a service from the descriptor of the corresponding application. It must not be null.

◻ Adds the specified ApplicationServiceListener object to this context application instance's list of listeners. The specified referenceName is a reference name specified in the descriptor of the corresponding application. The registered listener> will only receive the ApplicationServiceEvents realted to the referred service.

If the listener was already added, calling this method will overwrite the previous registration.

Throws IllegalStateException – If this context application instance has stopped.

NullPointerException – If listener or referenceName is null

IllegalArgumentException – If there is no service in the application descriptor with the specified referenceName.

120.7.2.2 **public void addServiceListener(ApplicationServiceListener listener, String[] referenceNames) throws IllegalArgumentException**

listener The org.osgi.application.ApplicationServiceListener to be added. It must not be null

referenceNames and array of service reference names from the descriptor of the corresponding application. It must not be null and it must not be empty.

◻ Adds the specified ApplicationServiceListener object to this context application instance's list of listeners. The referenceNames parameter is an array of reference name specified in the descriptor of the corresponding application. The registered listener> will only receive the ApplicationService-Events realted to the referred services.

If the listener was already added, calling this method will overwrite the previous registration.

Throws IllegalStateException – If this context application instance has stopped.

NullPointerException – If listener or referenceNames is null

IllegalArgumentException – If referenceNames array is empty or it contains unknown references

120.7.2.3 **public String getApplicationId( )**

◻ This method return the identifier of the correspondig application type. This identifier is the same for the different instances of the same application but it is different for different application type.

Note: this method can safely be called on an invalid ApplicationContext as well.

Returns the identifier of the application type.

See Also org.osgi.service.application.ApplicationDescriptor.getApplicationId()

120.7.2.4 **public String getInstanceId( )**

◻ This method returns the identifier of the corresponding application instace. This identifier is guaranteed to be unique within the scope of the device. Note: this method can safely be called on an invalid ApplicationContext as well.

Returns the unique identifier of the corresponding application instance

See Also org.osgi.service.application.ApplicationHandle.getInstanceId()

120.7.2.5 **public Map getServiceProperties(Object serviceObject)**

serviceObject A service object the application is bound to. It must not be null.

◻ Application can query the service properties of a service object it is bound to. Application gets bound to a service object when it fisrt obtains a reference to the service by calling locateService or locateServices methods.

Returns The service properties associated with the specified service object.

Throws NullPointerException – if the specified serviceObject is null

IllegalArgumentException – if the application is not bound to the specified service object or it is not a service object at all.

IllegalStateException – If this context application instance has stopped.

120.7.2.6   **public Map getStartupParameters( )**

☐ Returns the startup parameters specified when calling the org.osgi.service.application.Application-Descriptor.launch method.

Startup arguments can be specified as name, value pairs. The name must be of type java.lang.String, which must not be null or empty java.lang.String (""), the value can be any object including null.

Returns a java.util.Map containing the startup arguments. It can be null.

Throws IllegalStateException – If this context application instance has stopped.

120.7.2.7   **public Object locateService(String referenceName)**

referenceName The name of a reference as specified in a reference element in this context applications's description. It must not be null

☐ This method returns the service object for the specified referenceName. If the cardinality of the reference is 0..n or 1..n and multiple services are bound to the reference, the service with the highest ranking (as specified in its org.osgi.framework.Constants.SERVICE_RANKING property) is returned. If there is a tie in ranking, the service with the lowest service ID (as specified in its org.osgi.framework.Constants.SERVICE_ID property); that is, the service that was registered first is returned.

Returns A service object for the referenced service or null if the reference cardinality is 0..1 or 0..n and no bound service is available.

Throws NullPointerException – If referenceName is null.

IllegalArgumentException – If there is no service in the application descriptor with the specified referenceName.

IllegalStateException – If this context application instance has stopped.

120.7.2.8   **public Object[] locateServices(String referenceName)**

referenceName The name of a reference as specified in a reference element in this context applications's description. It must not be null.

☐ This method returns the service objects for the specified referenceName.

Returns An array of service object for the referenced service or null if the reference cardinality is 0..1 or 0..n and no bound service is available.

Throws NullPointerException – If referenceName is null.

IllegalArgumentException – If there is no service in the application descriptor with the specified referenceName.

IllegalStateException – If this context application instance has stopped.

120.7.2.9   **public ServiceRegistration registerService(String[] clazzes, Object service, Dictionary properties)**

clazzes The class names under which the service can be located. The class names in this array will be stored in the service's properties under the key org.osgi.framework.Constants.OBJECTCLASS. This parameter must not be null.

service The service object or a ServiceFactory object.

properties The properties for this service. The keys in the properties object must all be String objects. See org.osgi.framework.Constants for a list of standard service property keys. Changes should not be made to this object after calling this method. To update the service's properties the org.osgi.framework.ServiceRegistration.setProperties method must be called. The set of properties may be null if the service has no properties.

☐ Registers the specified service object with the specified properties under the specified class names into the Framework. A org.osgi.framework.ServiceRegistration object is returned. The org.osgi.framework.ServiceRegistration object is for the private use of the application registering the service and should not be shared with other applications. The registering application is defined to be the context application. Bundles can locate the service by using either the org.osgi.frame-work.BundleContext.getServiceReferences or org.osgi.framework.BundleContext.getServiceReference method. Other applications can locate this service by using locateService(String) or locateServices(String) method, if they declared their dependece on the registered service.

An application can register a service object that implements the org.osgi.framework.ServiceFactory interface to have more flexibility in providing service objects to other applications or bundles.

The following steps are required to register a service:

1   If service is not a ServiceFactory, an IllegalArgumentException is thrown if service is not an instanceof all the classes named.
2   The Framework adds these service properties to the specified Dictionary (which may be null): a property named org.osgi.framework.Constants.SERVICE_ID identifying the registration number of the service and a property named org.osgi.framework.Constants.OBJECTCLASS containing all the specified classes. If any of these properties have already been specified by the registering bundle, their values will be overwritten by the Framework.
3   The service is added to the Framework service registry and may now be used by others.
4   A service event of type org.osgi.framework.ServiceEvent.REGISTERED is fired. This event triggers the corresponding ApplicationServiceEvent to be delivered to the applications that registered the appropriate listener.
5   A ServiceRegistration object for this registration is returned.

Returns   A org.osgi.framework.ServiceRegistration object for use by the application registering the service to update the service's properties or to unregister the service.

Throws   IllegalArgumentException – If one of the following is true:
service is null.
service is not a ServiceFactory object and is not an instance of all the named classes in clazzes.
properties contains case variants of the same key name.

NullPointerException – if clazzes is null

SecurityException – If the caller does not have the ServicePermission to register the service for all the named classes and the Java Runtime Environment supports permissions.

IllegalStateException – If this ApplicationContext is no longer valid.

See Also   org.osgi.framework.BundleContext.registerService(java.lang.String[], java.lang.Object, java.util.Dictionary), org.osgi.framework.ServiceRegistration, org.osgi.framework.ServiceFactory

120.7.2.10   public ServiceRegistration registerService(String clazz, Object service, Dictionary properties)

clazz   The class name under which the service can be located. It must not be null

service   The service object or a ServiceFactory object.

properties   The properties for this service.

☐ Registers the specified service object with the specified properties under the specified class name with the Framework.

This method is otherwise identical to registerService(java.lang.String[], java.lang.Object, java.util.Dictionary) and is provided as a convenience when service will only be registered under a single class name. Note that even in this case the value of the service's Constants.OBJECTCLASS property will be an array of strings, rather than just a single string.

Returns A ServiceRegistration object for use by the application registering the service to update the service's properties or to unregister the service.

Throws IllegalArgumentException – If one of the following is true:
service is null.
service is not a ServiceFactory object and is not an instance of the named class in clazz.
properties contains case variants of the same key name.

NullPointerException – if clazz is null

SecurityException – If the caller does not have the ServicePermission to register the service the named class and the Java Runtime Environment supports permissions.

IllegalStateException – If this ApplicationContext is no longer valid.

See Also registerService(java.lang.String[], java.lang.Object, java.util.Dictionary)

120.7.2.11   **public void removeServiceListener(ApplicationServiceListener listener)**

listener The org.osgi.application.ApplicationServiceListener object to be removed.

☐ Removes the specified org.osgi.application.ApplicationServiceListener object from this context application instances's list of listeners.

If listener is not contained in this context application instance's list of listeners, this method does nothing.

Throws IllegalStateException – If this context application instance has stopped.

120.7.3   public class ApplicationServiceEvent
extends ServiceEvent

An event from the Framework describing a service lifecycle change.

ApplicationServiceEvent objects are delivered to a ApplicationServiceListener objects when a change occurs in this service's lifecycle. The delivery of an ApplicationServiceEvent is always triggered by a org.osgi.framework.ServiceEvent. ApplicationServiceEvent extends the content of ServiceEvent with the service object the event is referring to as applications has no means to find the corresponding service object for a org.osgi.framework.ServiceReference. A type code is used to identify the event type for future extendability. The available type codes are defined in org.osgi.framework.ServiceEvent.

OSGi Alliance reserves the right to extend the set of types.

See Also org.osgi.framework.ServiceEvent, ApplicationServiceListener

120.7.3.1   **public ApplicationServiceEvent(int type, ServiceReference reference, Object serviceObject)**

type The event type. Available type codes are defines in org.osgi.framework.ServiceEvent

reference A ServiceReference object to the service that had a lifecycle change. This reference will be used as the source in the java.util.EventObject baseclass, therefore, it must not be null.

serviceObject The service object bound to this application instance. It can be null if this application is not bound to this service yet.

☐ Creates a new application service event object.

Throws IllegalArgumentException – if the specified reference is null.

120.7.3.2   **public Object getServiceObject( )**

☐ This method returns the service object of this service bound to the listener application instance. A service object becomes bound to the application when it first obtains a service object reference to that service by calling the ApplicationContext.locateService or locateServices methods. If the application is not bound to the service yet, this method returns null.

Returns   the service object bound to the listener application or null if it isn't bound to this service yet.

120.7.4   **public interface ApplicationServiceListener**
extends EventListener

An ApplicationServiceEvent listener. When a ServiceEvent is fired, it is converted to an ApplictionServiceEvent and it is synchronously delivered to an ApplicationServiceListener.

ApplicationServiceListener is a listener interface that may be implemented by an application developer.

An ApplicationServiceListener object is registered with the Framework using the ApplicationContext.addServiceListener method. ApplicationServiceListener objects are called with an ApplicationServiceEvent object when a service is registered, modified, or is in the process of unregistering.

ApplicationServiceEvent object delivery to ApplicationServiceListener objects is filtered by the filter specified when the listener was registered. If the Java Runtime Environment supports permissions, then additional filtering is done. ApplicationServiceEvent objects are only delivered to the listener if the application which defines the listener object's class has the appropriate ServicePermission to get the service using at least one of the named classes the service was registered under, and the application specified its dependece on the corresponding service in the application metadata.

ApplicationServiceEvent object delivery to ApplicationServiceListener objects is further filtered according to package sources as defined in ServiceReference.isAssignableTo(Bundle, String).

See Also   ApplicationServiceEvent, ServicePermission

120.7.4.1   **public void serviceChanged(ApplicationServiceEvent event)**

event   The ApplicationServiceEvent object.

☐ Receives notification that a service has had a lifecycle change.

120.7.5   **public final class Framework**

Using this class, OSGi-aware applications can obtain their ApplicationContext.

120.7.5.1   **public static ApplicationContext getApplicationContext(Object applicationInstance)**

applicationInstance   is the activator object of an application instance

☐ This method needs an argument, an object that represents the application instance. An application consists of a set of object, however there is a single object, which is used by the corresponding application container to manage the lifecycle on the application instance. The lifetime of this object equals the lifetime of the application instance; therefore, it is suitable to represent the instance.

The returned ApplicationContext object is singleton for the specified application instance. Subsequent calls to this method with the same application instance must return the same context object

Returns   the ApplicationContext of the specified application instance.

Throws   NullPointerException – If applicationInstance is null

IllegalArgumentException – if called with an object that is not the activator object of an application.

120.8   References

[1]   *OSGi Core Specifications*
http://www.osgi.org/download

121 Blueprint Container Specification

Version 1.0

121.1 Introduction

One of the great promises of object oriented languages was the greater reuse it should enable. However, over time it turned out that reuse was still hard. One of the key reasons was *coupling*. Trying to reuse a few classes usually ended up in dragging in many more classes, that in their turn dragged in even more classes, ad nauseum.

One of the key innovations in the Java language to address this coupling issue were *interfaces*. Interfaces significantly could minimize coupling because they were void of any implementation details. Any class can use an interface, where that interface can be implemented by any other class. However, coupling was still necessary because objects need to be created, and for creating an object its concrete class is necessary.

One of the most successful insights in the software industry of late has been *inversion of control*, or more specific *dependency injection*. With dependency injection, an object is given the collaborators that it needs to work with. By not creating these dependencies itself, the object is not coupled to the concrete type of these implementations and their transitive implementation dependencies. However, these objects are not useful on their own, they can only function when an external party provides these objects with their collaborating objects.

An injection framework creates these objects, and also their concrete dependencies, and wires them together. Injection frameworks can significantly increase reuse and provide increased flexibility. For example, during testing it is possible to inject mocked up objects instead of the actual objects.

There exists a number of these injection frameworks in the market, for example [2] *Spring Framework*, [4] *Guice*, and [5] *Picocontainer*. These containers are configured with XML, Java annotations, or provide automatic configuration based on types.

Decoupling is one of the primary drivers for the OSGi specifications. The module layer provides many mechanisms to hide implementation details and explicitly defines any dependencies. The service layer provides a mechanism to collaborate with other bundles without caring about who that other bundle is. However, using the OSGi APIs to construct an application out of services and objects also implies coupling to these OSGi APIs.

This specification therefore defines a dependency injection framework, specifically for OSGi bundles, that understands the unique dynamic nature of services. It provides an OSGi bundle programming model with minimal implementation dependencies and virtually no accidental complexity in the Java code. Bundles in this programming model contain a number of XML definition resources which are used by the Blueprint Container to wire the application together and start it when the bundle is active.

This Blueprint Container specification is derived from the [3] *Spring Dynamic Modules* project.

121.1.1 Essentials

- *Dependency Injection Framework* – Provide an advanced dependency injection framework for bundles that can create and wire objects and services together into an application.

- *Inversion of Control* – (IOC) A pattern in which a framework/library provides the control over the component instances instead of the other way around. Dependency injection is a form of IOC.
- *Extender Model* – Enable the configuration of components inside a bundle based on configuration data provided by the bundle developer. The life cycle of these components is controlled by the extender based on the extended bundle's state.
- *Unencumbered* – Do not require any special bundle activator or other code to be written inside the bundle in order to have components instantiated and configured.
- *Services* – Enable the usage of OSGi services as injected dependencies.
- *Dependencies* – Allow components to depend on other components like services and beans as well as register as services, with the full breadth of the OSGi capabilities.
- *Dynamicity* – Minimize the complexity of using the dynamicity of services
- *Business Logic* – A focus on writing business logic in regular Java classes that are not required to implement certain framework APIs or contracts in order to integrate with a container.
- *Declarative* – This facilitates independent testing of components and reduces environment dependencies.
- *Familiarity* – Familiar to enterprise Java developers.

121.1.2 Entities

- *Blueprint Extender* – The bundle that creates and injects component instances for a Blueprint bundle as configured in that Blueprint bundle's XML definition resources.
- *Blueprint Container* – Represents the activities of the Blueprint Extender for a specific Blueprint Bundle.
- *Blueprint Bundle* – A bundle that is being constructed by the Blueprint Container because it has a Bundle-Blueprint header or it contains XML resources in the OSGI-INF/blueprint directory.
- *Manager* – A manager is responsible for the life cycle of all *component instances* for one *component definition.* There are the following types of managers. A manager is a *bean manager*, a *service reference manager*, or a *service manager*. A manager can have *explicit* and *implicit* dependencies on other manager. During instantiation and runtime, a manager can *provide* a component instance to be injected or used in other ways.
- *Component* – A loosely defined term for the application building blocks and their infrastructure. Components are instantiated into *component instances* by a *manager* that is configured with a *Component Metadata* subclass that is derived from a *Component Definition.*
- *Component Instance* – An object that is part of the application. Component Instances are created and managed by their component *manager.*
- *Component Definition* – Configuration data used by a manager to construct and manage component instances. This configuration data is represented in Metadata, an interface hierarchy starting with the *Metadata* interface.
- *Bean Manager* – A manager that has metadata for creating Java objects and injecting them with objects and component instances that come from other managers it implicitly depends on.
- *Service Manager* – A manager that handles the registration of a service object that is provided by a component instance.
- *Service Reference Manager* – The general name for the reference and reference-list managers.
- *Reference Manager* – A manager that handles the dependency on a single OSGi service.
- *Reference-list Manager* – A manager that handles the dependency on a list of OSGi services.
- *Environment Manager* – A manager that can provide information from the Bundle's environment. For example, the BlueprintContainer object is made available through an environment manager.
- *Target* – A manager type useful in a callback context. These are the ref (which is an indirection to), a reference, and a bean manager.
- *Property* – A conceptual instance variable of a component instance provided by a bean manager that is set on the component instance with a corresponding set<Name> method.
- *Argument* – Metadata for an argument in a constructor or method.
- *Type Converter* – A component instance defined, or referenced, in the type-converters section implementing the Converter interface.

Figure 121.1   *Blueprint Class and Service Overview*

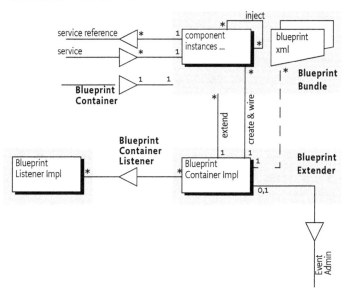

121.1.3   Synopsis

The Blueprint Extender bundle waits for Blueprint bundles. These are bundles that contain Blueprint XML resources called the definitions. These XML resources can be found in a fixed location or pointed to from a manifest header. When a Blueprint extender bundle detects that a Blueprint bundle is ready, it creates a Blueprint Container to manage that Blueprint bundle.

The Blueprint Container then parses the definitions into metadata objects. All top-level elements in the definitions are ComponentMetadata objects and are registered in the Blueprint Container by their id.

For each of the ComponentMetadata objects, the Blueprint Container has a corresponding component manager. For example, a BeanMetadata object relates to a Bean Manager instance. There are the following types of managers:

- *Bean Managers* – Can provide general objects that are properly constructed and configured
- *Service Managers* – Can register services
- *Service Reference Managers* – Provide proxies to one or more services. there are two sub-types: reference-list and reference.
- *Environment Managers* – Holding environment values like the Blueprint Bundle object

After creation, all managers are not yet activated. A manager is activated on demand when it has to provide a component instance for the first time.

All service reference managers track services in the service registry in order to determine if they are satisfied or not. If not, the Blueprint Container can optionally start a *grace* period. During the grace period, the Blueprint Container waits for all mandatory service reference managers to become satisfied. If this does not happen during the grace period, the Blueprint Container must abort the initialization.

From now on, the Blueprint Container is ready to provide component instances. Whenever a manager is asked to provide a component instance for the first time, the manager is activated. This activation will first request all its dependencies to provide a component instance, activating these managers if not already activated, recursively.

However, the activation needs a trigger to start. There are two triggers.

- *Service Request* – All service managers must have a Service Factory registered with the OSGi service registry whenever that service manager is enabled, see *Enabled* on page 559.
- *Eager Managers* – To kick start the application in the bundle, the Blueprint Container must ask all eager managers to provide a component instance, thereby activating these managers, see *Eager Instantiation* on page 542.

Service references must actuate their reference listeners when they are activated.

Bean managers have a scope. This scope can be `singleton`, where the manager always provides the same object, or `prototype`, where the manager creates a new object for each request.

Service reference managers provide proxies to the actual service objects and fetch the service object lazily. They provide a constant reference that dampen the dynamics of the underlying service objects.

If the Blueprint Container has successfully activated the eager managers, it will register a Blueprint Container service.

When the Blueprint Container must be destroyed because: the Blueprint bundle has stopped, there is a failure, or the Blueprint extender is stopped, then the Blueprint Container service is unregistered and all managers are deactivated. This will unregister any services and disable listeners, which release the component instances. Then all component instances are destroyed in reverse dependency order. That is, a component instance is destroyed when no other component instances depend on it.

121.2   Managers

The key feature of the Blueprint Container specification is to let the application in the bundle be constructed in the proper order from objects that are not required to be aware of Blueprint, OSGi, or even each other. These objects are called *component instances*. The active entity that orchestrates the life cycle of the bundle application is the *Blueprint Container*. It is configured by XML resources in the Blueprint bundle. The Blueprint Container is responsible for construction and configuration of the component instances as well as the interaction with the service registry.

Inside the Blueprint Container, component instances are managed by a *manager*. A manager is configured with one Component Definition, for example a bean definition, and can then provide one or more component instances. Such a configured manager instance is also loosely called a *component*.

A manager can have additional behavior associated with it. This behavior is controlled by the manager's *type*. This specification defines a number of manager types: bean, service, environment, reference, and reference-list. These types are further defined in the next section.

These managers are conceptual, they are not visible in the API of this specification. That is, an implementation is free to implement the specification without these objects as long as the externally observable behavior is the same.

As an example, a trivial echo service:

```
<blueprint>
    <service id="echoService"
         interface="com.acme.Echo" ref="echo"/>
    <bean id="echo" class="com.acme.EchoImpl">
      <property name="message" value="Echo: "/>
    </bean>
</blueprint>
```

```
public interface Echo {
  public String echo(String m);
}
public class EchoImpl implements Echo {
  String message;
  public void setMessage(String m) {
    this.message= m;
  }
  public void echo(String s) { return message + s; }
}
```

The example defines two *top-level* managers: echoService and echo. The echoService manager is of type *service*, and the echo manager is of type *bean*. The service manager is responsible for registering an OSGi service, where the service object will be the component instance provided by the echo manager. The echo component instance gets a message injected.

As seen from the example, managers can use component instances from other managers to construct their component instances. The use of other managers creates an *implicit dependency*. Managers can also declare *explicit dependencies*. Dependencies are transitive, see *Manager Dependencies* on page 533 for more information. In the previous example, the echoService service manager depends on the echo manager, this is an implicit dependency.

Managers have their own life cycle. They are conceptually created after the Blueprint Container has decided to run the application, see *Blueprint Life-Cycle* on page 537. However, the intention of this specification is to allow the bundle application to lazily *activate*. That is, no application code is used until there is an external trigger like a service request. Service reference and service managers exhibit side effects in their interaction with the service registry before activation, but they must not request component instances until they are activated. A manager must always be atomically activated before it provides its first component instance. During activation, listeners are actuated and notified, service objects are requested, etc. The details are described in the appropriate manager's type description.

Each manager type has an associated *component metadata* type. Component Metadata is used to configure a manager. XML definition resources in the bundle define the source for this Metadata. In the previous example, the service and bean XML element are translated to a ServiceMetadata and BeanMetadata object respectively.

The Blueprint Container maintains a registry of managers by their *id*. These are the managers that are called the *top-level* managers. Top level managers are managers defined as child elements of the top XML blueprint element or bean managers in the type-converters element. Their Metadata is registered under their id (or calculated id) in the Blueprint Container. All top level managers share a single namespace. That is, it is an error if the same id is used multiple times or attempts to override the built-in environment managers.

Top level managers can depend on other top level managers but there are many places where a manager can depend on an *inlined* manager. In these places, a complete manager can be defined inside another manager. Such inlined managers are always *anonymous*: they must not have an id and must not be registered as a top-level manager. Inlined beans are further constrained to always have prototype scope. That is, every time they are asked to provide a component instance, they must return a different object.

When the Blueprint Container must be *destroyed*, all singleton component instances that have been created must be destroyed. This must first *deactivate* all activated managers. All these managers must release their dependencies on any component instances they hold. Then the Blueprint Container must destroy all singleton component instances. The order of this destruction must be such that a component instance is only destroyed if there are no other component instances depending on it. See *Reverse Dependency Order* on page 534.

The relations between manager types, component instances, metadata and the Blueprint Container is schematically depicted in Figure 121.2 on page 532.

Figure 121.2   *Managers and Metadata*

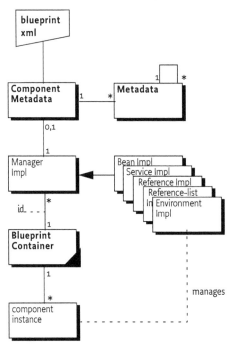

121.2.1   Manager Types

Blueprint only supports a fixed set of the following *manager types*:

- *Bean* – A bean manager provides regular Java objects as component instances. It has the following features:
  - Construction via class name, static factory method, or a factory method on a *target*. A *target* is a reference to a top level manager of type bean or service reference, or a referral to a top level manager of those types.
  - Can have *arguments* for a constructor or factory method.
  - Can have *properties* that are injected.
  - Manages a singleton or creates objects on demand depending on its *scope*.
  - Life cycle callbacks for end of initialization and destruction.

  See *Bean Manager* on page 548 for more details.
- *Reference* – Reference managers track a service in the OSGi service registry. When activated, they provide a proxy to a service object. See *Service Reference Managers* on page 560 for more details. A reference is satisfied when its selection matches a service in the registry.
- *Reference-list* – Reference-list managers track multiple services. A reference-list is satisfied when its selection matches one or more services in the registry. See *Service Reference Managers* on page 560 for more details.
- *Service* – Service managers maintain the registration of an OSGi service object. Service managers provide a proxied ServiceRegistration object so that the application code has a constant reference, even if the service is unregistered and then registered again. A service manager is *enabled* if all the mandatory service references in its dependencies are satisfied. See *Service Manager* on page 553.
- *Environment* – Environment managers provide access to the environment of the Blueprint bundle, for example its Bundle Context. See *Blueprint Container* on page 581 for more details.

121.2.2   ## Metadata Objects

Metadata objects hold the configuration information (from the Component Definition) for the managers. These metadata objects represent the element structure found in the XML definitions in canonical form. Each element in the XML has a corresponding Metadata sub-type that has a name that maps directly to the element. For example, the bean element represents the bean manager that has its configuration data defined in the BeanMetadata interface.

There are Metadata interfaces for all the manager types, except the environment type. Some dependency injections require the construction of arrays, maps, properties, simple objects, etc. For these type of objects, additional Metadata sub-interfaces are defined; these interfaces provide the information to construct the basic programming types. For example, the CollectionMetadata interface contains the information to construct an Array or Collection of a given type, where its member values are defined by other Metadata objects.

The set of Metadata types is fixed in this specification, just like the set of manager types. It is impossible to extend this set with user defined Metadata types. For more information about Metadata, see *Metadata* on page 585.

121.2.3   ## Activation and Deactivation

Managers are created after all the definitions are parsed. Some managers can already show some activity, for example service managers register a Service Factory with the OSGi service registry. However, in this state a manager should attempt to not use any resources from the Blueprint bundle. A manager must be atomically activated when it has to provide its first component instance. During activation it can perform a manager specific initialization that will actually consume resources from the Blueprint bundle. This activation must be atomic. That is, if a manager is being activated then other threads must block until the activation is completed.

Deactivation only happens during the destruction of the Blueprint Container. During deactivation, a manager must release any dependencies on resources of the Blueprint bundle. No components instances are destroyed during deactivation because the singleton component instance destruction must happen after all managers are deactivated.

Each manager type has a dedicated section that describes what must happen during its activation and deactivation.

121.2.4   ## Manager Dependencies

Managers that refer to other managers depend on these managers transitively. For example, a service manager depends directly on the manager that provides the service object. In its turn, that service object could depend on any provided objects that were used to construct and inject this service object, and so on. This transitive set of dependencies are called *implicit dependencies* because these dependencies are implicitly created by the use of other managers in the Component Definitions.

Managers can also be configured with *explicit dependencies*. The XML definitions for all managers have a depends-on attribute with a whitespace delimited list of manager ids. Each of these depends-on managers must provide an object, that will be ignored, before the component instance for the first manager is returned.

There is no ordering guarantee between independent sets of dependencies. The dependency graph is based on the managers, not the component instances. For example, the following definition:

```
<blueprint default-activation='eager'>
  <bean id='A'...>  <argument ref='B'> </bean>
  <bean id='B' depends-on='C E'...>
    <argument ref='C'>
  </bean>
  <bean id='C' scope='prototype' ...>
    <argument ref='D'>
```

```
        </bean>
        <bean id='D' .../>
        <bean id='E' ...> <argument ref='C'/> </bean>
        <bean id='F' depends-on='B' activation="lazy"/>
    </blueprint>
```

After initialization, there will be the following component instances: a, b, d, e, and three c's. Lower case names are used for instances, the corresponding upper case is its manager. The ordering guarantee is that manager D is activated before manager C, manager C is activated before manager E and B, manager E is activated before manager B, and manager B is activated before manager A. There will be no component instance f created because F is a lazy manager. There are three c's because manager E and B have an implicit dependency on C and manager B has an additional explicit dependency, totalling 3 dependencies. One of these c's is an orphan and will be garbage collected over time because it is not referred to by any component instance.

The example is depicted in Figure 121.3 on page 534.

Figure 121.3   *Dependency Graph after initialization*

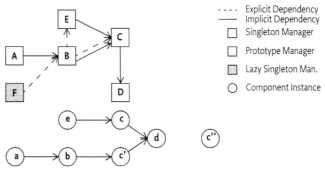

121.2.5   Reverse Dependency Order

The destruction of component instances must be done in *reverse dependency order*. This concept is defined as only destroying a singleton component instance (in a manager specific way) when no other activated singleton component instance has an implicit or explicit dependency on it. That is, a component instance has no more field references to other component instances. A component that never was activated does not have any dependencies.

This strategy will ensure that a component instance cannot have an instance field that refers to an component instance that has been destroyed.

Deactivating the manager will release its dependencies, which then frees up other component instances until all component instances are destroyed, or there are cyclic references. In the case of cyclic dependencies, the order of destruction is undefined.

In the example depicted in Figure 121.3 on page 534, the previous rules imply that component instance a can be immediately destroyed first because it has no clients. After component instance a is destroyed, component instance b becomes free because no other component instances refer to it. The explicit dependency from manager F to manager B was never activated, so it is not taken into account. The destruction of component instance b frees up component instance e and c because now the explicit dependency from manager B to manager E and manager B to manager C have been released. Manager C is deactivated but no component instances are destructed because it has prototype scope; these managers do not destroy their component instances. Then component instance d can be destructed.

121.2.6   **Cyclic Dependencies**

The implicit and explicit dependencies of a component form a dependency graph. In the ideal case, this graph should be free from *cycles*. A cycle occurs when a set of one or more managers find themselves in their own implicit or explicit dependencies. For example:

```
public class A { public A(B b); }
public class B { public void setA(A a); }

<bean id="a" class="A"> <argument ref="b"/> </bean>
<bean id="b" class="B"> <property name="a" ref="a"/> </bean>
```

In this example, the cycle is the set {a,b}. Managers can be part of multiple cycles.

When a member of a cycle is requested to provide a component instance, the Blueprint Container must break the cycle by finding one *breaking member* in the cycle's members. A breaking member must use property injection for the dependency that causes the cycle. The Blueprint Container can pick any suitable member of the cycle for breaking member, if no such member can be found, then initialization fails or the getComponentInstance method must throw a Component Definition Exception.

In the previous example, manager b can be a breaking member because it uses the property injection for the cyclic dependency on manager a. Manager a cannot be a breaking member because the cyclic dependency is caused by a constructor argument, a breaking member must use property injection for the cyclic dependency to be broken.

A breaking member must return a partially initialized component instance when it is asked to provide an object. A partially initialized object has done all possible initialization but has not yet been called with the initMethod (if specified) nor has it been injected any of the properties that causes a cycle. The *finalization* of the partially initialized component instance must be delayed until the breaking member has been injected in all referring members of the cycles. Finalization means injecting any remaining unset properties and calling of the initMethod, if specified.

The consequence of partially initialized component instances is that they can be used before they have all properties set, applications must be aware of this.

All partially initialized component instances must be finalized before the Blueprint Container enters the Runtime phase and before a call to the getComponentInstance method returns a component instance. User code that causes a dynamic cycle by recursively calling the getComponentInstance method must be detected and cause a failure, these cycles cannot be broken.

All detected cycles should be logged.

Consider the following example:

```
public class A {
 public A(B b) {}
}
public class B {
 public B(A a) {}
}
```

And the configuration:

```
<bean id="a" class="A"> <argument value="b"/>      </bean>
<bean id="b" class="B"> <argument value="a"/>      </bean>
```

In this case, the cycle cannot be broken because neither manager qualifies as breaking manager because they have a constructor/factory argument dependency. That is, it is impossible to construct an object without using the dependency. However, consider the following example:

```
public class A {
 public A(B b) {}
```

```
}
public class B {
 public B(C c) {}
}
public class C {
   public void setA(A a) {}
}
```

And the configuration:

```
<bean id="a" class="A"> <argument value="b"/>        </bean>
<bean id="b" class="B"> <argument value="c"/>        </bean>
<bean id="c" class="C" init-method="done">
    <property name="a" ref="a"/>
</bean>
```

This configuration is depicted in Figure 121.4 on page 536. This cycle {a,b,c} can be broken by selecting manager c as the breaking member. If manager a is requested to provide a component instance for the first time, then the following sequence takes place:

```
activate a
  activate b
    activate c
      c = new C()
    b = new B(c)
  a = new A(b)
  c.seta(a)
  c.done()
return a
```

Figure 121.4 *Cyclic Dependency*

Cycles must be broken, if possible, both for singleton managers as well as prototype beans. That is, the following definition is not allowed to attempt to create an infinite loop:

```
<bean id="a" scope="singleton" class="A">
    <property name="a" ref="a">
</bean>
```

The previous definition must create an A object that refers to itself.

121.2.7   **Eager Managers**

The Blueprint Container can force the activation of the application in the Blueprint bundle with *eager* managers. An eager manager is a manager that has the activation set to eager. A bean manager can only be eager if it has singleton scope.

Eager managers are explicitly activated by asking them to provide a component instance after all other initialization is done. A bundle that wants to be lazily initialized should not define any eager managers.

121.3   Blueprint Life-Cycle

A bundle is a *Blueprint bundle* if it contains one or more blueprint XML *definition* resources in the OSGI-INF/blueprint directory or it contains the Bundle-Blueprint manifest header referring to existing resources.

A *Blueprint extender* is an implementation of this specification and must track blueprint bundles that are *type compatible* for the Blueprint packages and initialize them appropriately. The timing and ordering of the initialization process is detailed in the following section.

There should be only one Blueprint extender present in an OSGi framework because this specification does not specify a way to resolve the conflicts that arise when two Blueprint extenders extend the same Blueprint bundle.

121.3.1   Class Space Compatibility

A Blueprint extender must not manage a Blueprint bundle if there is a class space incompatibility for the org.osgi.service.blueprint packages. For example, if the Blueprint bundle uses the BlueprintContainer class, then it must import the org.osgi.service.blueprint.container package. The Blueprint extender and the Blueprint bundle must then share the same class space for this package. Type compatibility can be verified by loading a class from the blueprint packages via the Blueprint extender bundle and the Blueprint bundle's loadClass methods. If the Blueprint bundle cannot load the class or the class is identical to the class loaded from the extender, then the two bundles are compatible for the given package. If the Blueprint extender is not class space compatible with the Blueprint bundle, then Blueprint extender must not start to manage the Blueprint bundle.

121.3.2   Initialization of a Blueprint Container

A Blueprint extender manages the application life cycle of Blueprint bundles based on:

- The Blueprint bundle state,
- The Blueprint definitions,
- The Blueprint extender's bundle state
- The class space compatibility

All activities on behalf of the Blueprint bundle must use the Bundle Context of the Blueprint bundle. All dynamic class loads must use the Blueprint bundle's Bundle loadClass method.

The following sections describe a linear process that handles one Blueprint bundle as if it was managed by a special thread, that is, waits are specified if the thread waits. Implementations are likely to use a state machine instead for each managed Blueprint bundle, the linear description is only used for simplicity.

In the following description of the initialization steps, the Blueprint Container will update its state. State changes are broadcast as events, see *Events* on page 582.

If any failure occurs during initialization, or the Blueprint bundle or Blueprint extender bundle is stopped, the Blueprint Container must be destroyed, see *Failure* on page 538. These checks are not indicated in the normal flow for clarity.

121.3.2.1   Initialization Steps

The initialization process of a Blueprint Container is defined in the following steps:

1   Wait until a blueprint bundle is *ready*. A blueprint bundle is ready when it is in the ACTIVE state, and for blueprint bundles that have a lazy activation policy, also in the STARTING state.
2   Prepare, verify if this Blueprint bundle must be managed, see *Preparing* on page 540.
3   State = CREATING
4   Parse the XML definition resources.
5   Service reference managers must start tracking their satisfiablity without actually activating. See *Tracking* on page 541.

6 If all mandatory service references are satisfied, or the blueprint.graceperiod is false, then go to step 9.

7 State = GRACE_PERIOD

8 Perform the *grace period*. This period waits until all mandatory service references are satisfied. See *Grace Period* on page 541. This step fails if the mandatory dependencies are not satisfied at the end of the grace period.

9 The Blueprint Container is now ready to provide component instances.

10 Service managers must have a Service Factory registered during the periods that they are enabled. See *Service Registration* on page 541.

11 Ask all eager managers to provide a component instance. See *Eager Instantiation* on page 542.

12 State = CREATED

13 Register the Blueprint Container

14 The components are now active and perform their function until the Blueprint bundle or the Blueprint extender bundle are stopped.

15 State = DESTROYING

16 Perform the Destroy phase, see *Destroy the Blueprint Container* on page 542.

17 State = DESTROYED

121.3.2.2 Failure

If at any time there is a failure, the Blueprint Container must:

1 State = FAILURE

2 Unregister the Blueprint Container service.

3 Destroy the Blueprint Container.

4 Wait for the Blueprint bundle to be stopped.

121.3.2.3 Diagram

This initialization process is depicted in Figure 121.5 on page 539.

Figure 121.5   *Blueprint Bundle Initialization*

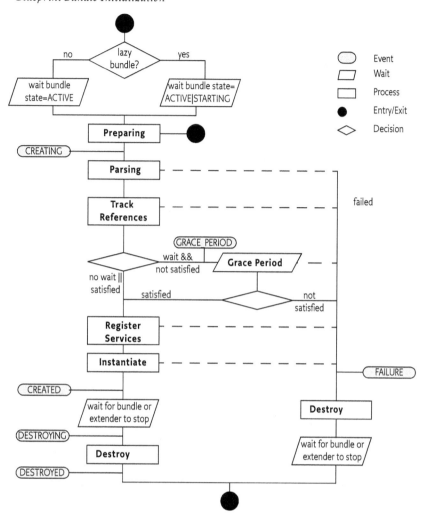

121.3.3 Extensions

A compliant implementation of this specification must follow the rules as outlined. However, implementations can provide functional extensions by including attributes or elements of other
namespaces. For example, a Blueprint extender implementation that supports proxying of certain
classes and a number of additional type converters could include a http://www.acme.com/
extensions namespace that adds an extensions attribute on the blueprint element:

```xml
<?xml version="1.0" encoding="UTF-8"?>
<blueprint
 xmlns="http://www.osgi.org/xmlns/blueprint/v1.0.0"
 xmlns:ext="http://www.acme.com/extensions"

  ext:extensions="proxyClasses"
>
  ...
</blueprint>
```

Blueprint extenders that detect the use of an unrecognized namespace must fail to signal a portability problem.

121.3.4   Preparing

Blueprint definitions are stored as resources in the Blueprint bundle. If a Bundle-Blueprint manifest header is defined, then this header contains a list of paths. The Bundle-Blueprint header has the following syntax:

```
Bundle-Blueprint   ::= header
                       // Core 3.2.4 Common Header Syntax
```

This specification does not define any attributes or directives for this header. Implementations can provide proprietary parameters that should be registered with the OSGi Alliance to prevent name collisions. The non-localized version of the header must be used.

The last component of each path in the Bundle-Blueprint header may use wildcards so that Bundle.findEntries can be used to locate the XML document within the bundle and its fragments. The findEndtries method must always be used in the non-recursive mode. Valid paths in the header have one of the following forms:

- *absolute path* – The path to a resource in the fragment or directory, this resource must exist. For example cnf/start.xml.
- *directory* – The path to directory in a fragment or main bundle, the path must end in a slash ('/'). The pattern used in the findEntries method must then be *.xml. The directory is allowed to be empty.
- *pattern* – The last component of the path specifies a filename with optional wildcards. The part before is the path of directory in the bundle or one of its fragments. These two parts specify the parameter to findEntries. It is allowed to have no matching resources. An example of a pattern is: cnf/*.xml.

If no resources can be found, then the Blueprint bundle will not be managed and the initialization exits.

For example, the following header will read the resources /lib/account.xml, /security.bp, and all resources which path ends in .xml in the /cnf directory:

```
Bundle-Blueprint: lib/account.xml, security.bp, cnf/*.xml
```

If the Bundle-Blueprint header is not defined, then its default value is:

```
OSGI-INF/blueprint/*.xml
```

A Bundle-Blueprint manifest header specified in a fragment is ignored by the Blueprint Container. However, XML documents referenced by a bundle's Bundle-Blueprint manifest header, or its default, may be contained in attached fragments, as defined by the findEntries method.

If the Bundle-Blueprint header is specified but empty, then the Blueprint bundle must not be managed. This can be used to temporarily disable a Blueprint bundle.

121.3.5   Parsing

The Blueprint Container must parse the XML definitions into the Blueprint Container's metadata registry. Parsing fails if:

- A path from the Bundle-Blueprint header cannot be found in the bundle or any of its fragments.
- An XML definition does not validate against its schema.
- The XML elements do not meet one or more of their constraints
- Any errors occur

For failure, see *Failure* on page 543.

121.3.6   Tracking

Service reference managers must track the service registry to see if they are satisfied or not. These managers must not be activated to register these service listeners. That is, no component instances for the reference listeners are obtained until the service reference manager is activated.

121.3.7   Grace Period

A Blueprint Container by default will wait for its dependencies in the *grace period*. However, this can be overridden with a directive on the Bundle-SymbolicName header of the Blueprint bundle:

*   blueprint.graceperiod (true|false) – If set to true, then the Blueprint Container must enter the grace period and wait for dependencies, this is the default. Otherwise, it must skip the grace period and progress to the next phase regardless if there are any unsatisfied service references.

The purpose of the grace period is to handle the initialization of multiple bundles *gracefully*. The grace period will first wait a configurable time for all mandatory service references to become satisfied, or for the bundle to stop. If these mandatory services are satisfied, then the grace period succeeds, otherwise it will fail. If the bundle is stopped during the grace period, then the Blueprint Container must be destroyed.

During the waiting period services can come and go. Each time such a service event takes place that involves any of the mandatory service references, the Blueprint Container must send out another GRACE_PERIOD event if that event does not result in ending the grace period. The event contains the complete filters of the unsatisfied service references, see *Blueprint Event* on page 583.

The wait time for the grace period is defined in a directive on the Bundle-SymbolicName header of the Blueprint bundle:

*   blueprint.timeout (Integer >= 0) – The time to wait in the grace period for dependencies to become satisfied in milliseconds. The default is 300000, which is 5 minutes. If the timeout is 0, an indefinite wait will take place.

OSGi services are dynamic, therefore the grace period does not guarantee that all mandatory service references are still available. It only guarantees that at one moment in time they were available. A mandatory reference can become *unsatisfied* at any moment in time when a service is not available. See the *Service Dynamics* on page 579 for a description of how this is handled.

For example, the following header will make the bundle wait a maximum of 10 seconds for its mandatory service references to be satisfied. These dependencies must be satisfied, or a failure occurs.

```
Bundle-SymbolicName: com.acme.foo;
    blueprint.graceperiod:=true;
    blueprint.timeout:= 10000
```

121.3.8   Service Registration

All service managers must ensure that a Service Factory object is registered as a service when that service is *enabled*. Enabled means that all of the mandatory service references in its dependencies are satisfied.

Once the Service Factory is registered, any bundle can get the corresponding service object. Such a request must activate the service manager, if it is not already activated. Activation of a service manager must obtain a component instance from the Blueprint Container for the service object and any registration listeners. The registration listeners are then actuated and notified of the initial state.

121.3.9   Eager Instantiation

After all initialization is done, the Blueprint Container is ready. It is now possible to request component instances. If a bundle needs immediate startup because they cannot wait until they are triggered, then it should set the activation of its bean managers to eager. The Blueprint Container must
request all eager managers to provide a component instance in this instantiation phase, see also *Lazy
and Eager* on page 547.

121.3.10   Runtime Phase

The Blueprint Container must be registered as a service with the following service properties:

- osgi.blueprint.container.symbolicname – The bundle symbolic name of the Blueprint bundle
- osgi.blueprint.container.version – The version of the Blueprint bundle

The Blueprint Container service must only be available during the runtime phase when initialization
has succeeded.

As long as the Blueprint extender and the Blueprint bundle are active, the application is in the runtime phase. The component instances perform their requested functionality in collaboration. The
Blueprint Container can be used to provide objects from the defined managers, get information about
the configuration, and general state information, see *Blueprint Container* on page 581.

121.3.11   Destroy the Blueprint Container

The Blueprint Container must be destroyed when any of the following conditions becomes true:

- The Blueprint bundle is stopped, that is, it is no longer ready.
- The Blueprint extender is stopped
- One of the initialization phases failed.

Destroying the Blueprint Container must occur synchronously with the Bundle STOPPING event if
that caused any of the previous conditions. For example, if the Blueprint extender is stopped, it must
synchronously destroy all Blueprint Containers it has created.

Destroying the Blueprint Container means:

1 Unregistering the Blueprint Container service
2 Deactivating all managers.
3 Destroying all component instances in reverse dependency order, see *Reverse Dependency Order* on
   page 534.

A Blueprint Container must continue to follow the destruction even when component instances
throw exceptions or other problems occur. These errors should be logged.

If the Blueprint extender is stopped, then all its active Blueprint Containers must be destroyed in an
orderly fashion, synchronously with the stopping of the Blueprint extender bundle. Blueprint Containers must use the following algorithm to destroy multiple Blueprint Containers:

1 Destroy Blueprint Containers that do not have any services registered that are in use by other
   bundles. More recently installed bundles must be destroyed before later installed bundles, that is,
   reverse bundle id order.
2 The previous step can have released services, therefore, repeat step 1 until no more Blueprint Containers can be destroyed.
3 If there are still Blueprint Containers that are not destroyed, then destroy the Blueprint Container
   with:
   - The highest ranking (lowest number) registered service, or if a tie
   - The highest registered service id
   If there are still Bundle Containers to be destroyed, retry step 1

During the shutting down of an OSGi framework, it is likely that many bundles are stopped near simultaneously. The Blueprint extender should be able to handle this case, without deadlock, when the stop of a Blueprint bundle overlaps with the stop of the Blueprint extender bundle.

121.3.12 Failure

If a failure occurs during the initialization of the Blueprint bundle, then first a FAILURE event must be posted, see *Events* on page 582. Then the Blueprint Container should be destroyed, ensuring that no uninitialized or half initialized objects are destroyed. Failures should be logged if a Log Service is present.

121.3.13 Lazy

The Blueprint Container specification specifically allows lazy initialization of the application in the Blueprint bundle. No component instances are created until an eager manager is activated, or a service request comes in.

If no eager managers are defined then no component instances are provided until an external trigger occurs. This trigger can be a service request or a call to the getComponentInstance method of the Blueprint Container, which is registered as a service. This allows a Blueprint bundle to not create component instances, and thereby load classes, until they are really needed. This can significantly reduce startup time.

Some features of the component definitions can only be verified by inspecting a class. This class loading can break the lazy initialization of a Blueprint bundle. It is therefore allowed to delay this kind of verification until the activation of a manager.

This lazy behavior is independent of the bundle's lazy activation policy. Though the Blueprint extender recognizes this policy to detect when the bundle is ready (for a lazy activated bundle the STARTING state is like the ACTIVE state), it is further ignored. That is, the relation between a Bundle Activator that is lazily activated and the Blueprint Container is not defined.

121.4 Blueprint Definitions

The Blueprint XML resources in a bundle are the *definitions*. Each definition can include multiple namespaces. Implementations of the Blueprint core namespace must strictly follow this specification, if they add additional behavior they must add additional namespaces that are actually used in the definitions to signal the deviation from this specification.

The namespace for the core Blueprint definition resources is:

```
http://www.osgi.org/xmlns/blueprint/v1.0.0
```

Blueprint resources that use this core specification must have as top the blueprint element. The following example shows the body of a Blueprint definition:

```
<?xml version="1.0" encoding="UTF-8"?>
<blueprint
 xmlns="http://www.osgi.org/xmlns/blueprint/v1.0.0">
  ...
</blueprint>
```

The recommended prefix for the Blueprint core namespace is bp.

All elements in the Blueprint namespace are prepared for future extensions and provide a description child element in most positions.

121.4.1   **XML**

In the following sections, the XML is explained using the normal syntax notation used for headers. There is, however, one addition to the normal usage specific to XML, and that is the use of the angled brackets (‹›). A term enclosed in angled brackets, indicates the use of a real element. Without the angled brackets it is the definition of a term that is expanded later to a one or more other terms or elements. For example:

```
people      ::= <person> *
person      ::= <child>* address?
address     ::= <fr> | <us> | <nl>
```

Describes for example the following XML:

```
<people>
    <person id="mieke">
        <child name="mischa"/>
        <child name="thomas"/>
        <fr zip="34160"/>
    </person>
</people>
```

Attributes are described in tables that define how they map to their corresponding Metadata. As a rule, the XML elements and attributes are expressed directly in the Metadata.

The text in the following sections is a normative description of the semantics of the schema. However, the structure information is illustrative. For example, all description elements have been ignored for brevity. The exact structure is described by the XML schema, see *Blueprint XML Schema* on page 586.

There are a number of convenient XML types used in the following sections. There schema types are defined here:

- fqn – A fully qualified Java class name in dotted form, for example java.lang.String.
- method – A valid Java method name, for example setFoo.
- NCName – A string syntax for names defined in [9] *XML Schema*.
- ID – A string syntax for ids defined in [9] *XML Schema*.
- type – A name of a Java type including arrays, see the next section *Syntax for Java types* on page 544.
- target – An inline bean, reference, or ref, see *Target* on page 547.
- object – An object value, see *Object Values* on page 566

In several cases, the actual syntax depends on the type conversion. This type of syntax is indicated with ‹‹type›› indicates that the syntax of the string depends on the type conversion, where ten type is usually given as a parameter on the same Metadata.

121.4.2   **Syntax for Java types**

A number of elements can refer to a Java type, for example the value element has a type attribute and a map element has a key-type attribute. The syntax for these types is as follows:

```
type        ::= fqn array
array       ::= '[]' *
```

Where fqn is the fully qualified name of a Java class or interface, or the name of a primitive type.

For example:

```
<value type="java.lang.String[]"/>
```

It is not possible to specify generic information in this syntax.

121.4.3   XML and Metadata

The Blueprint Container parses the XML into Metadata objects, see *Metadata* on page 585. During parsing, the XML parser validates against the detailed Blueprint schema and will therefore catch many errors. However, the XML schema and the Metadata type are not equivalent. The XML contains many conveniences that the Blueprint Container must convert to the canonical type in the Metadata. A number of general rules apply for this conversion:

- An absent attribute will result in null, unless the schema element provides a default value. In that case, the default must be returned from the Metadata object. That is, a default is indistinguishable from a specifically set value.
- Defaults from the blueprint element are filled in the Metadata objects, they are not available in any other way.
- Strings are trimmed from extraneous whitespace, as described in XML normalization.
- Child elements are represented by List objects, in the order of their definition. If no child elements are specified, the list will be empty.

For example, the activation feature reflects the total of default-activation and activation attributes but does not reflect that a prototype scope always makes a bean lazy. That is, even if activation is eager, the bean must still have lazy activation when it has prototype scope.

121.4.4   <blueprint>

The blueprint element is the top element. The definitions consist of two sections: the type-converter section and the managers section.

```
blueprint           ::= <type-converters> manager*
manager             ::= <bean> | <service>
                            | service-reference
service-reference   ::= <reference> | <reference-list>
type-converters     ::= <bean> | <ref>
```

In this specification, the reference and reference-list managers are referred to as *service references* when their differences are irrelevant. The blueprint element structure is visualized in Figure 121.6.

Figure 121.6   *Managers (bold = element name, plain=base type)*

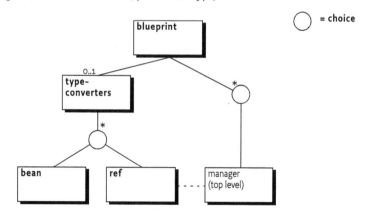

121.4.5   Metadata

The blueprint element has no corresponding Metadata class.

121.4.6   Defaults

The blueprint element supports the setting of the diverse defaults for the current definition resource with the following attributes:

- default-activation – Controls the default for the activation attribute on a manager. See *Lazy and Eager* on page 547. The default for this attribute is eager.
- default-availability – The default availability of the service reference elements, see *Service Reference Managers* on page 560. The default for this attribute is mandatory.
- default-timeout – The default for the reference element timeout attribute, see *Service Reference Managers* on page 560. The default for this attribute is is 30000, or 5 minutes.

These defaults are specific for one definition resource, they apply only to elements enclosed to any depth in the blueprint element. These defaults are not visible in the Metadata.

121.4.7   ‹type-converters›

The Blueprint definitions are text based but the component instances require actual classes for their construction and dependency injection. Component instances are injected with general objects the target type is not always compatible with the source type. This specification therefore allows for *type conversion*. Type conversion rules are specified in *Type Conversion* on page 574. This section provides beans, or referrals to beans, that can be used in this type conversion process. They are listed in a separate section so they can be registered as a type converter, pre-instantiated, and preventing dependencies that easily become cyclic. Beans defined in the type-converters element must be registered as top-level managers.

The structure of the type-converters element is:

```
type-converters ::= ( ‹bean› | ‹ref› )*
```

Type converters defined with the ref element can refer to bean managers or reference managers. Type converters must have ids distinct from any other manager and are available through the Blueprint Container's getComponentInstance method.

121.4.8   manager

The component XML schema type is the base type of the bean, service, reference-list, and reference elements. All manager sub-types share the following attributes:

- id – The manager and its Metadata are identified by its id as defined in its Component Definition. In general this id is therefore referred to as the *component id*. This is an optional attribute. If it is not defined, a default calculated unique id will be assigned to it for top-level managers. For inlined managers, the id attribute cannot be set, their Metadata must return null. All top level manager ids must be unique in a Blueprint Container.
  The id attribute must be of type ID as defined in XML Schema, see [9] *XML Schema*. The syntax for an id is therefore:

  ```
  id      ::= ID       // See [9] XML Schema #ID
  ```

  Ids generally use camel case, like myComponent, and they are case sensitive. That is, component id madHatter and madhatter are distinct ids. Applications should not use ids starting with the prefix blueprint.
  Ids are not required, if no component id is specified, the Blueprint Container must assign a unique id when it is a configured in a top level element. This calculated id must start with a dot ('.' \u002E).
- activation – Defines the activation mode to be lazy or eager. See *Eager Instantiation* on page 542.
- dependsOn – The list of explicit dependencies that must be activated before this manager is activated. See *Explicit Dependencies* on page 547.

The Metadata interface of top level managers will be a sub-interface of ComponentMetadata and is available from the Blueprint Container by its component id.

Figure 121.7   *Inheritance hierarchy for managers*

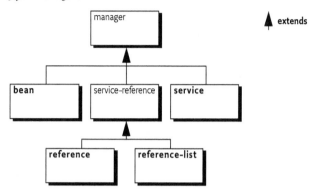

121.4.9   Explicit Dependencies

Before a manager is activated it must have asked all the managers referred to in dependsOn to provide an object. The dependsOn list contains the ids of the top-level managers the bean explicitly depends on.

For example:

```
<bean id="alice" class="com.acme.MadHatter"
      depends-on="cheshire rabbit queen"/>
```

This example will ask the top level managers cheshire, rabbit, and queen to provide an object before alice is activated. For a discussion about dependencies see *Manager Dependencies* on page 533.

121.4.10   Lazy and Eager

During initialization, all *eager* top level managers are requested to provide a component instance. Applications can use this request as an indication to start providing their intended functionality.

Managers that are *lazy*, that is, not singleton scope, activation is lazy, or inlined, are activated when they are first asked to provide a component instance. Therefore, even lazy managers can activate during initialization when they happen to be a dependency of another manager that gets activated.

Services and service references can also have lazy or eager activation. The eager activation will ensure that all listeners are properly actuated during the corresponding activation. For services, the service object is then also requested at startup.

The following example defines an eager bean by making it a singleton and setting the activation to eager:

```
<bean id="eager" scope="singleton"
      class="com.acme.FooImpl" activation="eager"/>
```

121.4.11   Target

In several places in the Blueprint schema it is necessary to refer to a *target*. A target is a:

- ref – Must reference one of the following managers
- reference – An inlined reference manager
- bean – An inlined bean manager

The target type is normally used for listeners, service objects, and other places where a general application component instance is required.

121.5   Bean Manager

A bean manager provides an arbitrary Java object. It constructs this object from a given class or factory and then configures the object by injecting its *properties* with other component instances or more general object values.

The provided component instance can be a singleton or a new object can be returned on every invocation (prototype), this behavior is defined with the scope attribute, see *Scope* on page 551.

The provided object can optionally be notified when all of its properties have been injected, and when the providing bean manager will be deactivated, see *Life Cycle Callbacks* on page 553.

121.5.1   Bean Component XML

The structure of a bean element is:

```
bean              ::= ( <argument> | <property> )*
```

Figure 121.8   Bean Structure

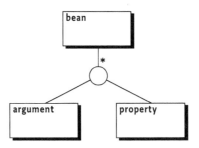

121.5.2   <bean>

The Metadata for a bean manager is represented in the BeanMetadata interface, which extends ComponentMetadata. Table 121.1 on page 548 provides an overview of the related XML definitions and the BeanMetadata interface. The table only provides a summary, the sometimes subtle interactions between the different features are discussed in later sections.

Table 121.1   *Bean Manager Features*

Attribute or Element	Syntax	Bean Metadata	Description
id	ID	id : String	The id of a top level manager, must be unique in the Blueprint Container. All inlined managers must return null for their id.
activation	lazy | eager	activation : int	Defines if this bean is lazily or eagerly activated. If not explicitly set, the blueprint element's value for the default-activation attributes is used. If this is also not set, the value is eager. See *Lazy and Eager* on page 547.

Table 121.1   *Bean Manager Features*

Attribute or Element	Syntax	Bean Metadata	Description
depends-on	NCName*	dependsOn : List<String>	Explicit list of ids that are the dependencies. These referred managers must be activated before this bean can provide an object. See *Explicit Dependencies* on page 547. This is a whitespace separated list.
class	fqn	className : String	Class name of the object to be provided or the class name for a static factory. See *Construction* on page 551.
scope	singleton | prototype	scope : String	The scope defines the construction strategy for the component instance. The default is singleton except for inlined bean managers, where it is prototype. There is no schema default, so if it is not explicitly set, the Metadata will be null. See *Scope* on page 551.
init-method	method	initMethod : String	The name of a method to invoke when a provided object has been injected with all its properties. If this is not set, it is null. See *Life Cycle Callbacks* on page 553.
destroy-method	method	destroyMethod : String	A name of a method to invoke on the provided objects with singleton scope when the Blueprint Container is destroyed. If this is not set, it is null. See *Life Cycle Callbacks* on page 553.
factory-method	method	factoryMethod : String	The name of the method on a static or component instance factory. See *Construction* on page 551.
factory-ref	NCName	factoryComponent : String	A reference to a manager that acts as the factory. See *Construction* on page 551.
<argument>	Table	arguments : List<BeanArgument>	Defined as sub-elements of the bean element. A BeanArgument object contains the value of an argument in the factory method or constructor. The order of the arguments is declaration order. See *Construction* on page 551.
<property>	Table	properties : List<BeanProperties>	Defined as sub-elements of the bean element. A BeanProperty object provides the property name and injection value. See *Properties* on page 552.

The bean element has the following constraints that are not enforced by the schema but must be enforced by the Blueprint Container:

- The destroyMethod must not be set when the scope is prototype.
- The activation must not be set to eager if the bean also has prototype scope.
- The following combinations of arguments are valid, all other combinations are invalid:
  - className
  - className, factory-method
  - factory-ref, factory-method

121.5.3 <argument>

The argument element holds a value for a constructor or factory method's parameters.

Table 121.2   Bean Argument Features

Attribute or Element	Syntax	Bean Argument	Description
index	int >= 0	index : int	The index of the argument in the constructor or factory-method signature. If this is not set, the Blueprint Container must use the type information to calculate it to match the disambiguation algorithm. The index will be -1 when not explicitly set.
type	fqn	valueType : String	The fully qualified class name of a Java type to match the argument to the signature against.
ref	NCName	value : RefMetadata	A reference to a top level manager that provides the value for the argument.
value	<<type>>	value : ValueMetadata	The Value Metadata based on the value property.
<...>	object	value : Metadata	An inlined value.

The argument element has the following additional constraints:

- Either all arguments have a specified index or none have a specified index.
- If indexes are specified, they must be unique and run from 0..(n-1), where n is the number of arguments.
- The following attributes and elements are mutually exclusive:
  - ref
  - value
  - An inlined object value

121.5.4 <property>

The property element holds the information to inject a bean property with an object value.

Table 121.3   Bean Property Features

Attribute or Element	Syntax	Bean Property	Description
name	method ('.' method)*	name : String	The property name, for example foo. The method name can consist of dot separated method names, indicating nested property access.
ref	NCName	value : RefMetadata	A reference to a top level manager.

Table 121.3   *Bean Property Features*

value	<<type>>	value : ValueMetadata	A Value Metadata where the type is null.
<...>	object	value : Metadata	An inlined object value.

The argument element has the following additional constraints:

- The following attributes/elements are mutually exclusive
  - ref
  - value
  - An inlined object value

121.5.5 Scope

A bean manager has a recipe for the construction and injection of an object value. However, there can be different strategies in constructing its component instance, this strategy is reflected in the scope. The following scopes are architected for this specification:

- singleton – The bean manager only holds a single component instance. This object is created and set when the bean is activated. Subsequent requests must provide the same instance. Singleton is the default scope. It is usually used for core component instances as well as stateless services.
- prototype – The object is created and configured anew each time the bean is requested to provide a component instance, that is, every call to getComponentInstance must result in a new component instance. This is usually the only possible scope for stateful objects. All inlined beans are always prototype scope.

Implementations can provide additional scope types. However, these types must only be allowed when a defining namespace is included in the definitions and is actually used in the definitions to specify the dependency on this feature.

121.5.6 Construction

The Blueprint specification supports a number of ways for a bean manager to construct an object. Each possibility is a combination of the following Metadata properties:

- className – Defines the fully qualified name of a class to construct, or the name of a class with a static factory method. The class must be loadable from the Blueprint bundle loadClass method.
- factoryMethod – A static or instance factory method name that corresponds to a publicly accessible method on the given class or factory manager.
- factoryComponent – The id of a top-level target manager in the Blueprint Container that is an instance factory.

The Bean manager can have a number of BeanArgument objects that specify arguments for the constructor or for the factory class/object method. The matching constructor or method must be publicly accessible. The argument's valueType can be used to disambiguate between multiple signatures of constructors or methods. See *Signature Disambiguation* on page 572.

The value of the argument is always a Metadata object. Such an object can be converted into a general object value, see *Object Values* on page 566.

The construction properties can be used in a rather large number of combinations, however, not all combinations are valid. Table 121.4 shows the different valid combinations. If none of the combinations matches, then the Bean Metadata is erroneous.

In Table 121.4, a variation of the following bean definition is assumed:

```
<bean class="C" factory-method="f" factory-ref="fc">
    <argument value="1"/>
    <argument value="2"/>
</bean>
```

This definition is invalid because it specifies an invalid combination of metadata properties. The only valid combinations are subsets, they are all specified in the following table.

Table 121.4   *Component Attributes and Construction*

className	factory-method	factory-ref	argument	Corresponding Java Code
C				new C
C	f			C.f()
C			1,2	new C(1,2)
C	f		1,2	C.f(1,2)
	f	$fc		$fc.f()
	f	$fc	1,2	$fc.f(1,2)
*	*	*	*	failure

The object created this way will be the provided object of the bean after any properties are injected. If the factoryMethod returns a primitive type, then this primitive must be converted to the corresponding wrapper type before any usage.

121.5.7   Properties

Dependency injection configures a constructed object with the help of the properties, which is a a List of BeanProperty objects. A Bean Property has the following features:

- name – The name of the bean property. This name refers to the set method on the constructed object as specified in the design pattern for beans getters and setters, see [6] *Java Beans Specification.* For example, if the property name is foo, then the public method setFoo(arg) will be used to set the value. There must only be one set method with a single argument for a specific property, that is, overloading of properties is not allowed.
  Nested property names are allowed when setting bean properties, as long as all parts of the path, except the property that is set, result in a non-null value. The parts of the path are separated with a dot ('.' \u002E). For example:

    ```
    <property name="foo.bar.baz" value="42"/>
    ```

  This example gets the foo property, from the constructed object, it then gets the bar property and then sets the baz property on that object with the given value.
- value – The value of the property is always a Metadata object. This Metadata object can be converted to a value object, see *Object Values* on page 566.

After the Metadata object is converted to an object value, it must be injected into the property. If the value object is not directly assignable to the property type (as defined by its only set method and the rules in *Type Compatibility* on page 573), then the Blueprint Container must use the type conversion mechanism to create a new object that matches the desired type, or fail. See *Dependency Injection* on page 572 for more information about dependency injection.

For example, the following bean creates an instance and then injects a three into a the foo property that it gets from the bar property. The string that holds the three is converted to a double:

```
<bean id="foo" class="com.acme.Foo">
  <property name="bar.foo" value="3"/>
</bean>

// Classes
package com.acme;
public class Bar {
    double v;
```

```
            public void setFoo(double v) { this.v = v; }
      }
      public class Foo {
         Bar bar = new Bar();
         public void getBar() { return bar; }
      }

      // Corresponding Java code
      Foo foo = new Foo();
      foo.getBar().setFoo(3.0);
```

121.5.8   Life Cycle Callbacks

The bean element provides two attributes that define the *callback* method names for initialization and destruction. A callback must be implemented as a publicly accessible method without any arguments. The callback method names must exist as void() methods.

The initMethod specifies the name of an initialization method that is called after all properties have been injected. The destroyMethod specifies the name of a destroy method that is called when the Blueprint Container has destroyed a component instance. Only bean managers with singleton scope support the destroyMethod. The destroy callback cannot be used for beans that have prototype scope, the responsibility for destroying those instances lies with the application.

121.5.9   Activation and Deactivation

A singleton bean manager must construct its single object during activation and then callback its initMethod method. Prototype scoped beans are created after activation and also have their initMethod invoked. The destroy method is called during the destruction of all the beans in singleton scope, this happens after deactivation.

A prototype bean manager has no special activities for deactivation.

121.6   Service Manager

The service manager defined by a service element is responsible for registering a service object with the service registry. It must ensure that this service is only registered when it is *enabled*. Where enabled means that all its mandatory service reference managers in its dependencies are satisfied.

121.6.1   <service>

The XML structure of the <service> manager is:

```
service                 ::=  <interfaces>?
                             <service-properties>?
                             <registration-listener>*
                             target?
interfaces              ::=  <value>+
service-properties      ::=  <entry>+
registration-listener   ::=  target
```

The service manager has the features outlined in Table 121.5 on page 554. The following additional constraints apply:

- The interface attribute and interfaces element are mutually exclusive.
- If the auto-export attribute is set to anything else but disabled, neither the interface attribute nor the interfaces element must be used.
- The ref attribute and inlined element are mutually exclusive

Table 121.5   *Service Manager Features*

Attribute or Element	Type	Service Metadata	Description
id	ID	id : String	Optional component id of the manager, if it is a top level manager.
activation	lazy | eager	activation : int	Defines if this service is lazily or eagerly initialized. If not explicitly set, the blueprint element's value for the default-activation attributes is used. If this is also not set, the value is eager. See also *Lazy and Eager* on page 547.
depends-on	NCName*	dependsOn : List<String>	Explicit list of ids that are the dependencies. These managers must be activated before this bean can provide an object. See *Explicit Dependencies* on page 547. This is a whitespace separated list.
interface	fqn	interfaces : List<String>	Name of the interface under which this service should be registered. See *Service Interfaces* on page 556.
auto-export	disabled | interfaces | class- hierarchy | all-classes	autoExport : int	Defines the way the class must be analyzed to find the interfaces under which the service must be registered. The schema default is disabled. See *Service Interfaces* on page 556
ranking	int	ranking : int	The service.ranking value. The schema default is 0, which implies no service property. See *Ranking* on page 558.
ref	NCName	value : RefMetadata	Reference to the manager that provides the service object. See *Service Object* on page 557.
<service- properties>	See <map> on page 569.	serviceProperties : List<MapEntry>	The service properties for this service. See *Service Properties* on page 556.
<registration- listener>	See Table 121.6	registrationListeners : List<Registration Listener>	The registration listeners. See *Registration Listener* on page 558.

Table 121.5   *Service Manager Features*

Attribute or Element	Type	Service Metadata	Description

<interfaces>	<value>*	interfaces
		: List<String>
			Names of interfaces under which this service should be registered. Each interface name must be listed as a child value element. This value element has no attributes. For example:
			
			`<interfaces>`
			`  <value>com.acme.Foo</value>`
			`  <value>com.acme.Bar</value>`
			`</interfaces>`
			
			The value element must only hold a string value. See *Service Interfaces* on page 556

<...>	target	value : Target	An inlined target manager that is used for the service object. See *Service Object* on page 557

121.6.2   <registration-listener>

The service element can contain zero or more registration-listener elements, that define registration listeners to be notified of service registration and unregistration events. This element has the following structure:

```
registration-listener ::= target*
```

The registration-listener element defines the callback methods for registration and unregistration.

Table 121.6   *Registration Listener Features*

Attribute or Element	Type	Registration Listener	Description
ref	NCName	registrationListener : Target	A reference to a top level manager.
registration-method	method	registrationMethod : String	The name of the method to call after the service has been registered. See *Registration Listener* on page 558.
unregistration-method	method	unregistrationMethod : String	The name of the method to call before the service will be unregistered. See *Registration Listener* on page 558.
<...>	target	registrationListener : Target	An inlined target manager

The additional constraint is:

- The ref attribute and the inlined manager are mutually exclusive.
- Either or both of the registrationMethod and unregistrationMethod must be set.
- For each method name set, there must be at least one method matching the possible prototypes in the registration listener object, see *Registration Listener* on page 558.

121.6.3   Provided Object

A service manager provides a proxy to a ServiceRegistration object. If this proxy is used when the dependencies are not met, and the service is therefore unregistered, an Illegal State Exception must be thrown. In all other cases, the proxy acts as if it was the ServiceRegistration object associated with the registration of its service object.

The unregister method on the returned object must not be used. If the application code calls unregister then this must result in an Unsupported Operation Exception.

121.6.4   Service Interfaces

Each service object is registered under one or more interface names. The list of interface names is provided by interfaces or autoExport.

The autoExport tells the Blueprint Container to calculate the interface(s) from the type of the service object. The autoExport can have the following values:

- disabled – No auto-detection of service interface names is undertaken, the interface names must be found in interfaces. This is the default mode.
- interfaces – The service object will be registered using all of its implemented public Java interface types, including any interfaces implemented by super classes.
- class-hierarchy – The service object will be registered using its actual type and any public super-types up to the Object class (not included).
- all-classes – The service object will be registered using its actual type, all public super-types up to the Object class (not including), as well as all public interfaces implemented by the service object and any of its super classes.

The autoExport requires the actual class object for introspection for all its modes except disabled, which can cause a bundle with a lazy activation policy to activate because a class will be loaded from the Blueprint bundle.

As an example:

```
<bean id="fooImpl" class="FooImpl"/>

public class FooImpl implements Foo { ... }
```

Then the following service definitions are equivalent:

```
<service id="foo">
    <interfaces>
        <value>com.acme.Foo</value>
    </interface>
</service>
<service id="foo" interface="com.acme.Foo" ref="fooImpl"/>
<service id="foo" auto-export="interfaces" ref="fooImpl"/>
```

121.6.5   Service Properties

Each service can optionally be registered with *service properties*. The serviceProperties is a list of MapEntry, see *<entry>* on page 570. This metadata must be used to create the service properties when the service is registered.

The service manager adds the following automatic service properties that cannot be overridden. When these properties are explicitly set, they must be ignored.

- osgi.service.blueprint.compname – This will reflect the id of the manager that provides the service object, unless it is inlined. Inlined beans are always anonymous and must not have this property set.

- service.ranking – If the ranking attribute is not zero, this property will be set and hold an Integer object with the given value, see *Ranking* on page 558.

For example, the following definition is followed by equivalent Java code needed to register the service:

```
<service ref="fooImpl" interface="com.acme.Foo">
  <service-properties>
    <entry key="size" value="42"/>
  </service-properties>
</service>

Dictionary d = new Hashtable();
d.put("size", "42");
d.put("osgi.service.blueprint.compname", "fooImpl");
ServiceRegistration sr =
  bundleContext.registerService("com.acme.Foo",
    blueprintContainer.getComponentInstance("fooImpl"),
    d);
```

Service properties should specify the valueType of the entry unless the value to be registered needs to be a String object. The service property types should be one of:

- *Primitives Number* – int, long, float, double, byte, short, char, boolean
- *Scalar* – String, Integer, Long, Float, Double, Byte, Short, Character, Boolean.
- *Array* – An array of either the allowable primitive or scalar types.
- *Collection* – An object implementing the Collection interface that contains scalar types.

See *‹entry›* on page 570 types for information how to create these types.

121.6.6   Service Object

The service manager must not request the Blueprint Container for the service object until it is actually needed because a bundle requests it. The service object is represented in the value. This is a Metadata object that can be used to construct an object value, see *Object Values* on page 566.

For example:

```
<service id="fooService" ref="fooImpl" .../>

<service id="fooService" ... >
  <bean class="com.acme.fooImpl"/>
</service>
```

121.6.7   Scope

A service manager must always register a Service Factory as service object and then dispatch the service requests to the service object. For every service request from a bundle, the service manager must request a component instance of the referred or inlined manager. If this component instance implements Service Factory, then no further component instances will be requested and all requests are forwarded to this single component instance regardless of the service object manager's scope.

Otherwise, if the manager that provided the service object has prototype scope, a new object will be provided for each bundle. A singleton manager will be shared between all bundles.

121.6.8   Ranking

When registering a service with the service registry, an optional *service ranking* can be specified that orders service references. The service ranking is registered as the SERVICE_RANKING property defined in the OSGi service layer. When a bundle looks up a service in the service registry, given two or more matching services, then the one with the highest number will be returned. The default ranking value for the OSGi service registry is zero, therefore, this property must not be registered when ranking is zero, which is also the default value.

For example:

```
<service ref="fooImpl" interface="com.acme.FooImpl"
        ranking="900" />
```

This will result in the following service property:

```
service.ranking=new Integer(900)
```

121.6.9   Registration Listener

The registrationListeners represent the objects that need to be called back after the service has been registered and just before it will be unregistered.

The listenerComponent must be a Target object; it is the target for the following callbacks:

- registrationMethod – The name of the notification method that is called after this service has been registered.
- unregistrationMethod – This method is called when this service will be unregistered.

The signatures for the callback methods depend on the scope and if the service object implements the ServiceFactory interface. The different possibilities are outlined in Table 121.7 on page 558.

Table 121.7   Interaction scopes and types for callback signature.

Scope	Type	Signature	Comment
singleton	ServiceFactory	void(ServiceFactory,Map)	All service requests are handled by the component instance.
singleton	T	void(? super T,Map)	T is assignable from the service object's type.
prototype	ServiceFactory	void(ServiceFactory,Map)	All service requests are handled by the first component instance.
prototype	T	void(?,Map)	The first argument must be null because for prototype service objects, the component instance is created when a bundle requests the service. Therefore, at registration time there is no service object available.

If multiple signatures match, then all methods must be called in indeterminate order. At least one method must match.

The service manager must provide the registration listener with the current registration state when the listener is registered. This initial notification must take place before any other callback methods are called on this listener on other threads. That is, if the service is registered at that time, it must call the registration method and otherwise the unregistration method.

The following example shows two registration listeners, one with a referred bean and another one with an inlined bean.

```
<service ref="fooImpl" interface="com.acme.Foo">
  <registration-listener registration-method="reg"
      unregistration-method="unreg">
    <bean class="com.acme.FooListener"/>
  </registration-listener>
</service>

<service ref="fooImpl" interface="com.acme.Foo">
  <registration-listener registration-method="reg"
      unregistration-method="unreg" ref="fooListener"/>
</service>
<bean id="fooListener" class="com.acme.FooListener"/>

package com.acme;
public class FooListener {
  public void reg( Foo foo, Map properties ) { ... }
  public void unreg( Foo foo, Map properties ) { ... }
}
```

The manager that provides the registration listener object is an implicit dependency of the enclosing service manager. However, the registration listener component instance is specifically allowed to use to the service manager though this is technically a cyclic dependency. Therefore, a bean is allowed to be both be injected with a ServiceRegistration object from the service manager as well as being a registered listener to the same service manager.

In the following example, the foo service manager uses manager main, both as a registration listener as well as top-level bean main being injected with reference foo.

```
<service id="foo" interface="com.acme.Foo" ref="main">
  <registration-listener
      registration-method="register" ref="main"/>
</service>

<bean id="main" class="com.acme.Main" init-method="done">
  <property name="foo" ref="foo"/>
</bean>
```

121.6.10   Enabled

A service manager needs a service object that is referred to by the value Metadata property. This value can in its turn depend on other managers transitively. If any of these managers are service reference managers, then they can be satisfied or not. If these service reference managers are marked to be mandatory, then they influence the *enabled* state of the first service manager. Only if all of these mandatory service reference managers in the dependency graph are satisfied, then the first service manager is enabled.

An service manager must have a Service Factory registered with the OSGi service registry after the primary initialization of the Blueprint Container has been done until the Blueprint Container is destroyed while it is enabled. See see *Service Registration* on page 541.

121.6.11   Activation and Deactivation

When a service manager is activated, it must actuate its registration listeners. Each registration listener must be called back during its actuation with the current service registration state as described in the *Registration Listener* on page 558. Normally, this will also request the container for a service object but this can be further delayed in certain circumstances. See *Service Object* on page 557 for more details.

During deactivation, a service manager must disable any registration listeners and release any dependencies it has on these component instances.

121.7   Service Reference Managers

The reference, and reference-list elements are all *service references*. They select a number of services in the service registry. The structure of these elements is as follows:

```
reference        ::= <reference-listener>*
reference-list   ::= <reference-listener>*
```

The inheritance hierarchy for service references is depicted in Figure 121.9 on page 560.

Figure 121.9   *Inheritance hierarchy for service references*

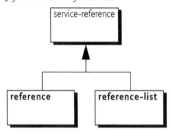

121.7.1   Service Reference

The service reference managers have almost identical Metadata and share most behavior. The only schema differences between a reference manager and a reference-list manager are:

- timeout – A reference manager supports a timeout.
- memberType – The reference-list can define its member-type

The features of the service references are explained in Table 121.8 on page 560.

Table 121.8   *Service Reference Manager Features*

Attribute or Element	Type	ServiceReference-Metadata	Description
id	ID	id : String	The component id of a top level manager
activation	lazy | eager	activation : int	Defines if this bean is lazily of eagerly initialized. If not explicitly set, the blueprint element's value for the default-activation attributes is used. If this is also not set, the value is eager. See also *Lazy and Eager* on page 547.

Table 121.8   *Service Reference Manager Features*

Attribute or Element	Type	ServiceReference-Metadata	Description
depends-on	NCName*	dependsOn : List<String>	Explicit list of component ids that are the dependencies. These managers must be activated before this service reference's activation. See *Explicit Dependencies* on page 547. This is a whitespace separated List.
availability	mandatory | optional	availability : int	Defines if a service reference is mandatory or optional. The default for the availability attribute is defined by the default-availability attribute in the blueprint element. If the default-availability attribute is not defined, the value is mandatory.
interface	fqn	interface : String	A single name of an interface class. It is allowed to not specify an interface name.
component-name	NCName	componentName : String	Points to another manager in another Blueprint Container registered in the service registry. If set, the component name must be part of the effective filter.
filter	filter	filter : String	The given filter string, can be null.
<reference-listener>	See *<reference-listener>* on page 562	referenceListeners : List<Listener>	The Metadata of the reference listeners

The additional constraints for service references are:

- The interface, if set, must refer to a public interface.

121.7.2   <reference>

A reference manager, selecting a single service, has the additional feature explained in Table 121.9 on page 561.

Table 121.9   *Reference Features*

Attribute or Element	Type	Reference Metadata	Description
timeout	long >= 0	timeout : long	The timeout in ms. Zero is indefinite.

An additional constraint on the reference is:

- The timeout must be equal or larger than zero.

121.7.3   <reference-list>

A reference-list manager, selecting multiple services, has the additional feature explained in Table 121.9 on page 561.

Table 121.10   Reference-list Features

Attribute or Element	Type	Reference List Metadata	Description
member-type	service-object | service-reference	memberType : int	Defines if the members of the list are ServiceReference objects or the proxies to the actual service objects.

121.7.4   <reference-listener>

The reference element can notify reference listeners of the service selection changes with the referenceListeners. The reference-listener element has the following structure:

```
reference-listener    ::= target*
```

The reference-listener element defines the callback methods for binding and unbinding a service.

Table 121.11   Reference Listener Features

Attribute or Element	Type	Reference Listener	Description
ref	NCName	listenerComponent : Target	A reference to a top level target manager.
bind-method	method	bindMethod : String	The name of the method to call after the service has been bound. See *Reference Listeners* on page 564.
bind-method	method	unbindMethod : String	The name of the method to call before the service will be unbound. See *Reference Listeners* on page 564.
<...>	target	listenerComponent : Target	An inlined target manager

The additional constraints are:

- The ref attribute and the inlined manager are mutually exclusive.
- Either or both bindMethod and unbindMethod must be specified.
- At least one specified method must exist with each given method name, see *Reference Listeners* on page 564.

121.7.5   Provided Object For a Reference

The provided object for a service reference manager is a *proxy* backed by a service object from the service registry. Therefore, even though the injected object will remain constant, it can change its reference to a backing service at any time, implying it can only be used with stateful services if reference listeners are used. If use when no suitable backing service is available, it will wait until it times out. See *Service Dynamics* on page 579 for more details. The model is depicted in Figure 121.10.

Figure 121.10   Constant references with dynamic selection

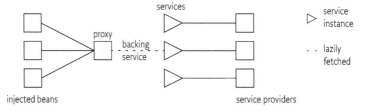

The following example shows how a property can be set to the service object.

```
public class C {
    public void setProxy(T ref) { ... }
}
<reference id="p" interface="T"/>
<bean id="c" class="C">
    <property name="proxy" ref="p"/>
</bean>
```

121.7.6   Provided Object For a Reference-list

The reference-list provided object implements the List interface; this List contains proxies to the backing services. These proxies do not have a timeout. That is, when a proxy from a reference-list is used, it must not wait when the backing service is no longer available but it must immediately throw a Service Unavailable Exception.

Changes to the list are dynamic. When a backing service is unregistered, the corresponding proxy is removed from the list synchronously with the service event. When a new service enters the selection, it is added synchronously with the service event. Proxies to newly discovered services must be added at the end of the list. The structure is depicted in Figure 121.11.

Figure 121.11   *Constant reference to list with dynamic selection*

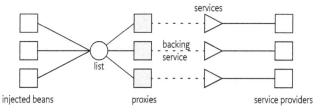

The member type of the list depends on the memberType. If this is set to:

- service-object – Inject a List of service objects, this is the default.
- service-reference – Inject a list of ServiceReference objects

If generics information is available, then it is an error if the generic member type of the target list is not assignable with the memberType. If the member target type is in itself specified with generic arguments, like List<T<U>>, then the assignment must fail because this would require conversion and no conversion can take place for this assignment. For information about generics, see *Generics* on page 577.

121.7.7   Read Only Lists

The list is a read-only view on the actual set of proxies to the service objects. This List object must only support the following methods:

```
contains(Object)
containsAll(Collection)
equals(Object)
get(int)
hashCode()
indexOf(Object)
isEmpty()
iterator()          // no remove method
lastIndexOf(Object)
listIterator()      // not supported
listIterator(int)   // not supported
```

```
size()
subList(int, int)  // same list type as parent
toArray()
toArray(T[])
```

All other methods must throw an Unsupported Operation Exception. The List Iterator is not supported for these lists.

121.7.8   Selection

A service reference must provide a *selection* of services from the service registry. The Blueprint Container must logically use a filter for the selection that is the and (&) of the following assertions:

- The interface, if specified
- If componentName is not null, a filter that asserts osgi.blueprint.compname=$componentName This is a convenience function to easily refer to managers in other Blueprint Containers. Registered Blueprint services will automatically get this property set to their blueprint name.
- If filter is not null, the filter

The selection is defined as the set of Service References selected by the given filter.

121.7.9   Availability

A service reference is *satisfied* when one or more services match the selection. The availability is used to specify whether a service reference needs to be satisfied before initialization, see *Grace Period* on page 541, or if it controls the registration state of any service managers that depend on this service reference manager (explicit and implicit), see *Mandatory Dependencies* on page 580. The availability can have the following values:

- mandatory – Mandatory indicates that the service reference needs to be satisfied.
- optional – Optional indicates that the satisfaction of this reference is not relevant for any registered services, or for the grace period.

It is an error to declare a mandatory reference to a service that is registered by the same bundle. Such a definition could cause either deadlock or a timeout.

The fact that Blueprint specification has mandatory service references gives no guarantee that a valid service object is available when the service reference is used, in the dynamic world of OSGi, services can get unregistered at any time.

The following example declares a mandatory service reference for a single service. The usage of the reference can stall a maximum of 5 seconds if no service matches the selection.

```
<reference
    id           ="log"
    interface    ="org.osgi.service.log.LogService"
    availability ="mandatory"
    timeout      ="5000" />
```

121.7.10   Reference Listeners

The referenceListeners are represented as ReferenceListener objects. They define the following callbacks:

- bindMethod – Called after a service is selected by the service reference manager. For a reference manager, this method can be called repeatedly without an intermediate unbind callback. This happens when a service is unregistered but a replacement can be found immediately.
- unbindMethod – Called when the service is no longer used by the service reference manager but before it has been returned to the service registry with the unget method. For a reference manager, no unbind method is called when the service can immediately be replaced with an alternative service when the service goes away.

A reference listener callback can have any of the following signatures:

- `public void(ServiceReference)` – Provide the `ServiceReference` object associated with this service reference. This callback type provides access to the service's properties without actually getting the service.
- `public void(? super T)` – Provide the proxy to the service object, where T is on of the types implemented by the service object proxy.
- `public void (? super T,Map)` – Provide the proxy to the service object. T is a type that is assignable from the service object. The `Map` object provides the service properties of the corresponding `ServiceReference` object.

All signatures must be supported regardless of the value of `memberType` that was specified in the reference-list. The service object given to the reference listeners must be the proxy to the service object.

The callbacks must be made synchronously with the corresponding OSGi service event. For reference-list callbacks, the service proxy is guaranteed to be available in the collection before a bind callback is invoked, and to remain in the collection until after an unbind callback has completed.

If a service listener defines multiple overloaded methods for a callback, then every method with a matching signature is invoked in an undefined order.

For example, the following definition will result in calling all the `setLog` methods on a `FooImpl` object:

```
<reference id="log"
      interface="org.osgi.service.log.LogService">
  <reference-listener
      bind-method="setLog">
      <bean class="com.acme.FooImpl"/>
  </reference-listener>
</reference>

public class FooImpl {
    public void setLog(Object o, Map m) { ... }
    public void setLog(LogService l, Map m) { ... }
    public void setLog(ServiceReference ref) { ... }
}
```

The manager that provides the reference listener object is treated as an implicit dependency of the enclosing service reference. This manager is specifically allowed to use to the service reference in a property injection or constructor argument, though this is technically a cyclic dependency. Therefore, a bean must be allowed to both be injected with a reference as well as listening to the bind and unbind callbacks of that same reference.

In the following example, the foo reference manager uses manager main, both as a reference listener as well as manager main being injected with reference foo.

```
<reference id="foo" interface="com.acme.Foo">
  <reference-listener bind-method="setL" ref="main"/>
</reference>
<bean id="main" class="com.acme.Main">
  <property name="r" ref="foo"/>
</bean>
```

121.7.11   Service Proxies

The Blueprint extender must generate proxies for the service reference managers. Reference managers provide proxies that dynamically select a *backing* service, which can change over time. A reference-list provides a list of proxies that have a fixed backing service, these proxies are added and removed from the list. based on the selection, they do not have a time-out.

The backing service for a reference proxy must not be gotten from the OSGi service registry until an actual service object is needed, that is, when an actual method is called on the proxy. If the backing service becomes unregistered, then the proxy must unget the reference to the backing service (if it had gotten it) and get another service object the next time a method on the proxy is called. If a replacement can be found immediately, the reference listener's bind method must be called without calling the unbind method. Other threads that need the same service object must block until the service object has become available or times out.

The proxies must implement all the methods that are defined in the interface. The interface must refer to an interface, not a class. The proxy must only support the methods in the given interface. That is, it must not proxy methods available on the service object that are not available in the given interface. If no interface is defined, the proxy must be implemented as if the interface had no methods defined.

Blueprint bundles must ensure that the proper semantics are maintained for hashCode and equals methods. If these methods are not defined in the interface, then the proxy must use the default semantics of the Object class for equals and hashCode methods.

121.7.12 Activation and Deactivation

Service reference managers are active before activation because they must handle the enable status of service managers.

During activation, a service reference must actuate its listeners and provide these listeners with the initial state of the reference. For a reference, if there is a selected object, the bind method must be called with the proxy object, otherwise the unbind method must be called with a null as proxy object. For a reference-list, the bind method must be called for each member of the list. If the list is empty, the unbind method must be called with a null as proxy object.

During deactivation, the listeners must be disabled.

121.8 Object Values

Top-level managers can use *object values* in different places. These object values are defined with XML elements and attributes. After parsing, they are all converted to sub-interfaces of the Metadata interface, transitively reachable from top-level managers. For example, the following definition creates a bean that is injected with the byte array: byte[] {7,42}:

```
<bean class="com.acme.FooImpl">
   <property name="array">
      <array value-type="byte">
         <value>7</value>
         <value>42</value>
      </array>
   </property>
</bean>
```

This definition provides the configuration data for an *array value*, which is represented by the CollectionMetadata interface. A Metadata object can be used to construct its object value during runtime whenever a new object must be constructed.

In most places where an object value can be used, it can be anything, including objects provided by a managers and even null. However, maps require non-null keys. The object values are therefore split in value and nonNullValue types.

The syntax for object values has the following structure:

```
nonNullValue::=    <ref>
           |       <idref>
```

```
                    |      <value>
                    |      <map>
                    |      <props>
                    |      collection
                    |      manager  // see manager on page 546
value               ::= nonNullValue | <null>
collection          ::= <list> | <set> | <array>
```

Object values also include inlined managers. The use of an inlined manager for an object value means that manager will provide a value every time the object value is constructed. Each of the object values is created anew and the types are mutable, except for the service references. The use of managers in object values must create an implicit dependency between the top level managers and any transitively reachable manager from their Metadata.

121.8.1   <ref>

The ref element is a reference to a top-level manager in the same Blueprint Container. The ref element has a single attribute component-id.

Table 121.12   Ref Features

Attribute	Type	Ref Metadata	Description
component-id	NCName	componentId : String	A reference to a top level manager.

For example, the following definition uses the foo manager to instantiate the service object.

```
<service id="fooService" interface="com.acme.Foo">
  <ref component-id="fooImpl"/>
</service>
<bean id="fooImpl" class="com.acme.FooImpl"/>

public class FooImpl implements Foo { }
```

121.8.2   <idref>

The idref element provides the component id of another manager in the same Blueprint Container. This reference can then be used by the application to look up a manager in the Blueprint Container during runtime. The idref element is a safe way to provide a component id because the Blueprint Container will verify that the component id exists, thereby showing errors early. The idref does not create an implicit dependency on the given manager.

Table 121.13   IdRef Features

Attribute	Type	Id Ref Metadata	Description
component-id	NCName	componentId : String	A reference to a top level manager.

The following example provides the foo object with the reference to the database.

```
<bean id="foo" class="com.acme.FooImpl">
  <property name="db">
    <idref component-id="jdbc"/>
  </property>
</bean>

<bean id="jdbc" ... />
```

The following definition is equivalent to except that a non existent component id will not be detected until the foo object access the Blueprint Container. In the previous example this was detected directly after the definitions were parsed.

```
<bean id="foo" class="com.acme.FooImpl">
  <property name="db" value="jdbc"/>
</bean>
<bean id="jdbc" ... />
```

121.8.3   <value>

A value element represents an object that can directly be constructed from a string formed by its text contents.

Table 121.14   *Value Features*

Attribute, Element	Type	Value Metadata	Description
type	type	type : String	The optional type name to be used in type converting the given string to a target type. This type can commit the conversion to a specific choice. If this type is not set, and the value is part of a collection, then it must return the value from the collection valueType. If this is also not available, then it must return null. For the type syntax, see *Syntax for Java types* on page 544.
...	<<type>>	stringValue : String	The string value that must be converted to the target type, if set.

If a value element is used as a member in a list, map, array, or set then the enclosing collection can define a default value for the type attribute of its value elements.

The following example creates a list of two OSGi version objects.

```
<list value-type="org.osgi.framework.Version">
  <value>1.3.4</value>
  <value>5.6.2.v200911121020</value>
</list>
```

The corresponding Java code is:

```
Arrays.asList( new Version("1.3.4"),
   new Version("5.6.2.v200911121020") )
```

121.8.4   <null>

A null element results in a Java null. It has no attributes and no elements. It corresponds to Null Metadata.

121.8.5   <list>, <set>, <array>

Lists, sets, and arrays are referred to as *collections*. List and array are ordered sequences of objects, where equal objects can occur multiple times. A set discards equal objects.

The structure of a collection element is:

```
collection ::= value *
```

Table 121.15   Collection Features

Attribute or Element	Type	Collection Metadata	Description
value-type	type	valueType : String	Optionally set the type for ValueMetadata children.
		collectionClass : Class< List | Set | Object[] >	The actual collection class to be used, derived from the appropriate definition.
<...>	object*	values : List<Metadata>	The Metadata for the children of the collection

The valueType sets the default for any contained ValueMetadata objects. The result of a collection element is an object that implements the given collection interface or is an Object[]. That is, the resulting object is mutable and can be used by the application. However, type conversion can create a copy of this list.

The following example creates a List of Lists of 2x2 of int values:

```
<list>
   <list value-type="int">
      <value >2</value>
      <value >7</value>
   </list>
   <list value-type="int">
      <value >9</value>
      <value >5</value>
   </list>
</list>
```

The corresponding Java code is:

```
Arrays.asList(
   new int[] {2,7},
   new int[]{9,5},
)
```

121.8.6   **<map>**

A map is a sequence of associations between a *key* and some object., this association is called an *entry*. The structure of a map element is therefore:

```
map        ::=   <entry> *
```

Table 121.16   Map Features

Attribute or Element	Type	Map Metadata	Description
key-type	type	keyType : String	Optional default type for keys. For the syntax see *Syntax for Java types* on page 544.
value-type	type	valueType : String	Optional default type for values. For the syntax see *Syntax for Java types* on page 544.
<entry>	See *<entry>* on page 570	values : List<MapEntry>	The MapEntry object for the children of the map or properties.

There are no additional constraints.

121.8.7   **<entry>**

The entry element provides an association between a key and a value. The structure of the element is:

```
entry      ::=    <key>? object
key        ::=    nonNullValue
```

Table 121.17   *Entry Features*

Attribute	Type	Map Entry	Description
key	<<type>>	key : NonNullMetadata	Specify the key of the entry.
key-ref	NCName	key : NonNullMetadata	Reference to a top-level manager
<key>	nonNull- Value	key : NonNullMetadata	Contains an inlined value that is never null.
value	<<type>>	value : Metadata	Specify the value directly, this will be a string type.
value-ref	NCName	value : RefMetadata	A reference to a top-level manager
<...>	object	value : Metadata	An inlined manager

Additional constraints:

- key, key-ref attributes and key element are mutually exclusive.
- value, value-ref attributes and value element are mutually exclusive.
- The resulting object of a key must not be a primitive type.

The following example shows the different way an entry can get its key. In this case the value is always a string.

```
<map>
    <entry key="bar"       value="..."/>   // 1
    <entry key-ref="bar" value="..."/>   // 2
    <entry value="...">                    // 3
       <key>
          <value type="org.osgi.framework.Version">
             2.71
          </value>
       </key>
    </entry>
</map>
```

The previous example is equivalent to the following Java code:

```
Map m = new HashMap();
m.put( "bar", "..." );
m.put( container.getComponentInstance("bar"), "..." );
m.put( new Version("2.71"), "..." );
```

The following examples shows the different ways a value of an entry can be defined.

```
<map>
    <entry key="1" value="1"/>
    <entry key="2" value-ref="foo"/>
    <entry key="3">
       <value type="org.osgi.framework.Version">3.14</value>
    </entry>
```

```
</map>
```

The previous code is equivalent to the following Java code.

```
Map m = new HashMap()
m.put("1", "1");
m.put("2", container.getComponentInstance("foo"))
m.put("3", new Version("3.14"));
```

121.8.8   <props>

The props element specifies a Properties object. The structure of a props element is as follows:

```
props        ::=       prop *
```

Each prop element is an association between two strings. It defines the following attributes:

- key – A string specifying the property key. This attribute is required.
- value – A string specifying the property value.

The following example initializes the same Properties object in two s ways.

```
<props>
    <prop key="1">one</prop>
    <prop key="2">two</prop>
</props>

<props>
    <prop key="1"    value="one"/>
    <prop key="2"    value="two"/>
</props>
```

This is equivalent to the following Java code:

```
Properties p = new Properties();
p.setProperty( "1", "one");
p.setProperty( "2", "two");
```

121.8.9   Manager as Value

Each manager can be the provider of component instances that act as object values. When a manager is used in an object value, then that is the manager asked to provide a component instance. The managers are specified in *manager* on page 546. The simple example is a bean. Any inlined bean can act as an object value. For example:

```
<list>
    <bean class="com.acme.FooImpl"/>
</list>
```

Some managers have side effects when they are instantiated. For example, a service manager will result in a ServiceRegistration object but it will also register a service.

```
<map>
    <entry key="foo">
        <service interface="com.acme.Foo">
            <bean class="com.acme.FooImpl"/>
        </service>
    </entry>
</map>
```

121.9   Dependency Injection

A bean has a recipe for constructing a component instance with a constructor or factory and then providing it with its *properties*. These properties are then injected with *object values*, see *Object Values* on page 566.

The following types of dependencies can be injected:

- *Constructor arguments* – The arguments specify the parameters for a constructor.
- *Static Factory arguments* – The arguments specify the parameters for a static method.
- *Instance Factory arguments* – The arguments specify the parameters for a method on an object provided by another manager.
- *Properties* – The value of the Bean Property specifies the single parameter for the property's set method.

In all the previous cases, the Blueprint Container must find an appropriate method or constructor to inject the dependent objects into the bean. The process of selecting the correct method or constructor is described in the following section, which assumes a Bean Argument as context, where a Bean Property acts as a Bean Argument without an index or type set.

121.9.1   Signature Disambiguation

Constructors, factory methods, and property set methods are described with Metadata. The Blueprint Container must map these descriptions to an actual method or constructor. In practice, there can be multiple methods/constructors that could potentially map to the same description. It is therefore necessary to disambiguate this selection. Both factory methods and constructors have the same concept of *signatures*. A signature consists of an ordered sequence of zero or more types. For methods, only publicly accessible methods with the appropriate name are considered. For constructors, all publicly accessible constructors are considered. The disambiguation process described here is valid for all constructors and methods because the signature concept applies to both of them.

1 Discard any signatures that have the wrong cardinality

2 Find the list of signatures that have *assignable* types for each argument in their corresponding positions. Assignable is defined in *Type Compatibility* on page 573. If a type was specified for an argument, then this type must match the name of the corresponding reified type in the signature exactly.

3 If this result list has one element, then this element is the answer. If this list has more than one element, then the disambiguation fails.

4 Otherwise, find the list of signatures that have *compatible* types for each argument in their corresponding positions. Compatibility is defined in *Type Compatibility* on page 573.

5 If this result list has one element, then this element is the answer. If the list has more than one element, then the disambiguation fails.

6 If the arguments cannot be reordered (the index of the argument is used and is thus not -1, or there are less than two arguments) then the disambiguation fails.

7 Find all signatures that match a re-ordered combination of the arguments. Reordering must begin with the first argument and match this argument against the first *assignable* types in a signature, going from position 0 to n. If the type is assignable from the argument, then it is locked in that position. If the argument has a type, then it must exactly match the name of the selected signature type. The same is done for the subsequent arguments. If all arguments can find an exclusive position in the signature this way, than the signature is added to the result.

8 If the result list contains one signature, then this is the resulting signature. If the list has more than one element, then the disambiguation fails.

9 Repeat step 6, but now look for *compatible* types instead of assignable types.

10 If the result list contains one signature, then this is the resulting signature.

11 Otherwise, the disambiguation fails

An example elucidates how the disambiguation works. Assuming the following definition and classes:

```
<bean ...>
  <argument>
    <bean class="Bar"/>
  </argument>
  <argument>
    <bean class="Foo"/>
  </argument>
<bean>

public class Bar extends Foo {}
public class Foo {}
```

The following bullets provide examples how signatures are matched against the previous definition.

- (Bar,Foo) – The arguments will be in the given order and the orderd match will succeed. This is the normal case.
- (Foo,Bar) – This will not match because in the re-ordered match, the Bar argument (which is a Foo sub-type) is matched against the first argument. The second Foo argument can then no longer find a compatible type because that slot is taken by the Bar instance.
- (Object,Object) – This will be called with (aBar,aFoo).

Multiple constructors on a class can require disambiguation with the arguments type. In the following example, the Multiple class has two constructors that would both match the constructor arguments because a String object can be converted to both a File object and a URL object.

```
public class Multiple {
    public Multiple(URL a);
    public Multiple(File a);
}
```

An attempt to configure a Multiple object without the type will fail, because it is not possible to determine the correct constructor. Therefore, the type should be set to disambiguate this:

```
<bean class="Multiple">
  <argument type="java.net.URL" value="http://www.acme.us"/>
</bean>
```

121.9.2   Type Compatibility

During injection, it is necessary to decide about type *assignability* or type *compatibility* in several places. If generics are present, a type must be *reified* in its class, see *Generics* on page 577. In this specification, the canonical representation for a type is $T<P_1..P_n>$, where n is zero for a non-parameterized type, which is always true in a VM less than Java 5. The ReifiedType class models this kind of type.

If type T or S is primitive, then they are treated as their corresponding wrapper class for deciding assignability and compatibility. Therefore, a type $T<P_1..P_n>$ (target) is *assignable* from an object s of type S (source) when the following is true:

- n == 0, and
- T.isAssignableFrom(S)

$T<P_1..P_n>$ is *compatible* with an object s of type S when it is assignable or it can be converted using the Blueprint built-in type converter. The convertability must be verified with the canConvert(s, $T<P_1..P_n>$) method. That is, type compatibility is defined as:

- assignable($T<P_1..P_n>$,S), and
- cs.canConvert(s,$T<P_1..P_n>$) returns true

Where cs is the Blueprint built in type converter that also uses the custom type converters.

121.9.3 Type Conversion

Strings in Blueprint definitions, object values, and component instances must be made compatible with the type expected by an injection target (method or constructor argument, or property) before being injected, which can require *type conversion*. The Blueprint Container supports a number of built-in type conversions, and provides an extension mechanism for configuring additional type converters. Custom type converters have priority over built-in converters.

The goal of the type conversion is to convert a source object s with type S to a target type $T<P_1..P_n>$. The conversion of the Blueprint built-in type converter must take place in the following order:

1   If $T<P_1..P_n>$ is assignable from S, which implies n=0, then no conversion is necessary, except that primitives must be converted to their wrapper types.
2   Try all type converters in declaration order with the canConvert(s,$T<P_1..P_n>$) method, exceptions are ignored and logged. The first converter that returns true is considered the converter, its result is obtained by calling convert(s,$T<P_1..P_n>$). Exceptions in this method must be treated as an error.
3   If T is an array, then S must be an array or it must implement Collection, otherwise the conversion fails. Each member of array s must be type converted to the component type of T using the generics information if available, see the getComponentType method on Class. This is a recursive process. The result must be stored in an array of type T.
4   If T implements Collection, then S must be an array or implement Collection, otherwise the conversion fails. If the platform supports generics, the members of object s must be converted to the member type of the collection if this is available from the generics information, or to Object otherwise. The Blueprint Container must create a target collection and add all members of s to this new object in the iteration order of s. The target collection depends on type T:
    - If T is one of the interfaces listed in *Concrete Types for Interfaces* on page 577, then the target collection must be the corresponding concrete class.
    - T must represent a public concrete class with an empty publicly accessible constructor, the target collection is then a new instance of T.
    - Otherwise T represents an interface and the conversion must fail.
5   If T implements Map or extends Dictionary, then S must implement Map or extend Dictionary as well, otherwise the conversion fails. If the platform supports generics, the members of map s must be converted to the key and value type of the target map. This is a recursive process. Without generics, the members are not converted and put as is.
    The target map depends on T:
    - If T is a public concrete class (not interface) with an empty publicly accessible constructor then the target map must be a new instance of T.
    - If T is one of the Map interfaces or Dictionary listed in *Concrete Types for Interfaces* on page 577, then the target map must be the corresponding concrete class.
    - Otherwise, the conversion fails.
6   If T is one of the primitive types (byte, char, short, int, long, float, double, boolean) then treat T as the corresponding wrapper class.
7   If T extends class Number and S extends also class Number then convert the source to a number of type T. If the target type cannot hold the value then the conversion fails. However, precision may be lost if a double or float is converted to one of the integer types.
8   If source type S is not class String, then the conversion fails.
9   The conversion is attempted based on the target type T from the string s. The following target types are supported:
    - boolean or Boolean – Construct the appropriate boolean type while accepting the following additional values for true and false respectively:
        - yes, no
        - on, off

- Character – The string s must have a length of 1, this single character is then converted to a Character object.
- Locale – The string s is converted to a Locale using the following syntax (no spaces are allowed between terms).

```
locale   ::=   <java language-code> ( '_' country)+
country ::=   <java country-code>
                      ('_' <java variant-code>)+
```

- Pattern – Create the Pattern object with Pattern.compile(String).
- Properties – Create a new Properties object and load the properties from the string. The string must follow the format described with the Properties.load method.
- Enum subclass – Convert the string s to the appropriate member of the given enum with the Enum.valueOf method. If the string is not one of the enum values, then the conversion must fail.
- Class – The string s must conform to the syntax in *Syntax for Java types* on page 544. This type must be loaded through the Bundle's loadClass method. The resulting class must match any generic constraints on T. If this fails, the conversion fails.

10 If target type T has a constructor (String), then use this constructor to create an instance with the source string s. This convention caters for many of the built-in Java types such as BigDecimal, BigInteger, File, URL, and so on, as well as for custom types.

If none of the above steps has found a proper conversion than the conversion fails. Failing a conversion must end with throwing an Illegal Argument Exception.

121.9.4   Type Converters

A type converter converts a source type to a target type. The source type for a type converter is not constrained. A type converter must support the following methods:

- canConvert(Object,ReifiedType) – A light weight method that inspects the object and returns true if it can convert it to the given Reified Type, false otherwise. Converters normally can convert a type S to a type T<...>. However, converters can convert to multiple types and the value of the source object can influence the returned type. For example, a converter could convert a string to a type based on its content.
- convert(Object,ReifiedType) – The actual conversion method. This method should not fail if the canConvert method has returned true.

The ReifiedType class provides access to the target class. In a Java 1.4 environment, the ReifiedType object will provide a Class object for conversion and no type arguments. In a Java 5 environment, the ReifiedType object provides access to the reified class as well as the type arguments. Generics and reified types are described in *Generics* on page 577.

Type converters are normal managers with some limitations due to the dependency handling. If they depend on general managers or services then there is a change that cyclic dependencies are created.

Converters must be defined in the type-converters element, see *<type-converters>* on page 546, to be registered as a converter. Component instances of managers in this section must implement the Converter interface. Converters must also only transitively depend on built-in converters. It must be possible to initialize all converters before any of them are used. Type converters should not use the type conversion before all type converters are fully configured.

Converters are ordered within one definition resource but there is no resource ordering, so the overall ordering is not defined, making it a good practice to concentrate all converters in a single XML definition. The definition ordering is used during type conversion. That is, converters are not ordered by their specialization, a converter that is earlier can convert a more general type will override a converter that is later in the list but could have converted to a more specific type.

Converters must always use the type arguments of the given Reified Type, even if they are running on Java 1.4. The default behavior of the Reified Type will automatically work.

The following example demonstrates how a converter can use generics to use an AtomicReference<T> whenever type T is supported. Such a type could be for a property like:

```
public void setInteger( AtomicReference<Integer> atomic );
```

The Atomic Converter uses the generic argument to convert a source object to an Integer and then creates an AtomicReference with this converted object. The definition of the type converter looks like:

```
<type-converters>
  <bean class="AtomicConverter">
    <argument ref="blueprintConverter"/>
  </bean>
</type-converters>
```

The Blueprint converter is injected in the constructor of the AtomicInteger class, in order to allow the conversion of the generic arguments. The Blueprint built-in type converter must not be used before all type converters are registered because a needed type converter might not have been registered yet. This is the reason type converters should not require type conversion in their initialization because the state of this converter is not well defined at this time.

The conversion class looks like:

```
public class AtomicConverter {
  Converter bpc;
  public AtomicConverter(Converter bpc) { this.bpc=bpc; }

  public boolean canConvert(Object s,ReifiedType T) {
    return T.getRawClass() == AtomicReference.class
    && bpc.canConvert(s, T.getActualTypeArgument(0));
  }

  public Object convert( Object s, ReifiedType T )
                                      throws Exception {
    Object obj = bpc.convert(
      s,T.getActualTypeArgument(0) );

    return new AtomicReference<Object>(obj);
  }
}
```

Any injection that now targets an AtomicReference<T> value will automatically be converted into an AtomicReference of the appropriate type because of the example converter. The following definitions test this behavior:

```
public class Foo<T extends Integer> {
  public Foo( AtomicReference<T> v) {}
}

<bean id="foo" class="Foo"> <argument value="6"/> </bean>
```

This definition will create an foo object with the Foo(AtomicReference<T>) constructor. The source type is a string and there is no assignability for an Atomic Reference, so the registered type converters are consulted. The Atomic Converter recognizes that the target T is an AtomicReference class and indicates it can convert. The convert method then uses the generic argument information, which is an Integer object in the example, to convert the string "6" to an Integer object and return the appropriate AtomicReference object.

121.9.5   Built-in Converter

A Blueprint Container must contain an environment manager called blueprintConverter. The related component instance must implement the Converter interface.

The built-in Converter provides access to the provided type converters as well as the built in types. This service provides the type conversion as defined in *Type Conversion* on page 574.

Injecting a reference to the blueprintConverter environment manager into a bean provides access to all the type conversions that the Blueprint Container and registered type converters are able to perform. However, if this converter is injected in a type converter, then by definition, not all custom type converters are yet registered with the built-in converter. Type converters should therefore in general not rely on type conversion during their construction.

121.9.6   Concrete Types for Interfaces

The Blueprint extender can choose an implementation class when it provides an instance during conversion to an interface as well as when it natively provides an object. The actual implementation class can make a noticeable difference in disambiguation, type conversion, and general behavior. Therefore this sections describe the concrete types an implementation must use for specific interfaces if the platform allows this.

Table 121.18   Implementation types for interfaces

	Interface/Abstract class	Implementation class
	Collection	ArrayList
	List	ArrayList
Java 5	Queue	LinkedList
	Set	LinkedHashSet
	SortedSet	TreeSet
	Map	LinkedHashMap
	SortedMap	TreeMap
Java 5	ConcurrentMap	ConcurrentHashMap
	Dictionary	Hashtable

If possible, the instances of these types must preserve the definition ordering.

121.9.7   Generics

Java 5 introduced the concept of *generics*. Before Java 5, a *type*, was simply a class or interface, both represented by the Class object. Generics augment these classes and interfaces with additional *type constraints*. These type constraints are not available on an instance because an instance always references a raw Class. For an instance all generic type constraints are *erased*. That is, a List<Integer> object is indistinguishable from a List<String> object, which are indistinguishable from a List object. Objects always refer to a raw Class object, this is the one returned from the getClass method. This Class object is shared between all instances and can therefore not have the actual type constraints (like String, Integer in the list examples).

When a class is used the compiler captures the type constraints and associates them with the specific use and encodes them in a Type object. For example, a field declaration captures the full generic type information:

```
List<String> strings;
```

A field has a getGenericType method that provides access to a Type object, which is a super interface for all type information in the Java 5 and later runtime. In the previous example, this would be a Parameterized Type that has a raw class of List and a type argument that is the String class. These constraints are reflectively available for:

- A superclass
- Implemented interfaces
- Fields
- For each method or constructor:
  - Return type
  - Exception types
  - Parameter types

Generics influence the type conversion rules because most of the time the Blueprint extender knows the actual Type object for an injection. Therefore, conversion must take place to a type like $T<P_1..P_n>$, where T is a raw Class object and $P_1..P_n$ form the available type parameters. For a non-parametrized class and for other VMs than 1.4, n is always zero, that is no type arguments are available. The P arguments are in itself instances of Type. The form $T<P_1..P_n>$ is called the *reified* form. It can be constructed by traversing the Type graph and calculating a class that matches the constraints. For example <? extends List<T>> defines a *wild card* constraint, that has a List<T> as reified type, where T is a Type Variable defined elsewhere that can have additional constraints. The resulting type must be an instance of List<T>. A reified type will use an object implementing List for such an example because that is the only class that is guaranteed to be compatible. The rules to reify the different Type interfaces are:

- Class – A Class represents unparameterized raw type and is reified into T<>. For example:

  ```
  String string;
  ```

- ParameterizedType – A Parameterized Type defines a raw type and 1..n typed parameters. The raw type of the Parameterized Type is also reified and represents T. The arguments map directly to the arguments of the reified form. An example of a Parameterized Type is:

  ```
  Map<String,Object> map;
  ```

- TypeVariable – Represents a Type Variable. A type variable is listed in a generics type declaration, for example in Map<K,V>, the K and V are the type variables. A type variable is bounded by a number of types because it is possible to declare a bounded type like: <A extends Readable&Closeable>. A Type Variable is reified by taking its first bound in reified form, this is the same as in Java 5 where the first bounds is the erasure type. However, this can fail if multiple bounds are present. An example of a Type Variable is:

  ```
  public <T extends ServiceTracker> void setMap(T st) {}
  ```

  In this example, the parameter st will have a reified type of ServiceTracker.
- WildcardType – A Wildcard Type constrains a type to a set of lower bounds and a set of upper bounds, at least in the reflective API. In the Java 5 and later syntax a Wildcard Type can only specify 0 or one lower and one upper bound, for example <T extends Number> constraints the Type Variable T to at least extend the Number class. A Wildcard Type is reified into its reified upper bound when no lower bound is set, and otherwise it is reified into its reified lower bound.

An example of a Wildcard Type is seen in the example of a Type Variable.

- GenericArrayType – A Generic Array Type represents an array. Its component type is reified and then converted to an array. The Reified Type will have the array class as reified class and the type arguments reflect the type arguments of the component type. For example:

```
public void setLists(List<String>[] lists) {}
```

This example will have a Reified Type of List[]<String>.

This specification is written to allow Java 1.4 implementations and clients, the API therefore has no generics. Therefore, the Type class in Java 5 and later cannot be used in the API. However, even if it could use the Type class, using the type classes to create the reified form is non-trivial and error prone. The API therefore provides a concrete class that gives convenient access to the reified form without requiring the usage of the Type class.

The ReifiedType class provides access to the reified form of Class, which is itself and has no type arguments. However, Blueprint extender implementations that recognize Java 5 generics should subclass the ReifiedType class and use this in the conversion process. The subclass can calculate the reified form of any Type subclasses.

121.10 Service Dynamics

The Blueprint Container specification handles the complexities of the dynamic nature of OSGi by *hiding* the dynamic behavior of the OSGi service registry, at least temporarily. This dynamic behavior is caused by service references that select one or more services that can come and go at runtime.

The Blueprint Container must handle the dynamics in the following way:

- *Proxied references* – Service reference managers must provide a proxy implementing the specified interfaces, instead of the actual service object it refers to. The proxy must fetch the real service lazily. For reference managers, when a proxy is used, and no candidate is available, a candidate must be found within a limited time. If no candidate service is available during this time, a Service Unavailable Exception must be thrown. The reference-list manager also maintains proxies but these proxies must throw a Service Unavailable Exception immediately when the proxy is used and the backing service is no longer available.
  When proxied references are used with stateful services, then the application code must register a reference listener to perform the necessary initialization and cleanup when a new backing service is bound.
- *Conditional Service Registrations* – The service manager is responsible for registering a service with the OSGi service registry. A service manager is statically dependent on the transitive set of managers that it depends on. If these static dependencies contain mandatory service references, then the manager's service must not be registered when any of these mandatory service references is unsatisfied, see *Enabled* on page 559.

121.10.1 Damping

When an operation is invoked on an unsatisfied proxy from a reference manager (either optional or mandatory), the invocation must block until either the reference becomes satisfied or a time-out expires (whichever comes first). During this wait, a WAITING event must be broadcast, see *Events* on page 582.

The default timeout for service invocations is 5 minutes. The optional timeout of the reference element specifies an alternate timeout (in milliseconds). If no matching service becomes available within the timeout, then a Service Unavailable Exception must be thrown. A timeout of zero means infinite and a negative timeout is an error.

For example:

```
<reference id="logService"
    interface="org.osgi.service.log.LogService"
    timeout="100000" />

<bean id="bar" class="BarImpl">
  <property name="log" ref="logService"/>
</bean>
```

When this Blueprint Container is instantiated, the reference manager provides a proxy for the Log Service, which gets injected in the log property. If no Log Service is available, then the proxy will have no backing service. If the bar object attempts to log, it will block and if the timeout expires the proxy must throw a Service Unavailable Exception.

If at some later point in time, a Log Service is registered then it becomes satisfied again. If bar now logs a message, the proxy will get the service object again and forward the method invocation to the actual Log Service implementation.

The damping ensures that a mandatory service reference that becomes unsatisfied does not cause the Blueprint Container to be destroyed. Temporary absences of mandatory services are tolerated to allow for administrative operations and continuous operation of as much of the system as possible.

A reference-list manager does not provide damping. It only removes the service proxy from the collection if its service goes away. Using a collection reference manager will never block, it will just have no members if its selection is empty. A timeout attribute is therefore not supported by the reference-list elements. However, the elements are proxied and it is possible that they throw a Service Unavailable Exception when used and the backing service has disappeared. The exceptions for a reference-list proxy will be thrown immediately when the proxy is used.

121.10.2   Iteration

The provided object of a reference-list manager implements the List interface. Depending on the memberType or the optional generics information, it provides a collection that contains the member objects, that is, either proxies to the service object, or ServiceReference objects. These collections are read-only for the receiver, however, their contents can dynamically change due to changes in the selection. The access to these collections with iterators must give a number of guarantees:

- *Safe* – All iterators of reference-list managers must be safe to traverse according to the Iterator interface contract, even while the underlying collection is being modified locally or in another thread. If the hasNext method returns true, the iterator must return a member object on the subsequent next method invocation. If there is no longer a service object available when requested, then a dummy proxy must be returned that throws a Service Unavailable Exception whenever it is used.
- *Visibility* – All the changes made to the collection that affect member objects not yet returned by the iterator must be visible in the iteration. Proxies for new services must be added at the end of the List. Proxies already returned can be affected by changes in the service registry after the iterator has returned them.

After the iterator has returned false for the hasNext method, no more objects can be obtained from it. A List Iterator must not be supported.

121.10.3   Mandatory Dependencies

A service manager can have mandatory service reference managers in its transitive dependencies. Such a service manager must ensure that the service object is registered with the OSGi service registry during the runtime phase when all its mandatory service references that it depends on are satisfied. This called *tracking* the dependency. A service manager is *enabled* when all its mandatory references in its dependencies are satisfied.

This tracking only works for dependencies declared directly in the definitions; dependencies established during runtime by calling the getComponentInstance method are not tracked.

In the following example, service manager S has a transitive dependency on the mandatory reference manager M, which means the Blueprint Container must ensure that the service object provided by bean A is registered when reference manager M is satisfied.

```
<service id="S" ref="A" interface="com.acme.Foo"/>
<bean id="A" class="com.acme.FooImpl">
   <property name="bar" ref="m"/>
</bean>
<reference id="M" interface="com.acme.Bar"
     availability="mandatory"/>
```

However, if the dependency from manager A on manager M is not declared but created through code that manipulates the Blueprint Container then the dependency is not tracked.

121.11 Blueprint Container

The Blueprint Container has a registry where all top-level managers, as well as *environment* managers, are registered by their component id. The Blueprint Container can be injected in application code with the environment blueprintContainer manager. For example:

```
<bean class="com.acme.FooImpl">
   <property name="container" ref="blueprintContainer"/>
</bean>
```

The Blueprint Container allows application code to get objects that are provided by the top-level managers through the getComponentInstance method. However, the Blueprint Container should not be required to get a component instance; the proper way to use Blueprint is to inject them. This declarative approach makes the Blueprint Container aware of any dependencies; one of the primary goals of a dependency injection framework. The Blueprint Container's introspective features are commonly used for management and other non-application purposes.

The Blueprint Container is registered as a service during the runtime phase so that other bundles can use it for these, and other, purposes.

121.11.1 Environment Managers

The Blueprint Container provides a number of *environment managers*. These managers have defined names and provide convenient access to information about the environment. Environment managers cannot be overridden by explicitly defined managers because it is invalid to define a manager with an existing component id. All component ids starting with blueprint are reserved for this specification and future incarnations.

There is no XML definition for environment managers but their Metadata must be provided as ComponentMetadata objects.

The following ids are used for the environment managers:

- blueprintContainer – The Blueprint Container.
- blueprintBundle – A manager that provides the Blueprint bundle's Bundle object.
- blueprintBundleContext – A manager that provides the Blueprint bundle's BundleContext object.
- blueprintConverter – A manager that provides an object implementing the Converter interface. This represents the built-in conversion facility that the Blueprint Container uses to convert objects. See *Built-in Converter* on page 577.

121.11.2   **Component Instances**

The Blueprint Container provides access to the component instances that the top level managers can provide, as well as their Metadata. The Blueprint Container has the following methods for requesting a component instance and to find out what managers are available:

- getComponentInstance(String) – This method will provide a component instance from the component id. If the manager has not been activated yet, it must atomically activate and ensure its explicit and implicit dependencies are activated transitively.
- getComponentIds() – Returns a set of component ids in this Blueprint Container. These ids must consist of all top level managers (including calculated ids) and environment managers.

121.11.3   **Access to Component Metadata**

Each of the manager types has specific Component Metadata subtypes associated with it. The Blueprint Container provides access by component id to the Component Metadata of the top level managers. However, managers can also be defined inline, in which case they do not have a component id. Therefore, the Blueprint Container can also enumerate all the managers that are represented by a Metadata sub-interface.

- getComponentMetadata(String) – Answer the Component Metadata sub-type for the given component id. Environment managers will return a ComponentMetadata object, the other managers each have their own specific Metadata type.
- getMetadata(Class) – Answer a collection with the Metadata of the given type, regardless if it is defined as/in a top-level or inlined manager. For example, getMetadata(ServiceMetadata.class) returns all Service Metadata in the Blueprint container. This includes all top level managers as well as any inlined managers. For Environment Managers, this method returns a ComponentMetadata object.

121.11.4   **Concurrency**

A Blueprint Container must be thread safe. Each method must handle the case when multiple threads access the underlying registry of managers. Activation of managers must be atomic. That is, other threads must be blocked until a manager is completely activated.

The Blueprint Container must handle reentrant calls.

121.12   Events

The Blueprint Container must track all Blueprint Listener services and keep these listeners updated of the progress or failure of all its managed bundles. The Blueprint Listener is kept informed by sending it events synchronously. These events are therefore normally delivered in order but in exceptional cases this can be seen out of order for a listener when new events are initiated synchronously from within a callback. Therefore, Blueprint Listener services should see the event as a notification, where actual work should be processed on another thread.

Blueprint Events must be sent to each registered Blueprint Listener service. This service has the following method:

- blueprintEvent(BlueprintEvent) – Notify the listener of a new Blueprint Event. These events are send synchronously with their cause. That is, all listeners must be notified before the Blueprint Container continues to the next step.

The events must be delivered as BlueprintEvent objects. The event types that they represent, and the data that these objects carry, is further described in *Blueprint Event* on page 583.

A Blueprint Listener services must be given the initial state of all managed bundles before normal processing starts, see *Replay* on page 583.

Blueprint Listener services that throw Exceptions or do not return in a reasonable time as judged by the Blueprint extender implementation, should be logged, if possible, and further ignored.

121.12.1   Blueprint Event

The Blueprint Event supports the following event types:

- CREATING – The Blueprint extender has started creating a Blueprint Container for the bundle.
- GRACE_PERIOD – The Blueprint Container enters the grace period. This event can be repeated multiple times when the list of dependencies changes due to changes in the service registry.
- CREATED – The Blueprint Container is ready. The application is now running.
- WAITING – A service reference is blocking because of unsatisfied mandatory dependencies. This event can happen multiple times in a row.
- DESTROYING – The Blueprint Container is being destroyed because the Blueprint bundle or Blueprint extender has stopped.
- DESTROYED – The Blueprint Container is completely destroyed.
- FAILURE – An error occurred during the creation of the Blueprint Container.

The Blueprint Event provides the following methods:

- getBundle() – The Blueprint bundle
- getCause() – Any occurred exception or null
- getDependencies() – A list of filters that specify the unsatisfied mandatory references.
- getExtenderBundle() – The Blueprint extender bundle.
- getTimestamp() – The time the event occurred
- getType() – The type of the event.
- isReplay() – Indicates if the event is a replay (true) or if it is a new event (false), see *Replay* on page 583.

121.12.2   Replay

The Blueprint Extender must remember the last Blueprint Event for each ready bundle that it manages, see *Initialization Steps* on page 537. During the (synchronous) service registration event of a Blueprint Listener service, the Blueprint extender must inform the Blueprint Listener service about all its managed bundles by sending it the last known event for each bundle the Blueprint extender manages. This initial event is called the *replay* event, and is marked as such.

The replay event must be delivered to the Blueprint Listener service as the first event, before any other event is delivered, during the registration of the Blueprint Listener service. That is, the blueprintEvent method must have returned before the first non-replay event can be delivered and no events must be lost. The replay events must be sent every time a Blueprint Listener service is registered.

The set of managed bundles is defined by bundles that are active and are managed by the Blueprint extender, even if their initialization ended in failure.

The BlueprintEvent object for a replay event must return true for the isReplay() method in this situation, and false in all other situations.

121.12.3   Event Admin Mapping

When the Event Admin service is present, the Blueprint extender must create an Event Admin event for each defined Blueprint Event. This Event Admin event must be asynchronously given to the Event Admin service with the postEvent method.

The topic of the Event Admin event is derived from the Blueprint event type with a fixed prefix. All topics must have the prefix of:

    TOPIC_BLUEPRINT_EVENTS

After this prefix, the name of the Blueprint Event type must be used as the suffix. That is, CREATING, GRACE_PERIOD, etc. For example, org/osgi/service/blueprint/container/GRACE_PERIOD.

For each Blueprint event the following properties must be included:

- TYPE – The type of the Event, see *Blueprint Event* on page 583.
- BUNDLE– (Bundle) The Bundle object of the Blueprint bundle
- BUNDLE_ID – (Long) The id of the Blueprint bundle.
- BUNDLE_SYMBOLICNAME – (String) The Bundle Symbolic Name of the Blueprint bundle.
- BUNDLE_VERSION - (Version) The version of the Blueprint bundle.
- EXTENDER_BUNDLE – (Bundle) the Bundle object of the Blueprint extender bundle.
- EXTENDER_BUNDLE_ID – (Long) The id of the Blueprint extender bundle
- EXTENDER_BUNDLE_SYMBOLICNAME – (String) The Bundle Symbolic Name of the Blueprint extender bundle.
- EXTENDER_BUNDLE_VERSION – (Version) The version of the Blueprint extender bundle
- TIMESTAMP – (Long) The time when the event occurred
- CAUSE – (Throwable) The failure cause, only included for a FAILURE event.
- DEPENDENCIES – (String[]) The filter of an unsatisfied service reference. Can only appear in a GRACE_PERIOD, WAITING or FAILURE event caused by a time-out.
- EVENT – (BlueprintEvent) The BlueprintEvent object that caused this event.

The property names for Blueprint Listener events may be conveniently referenced using the constants defined in the org.osgi.service.event.EventConstants and EventConstants interfaces.

The Event Admin events do not follow the replay model in use for Blueprint Listener services. That is, the Event Admin must only be kept informed about events as they occur.

121.13 Class Loading

The module layer in OSGi provides advanced class loading rules that potentially can cause bundles to live in different class spaces. This means that not all bundles can collaborate because the classes involved in the collaboration can come from different class loaders, which results in confusing Class Cast Exceptions on classes with the same name. It is therefore crucial that the Blueprint Container uses the Bundle Context and the bundle class loader of the Blueprint bundle for all actions that are made on behalf of the Blueprint bundle. Especially, access to the OSGi service registry must use the Bundle Context of the Blueprint bundle. Any dynamic class loading must use the Blueprint bundle's loadClass method. The normal OSGi mechanics will then ensure class space consistency for resolved bundles.

121.13.1 Blueprint Extender and Bundle Compatibility

For many Blueprint bundles, there is no class space compatibility issue. These bundles do not use any Blueprint classes and are therefore by definition compatible with any extender. However, if the Blueprint bundle uses some of the Blueprint packages, it must import these packages. Blueprint Containers must verify that they are *type compatible* with the Blueprint bundle before they attempt to manage it. See *Type Compatibility* on page 585.

121.13.2 XML and Class Loading

The Blueprint definition resources contain textual references to classes. These textual references will be loaded with the class loader of the Blueprint bundle. This implies that all the classes of provided component instances must be either imported or available from the bundle.

The Blueprint specification has the following attributes and elements that can cause imports:

- class
- value-type
- interface

- interfaces
- type
- key-type

All these attributes and elements are defined with the Tclass and Ttype XML Schema type for the Blueprint namespace. The Tclass defines simple class names, and Ttype defines types defined in *Syntax for Java types* on page 544.

121.13.3 Foreign Bundle Context

When using the Blueprint Container in its Blueprint bundle, the types that the managers provide are guaranteed to be compatible with the caller.

When using a Blueprint Container service in another bundle (for example, getting it as a service) then there is no guarantee of type compatibility or even visibility between the versions of the types of the returned managers, and the versions of the types visible to the caller. Care must therefore be taken when casting the return value of the getComponentInstance method to a more specific type.

121.13.4 Converters and Class Loading

A converter is closely coupled to its target class. If the converter comes from another bundle, then the converter bundle must ensure class space consistency between the converter implementation and the target class. This can be achieved by specifying the target class in the uses directive.

For example:

```
Export-Package:
    com.converters.ac;uses:="com.converters.dc"
```

A bundle that references a type converter defined in the Blueprint bundle does not need to export that type. When creating a Blueprint Container, the extender bundle uses the class loader of the Blueprint bundle.

121.13.5 Type Compatibility

Two bundles are type compatible for a given class if they both load the same class object, or if either bundle cannot load the given class.

To mitigate type incompatibility problems, a Blueprint extender must export the org.osgi.service.blueprint package. In the uses: directive, it should list any packages of classes that can be shared between the Blueprint extender and the Blueprint bundle. Blueprint bundles should import this package.

121.13.6 Visibility and Accessibility

The Blueprint Container must load any classes it needs through the Blueprint bundle's loadClass method. If a class can not be loaded, then the initialization fails. Class loading issues are further discussed in *Class Loading* on page 584.

The Blueprint Container must respect the accessibility of the class and any of its members. That is, the Blueprint Container must not use the setAccessibility method. All classes and reflected members must therefore be declared public or be implicitly public like the default constructor.

121.14 Metadata

An important aspect of the Blueprint specification is the so called *metadata* interfaces. These interfaces are used in the Blueprint Container to enable programmatic access to the XML definitions. During the parsing phase the Blueprint Container reads the XML and converts it to an object implementing the appropriate interface.

The XML elements and XML Schema types map to the Metadata interfaces. For example, <bean> maps to BeanMetadata. However, in several cases, the attributes and/or sub-elements in the Metadata interfaces are merged when possible. For example, the interface attribute and interfaces element in the service element are merged in the ServiceMetadata class' getInterfaces() method.

The interfaces are arranged in a comprehensive hierarchy that reflects their usage and constraints. This hierarchy is depicted inFigure 121.12 on page 586.

The hierarchy can roughly be divided in two parts. The first part is the sub-interfaces of the ComponentMetadata interface. These interfaces are defining the configuration data of the top-level and inlined managers. The manager's component instance(s) are injected with values during runtime. The configuration of how to create a specific value is also described with Metadata interfaces. For example, a Map object is described with configuration information in the MapMetadata interface. The hierarchy makes it clear that Component Metadata is also a value that can be injected. Keys in maps or properties can not be null. This is the reason the hierarchy is split at the top into a null value branch and a branch that can only generates non-null values.

The Target interface describes managers that can be used as the target for the reference listener or the registration listener, or a ref.

Figure 121.12   Metadata Interfaces Hierarchy

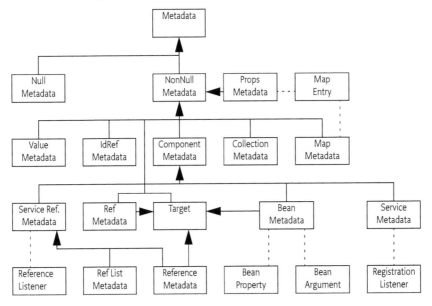

121.15   **Blueprint XML Schema**

The Blueprint schema included in this specification can be found in digital form at [10] *OSGi XML Schemas*. The schema listed here is not annotated, the digital form has annotations.

```xml
<?xml version="1.0" encoding="UTF-8"?>
<xsd:schema
    xmlns="http://www.osgi.org/xmlns/blueprint/v1.0.0"
    xmlns:xsd="http://www.w3.org/2001/XMLSchema"
    targetNamespace="http://www.osgi.org/xmlns/blueprint/v1.0.0"
    elementFormDefault="qualified"
    attributeFormDefault="unqualified"
    version="1.0.0">
    <xsd:complexType name="Tcomponent" abstract="true">
        <xsd:attribute name="id" type="xsd:ID"/>
```

```xsd
            <xsd:attribute name="activation" type="Tactivation"/>
            <xsd:attribute name="depends-on" type="TdependsOn"/>
    </xsd:complexType>
    <xsd:element name="blueprint" type="Tblueprint"/>
    <xsd:complexType name="Tblueprint">
        <xsd:sequence>
            <xsd:element name="description" type="Tdescription" minOccurs="0"/>
            <xsd:element name="type-converters" type="Ttype-converters"
                    minOccurs="0" maxOccurs="1"/>
            <xsd:choice minOccurs="0" maxOccurs="unbounded">
                <xsd:element name="service" type="Tservice"/>
                <xsd:element name="reference-list" type="Treference-list"/>
                <xsd:element name="bean" type="Tbean"/>
                <xsd:element name="reference" type="Treference"/>
                <xsd:any namespace="##other" processContents="strict"/>
            </xsd:choice>
        </xsd:sequence>
        <xsd:attribute name="default-activation" default="eager" type="Tactivation"/>
        <xsd:attribute name="default-timeout" type="Ttimeout" default="300000"/>
        <xsd:attribute name="default-availability" type="Tavailability" default="mandatory"/>
        <xsd:anyAttribute namespace="##other" processContents="strict"/>
    </xsd:complexType>
    <xsd:complexType name="Ttype-converters">
        <xsd:choice minOccurs="0" maxOccurs="unbounded">
            <xsd:element name="bean" type="Tbean"/>
            <xsd:element name="reference" type="Treference"/>
            <xsd:element name="ref" type="Tref"/>
            <xsd:any namespace="##other" processContents="strict"/>
        </xsd:choice>
    </xsd:complexType>
    <xsd:group name="GtargetComponent">
        <xsd:choice>
            <xsd:element name="bean" type="Tinlined-bean"/>
            <xsd:element name="reference" type="Tinlined-reference"/>
            <xsd:element name="ref" type="Tref"/>
            <xsd:any namespace="##other" processContents="strict"/>
        </xsd:choice>
    </xsd:group>
    <xsd:group name="GallComponents">
        <xsd:choice>
            <xsd:element name="service" type="Tinlined-service"/>
            <xsd:element name="reference-list" type="Tinlined-reference-list"/>
            <xsd:group ref="GtargetComponent"/>
        </xsd:choice>
    </xsd:group>
    <xsd:group name="GbeanElements">
        <xsd:sequence>
            <xsd:element name="description" type="Tdescription" minOccurs="0"/>
            <xsd:choice minOccurs="0" maxOccurs="unbounded">
                <xsd:element name="argument" type="Targument"/>
                <xsd:element name="property" type="Tproperty"/>
                <xsd:any namespace="##other" processContents="strict"/>
            </xsd:choice>
        </xsd:sequence>
    </xsd:group>
    <xsd:complexType name="Tbean">
        <xsd:complexContent>
            <xsd:extension base="Tcomponent">
                <xsd:group ref="GbeanElements"/>
                <xsd:attribute name="class" type="Tclass"/>
                <xsd:attribute name="init-method" type="Tmethod"/>
                <xsd:attribute name="destroy-method" type="Tmethod"/>
                <xsd:attribute name="factory-method" type="Tmethod"/>
                <xsd:attribute name="factory-ref" type="Tidref"/>
                <xsd:attribute name="scope" type="Tscope"/>
                <xsd:anyAttribute namespace="##other" processContents="strict"/>
            </xsd:extension>
        </xsd:complexContent>
    </xsd:complexType>
    <xsd:complexType name="Tinlined-bean">
        <xsd:complexContent>
            <xsd:restriction base="Tbean">
                <xsd:group ref="GbeanElements"/>
                <xsd:attribute name="id" use="prohibited"/>
```

```xml
                    <xsd:attribute name="depends-on" type="TdependsOn"/>
                    <xsd:attribute name="activation" use="prohibited" fixed="lazy"/>
                    <xsd:attribute name="class" type="Tclass"/>
                    <xsd:attribute name="init-method" type="Tmethod"/>
                    <xsd:attribute name="destroy-method" use="prohibited"/>
                    <xsd:attribute name="factory-method" type="Tmethod"/>
                    <xsd:attribute name="factory-ref" type="Tidref"/>
                    <xsd:attribute name="scope" use="prohibited" fixed="prototype"/>
                    <xsd:anyAttribute namespace="##other" processContents="strict"/>
                </xsd:restriction>
            </xsd:complexContent>
        </xsd:complexType>
        <xsd:complexType name="Targument">
            <xsd:sequence>
                <xsd:element name="description" type="Tdescription" minOccurs="0"/>
                <xsd:group ref="Gvalue" minOccurs="0"/>
            </xsd:sequence>
            <xsd:attribute name="index" type="xsd:nonNegativeInteger"/>
            <xsd:attribute name="type" type="Ttype"/>
            <xsd:attribute name="ref" type="Tidref"/>
            <xsd:attribute name="value" type="TstringValue"/>
        </xsd:complexType>
        <xsd:complexType name="Tproperty">
            <xsd:sequence>
                <xsd:element name="description" type="Tdescription" minOccurs="0"/>
                <xsd:group ref="Gvalue" minOccurs="0"/>
            </xsd:sequence>
            <xsd:attribute name="name" type="Tmethod" use="required"/>
            <xsd:attribute name="ref" type="Tidref"/>
            <xsd:attribute name="value" type="TstringValue"/>
        </xsd:complexType>
        <xsd:complexType name="Tkey">
            <xsd:group ref="GnonNullValue"/>
        </xsd:complexType>
        <xsd:complexType name="Treference">
            <xsd:complexContent>
                <xsd:extension base="TserviceReference">
                    <xsd:sequence>
                        <xsd:any namespace="##other"
                            minOccurs="0" maxOccurs="unbounded" processContents="strict"/>
                    </xsd:sequence>
                    <xsd:attribute name="timeout" type="Ttimeout"/>
                </xsd:extension>
            </xsd:complexContent>
        </xsd:complexType>
        <xsd:complexType name="Tinlined-reference">
            <xsd:complexContent>
                <xsd:restriction base="Treference">
                    <xsd:sequence>
                        <xsd:group ref="GserviceReferenceElements"/>
                        <xsd:any namespace="##other"
                            minOccurs="0" maxOccurs="unbounded" processContents="strict"/>
                    </xsd:sequence>
                    <xsd:attribute name="id" use="prohibited"/>
                    <xsd:attribute name="depends-on" type="TdependsOn"/>
                    <xsd:attribute name="activation" use="prohibited" fixed="lazy"/>
                    <xsd:attribute name="interface" type="Tclass"/>
                    <xsd:attribute name="filter" type="xsd:normalizedString"/>
                    <xsd:attribute name="component-name" type="Tidref"/>
                    <xsd:attribute name="availability" type="Tavailability"/>
                    <xsd:attribute name="timeout" type="Ttimeout"/>
                    <xsd:anyAttribute namespace="##other" processContents="strict"/>
                </xsd:restriction>
            </xsd:complexContent>
        </xsd:complexType>
        <xsd:complexType name="Treference-list">
            <xsd:complexContent>
                <xsd:extension base="TserviceReference">
                    <xsd:sequence>
                        <xsd:any namespace="##other"
                            minOccurs="0" maxOccurs="unbounded" processContents="strict"/>
                    </xsd:sequence>
                    <xsd:attribute name="member-type" type="Tservice-use" default="service-object"/>
                </xsd:extension>
            </xsd:complexContent>
```

```
        </xsd:complexType>
    <xsd:complexType name="Tinlined-reference-list">
        <xsd:complexContent>
            <xsd:restriction base="Treference-list">
                <xsd:sequence>
                    <xsd:group ref="GserviceReferenceElements"/>
                    <xsd:any namespace="##other"
                            minOccurs="0" maxOccurs="unbounded" processContents="strict"/>
                </xsd:sequence>
                <xsd:attribute name="id" use="prohibited"/>
                <xsd:attribute name="depends-on" type="TdependsOn"/>
                <xsd:attribute name="activation" use="prohibited" fixed="lazy"/>
                <xsd:attribute name="interface" type="Tclass"/>
                <xsd:attribute name="filter" type="xsd:normalizedString"/>
                <xsd:attribute name="component-name" type="Tidref"/>
                <xsd:attribute name="availability" type="Tavailability"/>
                <xsd:attribute name="member-type" type="Tservice-use" default="service-object"/>
                <xsd:anyAttribute namespace="##other" processContents="strict"/>
            </xsd:restriction>
        </xsd:complexContent>
    </xsd:complexType>
    <xsd:complexType name="TserviceReference">
        <xsd:complexContent>
            <xsd:extension base="Tcomponent">
                <xsd:sequence>
                    <xsd:group ref="GserviceReferenceElements"/>
                </xsd:sequence>
                <xsd:attribute name="interface" type="Tclass"/>
                <xsd:attribute name="filter" type="xsd:normalizedString"/>
                <xsd:attribute name="component-name" type="Tidref"/>
                <xsd:attribute name="availability" type="Tavailability"/>
                <xsd:anyAttribute namespace="##other" processContents="strict"/>
            </xsd:extension>
        </xsd:complexContent>
    </xsd:complexType>
    <xsd:group name="GserviceReferenceElements">
        <xsd:sequence>
            <xsd:element name="description" type="Tdescription" minOccurs="0"/>
            <xsd:element name="reference-listener"
                    type="TreferenceListener" minOccurs="0" maxOccurs="unbounded"/>
        </xsd:sequence>
    </xsd:group>
    <xsd:complexType name="TreferenceListener">
        <xsd:sequence>
            <xsd:group ref="GtargetComponent" minOccurs="0"/>
        </xsd:sequence>
        <xsd:attribute name="ref" type="Tidref"/>
        <xsd:attribute name="bind-method" type="Tmethod"/>
        <xsd:attribute name="unbind-method" type="Tmethod"/>
    </xsd:complexType>
    <xsd:simpleType name="Tactivation">
        <xsd:restriction base="xsd:NMTOKEN">
            <xsd:enumeration value="eager"/>
            <xsd:enumeration value="lazy"/>
        </xsd:restriction>
    </xsd:simpleType>
    <xsd:simpleType name="Tavailability">
        <xsd:restriction base="xsd:NMTOKEN">
            <xsd:enumeration value="mandatory"/>
            <xsd:enumeration value="optional"/>
        </xsd:restriction>
    </xsd:simpleType>
    <xsd:complexType name="Tservice">
        <xsd:complexContent>
            <xsd:extension base="Tcomponent">
                <xsd:sequence>
                    <xsd:group ref="GserviceElements"/>
                </xsd:sequence>
                <xsd:attribute name="interface" type="Tclass"/>
                <xsd:attribute name="ref" type="Tidref"/>
                <xsd:attribute name="auto-export" type="TautoExportModes" default="disabled"/>
                <xsd:attribute name="ranking" type="xsd:int" default="0"/>
                <xsd:anyAttribute namespace="##other" processContents="strict"/>
            </xsd:extension>
        </xsd:complexContent>
```

```
      </xsd:complexType>
      <xsd:complexType name="Tinlined-service">
         <xsd:complexContent>
            <xsd:restriction base="Tservice">
               <xsd:sequence>
                  <xsd:group ref="GserviceElements"/>
               </xsd:sequence>
               <xsd:attribute name="id" use="prohibited"/>
               <xsd:attribute name="depends-on" type="TdependsOn"/>
               <xsd:attribute name="activation" use="prohibited" fixed="lazy"/>
               <xsd:attribute name="interface" type="Tclass"/>
               <xsd:attribute name="ref" type="Tidref"/>
               <xsd:attribute name="auto-export" type="TautoExportModes" default="disabled"/>
               <xsd:attribute name="ranking" type="xsd:int" default="0"/>
               <xsd:anyAttribute namespace="##other" processContents="strict"/>
            </xsd:restriction>
         </xsd:complexContent>
      </xsd:complexType>
      <xsd:group name="GbaseServiceElements">
         <xsd:sequence>
            <xsd:element name="description" type="Tdescription" minOccurs="0"/>
            <xsd:element name="interfaces" type="Tinterfaces" minOccurs="0"/>
            <xsd:element name="service-properties" type="TserviceProperties" minOccurs="0"/>
            <xsd:element name="registration-listener"
                  type="TregistrationListener" minOccurs="0" maxOccurs="unbounded"/>
         </xsd:sequence>
      </xsd:group>
      <xsd:group name="GserviceElements">
         <xsd:sequence>
            <xsd:group ref="GbaseServiceElements"/>
            <xsd:group ref="GtargetComponent" minOccurs="0"/>
         </xsd:sequence>
      </xsd:group>
      <xsd:complexType name="TregistrationListener">
         <xsd:sequence>
            <xsd:group ref="GtargetComponent" minOccurs="0"/>
         </xsd:sequence>
         <xsd:attribute name="ref" type="Tidref"/>
         <xsd:attribute name="registration-method" type="Tmethod"/>
         <xsd:attribute name="unregistration-method" type="Tmethod"/>
      </xsd:complexType>
      <xsd:group name="Gvalue">
         <xsd:choice>
            <xsd:group ref="GnonNullValue"/>
            <xsd:element name="null" type="Tnull"/>
         </xsd:choice>
      </xsd:group>
      <xsd:complexType name="Tnull"/>
      <xsd:group name="GnonNullValue">
         <xsd:choice>
            <xsd:group ref="GallComponents"/>
            <xsd:element name="idref" type="Tref"/>
            <xsd:element name="value" type="Tvalue"/>
            <xsd:element name="list" type="Tcollection"/>
            <xsd:element name="set" type="Tcollection"/>
            <xsd:element name="map" type="Tmap"/>
            <xsd:element name="array" type="Tcollection"/>
            <xsd:element name="props" type="Tprops"/>
         </xsd:choice>
      </xsd:group>
      <xsd:complexType name="Tref">
         <xsd:attribute name="component-id" type="Tidref" use="required"/>
      </xsd:complexType>
      <xsd:complexType name="Tvalue" mixed="true">
         <xsd:attribute name="type" type="Ttype"/>
      </xsd:complexType>
      <xsd:complexType name="TtypedCollection">
         <xsd:attribute name="value-type" type="Ttype"/>
      </xsd:complexType>
      <xsd:complexType name="Tcollection">
         <xsd:complexContent>
            <xsd:extension base="TtypedCollection">
               <xsd:group ref="Gvalue" minOccurs="0" maxOccurs="unbounded"/>
            </xsd:extension>
         </xsd:complexContent>
```

```xml
  </xsd:complexType>
  <xsd:complexType name="Tprops">
    <xsd:sequence>
      <xsd:element name="prop" type="Tprop" minOccurs="0" maxOccurs="unbounded"/>
    </xsd:sequence>
  </xsd:complexType>
  <xsd:complexType name="Tprop" mixed="true">
    <xsd:attribute name="key" type="TstringValue" use="required"/>
    <xsd:attribute name="value" type="TstringValue"/>
  </xsd:complexType>
  <xsd:complexType name="Tmap">
    <xsd:complexContent>
      <xsd:extension base="TtypedCollection">
        <xsd:sequence>
          <xsd:element name="entry" type="TmapEntry" minOccurs="0" maxOccurs="unbounded"/>
        </xsd:sequence>
        <xsd:attribute name="key-type" type="Ttype"/>
      </xsd:extension>
    </xsd:complexContent>
  </xsd:complexType>
  <xsd:complexType name="TmapEntry">
    <xsd:sequence>
      <xsd:element name="key" type="Tkey" minOccurs="0"/>
      <xsd:group ref="Gvalue" minOccurs="0"/>
    </xsd:sequence>
    <xsd:attribute name="key" type="TstringValue"/>
    <xsd:attribute name="key-ref" type="Tidref"/>
    <xsd:attribute name="value" type="TstringValue"/>
    <xsd:attribute name="value-ref" type="Tidref"/>
  </xsd:complexType>
  <xsd:complexType name="TserviceProperties">
    <xsd:sequence>
      <xsd:element name="entry"
          type="TservicePropertyEntry" minOccurs="0" maxOccurs="unbounded"/>
      <xsd:any namespace="##other"
          processContents="strict" minOccurs="0" maxOccurs="unbounded"/>
    </xsd:sequence>
  </xsd:complexType>
  <xsd:complexType name="TservicePropertyEntry">
    <xsd:sequence>
      <xsd:group ref="Gvalue" minOccurs="0"/>
    </xsd:sequence>
    <xsd:attribute name="key" type="TstringValue" use="required"/>
    <xsd:attribute name="value" type="TstringValue"/>
  </xsd:complexType>
  <xsd:complexType name="Tdescription" mixed="true">
    <xsd:choice minOccurs="0" maxOccurs="unbounded"/>
  </xsd:complexType>
  <xsd:complexType name="Tinterfaces">
    <xsd:choice minOccurs="1" maxOccurs="unbounded">
      <xsd:element name="value" type="TinterfaceValue"/>
    </xsd:choice>
  </xsd:complexType>
  <xsd:simpleType name="TinterfaceValue">
    <xsd:restriction base="Tclass"/>
  </xsd:simpleType>
  <xsd:simpleType name="Tclass">
    <xsd:restriction base="xsd:NCName"/>
  </xsd:simpleType>
  <xsd:simpleType name="Ttype">
    <xsd:restriction base="xsd:token">
      <xsd:pattern value="[\i-[:]][\c-[:]]*(\[\])*"/>
    </xsd:restriction>
  </xsd:simpleType>
  <xsd:simpleType name="Tmethod">
    <xsd:restriction base="xsd:NCName"/>
  </xsd:simpleType>
  <xsd:simpleType name="Tidref">
    <xsd:restriction base="xsd:NCName"/>
  </xsd:simpleType>
  <xsd:simpleType name="TstringValue">
    <xsd:restriction base="xsd:normalizedString"/>
  </xsd:simpleType>
  <xsd:simpleType name="TautoExportModes">
    <xsd:restriction base="xsd:NMTOKEN">
```

```
            <xsd:enumeration value="disabled"/>
            <xsd:enumeration value="interfaces"/>
            <xsd:enumeration value="class-hierarchy"/>
            <xsd:enumeration value="all-classes"/>
        </xsd:restriction>
    </xsd:simpleType>
    <xsd:simpleType name="Ttimeout">
        <xsd:restriction base="xsd:unsignedLong"/>
    </xsd:simpleType>
    <xsd:simpleType name="TdependsOn">
        <xsd:restriction>
            <xsd:simpleType>
                <xsd:list itemType="Tidref"/>
            </xsd:simpleType>
            <xsd:minLength value="1"/>
        </xsd:restriction>
    </xsd:simpleType>
    <xsd:simpleType name="Tscope">
        <xsd:restriction base="xsd:NMTOKEN">
            <xsd:enumeration value="singleton"/>
            <xsd:enumeration value="prototype"/>
        </xsd:restriction>
    </xsd:simpleType>
    <xsd:simpleType name="Tservice-use">
        <xsd:restriction base="xsd:NMTOKEN">
            <xsd:enumeration value="service-object"/>
            <xsd:enumeration value="service-reference"/>
        </xsd:restriction>
    </xsd:simpleType>
</xsd:schema>
```

121.16 Security

121.16.1 Blueprint Extender

A Blueprint Extender must use the Bundle Context of the Blueprint bundle. This will ensure that much of the resources allocated will be used on behalf of the Blueprint bundle. However, most Java 2 permissions will also verify the stack and this will inevitably include the Blueprint extender's code. Therefore, the Blueprint extender will require the combined set of permissions needed by all Blueprint bundles. It is therefore likely that in practical situations the Blueprint extender requires All Permission.

The Blueprint bundle requires permission for all actions that are done by the Blueprint Container on behalf of this bundle. That is, the Blueprint Container must not give any extra permissions to the Blueprint bundle because it is being extended.

A Blueprint Container must therefore use a doPriviliged block around all actions that execute code on behalf of the Blueprint bundle. This doPrivileged block must use an Access Control Context that represents the permissions of the Blueprint bundle. This Access Control Context for the Blueprint bundle can be obtained from the Conditional Permission Admin.

For example, if a Blueprint bundle defines the following bean:

```
<bean class="java.lang.System" factory-method="exit">
    <argument value="1"/>
</bean>
```

Then the Blueprint bundle must have the proper permission to exit the system or the Blueprint bundle must fail when the bean is constructed. At the same time, a Blueprint bundle must not be required to have any permission needed by the Blueprint Container to performs its tasks.

A Blueprint Container must never use the setAccessibility method on a returned member. Only publicly accessible members must be used. Using a non-publicly accessible member must initiate failure, resulting in the destruction of the container.

121.17   org.osgi.service.blueprint.container

Blueprint Container Package Version 1.0.

Bundles wishing to use this package must list the package in the Import-Package header of the bundle's manifest. For example:

```
Import-Package: org.osgi.service.blueprint.container; version="[1.0,2.0)"
```

This package defines the primary interface to a Blueprint Container, BlueprintContainer. An instance of this type is available inside a Blueprint Container as an implicitly defined component with the name "blueprintContainer".

This package also declares the supporting exception types, listener, and constants for working with a Blueprint Container.

121.17.1   Summary

- *BlueprintContainer* - A Blueprint Container represents the managed state of a Blueprint bundle.
- *BlueprintEvent* - A Blueprint Event.
- *BlueprintListener* - A BlueprintEvent Listener.
- *ComponentDefinitionException* - A Blueprint exception indicating that a component definition is in error.
- *Converter* - Type converter to convert an object to a target type.
- *EventConstants* - Event property names used in Event Admin events published by a Blueprint Container.
- *NoSuchComponentException* - A Blueprint exception indicating that a component does not exist in a Blueprint Container.
- *ReifiedType* - Provides access to a concrete type and its optional generic type parameters.
- *ServiceUnavailableException* - A Blueprint exception indicating that a service is unavailable.

121.17.2   public interface BlueprintContainer

A Blueprint Container represents the managed state of a Blueprint bundle. A Blueprint Container provides access to all managed components. These are the beans, services, and service references. Only bundles in the ACTIVE state (and also the STARTING state for bundles awaiting lazy activation) can have an associated Blueprint Container. A given Bundle Context has at most one associated Blueprint Container. A Blueprint Container can be obtained by injecting the predefined "blueprintContainer" component id. The Blueprint Container is also registered as a service and its managed components can be queried.

Concurrency   Thread-safe

121.17.2.1   public Set getComponentIds( )

□ Returns the set of component ids managed by this Blueprint Container.

Returns   An immutable Set of Strings, containing the ids of all of the components managed within this Blueprint Container.

121.17.2.2   public Object getComponentInstance(String id)

id   The component id for the requested component instance.

□ Return the component instance for the specified component id. If the component's manager has not yet been activated, calling this operation will atomically activate it. If the component has singleton scope, the activation will cause the component instance to be created and initialized. If the component has prototype scope, then each call to this method will return a new component instance.

Returns   A component instance for the component with the specified component id.

Throws NoSuchComponentException – If no component with the specified component id is managed by this Blueprint Container.

121.17.2.3   **public ComponentMetadata getComponentMetadata(String id)**

id The component id for the requested Component Metadata.

☐ Return the Component Metadata object for the component with the specified component id.

Returns The Component Metadata object for the component with the specified component id.

Throws NoSuchComponentException – If no component with the specified component id is managed by this Blueprint Container.

121.17.2.4   **public Collection getMetadata(Class type)**

type The super type or type of the requested Component Metadata objects.

☐ Return all ComponentMetadata objects of the specified Component Metadata type. The supported Component Metadata types are ComponentMetadata (which returns the Component Metadata for all defined manager types), BeanMetadata , ServiceReferenceMetadata (which returns both ReferenceMetadata and ReferenceListMetadata objects), and ServiceMetadata. The collection will include all Component Metadata objects of the requested type, including components that are declared inline.

Returns An immutable collection of Component Metadata objects of the specified type.

121.17.3   public class BlueprintEvent

A Blueprint Event.

BlueprintEvent objects are delivered to all registered BlueprintListener services. Blueprint Events must be asynchronously delivered in chronological order with respect to each listener.

In addition, after a Blueprint Listener is registered, the Blueprint extender will synchronously send to this Blueprint Listener the last Blueprint Event for each ready Blueprint bundle managed by this extender. This *replay* of Blueprint Events is designed so that the new Blueprint Listener can be informed of the state of each Blueprint bundle. Blueprint Events sent during this replay will have the isReplay() flag set. The Blueprint extender must ensure that this replay phase does not interfere with new Blueprint Events so that the chronological order of all Blueprint Events received by the Blueprint Listener is preserved. If the last Blueprint Event for a given Blueprint bundle is DESTROYED, the extender must not send it during this replay phase.

A type code is used to identify the type of event. The following event types are defined:

- CREATING
- CREATED
- DESTROYING
- DESTROYED
- FAILURE
- GRACE_PERIOD
- WAITING

In addition to calling the registered BlueprintListener services, the Blueprint extender must also send those events to the Event Admin service, if it is available.

See Also BlueprintListener, EventConstants

Concurrency Immutable

121.17.3.1   **public static final int CREATED = 2**

The Blueprint extender has created a Blueprint Container for the bundle. This event is sent after the Blueprint Container has been registered as a service.

121.17.3.2   **public static final int CREATING = 1**

The Blueprint extender has started creating a Blueprint Container for the bundle.

121.17.3.3   **public static final int DESTROYED = 4**

The Blueprint Container for the bundle has been completely destroyed. This event is sent after the Blueprint Container has been unregistered as a service.

121.17.3.4   **public static final int DESTROYING = 3**

The Blueprint extender has started destroying the Blueprint Container for the bundle.

121.17.3.5   **public static final int FAILURE = 5**

The Blueprint Container creation for the bundle has failed. If this event is sent after a timeout in the Grace Period, the getDependencies() method must return an array of missing mandatory dependencies. The event must also contain the cause of the failure as a Throwable through the getCause() method.

121.17.3.6   **public static final int GRACE_PERIOD = 6**

The Blueprint Container has entered the grace period. The list of missing dependencies must be made available through the getDependencies() method. During the grace period, a GRACE_PERIOD event is sent each time the set of unsatisfied dependencies changes.

121.17.3.7   **public static final int WAITING = 7**

The Blueprint Container is waiting on the availability of a service to satisfy an invocation on a referenced service. The missing dependency must be made available through the getDependencies() method which will return an array containing one filter object as a String.

121.17.3.8   **public BlueprintEvent(int type, Bundle bundle, Bundle extenderBundle)**

type The type of this event.

bundle The Blueprint bundle associated with this event. This parameter must not be null.

extenderBundle The Blueprint extender bundle that is generating this event. This parameter must not be null.

☐ Create a simple BlueprintEvent object.

121.17.3.9   **public BlueprintEvent(int type, Bundle bundle, Bundle extenderBundle, String[] dependencies)**

type The type of this event.

bundle The Blueprint bundle associated with this event. This parameter must not be null.

extenderBundle The Blueprint extender bundle that is generating this event. This parameter must not be null.

dependencies An array of String filters for each dependency associated with this event. Must be a non-empty array for event types FAILURE, GRACE_PERIOD and WAITING. Must be null for other event types.

☐ Create a BlueprintEvent object associated with a set of dependencies.

121.17.3.10   **public BlueprintEvent(int type, Bundle bundle, Bundle extenderBundle, Throwable cause)**

type The type of this event.

bundle The Blueprint bundle associated with this event. This parameter must not be null.

extenderBundle The Blueprint extender bundle that is generating this event. This parameter must not be null.

cause A Throwable object describing the root cause of the event. May be null.

☐ Create a BlueprintEvent object associated with a failure cause.

121.17.3.11   **public BlueprintEvent(int type, Bundle bundle, Bundle extenderBundle, String[] dependencies, Throwable cause)**

type   The type of this event.

bundle   The Blueprint bundle associated with this event. This parameter must not be null.

extenderBundle   The Blueprint extender bundle that is generating this event. This parameter must not be null.

dependencies   An array of String filters for each dependency associated with this event. Must be a non-empty array for event types FAILURE, GRACE_PERIOD and WAITING. Must be null for other event types.

cause   A Throwable object describing the root cause of this event. May be null.

□ Create a BlueprintEvent object associated with a failure cause and a set of dependencies.

121.17.3.12   **public BlueprintEvent(BlueprintEvent event, boolean replay)**

event   The original BlueprintEvent to copy. Must not be null.

replay   true if this event should be used as a replay event.

□ Create a new BlueprintEvent from the specified BlueprintEvent. The timestamp property will be copied from the original event and only the replay property will be overridden with the given value.

121.17.3.13   **public Bundle getBundle( )**

□ Return the Blueprint bundle associated with this event.

Returns   The Blueprint bundle associated with this event.

121.17.3.14   **public Throwable getCause( )**

□ Return the cause for this FAILURE event.

Returns   The cause of the failure for this event. May be null .

121.17.3.15   **public String[] getDependencies( )**

□ Return the filters identifying the missing dependencies that caused this event.

Returns   The filters identifying the missing dependencies that caused this event if the event type is one of WAITING, GRACE_PERIOD or FAILURE or null for the other event types.

121.17.3.16   **public Bundle getExtenderBundle( )**

□ Return the Blueprint extender bundle that is generating this event.

Returns   The Blueprint extender bundle that is generating this event.

121.17.3.17   **public long getTimestamp( )**

□ Return the time at which this event was created.

Returns   The time at which this event was created.

121.17.3.18   **public int getType( )**

□ Return the type of this event.

The type values are:

- CREATING
- CREATED
- DESTROYING
- DESTROYED
- FAILURE
- GRACE_PERIOD
- WAITING

Returns The type of this event.

121.17.3.19　　**public boolean isReplay( )**

　　　　□ Return whether this event is a replay event.

Returns true if this event is a replay event and false otherwise.

121.17.4　public interface BlueprintListener

A BlueprintEvent Listener.

To receive Blueprint Events, a bundle must register a Blueprint Listener service. After a Blueprint Listener is registered, the Blueprint extender must synchronously send to this Blueprint Listener the last Blueprint Event for each ready Blueprint bundle managed by this extender. This replay of Blueprint Events is designed so that the new Blueprint Listener can be informed of the state of each Blueprint bundle. Blueprint Events sent during this replay will have the isReplay() flag set. The Blueprint extender must ensure that this replay phase does not interfere with new Blueprint Events so that the chronological order of all Blueprint Events received by the Blueprint Listener is preserved. If the last Blueprint Event for a given Blueprint bundle is DESTROYED, the extender must not send it during this replay phase.

See Also BlueprintEvent

Concurrency Thread-safe

121.17.4.1　　**public void blueprintEvent(BlueprintEvent event)**

event The BlueprintEvent.

　　　　□ Receives notifications of a Blueprint Event. Implementers should quickly process the event and return.

121.17.5　public class ComponentDefinitionException
extends RuntimeException

A Blueprint exception indicating that a component definition is in error. This exception is thrown when a configuration-related error occurs during creation of a Blueprint Container.

121.17.5.1　　**public ComponentDefinitionException( )**

　　　　□ Creates a Component Definition Exception with no message or exception cause.

121.17.5.2　　**public ComponentDefinitionException(String explanation)**

explanation The associated message.

　　　　□ Creates a Component Definition Exception with the specified message

121.17.5.3　　**public ComponentDefinitionException(String explanation, Throwable cause)**

explanation The associated message.

cause The cause of this exception.

　　　　□ Creates a Component Definition Exception with the specified message and exception cause.

121.17.5.4　　**public ComponentDefinitionException(Throwable cause)**

cause The cause of this exception.

　　　　□ Creates a Component Definition Exception with the exception cause.

121.17.6　public interface Converter

Type converter to convert an object to a target type.

Concurrency　Thread-safe

121.17.6.1　public boolean canConvert(Object sourceObject, ReifiedType targetType)

sourceObject　The source object s to convert.

targetType　The target type T.

□　Return if this converter is able to convert the specified object to the specified type.

Returns　true if the conversion is possible, false otherwise.

121.17.6.2　public Object convert(Object sourceObject, ReifiedType targetType) throws Exception

sourceObject　The source object s to convert.

targetType　The target type T.

□　Convert the specified object to an instance of the specified type.

Returns　An instance with a type that is assignable from targetType's raw class

Throws　Exception – If the conversion cannot succeed. This exception should not be thrown when the can-Convert method has returned true.

121.17.7　public class EventConstants

Event property names used in Event Admin events published by a Blueprint Container.

Each type of event is sent to a different topic:

org/osgi/service/blueprint/container/ *<event-type>*

where *<event-type>* can have the values CREATING, CREATED, DESTROYING, DESTROYED, FAILURE, GRACE_PERIOD, or WAITING.

Such events have the following properties:

- type
- event
- timestamp
- bundle
- bundle.symbolicName
- bundle.id
- bundle.version
- extender.bundle.symbolicName
- extender.bundle.id
- extender.bundle.version
- dependencies
- cause

Concurrency　Immutable

121.17.7.1　public static final String BUNDLE = "bundle"

The Blueprint bundle associated with this event. This property is of type Bundle.

121.17.7.2　public static final String BUNDLE_ID = "bundle.id"

The bundle id of the Blueprint bundle associated with this event. This property is of type Long.

121.17.7.3   **public static final String BUNDLE_SYMBOLICNAME = "bundle.symbolicName"**

The bundle symbolic name of the Blueprint bundle associated with this event. This property is of type String.

121.17.7.4   **public static final String BUNDLE_VERSION = "bundle.version"**

The bundle version of the Blueprint bundle associated with this event. This property is of type Version.

121.17.7.5   **public static final String CAUSE = "cause"**

The cause for a FAILURE event. This property is of type Throwable.

121.17.7.6   **public static final String DEPENDENCIES = "dependencies"**

The filters identifying the missing dependencies that caused this event for a FAILURE, GRACE_PERIOD, or WAITING event. This property type is an array of String.

121.17.7.7   **public static final String EVENT = "event"**

The BlueprintEvent object that caused this event. This property is of type BlueprintEvent.

121.17.7.8   **public static final String EXTENDER_BUNDLE = "extender.bundle"**

The Blueprint extender bundle that is generating this event. This property is of type Bundle.

121.17.7.9   **public static final String EXTENDER_BUNDLE_ID = "extender.bundle.id"**

The bundle id of the Blueprint extender bundle that is generating this event. This property is of type Long.

121.17.7.10   **public static final String EXTENDER_BUNDLE_SYMBOLICNAME = "extender.bundle.symbolicName"**

The bundle symbolic of the Blueprint extender bundle that is generating this event. This property is of type String.

121.17.7.11   **public static final String EXTENDER_BUNDLE_VERSION = "extender.bundle.version"**

The bundle version of the Blueprint extender bundle that is generating this event. This property is of type Version.

121.17.7.12   **public static final String TIMESTAMP = "timestamp"**

The time the event was created. This property is of type Long.

121.17.7.13   **public static final String TOPIC_BLUEPRINT_EVENTS = "org/osgi/service/blueprint/container"**

Topic prefix for all events issued by the Blueprint Container

121.17.7.14   **public static final String TOPIC_CREATED = "org/osgi/service/blueprint/container/CREATED"**

Topic for Blueprint Container CREATED events

121.17.7.15   **public static final String TOPIC_CREATING = "org/osgi/service/blueprint/container/CREATING"**

Topic for Blueprint Container CREATING events

121.17.7.16   **public static final String TOPIC_DESTROYED = "org/osgi/service/blueprint/container/ DESTROYED"**

Topic for Blueprint Container DESTROYED events

121.17.7.17 **public static final String TOPIC_DESTROYING = "org/osgi/service/blueprint/container/ DESTROYING"**

Topic for Blueprint Container DESTROYING events

121.17.7.18 **public static final String TOPIC_FAILURE = "org/osgi/service/blueprint/container/FAILURE"**

Topic for Blueprint Container FAILURE events

121.17.7.19 **public static final String TOPIC_GRACE_PERIOD = "org/osgi/service/blueprint/container/ GRACE_PERIOD"**

Topic for Blueprint Container GRACE_PERIOD events

121.17.7.20 **public static final String TOPIC_WAITING = "org/osgi/service/blueprint/container/WAITING"**

Topic for Blueprint Container WAITING events

121.17.7.21 **public static final String TYPE = "type"**

The type of the event that has been issued. This property is of type Integer and can take one of the values defined in BlueprintEvent.

121.17.8 public class NoSuchComponentException extends RuntimeException

A Blueprint exception indicating that a component does not exist in a Blueprint Container. This exception is thrown when an attempt is made to create a component instance or lookup Component Metadata using a component id that does not exist in the Blueprint Container.

121.17.8.1 **public NoSuchComponentException(String msg, String id)**

msg The associated message.

id The id of the non-existent component.

☐ Create a No Such Component Exception for a non-existent component.

121.17.8.2 **public NoSuchComponentException(String id)**

id The id of the non-existent component.

☐ Create a No Such Component Exception for a non-existent component.

121.17.8.3 **public String getComponentId( )**

☐ Returns the id of the non-existent component.

Returns The id of the non-existent component.

121.17.9 public class ReifiedType

Provides access to a concrete type and its optional generic type parameters.

Java 5 and later support generic types. These types consist of a raw class with type parameters. This class models such a Type class but ensures that the type is *reified*. Reification means that the Type graph associated with a Java 5 Type instance is traversed until the type becomes a concrete class. This class is available with the getRawClass() method. The optional type parameters are recursively represented as Reified Types.

In Java 1.4, a class has by definition no type parameters. This class implementation provides the Reified Type for Java 1.4 by making the raw class the Java 1.4 class and using a Reified Type based on the Object class for any requested type parameter.

A Blueprint extender implementations can subclass this class and provide access to the generic type parameter graph for conversion. Such a subclass must *reify* the different Java 5 Type instances into the reified form. That is, a form where the raw Class is available with its optional type parameters as Reified Types.

Concurrency Immutable

121.17.9.1   **public ReifiedType(Class clazz)**

clazz The raw class of the Reified Type.

☐ Create a Reified Type for a raw Java class without any generic type parameters. Subclasses can provide the optional generic type parameter information. Without subclassing, this instance has no type parameters.

121.17.9.2   **public ReifiedType getActualTypeArgument(int i)**

i The zero-based index of the requested type parameter.

☐ Return a type parameter for this type. The type parameter refers to a parameter in a generic type declaration given by the zero-based index i. For example, in the following example:

   Map<String, ? extends Metadata>

type parameter 0 is String, and type parameter 1 is Metadata.

This implementation returns a Reified Type that has Object as class. Any object is assignable to Object and therefore no conversion is then necessary. This is compatible with versions of Java language prior to Java 5. This method should be overridden by a subclass that provides access to the generic type parameter information for Java 5 and later.

Returns The ReifiedType for the generic type parameter at the specified index.

121.17.9.3   **public Class getRawClass( )**

☐ Return the raw class represented by this type. The raw class represents the concrete class that is associated with a type declaration. This class could have been deduced from the generics type parameter graph of the declaration. For example, in the following example:

   Map<String, ? extends Metadata>

The raw class is the Map class.

Returns The raw class represented by this type.

121.17.9.4   **public int size( )**

☐ Return the number of type parameters for this type.

This implementation returns 0. This method should be overridden by a subclass that provides access to the generic type parameter information for Java 5 and later.

Returns The number of type parameters for this type.

121.17.10   public class ServiceUnavailableException extends ServiceException

A Blueprint exception indicating that a service is unavailable. This exception is thrown when an invocation is made on a service reference and a backing service is not available.

121.17.10.1   **public ServiceUnavailableException(String message, String filter)**

message The associated message.

filter The filter used for the service lookup.

☐ Creates a Service Unavailable Exception with the specified message.

121.17.10.2　　　**public ServiceUnavailableException(String message, String filter, Throwable cause)**

message　The associated message.

filter　The filter used for the service lookup.

cause　The cause of this exception.

　　☐　Creates a Service Unavailable Exception with the specified message and exception cause.

121.17.10.3　　　**public String getFilter( )**

　　☐　Returns the filter expression that a service would have needed to satisfy in order for the invocation to proceed.

Returns　The failing filter.

121.18　org.osgi.service.blueprint.reflect

Blueprint Reflection Package Version 1.0.

Bundles wishing to use this package must list the package in the Import-Package header of the bundle's manifest. For example:

```
Import-Package: org.osgi.service.blueprint.reflect; version="[1.0,2.0)"
```

This package provides a reflection-based view of the configuration information for a Blueprint Container.

121.18.1　Summary

- *BeanArgument* - Metadata for a factory method or constructor argument of a bean.
- *BeanMetadata* - Metadata for a Bean component.
- *BeanProperty* - Metadata for a property to be injected into a bean.
- *CollectionMetadata* - Metadata for a collection based value.
- *ComponentMetadata* - Metadata for managed components.
- *IdRefMetadata* - Metadata for the verified id of another component managed by the Blueprint Container.
- *MapEntry* - Metadata for a map entry.
- *MapMetadata* - Metadata for a Map based value.
- *Metadata* - Top level Metadata type.
- *NonNullMetadata* - Metadata for a value that cannot null.
- *NullMetadata* - Metadata for a value specified to be null via the ‹null› element.
- *PropsMetadata* - Metadata for a java.util.Properties based value.
- *ReferenceListener* - Metadata for a reference listener interested in the reference bind and unbind events for a service reference.
- *ReferenceListMetadata* - Metadata for a list of service references.
- *ReferenceMetadata* - Metadata for a reference that will bind to a single matching service in the service registry.
- *RefMetadata* - Metadata for a reference to another component managed by the Blueprint Container.
- *RegistrationListener* - Metadata for a registration listener interested in service registration and unregistration events for a service.
- *ServiceMetadata* - Metadata for a service to be registered by the Blueprint Container when enabled.
- *ServiceReferenceMetadata* - Metadata for a reference to an OSGi service.
- *Target* - A common interface for managed components that can be used as a direct target for method calls.

- *ValueMetadata* - Metadata for a simple String value that will be type-converted if necessary before injecting.

121.18.2   public interface BeanArgument

Metadata for a factory method or constructor argument of a bean. The arguments of a bean are obtained from BeanMetadata.getArguments(). This is specified by the argument elements of a bean.

Concurrency Thread-safe

121.18.2.1   public int getIndex( )

❏ Return the zero-based index into the parameter list of the factory method or constructor to be invoked for this argument. This is determined by specifying the index attribute for the bean. If not explicitly set, this will return -1 and the initial ordering is defined by its position in the BeanMetadata.getArguments() list. This is specified by the index attribute.

Returns The zero-based index of the parameter, or -1 if no index is specified.

121.18.2.2   public Metadata getValue( )

❏ Return the Metadata for the argument value. This is specified by the value attribute.

Returns The Metadata for the argument value.

121.18.2.3   public String getValueType( )

❏ Return the name of the value type to match the argument and convert the value into when invoking the constructor or factory method. This is specified by the type attribute.

Returns The name of the value type to convert the value into, or null if no type is specified.

121.18.3   public interface BeanMetadata
extends Target , ComponentMetadata

Metadata for a Bean component.

This is specified by the bean element.

Concurrency Thread-safe

121.18.3.1   public static final String SCOPE_PROTOTYPE = "prototype"

The bean has prototype scope.

See Also getScope ()

121.18.3.2   public static final String SCOPE_SINGLETON = "singleton"

The bean has singleton scope.

See Also getScope ()

121.18.3.3   public List getArguments( )

❏ Return the arguments for the factory method or constructor of the bean. This is specified by the child argument elements.

Returns An immutable List of BeanArgument objects for the factory method or constructor of the bean. The List is empty if no arguments are specified for the bean.

121.18.3.4   public String getClassName( )

❏ Return the name of the class specified for the bean. This is specified by the class attribute of the bean definition.

Returns The name of the class specified for the bean. If no class is specified in the bean definition, because the a factory component is used instead, then this method will return null.

121.18.3.5   **public String getDestroyMethod( )**

☐ Return the name of the destroy method specified for the bean. This is specified by the destroy-method attribute of the bean definition.

Returns The name of the destroy method specified for the bean, or null if no destroy method is specified.

121.18.3.6   **public Target getFactoryComponent( )**

☐ Return the Metadata for the factory component on which to invoke the factory method for the bean. This is specified by the factory-ref attribute of the bean.

When a factory method and factory component have been specified for the bean, this method returns the factory component on which to invoke the factory method for the bean. When no factory component has been specified this method will return null. When a factory method has been specified for the bean but a factory component has not been specified, the factory method must be invoked as a static method on the bean's class.

Returns The Metadata for the factory component on which to invoke the factory method for the bean or null if no factory component is specified.

121.18.3.7   **public String getFactoryMethod( )**

☐ Return the name of the factory method for the bean. This is specified by the factory-method attribute of the bean.

Returns The name of the factory method of the bean or null if no factory method is specified for the bean.

121.18.3.8   **public String getInitMethod( )**

☐ Return the name of the init method specified for the bean. This is specified by the init-method attribute of the bean definition.

Returns The name of the init method specified for the bean, or null if no init method is specified.

121.18.3.9   **public List getProperties( )**

☐ Return the properties for the bean. This is specified by the child property elements.

Returns An immutable List of BeanProperty objects, with one entry for each property to be injected in the bean. The List is empty if no property injection is specified for the bean.

121.18.3.10   **public String getScope( )**

☐ Return the scope for the bean.

Returns The scope for the bean.

See Also SCOPE_SINGLETON, SCOPE_PROTOTYPE

121.18.4   public interface BeanProperty

Metadata for a property to be injected into a bean. The properties of a bean are obtained from Bean-Metadata.getProperties(). This is specified by the property elements of a bean. Properties are defined according to the Java Beans conventions.

Concurrency Thread-safe

121.18.4.1   **public String getName( )**

☐ Return the name of the property to be injected. The name follows Java Beans conventions. This is specified by the name attribute.

Returns The name of the property to be injected.

121.18.4.2   **public Metadata getValue( )**

☐ Return the Metadata for the value to be injected into a bean. This is specified by the value attribute or in inlined text.

Returns The Metadata for the value to be injected into a bean.

121.18.5   public interface CollectionMetadata
extends NonNullMetadata

Metadata for a collection based value. Values of the collection are defined by Metadata objects. This Collection Metadata can constrain the values of the collection to a specific type.

Concurrency Thread-safe

121.18.5.1   public Class getCollectionClass( )

☐ Return the type of the collection. The possible types are: array (Object[]), Set, and List. This information is specified in the element name.

Returns The type of the collection. Object[] is returned to indicate an array.

121.18.5.2   public List getValues( )

☐ Return Metadata for the values of the collection.

Returns A List of Metadata for the values of the collection.

121.18.5.3   public String getValueType( )

☐ Return the type specified for the values of the collection. The value-type attribute specified this information.

Returns The type specified for the values of the collection.

121.18.6   public interface ComponentMetadata
extends NonNullMetadata

Metadata for managed components. This is the base type for BeanMetadata, ServiceMetadata and ServiceReferenceMetadata.

Concurrency Thread-safe

121.18.6.1   public static final int ACTIVATION_EAGER = 1

The component's manager must eagerly activate the component.

See Also getActivation()

121.18.6.2   public static final int ACTIVATION_LAZY = 2

The component's manager must lazily activate the component.

See Also getActivation()

121.18.6.3   public int getActivation( )

☐ Return the activation strategy for the component. This is specified by the activation attribute of a component definition. If this is not set, then the default-activation in the blueprint element is used. If that is also not set, then the activation strategy is ACTIVATION_EAGER.

Returns The activation strategy for the component.

See Also ACTIVATION_EAGER, ACTIVATION_LAZY

121.18.6.4   public List getDependsOn( )

☐ Return the ids of any components listed in a depends-on attribute for the component.

Returns An immutable List of component ids that are explicitly declared as a dependency, or an empty List if none.

121.18.6.5   public String getId( )

☐ Return the id of the component.

Returns   The id of the component. The component id can be null if this is an anonymously defined and/or in-lined component.

121.18.7   public interface IdRefMetadata
extends NonNullMetadata

Metadata for the verified id of another component managed by the Blueprint Container. The id itself will be injected, not the component to which the id refers. No implicit dependency is created.

Concurrency   Thread-safe

121.18.7.1   public String getComponentId( )

☐ Return the id of the referenced component. This is specified by the component-id attribute of a component.

Returns   The id of the referenced component.

121.18.8   public interface MapEntry

Metadata for a map entry. This type is used by MapMetadata, PropsMetadata and ServiceMetadata.

Concurrency   Thread-safe

121.18.8.1   public NonNullMetadata getKey( )

☐ Return the Metadata for the key of the map entry. This is specified by the key attribute or element.

Returns   The Metadata for the key of the map entry. This must not be null.

121.18.8.2   public Metadata getValue( )

☐ Return the Metadata for the value of the map entry. This is specified by the value attribute or element.

Returns   The Metadata for the value of the map entry. This must not be null.

121.18.9   public interface MapMetadata
extends NonNullMetadata

Metadata for a Map based value.

This is specified by the map element.

Concurrency   Thread-safe

121.18.9.1   public List getEntries( )

☐ Return the entries for the map.

Returns   An immutable List of MapEntry objects for each entry in the map. The List is empty if no entries are specified for the map.

121.18.9.2   public String getKeyType( )

☐ Return the name of the type of the map keys. This is specified by the key-type attribute of the map.

Returns   The name of the type of the map keys, or null if none is specified.

121.18.9.3   public String getValueType( )

☐ Return the name of the type of the map values. This is specified by the value-type attribute of the map.

Returns   The name of the type of the map values, or null if none is specified.

121.18.10 public interface Metadata

Top level Metadata type. All Metdata types extends this base type.

Concurrency Thread-safe

121.18.11 public interface NonNullMetadata
extends Metadata

Metadata for a value that cannot null. All Metadata subtypes extend this type except for NullMetadata.

This Metadata type is used for keys in Maps because they cannot be null.

Concurrency Thread-safe

121.18.12 public interface NullMetadata
extends Metadata

Metadata for a value specified to be null via the ‹null› element.

Concurrency Thread-safe

121.18.12.1 public static final NullMetadata NULL

Singleton instance of NullMetadata.

121.18.13 public interface PropsMetadata
extends NonNullMetadata

Metadata for a java.util.Properties based value.

The MapEntry objects of properties are defined with keys and values of type String.

This is specified by the props element.

Concurrency Thread-safe

121.18.13.1 public List getEntries( )

☐ Return the entries for the properties.

Returns An immutable List of MapEntry objects for each entry in the properties. The List is empty if no entries are specified for the properties.

121.18.14 public interface ReferenceListener

Metadata for a reference listener interested in the reference bind and unbind events for a service reference.

Concurrency Thread-safe

121.18.14.1 public String getBindMethod( )

☐ Return the name of the bind method. The bind method will be invoked when a matching service is bound to the reference. This is specified by the bind-method attribute of the reference listener.

Returns The name of the bind method.

121.18.14.2 public Target getListenerComponent( )

☐ Return the Metadata for the component that will receive bind and unbind events. This is specified by the ref attribute or via an inlined component.

Returns The Metadata for the component that will receive bind and unbind events.

121.18.14.3   **public String getUnbindMethod( )**

☐ Return the name of the unbind method. The unbind method will be invoked when a matching service is unbound from the reference. This is specified by the unbind-method attribute of the reference listener.

Returns   The name of the unbind method.

121.18.15   public interface ReferenceListMetadata extends ServiceReferenceMetadata

Metadata for a list of service references.

This is specified by the reference-list element.

Concurrency   Thread-safe

121.18.15.1   **public static final int USE_SERVICE_OBJECT = 1**

Reference list values must be proxies to the actual service objects.

See Also   getMemberType( )

121.18.15.2   **public static final int USE_SERVICE_REFERENCE = 2**

Reference list values must be ServiceReference objects.

See Also   getMemberType( )

121.18.15.3   **public int getMemberType( )**

☐ Return whether the List will contain service object proxies or ServiceReference objects. This is specified by the member-type attribute of the reference list.

Returns   Whether the List will contain service object proxies or ServiceReference objects.

See Also   USE_SERVICE_OBJECT, USE_SERVICE_REFERENCE

121.18.16   public interface ReferenceMetadata extends Target , ServiceReferenceMetadata

Metadata for a reference that will bind to a single matching service in the service registry.

This is specified by the reference element.

Concurrency   Thread-safe

121.18.16.1   **public long getTimeout( )**

☐ Return the timeout for service invocations when a backing service is is unavailable. This is specified by the timeout attribute of the reference.

Returns   The timeout, in milliseconds, for service invocations when a backing service is is unavailable.

121.18.17   public interface RefMetadata extends Target , NonNullMetadata

Metadata for a reference to another component managed by the Blueprint Container.

Concurrency   Thread-safe

121.18.17.1   **public String getComponentId( )**

☐ Return the id of the referenced component. This is specified by the component-id attribute of a component.

Returns   The id of the referenced component.

121.18.18   public interface RegistrationListener

Metadata for a registration listener interested in service registration and unregistration events for a service.

The registration listener is called with the initial state of the service when the registration listener is actuated.

Concurrency   Thread-safe

121.18.18.1   public Target getListenerComponent( )

☐ Return the Metadata for the component that will receive registration and unregistration events. This is specified by the ref attribute or via an inlined component.

Returns   The Metadata for the component that will receive registration and unregistration events.

121.18.18.2   public String getRegistrationMethod( )

☐ Return the name of the registration method. The registration method will be invoked when the associated service is registered with the service registry. This is specified by the registration-method attribute of the registration listener.

Returns   The name of the registration method.

121.18.18.3   public String getUnregistrationMethod( )

☐ Return the name of the unregistration method. The unregistration method will be invoked when the associated service is unregistered from the service registry. This is specified by the unregistration-method attribute of the registration listener.

Returns   The name of the unregistration method.

121.18.19   public interface ServiceMetadata
extends ComponentMetadata

Metadata for a service to be registered by the Blueprint Container when enabled.

This is specified by the service element.

Concurrency   Thread-safe

121.18.19.1   public static final int AUTO_EXPORT_ALL_CLASSES = 4

Advertise all Java classes and interfaces in the component instance type as service interfaces.

See Also   getAutoExport()

121.18.19.2   public static final int AUTO_EXPORT_CLASS_HIERARCHY = 3

Advertise all Java classes in the hierarchy of the component instance type as service interfaces.

See Also   getAutoExport()

121.18.19.3   public static final int AUTO_EXPORT_DISABLED = 1

Do not auto-detect types for advertised service interfaces

See Also   getAutoExport()

121.18.19.4   public static final int AUTO_EXPORT_INTERFACES = 2

Advertise all Java interfaces implemented by the component instance type as service interfaces.

See Also   getAutoExport()

121.18.19.5   public int getAutoExport( )

☐ Return the auto-export mode for the service. This is specified by the auto-export attribute of the service.

Returns   The auto-export mode for the service.

See Also   AUTO_EXPORT_DISABLED, AUTO_EXPORT_INTERFACES, AUTO_EXPORT_CLASS_HIERARCHY, AUTO_EXPORT_ALL_CLASSES

121.18.19.6   **public List getInterfaces( )**

    □   Return the type names of the interfaces that the service should be advertised as supporting. This is specified in the interface attribute or child interfaces element of the service.

Returns   An immutable List of String for the type names of the interfaces that the service should be advertised as supporting. The List is empty if using auto-export or no interface names are specified for the service.

121.18.19.7   **public int getRanking( )**

    □   Return the ranking value to use when advertising the service. If the ranking value is zero, the service must be registered without a service.ranking service property. This is specified by the ranking attribute of the service.

Returns   The ranking value to use when advertising the service.

121.18.19.8   **public Collection getRegistrationListeners( )**

    □   Return the registration listeners to be notified when the service is registered and unregistered with the framework. This is specified by the registration-listener elements of the service.

Returns   An immutable Collection of RegistrationListener objects to be notified when the service is registered and unregistered with the framework. The Collection is empty if no registration listeners are specified for the service.

121.18.19.9   **public Target getServiceComponent( )**

    □   Return the Metadata for the component to be exported as a service. This is specified inline or via the ref attribute of the service.

Returns   The Metadata for the component to be exported as a service.

121.18.19.10   **public List getServiceProperties( )**

    □   Return the user declared properties to be advertised with the service. This is specified by the service-properties element of the service.

Returns   An immutable List of MapEntry objects for the user declared properties to be advertised with the service. The List is empty if no service properties are specified for the service.

121.18.20   public interface ServiceReferenceMetadata extends ComponentMetadata

Metadata for a reference to an OSGi service. This is the base type for ReferenceListMetadata and ReferenceMetadata.

Concurrency   Thread-safe

121.18.20.1   **public static final int AVAILABILITY_MANDATORY = 1**

A matching service is required at all times.

See Also   getAvailability()

121.18.20.2   **public static final int AVAILABILITY_OPTIONAL = 2**

A matching service is not required to be present.

See Also   getAvailability()

121.18.20.3   **public int getAvailability( )**

    ☐ Return whether or not a matching service is required at all times. This is specified in the availability attribute of the service reference.

Returns Whether or not a matching service is required at all times.

See Also AVAILABILITY_MANDATORY, AVAILABILITY_OPTIONAL

121.18.20.4   **public String getComponentName( )**

    ☐ Return the value of the component-name attribute of the service reference. This specifies the id of a component that is registered in the service registry. This will create an automatic filter, appended with the filter if set, to select this component based on its automatic id attribute.

Returns The value of the component-name attribute of the service reference or null if the attribute is not specified.

121.18.20.5   **public String getFilter( )**

    ☐ Return the filter expression that a matching service must match. This is specified by the filter attribute of the service reference.

Returns The filter expression that a matching service must match or null if a filter is not specified.

121.18.20.6   **public String getInterface( )**

    ☐ Return the name of the interface type that a matching service must support. This is specified in the interface attribute of the service reference.

Returns The name of the interface type that a matching service must support or null when no interface name is specified.

121.18.20.7   **public Collection getReferenceListeners( )**

    ☐ Return the reference listeners to receive bind and unbind events. This is specified by the reference-listener elements of the service reference.

Returns An immutable Collection of ReferenceListener objects to receive bind and unbind events. The Collection is empty if no reference listeners are specified for the service reference.

121.18.21   public interface Target
extends NonNullMetadata

A common interface for managed components that can be used as a direct target for method calls. These are bean, reference, and ref, where the ref must refer to a bean or reference component.

See Also BeanMetadata, ReferenceMetadata, RefMetadata

Concurrency Thread-safe

121.18.22   public interface ValueMetadata
extends NonNullMetadata

Metadata for a simple String value that will be type-converted if necessary before injecting.

Concurrency Thread-safe

121.18.22.1   **public String getStringValue( )**

    ☐ Return the unconverted string representation of the value. This is specified by the value attribute or text part of the value element.

Returns The unconverted string representation of the value.

121.18.22.2   **public String getType( )**

      ☐ Return the name of the type to which the value should be converted. This is specified by the type attribute.

Returns   The name of the type to which the value should be converted or null if no type is specified.

121.19   References

[1]   *OSGi Core Specifications*
http://www.osgi.org/download

[2]   *Spring Framework*
http://www.springsource.org/

[3]   *Spring Dynamic Modules*
http://www.springsource.org/osgi

[4]   *Guice*
http://code.google.com/p/google-guice/

[5]   *Picocontainer*
http://www.picocontainer.org/

[6]   *Java Beans Specification*
http://java.sun.com/javase/technologies/desktop/javabeans/docs/spec.html

[7]   *XML Namespaces*
http://www.w3.org/TR/REC-xml-names

[8]   *Properties format*
http://tiny.cc/uu2Js

[9]   *XML Schema*
http://www.w3.org/XML/Schema

[10]   *OSGi XML Schemas*
http://www.osgi.org/Release4/XMLSchemas

701 Tracker Specification

Version 1.4

701.1 Introduction

The Framework provides a powerful and very dynamic programming environment: Bundles are installed, started, stopped, updated, and uninstalled without shutting down the Framework. Dependencies between bundles are monitored by the Framework, but bundles *must* cooperate in handling these dependencies correctly. Two important *dynamic* aspects of the Framework are the service registry and the set of installed bundles.

Bundle developers must be careful not to use service objects that have been unregistered and are therefore stale. The dynamic nature of the Framework service registry makes it necessary to track the service objects as they are registered and unregistered to prevent problems. It is easy to overlook race conditions or boundary conditions that will lead to random errors. Similar problems exist when tracking the set of installed bundles and their state.

This specification defines two utility classes, ServiceTracker and BundleTracker, that make tracking services and bundles easier. A ServiceTracker class can be customized by implementing the ServiceTrackerCustomizer interface or by sub-classing the ServiceTracker class. Similarly, a BundleTracker class can be customized by sub-classing or implementing the BundleTrackerCustomizer interface.

These utility classes significantly reduce the complexity of tracking services in the service registry and the set of installed bundles.

701.1.1 Essentials

- *Simplify* – Simplify the tracking of services or bundles.
- *Customizable* – Allow a default implementation to be customized so that bundle developers can start simply and later extend the implementation to meet their needs.
- *Small* – Every Framework implementation should have this utility implemented. It should therefore be very small because some Framework implementations target minimal OSGi Service Platforms.
- *Services* – Track a set of services, optionally filtered, or track a single service.
- *Bundles* – Track bundles based on their state.
- *Cleanup* – Properly clean up when tracking is no longer necessary

701.1.2 Operation

The fundamental tasks of a tracker are:

- To create an initial list of *targets* (service or bundle).
- To listen to the appropriate events so that the targets are properly tracked.
- To allow the client to customize the tracking process through programmatic selection of the services/bundles to be tracked, as well as to perform client code when a service/bundle is added or removed.

A ServiceTracker object is populated with a set of services that match given search criteria, and then listens to ServiceEvent objects which correspond to those services. A Bundle Tracker is populated with the set of installed bundles and then listens to BundleEvent objects to notify the customizer of changes in the state of the bundles.

701.1.3   Entities

Figure 701.1   *Class diagram of org.osgi.util.tracker*

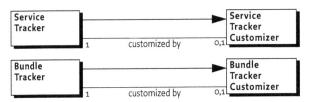

701.2   Tracking

The OSGi Framework is a dynamic multi-threaded environment. In such an environments callbacks can occur on different threads at the same time. This dynamism causes many complexities. One of the surprisingly hard aspects of this environment is to reliably track services and bundles (called *targets* from now on).

The complexity is caused by the fact that the BundleListener and ServiceListener interfaces are only providing access to the *changed* state, not to the existing state when the listener is registered. This leaves the programmer with the problem to merge the set of existing targets with the changes to the state as signified by the events, without unwantedly duplicating a target or missing a remove event that would leave a target in the tracked map while it is in reality gone. These problems are caused by the multi-threaded nature of an OSGi service platform.

The problem is illustrated with the following (quite popular) code:

```
// Bad Example! Do not do this!
Bundle[] bundles = context.getBundles();
for ( Bundle bundle : bundles ) {
    map.put(bundle.getLocation(), bundle );
}

context.addBundleListener( new BundleListener() {
    public void bundleChanged(BundleEvent event) {
        Bundle bundle = event.getBundle();
        switch(event.getType()) {
        case BundleEvent.INSTALLED:
            map.put(bundle.getLocation(), bundle );
            break;

        case BundleEvent.UNINSTALLED:
            map.remove(bundle.getLocation());
            break;

        default:
            // ignore
        }
    }
}
```

```
});
```

Assume the code runs the first part, getting the existing targets. If during this time a targets state changes, for example bundle is installed or uninstalled, then the event is missed and the map will miss a bundle or it will contain a bundle that is already gone. An easy solution seems to be to first register the listener and then get the existing targets. This solves the earlier problem but will be introduce other problems. In this case, an uninstall event can occur before the bundle has been discovered.

Proper locking can alleviate the problem but it turns out that this easily create solutions that are very prone to deadlocks. Solving this tracking problem is surprisingly hard. For this reason, the OSGi specifications contain a *bundle tracker* and a *service tracker* that are properly implemented. These classes significantly reduce the complexity of the dynamics in an OSGi Service Platform.

701.2.1   Usage

Trackers can be used with the following patterns:

- *As-is* – Each tracker can be used without further customizing. A tracker actively tracks a map of targets and this map can be consulted with a number of methods when the information is needed. This is especially useful for the Service Tracker because it provides convenience methods to wait for services to arrive.
- *Callback object* – Each tracker provides a call back interface that can be implemented by the client code.
- *Sub-classing* – The trackers are designed to be sub-classed. Sub-classes have access to the bundle context and only have to override the callback methods they need.

701.2.2   General API

A tracker hides the mechanisms in the way the targets are stored and evented. From a high level, a tracker maintains a *map* of targets to *wrapper* objects. The wrapper object can be defined by the client, though the Bundle Tracker uses the Bundle object and the Service Tracker uses the service object as default wrapper. The tracker notifies the client of any changes in the state of the target.

A tracker must be constructed with a Bundle Context. This context is used to register listeners and obtain the initial list of targets during the call to the open method. At the end of the life of a tracker it must be closed to release any remaining objects. It is advised to properly close all trackers in the bundle activator's stop method.

A tracker provides a uniform callback interface, which has 3 different methods.

- *Adding* – Provide a new object, obtained from the store or from an event and return the wrapper or a related object. The adding method can decide not to track the target by returning a null object. When null is returned, no modified or remove methods are further called. However, it is possible that the adding method is called again for the same target.
- *Modified* –The target is modified. For example, the service properties have changed or the bundle has changed state. This callback provides a mechanism for the client to update its internal structures. The callback provides the wrapper object.
- *Removing* – The target is no longer tracked. This callback is provided the wrapper object returned from the adding method. This allows for simplified cleanup if the client maintains state about the target.

Each tracker is associated with a callback interface, which it implements itself. That is, a Service Tracker implements the ServiceTrackerCustomizer interface. By implementing this customizer, the tracker can also be sub-classed, this can be quite useful in many cases. Sub-classing can override only one or two of the methods instead of having to implement all methods. When overriding the callback methods, it must be ensured that the wrapper object is treated accordingly to the base implementation in all methods. For example, the Service Tracker's default implementation for the adding method checks out the service and therefore the remove method must unget this same service. Changing the wrapper object type to something else can therefore clash with the default implementations.

Trackers can provide all the objects that are tracked, return the mapped wrapper from the target, and deliver the number of tracked targets.

701.2.3 Tracking Count

The tracker also maintains a count that is updated each time that an object is added, modified, or removed, that is any change to the implied map. This tracking count makes it straightforward to verify that a tracker has changed; just store the tracking count and compare it later to see if it has changed.

701.2.4 Multi Threading

The dynamic environment of OSGi requires that tracker are thread safe. However, the tracker closely interacts with the client through a callback interface. The tracker implementation must provide the following guarantees:

- The tracker code calling a callback must not hold any locks

Clients must be aware that their callbacks are reentrant though the tracker implementations guarantee that the add/modified/remove methods can only called in this order for a specific target. A tracker must not call these methods out of order.

701.2.5 Synchronous

Trackers use *synchronous* listeners; the callbacks are called on the same thread as that of the initiating event. Care should be taken to not linger in the callback and perform non-trivial work. Callbacks should return immediately and move substantial work to other threads.

701.3 Service Tracker Class

The purpose of a Service Tracker is to track *service references*, that is, the target is the ServiceReference object. The ServiceTracker interface defines three constructors to create ServiceTracker objects, each providing different search criteria:

- ServiceTracker(BundleContext,String,ServiceTrackerCustomizer) – This constructor takes a service interface name as the search criterion. The ServiceTracker object must then track all services that are registered under the specified service interface name.
- ServiceTracker(BundleContext,Filter,ServiceTrackerCustomizer) – This constructor uses a Filter object to specify the services to be tracked. The ServiceTracker must then track all services that match the specified filter.
- ServiceTracker(BundleContext,ServiceReference,ServiceTrackerCustomizer) – This constructor takes a ServiceReference object as the search criterion. The ServiceTracker must then track only the service that corresponds to the specified ServiceReference. Using this constructor, no more than one service must ever be tracked, because a ServiceReference refers to a specific service.

Each of the ServiceTracker constructors takes a BundleContext object as a parameter. This BundleContext object must be used by a ServiceTracker object to track, get, and unget services.

A new ServiceTracker object must not begin tracking services until its open method is called. There are 2 versions of the open method:

- open() – This method is identical to open(false). It is provided for backward compatibility reasons.

- open(boolean) – The tracker must start tracking the services as were specified in its constructor. If the boolean parameter is true, it must track all services, regardless if they are compatible with the bundle that created the Service Tracker or not. See Section 5.9 "Multiple Version Export Considerations" for a description of the compatibility issues when multiple variations of the same package can exist. If the parameter is false, the Service Tracker must only track compatible versions.

701.3.1   Using a Service Tracker

Once a ServiceTracker object is opened, it begins tracking services immediately. A number of methods are available to the bundle developer to monitor the services that are being tracked, including the ones that are in the service registry at that time. The ServiceTracker class defines these methods:

- getService() – Returns one of the services being tracked or null if there are no active services being tracked.
- getServices() – Returns an array of all the tracked services. The number of tracked services is returned by the size method.
- getServiceReference() – Returns a ServiceReference object for one of the services being tracked. The service object for this service may be returned by calling the ServiceTracker object's getService() method.
- getServiceReferences() – Returns a list of the ServiceReference objects for services being tracked. The service object for a specific tracked service may be returned by calling the ServiceTracker object's getService(ServiceReference) method.
- waitForService(long) – Allows the caller to wait until at least one instance of a service is tracked or until the time-out expires. If the time-out is zero, the caller must wait until at least one instance of a service is tracked. waitForService must not used within the BundleActivator methods, as these methods are expected to complete in a short period of time. A Framework could wait for the start method to complete before starting the bundle that registers the service for which the caller is waiting, creating a deadlock situation.
- remove(ServiceReference) – This method may be used to remove a specific service from being tracked by the ServiceTracker object, causing removedService to be called for that service.
- close() – This method must remove all services being tracked by the ServiceTracker object, causing removedService to be called for all tracked services.
- getTrackingCount() – A Service Tracker can have services added, modified, or removed at any moment in time. The getTrackingCount method is intended to efficiently detect changes in a Service Tracker. Every time the Service Tracker is changed, it must increase the tracking count.

701.3.2   Customizing the Service Tracker class

The behavior of the ServiceTracker class can be customized either by providing a ServiceTrackerCustomizer object, implementing the desired behavior when the ServiceTracker object is constructed, or by sub-classing the ServiceTracker class and overriding the ServiceTrackerCustomizer methods.

The ServiceTrackerCustomizer interface defines these methods:

- addingService(ServiceReference) – Called whenever a service is being added to the ServiceTracker object.
- modifiedService(ServiceReference,Object) – Called whenever a tracked service is modified.
- removedService(ServiceReference,Object) – Called whenever a tracked service is removed from the ServiceTracker object.

When a service is being added to the ServiceTracker object or when a tracked service is modified or removed from the ServiceTracker object, it must call addingService, modifiedService, or removedService, respectively, on the ServiceTrackerCustomizer object (if specified when the ServiceTracker object was created); otherwise it must call these methods on itself.

A bundle developer may customize the action when a service is tracked. Another reason for customizing the ServiceTracker class is to programmatically select which services are tracked. A filter may not sufficiently specify the services that the bundle developer is interested in tracking. By implementing addingService, the bundle developer can use additional runtime information to determine if the service should be tracked. If null is returned by the addingService method, the service must not be tracked.

Finally, the bundle developer can return a specialized object from addingService that differs from the service object. This specialized object could contain the service object and any associated information. This returned object is then tracked instead of the service object. When the removedService method is called, the object that is passed along with the ServiceReference object is the one that was returned from the earlier call to the addingService method.

701.3.3 Customizing Example

An example of customizing the action taken when a service is tracked might be registering a Servlet object with each Http Service that is tracked. This customization could be done by sub-classing the ServiceTracker class and overriding the addingService and removedService methods as follows:

```
public Object addingService( ServiceReference reference) {
    Object obj = context.getService(reference);
    HttpService svc = (HttpService)obj;
    // Register the Servlet using svc
    ...
    return svc;
}
public void removedService( ServiceReference reference,
    Object obj ){
    HttpService svc = (HttpService)obj;
    // Unregister the Servlet using svc
    ...
    context.ungetService(reference);
}
```

701.4 Bundle Tracker

The purpose of the Bundle Tracker is to simplify tracking bundles. A popular example where bundles need to be tracked is the *extender* pattern. An extender uses information in other bundles to provide its function. For example, a Declarative Services implementation reads the component XML file from the bundle to learn of the presence of any components in that bundle.

There are, however, other places where it is necessary to track bundles. The Bundle Tracker significantly simplifies this task.

701.4.1 Bundle States

The state diagram of a Bundle is significantly more complex than that of a service. However, the interface is simpler because there is only a need to specify for which states the bundle tracker should track a service.

Bundle states are defined as a bit in an integer, allowing the specifications of multiple states by setting multiple bits. The Bundle Tracker therefore uses a *bit mask* to specify which states are of interest. For example, if a client is interested in active and resolved bundles, it is possible to specify the Bundle ACTIVE | RESOLVED | STARTING states in the mask.

The Bundle Tracker tracks bundles whose state matches the mask. That is, when a bundle is not tracked it adds that bundle to the tracked map when its state matches the mask. If the bundle reaches a new state that is not listed in the mask, the bundle will be removed from the tracked map. If the state changes but the bundle should still be tracked, then the bundle is considered to be modified.

701.4.2 Constructor

The BundleTracker interface defines the following constructors to create BundleTracker objects:

- BundleTracker(BundleContext,int,BundleTrackerCustomizer) – Create a Bundle Tracker that tracks the bundles which state is listed in the mask. The customizer may be null, in that case the callbacks can be implemented in a subclass.

A new BundleTracker object must not begin tracking services until its open method is called.

- open() – Start tracking the bundles, callbacks can occur before this method is called.

701.4.3 Using a Bundle Tracker

Once a BundleTracker object is opened, it begins tracking bundles immediately. A number of methods are available to the bundle developer to monitor the bundles that are being tracked. The BundleTracker class defines the following methods:

- getBundles() – Returns an array of all the tracked bundles.
- getObject(Bundle) – Returns the wrapper object that was returned from the addingBundle method.
- remove(Bundle) – Removes the bundle from the tracked bundles. The removedBundle method is called when the bundle is not in the tracked map.
- size() – Returns the number of bundles being tracked.
- getTrackingCount() – A Bundle Tracker can have bundles added, modified, or removed at any moment in time. The getTrackingCount method is intended to efficiently detect changes in a Bundle Tracker. Every time the Bundle Tracker is changed, it must increase the tracking count.

701.4.4 Customizing the Bundle Tracker class

The behavior of the BundleTracker class can be customized either by providing a BundleTrackerCustomizer object when the BundleTracker object is constructed, or by sub-classing the BundleTracker class and overriding the BundleTrackerCustomizer methods on the BundleTracker class.

The BundleTrackerCustomizer interface defines these methods:

- addingBundle(Bundle,BundleEvent) – Called whenever a bundle is being added to the BundleTracker object. This method should return a wrapper object, which can be the Bundle object itself. If null is returned, the Bundle must not be further tracked.
- modifiedBundle(Bundle,BundleEvent,Object) – Called whenever a tracked bundle is modified. The object that is passed is the object returned from the addingBundle method, the wrapper object.
- removedBundle(Bundle,BundleEvent,Object) – Called whenever a tracked bundle is removed from the BundleTracker object. The passed object is the wrapper returned from the addingBundle method.

The BundleEvent object in the previous methods can be null.

When a bundle is being added the OSGi Framework, or when a tracked bundle is modified or uninstalled from the OSGi Framework, the Bundle Tracker must call addingBundle, modifiedBundle, or removedBundle, respectively, on the BundleTrackerCustomizer object (if specified when the BundleTracker object was created); otherwise it must call these methods on itself, allowing them to be overridden in a subclass.

The bundle developer can return a specialized object from addingBundle that differs from the Bundle object. This wrapper object could contain the Bundle object and any associated client specific information. This returned object is then used as the wrapper instead of the Bundle object. When the removedBundle method is called, the wrapper is passed as an argument.

701.4.5 Extender Model

The Bundle Tracker allows the implementation of extenders with surprisingly little effort. The following example checks a manifest header (Http-Mapper) in all active bundles to see if the bundle has resources that need to be mapped to the HTTP service. This extender enables bundles that have no code, just content.

This example is implemented with a BundleTrackerCustomizer implementation, though sub-classing the BundleTracker class is slightly simpler because the open/close methods would be inherited, the tracker field is not necessary and it is not necessary to provide a dummy implementation of modifiedBundle method. However, the Service Tracker example already showed how to use inheritance.

The Extender class must implement the customizer and declare fields for the Http Service and a Bundle Tracker.

```
public class Extender implements BundleTrackerCustomizer {
    final HttpService    http;
    final BundleTracker  tracker;
```

It is necessary to parse the Http-Mapper header. Regular expression allow this to be done very concise.

```
final static Pattern HTTPMAPPER=
    Pattern.compile(
      "\\s*([-/\\w.]+)\\s*=\\s*([-/\\w.]+)\\s*");
```

The Bundle Tracker requires a specialized constructor. This example only works for *active* bundles. This implies that a bundle only provides contents when it is started, enabling an administrator to control the availability.

```
Extender(BundleContext context, HttpService http) {
    tracker = new BundleTracker(
        context,Bundle.ACTIVE, this );
    this.http = http;
}
```

The following method implements the callback from the Bundle Tracker when a new bundle is discovered. In this method a specialized HttpContext object is created that knows how to retrieve its resources from the bundle that was just discovered. This context is registered with the Http Service. If no header is found null is returned so that non-participating bundles are no longer tracked.

```
public Object addingBundle(Bundle bundle,
    BundleEvent event) {
    String header = bundle.getHeaders()
      .get("Http-Mapper") + "";
    Matcher match = HTTPMAPPER.matcher(header);
    if (match.matches()) {
        try {
          ExtenderContext wrapper =
              new ExtenderContext(bundle, match.group(1));
          http.registerResources(
            match.group(1), // alias
```

```
            match.group(2), // resource path
            wrapper         // the http context
          );
          return wrapper;
        } catch (NamespaceException nspe) {
          // error is handled in the fall through
        }
      }
      System.err.println(
        "Invalid header for Http-Mapper: " + header);
      return null;
    }
```

The modifiedBundle method does not have to be implemented because this example is not interested in state changes because the only state of interest is the ACTIVE state. Therefore, the remaining method left to implement is the removedBundle method. If the wrapper object is non-null then we need to unregister the alias to prevent collisions in the http namespace when the bundle is reinstalled or updated.

```
    public void removedBundle(
      Bundle bundle, BundleEvent event,
      Object object) {
        ExtenderContext wrapper = (ExtenderContext) object;
        http.unregister(wrapper.alias);
    }
```

The remaining methods would be unnecessary if the Extender class had extended the BundleTracker class. The BundleTrackerCustomizer interface requires a dummy implementation of the modifiedBundle method:

```
    public void modifiedBundle(
      Bundle bundle, BundleEvent event, Object object) {
      // Nothing to do
    }
```

It is usually not a good idea to start a tracker in a constructor because opening a service tracker will immediately cause a number of callbacks for the existing bundles. If the Extender class was subclassed, then this could call back the uninitialized sub class methods. It is therefore better to separate the initialization from the opening. There is therefore a need for an open and close method.

```
    public void close() {
      tracker.close();
    }
    public void open() {
      tracker.open();
    }
  }
```

The previous example uses an HttpContext subclass that can retrieve resources from the target bundle:

```
  public class ExtenderContext implements HttpContext {
    final Bundle    bundle;
    final String    alias;

    ExtenderContext(Bundle bundle, String alias) {
      this.bundle = bundle;
      this.alias = alias;
    }
```

```
    public boolean handleSecurity(
      HttpServletRequest rq, HttpServletResponse rsp) {
      return true;
    }
    public String getMimeType(String name) {
      return null;
    }
    public URL getResource(String name) {
      return bundle.getResource(name);
    }
  }
```

701.5   Security

A tracker contains a BundleContext instance variable that is accessible to the methods in a subclass. A BundleContext object should never be given to other bundles because it is a *capability*. The framework makes allocations based on the bundle context with respect to security and resource management.

The tracker implementations do not have a method to get the BundleContext object, however, subclasses should be careful not to provide such a method if the tracker is given to other bundles.

The services that are being tracked are available via a ServiceTracker. These services are dependent on the BundleContext as well. It is therefore necessary to do a careful security analysis when ServiceTracker objects are given to other bundles. The same counts for the Bundle Tracker. It is strongly advised to not pass trackers to other bundles.

701.5.1   Synchronous Bundle Listener

The Bundle Tracker uses the synchronous bundle listener because it is impossible to provide some of the guarantees the Bundle Tracker provides without handling the events synchronously. Synchronous events can block the complete system, therefore Synchronous Bundle Listeners require AdminPermission[*,LISTENER]. The wildcard * can be replaced with a specifier for the bundles that should be visible to the Bundle Tracker. See *Admin Permission* on page 117 for more information.

Code that calls the open and close methods of Bundle Trackers must therefore have the appropriate Admin Permission.

701.6   org.osgi.util.tracker

Tracker Package Version 1.4.

Bundles wishing to use this package must list the package in the Import-Package header of the bundle's manifest. For example:

```
Import-Package: org.osgi.util.tracker; version="[1.4,2.0)"
```

701.6.1   Summary

- *BundleTracker* - The BundleTracker class simplifies tracking bundles much like the ServiceTracker simplifies tracking services.
- *BundleTrackerCustomizer* - The BundleTrackerCustomizer interface allows a BundleTracker to customize the Bundles that are tracked.
- *ServiceTracker* - The ServiceTracker class simplifies using services from the Framework's service registry.

  • *ServiceTrackerCustomizer* - The ServiceTrackerCustomizer interface allows a ServiceTracker to customize the service objects that are tracked.

701.6.2   public class BundleTracker
implements BundleTrackerCustomizer

The BundleTracker class simplifies tracking bundles much like the ServiceTracker simplifies tracking services.

A BundleTracker is constructed with state criteria and a BundleTrackerCustomizer object. A BundleTracker can use the BundleTrackerCustomizer to select which bundles are tracked and to create a customized object to be tracked with the bundle. The BundleTracker can then be opened to begin tracking all bundles whose state matches the specified state criteria.

The getBundles method can be called to get the Bundle objects of the bundles being tracked. The getObject method can be called to get the customized object for a tracked bundle.

The BundleTracker class is thread-safe. It does not call a BundleTrackerCustomizer while holding any locks. BundleTrackerCustomizer implementations must also be thread-safe.

Since 1.4

Concurrency Thread-safe

701.6.2.1   protected final BundleContext context

The Bundle Context used by this BundleTracker.

701.6.2.2   public BundleTracker(BundleContext context, int stateMask, BundleTrackerCustomizer customizer)

context The BundleContext against which the tracking is done.

stateMask The bit mask of the ORing of the bundle states to be tracked.

customizer The customizer object to call when bundles are added, modified, or removed in this BundleTracker. If customizer is null, then this BundleTracker will be used as the BundleTrackerCustomizer and this BundleTracker will call the BundleTrackerCustomizer methods on itself.

  ☐ Create a BundleTracker for bundles whose state is present in the specified state mask.

Bundles whose state is present on the specified state mask will be tracked by this BundleTracker.

See Also Bundle.getState()

701.6.2.3   public Object addingBundle(Bundle bundle, BundleEvent event)

bundle The Bundle being added to this BundleTracker object.

event The bundle event which caused this customizer method to be called or null if there is no bundle event associated with the call to this method.

  ☐ Default implementation of the BundleTrackerCustomizer.addingBundle method.

This method is only called when this BundleTracker has been constructed with a null BundleTrackerCustomizer argument.

This implementation simply returns the specified Bundle.

This method can be overridden in a subclass to customize the object to be tracked for the bundle being added.

Returns The specified bundle.

See Also BundleTrackerCustomizer.addingBundle(Bundle, BundleEvent)

701.6.2.4 **public void close( )**

☐ Close this BundleTracker.

This method should be called when this BundleTracker should end the tracking of bundles.

This implementation calls getBundles() to get the list of tracked bundles to remove.

701.6.2.5 **public Bundle[] getBundles( )**

☐ Return an array of Bundles for all bundles being tracked by this BundleTracker.

Returns An array of Bundles or null if no bundles are being tracked.

701.6.2.6 **public Object getObject(Bundle bundle)**

bundle The Bundle being tracked.

☐ Returns the customized object for the specified Bundle if the specified bundle is being tracked by this BundleTracker.

Returns The customized object for the specified Bundle or null if the specified Bundle is not being tracked.

701.6.2.7 **public int getTrackingCount( )**

☐ Returns the tracking count for this BundleTracker. The tracking count is initialized to 0 when this BundleTracker is opened. Every time a bundle is added, modified or removed from this BundleTracker the tracking count is incremented.

The tracking count can be used to determine if this BundleTracker has added, modified or removed a bundle by comparing a tracking count value previously collected with the current tracking count value. If the value has not changed, then no bundle has been added, modified or removed from this BundleTracker since the previous tracking count was collected.

Returns The tracking count for this BundleTracker or -1 if this BundleTracker is not open.

701.6.2.8 **public void modifiedBundle(Bundle bundle, BundleEvent event, Object object)**

bundle The Bundle whose state has been modified.

event The bundle event which caused this customizer method to be called or null if there is no bundle event associated with the call to this method.

object The customized object for the specified Bundle.

☐ Default implementation of the BundleTrackerCustomizer.modifiedBundle method.

This method is only called when this BundleTracker has been constructed with a null BundleTrackerCustomizer argument.

This implementation does nothing.

See Also BundleTrackerCustomizer.modifiedBundle(Bundle, BundleEvent, Object)

701.6.2.9 **public void open( )**

☐ Open this BundleTracker and begin tracking bundles.

Bundle which match the state criteria specified when this BundleTracker was created are now tracked by this BundleTracker.

Throws IllegalStateException – If the BundleContext with which this BundleTracker was created is no longer valid.

SecurityException – If the caller and this class do not have the appropriate AdminPermission[context bundle,LISTENER], and the Java Runtime Environment supports permissions.

701.6.2.10   **public void remove(Bundle bundle)**

bundle The Bundle to be removed.

☐ Remove a bundle from this BundleTracker. The specified bundle will be removed from this BundleTracker . If the specified bundle was being tracked then the BundleTrackerCustomizer.removedBundle method will be called for that bundle.

701.6.2.11   **public void removedBundle(Bundle bundle, BundleEvent event, Object object)**

bundle The Bundle being removed.

event The bundle event which caused this customizer method to be called or null if there is no bundle event associated with the call to this method.

object The customized object for the specified bundle.

☐ Default implementation of the BundleTrackerCustomizer.removedBundle method.

This method is only called when this BundleTracker has been constructed with a null BundleTrackerCustomizer argument.

This implementation does nothing.

See Also BundleTrackerCustomizer.removedBundle(Bundle, BundleEvent, Object)

701.6.2.12   **public int size( )**

☐ Return the number of bundles being tracked by this BundleTracker.

Returns The number of bundles being tracked.

701.6.3   public interface BundleTrackerCustomizer

The BundleTrackerCustomizer interface allows a BundleTracker to customize the Bundles that are tracked. A BundleTrackerCustomizer is called when a bundle is being added to a BundleTracker. The BundleTrackerCustomizer can then return an object for the tracked bundle. A BundleTrackerCustomizer is also called when a tracked bundle is modified or has been removed from a BundleTracker.

The methods in this interface may be called as the result of a BundleEvent being received by a BundleTracker. Since BundleEvents are received synchronously by the BundleTracker, it is highly recommended that implementations of these methods do not alter bundle states while being synchronized on any object.

The BundleTracker class is thread-safe. It does not call a BundleTrackerCustomizer while holding any locks. BundleTrackerCustomizer implementations must also be thread-safe.

Since 1.4

Concurrency Thread-safe

701.6.3.1   **public Object addingBundle(Bundle bundle, BundleEvent event)**

bundle The Bundle being added to the BundleTracker.

event The bundle event which caused this customizer method to be called or null if there is no bundle event associated with the call to this method.

☐ A bundle is being added to the BundleTracker.

This method is called before a bundle which matched the search parameters of the BundleTracker is added to the BundleTracker. This method should return the object to be tracked for the specified Bundle. The returned object is stored in the BundleTracker and is available from the getObject method.

Returns The object to be tracked for the specified Bundle object or null if the specified Bundle object should not be tracked.

701.6.3.2   **public void modifiedBundle(Bundle bundle, BundleEvent event, Object object)**

bundle The Bundle whose state has been modified.

event The bundle event which caused this customizer method to be called or null if there is no bundle event associated with the call to this method.

object The tracked object for the specified bundle.

☐ A bundle tracked by the BundleTracker has been modified.

This method is called when a bundle being tracked by the BundleTracker has had its state modified.

701.6.3.3   **public void removedBundle(Bundle bundle, BundleEvent event, Object object)**

bundle The Bundle that has been removed.

event The bundle event which caused this customizer method to be called or null if there is no bundle event associated with the call to this method.

object The tracked object for the specified bundle.

☐ A bundle tracked by the BundleTracker has been removed.

This method is called after a bundle is no longer being tracked by the BundleTracker.

701.6.4   public class ServiceTracker
implements ServiceTrackerCustomizer

The ServiceTracker class simplifies using services from the Framework's service registry.

A ServiceTracker object is constructed with search criteria and a ServiceTrackerCustomizer object. A ServiceTracker can use a ServiceTrackerCustomizer to customize the service objects to be tracked. The ServiceTracker can then be opened to begin tracking all services in the Framework's service registry that match the specified search criteria. The ServiceTracker correctly handles all of the details of listening to ServiceEvents and getting and ungetting services.

The getServiceReferences method can be called to get references to the services being tracked. The getService and getServices methods can be called to get the service objects for the tracked service.

The ServiceTracker class is thread-safe. It does not call a ServiceTrackerCustomizer while holding any locks. ServiceTrackerCustomizer implementations must also be thread-safe.

Concurrency Thread-safe

701.6.4.1   **protected final BundleContext context**

The Bundle Context used by this ServiceTracker.

701.6.4.2   **protected final Filter filter**

The Filter used by this ServiceTracker which specifies the search criteria for the services to track.

Since 1.1

701.6.4.3   **public ServiceTracker(BundleContext context, ServiceReference reference,
ServiceTrackerCustomizer customizer)**

context The BundleContext against which the tracking is done.

reference The ServiceReference for the service to be tracked.

customizer The customizer object to call when services are added, modified, or removed in this ServiceTracker. If customizer is null, then this ServiceTracker will be used as the ServiceTrackerCustomizer and this

ServiceTracker will call the ServiceTrackerCustomizer methods on itself.

☐ Create a ServiceTracker on the specified ServiceReference.

The service referenced by the specified ServiceReference will be tracked by this ServiceTracker.

701.6.4.4   **public ServiceTracker(BundleContext context, String clazz, ServiceTrackerCustomizer customizer)**

context The BundleContext against which the tracking is done.

clazz The class name of the services to be tracked.

customizer The customizer object to call when services are added, modified, or removed in this ServiceTracker. If customizer is null, then this ServiceTracker will be used as the ServiceTrackerCustomizer and this ServiceTracker will call the ServiceTrackerCustomizer methods on itself.

☐ Create a ServiceTracker on the specified class name.

Services registered under the specified class name will be tracked by this ServiceTracker.

701.6.4.5   **public ServiceTracker(BundleContext context, Filter filter, ServiceTrackerCustomizer customizer)**

context The BundleContext against which the tracking is done.

filter The Filter to select the services to be tracked.

customizer The customizer object to call when services are added, modified, or removed in this ServiceTracker. If customizer is null, then this ServiceTracker will be used as the ServiceTrackerCustomizer and this ServiceTracker will call the ServiceTrackerCustomizer methods on itself.

☐ Create a ServiceTracker on the specified Filter object.

Services which match the specified Filter object will be tracked by this ServiceTracker.

Since 1.1

701.6.4.6   **public Object addingService(ServiceReference reference)**

reference The reference to the service being added to this ServiceTracker.

☐ Default implementation of the ServiceTrackerCustomizer.addingService method.

This method is only called when this ServiceTracker has been constructed with a null ServiceTrackerCustomizer argument.

This implementation returns the result of calling getService on the BundleContext with which this ServiceTracker was created passing the specified ServiceReference.

This method can be overridden in a subclass to customize the service object to be tracked for the service being added. In that case, take care not to rely on the default implementation of removedService to unget the service.

Returns The service object to be tracked for the service added to this ServiceTracker.

See Also ServiceTrackerCustomizer. addingService(ServiceReference)

701.6.4.7   **public void close( )**

☐ Close this ServiceTracker.

This method should be called when this ServiceTracker should end the tracking of services.

This implementation calls getServiceReferences() to get the list of tracked services to remove.

701.6.4.8   **public Object getService(ServiceReference reference)**

reference The reference to the desired service.

☐ Returns the service object for the specified ServiceReference if the specified referenced service is being tracked by this ServiceTracker.

Returns A service object or null if the service referenced by the specified ServiceReference is not being tracked.

701.6.4.9 **public Object getService( )**

☐ Returns a service object for one of the services being tracked by this ServiceTracker.

If any services are being tracked, this implementation returns the result of calling getService(getServiceReference()).

Returns A service object or null if no services are being tracked.

701.6.4.10 **public ServiceReference getServiceReference( )**

☐ Returns a ServiceReference for one of the services being tracked by this ServiceTracker.

If multiple services are being tracked, the service with the highest ranking (as specified in its service.ranking property) is returned. If there is a tie in ranking, the service with the lowest service ID (as specified in its service.id property); that is, the service that was registered first is returned. This is the same algorithm used by BundleContext.getServiceReference.

This implementation calls getServiceReferences() to get the list of references for the tracked services.

Returns A ServiceReference or null if no services are being tracked.

Since 1.1

701.6.4.11 **public ServiceReference[] getServiceReferences( )**

☐ Return an array of ServiceReferences for all services being tracked by this ServiceTracker.

Returns Array of ServiceReferences or null if no services are being tracked.

701.6.4.12 **public Object[] getServices( )**

☐ Return an array of service objects for all services being tracked by this ServiceTracker.

This implementation calls getServiceReferences() to get the list of references for the tracked services and then calls getService(ServiceReference) for each reference to get the tracked service object.

Returns An array of service objects or null if no services are being tracked.

701.6.4.13 **public int getTrackingCount( )**

☐ Returns the tracking count for this ServiceTracker. The tracking count is initialized to 0 when this ServiceTracker is opened. Every time a service is added, modified or removed from this ServiceTracker, the tracking count is incremented.

The tracking count can be used to determine if this ServiceTracker has added, modified or removed a service by comparing a tracking count value previously collected with the current tracking count value. If the value has not changed, then no service has been added, modified or removed from this ServiceTracker since the previous tracking count was collected.

Returns The tracking count for this ServiceTracker or -1 if this ServiceTracker is not open.

Since 1.2

701.6.4.14 **public void modifiedService(ServiceReference reference, Object service)**

reference The reference to modified service.

service The service object for the modified service.

☐ Default implementation of the ServiceTrackerCustomizer.modifiedService method.

This method is only called when this ServiceTracker has been constructed with a null ServiceTrackerCustomizer argument.

This implementation does nothing.

See Also ServiceTrackerCustomizer.modifiedService(ServiceReference, Object)

701.6.4.15   **public void open( )**

□ Open this ServiceTracker and begin tracking services.

This implementation calls open(false).

Throws IllegalStateException – If the BundleContext with which this ServiceTracker was created is no longer valid.

See Also open(boolean)

701.6.4.16   **public void open(boolean trackAllServices)**

trackAllServices If true, then this ServiceTracker will track all matching services regardless of class loader accessibility. If false, then this ServiceTracker will only track matching services which are class loader accessible to the bundle whose BundleContext is used by this ServiceTracker.

□ Open this ServiceTracker and begin tracking services.

Services which match the search criteria specified when this ServiceTracker was created are now tracked by this ServiceTracker.

Throws IllegalStateException – If the BundleContext with which this ServiceTracker was created is no longer valid.

Since 1.3

701.6.4.17   **public void remove(ServiceReference reference)**

reference The reference to the service to be removed.

□ Remove a service from this ServiceTracker. The specified service will be removed from this ServiceTracker. If the specified service was being tracked then the ServiceTrackerCustomizer.removedService method will be called for that service.

701.6.4.18   **public void removedService(ServiceReference reference, Object service)**

reference The reference to removed service.

service The service object for the removed service.

□ Default implementation of the ServiceTrackerCustomizer.removedService method.

This method is only called when this ServiceTracker has been constructed with a null ServiceTrackerCustomizer argument.

This implementation calls ungetService, on the BundleContext with which this ServiceTracker was created, passing the specified ServiceReference.

This method can be overridden in a subclass. If the default implementation of addingService method was used, this method must unget the service.

See Also ServiceTrackerCustomizer.removedService(ServiceReference, Object)

701.6.4.19   **public int size( )**

□ Return the number of services being tracked by this ServiceTracker.

Returns The number of services being tracked.

701.6.4.20   **public Object waitForService(long timeout) throws InterruptedException**

timeout The time interval in milliseconds to wait. If zero, the method will wait indefinitely.

    ☐ Wait for at least one service to be tracked by this ServiceTracker. This method will also return when this ServiceTracker is closed.

It is strongly recommended that waitForService is not used during the calling of the BundleActivator methods. BundleActivator methods are expected to complete in a short period of time.

This implementation calls getService() to determine if a service is being tracked.

Returns Returns the result of getService().

Throws InterruptedException – If another thread has interrupted the current thread.

IllegalArgumentException – If the value of timeout is negative.

701.6.5 public interface ServiceTrackerCustomizer

The ServiceTrackerCustomizer interface allows a ServiceTracker to customize the service objects that are tracked. A ServiceTrackerCustomizer is called when a service is being added to a ServiceTracker. The ServiceTrackerCustomizer can then return an object for the tracked service. A ServiceTrackerCustomizer is also called when a tracked service is modified or has been removed from a ServiceTracker.

The methods in this interface may be called as the result of a ServiceEvent being received by a ServiceTracker. Since ServiceEvents are synchronously delivered by the Framework, it is highly recommended that implementations of these methods do not register (BundleContext.registerService), modify (ServiceRegistration.setProperties) or unregister (ServiceRegistration.unregister) a service while being synchronized on any object.

The ServiceTracker class is thread-safe. It does not call a ServiceTrackerCustomizer while holding any locks. ServiceTrackerCustomizer implementations must also be thread-safe.

Concurrency Thread-safe

701.6.5.1 public Object addingService(ServiceReference reference)

reference The reference to the service being added to the ServiceTracker.

    ☐ A service is being added to the ServiceTracker.

This method is called before a service which matched the search parameters of the ServiceTracker is added to the ServiceTracker. This method should return the service object to be tracked for the specified ServiceReference. The returned service object is stored in the ServiceTracker and is available from the getService and getServices methods.

Returns The service object to be tracked for the specified referenced service or null if the specified referenced service should not be tracked.

701.6.5.2 public void modifiedService(ServiceReference reference, Object service)

reference The reference to the service that has been modified.

service The service object for the specified referenced service.

    ☐ A service tracked by the ServiceTracker has been modified.

This method is called when a service being tracked by the ServiceTracker has had it properties modified.

701.6.5.3 public void removedService(ServiceReference reference, Object service)

reference The reference to the service that has been removed.

service The service object for the specified referenced service.

    ☐ A service tracked by the ServiceTracker has been removed.

This method is called after a service is no longer being tracked by the ServiceTracker.

702 XML Parser Service Specification

Version 1.0

702.1 Introduction

The Extensible Markup Language (XML) has become a popular method of describing data. As more bundles use XML to describe their data, a common XML Parser becomes necessary in an embedded environment in order to reduce the need for space. Not all XML Parsers are equivalent in function, however, and not all bundles have the same requirements on an XML parser.

This problem was addressed in the Java API for XML Processing, see [4] *JAXP* for Java 2 Standard Edition and Enterprise Edition. This specification addresses how the classes defined in JAXP can be used in an OSGi Service Platform. It defines how:

- Implementations of XML parsers can become available to other bundles
- Bundles can find a suitable parser
- A standard parser in a JAR can be transformed to a bundle

702.1.1 Essentials

- *Standards* – Leverage existing standards in Java based XML parsing: JAXP, SAX and DOM
- *Unmodified JAXP code* – Run unmodified JAXP code
- *Simple* – It should be easy to provide a SAX or DOM parser as well as easy to find a matching parser
- *Multiple* – It should be possible to have multiple implementations of parsers available
- *Extendable* – It is likely that parsers will be extended in the future with more functionality

702.1.2 Entities

- *XMLParserActivator* – A utility class that registers a parser factory from declarative information in the Manifest file.
- *SAXParserFactory* – A class that can create an instance of a SAXParser class.
- *DocumentBuilderFactory* – A class that can create an instance of a DocumentBuilder class.
- *SAXParser* – A parser, instantiated by a SaxParserFactory object, that parses according to the SAX specifications.
- *DocumentBuilder* – A parser, instantiated by a DocumentBuilderFactory, that parses according to the DOM specifications.

Figure 702.1   *XML Parsing diagram*

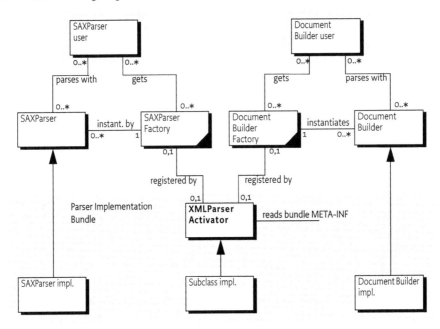

702.1.3   **Operations**

A bundle containing a SAX or DOM parser is started. This bundle registers a SAXParserFactory and/or a DocumentBuilderFactory service object with the Framework. Service registration properties describe the features of the parsers to other bundles. A bundle that needs an XML parser will get a SAXParserFactory or DocumentBuilderFactory service object from the Framework service registry. This object is then used to instantiate the requested parsers according to their specifications.

702.2   **JAXP**

XML has become very popular in the last few years because it allows the interchange of complex information between different parties. Though only a single XML standard exists, there are multiple APIs to XML parsers, primarily of two types:

- The Simple API for XML (SAX1 and SAX2)
- Based on the Document Object Model (DOM 1 and 2)

Both standards, however, define an abstract API that can be implemented by different vendors.

A given XML Parser implementation may support either or both of these parser types by implementing the org.w3c.dom and/or org.xml.sax packages. In addition, parsers have characteristics such as whether they are validating or non-validating parsers and whether or not they are name-space aware.

An application which uses a specific XML Parser must code to that specific parser and become coupled to that specific implementation. If the parser has implemented [4] *JAXP*, however, the application developer can code against SAX or DOM and let the runtime environment decide which parser implementation is used.

JAXP uses the concept of a *factory*. A factory object is an object that abstracts the creation of another object. JAXP defines a DocumentBuilderFactory and a SAXParserFactory class for this purpose.

JAXP is implemented in the javax.xml.parsers package and provides an abstraction layer between an application and a specific XML Parser implementation. Using JAXP, applications can choose to use any JAXP compliant parser without changing any code, simply by changing a System property which specifies the SAX- and DOM factory class names.

In JAXP, the default factory is obtained with a static method in the SAXParserFactory or DocumentBuilderFactory class. This method will inspect the associated System property and create a new instance of that class.

702.3   XML Parser service

The current specification of JAXP has the limitation that only one of each type of parser factories can be registered. This specification specifies how multiple SAXParserFactory objects and DocumentBuilderFactory objects can be made available to bundles simultaneously.

Providers of parsers should register a JAXP factory object with the OSGi service registry under the factory class name. Service properties are used to describe whether the parser:

- Is validating
- Is name-space aware
- Has additional features

With this functionality, bundles can query the OSGi service registry for parsers supporting the specific functionality that they require.

702.4   Properties

Parsers must be registered with a number of properties that qualify the service. In this specification, the following properties are specified:

- PARSER_NAMESPACEAWARE – The registered parser is aware of name-spaces. Name-spaces allow an XML document to consist of independently developed DTDs. In an XML document, they are recognized by the xmlns attribute and names prefixed with an abbreviated name-space identifier, like: <xsl:if ...>. The type is a Boolean object that must be true when the parser supports name-spaces. All other values, or the absence of the property, indicate that the parser does not implement name-spaces.
- PARSER_VALIDATING – The registered parser can read the DTD and can validate the XML accordingly. The type is a Boolean object that must true when the parser is validating. All other values, or the absence of the property, indicate that the parser does not validate.

702.5   Getting a Parser Factory

Getting a parser factory requires a bundle to get the appropriate factory from the service registry. In a simple case in which a non-validating, non-name-space aware parser would suffice, it is best to use getServiceReference(String).

```
DocumentBuilder getParser(BundleContext context)
  throws Exception {
  ServiceReference ref = context.getServiceReference(
    DocumentBuilderFactory.class.getName() );
  if ( ref == null )
    return null;
  DocumentBuilderFactory factory =
    (DocumentBuilderFactory) context.getService(ref);
  return factory.newDocumentBuilder();
}
```

In a more demanding case, the filtered version allows the bundle to select a parser that is validating and name-space aware:

```
SAXParser getParser(BundleContext context)
    throws Exception {
    ServiceReference refs[] = context.getServiceReferences(
        SAXParserFactory.class.getName(),
            "(&(parser.namespaceAware=true)"
    +   "(parser.validating=true))" );
    if ( refs == null )
        return null;
    SAXParserFactory factory =
        (SAXParserFactory) context.getService(refs[0]);
    return factory.newSAXParser();
}
```

702.6   Adapting a JAXP Parser to OSGi

If an XML Parser supports JAXP, then it can be converted to an OSGi aware bundle by adding a BundleActivator class which registers an XML Parser Service. The utility org.osgi.util.xml.XMLParserActivator class provides this function and can be added (copied, not referenced) to any XML Parser bundle, or it can be extended and customized if desired.

702.6.1   JAR Based Services

Its functionality is based on the definition of the [5] *JAR File specification, services directory.* This specification defines a concept for service providers. A JAR file can contain an implementation of an abstractly defined service. The class (or classes) implementing the service are designated from a file in the META-INF/services directory. The name of this file is the same as the abstract service class.

The content of the UTF-8 encoded file is a list of class names separated by new lines. White space is ignored and the number sign ('#' or \u0023) is the comment character.

JAXP uses this service provider mechanism. It is therefore likely that vendors will place these service files in the META-INF/services directory.

702.6.2   XMLParserActivator

To support this mechanism, the XML Parser service provides a utility class that should be normally delivered with the OSGi Service Platform implementation. This class is a Bundle Activator and must start when the bundle is started. This class is copied into the parser bundle, and *not* imported.

The start method of the utility BundleActivator class will look in the META-INF/services service provider directory for the files javax.xml.parsers.SAXParserFactory (SAXFACTORYNAME) or javax.xml.parsers.DocumentBuilderFactory (DOMFACTORYNAME). The full path name is specified in the constants SAXCLASSFILE and DOMCLASSFILE respectively.

If either of these files exist, the utility BundleActivator class will parse the contents according to the specification. A service provider file can contain multiple class names. Each name is read and a new instance is created. The following example shows the possible content of such a file:

```
# ACME example SAXParserFactory file
com.acme.saxparser.SAXParserFast        # Fast
com.acme.saxparser.SAXParserValidating  # Validates
```

Both the javax.xml.parsers.SAXParserFactory and the javax.xml.parsers.DocumentBuilderFactory provide methods that describe the features of the parsers they can create. The XMLParserActivator activator will use these methods to set the values of the properties, as defined in *Properties* on page 635, that describe the instances.

702.6.3 Adapting an Existing JAXP Compatible Parser

To incorporate this bundle activator into a XML Parser Bundle, do the following:

- If SAX parsing is supported, create a /META-INF/services/javax.xml.parsers.SAXParserFactory resource file containing the class names of the SAXParserFactory classes.
- If DOM parsing is supported, create a /META-INF/services/ javax.xml.parsers.DocumentBuilderFactory file containing the fully qualified class names of the DocumentBuilderFactory classes.
- Create manifest file which imports the packages org.w3c.dom, org.xml.sax, and javax.xml.parsers.
- Add a Bundle-Activator header to the manifest pointing to the XMLParserActivator, the sub-class that was created, or a fully custom one.
- If the parsers support attributes, properties, or features that should be registered as properties so they can be searched, extend the XMLParserActivator class and override setSAXProperties(javax.xml.parsers.SAXParserFactory,Hashtable) and setDOMProperties(javax.xml.parsers.DocumentBuilderFactory,Hashtable).
- Ensure that custom properties are put into the Hashtable object. JAXP does not provide a way for XMLParserActivator to query the parser to find out what properties were added.
- Bundles that extend the XMLParserActivator class must call the original methods via super to correctly initialize the XML Parser Service properties.
- Compile this class into the bundle.
- Install the new XML Parser Service bundle.
- Ensure that the org.osgi.util.xml.XMLParserActivator class is contained in the bundle.

702.7 Usage of JAXP

A single bundle should export the JAXP, SAX, and DOM APIs. The version of contained packages must be appropriately labeled. JAXP 1.1 or later is required which references SAX 2 and DOM 2. See [4] *JAXP* for the exact version dependencies.

This specification is related to related packages as defined in the JAXP 1.1 document. Table 702.1 con-
Table 702.1   JAXP 1.1 minimum package versions

Package	Minimum Version
javax.xml.parsers	1.1
org.xml.sax	2.0
org.xml.sax.helpers	2.0
org.xsml.sax.ext	1.0
org.w3c.dom	2.0

tains the expected minimum versions.

The Xerces project from the Apache group, [6] *Xerces 2 Java Parser*, contains a number libraries that implement the necessary APIs. These libraries can be wrapped in a bundle to provide the relevant packages.

702.8   Security

A centralized XML parser is likely to see sensitive information from other bundles. Provisioning an XML parser should therefore be limited to trusted bundles. This security can be achieved by providing ServicePermission[javax.xml.parsers.DocumentBuilderFactory | javax.xml.parsers.SAXFactory, REGISTER] to only trusted bundles.

Using an XML parser is a common function, and ServicePermission[javax.xml.parsers.DOMParserFactory | javax.xml.parsers.SAXFactory, GET] should not be restricted.

The XML parser bundle will need FilePermission[<<ALL FILES>>,READ] for parsing of files because it is not known beforehand where those files will be located. This requirement further implies that the XML parser is a system bundle that must be fully trusted.

702.9   org.osgi.util.xml

XML Parser Package Version 1.0.

Bundles wishing to use this package must list the package in the Import-Package header of the bundle's manifest. For example:

```
Import-Package: org.osgi.util.xml; version="[1.0,2.0)"
```

702.9.1   public class XMLParserActivator
implements BundleActivator , ServiceFactory

A BundleActivator class that allows any JAXP compliant XML Parser to register itself as an OSGi parser service. Multiple JAXP compliant parsers can concurrently register by using this BundleActivator class. Bundles who wish to use an XML parser can then use the framework's service registry to locate available XML Parsers with the desired characteristics such as validating and namespace-aware.

The services that this bundle activator enables a bundle to provide are:

- javax.xml.parsers.SAXParserFactory(SAXFACTORYNAME)
- javax.xml.parsers.DocumentBuilderFactory(DOMFACTORYNAME)

The algorithm to find the implementations of the abstract parsers is derived from the JAR file specifications, specifically the Services API.

An XMLParserActivator assumes that it can find the class file names of the factory classes in the following files:

- /META-INF/services/javax.xml.parsers.SAXParserFactory is a file contained in a jar available to the runtime which contains the implementation class name(s) of the SAXParserFactory.
- /META-INF/services/javax.xml.parsers.DocumentBuilderFactory is a file contained in a jar available to the runtime which contains the implementation class name(s) of the DocumentBuilderFactory

If either of the files does not exist, XMLParserActivator assumes that the parser does not support that parser type.

XMLParserActivator attempts to instantiate both the SAXParserFactory and the DocumentBuilderFactory. It registers each factory with the framework along with service properties:

- PARSER_VALIDATING- indicates if this factory supports validating parsers. It's value is a Boolean.
- PARSER_NAMESPACEAWARE- indicates if this factory supports namespace aware parsers It's value is a Boolean.

Individual parser implementations may have additional features, properties, or attributes which could be used to select a parser with a filter. These can be added by extending this class and overriding the setSAXProperties and setDOMProperties methods.

Concurrency Thread-safe

702.9.1.1 **public static final String DOMCLASSFILE = "/META-INF/services/ javax.xml.parsers.DocumentBuilderFactory"**

Fully qualified path name of DOM Parser Factory Class Name file

702.9.1.2 **public static final String DOMFACTORYNAME = "javax.xml.parsers.DocumentBuilderFactory"**

Filename containing the DOM Parser Factory Class name. Also used as the basis for the SERVICE_PID registration property.

702.9.1.3 **public static final String PARSER_NAMESPACEAWARE = "parser.namespaceAware"**

Service property specifying if factory is configured to support namespace aware parsers. The value is of type Boolean.

702.9.1.4 **public static final String PARSER_VALIDATING = "parser.validating"**

Service property specifying if factory is configured to support validating parsers. The value is of type Boolean.

702.9.1.5 **public static final String SAXCLASSFILE = "/META-INF/services/ javax.xml.parsers.SAXParserFactory"**

Fully qualified path name of SAX Parser Factory Class Name file

702.9.1.6 **public static final String SAXFACTORYNAME = "javax.xml.parsers.SAXParserFactory"**

Filename containing the SAX Parser Factory Class name. Also used as the basis for the SERVICE_PID registration property.

702.9.1.7 **public XMLParserActivator( )**

702.9.1.8 **public Object getService(Bundle bundle, ServiceRegistration registration)**

bundle The bundle using the service.

registration The ServiceRegistration object for the service.

□ Creates a new XML Parser Factory object.

A unique XML Parser Factory object is returned for each call to this method.

The returned XML Parser Factory object will be configured for validating and namespace aware support as specified in the service properties of the specified ServiceRegistration object. This method can be overridden to configure additional features in the returned XML Parser Factory object.

Returns A new, configured XML Parser Factory object or null if a configuration error was encountered

702.9.1.9 **public void setDOMProperties(DocumentBuilderFactory factory, Hashtable props)**

factory - the DocumentBuilderFactory object

props - Hashtable of service properties.

□ Set the customizable DOM Parser Service Properties.

This method attempts to instantiate a validating parser and a namespace aware parser to determine if the parser can support those features. The appropriate properties are then set in the specified props object.

This method can be overridden to add additional DOM2 features and properties. If you want to be able to filter searches of the OSGi service registry, this method must put a key, value pair into the properties object for each feature or property. For example, properties.put("http://www.acme.com/features/foo", Boolean.TRUE);

702.9.1.10   **public void setSAXProperties(SAXParserFactory factory, Hashtable properties)**

factory - the SAXParserFactory object

properties - the properties object for the service

☐ Set the customizable SAX Parser Service Properties.

This method attempts to instantiate a validating parser and a namespace aware parser to determine if the parser can support those features. The appropriate properties are then set in the specified properties object.

This method can be overridden to add additional SAX2 features and properties. If you want to be able to filter searches of the OSGi service registry, this method must put a key, value pair into the properties object for each feature or property. For example, properties.put("http://www.acme.com/features/foo", Boolean.TRUE);

702.9.1.11   **public void start(BundleContext context) throws Exception**

context The execution context of the bundle being started.

☐ Called when this bundle is started so the Framework can perform the bundle-specific activities necessary to start this bundle. This method can be used to register services or to allocate any resources that this bundle needs.

This method must complete and return to its caller in a timely manner.

This method attempts to register a SAX and DOM parser with the Framework's service registry.

Throws Exception– If this method throws an exception, this bundle is marked as stopped and the Framework will remove this bundle's listeners, unregister all services registered by this bundle, and release all services used by this bundle.

702.9.1.12   **public void stop(BundleContext context) throws Exception**

context The execution context of the bundle being stopped.

☐ This method has nothing to do as all active service registrations will automatically get unregistered when the bundle stops.

Throws Exception– If this method throws an exception, the bundle is still marked as stopped, and the Framework will remove the bundle's listeners, unregister all services registered by the bundle, and release all services used by the bundle.

702.9.1.13   **public void ungetService(Bundle bundle, ServiceRegistration registration, Object service)**

bundle The bundle releasing the service.

registration The ServiceRegistration object for the service.

service The XML Parser Factory object returned by a previous call to the getService method.

☐ Releases a XML Parser Factory object.

702.10 References

[1] *XML*
http://www.w3.org/XML

[2] *SAX*
http://www.saxproject.org/

[3] *DOM Java Language Binding*
http://www.w3.org/TR/REC-DOM-Level-1/java-language-binding.html

[4] *JAXP*
http://java.sun.com/xml/jaxp

[5] *JAR File specification, services directory*
http://java.sun.com/j2se/1.4/docs/guide/jar/jar.html

[6] *Xerces 2 Java Parser*
http://xml.apache.org/xerces2-j

703   Position Specification

Version 1.0

703.1   Introduction

The Position class is a utility providing bundle developers with a consistent way of handling geographic positions in OSGi applications. The Position class is intended to be used with the Wire Admin service but has wider applicability.

The Position class is designed to be compatible with the Global Positioning System (GPS). This specification will not define or explain the complexities of positioning information. It is assumed that the reader has the appropriate background to understand this information.

703.1.1   Essentials

- *Position* – Provide an information object that has well defined semantics for a position.
- *WGS-84* – Use the World Geodetic System 84 as the datum.
- *Speed* – Provide speed and track information.
- *Errors* – Position information always has certain errors or cannot be measured at all. This information must be available to the users of the information.
- *Units* – Use SI units for all measurements.
- *Wire Admin* – This specification must work within the Wire Admin service.

703.1.2   Entities

- *Position* – An object containing the different aspects of a position.
- *Measurement* – Contains a typed measurement made at a certain time and with a specified error.

Figure 703.1   *Class Diagram, org.osgi.util.position*

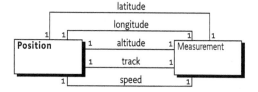

703.2   Positioning

The Position class is used to give information about the position and movement of a vehicle with a specified amount of uncertainty. The position is based on WGS-84.

The Position class offers the following information:

- getLatitude() – The WGS-84 latitude of the current position. The unit of a latitude must be rad (radians).
- getLongitude() – The WGS-84 longitude of the current position. The unit of a longitude must be rad (radians).
- getAltitude() – Altitude is expressed as height in meters above the WGS-84 ellipsoid. This value can differ from the actual height above mean sea level depending on the place on earth where the

measurement is taken place. This value is not corrected for the geoid.
- getTrack() – The true north course of the vehicle in radians.
- getSpeed() – The ground speed. This speed must not include vertical speed.

703.3 Units

Longitude and latitude are represented in radians, not degrees. This is consistent with the use of the Measurement object. Radians can be converted to degrees with the following formula, when lonlat is the longitude or latitude:

    degrees = (lonlat / π) * 180

Calculation errors are significantly reduced when all calculations are done with a single unit system. This approach increases the complexity of presentation, but presentations are usually localized and require conversion anyway. Also, the radians are the units in the SI system and the java.lang.Math class uses only radians for angles.

703.4 Optimizations

A Position object must be immutable. It must remain its original values after it is created.

The Position class is not final. This approach implies that developers are allowed to sub-class it and provide optimized implementations. For example, it is possible that the Measurement objects are only constructed when actually requested.

703.5 Errors

Positioning information is never exact. Even large errors can exist in certain conditions. For this reason, the Position class returns all its measurements as Measurement objects. The Measurement class maintains an error value for each measurement.

In certain cases it is not possible to supply a value; in those cases, the method should return a NaN as specified in the Measurement class.

703.6 Using Position With Wire Admin

The primary reason the Position is specified, is to use it with the *Wire Admin Service Specification* on page 161. A bundle that needs position information should register a Consumer service and the configuration should connect this service to an appropriate Producer service.

703.7 Related Standards

703.7.1 JSR 179

In JCP, started [3] *Location API for J2ME*. This API is targeted at embedded systems and is likely to not contain some of the features found in this API. This API is targeted to be reviewed at Q4 of 2002. This API should be considered in a following release.

703.8   Security

The security aspects of the Position class are delegated to the security aspects of the Wire Admin service. The Position object only carries the information. The Wire Admin service will define what Consumer services will receive position information from what Producer services. It is therefore up to the administrator of the Wire Admin service to assure that only trusted bundles receive this information, or can supply it.

703.9   org.osgi.util.position

Position Package Version 1.0.

Bundles wishing to use this package must list the package in the Import-Package header of the bundle's manifest. For example:

```
Import-Package: org.osgi.util.position; version="[1.0,2.0)"
```

703.9.1   public class Position

Position represents a geographic location, based on the WGS84 System (World Geodetic System 1984).

The org.osgi.util.measurement.Measurement class is used to represent the values that make up a position.

A given position object may lack any of it's components, i.e. the altitude may not be known. Such missing values will be represented by null.

Position does not override the implementation of either equals() or hashCode() because it is not clear how missing values should be handled. It is up to the user of a position to determine how best to compare two position objects. A Position object is immutable.

Concurrency Immutable

703.9.1.1   public Position(Measurement lat, Measurement lon, Measurement alt, Measurement speed, Measurement track)

lat a Measurement object specifying the latitude in radians, or null

lon a Measurement object specifying the longitude in radians, or null

alt a Measurement object specifying the altitude in meters, or null

speed a Measurement object specifying the speed in meters per second, or null

track a Measurement object specifying the track in radians, or null

☐ Constructs a Position object with the given values.

703.9.1.2   public Measurement getAltitude( )

☐ Returns the altitude of this position in meters.

Returns a Measurement object in Unit.m representing the altitude in meters above the ellipsoid null if the altitude is not known.

703.9.1.3   public Measurement getLatitude( )

☐ Returns the latitude of this position in radians.

Returns a Measurement object in Unit.rad representing the latitude, or null if the latitude is not known..

703.9.1.4   public Measurement getLongitude( )

☐ Returns the longitude of this position in radians.

Returns a Measurement object in Unit.rad representing the longitude, or null if the longitude is not known.

703.9.1.5   **public Measurement getSpeed( )**

☐ Returns the ground speed of this position in meters per second.

Returns a Measurement object in Unit.m_s representing the speed, or null if the speed is not known..

703.9.1.6   **public Measurement getTrack( )**

☐ Returns the track of this position in radians as a compass heading. The track is the extrapolation of previous previously measured positions to a future position.

Returns a Measurement object in Unit.rad representing the track, or null if the track is not known..

703.10   References

[1]   *World Geodetic System 84 (WGS-84)*
http://www.wgs84.com

[2]   *Location Interoperability Forum*
http://www.locationforum.org/

[3]   *Location API for J2ME*
http://www.jcp.org/jsr/detail/179.jsp

704 Measurement and State Specification

Version 1.0

704.1 Introduction

The Measurement class is a utility that provides a consistent way of handling a diverse range of measurements for bundle developers. Its purpose is to simplify the correct handling of measurements in OSGi Service Platforms.

OSGi bundle developers from all over the world have different preferences for measurement units, such as feet versus meters. In an OSGi environment, bundles developed in different parts of the world can and will exchange measurements when collaborating.

Distributing a measurement such as a simple floating point number requires the correct and equal understanding of the measurement's semantic by both the sender and the receiver. Numerous accidents have occurred due to misunderstandings between the sender and receiver because there are so many different ways to represent the same value. For example, on September 23, 1999, the Mars Polar Lander was lost because calculations used to program the craft's trajectory were input with English units while the operation documents specified metric units. See [5] *Mars Polar Lander failure* for more information.

This Measurement and State Specification defines the norm that should be used by all applications that execute in an OSGi Service Platform. This specification also provides utility classes.

704.1.1 Measurement Essentials

- *Numerical error* – All floating point measurements should be able to have a numerical error.
- *Numerical error calculations simplification* – Support should be provided to simplify measurements calculations.
- *Unit conflict resolution* – It must not be possible to perform addition or subtraction with different units when they are not compatible. For example, it must not be possible to add meters to amperes or watts to pascals.
- *Unit coercion* – Multiplication and division operations involving more than one type of measurement must result in a different unit. For example, if meters are divided by seconds, the result must be a new unit that represents m/s.
- *Time-stamp* – Measurements should contain a time-stamp so that bundles can determine the age of a particular measurement.
- *Support for floating and discrete values* – Both floating point values (64 bit Java double floats) and discrete measurements (32 bit Java int) should be supported.
- *Consistency* – The method of error calculation and handling of unit types should be consistent.
- *Presentation* – The format of measurements and specified units should be easy to read and understand.

704.1.2 Measurement Entities

- *Measurement object* – A Measurement object contains a double value, a double error, and a long time-stamp. It is associated with a Unit object that represents its *type*.
- *State object* – A State object contains a discrete measurement (int) with a time-stamp and a name.

- *Unit object* – A Unit object represents a unit such as meter, second, mol, or Pascal. A number of Unit objects are predefined and have common names. Other Unit objects are created as needed from the 7 basic Système International d'Unité (SI) units. Different units are *not* used when a conversion is sufficient. For example, the unit of a Measurement object for length is *always* meters. If the length is needed in feet, then the number of feet is calculated by multiplying the value of the Measurement object in meters with the necessary conversion factor.
- *Error* – When a measurement is taken, it is *never* accurate. This specification defines the error as the value that is added and subtracted to the value to produce an interval, where the probability is 95% that the actual value falls within this interval.
- *Unit* – A unit is the *type* of a measurement: meter, feet, liter, gallon etc.
- *Base Unit* – One of the 7 base units defined in the SI.
- *Derived SI unit* – A unit is a derived SI unit when it is a combination of exponentiated base units. For example, a volt (V) is a derived unit because it can be expressed as $(m^2 \times kg) / (s^3 \times A)$, where m, kg, s and A are all base units.
- *Quantitative derivation* – A unit is quantitatively derived when it is converted to one of the base units or derived units using a conversion formula. For example, kilometers (km) can be converted to meters (m), gallons can be converted to liters, or horsepower can be converted to watts.

Figure 704.1   *Class Diagram, org.osgi.util.measurement*

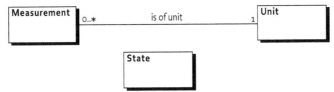

704.2   **Measurement Object**

A Measurement object contains a value, an error, and a time-stamp It is linked to a Unit object that describes the measurement unit in an SI Base Unit or Derived SI Unit.

704.2.1   **Value**

The value of the Measurement object is the measured value. It is set in a constructor. The type of the value is double.

704.2.2   **Error**

The Measurement object can contain a numerical error. This error specifies an interval by adding and subtracting the error value from the measured value. The type of the error is double. A valid error value indicates that the actual measured value has a 95% chance of falling within this interval (see Figure 2). If the error is not known it should be represented as a Double.NaN.

Figure 704.2   *The Error Interval*

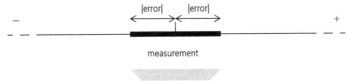

704.2.3   Time-stamp

When a Measurement object is created, the time-stamp can be set. A time-stamp is a long value representing the number of milliseconds since the epoch midnight of January 1, 1970, UTC (this is the value from System.currentTimeMillis() method).

By default, a time-stamp is not set because the call to System.currentTimeMillis() incurs overhead. If the time-stamp is not set when the Measurement object is created, then its default value is zero. If the time-stamp is set, the creator of the Measurement object must give the time as an argument to the constructor. For example:

```
Measurement m = new Measurement(
    v, e, null, System.currentTimeMillis() );
```

704.3   Error Calculations

Once a measurement is taken, it often is used in calculations. The error value assigned to the result of a calculation depends largely on the error values of the operands. Therefore, the Measurement class offers addition, subtraction, multiplication, and division functions for measurements and constants. These functions take the error into account when performing the specific operation.

The Measurement class uses absolute errors and has methods to calculate a new absolute error when multiplication, division, addition, or subtraction is performed. Error calculations must therefore adhere to the rules listed in Table 704.1. In this table, Δa is the absolute positive error in a value a and Δb is the absolute positive error in a value b. c is a constant floating point value without an error.

Table 704.1   Error Calculation Rules

Calculation	Function	Error
$a \times b$	mul(Measurement)	$\lvert \Delta a \times b \rvert + \lvert a \times \Delta b \rvert$
a / b	div(Measurement)	$(\lvert \Delta a \times b \rvert + \lvert a \times \Delta b \rvert) / b^2$
$a + b$	add(Measurement)	$\Delta a + \Delta b$
$a - b$	sub(Measurement)	$\Delta a + \Delta b$
$a \times c$	mul(double)	$\lvert \Delta a \times c \rvert$
a / c	div(double)	$\lvert \Delta a / c \rvert$
$a + c$	add(double)	Δa
$a - c$	sub(double)	Δa

704.4   Constructing and Comparing Measurements

Measurement objects have a value and an error range, making comparing and constructing these objects more complicated than normal scalars.

704.4.1   Constructors

The Measurements object has the following constructors that the value, error, unit and timestamp:

- Measurement(double,double,Unit,long)
- Measurement(double,double,Unit)
- Measurement(double,Unit)
- Measurement(double)

704.4.2   Identity and Equality

Both equals(Object) and hashCode() methods are overridden to provide value-based equality. Two Measurement objects are equal when the unit, error, and value are the same. The time-stamp is not relevant for equality or the hash code.

704.4.3   Comparing Measurement Objects

The Measurement class implements the java.lang.Comparable interface and thus implements the compareTo(Object) method. Comparing two Measurement objects is not straightforward, however, due to the associated error. The error effectively creates a range, so comparing two Measurement objects is actually comparing intervals.

Two Measurement objects are considered to be equal when their intervals overlap. In all other cases, the value is used in the comparison.

Figure 704.3   *Comparing Measurement Objects*

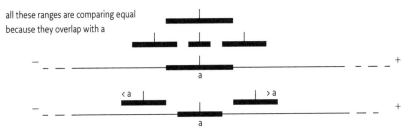

This comparison implies that the equals(Object) method may return false while the compareTo(Object) method returns 0 for the same Measurement object.

704.5   Unit Object

Each Measurement object is related to a Unit object. The Unit object defines the unit of the measurement value and error. For example, the Unit object might define the unit of the measurement value and the error as meters (m). For convenience, the Unit class defines a number of standard units as constants. Measurement objects are given a specific Unit with the constructor. The following example shows how a measurement can be associated with meters (m):

```
Measurement length = new Measurement( v, 0.01, Unit.m );
```

Units are based on the Système International d'Unité (SI), developed after the French Revolution. The SI consists of 7 different units that can be combined in many ways to form a large series of derived units. The basic 7 units are listed in Table 704.2. For more information, see [2] *General SI index.*

Table 704.2   *Basic SI units.*

Description	Unit name	Symbol
length	meter	m
mass	kilogram	kg
time	second	s
electric current	ampere	A
thermodynamic temperature	kelvin	K
amount of substance	mole	mol
luminous intensity	candela	cd

Additional units are derived in the following ways:

Derived units can be a combination of exponentiated base units. For example, Hz (Hertz) is the unit for frequencies and is actually derived from the calculation of 1/s. A more complicated derived unit is volt (V). A volt is actually:

$$(m^2 \times kg) / (s^3 \times A)$$

The SI defines various derived units with their own name, for example pascal (Pa), watt (W), volt (V), and many more.

The Measurement class must maintain its unit by keeping track of the exponents of the 7 basic SI units.

If different units are used in addition or subtraction of Measurement objects, an ArithmeticException must be thrown.

```
Measurement length = new Measurement( v1, 0.01, Unit.m );
Measurement duration = new Measurement( v2, 0, Unit.s );
try {
    Measurement r = length.add( duration );
}
catch( ArithmeticException e ) {
    // This must be thrown
}
```

When two Measurement objects are multiplied, the Unit object of the result contains the sum of the exponents. When two Measurement objects are divided, the exponents of the Unit object of the result are calculated by subtraction of the exponents.

The Measurement class must support exponents of -64 to +63. Overflow must not be reported but must result in an invalid Unit object. All calculations with an invalid Unit object should result in an invalid Unit object. Typical computations generate exponents for units between +/- 4.

704.5.1   Quantitative Differences

The base and derived units can be converted to other units that are of the same *quality*, but require a conversion because their scales and offsets may differ. For example, degrees Fahrenheit, kelvin, and Celsius are all temperatures and, therefore, only differ in their quantity. Kelvin and Celsius are the same scale and differ only in their starting points. Fahrenheit differs from kelvin in that both scale and starting point differ.

Using different Unit objects for the units that differ only in quantity can easily introduce serious software bugs. Therefore, the Unit class utilizes the SI units. Any exchange of measurements should be done using SI units to prevent these errors. When a measurement needs to be displayed, the presentation logic should perform the necessary conversions to present it in a localized form. For example, when speed is presented in a car purchased in the United States, it should be presented as miles instead of meters.

704.5.2   Why Use SI Units?

The adoption of the SI in the United States and the United Kingdom has met with resistance. This issue raises the question why the SI system has to be the preferred measurement system in the OSGi Specifications.

The SI system is utilized because it is the only measurement *system* that has a consistent set of base units. The base units can be combined to create a large number of derived units without requiring a large number of complicated conversion formulas. For example, a watt is simply a combination of meters, kilograms, and seconds ($m^2 \times kg/s^3$). In contrast, horsepower is not easily related to inches, feet, fathoms, yards, furlongs, ounces, pounds, stones, or miles. This difficulty is the reason that science has utilized the SI for a long time. It is also the reason that the SI has been chosen as the system used for the Measurement class.

The purpose of the Measurement class is internal, however, and should not restrict the usability of the OSGi environment. Users should be able to use the local measurement units when data is input or displayed. This choice is the responsibility of the application developer.

704.6 State Object

The State object is used to represent discrete states. It contains a time-stamp but does not contain an error or Unit object. The Measurement object is not suitable to maintain discrete states. For example, a car door can be LOCKED, UNLOCKED, or CHILDLOCKED. Measuring and operating with these values does not require error calculations, nor does it require SI units. Therefore, the State object is a simple, named object that holds an integer value.

704.7 Related Standards

704.7.1 GNU Math Library in Kawa

The open source project Kawa, a scheme-based Java environment, has included a gnu.math library that contains unit handling similar to this specification. It can be found at [4] *A Math Library containing unit handling in Kawa*.

The library seems considerably more complex without offering much more functionality than this specification. It also does not strictly separate basic SI units such as meter from quantitatively derived units such as pica.

704.8 Security Considerations

The Measurement, Unit, and State classes have been made immutable. Instances of these classes can be freely handed out to other bundles because they cannot be extended, nor can the value, error, or time-stamp be altered after the object is created.

704.9 org.osgi.util.measurement

Measurement Package Version 1.0.

Bundles wishing to use this package must list the package in the Import-Package header of the bundle's manifest. For example:

```
Import-Package: org.osgi.util.measurement; version="[1.0,2.0)"
```

704.9.1 Summary

- *Measurement* - Represents a value with an error, a unit and a time-stamp.
- *State* - Groups a state name, value and timestamp.
- *Unit* - A unit system for measurements.

704.9.2 public class Measurement
implements Comparable

Represents a value with an error, a unit and a time-stamp.

A Measurement object is used for maintaining the tuple of value, error, unit and time-stamp. The value and error are represented as doubles and the time is measured in milliseconds since midnight, January 1, 1970 UTC.

Mathematic methods are provided that correctly calculate taking the error into account. A runtime error will occur when two measurements are used in an incompatible way. E.g., when a speed (m/s) is added to a distance (m). The measurement class will correctly track changes in unit during multiplication and division, always coercing the result to the most simple form. See Unit for more information on the supported units.

Errors in the measurement class are absolute errors. Measurement errors should use the P95 rule. Actual values must fall in the range value +/- error 95% or more of the time.

A Measurement object is immutable in order to be easily shared.

Note: This class has a natural ordering that is inconsistent with equals. See compareTo.

Concurrency Immutable

704.9.2.1   **public Measurement(double value, double error, Unit unit, long time)**

value The value of the Measurement.

error The error of the Measurement.

unit The Unit object in which the value is measured. If this argument is null, then the unit will be set to Unit.unity.

time The time measured in milliseconds since midnight, January 1, 1970 UTC.

☐ Create a new Measurement object.

704.9.2.2   **public Measurement(double value, double error, Unit unit)**

value The value of the Measurement.

error The error of the Measurement.

unit The Unit object in which the value is measured. If this argument is null, then the unit will be set to Unit.unity.

☐ Create a new Measurement object with a time of zero.

704.9.2.3   **public Measurement(double value, Unit unit)**

value The value of the Measurement.

unit The Unit in which the value is measured. If this argument is null, then the unit will be set to Unit.unity.

☐ Create a new Measurement object with an error of 0.0 and a time of zero.

704.9.2.4   **public Measurement(double value)**

value The value of the Measurement.

☐ Create a new Measurement object with an error of 0.0, a unit of Unit.unity and a time of zero.

704.9.2.5   **public Measurement add(Measurement m)**

m The Measurement object that will be added with this object.

☐ Returns a new Measurement object that is the sum of this object added to the specified object. The error and unit of the new object are computed. The time of the new object is set to the time of this object.

Returns A new Measurement object that is the sum of this and m.

Throws ArithmeticException – If the Unit objects of this object and the specified object cannot be added.

See Also Unit

704.9.2.6   **public Measurement add(double d, Unit u)**

    d The value that will be added with this object.

    u The Unit object of the specified value.

    □ Returns a new Measurement object that is the sum of this object added to the specified value.

Returns A new Measurement object that is the sum of this object added to the specified value. The unit of the new object is computed. The error and time of the new object is set to the error and time of this object.

Throws ArithmeticException – If the Unit objects of this object and the specified value cannot be added.

See Also Unit

704.9.2.7   **public Measurement add(double d)**

    d The value that will be added with this object.

    □ Returns a new Measurement object that is the sum of this object added to the specified value.

Returns A new Measurement object that is the sum of this object added to the specified value. The error, unit, and time of the new object is set to the error, Unit and time of this object.

704.9.2.8   **public int compareTo(Object obj)**

    obj The object to be compared.

    □ Compares this object with the specified object for order. Returns a negative integer, zero, or a positive integer if this object is less than, equal to, or greater than the specified object.

    Note: This class has a natural ordering that is inconsistent with equals. For this method, another Measurement object is considered equal if there is some x such that

      getValue() - getError() <= x <= getValue() + getError()

    for both Measurement objects being compared.

Returns A negative integer, zero, or a positive integer if this object is less than, equal to, or greater than the specified object.

Throws ClassCastException – If the specified object is not of type Measurement.

    ArithmeticException – If the unit of the specified Measurement object is not equal to the Unit object of this object.

704.9.2.9   **public Measurement div(Measurement m)**

    m The Measurement object that will be the divisor of this object.

    □ Returns a new Measurement object that is the quotient of this object divided by the specified object.

Returns A new Measurement object that is the quotient of this object divided by the specified object. The error and unit of the new object are computed. The time of the new object is set to the time of this object.

Throws ArithmeticException – If the Unit objects of this object and the specified object cannot be divided.

See Also Unit

704.9.2.10   **public Measurement div(double d, Unit u)**

    d The value that will be the divisor of this object.

    u The Unit object of the specified value.

    □ Returns a new Measurement object that is the quotient of this object divided by the specified value.

Returns A new Measurement that is the quotient of this object divided by the specified value. The error and unit of the new object are computed. The time of the new object is set to the time of this object.

Throws ArithmeticException – If the Unit objects of this object and the specified object cannot be divided.

See Also Unit

704.9.2.11   **public Measurement div(double d)**

d The value that will be the divisor of this object.

□ Returns a new Measurement object that is the quotient of this object divided by the specified value.

Returns A new Measurement object that is the quotient of this object divided by the specified value. The error of the new object is computed. The unit and time of the new object is set to the Unit and time of this object.

704.9.2.12   **public boolean equals(Object obj)**

obj The object to compare with this object.

□ Returns whether the specified object is equal to this object. Two Measurement objects are equal if they have same value, error and Unit.

Note: This class has a natural ordering that is inconsistent with equals. See compareTo.

Returns true if this object is equal to the specified object; false otherwise.

704.9.2.13   **public final double getError( )**

□ Returns the error of this Measurement object. The error is always a positive value.

Returns The error of this Measurement as a double.

704.9.2.14   **public final long getTime( )**

□ Returns the time at which this Measurement object was taken. The time is measured in milliseconds since midnight, January 1, 1970 UTC, or zero when not defined.

Returns The time at which this Measurement object was taken or zero.

704.9.2.15   **public final Unit getUnit( )**

□ Returns the Unit object of this Measurement object.

Returns The Unit object of this Measurement object.

See Also Unit

704.9.2.16   **public final double getValue( )**

□ Returns the value of this Measurement object.

Returns The value of this Measurement object as a double.

704.9.2.17   **public int hashCode( )**

□ Returns a hash code value for this object.

Returns A hash code value for this object.

704.9.2.18   **public Measurement mul(Measurement m)**

m The Measurement object that will be multiplied with this object.

□ Returns a new Measurement object that is the product of this object multiplied by the specified object.

Returns A new Measurement that is the product of this object multiplied by the specified object. The error and unit of the new object are computed. The time of the new object is set to the time of this object.

Throws ArithmeticException – If the Unit objects of this object and the specified object cannot be multiplied.

See Also Unit

704.9.2.19   **public Measurement mul(double d, Unit u)**

    d The value that will be multiplied with this object.

    u The Unit of the specified value.

    □ Returns a new Measurement object that is the product of this object multiplied by the specified value.

Returns A new Measurement object that is the product of this object multiplied by the specified value. The error and unit of the new object are computed. The time of the new object is set to the time of this object.

Throws ArithmeticException – If the units of this object and the specified value cannot be multiplied.

See Also Unit

704.9.2.20   **public Measurement mul(double d)**

    d The value that will be multiplied with this object.

    □ Returns a new Measurement object that is the product of this object multiplied by the specified value.

Returns A new Measurement object that is the product of this object multiplied by the specified value. The error of the new object is computed. The unit and time of the new object is set to the unit and time of this object.

704.9.2.21   **public Measurement sub(Measurement m)**

    m The Measurement object that will be subtracted from this object.

    □ Returns a new Measurement object that is the subtraction of the specified object from this object.

Returns A new Measurement object that is the subtraction of the specified object from this object. The error and unit of the new object are computed. The time of the new object is set to the time of this object.

Throws ArithmeticException – If the Unit objects of this object and the specified object cannot be subtracted.

See Also Unit

704.9.2.22   **public Measurement sub(double d, Unit u)**

    d The value that will be subtracted from this object.

    u The Unit object of the specified value.

    □ Returns a new Measurement object that is the subtraction of the specified value from this object.

Returns A new Measurement object that is the subtraction of the specified value from this object. The unit of the new object is computed. The error and time of the new object is set to the error and time of this object.

Throws ArithmeticException – If the Unit objects of this object and the specified object cannot be subtracted.

See Also Unit

704.9.2.23   **public Measurement sub(double d)**

    d The value that will be subtracted from this object.

    □ Returns a new Measurement object that is the subtraction of the specified value from this object.

Returns A new Measurement object that is the subtraction of the specified value from this object. The error, unit and time of the new object is set to the error, Unit object and time of this object.

704.9.2.24   **public String toString( )**

    □ Returns a String object representing this Measurement object.

Returns a String object representing this Measurement object.

704.9.3 public class State

Groups a state name, value and timestamp.

The state itself is represented as an integer and the time is measured in milliseconds since midnight, January 1, 1970 UTC.

A State object is immutable so that it may be easily shared.

Concurrency Immutable

704.9.3.1 public State(int value, String name, long time)

value The value of the state.

name The name of the state.

time The time measured in milliseconds since midnight, January 1, 1970 UTC.

□ Create a new State object.

704.9.3.2 public State(int value, String name)

value The value of the state.

name The name of the state.

□ Create a new State object with a time of 0.

704.9.3.3 public boolean equals(Object obj)

obj The object to compare with this object.

□ Return whether the specified object is equal to this object. Two State objects are equal if they have same value and name.

Returns true if this object is equal to the specified object; false otherwise.

704.9.3.4 public final String getName( )

□ Returns the name of this State.

Returns The name of this State object.

704.9.3.5 public final long getTime( )

□ Returns the time with which this State was created.

Returns The time with which this State was created. The time is measured in milliseconds since midnight, January 1, 1970 UTC.

704.9.3.6 public final int getValue( )

□ Returns the value of this State.

Returns The value of this State object.

704.9.3.7 public int hashCode( )

□ Returns a hash code value for this object.

Returns A hash code value for this object.

704.9.3.8 public String toString( )

□ Returns a String object representing this object.

Returns a String object representing this object.

704.9.4   **public class Unit**

A unit system for measurements. This class contains definitions of the most common SI units.

This class only support exponents for the base SI units in the range -64 to +63. Any operation which produces an exponent outside of this range will result in a Unit object with undefined exponents.

Concurrency Immutable

704.9.4.1   **public static final Unit A**

The electric current unit ampere (A)

704.9.4.2   **public static final Unit C**

The electric charge unit coulomb (C).

coulomb is expressed in SI units as s· A

704.9.4.3   **public static final Unit cd**

The luminous intensity unit candela (cd)

704.9.4.4   **public static final Unit F**

The capacitance unit farad (F).

farad is equal to C/V or is expressed in SI units as s 4 · A 2 /m 2 · kg

704.9.4.5   **public static final Unit Gy**

The absorbed dose unit gray (Gy).

Gy is equal to J/kg or is expressed in SI units as m 2 /s 2

704.9.4.6   **public static final Unit Hz**

The frequency unit hertz (Hz).

hertz is expressed in SI units as 1/s

704.9.4.7   **public static final Unit J**

The energy unit joule (J).

joule is equal to N· m or is expressed in SI units as m 2 · kg/s 2

704.9.4.8   **public static final Unit K**

The temperature unit kelvin (K)

704.9.4.9   **public static final Unit kat**

The catalytic activity unit katal (kat).

katal is expressed in SI units as mol/s

704.9.4.10   **public static final Unit kg**

The mass unit kilogram (kg)

704.9.4.11   **public static final Unit lx**

The illuminance unit lux (lx).

lux is expressed in SI units as cd/m 2

704.9.4.12   **public static final Unit m**

The length unit meter (m)

704.9.4.13   **public static final Unit m2**

The area unit square meter(m 2)

704.9.4.14   **public static final Unit m3**

The volume unit cubic meter (m 3)

704.9.4.15   **public static final Unit m_s**

The speed unit meter per second (m/s)

704.9.4.16   **public static final Unit m_s2**

The acceleration unit meter per second squared (m/s 2)

704.9.4.17   **public static final Unit mol**

The amount of substance unit mole (mol)

704.9.4.18   **public static final Unit N**

The force unit newton (N).

N is expressed in SI units as m· kg/s 2

704.9.4.19   **public static final Unit Ohm**

The electric resistance unit ohm.

ohm is equal to V/A or is expressed in SI units as m 2 · kg/s 3 · A 2

704.9.4.20   **public static final Unit Pa**

The pressure unit pascal (Pa).

Pa is equal to N/m 2 or is expressed in SI units as kg/m· s 2

704.9.4.21   **public static final Unit rad**

The angle unit radians (rad)

704.9.4.22   **public static final Unit S**

The electric conductance unit siemens (S).

siemens is equal to A/V or is expressed in SI units as s 3 · A 2 /m 2 · kg

704.9.4.23   **public static final Unit s**

The time unit second (s)

704.9.4.24   **public static final Unit T**

The magnetic flux density unit tesla (T).

tesla is equal to Wb/m 2 or is expressed in SI units as kg/s 2 · A

704.9.4.25   **public static final Unit unity**

No Unit (Unity)

704.9.4.26 **public static final Unit V**

The electric potential difference unit volt (V).

volt is equal to W/A or is expressed in SI units as m 2 · kg/s 3 · A

704.9.4.27 **public static final Unit W**

The power unit watt (W).

watt is equal to J/s or is expressed in SI units as m 2 · kg/s 3

704.9.4.28 **public static final Unit Wb**

The magnetic flux unit weber (Wb).

weber is equal to V· s or is expressed in SI units as m 2 · kg/s 2 · A

704.9.4.29 **public boolean equals(Object obj)**

obj the Unit object that should be checked for equality

☐ Checks whether this Unit object is equal to the specified Unit object. The Unit objects are considered equal if their exponents are equal.

Returns true if the specified Unit object is equal to this Unit object.

704.9.4.30 **public int hashCode( )**

☐ Returns the hash code for this object.

Returns This object's hash code.

704.9.4.31 **public String toString( )**

☐ Returns a String object representing the Unit

Returns A String object representing the Unit

704.10   References

[1]   *SI Units information*
      http://physics.nist.gov/cuu/Units

[2]   *General SI index*
      http://directory.google.com/Top/Science/Reference/Units_of_Measurement

[3]   *JSR 108 Units Specification*
      http://www.jcp.org/jsr/detail/108.jsp

[4]   *A Math Library containing unit handling in Kawa*
      http://www.gnu.org/software/kawa

[5]   *Mars Polar Lander failure*
      http://mars.jpl.nasa.gov/msp98/news/mco990930.html

999 Execution Environment Specification

Version 1.3

999.1 Introduction

This specification defines two different execution environments for OSGi Server Platform Servers. One is based on a minimal environment that supports OSGi Framework and basic services implementations. The other is derived from [6] *Foundation Profile*. Care has been taken to make the minimum requirements a proper subset of Foundation Profile.

This chapter contains a detailed listing of the Execution Environments. This list is the actual specification and is normative. However, this list is not suited for tools. Therefore, the OSGi web site provides the JAR files that contain all the signatures of the Execution Environments on the OSGi web site, see [2] *Downloadable Execution Environments*.

Please note that the OSGi Minimum Execution Requirements do not constitute a specification for a Java technology profile or platform under the Java Community Process, but rather are a list of dependencies on certain elements of the presumed underlying Java profile(s) or platform(s).

999.1.1 Essentials

- *Bundle Environment* – A well defined format with handling rules for defining the classes and methods that a bundle can rely on.
- *Machine Processable* – It should be easy to process the specification with tools to verify bundles and Service Platforms.
- *Standards* – It should be based on standards as much as possible. It must be compatible with [3] *J2ME, Java 2 Micro Edition*.

999.1.2 Entities

- *Execution Environment* – A collection of classes.
- *Class* – Contains a set of qualifiers and a set of signature for each method and field in that class.
- *Signature* – A unique identifier for the type associated with a field or the return type and argument types of a function.
- *Qualifiers* – A set of attributes that further define a signature.
- *Profile* – A SUN/JCP defined set of classes, based on a configuration.
- *Configuration* – A SUN/JCP defined set of classes and VM specification.

Figure 999.1   *Entities involved in an Execution Environment*

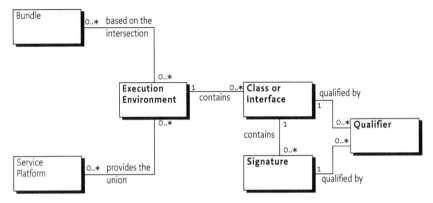

999.2   About Execution Environments

999.2.1   Signatures

An Execution Environment consists of a set of public and protected *signatures*. A signature is defined to be a unique identifier for a field or method with class and type information. For example, the signature of the wait(long) method in Object would be:

    java/lang/Object.wait(J)V

The encoding of the signature is defined in [1] *The Java Virtual Machine Specification.*

For this specification, each signature includes a set of *qualifiers* that further qualify the field or method. These are the access qualifiers (like public, private, and protected), and informational qualifiers like synchronized, volatile, strictfp, interface, native, and abstract. These informational qualifiers are not included in the EE listings.

An Execution Environment consists of a set of classes and interfaces with their access qualifiers. Each class consist of a set of signatures.

999.2.2   Semantics

An Execution environment is solely based on the signatures of the methods and fields. An OSGi Execution Environment relies on the appropriate SUN Java documents to define the semantics of a methods or fields.

999.3   OSGi Defined Execution Environments

This specification contains two Execution Environments. They are listed in the following sections. Each signature is printed in the normal Java format except that public modifiers are not shown to save space (all fields or methods must be public or protected to be included in this list).

Before each signature there are two columns.

1. OSGi/Minimum-1.2 execution requirements

2. CDC-1.1/Foundation-1.1 execution environment.

If the column contains a ■, it means that the signature has been *included* in that Execution Environment. A □ indicates that the signature is missing from the EE.

The information is included here for completeness. However, it is likely that tools will be developed by vendors that validate the compliance of Service Platforms and bundles in relation to an Execution Environment. For that reason, it is possible to download a JAR file containing all the signatures as Java class files from the OSGi web site, see [2] *Downloadable Execution Environments*.

999.3.1　java.io

■ ■ **package java.io**
■ ■ **class BufferedInputStream extends FilterInputStream**
■ ■ BufferedInputStream(InputStream)
■ ■ BufferedInputStream(InputStream,int)
■ ■ protected byte[] buf
■ ■ protected int count

■ ■ protected int marklimit
■ ■ protected int markpos
■ ■ protected int pos

■ ■ **class BufferedOutputStream extends FilterOutputStream**
■ ■ BufferedOutputStream(OutputStream)
■ ■ BufferedOutputStream(OutputStream,int)

■ ■ protected byte[] buf
■ ■ protected int count

■ ■ **class BufferedReader extends Reader**
■ ■ BufferedReader(Reader)
■ ■ BufferedReader(Reader,int)
■ ■ void close() throws IOException

■ ■ int read(char[],int,int) throws IOException
■ ■ String readLine() throws IOException

■ ■ **class BufferedWriter extends Writer**
■ ■ BufferedWriter(Writer)
■ ■ BufferedWriter(Writer,int)
■ ■ void close() throws IOException

■ ■ void flush() throws IOException
■ ■ void newLine() throws IOException
■ ■ void write(char[],int,int) throws IOException

■ ■ **class ByteArrayInputStream extends InputStream**
■ ■ ByteArrayInputStream(byte[])
■ ■ ByteArrayInputStream(byte[],int,int)
■ ■ int available()
■ ■ protected byte[] buf
■ ■ protected int count
■ ■ protected int mark

■ ■ protected int pos
■ ■ int read()
■ ■ int read(byte[],int,int)
■ ■ void reset()
■ ■ long skip(long)

■ ■ **class ByteArrayOutputStream extends OutputStream**
■ ■ ByteArrayOutputStream()
■ ■ ByteArrayOutputStream(int)
■ ■ protected byte[] buf
■ ■ protected int count
■ ■ void reset()
■ ■ int size()

■ ■ byte[] toByteArray()
■ ■ String toString(String) throws UnsupportedEncodingException
■ ■ void write(byte[],int,int)
■ ■ void write(int)
■ ■ void writeTo(OutputStream) throws IOException

■ ■ **class CharArrayReader extends Reader**
■ ■ CharArrayReader(char[])
■ ■ CharArrayReader(char[],int,int)
■ ■ protected char[] buf
■ ■ void close()

■ ■ protected int count
■ ■ protected int markedPos
■ ■ protected int pos
■ ■ int read(char[],int,int) throws IOException

■ ■ **class CharArrayWriter extends Writer**
■ ■ CharArrayWriter()
■ ■ CharArrayWriter(int)
■ ■ protected char[] buf
■ ■ void close()
■ ■ protected int count
■ ■ void flush()
■ ■ void reset()

■ ■ int size()
■ ■ char[] toCharArray()
■ ■ void write(char[],int,int)
■ ■ void write(int)
■ ■ void write(String,int,int)
■ ■ void writeTo(Writer) throws IOException

■ ■ **class CharConversionException extends IOException**
■ ■ CharConversionException()

■ ■ CharConversionException(String)

■ ■ **interface DataInput**
■ ■ abstract boolean readBoolean() throws IOException
■ ■ abstract byte readByte() throws IOException
■ ■ abstract char readChar() throws IOException
■ ■ abstract double readDouble() throws IOException
■ ■ abstract float readFloat() throws IOException
■ ■ abstract void readFully(byte[]) throws IOException
■ ■ abstract void readFully(byte[],int,int) throws IOException
■ ■ abstract int readInt() throws IOException

■ ■ abstract String readLine() throws IOException
■ ■ abstract long readLong() throws IOException
■ ■ abstract short readShort() throws IOException
■ ■ abstract int readUnsignedByte() throws IOException
■ ■ abstract int readUnsignedShort() throws IOException
■ ■ abstract String readUTF() throws IOException
■ ■ abstract int skipBytes(int) throws IOException

■ ■ **class DataInputStream extends FilterInputStream implements DataInput**
■ ■ DataInputStream(InputStream)
■ ■ final int read(byte[]) throws IOException
■ ■ final int read(byte[],int,int) throws IOException
■ ■ final boolean readBoolean() throws IOException
■ ■ final byte readByte() throws IOException
■ ■ final char readChar() throws IOException
■ ■ final double readDouble() throws IOException
■ ■ final float readFloat() throws IOException
■ ■ final void readFully(byte[]) throws IOException

■ ■ final void readFully(byte[],int,int) throws IOException
■ ■ final int readInt() throws IOException
■ ■ final String readLine() throws IOException
■ ■ final long readLong() throws IOException
■ ■ final short readShort() throws IOException
■ ■ final int readUnsignedByte() throws IOException
■ ■ final int readUnsignedShort() throws IOException
■ ■ final String readUTF() throws IOException
■ ■ final static String readUTF(DataInput) throws IOException

■ ■ final int skipBytes(int) throws IOException

■ ■ **interface DataOutput**
■ ■ abstract void write(byte[]) throws IOException
■ ■ abstract void write(byte[],int,int) throws IOException
■ ■ abstract void write(int) throws IOException
■ ■ abstract void writeBoolean(boolean) throws IOException
■ ■ abstract void writeByte(int) throws IOException
■ ■ abstract void writeBytes(String) throws IOException
■ ■ abstract void writeChar(int) throws IOException

■ ■ abstract void writeChars(String) throws IOException
■ ■ abstract void writeDouble(double) throws IOException
■ ■ abstract void writeFloat(float) throws IOException
■ ■ abstract void writeInt(int) throws IOException
■ ■ abstract void writeLong(long) throws IOException
■ ■ abstract void writeShort(int) throws IOException
■ ■ abstract void writeUTF(String) throws IOException

■ ■ **class DataOutputStream extends FilterOutputStream implements DataOutput**
■ ■ DataOutputStream(OutputStream)
■ ■ final int size()
■ ■ final void writeBoolean(boolean) throws IOException
■ ■ final void writeByte(int) throws IOException
■ ■ final void writeBytes(String) throws IOException
■ ■ final void writeChar(int) throws IOException
■ ■ final void writeChars(String) throws IOException

■ ■ final void writeDouble(double) throws IOException
■ ■ final void writeFloat(float) throws IOException
■ ■ final void writeInt(int) throws IOException
■ ■ final void writeLong(long) throws IOException
■ ■ final void writeShort(int) throws IOException
■ ■ final void writeUTF(String) throws IOException
■ ■ protected int written

■ ■ **class EOFException extends IOException**
■ ■ EOFException()

■ ■ EOFException(String)

■ ■ **interface Externalizable extends Serializable**
■ ■ abstract void readExternal(ObjectInput) throws IOException,
ClassNotFoundException

■ ■ abstract void writeExternal(ObjectOutput) throws IOException

■ ■ **class File implements Serializable , Comparable**
■ ■ File(File,String)
■ ■ File(String)
■ ■ File(String,String)
■ ■ File(java.net.URI)
■ ■ boolean canRead()
■ ■ boolean canWrite()
■ ■ int compareTo(File)
■ ■ int compareTo(Object)
■ ■ boolean createNewFile() throws IOException
■ ■ static File createTempFile(String,String) throws IOException
■ ■ static File createTempFile(String,String,File) throws IOException
■ ■ boolean delete()
■ ■ void deleteOnExit()
■ ■ boolean exists()
■ ■ File getAbsoluteFile()
■ ■ String getAbsolutePath()
■ ■ File getCanonicalFile() throws IOException
■ ■ String getCanonicalPath() throws IOException
■ ■ String getName()
■ ■ String getParent()
■ ■ File getParentFile()
■ ■ String getPath()
■ ■ boolean isAbsolute()

■ ■ boolean isDirectory()
■ ■ boolean isFile()
■ ■ boolean isHidden()
■ ■ long lastModified()
■ ■ long length()
■ ■ String[] list()
■ ■ String[] list(FilenameFilter)
■ ■ File[] listFiles()
■ ■ File[] listFiles(FileFilter)
■ ■ File[] listFiles(FilenameFilter)
■ ■ static File[] listRoots()
■ ■ boolean mkdir()
■ ■ boolean mkdirs()
■ ■ final static String pathSeparator
■ ■ final static char pathSeparatorChar
■ ■ boolean renameTo(File)
■ ■ final static String separator
■ ■ final static char separatorChar
■ ■ boolean setLastModified(long)
■ ■ boolean setReadOnly()
■ ■ java.net.URI toURI()
■ ■ java.net.URL toURL() throws java.net.MalformedURLException

■ ■ **final class FileDescriptor**
■ ■ FileDescriptor()
■ ■ final static FileDescriptor err
■ ■ final static FileDescriptor in

■ ■ final static FileDescriptor out
■ ■ void sync() throws SyncFailedException
■ ■ boolean valid()

■ ■ **interface FileFilter**
■ ■ abstract boolean accept(File)

■ ■ **class FileInputStream extends InputStream**
■ ■ FileInputStream(File) throws FileNotFoundException
■ ■ FileInputStream(FileDescriptor)
■ ■ FileInputStream(String) throws FileNotFoundException

■ ■ protected void finalize() throws IOException
■ ■ final FileDescriptor getFD() throws IOException
■ ■ int read() throws IOException

■ ■ **interface FilenameFilter**
■ ■ abstract boolean accept(File,String)

■ ■ **class FileNotFoundException extends IOException**
■ ■ FileNotFoundException()

■ ■ FileNotFoundException(String)

■ ■ **class FileOutputStream extends OutputStream**
■ ■ FileOutputStream(File) throws FileNotFoundException
■ ■ FileOutputStream(File,boolean) throws FileNotFoundException
■ ■ FileOutputStream(FileDescriptor)
■ ■ FileOutputStream(String) throws FileNotFoundException

■ ■ FileOutputStream(String,boolean) throws FileNotFoundException
■ ■ protected void finalize() throws IOException
■ ■ final FileDescriptor getFD() throws IOException
■ ■ void write(int) throws IOException

■ ■ **final class FilePermission extends java.security.Permission implements Serializable**
■ ■ FilePermission(String,String)
■ ■ boolean equals(Object)
■ ■ String getActions()

■ ■ int hashCode()
■ ■ boolean implies(java.security.Permission)

■ ■ **class FileReader extends InputStreamReader**
■ ■ FileReader(File) throws FileNotFoundException
■ ■ FileReader(FileDescriptor)

■ ■ FileReader(String) throws FileNotFoundException

■ ■ **class FileWriter extends OutputStreamWriter**

■ ■ FileWriter(File) throws IOException
■ ■ FileWriter(File,boolean) throws IOException
■ ■ FileWriter(FileDescriptor)

■ ■ FileWriter(String) throws IOException
■ ■ FileWriter(String,boolean) throws IOException

■ ■ **class FilterInputStream extends InputStream**
■ ■ protected FilterInputStream(InputStream)
■ ■ protected InputStream in

■ ■ int read() throws IOException

■ ■ **class FilterOutputStream extends OutputStream**
■ ■ FilterOutputStream(OutputStream)
■ ■ protected OutputStream out

■ ■ void write(int) throws IOException

■ ■ **abstract class FilterReader extends Reader**
■ ■ protected FilterReader(Reader)
■ ■ void close() throws IOException

■ ■ protected Reader in
■ ■ int read(char[],int,int) throws IOException

■ ■ **abstract class FilterWriter extends Writer**
■ ■ protected FilterWriter(Writer)
■ ■ void close() throws IOException
■ ■ void flush() throws IOException

■ ■ protected Writer out
■ ■ void write(char[],int,int) throws IOException

■ ■ **abstract class InputStream**
■ ■ InputStream()
■ ■ int available() throws IOException
■ ■ void close() throws IOException
■ ■ void mark(int)
■ ■ boolean markSupported()

■ ■ abstract int read() throws IOException
■ ■ int read(byte[]) throws IOException
■ ■ int read(byte[],int,int) throws IOException
■ ■ void reset() throws IOException
■ ■ long skip(long) throws IOException

■ ■ **class InputStreamReader extends Reader**
■ ■ InputStreamReader(InputStream)
■ ■ InputStreamReader(InputStream,String) throws
UnsupportedEncodingException

■ ■ void close() throws IOException
■ ■ String getEncoding()
■ ■ int read(char[],int,int) throws IOException

■ ■ **class InterruptedIOException extends IOException**
■ ■ InterruptedIOException()
■ ■ InterruptedIOException(String)

■ ■ int bytesTransferred

■ ■ **class InvalidClassException extends ObjectStreamException**
■ ■ InvalidClassException(String)
■ ■ InvalidClassException(String,String)

■ ■ String classname

■ ■ **class InvalidObjectException extends ObjectStreamException**
■ ■ InvalidObjectException(String)

■ ■ **class IOException extends Exception**
■ ■ IOException()

■ ■ IOException(String)

■ ■ **class LineNumberReader extends BufferedReader**
■ ■ LineNumberReader(Reader)
■ ■ LineNumberReader(Reader,int)

■ ■ int getLineNumber()
■ ■ void setLineNumber(int)

■ ■ **class NotActiveException extends ObjectStreamException**
■ ■ NotActiveException()

■ ■ NotActiveException(String)

■ ■ **class NotSerializableException extends ObjectStreamException**
■ ■ NotSerializableException()

■ ■ NotSerializableException(String)

■ ■ **interface ObjectInput extends DataInput**
■ ■ abstract int available() throws IOException
■ ■ abstract void close() throws IOException
■ ■ abstract int read() throws IOException
■ ■ abstract int read(byte[]) throws IOException

■ ■ abstract int read(byte[],int,int) throws IOException
■ ■ abstract Object readObject() throws IOException,
ClassNotFoundException
■ ■ abstract long skip(long) throws IOException

■ ■ **class ObjectInputStream extends InputStream implements ObjectInput , ObjectStreamConstants**
■ ■ protected ObjectInputStream() throws IOException
■ ■ ObjectInputStream(InputStream) throws IOException
■ ■ void defaultReadObject() throws IOException,
ClassNotFoundException
■ ■ protected boolean enableResolveObject(boolean)
■ ■ int read() throws IOException
■ ■ boolean readBoolean() throws IOException
■ ■ byte readByte() throws IOException
■ ■ char readChar() throws IOException
■ ■ protected ObjectStreamClass readClassDescriptor() throws
IOException, ClassNotFoundException
■ ■ double readDouble() throws IOException
■ ■ ObjectInputStream.GetField readFields() throws IOException,
ClassNotFoundException
■ ■ float readFloat() throws IOException
■ ■ void readFully(byte[]) throws IOException
■ ■ void readFully(byte[],int,int) throws IOException
■ ■ int readInt() throws IOException
■ ■ String readLine() throws IOException
■ ■ long readLong() throws IOException

■ ■ final Object readObject() throws IOException,
ClassNotFoundException
■ ■ protected Object readObjectOverride() throws IOException,
ClassNotFoundException
■ ■ short readShort() throws IOException
■ ■ protected void readStreamHeader() throws IOException
■ ■ Object readUnshared() throws IOException,
ClassNotFoundException
■ ■ int readUnsignedByte() throws IOException
■ ■ int readUnsignedShort() throws IOException
■ ■ String readUTF() throws IOException
■ ■ void registerValidation(ObjectInputValidation,int) throws
InvalidObjectException, NotActiveException
■ ■ protected Class resolveClass(ObjectStreamClass) throws
IOException, ClassNotFoundException
■ ■ protected Object resolveObject(Object) throws IOException
■ ■ protected Class resolveProxyClass(String[]) throws IOException,
ClassNotFoundException
■ ■ int skipBytes(int) throws IOException

■ ■ **abstract class ObjectInputStream.GetField**
■ ■ ObjectInputStream.GetField()
■ ■ abstract boolean defaulted(String) throws IOException
■ ■ abstract byte get(String,byte) throws IOException

■ ■ abstract char get(String,char) throws IOException
■ ■ abstract double get(String,double) throws IOException
■ ■ abstract float get(String,float) throws IOException

- ■ abstract int get(String,int) throws IOException
- ■ abstract long get(String,long) throws IOException
- ■ abstract Object get(String,Object) throws IOException

- ■ abstract short get(String,short) throws IOException
- ■ abstract boolean get(String,boolean) throws IOException
- ■ abstract ObjectStreamClass getObjectStreamClass()

■ ■ **interface ObjectInputValidation**
- ■ abstract void validateObject() throws InvalidObjectException

■ ■ **interface ObjectOutput extends DataOutput**
- ■ abstract void close() throws IOException
- ■ abstract void flush() throws IOException

- ■ abstract void writeObject(Object) throws IOException

■ ■ **class ObjectOutputStream extends OutputStream implements ObjectOutput , ObjectStreamConstants**
- ■ protected ObjectOutputStream() throws IOException
- ■ ObjectOutputStream(OutputStream) throws IOException
- ■ protected void annotateClass(Class) throws IOException
- ■ protected void annotateProxyClass(Class) throws IOException
- ■ void defaultWriteObject() throws IOException
- ■ protected void drain() throws IOException
- ■ protected boolean enableReplaceObject(boolean)
- ■ ObjectOutputStream.PutField putFields() throws IOException
- ■ protected Object replaceObject(Object) throws IOException
- ■ void reset() throws IOException
- ■ void useProtocolVersion(int) throws IOException
- ■ void write(int) throws IOException
- ■ void writeBoolean(boolean) throws IOException
- ■ void writeByte(int) throws IOException
- ■ void writeBytes(String) throws IOException

- ■ void writeChar(int) throws IOException
- ■ void writeChars(String) throws IOException
- ■ protected void writeClassDescriptor(ObjectStreamClass) throws IOException
- ■ void writeDouble(double) throws IOException
- ■ void writeFields() throws IOException
- ■ void writeFloat(float) throws IOException
- ■ void writeInt(int) throws IOException
- ■ void writeLong(long) throws IOException
- ■ final void writeObject(Object) throws IOException
- ■ protected void writeObjectOverride(Object) throws IOException
- ■ void writeShort(int) throws IOException
- ■ protected void writeStreamHeader() throws IOException
- ■ void writeUnshared(Object) throws IOException
- ■ void writeUTF(String) throws IOException

■ ■ **abstract class ObjectOutputStream.PutField**
- ■ ObjectOutputStream.PutField()
- ■ abstract void put(String,byte)
- ■ abstract void put(String,char)
- ■ abstract void put(String,double)
- ■ abstract void put(String,float)
- ■ abstract void put(String,int)

- ■ abstract void put(String,long)
- ■ abstract void put(String,Object)
- ■ abstract void put(String,short)
- ■ abstract void put(String,boolean)
- ■ abstract void write(ObjectOutput) throws IOException

■ ■ **class ObjectStreamClass implements Serializable**
- ■ Class forClass()
- ■ ObjectStreamField getField(String)
- ■ ObjectStreamField[] getFields()
- ■ String getName()

- ■ long getSerialVersionUID()
- ■ static ObjectStreamClass lookup(Class)
- ■ final static ObjectStreamField[] NO_FIELDS

■ ■ **interface ObjectStreamConstants**
- ■ final static int baseWireHandle
- ■ final static int PROTOCOL_VERSION_1
- ■ final static int PROTOCOL_VERSION_2
- ■ final static byte SC_BLOCK_DATA
- ■ final static byte SC_EXTERNALIZABLE
- ■ final static byte SC_SERIALIZABLE
- ■ final static byte SC_WRITE_METHOD
- ■ final static short STREAM_MAGIC
- ■ final static short STREAM_VERSION
- ■ final static SerializablePermission
SUBCLASS_IMPLEMENTATION_PERMISSION
- ■ final static SerializablePermission SUBSTITUTION_PERMISSION
- ■ final static byte TC_ARRAY
- ■ final static byte TC_BASE

- ■ final static byte TC_BLOCKDATA
- ■ final static byte TC_BLOCKDATALONG
- ■ final static byte TC_CLASS
- ■ final static byte TC_CLASSDESC
- ■ final static byte TC_ENDBLOCKDATA
- ■ final static byte TC_EXCEPTION
- ■ final static byte TC_LONGSTRING
- ■ final static byte TC_MAX
- ■ final static byte TC_NULL
- ■ final static byte TC_OBJECT
- ■ final static byte TC_PROXYCLASSDESC
- ■ final static byte TC_REFERENCE
- ■ final static byte TC_RESET
- ■ final static byte TC_STRING

■ ■ **abstract class ObjectStreamException extends IOException**
- ■ protected ObjectStreamException()

- ■ protected ObjectStreamException(String)

■ ■ **class ObjectStreamField implements Comparable**
- ■ ObjectStreamField(String,Class)
- ■ ObjectStreamField(String,Class,boolean)
- ■ int compareTo(Object)
- ■ String getName()
- ■ int getOffset()

- ■ Class getType()
- ■ char getTypeCode()
- ■ String getTypeString()
- ■ boolean isPrimitive()
- ■ protected void setOffset(int)

■ ■ **class OptionalDataException extends ObjectStreamException**
- ■ boolean eof

- ■ int length

■ ■ **abstract class OutputStream**
- ■ OutputStream()
- ■ void close() throws IOException
- ■ void flush() throws IOException

- ■ void write(byte[]) throws IOException
- ■ void write(byte[],int,int) throws IOException
- ■ abstract void write(int) throws IOException

■ ■ **class OutputStreamWriter extends Writer**
- ■ OutputStreamWriter(OutputStream)
- ■ OutputStreamWriter(OutputStream,String) throws
UnsupportedEncodingException
- ■ void close() throws IOException

- ■ void flush() throws IOException
- ■ String getEncoding()
- ■ void write(char[],int,int) throws IOException

■ ■ **class PipedInputStream extends InputStream**
- ■ PipedInputStream()
- ■ PipedInputStream(PipedOutputStream) throws IOException

- ■ protected byte[] buffer
- ■ void connect(PipedOutputStream) throws IOException

■ ■ protected int in
■ ■ protected int out
■ ■ final protected static int PIPE_SIZE

■ ■ **class PipedOutputStream extends OutputStream**
■ ■ PipedOutputStream()
■ ■ PipedOutputStream(PipedInputStream) throws IOException

■ ■ **class PipedReader extends Reader**
■ ■ PipedReader()
■ ■ PipedReader(PipedWriter) throws IOException
■ ■ void close() throws IOException

■ ■ **class PipedWriter extends Writer**
■ ■ PipedWriter()
■ ■ PipedWriter(PipedReader) throws IOException
■ ■ void close() throws IOException

■ ■ **class PrintStream extends FilterOutputStream**
■ ■ PrintStream(OutputStream)
■ ■ PrintStream(OutputStream,boolean)
■ ■ PrintStream(OutputStream,boolean,String) throws
UnsupportedEncodingException
■ ■ boolean checkError()
■ ■ void close()
■ ■ void flush()
■ ■ void print(char[])
■ ■ void print(char)
■ ■ void print(double)
■ ■ void print(float)
■ ■ void print(int)
■ ■ void print(long)
■ ■ void print(Object)
■ ■ void print(String)

■ ■ **class PrintWriter extends Writer**
■ ■ PrintWriter(OutputStream)
■ ■ PrintWriter(OutputStream,boolean)
■ ■ PrintWriter(Writer)
■ ■ PrintWriter(Writer,boolean)
■ ■ boolean checkError()
■ ■ void close()
■ ■ void flush()
■ ■ protected Writer out
■ ■ void print(char[])
■ ■ void print(char)
■ ■ void print(double)
■ ■ void print(float)
■ ■ void print(int)
■ ■ void print(long)
■ ■ void print(Object)
■ ■ void print(String)
■ ■ void print(boolean)

■ ■ **class PushbackInputStream extends FilterInputStream**
■ ■ PushbackInputStream(InputStream)
■ ■ PushbackInputStream(InputStream,int)
■ ■ protected byte[] buf
■ ■ protected int pos

■ ■ **class PushbackReader extends FilterReader**
■ ■ PushbackReader(Reader)
■ ■ PushbackReader(Reader,int)
■ ■ void unread(char[]) throws IOException

■ ■ **class RandomAccessFile implements DataInput , DataOutput**
■ ■ RandomAccessFile(File,String) throws FileNotFoundException
■ ■ RandomAccessFile(String,String) throws FileNotFoundException
■ ■ void close() throws IOException
■ ■ final FileDescriptor getFD() throws IOException
■ ■ long getFilePointer() throws IOException
■ ■ long length() throws IOException
■ ■ int read() throws IOException
■ ■ int read(byte[]) throws IOException
■ ■ int read(byte[],int,int) throws IOException
■ ■ final boolean readBoolean() throws IOException
■ ■ final byte readByte() throws IOException
■ ■ final char readChar() throws IOException
■ ■ final double readDouble() throws IOException
■ ■ final float readFloat() throws IOException
■ ■ final void readFully(byte[]) throws IOException
■ ■ final void readFully(byte[],int,int) throws IOException

■ ■ int read() throws IOException
■ ■ protected void receive(int) throws IOException

■ ■ void connect(PipedInputStream) throws IOException
■ ■ void write(int) throws IOException

■ ■ void connect(PipedWriter) throws IOException
■ ■ int read(char[],int,int) throws IOException

■ ■ void connect(PipedReader) throws IOException
■ ■ void flush() throws IOException
■ ■ void write(char[],int,int) throws IOException

■ ■ void print(boolean)
■ ■ void println()
■ ■ void println(char[])
■ ■ void println(char)
■ ■ void println(double)
■ ■ void println(float)
■ ■ void println(int)
■ ■ void println(long)
■ ■ void println(Object)
■ ■ void println(String)
■ ■ void println(boolean)
■ ■ protected void setError()
■ ■ void write(byte[],int,int)
■ ■ void write(int)

■ ■ void println()
■ ■ void println(char[])
■ ■ void println(char)
■ ■ void println(double)
■ ■ void println(float)
■ ■ void println(int)
■ ■ void println(long)
■ ■ void println(Object)
■ ■ void println(String)
■ ■ void println(boolean)
■ ■ protected void setError()
■ ■ void write(char[])
■ ■ void write(char[],int,int)
■ ■ void write(int)
■ ■ void write(String)
■ ■ void write(String,int,int)

■ ■ void unread(byte[]) throws IOException
■ ■ void unread(byte[],int,int) throws IOException
■ ■ void unread(int) throws IOException

■ ■ void unread(char[],int,int) throws IOException
■ ■ void unread(int) throws IOException

■ ■ final int readInt() throws IOException
■ ■ final String readLine() throws IOException
■ ■ final long readLong() throws IOException
■ ■ final short readShort() throws IOException
■ ■ final int readUnsignedByte() throws IOException
■ ■ final int readUnsignedShort() throws IOException
■ ■ final String readUTF() throws IOException
■ ■ void seek(long) throws IOException
■ ■ void setLength(long) throws IOException
■ ■ int skipBytes(int) throws IOException
■ ■ void write(byte[]) throws IOException
■ ■ void write(byte[],int,int) throws IOException
■ ■ void write(int) throws IOException
■ ■ final void writeBoolean(boolean) throws IOException
■ ■ final void writeByte(int) throws IOException
■ ■ final void writeBytes(String) throws IOException

■ ■ final void writeChar(int) throws IOException
■ ■ final void writeChars(String) throws IOException
■ ■ final void writeDouble(double) throws IOException
■ ■ final void writeFloat(float) throws IOException

■ ■ final void writeInt(int) throws IOException
■ ■ final void writeLong(long) throws IOException
■ ■ final void writeShort(int) throws IOException
■ ■ final void writeUTF(String) throws IOException

■ ■ **abstract class Reader**
■ ■ protected Reader()
■ ■ protected Reader(Object)
■ ■ abstract void close() throws IOException
■ ■ protected Object lock
■ ■ void mark(int) throws IOException
■ ■ boolean markSupported()

■ ■ int read() throws IOException
■ ■ int read(char[]) throws IOException
■ ■ abstract int read(char[],int,int) throws IOException
■ ■ boolean ready() throws IOException
■ ■ void reset() throws IOException
■ ■ long skip(long) throws IOException

■ ■ **class SequenceInputStream extends InputStream**
■ ■ SequenceInputStream(InputStream,InputStream)
■ ■ SequenceInputStream(java.util.Enumeration)

■ ■ int read() throws IOException

■ ■ **interface Serializable**
■ ■ **final class SerializablePermission extends java.security.BasicPermission**
■ ■ SerializablePermission(String)

■ ■ SerializablePermission(String,String)

■ ■ **class StreamCorruptedException extends ObjectStreamException**
■ ■ StreamCorruptedException()

■ ■ StreamCorruptedException(String)

■ ■ **class StreamTokenizer**
■ ■ StreamTokenizer(Reader)
■ ■ void commentChar(int)
■ ■ void eolIsSignificant(boolean)
■ ■ int lineno()
■ ■ void lowerCaseMode(boolean)
■ ■ int nextToken() throws IOException
■ ■ double nval
■ ■ void ordinaryChar(int)
■ ■ void ordinaryChars(int,int)
■ ■ void parseNumbers()
■ ■ void pushBack()
■ ■ void quoteChar(int)

■ ■ void resetSyntax()
■ ■ void slashSlashComments(boolean)
■ ■ void slashStarComments(boolean)
■ ■ String sval
■ ■ final static int TT_EOF
■ ■ final static int TT_EOL
■ ■ final static int TT_NUMBER
■ ■ final static int TT_WORD
■ ■ int ttype
■ ■ void whitespaceChars(int,int)
■ ■ void wordChars(int,int)

■ ■ **class StringReader extends Reader**
■ ■ StringReader(String)
■ ■ void close()

■ ■ int read(char[],int,int) throws IOException

■ ■ **class StringWriter extends Writer**
■ ■ StringWriter()
■ ■ StringWriter(int)
■ ■ void close() throws IOException
■ ■ void flush()
■ ■ StringBuffer getBuffer()

■ ■ void write(char[],int,int)
■ ■ void write(int)
■ ■ void write(String)
■ ■ void write(String,int,int)

■ ■ **class SyncFailedException extends IOException**
■ ■ SyncFailedException(String)

■ ■ **class UnsupportedEncodingException extends IOException**
■ ■ UnsupportedEncodingException()

■ ■ UnsupportedEncodingException(String)

■ ■ **class UTFDataFormatException extends IOException**
■ ■ UTFDataFormatException()

■ ■ UTFDataFormatException(String)

■ ■ **class WriteAbortedException extends ObjectStreamException**
■ ■ WriteAbortedException(String,Exception)

■ ■ Exception detail

■ ■ **abstract class Writer**
■ ■ protected Writer()
■ ■ protected Writer(Object)
■ ■ abstract void close() throws IOException
■ ■ abstract void flush() throws IOException
■ ■ protected Object lock

■ ■ void write(char[]) throws IOException
■ ■ abstract void write(char[],int,int) throws IOException
■ ■ void write(int) throws IOException
■ ■ void write(String) throws IOException
■ ■ void write(String,int,int) throws IOException

999.3.2   **java.lang**

■ ■ **package java.lang**
■ ■ **class AbstractMethodError extends IncompatibleClassChangeError**
■ ■ AbstractMethodError()

■ ■ AbstractMethodError(String)

■ ■ **class ArithmeticException extends RuntimeException**
■ ■ ArithmeticException()

■ ■ ArithmeticException(String)

■ ■ **class ArrayIndexOutOfBoundsException extends IndexOutOfBoundsException**
■ ■ ArrayIndexOutOfBoundsException()
■ ■ ArrayIndexOutOfBoundsException(int)

■ ■ ArrayIndexOutOfBoundsException(String)

■ ■ **class ArrayStoreException extends RuntimeException**
■ ■ ArrayStoreException()

■ ■ ArrayStoreException(String)

■ ■ **class AssertionError extends Error**
■ ■ AssertionError()
■ ■ AssertionError(char)
■ ■ AssertionError(double)
■ ■ AssertionError(float)

■ ■ AssertionError(int)
■ ■ AssertionError(long)
■ ■ AssertionError(Object)
■ ■ AssertionError(boolean)

■ ■ **final class Boolean implements java.io.Serializable**
■ ■ Boolean(String)
■ ■ Boolean(boolean)
■ ■ boolean booleanValue()
■ ■ final static Boolean FALSE
■ ■ static boolean getBoolean(String)

■ ■ static String toString(boolean)
■ ■ final static Boolean TRUE
■ ■ final static Class TYPE
■ ■ static Boolean valueOf(String)
■ ■ static Boolean valueOf(boolean)

■ ■ **final class Byte extends Number implements Comparable**
■ ■ Byte(byte)
■ ■ Byte(String)
■ ■ int compareTo(Byte)
■ ■ int compareTo(Object)
■ ■ static Byte decode(String)
■ ■ double doubleValue()
■ ■ float floatValue()
■ ■ int intValue()
■ ■ long longValue()

■ ■ final static byte MAX_VALUE
■ ■ final static byte MIN_VALUE
■ ■ static byte parseByte(String)
■ ■ static byte parseByte(String,int)
■ ■ static String toString(byte)
■ ■ final static Class TYPE
■ ■ static Byte valueOf(String)
■ ■ static Byte valueOf(String,int)

■ ■ **final class Character implements java.io.Serializable , Comparable**
■ ■ Character(char)
■ ■ char charValue()
■ ■ final static byte COMBINING_SPACING_MARK
■ ■ int compareTo(Character)
■ ■ int compareTo(Object)
■ ■ final static byte CONNECTOR_PUNCTUATION
■ ■ final static byte CONTROL
■ ■ final static byte CURRENCY_SYMBOL
■ ■ final static byte DASH_PUNCTUATION
■ ■ final static byte DECIMAL_DIGIT_NUMBER
■ ■ static int digit(char,int)
■ ■ final static byte DIRECTIONALITY_ARABIC_NUMBER
■ ■ final static byte DIRECTIONALITY_BOUNDARY_NEUTRAL
■ ■ final static byte DIRECTIONALITY_COMMON_NUMBER_SEPARATOR
■ ■ final static byte DIRECTIONALITY_EUROPEAN_NUMBER
■ ■ final static byte DIRECTIONALITY_EUROPEAN_NUMBER_SEPARATOR
■ ■ final static byte DIRECTIONALITY_EUROPEAN_NUMBER_TERMINATOR
■ ■ final static byte DIRECTIONALITY_LEFT_TO_RIGHT
■ ■ final static byte DIRECTIONALITY_LEFT_TO_RIGHT_EMBEDDING
■ ■ final static byte DIRECTIONALITY_LEFT_TO_RIGHT_OVERRIDE
■ ■ final static byte DIRECTIONALITY_NONSPACING_MARK
■ ■ final static byte DIRECTIONALITY_OTHER_NEUTRALS
■ ■ final static byte DIRECTIONALITY_PARAGRAPH_SEPARATOR
■ ■ final static byte DIRECTIONALITY_POP_DIRECTIONAL_FORMAT
■ ■ final static byte DIRECTIONALITY_RIGHT_TO_LEFT
■ ■ final static byte DIRECTIONALITY_RIGHT_TO_LEFT_ARABIC
■ ■ final static byte DIRECTIONALITY_RIGHT_TO_LEFT_EMBEDDING
■ ■ final static byte DIRECTIONALITY_RIGHT_TO_LEFT_OVERRIDE
■ ■ final static byte DIRECTIONALITY_SEGMENT_SEPARATOR
■ ■ final static byte DIRECTIONALITY_UNDEFINED
■ ■ final static byte DIRECTIONALITY_WHITESPACE
■ ■ final static byte ENCLOSING_MARK
■ ■ final static byte END_PUNCTUATION
■ ■ final static byte FINAL_QUOTE_PUNCTUATION
■ ■ static char forDigit(int,int)
■ ■ final static byte FORMAT
■ ■ static byte getDirectionality(char)
■ ■ static int getNumericValue(char)
■ ■ static int getType(char)
■ ■ final static byte INITIAL_QUOTE_PUNCTUATION
■ ■ static boolean isDefined(char)
■ ■ static boolean isDigit(char)

■ ■ static boolean isIdentifierIgnorable(char)
■ ■ static boolean isISOControl(char)
■ ■ static boolean isJavaIdentifierPart(char)
■ ■ static boolean isJavaIdentifierStart(char)
■ ■ static boolean isLetter(char)
■ ■ static boolean isLetterOrDigit(char)
■ ■ static boolean isLowerCase(char)
■ ■ static boolean isMirrored(char)
■ ■ static boolean isSpaceChar(char)
■ ■ static boolean isTitleCase(char)
■ ■ static boolean isUnicodeIdentifierPart(char)
■ ■ static boolean isUnicodeIdentifierStart(char)
■ ■ static boolean isUpperCase(char)
■ ■ static boolean isWhitespace(char)
■ ■ final static byte LETTER_NUMBER
■ ■ final static byte LINE_SEPARATOR
■ ■ final static byte LOWERCASE_LETTER
■ ■ final static byte MATH_SYMBOL
■ ■ final static int MAX_RADIX
■ ■ final static char MAX_VALUE
■ ■ final static int MIN_RADIX
■ ■ final static char MIN_VALUE
■ ■ final static byte MODIFIER_LETTER
■ ■ final static byte MODIFIER_SYMBOL
■ ■ final static byte NON_SPACING_MARK
■ ■ final static byte OTHER_LETTER
■ ■ final static byte OTHER_NUMBER
■ ■ final static byte OTHER_PUNCTUATION
■ ■ final static byte OTHER_SYMBOL
■ ■ final static byte PARAGRAPH_SEPARATOR
■ ■ final static byte PRIVATE_USE
■ ■ final static byte SPACE_SEPARATOR
■ ■ final static byte START_PUNCTUATION
■ ■ final static byte SURROGATE
■ ■ final static byte TITLECASE_LETTER
■ ■ static char toLowerCase(char)
■ ■ static String toString(char)
■ ■ static char toTitleCase(char)
■ ■ static char toUpperCase(char)
■ ■ final static Class TYPE
■ ■ final static byte UNASSIGNED
■ ■ final static byte UPPERCASE_LETTER

■ ■ **class Character.Subset**
■ ■ protected Character.Subset(String)
■ ■ final boolean equals(Object)

■ ■ final int hashCode()
■ ■ final String toString()

■ ■ **final class Character.UnicodeBlock extends Character.Subset**
■ ■ final static Character.UnicodeBlock ALPHABETIC_PRESENTATION_FORMS
■ ■ final static Character.UnicodeBlock ARABIC
■ ■ final static Character.UnicodeBlock ARABIC_PRESENTATION_FORMS_A
■ ■ final static Character.UnicodeBlock ARABIC_PRESENTATION_FORMS_B
■ ■ final static Character.UnicodeBlock ARMENIAN
■ ■ final static Character.UnicodeBlock ARROWS
■ ■ final static Character.UnicodeBlock BASIC_LATIN
■ ■ final static Character.UnicodeBlock BENGALI

■ ■ final static Character.UnicodeBlock BLOCK_ELEMENTS
■ ■ final static Character.UnicodeBlock BOPOMOFO
■ ■ final static Character.UnicodeBlock BOPOMOFO_EXTENDED
■ ■ final static Character.UnicodeBlock BOX_DRAWING
■ ■ final static Character.UnicodeBlock BRAILLE_PATTERNS
■ ■ final static Character.UnicodeBlock CHEROKEE
■ ■ final static Character.UnicodeBlock CJK_COMPATIBILITY
■ ■ final static Character.UnicodeBlock CJK_COMPATIBILITY_FORMS
■ ■ final static Character.UnicodeBlock CJK_COMPATIBILITY_IDEOGRAPHS
■ ■ final static Character.UnicodeBlock CJK_RADICALS_SUPPLEMENT

■ ■ final static Character.UnicodeBlock
CJK_SYMBOLS_AND_PUNCTUATION
■ ■ final static Character.UnicodeBlock CJK_UNIFIED_IDEOGRAPHS
■ ■ final static Character.UnicodeBlock
CJK_UNIFIED_IDEOGRAPHS_EXTENSION_A
■ ■ final static Character.UnicodeBlock
COMBINING_DIACRITICAL_MARKS
■ ■ final static Character.UnicodeBlock COMBINING_HALF_MARKS
■ ■ final static Character.UnicodeBlock
COMBINING_MARKS_FOR_SYMBOLS
■ ■ final static Character.UnicodeBlock CONTROL_PICTURES
■ ■ final static Character.UnicodeBlock CURRENCY_SYMBOLS
■ ■ final static Character.UnicodeBlock CYRILLIC
■ ■ final static Character.UnicodeBlock DEVANAGARI
■ ■ final static Character.UnicodeBlock DINGBATS
■ ■ final static Character.UnicodeBlock ENCLOSED_ALPHANUMERICS
■ ■ final static Character.UnicodeBlock
ENCLOSED_CJK_LETTERS_AND_MONTHS
■ ■ final static Character.UnicodeBlock ETHIOPIC
■ ■ final static Character.UnicodeBlock GENERAL_PUNCTUATION
■ ■ final static Character.UnicodeBlock GEOMETRIC_SHAPES
■ ■ final static Character.UnicodeBlock GEORGIAN
■ ■ final static Character.UnicodeBlock GREEK
■ ■ final static Character.UnicodeBlock GREEK_EXTENDED
■ ■ final static Character.UnicodeBlock GUJARATI
■ ■ final static Character.UnicodeBlock GURMUKHI
■ ■ final static Character.UnicodeBlock
HALFWIDTH_AND_FULLWIDTH_FORMS
■ ■ final static Character.UnicodeBlock HANGUL_COMPATIBILITY_JAMO
■ ■ final static Character.UnicodeBlock HANGUL_JAMO
■ ■ final static Character.UnicodeBlock HANGUL_SYLLABLES
■ ■ final static Character.UnicodeBlock HEBREW
■ ■ final static Character.UnicodeBlock HIRAGANA
■ ■ final static Character.UnicodeBlock
IDEOGRAPHIC_DESCRIPTION_CHARACTERS
■ ■ final static Character.UnicodeBlock IPA_EXTENSIONS
■ ■ final static Character.UnicodeBlock KANBUN
■ ■ final static Character.UnicodeBlock KANGXI_RADICALS
■ ■ final static Character.UnicodeBlock KANNADA

■ ■ **interface CharSequence**
■ ■ abstract char charAt(int)
■ ■ abstract int length()

■ ■ **final class Class implements java.io.Serializable**
■ ■ boolean desiredAssertionStatus()
■ ■ static Class forName(String) throws ClassNotFoundException
■ ■ static Class forName(String,boolean,ClassLoader) throws
ClassNotFoundException
■ ■ Class[] getClasses()
■ ■ ClassLoader getClassLoader()
■ ■ Class getComponentType()
■ ■ Constructor getConstructor(Class[]) throws
NoSuchMethodException
■ ■ Constructor[] getConstructors()
■ ■ Class[] getDeclaredClasses()
■ ■ Constructor getDeclaredConstructor(Class[]) throws
NoSuchMethodException
■ ■ Constructor[] getDeclaredConstructors()
■ ■ Field getDeclaredField(String) throws NoSuchFieldException
■ ■ Field[] getDeclaredFields()
■ ■ Method getDeclaredMethod(String,Class[]) throws
NoSuchMethodException
■ ■ Method[] getDeclaredMethods()
■ ■ Class getDeclaringClass()

■ ■ **class ClassCastException extends RuntimeException**
■ ■ ClassCastException()

■ ■ **class ClassCircularityError extends LinkageError**
■ ■ ClassCircularityError()

■ ■ **class ClassFormatError extends LinkageError**
■ ■ ClassFormatError()

■ ■ **abstract class ClassLoader**
■ ■ protected ClassLoader()
■ ■ protected ClassLoader(ClassLoader)
■ ■ void clearAssertionStatus()

■ ■ final static Character.UnicodeBlock KATAKANA
■ ■ final static Character.UnicodeBlock KHMER
■ ■ final static Character.UnicodeBlock LAO
■ ■ final static Character.UnicodeBlock LATIN_1_SUPPLEMENT
■ ■ final static Character.UnicodeBlock LATIN_EXTENDED_A
■ ■ final static Character.UnicodeBlock LATIN_EXTENDED_ADDITIONAL
■ ■ final static Character.UnicodeBlock LATIN_EXTENDED_B
■ ■ final static Character.UnicodeBlock LETTERLIKE_SYMBOLS
■ ■ final static Character.UnicodeBlock MALAYALAM
■ ■ final static Character.UnicodeBlock MATHEMATICAL_OPERATORS
■ ■ final static Character.UnicodeBlock MISCELLANEOUS_SYMBOLS
■ ■ final static Character.UnicodeBlock MISCELLANEOUS_TECHNICAL
■ ■ final static Character.UnicodeBlock MONGOLIAN
■ ■ final static Character.UnicodeBlock MYANMAR
■ ■ final static Character.UnicodeBlock NUMBER_FORMS
■ ■ static Character.UnicodeBlock of(char)
■ ■ final static Character.UnicodeBlock OGHAM
■ ■ final static Character.UnicodeBlock
OPTICAL_CHARACTER_RECOGNITION
■ ■ final static Character.UnicodeBlock ORIYA
■ ■ final static Character.UnicodeBlock PRIVATE_USE_AREA
■ ■ final static Character.UnicodeBlock RUNIC
■ ■ final static Character.UnicodeBlock SINHALA
■ ■ final static Character.UnicodeBlock SMALL_FORM_VARIANTS
■ ■ final static Character.UnicodeBlock SPACING_MODIFIER_LETTERS
■ ■ final static Character.UnicodeBlock SPECIALS
■ ■ final static Character.UnicodeBlock
SUPERSCRIPTS_AND_SUBSCRIPTS
■ ■ final static Character.UnicodeBlock SURROGATES_AREA
■ ■ final static Character.UnicodeBlock SYRIAC
■ ■ final static Character.UnicodeBlock TAMIL
■ ■ final static Character.UnicodeBlock TELUGU
■ ■ final static Character.UnicodeBlock THAANA
■ ■ final static Character.UnicodeBlock THAI
■ ■ final static Character.UnicodeBlock TIBETAN
■ ■ final static Character.UnicodeBlock
UNIFIED_CANADIAN_ABORIGINAL_SYLLABICS
■ ■ final static Character.UnicodeBlock YI_RADICALS
■ ■ final static Character.UnicodeBlock YI_SYLLABLES

■ ■ abstract CharSequence subSequence(int,int)
■ ■ abstract String toString()

■ ■ Field getField(String) throws NoSuchFieldException
■ ■ Field[] getFields()
■ ■ Class[] getInterfaces()
■ ■ Method getMethod(String,Class[]) throws NoSuchMethodException
■ ■ Method[] getMethods()
■ ■ int getModifiers()
■ ■ String getName()
■ ■ Package getPackage()
■ ■ java.security.ProtectionDomain getProtectionDomain()
■ ■ java.net.URL getResource(String)
■ ■ java.io.InputStream getResourceAsStream(String)
■ ■ Object[] getSigners()
■ ■ Class getSuperclass()
■ ■ boolean isArray()
■ ■ boolean isAssignableFrom(Class)
■ ■ boolean isInstance(Object)
■ ■ boolean isInterface()
■ ■ boolean isPrimitive()
■ ■ Object newInstance() throws IllegalAccessException,
InstantiationException

■ ■ ClassCastException(String)

■ ■ ClassCircularityError(String)

■ ■ ClassFormatError(String)

■ ■ final protected Class defineClass(String,byte[],int,int) throws
ClassFormatError
■ ■ final protected Class defineClass(String,byte[],int,int,
java.security.ProtectionDomain) throws ClassFormatError

■ ■ protected Package definePackage(String,String,String,String,String, String,String,java.net.URL)
■ ■ protected Class findClass(String) throws ClassNotFoundException
■ ■ protected String findLibrary(String)
■ ■ final protected Class findLoadedClass(String)
■ ■ protected java.net.URL findResource(String)
■ ■ protected java.util.Enumeration findResources(String) throws java.io.IOException
■ ■ final protected Class findSystemClass(String) throws ClassNotFoundException
■ ■ protected Package getPackage(String)
■ ■ protected Package[] getPackages()
■ ■ final ClassLoader getParent()
■ ■ java.net.URL getResource(String)
■ ■ java.io.InputStream getResourceAsStream(String)
■ ■ **class ClassNotFoundException extends Exception**
■ ■ ClassNotFoundException()
■ ■ ClassNotFoundException(String)
■ ■ **interface Cloneable**
■ ■ **class CloneNotSupportedException extends Exception**
■ ■ CloneNotSupportedException()
■ ■ **interface Comparable**
■ ■ abstract int compareTo(Object)
■ ■ **final class Compiler**
■ ■ static Object command(Object)
■ ■ static boolean compileClass(Class)
■ ■ static boolean compileClasses(String)
■ ■ **final class Double extends Number implements Comparable**
■ ■ Double(double)
■ ■ Double(String)
■ ■ static int compare(double,double)
■ ■ int compareTo(Double)
■ ■ int compareTo(Object)
■ ■ static long doubleToLongBits(double)
■ ■ static long doubleToRawLongBits(double)
■ ■ double doubleValue()
■ ■ float floatValue()
■ ■ int intValue()
■ ■ boolean isInfinite()
■ ■ static boolean isInfinite(double)
■ ■ boolean isNaN()
■ ■ **class Error extends Throwable**
■ ■ Error()
■ ■ Error(String)
■ ■ **class Exception extends Throwable**
■ ■ Exception()
■ ■ Exception(String)
■ ■ **class ExceptionInInitializerError extends LinkageError**
■ ■ ExceptionInInitializerError()
■ ■ ExceptionInInitializerError(String)
■ ■ **final class Float extends Number implements Comparable**
■ ■ Float(double)
■ ■ Float(float)
■ ■ Float(String)
■ ■ static int compare(float,float)
■ ■ int compareTo(Float)
■ ■ int compareTo(Object)
■ ■ double doubleValue()
■ ■ static int floatToIntBits(float)
■ ■ static int floatToRawIntBits(float)
■ ■ float floatValue()
■ ■ static float intBitsToFloat(int)
■ ■ int intValue()
■ ■ boolean isInfinite()
■ ■ **class IllegalAccessError extends IncompatibleClassChangeError**
■ ■ IllegalAccessError()
■ ■ **class IllegalAccessException extends Exception**
■ ■ IllegalAccessException()
■ ■ **class IllegalArgumentException extends RuntimeException**
■ ■ IllegalArgumentException()
■ ■ **class IllegalMonitorStateException extends RuntimeException**
■ ■ IllegalMonitorStateException()
■ ■ **class IllegalStateException extends RuntimeException**
■ ■ IllegalStateException()

■ ■ final java.util.Enumeration getResources(String) throws java.io.IOException
■ ■ static ClassLoader getSystemClassLoader()
■ ■ static java.net.URL getSystemResource(String)
■ ■ static java.io.InputStream getSystemResourceAsStream(String)
■ ■ static java.util.Enumeration getSystemResources(String) throws java.io.IOException
■ ■ Class loadClass(String) throws ClassNotFoundException
■ ■ protected Class loadClass(String,boolean) throws ClassNotFoundException
■ ■ final protected void resolveClass(Class)
■ ■ void setClassAssertionStatus(String,boolean)
■ ■ void setDefaultAssertionStatus(boolean)
■ ■ void setPackageAssertionStatus(String,boolean)
■ ■ final protected void setSigners(Class,Object[])

■ ■ ClassNotFoundException(String,Throwable)
■ ■ Throwable getException()

■ ■ CloneNotSupportedException(String)

■ ■ static void disable()
■ ■ static void enable()

■ ■ static boolean isNaN(double)
■ ■ static double longBitsToDouble(long)
■ ■ long longValue()
■ ■ final static double MAX_VALUE
■ ■ final static double MIN_VALUE
■ ■ final static double NaN
■ ■ final static double NEGATIVE_INFINITY
■ ■ static double parseDouble(String)
■ ■ final static double POSITIVE_INFINITY
■ ■ static String toString(double)
■ ■ final static Class TYPE
■ ■ static Double valueOf(String)

■ ■ Error(String,Throwable)
■ ■ Error(Throwable)

■ ■ Exception(String,Throwable)
■ ■ Exception(Throwable)

■ ■ ExceptionInInitializerError(Throwable)
■ ■ Throwable getException()

■ ■ static boolean isInfinite(float)
■ ■ boolean isNaN()
■ ■ static boolean isNaN(float)
■ ■ long longValue()
■ ■ final static float MAX_VALUE
■ ■ final static float MIN_VALUE
■ ■ final static float NaN
■ ■ final static float NEGATIVE_INFINITY
■ ■ static float parseFloat(String)
■ ■ final static float POSITIVE_INFINITY
■ ■ static String toString(float)
■ ■ final static Class TYPE
■ ■ static Float valueOf(String)

■ ■ IllegalAccessError(String)

■ ■ IllegalAccessException(String)

■ ■ IllegalArgumentException(String)

■ ■ IllegalMonitorStateException(String)

■ ■ IllegalStateException(String)

■ ■ **class IllegalThreadStateException extends IllegalArgumentException**
■ ■ IllegalThreadStateException()　　　　　　　　　　　　　■ ■ IllegalThreadStateException(String)

■ ■ **class IncompatibleClassChangeError extends LinkageError**
■ ■ IncompatibleClassChangeError()　　　　　　　　　　　　■ ■ IncompatibleClassChangeError(String)

■ ■ **class IndexOutOfBoundsException extends RuntimeException**
■ ■ IndexOutOfBoundsException()　　　　　　　　　　　　　■ ■ IndexOutOfBoundsException(String)

■ ■ **class InheritableThreadLocal extends ThreadLocal**
■ ■ InheritableThreadLocal()　　　　　　　　　　　　　　■ ■ protected Object childValue(Object)

■ ■ **class InstantiationError extends IncompatibleClassChangeError**
■ ■ InstantiationError()　　　　　　　　　　　　　　　　■ ■ InstantiationError(String)

■ ■ **class InstantiationException extends Exception**
■ ■ InstantiationException()　　　　　　　　　　　　　　■ ■ InstantiationException(String)

■ ■ **final class Integer extends Number implements Comparable**
■ ■ Integer(int)	■ ■ final static int MAX_VALUE
■ ■ Integer(String)	■ ■ final static int MIN_VALUE
■ ■ int compareTo(Integer)	■ ■ static int parseInt(String)
■ ■ int compareTo(Object)	■ ■ static int parseInt(String,int)
■ ■ static Integer decode(String)	■ ■ static String toBinaryString(int)
■ ■ double doubleValue()	■ ■ static String toHexString(int)
■ ■ float floatValue()	■ ■ static String toOctalString(int)
■ ■ static Integer getInteger(String)	■ ■ static String toString(int)
■ ■ static Integer getInteger(String,int)	■ ■ static String toString(int,int)
■ ■ static Integer getInteger(String,Integer)	■ ■ final static Class TYPE
■ ■ int intValue()	■ ■ static Integer valueOf(String)
■ ■ long longValue()	■ ■ static Integer valueOf(String,int)

■ ■ **class InternalError extends VirtualMachineError**
■ ■ InternalError()　　　　　　　　　　　　　　　　　　■ ■ InternalError(String)

■ ■ **class InterruptedException extends Exception**
■ ■ InterruptedException()　　　　　　　　　　　　　　　■ ■ InterruptedException(String)

■ ■ **class LinkageError extends Error**
■ ■ LinkageError()　　　　　　　　　　　　　　　　　　■ ■ LinkageError(String)

■ ■ **final class Long extends Number implements Comparable**
■ ■ Long(long)	■ ■ final static long MAX_VALUE
■ ■ Long(String)	■ ■ final static long MIN_VALUE
■ ■ int compareTo(Long)	■ ■ static long parseLong(String)
■ ■ int compareTo(Object)	■ ■ static long parseLong(String,int)
■ ■ static Long decode(String)	■ ■ static String toBinaryString(long)
■ ■ double doubleValue()	■ ■ static String toHexString(long)
■ ■ float floatValue()	■ ■ static String toOctalString(long)
■ ■ static Long getLong(String)	■ ■ static String toString(long)
■ ■ static Long getLong(String,long)	■ ■ static String toString(long,int)
■ ■ static Long getLong(String,Long)	■ ■ final static Class TYPE
■ ■ int intValue()	■ ■ static Long valueOf(String)
■ ■ long longValue()	■ ■ static Long valueOf(String,int)

■ ■ **final class Math**
■ ■ static double abs(double)	■ ■ static int max(int,int)
■ ■ static float abs(float)	■ ■ static long max(long,long)
■ ■ static int abs(int)	■ ■ static double min(double,double)
■ ■ static long abs(long)	■ ■ static float min(float,float)
■ ■ static double acos(double)	■ ■ static int min(int,int)
■ ■ static double asin(double)	■ ■ static long min(long,long)
■ ■ static double atan(double)	■ ■ final static double PI
■ ■ static double atan2(double,double)	■ ■ static double pow(double,double)
■ ■ static double ceil(double)	■ ■ static double random()
■ ■ static double cos(double)	■ ■ static double rint(double)
■ ■ final static double E	■ ■ static long round(double)
■ ■ static double exp(double)	■ ■ static int round(float)
■ ■ static double floor(double)	■ ■ static double sin(double)
■ ■ static double IEEEremainder(double,double)	■ ■ static double sqrt(double)
■ ■ static double log(double)	■ ■ static double tan(double)
■ ■ static double max(double,double)	■ ■ static double toDegrees(double)
■ ■ static float max(float,float)	■ ■ static double toRadians(double)

■ ■ **class NegativeArraySizeException extends RuntimeException**
■ ■ NegativeArraySizeException()　　　　　　　　　　　　■ ■ NegativeArraySizeException(String)

■ ■ **class NoClassDefFoundError extends LinkageError**
■ ■ NoClassDefFoundError()　　　　　　　　　　　　　　■ ■ NoClassDefFoundError(String)

■ ■ **class NoSuchFieldError extends IncompatibleClassChangeError**
■ ■ NoSuchFieldError()　　　　　　　　　　　　　　　　■ ■ NoSuchFieldError(String)

■ ■ **class NoSuchFieldException extends Exception**
■ ■ NoSuchFieldException()　　　　　　　　　　　　　　■ ■ NoSuchFieldException(String)

■ ■ **class NoSuchMethodError extends IncompatibleClassChangeError**
■ ■ NoSuchMethodError()　　　　　　　　　　　　　　　■ ■ NoSuchMethodError(String)

■ ■ **class NoSuchMethodException extends Exception**

■ ■ NoSuchMethodException()

■ ■ **class NullPointerException extends RuntimeException**
■ ■ NullPointerException()

■ ■ **abstract class Number implements java.io.Serializable**
■ ■ Number()
■ ■ byte byteValue()
■ ■ abstract double doubleValue()
■ ■ abstract float floatValue()

■ ■ **class NumberFormatException extends IllegalArgumentException**
■ ■ NumberFormatException()

■ ■ **class Object**
■ ■ Object()
■ ■ protected Object clone() throws CloneNotSupportedException
■ ■ boolean equals(Object)
■ ■ protected void finalize() throws Throwable
■ ■ final Class getClass()
■ ■ int hashCode()

■ ■ **class OutOfMemoryError extends VirtualMachineError**
■ ■ OutOfMemoryError()

■ ■ **class Package**
■ ■ String getImplementationTitle()
■ ■ String getImplementationVendor()
■ ■ String getImplementationVersion()
■ ■ String getName()
■ ■ static Package getPackage(String)
■ ■ static Package[] getPackages()

■ ■ **abstract class Process**
■ ■ Process()
■ ■ abstract void destroy()
■ ■ abstract int exitValue()
■ ■ abstract java.io.InputStream getErrorStream()

■ ■ **interface Runnable**
■ ■ abstract void run()

■ ■ **class Runtime**
■ ■ void addShutdownHook(Thread)
■ ■ int availableProcessors()
■ ■ Process exec(String[]) throws java.io.IOException
■ ■ Process exec(String[],String[]) throws java.io.IOException
■ ■ Process exec(String[],String[],java.io.File) throws java.io.IOException
■ ■ Process exec(String) throws java.io.IOException
■ ■ Process exec(String,String[]) throws java.io.IOException
■ ■ Process exec(String,String[],java.io.File) throws java.io.IOException
■ ■ void exit(int)
■ ■ long freeMemory()
■ ■ void gc()

■ ■ **class RuntimeException extends Exception**
■ ■ RuntimeException()
■ ■ RuntimeException(String)

■ ■ **final class RuntimePermission extends java.security.BasicPermission**
■ ■ RuntimePermission(String)

■ ■ **class SecurityException extends RuntimeException**
■ ■ SecurityException()

■ ■ **class SecurityManager**
■ ■ SecurityManager()
■ ■ void checkAccept(String,int)
■ ■ void checkAccess(Thread)
■ ■ void checkAccess(ThreadGroup)
■ ■ void checkAwtEventQueueAccess()
■ ■ void checkConnect(String,int)
■ ■ void checkConnect(String,int,Object)
■ ■ void checkCreateClassLoader()
■ ■ void checkDelete(String)
■ ■ void checkExec(String)
■ ■ void checkExit(int)
■ ■ void checkLink(String)
■ ■ void checkListen(int)
■ ■ void checkMemberAccess(Class,int)
■ ■ void checkMulticast(java.net.InetAddress)
■ ■ void checkMulticast(java.net.InetAddress,byte)
■ ■ void checkPackageAccess(String)
■ ■ void checkPackageDefinition(String)

■ ■ **final class Short extends Number implements Comparable**
■ ■ Short(String)
■ ■ Short(short)

■ ■ NoSuchMethodException(String)

■ ■ NullPointerException(String)

■ ■ abstract int intValue()
■ ■ abstract long longValue()
■ ■ short shortValue()

■ ■ NumberFormatException(String)

■ ■ final void notify()
■ ■ final void notifyAll()
■ ■ String toString()
■ ■ final void wait() throws InterruptedException
■ ■ final void wait(long) throws InterruptedException
■ ■ final void wait(long,int) throws InterruptedException

■ ■ OutOfMemoryError(String)

■ ■ String getSpecificationTitle()
■ ■ String getSpecificationVendor()
■ ■ String getSpecificationVersion()
■ ■ boolean isCompatibleWith(String)
■ ■ boolean isSealed()
■ ■ boolean isSealed(java.net.URL)

■ ■ abstract java.io.InputStream getInputStream()
■ ■ abstract java.io.OutputStream getOutputStream()
■ ■ abstract int waitFor() throws InterruptedException

■ ■ static Runtime getRuntime()
■ ■ void halt(int)
■ ■ void load(String)
■ ■ void loadLibrary(String)
■ ■ long maxMemory()
■ ■ boolean removeShutdownHook(Thread)
■ ■ void runFinalization()
■ ■ long totalMemory()
■ ■ void traceInstructions(boolean)
■ ■ void traceMethodCalls(boolean)

■ ■ RuntimeException(String,Throwable)
■ ■ RuntimeException(Throwable)

■ ■ RuntimePermission(String,String)

■ ■ SecurityException(String)

■ ■ void checkPermission(java.security.Permission)
■ ■ void checkPermission(java.security.Permission,Object)
■ ■ void checkPrintJobAccess()
■ ■ void checkPropertiesAccess()
■ ■ void checkPropertyAccess(String)
■ ■ void checkRead(java.io.FileDescriptor)
■ ■ void checkRead(String)
■ ■ void checkRead(String,Object)
■ ■ void checkSecurityAccess(String)
■ ■ void checkSetFactory()
■ ■ void checkSystemClipboardAccess()
■ ■ boolean checkTopLevelWindow(Object)
■ ■ void checkWrite(java.io.FileDescriptor)
■ ■ void checkWrite(String)
■ ■ protected Class[] getClassContext()
■ ■ Object getSecurityContext()
■ ■ ThreadGroup getThreadGroup()

■ ■ int compareTo(Object)
■ ■ int compareTo(Short)

- ■ ■ static Short decode(String)
- ■ ■ double doubleValue()
- ■ ■ float floatValue()
- ■ ■ int intValue()
- ■ ■ long longValue()
- ■ ■ final static short MAX_VALUE
- ■ ■ final static short MIN_VALUE

- ■ ■ **class StackOverflowError extends VirtualMachineError**
- ■ ■ StackOverflowError()

- ■ ■ **final class StackTraceElement implements java.io.Serializable**
- ■ ■ String getClassName()
- ■ ■ String getFileName()
- ■ ■ int getLineNumber()

- ■ ■ **final class StrictMath**
- ■ ■ static double abs(double)
- ■ ■ static float abs(float)
- ■ ■ static int abs(int)
- ■ ■ static long abs(long)
- ■ ■ static double acos(double)
- ■ ■ static double asin(double)
- ■ ■ static double atan(double)
- ■ ■ static double atan2(double,double)
- ■ ■ static double ceil(double)
- ■ ■ static double cos(double)
- ■ ■ final static double E
- ■ ■ static double exp(double)
- ■ ■ static double floor(double)
- ■ ■ static double IEEEremainder(double,double)
- ■ ■ static double log(double)
- ■ ■ static double max(double,double)
- ■ ■ static float max(float,float)

- ■ ■ **final class String implements java.io.Serializable , CharSequence , Comparable**
- ■ ■ String()
- ■ ■ String(byte[])
- ■ ■ String(byte[],int,int)
- ■ ■ String(byte[],int,int,String) throws java.io.UnsupportedEncodingException
- ■ ■ String(byte[],String) throws java.io.UnsupportedEncodingException
- ■ ■ String(char[])
- ■ ■ String(char[],int,int)
- ■ ■ String(String)
- ■ ■ String(StringBuffer)
- ■ ■ final static java.util.Comparator CASE_INSENSITIVE_ORDER
- ■ ■ char charAt(int)
- ■ ■ int compareTo(Object)
- ■ ■ int compareTo(String)
- ■ ■ int compareToIgnoreCase(String)
- ■ ■ String concat(String)
- ■ ■ boolean contentEquals(StringBuffer)
- ■ ■ static String copyValueOf(char[])
- ■ ■ static String copyValueOf(char[],int,int)
- ■ ■ boolean endsWith(String)
- ■ ■ boolean equalsIgnoreCase(String)
- ■ ■ byte[] getBytes()
- ■ ■ byte[] getBytes(String) throws java.io.UnsupportedEncodingException
- ■ ■ void getChars(int,int,char[],int)
- ■ ■ int indexOf(int)
- ■ ■ int indexOf(int,int)
- ■ ■ int indexOf(String)
- ■ ■ int indexOf(String,int)

- ■ ■ **final class StringBuffer implements java.io.Serializable , CharSequence**
- ■ ■ StringBuffer()
- ■ ■ StringBuffer(int)
- ■ ■ StringBuffer(String)
- ■ ■ StringBuffer append(char[])
- ■ ■ StringBuffer append(char[],int,int)
- ■ ■ StringBuffer append(char)
- ■ ■ StringBuffer append(double)
- ■ ■ StringBuffer append(float)
- ■ ■ StringBuffer append(int)
- ■ ■ StringBuffer append(long)
- ■ ■ StringBuffer append(Object)
- ■ ■ StringBuffer append(String)

- ■ ■ static short parseShort(String)
- ■ ■ static short parseShort(String,int)
- ■ ■ static String toString(short)
- ■ ■ final static Class TYPE
- ■ ■ static Short valueOf(String)
- ■ ■ static Short valueOf(String,int)

- ■ ■ StackOverflowError(String)

- ■ ■ String getMethodName()
- ■ ■ boolean isNativeMethod()

- ■ ■ static int max(int,int)
- ■ ■ static long max(long,long)
- ■ ■ static double min(double,double)
- ■ ■ static float min(float,float)
- ■ ■ static int min(int,int)
- ■ ■ static long min(long,long)
- ■ ■ final static double PI
- ■ ■ static double pow(double,double)
- ■ ■ static double random()
- ■ ■ static double rint(double)
- ■ ■ static long round(double)
- ■ ■ static int round(float)
- ■ ■ static double sin(double)
- ■ ■ static double sqrt(double)
- ■ ■ static double tan(double)
- ■ ■ static double toDegrees(double)
- ■ ■ static double toRadians(double)

- ■ ■ String intern()
- ■ ■ int lastIndexOf(int)
- ■ ■ int lastIndexOf(int,int)
- ■ ■ int lastIndexOf(String)
- ■ ■ int lastIndexOf(String,int)
- ■ ■ int length()
- ■ ■ boolean regionMatches(int,String,int,int)
- ■ ■ boolean regionMatches(boolean,int,String,int,int)
- ■ ■ String replace(char,char)
- ■ ■ boolean startsWith(String)
- ■ ■ boolean startsWith(String,int)
- ■ ■ CharSequence subSequence(int,int)
- ■ ■ String substring(int)
- ■ ■ String substring(int,int)
- ■ ■ char[] toCharArray()
- ■ ■ String toLowerCase()
- ■ ■ String toLowerCase(java.util.Locale)
- ■ ■ String toUpperCase()
- ■ ■ String toUpperCase(java.util.Locale)
- ■ ■ String trim()
- ■ ■ static String valueOf(char[])
- ■ ■ static String valueOf(char[],int,int)
- ■ ■ static String valueOf(char)
- ■ ■ static String valueOf(double)
- ■ ■ static String valueOf(float)
- ■ ■ static String valueOf(int)
- ■ ■ static String valueOf(long)
- ■ ■ static String valueOf(Object)
- ■ ■ static String valueOf(boolean)

- ■ ■ StringBuffer append(StringBuffer)
- ■ ■ StringBuffer append(boolean)
- ■ ■ int capacity()
- ■ ■ char charAt(int)
- ■ ■ StringBuffer delete(int,int)
- ■ ■ StringBuffer deleteCharAt(int)
- ■ ■ void ensureCapacity(int)
- ■ ■ void getChars(int,int,char[],int)
- ■ ■ int indexOf(String)
- ■ ■ int indexOf(String,int)
- ■ ■ StringBuffer insert(int,char[])
- ■ ■ StringBuffer insert(int,char[],int,int)

■ ■ StringBuffer insert(int,char)
■ ■ StringBuffer insert(int,double)
■ ■ StringBuffer insert(int,float)
■ ■ StringBuffer insert(int,int)
■ ■ StringBuffer insert(int,long)
■ ■ StringBuffer insert(int,Object)
■ ■ StringBuffer insert(int,String)
■ ■ StringBuffer insert(int,boolean)
■ ■ int lastIndexOf(String)

■ ■ int lastIndexOf(String,int)
■ ■ int length()
■ ■ StringBuffer replace(int,int,String)
■ ■ StringBuffer reverse()
■ ■ void setCharAt(int,char)
■ ■ void setLength(int)
■ ■ CharSequence subSequence(int,int)
■ ■ String substring(int)
■ ■ String substring(int,int)

■ ■ **class StringIndexOutOfBoundsException extends IndexOutOfBoundsException**
■ ■ StringIndexOutOfBoundsException()
■ ■ StringIndexOutOfBoundsException(int)

■ ■ StringIndexOutOfBoundsException(String)

■ ■ **final class System**
■ ■ static void arraycopy(Object,int,Object,int,int)
■ ■ static long currentTimeMillis()
■ ■ final static java.io.PrintStream err
■ ■ static void exit(int)
■ ■ static void gc()
■ ■ static java.util.Properties getProperties()
■ ■ static String getProperty(String)
■ ■ static String getProperty(String,String)
■ ■ static SecurityManager getSecurityManager()
■ ■ static int identityHashCode(Object)
■ ■ final static java.io.InputStream in

■ ■ static void load(String)
■ ■ static void loadLibrary(String)
■ ■ static String mapLibraryName(String)
■ ■ final static java.io.PrintStream out
■ ■ static void runFinalization()
■ ■ static void setErr(java.io.PrintStream)
■ ■ static void setIn(java.io.InputStream)
■ ■ static void setOut(java.io.PrintStream)
■ ■ static void setProperties(java.util.Properties)
■ ■ static String setProperty(String,String)
■ ■ static void setSecurityManager(SecurityManager)

■ ■ **class Thread implements Runnable**
■ ■ Thread()
■ ■ Thread(Runnable)
■ ■ Thread(Runnable,String)
■ ■ Thread(String)
■ ■ Thread(ThreadGroup,Runnable)
■ ■ Thread(ThreadGroup,Runnable,String)
■ ■ Thread(ThreadGroup,Runnable,String,long)
■ ■ Thread(ThreadGroup,String)
■ ■ static int activeCount()
■ ■ final void checkAccess()
■ ■ static Thread currentThread()
■ ■ void destroy()
■ ■ static void dumpStack()
■ ■ static int enumerate(Thread[])
■ ■ ClassLoader getContextClassLoader()
■ ■ final String getName()
■ ■ final int getPriority()
■ ■ final ThreadGroup getThreadGroup()
■ ■ static boolean holdsLock(Object)
■ ■ void interrupt()

■ ■ static boolean interrupted()
■ ■ final boolean isAlive()
■ ■ final boolean isDaemon()
■ ■ boolean isInterrupted()
■ ■ final void join() throws InterruptedException
■ ■ final void join(long) throws InterruptedException
■ ■ final void join(long,int) throws InterruptedException
■ ■ final static int MAX_PRIORITY
■ ■ final static int MIN_PRIORITY
■ ■ final static int NORM_PRIORITY
■ ■ void run()
■ ■ void setContextClassLoader(ClassLoader)
■ ■ final void setDaemon(boolean)
■ ■ final void setName(String)
■ ■ final void setPriority(int)
■ ■ static void sleep(long) throws InterruptedException
■ ■ static void sleep(long,int) throws InterruptedException
■ ■ void start()
■ ■ static void yield()

■ ■ **class ThreadDeath extends Error**
■ ■ ThreadDeath()

■ ■ **class ThreadGroup**
■ ■ ThreadGroup(String)
■ ■ ThreadGroup(ThreadGroup,String)
■ ■ int activeCount()
■ ■ int activeGroupCount()
■ ■ final void checkAccess()
■ ■ final void destroy()
■ ■ int enumerate(Thread[])
■ ■ int enumerate(Thread[],boolean)
■ ■ int enumerate(ThreadGroup[])
■ ■ int enumerate(ThreadGroup[],boolean)
■ ■ final int getMaxPriority()

■ ■ final String getName()
■ ■ final ThreadGroup getParent()
■ ■ final void interrupt()
■ ■ final boolean isDaemon()
■ ■ boolean isDestroyed()
■ ■ void list()
■ ■ final boolean parentOf(ThreadGroup)
■ ■ final void setDaemon(boolean)
■ ■ final void setMaxPriority(int)
■ ■ void uncaughtException(Thread,Throwable)

■ ■ **class ThreadLocal**
■ ■ ThreadLocal()
■ ■ Object get()

■ ■ protected Object initialValue()
■ ■ void set(Object)

■ ■ **class Throwable implements java.io.Serializable**
■ ■ Throwable()
■ ■ Throwable(String)
■ ■ Throwable(String,Throwable)
■ ■ Throwable(Throwable)
■ ■ Throwable fillInStackTrace()
■ ■ Throwable getCause()
■ ■ String getLocalizedMessage()

■ ■ String getMessage()
■ ■ StackTraceElement[] getStackTrace()
■ ■ Throwable initCause(Throwable)
■ ■ void printStackTrace()
■ ■ void printStackTrace(java.io.PrintStream)
■ ■ void printStackTrace(java.io.PrintWriter)
■ ■ void setStackTrace(StackTraceElement[])

■ ■ **class UnknownError extends VirtualMachineError**
■ ■ UnknownError()

■ ■ UnknownError(String)

■ ■ **class UnsatisfiedLinkError extends LinkageError**
■ ■ UnsatisfiedLinkError()

■ ■ UnsatisfiedLinkError(String)

■ ■ **class UnsupportedClassVersionError extends ClassFormatError**
■ ■ UnsupportedClassVersionError()

■ ■ UnsupportedClassVersionError(String)

■ ■ **class UnsupportedOperationException extends RuntimeException**
■ ■ UnsupportedOperationException()

■ ■ UnsupportedOperationException(String)

■ ■ **class VerifyError extends LinkageError**
■ ■ VerifyError()

■ ■ VerifyError(String)

■ ■ **abstract class VirtualMachineError extends Error**
■ ■ VirtualMachineError()

■ ■ VirtualMachineError(String)

■ ■ **final class Void**
■ ■ final static Class TYPE

999.3.3 java.lang.ref

■ ■ **package java.lang.ref**
■ ■ **class PhantomReference extends Reference**
■ ■ PhantomReference(Object,ReferenceQueue)

■ ■ **abstract class Reference**
■ ■ void clear()

■ ■ Object get()

■ ■ boolean enqueue()

■ ■ boolean isEnqueued()

■ ■ **class ReferenceQueue**
■ ■ ReferenceQueue()

■ ■ Reference remove() throws InterruptedException

■ ■ Reference poll()

■ ■ Reference remove(long) throws InterruptedException

■ ■ **class SoftReference extends Reference**
■ ■ SoftReference(Object)

■ ■ SoftReference(Object,ReferenceQueue)

■ ■ **class WeakReference extends Reference**
■ ■ WeakReference(Object)

■ ■ WeakReference(Object,ReferenceQueue)

999.3.4 java.lang.reflect

■ ■ **package java.lang.reflect**
■ ■ **class AccessibleObject**
■ ■ protected AccessibleObject()

■ ■ static void setAccessible(AccessibleObject[],boolean)

■ ■ boolean isAccessible()

■ ■ void setAccessible(boolean)

■ ■ **final class Array**
■ ■ static Object get(Object,int)

■ ■ static Object newInstance(Class,int)

■ ■ static boolean getBoolean(Object,int)

■ ■ static void set(Object,int,Object)

■ ■ static byte getByte(Object,int)

■ ■ static void setBoolean(Object,int,boolean)

■ ■ static char getChar(Object,int)

■ ■ static void setByte(Object,int,byte)

■ ■ static double getDouble(Object,int)

■ ■ static void setChar(Object,int,char)

■ ■ static float getFloat(Object,int)

■ ■ static void setDouble(Object,int,double)

■ ■ static int getInt(Object,int)

■ ■ static void setFloat(Object,int,float)

■ ■ static int getLength(Object)

■ ■ static void setInt(Object,int,int)

■ ■ static long getLong(Object,int)

■ ■ static void setLong(Object,int,long)

■ ■ static short getShort(Object,int)

■ ■ static void setShort(Object,int,short)

■ ■ static Object newInstance(Class,int[])

■ ■ **final class Constructor extends AccessibleObject implements Member**
■ ■ Class getDeclaringClass()

■ ■ Class[] getParameterTypes()

■ ■ Class[] getExceptionTypes()

■ ■ Object newInstance(Object[]) throws IllegalAccessException,
InstantiationException, InvocationTargetException

■ ■ int getModifiers()

■ ■ String getName()

■ ■ **final class Field extends AccessibleObject implements Member**
■ ■ Object get(Object) throws IllegalAccessException

■ ■ short getShort(Object) throws IllegalAccessException

■ ■ boolean getBoolean(Object) throws IllegalAccessException

■ ■ Class getType()

■ ■ byte getByte(Object) throws IllegalAccessException

■ ■ void set(Object,Object) throws IllegalAccessException

■ ■ char getChar(Object) throws IllegalAccessException

■ ■ void setBoolean(Object,boolean) throws IllegalAccessException

■ ■ Class getDeclaringClass()

■ ■ void setByte(Object,byte) throws IllegalAccessException

■ ■ double getDouble(Object) throws IllegalAccessException

■ ■ void setChar(Object,char) throws IllegalAccessException

■ ■ float getFloat(Object) throws IllegalAccessException

■ ■ void setDouble(Object,double) throws IllegalAccessException

■ ■ int getInt(Object) throws IllegalAccessException

■ ■ void setFloat(Object,float) throws IllegalAccessException

■ ■ long getLong(Object) throws IllegalAccessException

■ ■ void setInt(Object,int) throws IllegalAccessException

■ ■ int getModifiers()

■ ■ void setLong(Object,long) throws IllegalAccessException

■ ■ String getName()

■ ■ void setShort(Object,short) throws IllegalAccessException

■ ■ **interface InvocationHandler**
■ ■ abstract Object invoke(Object,Method,Object[]) throws Throwable

■ ■ **class InvocationTargetException extends Exception**
■ ■ protected InvocationTargetException()

■ ■ InvocationTargetException(Throwable,String)

■ ■ InvocationTargetException(Throwable)

■ ■ Throwable getTargetException()

■ ■ **interface Member**
■ ■ final static int DECLARED

■ ■ abstract String getName()

■ ■ abstract Class getDeclaringClass()

■ ■ final static int PUBLIC

■ ■ abstract int getModifiers()

■ ■ **final class Method extends AccessibleObject implements Member**
■ ■ Class getDeclaringClass()

■ ■ Class[] getExceptionTypes()

■ ■ int getModifiers()
■ ■ String getName()
■ ■ Class[] getParameterTypes()

■ ■ **class Modifier**
■ ■ Modifier()
■ ■ final static int ABSTRACT
■ ■ final static int FINAL
■ ■ final static int INTERFACE
■ ■ static boolean isAbstract(int)
■ ■ static boolean isFinal(int)
■ ■ static boolean isInterface(int)
■ ■ static boolean isNative(int)
■ ■ static boolean isPrivate(int)
■ ■ static boolean isProtected(int)
■ ■ static boolean isPublic(int)
■ ■ static boolean isStatic(int)
■ ■ static boolean isStrict(int)

■ ■ **class Proxy implements java.io.Serializable**
■ ■ protected Proxy(InvocationHandler)
■ ■ static InvocationHandler getInvocationHandler(Object)
■ ■ static Class getProxyClass(ClassLoader,Class[])
■ ■ protected InvocationHandler h

■ ■ **final class ReflectPermission extends java.security.BasicPermission**
■ ■ ReflectPermission(String)

■ ■ **class UndeclaredThrowableException extends RuntimeException**
■ ■ UndeclaredThrowableException(Throwable)
■ ■ UndeclaredThrowableException(Throwable,String)

■ ■ Class getReturnType()
■ ■ Object invoke(Object,Object[]) throws IllegalAccessException, InvocationTargetException

■ ■ static boolean isSynchronized(int)
■ ■ static boolean isTransient(int)
■ ■ static boolean isVolatile(int)
■ ■ final static int NATIVE
■ ■ final static int PRIVATE
■ ■ final static int PROTECTED
■ ■ final static int PUBLIC
■ ■ final static int STATIC
■ ■ final static int STRICT
■ ■ final static int SYNCHRONIZED
■ ■ static String toString(int)
■ ■ final static int TRANSIENT
■ ■ final static int VOLATILE

■ ■ static boolean isProxyClass(Class)
■ ■ static Object newProxyInstance(ClassLoader,Class[], InvocationHandler)

■ ■ ReflectPermission(String,String)

■ ■ Throwable getUndeclaredThrowable()

999.3.5　java.math

■ ■ **package java.math**
■ ■ **class BigDecimal extends Number implements Comparable**
■ ■ BigDecimal(double)
■ ■ BigDecimal(String)
■ ■ BigDecimal(BigInteger)
■ ■ BigDecimal(BigInteger,int)
■ ■ BigDecimal abs()
■ ■ BigDecimal add(BigDecimal)
■ ■ int compareTo(Object)
■ ■ int compareTo(BigDecimal)
■ ■ BigDecimal divide(BigDecimal,int)
■ ■ BigDecimal divide(BigDecimal,int,int)
■ ■ double doubleValue()
■ ■ float floatValue()
■ ■ int intValue()
■ ■ long longValue()
■ ■ BigDecimal max(BigDecimal)
■ ■ BigDecimal min(BigDecimal)
■ ■ BigDecimal movePointLeft(int)
■ ■ BigDecimal movePointRight(int)
■ ■ BigDecimal multiply(BigDecimal)

■ ■ BigDecimal negate()
■ ■ final static int ROUND_CEILING
■ ■ final static int ROUND_DOWN
■ ■ final static int ROUND_FLOOR
■ ■ final static int ROUND_HALF_DOWN
■ ■ final static int ROUND_HALF_EVEN
■ ■ final static int ROUND_HALF_UP
■ ■ final static int ROUND_UNNECESSARY
■ ■ final static int ROUND_UP
■ ■ int scale()
■ ■ BigDecimal setScale(int)
■ ■ BigDecimal setScale(int,int)
■ ■ int signum()
■ ■ BigDecimal subtract(BigDecimal)
■ ■ BigInteger toBigInteger()
■ ■ BigInteger unscaledValue()
■ ■ static BigDecimal valueOf(long)
■ ■ static BigDecimal valueOf(long,int)

■ ■ **class BigInteger extends Number implements Comparable**
■ ■ BigInteger(byte[])
■ ■ BigInteger(int,byte[])
■ ■ BigInteger(int,int,java.util.Random)
■ ■ BigInteger(int,java.util.Random)
■ ■ BigInteger(String)
■ ■ BigInteger(String,int)
■ ■ BigInteger abs()
■ ■ BigInteger add(BigInteger)
■ ■ BigInteger and(BigInteger)
■ ■ BigInteger andNot(BigInteger)
■ ■ int bitCount()
■ ■ int bitLength()
■ ■ BigInteger clearBit(int)
■ ■ int compareTo(Object)
■ ■ int compareTo(BigInteger)
■ ■ BigInteger divide(BigInteger)
■ ■ BigInteger[] divideAndRemainder(BigInteger)
■ ■ double doubleValue()
■ ■ BigInteger flipBit(int)
■ ■ float floatValue()
■ ■ BigInteger gcd(BigInteger)
■ ■ int getLowestSetBit()
■ ■ int intValue()

■ ■ boolean isProbablePrime(int)
■ ■ long longValue()
■ ■ BigInteger max(BigInteger)
■ ■ BigInteger min(BigInteger)
■ ■ BigInteger mod(BigInteger)
■ ■ BigInteger modInverse(BigInteger)
■ ■ BigInteger modPow(BigInteger,BigInteger)
■ ■ BigInteger multiply(BigInteger)
■ ■ BigInteger negate()
■ ■ BigInteger not()
■ ■ final static BigInteger ONE
■ ■ BigInteger or(BigInteger)
■ ■ BigInteger pow(int)
■ ■ BigInteger remainder(BigInteger)
■ ■ BigInteger setBit(int)
■ ■ BigInteger shiftLeft(int)
■ ■ BigInteger shiftRight(int)
■ ■ int signum()
■ ■ BigInteger subtract(BigInteger)
■ ■ boolean testBit(int)
■ ■ byte[] toByteArray()
■ ■ String toString(int)
■ ■ static BigInteger valueOf(long)

■ ■ BigInteger xor(BigInteger)   ■ ■ final static BigInteger ZERO

999.3.6   java.net

■ ■ **package java.net**
■ ■ **abstract class Authenticator**
■ ■ Authenticator()
■ ■ protected PasswordAuthentication getPasswordAuthentication()
■ ■ final protected String getRequestingHost()
■ ■ final protected int getRequestingPort()
■ ■ final protected String getRequestingPrompt()
■ ■ final protected String getRequestingProtocol()
■ ■ final protected String getRequestingScheme()

■ ■ final protected InetAddress getRequestingSite()
■ ■ static PasswordAuthentication
requestPasswordAuthentication(String,InetAddress,int,String,String,
String)
■ ■ static PasswordAuthentication
requestPasswordAuthentication(InetAddress,int,String,String,String)
■ ■ static void setDefault(Authenticator)

■ ■ **class BindException extends SocketException**
■ ■ BindException()

■ ■ BindException(String)

■ ■ **class ConnectException extends SocketException**
■ ■ ConnectException()

■ ■ ConnectException(String)

■ ■ **abstract class ContentHandler**
■ ■ ContentHandler()
■ ■ abstract Object getContent(URLConnection) throws
java.io.IOException

■ ■ Object getContent(URLConnection,Class[]) throws
java.io.IOException

■ ■ **interface ContentHandlerFactory**
■ ■ abstract ContentHandler createContentHandler(String)

■ ■ **final class DatagramPacket**
■ ■ DatagramPacket(byte[],int)
■ ■ DatagramPacket(byte[],int,int)
■ ■ DatagramPacket(byte[],int,int,InetAddress,int)
■ ■ DatagramPacket(byte[],int,int,SocketAddress) throws
SocketException
■ ■ DatagramPacket(byte[],int,InetAddress,int)
■ ■ DatagramPacket(byte[],int,SocketAddress) throws SocketException
■ ■ InetAddress getAddress()
■ ■ byte[] getData()
■ ■ int getLength()

■ ■ int getOffset()
■ ■ int getPort()
■ ■ SocketAddress getSocketAddress()
■ ■ void setAddress(InetAddress)
■ ■ void setData(byte[])
■ ■ void setData(byte[],int,int)
■ ■ void setLength(int)
■ ■ void setPort(int)
■ ■ void setSocketAddress(SocketAddress)

■ ■ **class DatagramSocket**
■ ■ DatagramSocket() throws SocketException
■ ■ DatagramSocket(int) throws SocketException
■ ■ DatagramSocket(int,InetAddress) throws SocketException
■ ■ protected DatagramSocket(DatagramSocketImpl)
■ ■ DatagramSocket(SocketAddress) throws SocketException
■ ■ void bind(SocketAddress) throws SocketException
■ ■ void close()
■ ■ void connect(InetAddress,int)
■ ■ void connect(SocketAddress) throws SocketException
■ ■ void disconnect()
■ ■ boolean getBroadcast() throws SocketException
■ ■ InetAddress getInetAddress()
■ ■ InetAddress getLocalAddress()
■ ■ int getLocalPort()
■ ■ SocketAddress getLocalSocketAddress()
■ ■ int getPort()
■ ■ int getReceiveBufferSize() throws SocketException
■ ■ SocketAddress getRemoteSocketAddress()

■ ■ boolean getReuseAddress() throws SocketException
■ ■ int getSendBufferSize() throws SocketException
■ ■ int getSoTimeout() throws SocketException
■ ■ int getTrafficClass() throws SocketException
■ ■ boolean isBound()
■ ■ boolean isClosed()
■ ■ boolean isConnected()
■ ■ void receive(DatagramPacket) throws java.io.IOException
■ ■ void send(DatagramPacket) throws java.io.IOException
■ ■ void setBroadcast(boolean) throws SocketException
■ ■ static void
setDatagramSocketImplFactory(DatagramSocketImplFactory) throws
java.io.IOException
■ ■ void setReceiveBufferSize(int) throws SocketException
■ ■ void setReuseAddress(boolean) throws SocketException
■ ■ void setSendBufferSize(int) throws SocketException
■ ■ void setSoTimeout(int) throws SocketException
■ ■ void setTrafficClass(int) throws SocketException

■ ■ **abstract class DatagramSocketImpl implements SocketOptions**
■ ■ DatagramSocketImpl()
■ ■ abstract protected void bind(int,InetAddress) throws
SocketException
■ ■ abstract protected void close()
■ ■ protected void connect(InetAddress,int) throws SocketException
■ ■ abstract protected void create() throws SocketException
■ ■ protected void disconnect()
■ ■ protected java.io.FileDescriptor fd
■ ■ protected java.io.FileDescriptor getFileDescriptor()
■ ■ protected int getLocalPort()
■ ■ abstract protected int getTimeToLive() throws java.io.IOException
■ ■ abstract protected void join(InetAddress) throws java.io.IOException
■ ■ abstract protected void joinGroup(SocketAddress,NetworkInterface)
throws java.io.IOException

■ ■ abstract protected void leave(InetAddress) throws
java.io.IOException
■ ■ abstract protected void leaveGroup(SocketAddress,
NetworkInterface) throws java.io.IOException
■ ■ protected int localPort
■ ■ abstract protected int peek(InetAddress) throws java.io.IOException
■ ■ abstract protected int peekData(DatagramPacket) throws
java.io.IOException
■ ■ abstract protected void receive(DatagramPacket) throws
java.io.IOException
■ ■ abstract protected void send(DatagramPacket) throws
java.io.IOException
■ ■ abstract protected void setTimeToLive(int) throws
java.io.IOException

■ ■ **interface DatagramSocketImplFactory**
■ ■ abstract DatagramSocketImpl createDatagramSocketImpl()

■ ■ **interface FileNameMap**
■ ■ abstract String getContentTypeFor(String)

■ ■ **abstract class HttpURLConnection extends URLConnection**
■ ■ protected HttpURLConnection(URL)

■ ■ abstract void disconnect()

■ ■ java.io.InputStream getErrorStream()
■ ■ static boolean getFollowRedirects()
■ ■ boolean getInstanceFollowRedirects()
■ ■ String getRequestMethod()
■ ■ int getResponseCode() throws java.io.IOException
■ ■ String getResponseMessage() throws java.io.IOException
■ ■ final static int HTTP_ACCEPTED
■ ■ final static int HTTP_BAD_GATEWAY
■ ■ final static int HTTP_BAD_METHOD
■ ■ final static int HTTP_BAD_REQUEST
■ ■ final static int HTTP_CLIENT_TIMEOUT
■ ■ final static int HTTP_CONFLICT
■ ■ final static int HTTP_CREATED
■ ■ final static int HTTP_ENTITY_TOO_LARGE
■ ■ final static int HTTP_FORBIDDEN
■ ■ final static int HTTP_GATEWAY_TIMEOUT
■ ■ final static int HTTP_GONE
■ ■ final static int HTTP_INTERNAL_ERROR
■ ■ final static int HTTP_LENGTH_REQUIRED
■ ■ final static int HTTP_MOVED_PERM
■ ■ final static int HTTP_MOVED_TEMP
■ ■ final static int HTTP_MULT_CHOICE
■ ■ final static int HTTP_NO_CONTENT
■ ■ final static int HTTP_NOT_ACCEPTABLE
■ ■ final static int HTTP_NOT_AUTHORITATIVE

■ ■ final static int HTTP_NOT_FOUND
■ ■ final static int HTTP_NOT_IMPLEMENTED
■ ■ final static int HTTP_NOT_MODIFIED
■ ■ final static int HTTP_OK
■ ■ final static int HTTP_PARTIAL
■ ■ final static int HTTP_PAYMENT_REQUIRED
■ ■ final static int HTTP_PRECON_FAILED
■ ■ final static int HTTP_PROXY_AUTH
■ ■ final static int HTTP_REQ_TOO_LONG
■ ■ final static int HTTP_RESET
■ ■ final static int HTTP_SEE_OTHER
■ ■ final static int HTTP_UNAUTHORIZED
■ ■ final static int HTTP_UNAVAILABLE
■ ■ final static int HTTP_UNSUPPORTED_TYPE
■ ■ final static int HTTP_USE_PROXY
■ ■ final static int HTTP_VERSION
■ ■ protected boolean instanceFollowRedirects
■ ■ protected String method
■ ■ protected int responseCode
■ ■ protected String responseMessage
■ ■ static void setFollowRedirects(boolean)
■ ■ void setInstanceFollowRedirects(boolean)
■ ■ void setRequestMethod(String) throws ProtocolException
■ ■ abstract boolean usingProxy()

■ ■ **final class Inet4Address extends InetAddress**
■ ■ **final class Inet6Address extends InetAddress**
■ ■ boolean isIPv4CompatibleAddress()

■ ■ **class InetAddress implements java.io.Serializable**
■ ■ byte[] getAddress()
■ ■ static InetAddress[] getAllByName(String) throws UnknownHostException
■ ■ static InetAddress getByAddress(byte[]) throws UnknownHostException
■ ■ static InetAddress getByAddress(String,byte[]) throws UnknownHostException
■ ■ static InetAddress getByName(String) throws UnknownHostException
■ ■ String getCanonicalHostName()
■ ■ String getHostAddress()
■ ■ String getHostName()

■ ■ static InetAddress getLocalHost() throws UnknownHostException
■ ■ boolean isAnyLocalAddress()
■ ■ boolean isLinkLocalAddress()
■ ■ boolean isLoopbackAddress()
■ ■ boolean isMCGlobal()
■ ■ boolean isMCLinkLocal()
■ ■ boolean isMCNodeLocal()
■ ■ boolean isMCOrgLocal()
■ ■ boolean isMCSiteLocal()
■ ■ boolean isMulticastAddress()
■ ■ boolean isSiteLocalAddress()

■ ■ **class InetSocketAddress extends SocketAddress**
■ ■ InetSocketAddress(int)
■ ■ InetSocketAddress(String,int)
■ ■ InetSocketAddress(InetAddress,int)
■ ■ final boolean equals(Object)
■ ■ final InetAddress getAddress()

■ ■ final String getHostName()
■ ■ final int getPort()
■ ■ final int hashCode()
■ ■ final boolean isUnresolved()

■ ■ **abstract class JarURLConnection extends URLConnection**
■ ■ protected JarURLConnection(URL) throws MalformedURLException
■ ■ java.util.jar.Attributes getAttributes() throws java.io.IOException
■ ■ java.security.cert.Certificate[] getCertificates() throws java.io.IOException
■ ■ String getEntryName()
■ ■ java.util.jar.JarEntry getJarEntry() throws java.io.IOException

■ ■ abstract java.util.jar.JarFile getJarFile() throws java.io.IOException
■ ■ URL getJarFileURL()
■ ■ java.util.jar.Attributes getMainAttributes() throws java.io.IOException
■ ■ java.util.jar.Manifest getManifest() throws java.io.IOException
■ ■ protected URLConnection jarFileURLConnection

■ ■ **class MalformedURLException extends java.io.IOException**
■ ■ MalformedURLException()

■ ■ MalformedURLException(String)

■ ■ **class MulticastSocket extends DatagramSocket**
■ ■ MulticastSocket() throws java.io.IOException
■ ■ MulticastSocket(int) throws java.io.IOException
■ ■ MulticastSocket(SocketAddress) throws java.io.IOException
■ ■ InetAddress getInterface() throws SocketException
■ ■ boolean getLoopbackMode() throws SocketException
■ ■ NetworkInterface getNetworkInterface() throws SocketException
■ ■ int getTimeToLive() throws java.io.IOException
■ ■ void joinGroup(InetAddress) throws java.io.IOException
■ ■ void joinGroup(SocketAddress,NetworkInterface) throws java.io.IOException

■ ■ void leaveGroup(InetAddress) throws java.io.IOException
■ ■ void leaveGroup(SocketAddress,NetworkInterface) throws java.io.IOException
■ ■ void send(DatagramPacket,byte) throws java.io.IOException
■ ■ void setInterface(InetAddress) throws SocketException
■ ■ void setLoopbackMode(boolean) throws SocketException
■ ■ void setNetworkInterface(NetworkInterface) throws SocketException
■ ■ void setTimeToLive(int) throws java.io.IOException

■ ■ **final class NetPermission extends java.security.BasicPermission**
■ ■ NetPermission(String)

■ ■ NetPermission(String,String)

■ ■ **final class NetworkInterface**
■ ■ static NetworkInterface getByInetAddress(InetAddress) throws SocketException
■ ■ static NetworkInterface getByName(String) throws SocketException
■ ■ String getDisplayName()

■ ■ java.util.Enumeration getInetAddresses()
■ ■ String getName()
■ ■ static java.util.Enumeration getNetworkInterfaces() throws SocketException

■ ■ class NoRouteToHostException extends SocketException
■ ■ NoRouteToHostException()

■ ■ NoRouteToHostException(String)

■ ■ final class PasswordAuthentication
■ ■ PasswordAuthentication(String,char[])

■ ■ String getUserName()

■ ■ char[] getPassword()

■ ■ class PortUnreachableException extends SocketException
■ ■ PortUnreachableException()

■ ■ PortUnreachableException(String)

■ ■ class ProtocolException extends java.io.IOException
■ ■ ProtocolException()

■ ■ ProtocolException(String)

■ ■ class ServerSocket
■ ■ ServerSocket() throws java.io.IOException
■ ■ ServerSocket(int) throws java.io.IOException
■ ■ ServerSocket(int,int) throws java.io.IOException
■ ■ ServerSocket(int,int,InetAddress) throws java.io.IOException
■ ■ Socket accept() throws java.io.IOException
■ ■ void bind(SocketAddress) throws java.io.IOException
■ ■ void bind(SocketAddress,int) throws java.io.IOException
■ ■ void close() throws java.io.IOException
■ ■ InetAddress getInetAddress()
■ ■ int getLocalPort()
■ ■ SocketAddress getLocalSocketAddress()

■ ■ int getReceiveBufferSize() throws SocketException
■ ■ boolean getReuseAddress() throws SocketException
■ ■ int getSoTimeout() throws java.io.IOException
■ ■ final protected void implAccept(Socket) throws java.io.IOException
■ ■ boolean isBound()
■ ■ boolean isClosed()
■ ■ void setReceiveBufferSize(int) throws SocketException
■ ■ void setReuseAddress(boolean) throws SocketException
■ ■ static void setSocketFactory(SocketImplFactory) throws java.io.IOException
■ ■ void setSoTimeout(int) throws SocketException

■ ■ class Socket
■ ■ Socket()
■ ■ Socket(String,int) throws java.io.IOException
■ ■ Socket(String,int,InetAddress,int) throws java.io.IOException
■ ■ Socket(InetAddress,int) throws java.io.IOException
■ ■ Socket(InetAddress,int,InetAddress,int) throws java.io.IOException
■ ■ protected Socket(SocketImpl) throws SocketException
■ ■ void bind(SocketAddress) throws java.io.IOException
■ ■ void close() throws java.io.IOException
■ ■ void connect(SocketAddress) throws java.io.IOException
■ ■ void connect(SocketAddress,int) throws java.io.IOException
■ ■ InetAddress getInetAddress()
■ ■ java.io.InputStream getInputStream() throws java.io.IOException
■ ■ boolean getKeepAlive() throws SocketException
■ ■ InetAddress getLocalAddress()
■ ■ int getLocalPort()
■ ■ SocketAddress getLocalSocketAddress()
■ ■ boolean getOOBInline() throws SocketException
■ ■ java.io.OutputStream getOutputStream() throws java.io.IOException
■ ■ int getPort()
■ ■ int getReceiveBufferSize() throws SocketException
■ ■ SocketAddress getRemoteSocketAddress()
■ ■ boolean getReuseAddress() throws SocketException
■ ■ int getSendBufferSize() throws SocketException

■ ■ int getSoLinger() throws SocketException
■ ■ int getSoTimeout() throws SocketException
■ ■ boolean getTcpNoDelay() throws SocketException
■ ■ int getTrafficClass() throws SocketException
■ ■ boolean isBound()
■ ■ boolean isClosed()
■ ■ boolean isConnected()
■ ■ boolean isInputShutdown()
■ ■ boolean isOutputShutdown()
■ ■ void sendUrgentData(int) throws java.io.IOException
■ ■ void setKeepAlive(boolean) throws SocketException
■ ■ void setOOBInline(boolean) throws SocketException
■ ■ void setReceiveBufferSize(int) throws SocketException
■ ■ void setReuseAddress(boolean) throws SocketException
■ ■ void setSendBufferSize(int) throws SocketException
■ ■ static void setSocketImplFactory(SocketImplFactory) throws java.io.IOException
■ ■ void setSoLinger(boolean,int) throws SocketException
■ ■ void setSoTimeout(int) throws SocketException
■ ■ void setTcpNoDelay(boolean) throws SocketException
■ ■ void setTrafficClass(int) throws SocketException
■ ■ void shutdownInput() throws java.io.IOException
■ ■ void shutdownOutput() throws java.io.IOException

■ ■ abstract class SocketAddress implements java.io.Serializable
■ ■ SocketAddress()

■ ■ class SocketException extends java.io.IOException
■ ■ SocketException()

■ ■ SocketException(String)

■ ■ abstract class SocketImpl implements SocketOptions
■ ■ SocketImpl()
■ ■ abstract protected void accept(SocketImpl) throws java.io.IOException
■ ■ protected InetAddress address
■ ■ abstract protected int available() throws java.io.IOException
■ ■ abstract protected void bind(InetAddress,int) throws java.io.IOException
■ ■ abstract protected void close() throws java.io.IOException
■ ■ abstract protected void connect(String,int) throws java.io.IOException
■ ■ abstract protected void connect(InetAddress,int) throws java.io.IOException
■ ■ abstract protected void connect(SocketAddress,int) throws java.io.IOException
■ ■ abstract protected void create(boolean) throws java.io.IOException
■ ■ protected java.io.FileDescriptor fd

■ ■ protected java.io.FileDescriptor getFileDescriptor()
■ ■ protected InetAddress getInetAddress()
■ ■ abstract protected java.io.InputStream getInputStream() throws java.io.IOException
■ ■ protected int getLocalPort()
■ ■ abstract protected java.io.OutputStream getOutputStream() throws java.io.IOException
■ ■ protected int getPort()
■ ■ abstract protected void listen(int) throws java.io.IOException
■ ■ protected int localport
■ ■ protected int port
■ ■ abstract protected void sendUrgentData(int) throws java.io.IOException
■ ■ protected void shutdownInput() throws java.io.IOException
■ ■ protected void shutdownOutput() throws java.io.IOException
■ ■ protected boolean supportsUrgentData()

■ ■ interface SocketImplFactory
■ ■ abstract SocketImpl createSocketImpl()

■ ■ interface SocketOptions
■ ■ abstract Object getOption(int) throws SocketException
■ ■ final static int IP_MULTICAST_IF
■ ■ final static int IP_MULTICAST_IF2
■ ■ final static int IP_MULTICAST_LOOP
■ ■ final static int IP_TOS

■ ■ abstract void setOption(int,Object) throws SocketException
■ ■ final static int SO_BINDADDR
■ ■ final static int SO_BROADCAST
■ ■ final static int SO_KEEPALIVE
■ ■ final static int SO_LINGER

■ ■ final static int SO_OOBINLINE
■ ■ final static int SO_RCVBUF
■ ■ final static int SO_REUSEADDR

■ ■ final static int SO_SNDBUF
■ ■ final static int SO_TIMEOUT
■ ■ final static int TCP_NODELAY

■ ■ **final class SocketPermission extends java.security.Permission implements java.io.Serializable**
■ ■ SocketPermission(String,String)
■ ■ boolean equals(Object)
■ ■ String getActions()

■ ■ int hashCode()
■ ■ boolean implies(java.security.Permission)

■ ■ **class SocketTimeoutException extends java.io.InterruptedIOException**
■ ■ SocketTimeoutException()

■ ■ SocketTimeoutException(String)

■ ■ **class UnknownHostException extends java.io.IOException**
■ ■ UnknownHostException()

■ ■ UnknownHostException(String)

■ ■ **class UnknownServiceException extends java.io.IOException**
■ ■ UnknownServiceException()

■ ■ UnknownServiceException(String)

■ ■ **final class URI implements java.io.Serializable , Comparable**
■ ■ URI(String) throws URISyntaxException
■ ■ URI(String,String,String) throws URISyntaxException
■ ■ URI(String,String,String,int,String,String,String) throws URISyntaxException
■ ■ URI(String,String,String,String) throws URISyntaxException
■ ■ URI(String,String,String,String) throws URISyntaxException
■ ■ int compareTo(Object)
■ ■ static URI create(String)
■ ■ String getAuthority()
■ ■ String getFragment()
■ ■ String getHost()
■ ■ String getPath()
■ ■ int getPort()
■ ■ String getQuery()
■ ■ String getRawAuthority()
■ ■ String getRawFragment()

■ ■ String getRawPath()
■ ■ String getRawQuery()
■ ■ String getRawSchemeSpecificPart()
■ ■ String getRawUserInfo()
■ ■ String getScheme()
■ ■ String getSchemeSpecificPart()
■ ■ String getUserInfo()
■ ■ boolean isAbsolute()
■ ■ boolean isOpaque()
■ ■ URI normalize()
■ ■ URI parseServerAuthority() throws URISyntaxException
■ ■ URI relativize(URI)
■ ■ URI resolve(String)
■ ■ URI resolve(URI)
■ ■ String toASCIIString()
■ ■ URL toURL() throws MalformedURLException

■ ■ **class URISyntaxException extends Exception**
■ ■ URISyntaxException(String,String)
■ ■ URISyntaxException(String,String,int)
■ ■ int getIndex()

■ ■ String getInput()
■ ■ String getReason()

■ ■ **final class URL implements java.io.Serializable**
■ ■ URL(String) throws MalformedURLException
■ ■ URL(String,String,int,String) throws MalformedURLException
■ ■ URL(String,String,int,String,URLStreamHandler) throws MalformedURLException
■ ■ URL(String,String,String) throws MalformedURLException
■ ■ URL(URL,String) throws MalformedURLException
■ ■ URL(URL,String,URLStreamHandler) throws MalformedURLException
■ ■ String getAuthority()
■ ■ final Object getContent() throws java.io.IOException
■ ■ final Object getContent(Class[]) throws java.io.IOException
■ ■ int getDefaultPort()
■ ■ String getFile()
■ ■ String getHost()

■ ■ String getPath()
■ ■ int getPort()
■ ■ String getProtocol()
■ ■ String getQuery()
■ ■ String getRef()
■ ■ String getUserInfo()
■ ■ URLConnection openConnection() throws java.io.IOException
■ ■ final java.io.InputStream openStream() throws java.io.IOException
■ ■ boolean sameFile(URL)
■ ■ protected void set(String,String,int,String,String)
■ ■ protected void set(String,String,int,String,String,String,String,String)
■ ■ static void setURLStreamHandlerFactory(URLStreamHandlerFactory)
■ ■ String toExternalForm()

■ ■ **class URLClassLoader extends java.security.SecureClassLoader**
■ ■ URLClassLoader(URL[])
■ ■ URLClassLoader(URL[],ClassLoader)
■ ■ URLClassLoader(URL[],ClassLoader,URLStreamHandlerFactory)
■ ■ protected void addURL(URL)
■ ■ protected Package definePackage(String,java.util.jar.Manifest,URL)
■ ■ URL findResource(String)

■ ■ java.util.Enumeration findResources(String) throws java.io.IOException
■ ■ URL[] getURLs()
■ ■ static URLClassLoader newInstance(URL[])
■ ■ static URLClassLoader newInstance(URL[],ClassLoader)

■ ■ **abstract class URLConnection**
■ ■ protected URLConnection(URL)
■ ■ void addRequestProperty(String,String)
■ ■ protected boolean allowUserInteraction
■ ■ abstract void connect() throws java.io.IOException
■ ■ protected boolean connected
■ ■ protected boolean doInput
■ ■ protected boolean doOutput
■ ■ boolean getAllowUserInteraction()
■ ■ Object getContent() throws java.io.IOException
■ ■ Object getContent(Class[]) throws java.io.IOException
■ ■ String getContentEncoding()
■ ■ int getContentLength()
■ ■ String getContentType()
■ ■ long getDate()
■ ■ static boolean getDefaultAllowUserInteraction()
■ ■ boolean getDefaultUseCaches()
■ ■ boolean getDoInput()
■ ■ boolean getDoOutput()

■ ■ long getExpiration()
■ ■ static FileNameMap getFileNameMap()
■ ■ String getHeaderField(int)
■ ■ String getHeaderField(String)
■ ■ long getHeaderFieldDate(String,long)
■ ■ int getHeaderFieldInt(String,int)
■ ■ String getHeaderFieldKey(int)
■ ■ java.util.Map getHeaderFields()
■ ■ long getIfModifiedSince()
■ ■ java.io.InputStream getInputStream() throws java.io.IOException
■ ■ long getLastModified()
■ ■ java.io.OutputStream getOutputStream() throws java.io.IOException
■ ■ java.security.Permission getPermission() throws java.io.IOException
■ ■ java.util.Map getRequestProperties()
■ ■ String getRequestProperty(String)
■ ■ URL getURL()
■ ■ boolean getUseCaches()
■ ■ static String guessContentTypeFromName(String)

■ ■ static String guessContentTypeFromStream(java.io.InputStream) throws java.io.IOException
■ ■ protected long ifModifiedSince
■ ■ void setAllowUserInteraction(boolean)
■ ■ static void setContentHandlerFactory(ContentHandlerFactory)
■ ■ static void setDefaultAllowUserInteraction(boolean)
■ ■ void setDefaultUseCaches(boolean)
■ ■ void setDoInput(boolean)

■ ■ **class URLDecoder**
■ ■ URLDecoder()
■ ■ static String decode(String)

■ ■ **class URLEncoder**
■ ■ static String encode(String)

■ ■ **abstract class URLStreamHandler**
■ ■ URLStreamHandler()
■ ■ protected boolean equals(URL,URL)
■ ■ protected int getDefaultPort()
■ ■ protected InetAddress getHostAddress(URL)
■ ■ protected int hashCode(URL)
■ ■ protected boolean hostsEqual(URL,URL)

■ ■ **interface URLStreamHandlerFactory**
■ ■ abstract URLStreamHandler createURLStreamHandler(String)

■ ■ void setDoOutput(boolean)
■ ■ static void setFileNameMap(FileNameMap)
■ ■ void setIfModifiedSince(long)
■ ■ void setRequestProperty(String,String)
■ ■ void setUseCaches(boolean)
■ ■ protected URL url
■ ■ protected boolean useCaches

■ ■ static String decode(String,String) throws java.io.UnsupportedEncodingException

■ ■ static String encode(String,String) throws java.io.UnsupportedEncodingException

■ ■ abstract protected URLConnection openConnection(URL) throws java.io.IOException
■ ■ protected void parseURL(URL,String,int,int)
■ ■ protected boolean sameFile(URL,URL)
■ ■ protected void setURL(URL,String,String,int,String,String,String, String,String)
■ ■ protected String toExternalForm(URL)

999.3.7 java.security

■ ■ **package java.security**
■ ■ **final class AccessControlContext**
■ ■ AccessControlContext(ProtectionDomain[])
■ ■ AccessControlContext(AccessControlContext,DomainCombiner)
■ ■ **class AccessControlException extends SecurityException**
■ ■ AccessControlException(String)
■ ■ AccessControlException(String,Permission)
■ ■ **final class AccessController**
■ ■ static void checkPermission(Permission)
■ ■ static Object doPrivileged(PrivilegedAction)
■ ■ static Object doPrivileged(PrivilegedAction,AccessControlContext)
■ ■ static Object doPrivileged(PrivilegedExceptionAction) throws PrivilegedActionException

■ ■ void checkPermission(Permission)
■ ■ DomainCombiner getDomainCombiner()

■ ■ Permission getPermission()

■ ■ static Object doPrivileged(PrivilegedExceptionAction, AccessControlContext) throws PrivilegedActionException
■ ■ static AccessControlContext getContext()

■ ■ **class AlgorithmParameterGenerator**
■ ■ protected AlgorithmParameterGenerator(AlgorithmParameterGeneratorSpi, Provider,String)
■ ■ final AlgorithmParameters generateParameters()
■ ■ final String getAlgorithm()
■ ■ static AlgorithmParameterGenerator getInstance(String) throws NoSuchAlgorithmException
■ ■ static AlgorithmParameterGenerator getInstance(String,String) throws NoSuchAlgorithmException, NoSuchProviderException

■ ■ static AlgorithmParameterGenerator getInstance(String,Provider) throws NoSuchAlgorithmException
■ ■ final Provider getProvider()
■ ■ final void init(int)
■ ■ final void init(int,SecureRandom)
■ ■ final void init(AlgorithmParameterSpec) throws InvalidAlgorithmParameterException
■ ■ final void init(AlgorithmParameterSpec,SecureRandom) throws InvalidAlgorithmParameterException

■ ■ **abstract class AlgorithmParameterGeneratorSpi**
■ ■ AlgorithmParameterGeneratorSpi()
■ ■ abstract protected AlgorithmParameters engineGenerateParameters()

■ ■ abstract protected void engineInit(int,SecureRandom)
■ ■ abstract protected void engineInit(AlgorithmParameterSpec, SecureRandom) throws InvalidAlgorithmParameterException

■ ■ **class AlgorithmParameters**
■ ■ protected AlgorithmParameters(AlgorithmParametersSpi,Provider, String)
■ ■ final String getAlgorithm()
■ ■ final byte[] getEncoded() throws java.io.IOException
■ ■ final byte[] getEncoded(String) throws java.io.IOException
■ ■ static AlgorithmParameters getInstance(String) throws NoSuchAlgorithmException
■ ■ static AlgorithmParameters getInstance(String,String) throws NoSuchAlgorithmException, NoSuchProviderException

■ ■ static AlgorithmParameters getInstance(String,Provider) throws NoSuchAlgorithmException
■ ■ final AlgorithmParameterSpec getParameterSpec(Class) throws InvalidParameterSpecException
■ ■ final Provider getProvider()
■ ■ final void init(byte[]) throws java.io.IOException
■ ■ final void init(byte[],String) throws java.io.IOException
■ ■ final void init(AlgorithmParameterSpec) throws InvalidParameterSpecException
■ ■ final String toString()

■ ■ **abstract class AlgorithmParametersSpi**
■ ■ AlgorithmParametersSpi()
■ ■ abstract protected byte[] engineGetEncoded() throws java.io.IOException
■ ■ abstract protected byte[] engineGetEncoded(String) throws java.io.IOException
■ ■ abstract protected AlgorithmParameterSpec engineGetParameterSpec(Class) throws InvalidParameterSpecException
■ ■ abstract protected void engineInit(byte[]) throws java.io.IOException

■ ■ abstract protected void engineInit(byte[],String) throws java.io.IOException
■ ■ abstract protected void engineInit(AlgorithmParameterSpec) throws InvalidParameterSpecException
■ ■ abstract protected String engineToString()

■ ■ final class AllPermission extends Permission
■ ■ AllPermission()
■ ■ AllPermission(String,String)
■ ■ boolean equals(Object)
■ ■ String getActions()
■ ■ int hashCode()
■ ■ boolean implies(Permission)

■ ■ abstract class BasicPermission extends Permission implements java.io.Serializable
■ ■ BasicPermission(String)
■ ■ BasicPermission(String,String)
■ ■ boolean equals(Object)
■ ■ String getActions()
■ ■ int hashCode()
■ ■ boolean implies(Permission)

■ ■ interface Certificate
■ ■ abstract void decode(java.io.InputStream) throws java.io.IOException, KeyException
■ ■ abstract void encode(java.io.OutputStream) throws java.io.IOException, KeyException
■ ■ abstract String getFormat()
■ ■ abstract Principal getGuarantor()
■ ■ abstract Principal getPrincipal()
■ ■ abstract PublicKey getPublicKey()
■ ■ abstract String toString(boolean)

■ ■ class CodeSource implements java.io.Serializable
■ ■ CodeSource(java.net.URL,Certificate[])
■ ■ final Certificate[] getCertificates()
■ ■ final java.net.URL getLocation()
■ ■ boolean implies(CodeSource)

■ ■ class DigestException extends GeneralSecurityException
■ ■ DigestException()
■ ■ DigestException(String)

■ ■ class DigestInputStream extends java.io.FilterInputStream
■ ■ DigestInputStream(java.io.InputStream,MessageDigest)
■ ■ protected MessageDigest digest
■ ■ MessageDigest getMessageDigest()
■ ■ void on(boolean)
■ ■ void setMessageDigest(MessageDigest)

■ ■ class DigestOutputStream extends java.io.FilterOutputStream
■ ■ DigestOutputStream(java.io.OutputStream,MessageDigest)
■ ■ protected MessageDigest digest
■ ■ MessageDigest getMessageDigest()
■ ■ void on(boolean)
■ ■ void setMessageDigest(MessageDigest)

■ ■ interface DomainCombiner
■ ■ abstract ProtectionDomain[] combine(ProtectionDomain[], ProtectionDomain[])

■ ■ class GeneralSecurityException extends Exception
■ ■ GeneralSecurityException()
■ ■ GeneralSecurityException(String)

■ ■ interface Guard
■ ■ abstract void checkGuard(Object)

■ ■ class GuardedObject implements java.io.Serializable
■ ■ GuardedObject(Object,Guard)
■ ■ Object getObject()

■ ■ abstract class Identity implements java.io.Serializable , Principal
■ ■ protected Identity()
■ ■ Identity(String)
■ ■ Identity(String,IdentityScope) throws KeyManagementException
■ ■ void addCertificate(Certificate) throws KeyManagementException
■ ■ Certificate[] certificates()
■ ■ final boolean equals(Object)
■ ■ String getInfo()
■ ■ final String getName()
■ ■ PublicKey getPublicKey()
■ ■ final IdentityScope getScope()
■ ■ protected boolean identityEquals(Identity)
■ ■ void removeCertificate(Certificate) throws KeyManagementException
■ ■ void setInfo(String)
■ ■ void setPublicKey(PublicKey) throws KeyManagementException
■ ■ String toString(boolean)

■ ■ abstract class IdentityScope extends Identity
■ ■ protected IdentityScope()
■ ■ IdentityScope(String)
■ ■ IdentityScope(String,IdentityScope) throws KeyManagementException
■ ■ abstract void addIdentity(Identity) throws KeyManagementException
■ ■ abstract Identity getIdentity(String)
■ ■ Identity getIdentity(Principal)
■ ■ abstract Identity getIdentity(PublicKey)
■ ■ static IdentityScope getSystemScope()
■ ■ abstract java.util.Enumeration identities()
■ ■ abstract void removeIdentity(Identity) throws KeyManagementException
■ ■ protected static void setSystemScope(IdentityScope)
■ ■ abstract int size()

■ ■ class InvalidAlgorithmParameterException extends GeneralSecurityException
■ ■ InvalidAlgorithmParameterException()
■ ■ InvalidAlgorithmParameterException(String)

■ ■ class InvalidKeyException extends KeyException
■ ■ InvalidKeyException()
■ ■ InvalidKeyException(String)

■ ■ class InvalidParameterException extends IllegalArgumentException
■ ■ InvalidParameterException()
■ ■ InvalidParameterException(String)

■ ■ interface Key extends java.io.Serializable
■ ■ abstract String getAlgorithm()
■ ■ abstract byte[] getEncoded()
■ ■ abstract String getFormat()
■ ■ final static long serialVersionUID

■ ■ class KeyException extends GeneralSecurityException
■ ■ KeyException()
■ ■ KeyException(String)

■ ■ class KeyFactory
■ ■ protected KeyFactory(KeyFactorySpi,Provider,String)
■ ■ final PrivateKey generatePrivate(KeySpec) throws InvalidKeySpecException
■ ■ final PublicKey generatePublic(KeySpec) throws InvalidKeySpecException
■ ■ final String getAlgorithm()
■ ■ static KeyFactory getInstance(String) throws NoSuchAlgorithmException
■ ■ static KeyFactory getInstance(String,String) throws NoSuchAlgorithmException, NoSuchProviderException
■ ■ static KeyFactory getInstance(String,Provider) throws NoSuchAlgorithmException
■ ■ final KeySpec getKeySpec(Key,Class) throws InvalidKeySpecException
■ ■ final Provider getProvider()
■ ■ final Key translateKey(Key) throws InvalidKeyException

■ ■ abstract class **KeyFactorySpi**
■ ■ KeyFactorySpi()
■ ■ abstract protected PrivateKey engineGeneratePrivate(KeySpec) throws InvalidKeySpecException
■ ■ abstract protected PublicKey engineGeneratePublic(KeySpec) throws InvalidKeySpecException

■ ■ abstract protected KeySpec engineGetKeySpec(Key,Class) throws InvalidKeySpecException
■ ■ abstract protected Key engineTranslateKey(Key) throws InvalidKeyException

■ ■ class **KeyManagementException extends KeyException**
■ ■ KeyManagementException()

■ ■ KeyManagementException(String)

■ ■ final class **KeyPair implements java.io.Serializable**
■ ■ KeyPair(PublicKey,PrivateKey)
■ ■ PrivateKey getPrivate()

■ ■ PublicKey getPublic()

■ ■ abstract class **KeyPairGenerator extends KeyPairGeneratorSpi**
■ ■ protected KeyPairGenerator(String)
■ ■ KeyPair generateKeyPair()
■ ■ final KeyPair genKeyPair()
■ ■ String getAlgorithm()
■ ■ static KeyPairGenerator getInstance(String) throws NoSuchAlgorithmException
■ ■ static KeyPairGenerator getInstance(String,String) throws NoSuchAlgorithmException, NoSuchProviderException

■ ■ static KeyPairGenerator getInstance(String,Provider) throws NoSuchAlgorithmException
■ ■ final Provider getProvider()
■ ■ void initialize(int)
■ ■ void initialize(int,SecureRandom)
■ ■ void initialize(AlgorithmParameterSpec) throws InvalidAlgorithmParameterException

■ ■ abstract class **KeyPairGeneratorSpi**
■ ■ KeyPairGeneratorSpi()
■ ■ abstract KeyPair generateKeyPair()
■ ■ abstract void initialize(int,SecureRandom)

■ ■ void initialize(AlgorithmParameterSpec,SecureRandom) throws InvalidAlgorithmParameterException

■ ■ class **KeyStore**
■ ■ protected KeyStore(KeyStoreSpi,Provider,String)
■ ■ final java.util.Enumeration aliases() throws KeyStoreException
■ ■ final boolean containsAlias(String) throws KeyStoreException
■ ■ final void deleteEntry(String) throws KeyStoreException
■ ■ final Certificate getCertificate(String) throws KeyStoreException
■ ■ final String getCertificateAlias(Certificate) throws KeyStoreException
■ ■ final Certificate[] getCertificateChain(String) throws KeyStoreException
■ ■ final java.util.Date getCreationDate(String) throws KeyStoreException
■ ■ final static String getDefaultType()
■ ■ static KeyStore getInstance(String) throws KeyStoreException
■ ■ static KeyStore getInstance(String,String) throws KeyStoreException, NoSuchProviderException
■ ■ static KeyStore getInstance(String,Provider) throws KeyStoreException
■ ■ final Key getKey(String,char[]) throws KeyStoreException, NoSuchAlgorithmException, UnrecoverableKeyException

■ ■ final Provider getProvider()
■ ■ final String getType()
■ ■ final boolean isCertificateEntry(String) throws KeyStoreException
■ ■ final boolean isKeyEntry(String) throws KeyStoreException
■ ■ final void load(java.io.InputStream,char[]) throws java.io.IOException, NoSuchAlgorithmException, CertificateException
■ ■ final void setCertificateEntry(String,Certificate) throws KeyStoreException
■ ■ final void setKeyEntry(String,byte[],Certificate[]) throws KeyStoreException
■ ■ final void setKeyEntry(String,Key,char[],Certificate[]) throws KeyStoreException
■ ■ final int size() throws KeyStoreException
■ ■ final void store(java.io.OutputStream,char[]) throws java.io.IOException, KeyStoreException, NoSuchAlgorithmException, CertificateException

■ ■ class **KeyStoreException extends GeneralSecurityException**
■ ■ KeyStoreException()

■ ■ KeyStoreException(String)

■ ■ abstract class **KeyStoreSpi**
■ ■ KeyStoreSpi()
■ ■ abstract java.util.Enumeration engineAliases()
■ ■ abstract boolean engineContainsAlias(String)
■ ■ abstract void engineDeleteEntry(String) throws KeyStoreException
■ ■ abstract Certificate engineGetCertificate(String)
■ ■ abstract String engineGetCertificateAlias(Certificate)
■ ■ abstract Certificate[] engineGetCertificateChain(String)
■ ■ abstract java.util.Date engineGetCreationDate(String)
■ ■ abstract Key engineGetKey(String,char[]) throws NoSuchAlgorithmException, UnrecoverableKeyException
■ ■ abstract boolean engineIsCertificateEntry(String)
■ ■ abstract boolean engineIsKeyEntry(String)

■ ■ abstract void engineLoad(java.io.InputStream,char[]) throws java.io.IOException, NoSuchAlgorithmException, CertificateException
■ ■ abstract void engineSetCertificateEntry(String,Certificate) throws KeyStoreException
■ ■ abstract void engineSetKeyEntry(String,byte[],Certificate[]) throws KeyStoreException
■ ■ abstract void engineSetKeyEntry(String,Key,char[],Certificate[]) throws KeyStoreException
■ ■ abstract int engineSize()
■ ■ abstract void engineStore(java.io.OutputStream,char[]) throws java.io.IOException, NoSuchAlgorithmException, CertificateException

■ ■ abstract class **MessageDigest extends MessageDigestSpi**
■ ■ protected MessageDigest(String)
■ ■ byte[] digest()
■ ■ byte[] digest(byte[])
■ ■ int digest(byte[],int,int) throws DigestException
■ ■ final String getAlgorithm()
■ ■ final int getDigestLength()
■ ■ static MessageDigest getInstance(String) throws NoSuchAlgorithmException
■ ■ static MessageDigest getInstance(String,String) throws NoSuchAlgorithmException, NoSuchProviderException

■ ■ static MessageDigest getInstance(String,Provider) throws NoSuchAlgorithmException
■ ■ final Provider getProvider()
■ ■ static boolean isEqual(byte[],byte[])
■ ■ void reset()
■ ■ void update(byte[])
■ ■ void update(byte[],int,int)
■ ■ void update(byte)

■ ■ abstract class **MessageDigestSpi**
■ ■ MessageDigestSpi()
■ ■ Object clone() throws CloneNotSupportedException
■ ■ abstract protected byte[] engineDigest()
■ ■ protected int engineDigest(byte[],int,int) throws DigestException

■ ■ protected int engineGetDigestLength()
■ ■ abstract protected void engineReset()
■ ■ abstract protected void engineUpdate(byte[],int,int)
■ ■ abstract protected void engineUpdate(byte)

■ ■ **class NoSuchAlgorithmException extends GeneralSecurityException**
■ ■ NoSuchAlgorithmException()　　　　　　　　　■ ■ NoSuchAlgorithmException(String)

■ ■ **class NoSuchProviderException extends GeneralSecurityException**
■ ■ NoSuchProviderException()　　　　　　　　　■ ■ NoSuchProviderException(String)

■ ■ **abstract class Permission implements java.io.Serializable , Guard**
■ ■ Permission(String)　　　　　　　　　　　　　■ ■ final String getName()
■ ■ void checkGuard(Object)　　　　　　　　　　■ ■ abstract int hashCode()
■ ■ abstract boolean equals(Object)　　　　　　■ ■ abstract boolean implies(Permission)
■ ■ abstract String getActions()　　　　　　　　■ ■ PermissionCollection newPermissionCollection()

■ ■ **abstract class PermissionCollection implements java.io.Serializable**
■ ■ PermissionCollection()　　　　　　　　　　　■ ■ abstract boolean implies(Permission)
■ ■ abstract void add(Permission)　　　　　　　■ ■ boolean isReadOnly()
■ ■ abstract java.util.Enumeration elements()　■ ■ void setReadOnly()

■ ■ **final class Permissions extends PermissionCollection implements java.io.Serializable**
■ ■ Permissions()　　　　　　　　　　　　　　　■ ■ java.util.Enumeration elements()
■ ■ void add(Permission)　　　　　　　　　　　■ ■ boolean implies(Permission)

■ ■ **abstract class Policy**
■ ■ Policy()　　　　　　　　　　　　　　　　　　■ ■ boolean implies(ProtectionDomain,Permission)
■ ■ abstract PermissionCollection getPermissions(CodeSource)　■ ■ abstract void refresh()
■ ■ PermissionCollection getPermissions(ProtectionDomain)　　■ ■ static void setPolicy(Policy)
■ ■ static Policy getPolicy()

■ ■ **interface Principal**
■ ■ abstract boolean equals(Object)　　　　　　■ ■ abstract int hashCode()
■ ■ abstract String getName()　　　　　　　　　■ ■ abstract String toString()

■ ■ **interface PrivateKey extends Key**
■ ■ final static long serialVersionUID

■ ■ **interface PrivilegedAction**
■ ■ abstract Object run()

■ ■ **class PrivilegedActionException extends Exception**
■ ■ PrivilegedActionException(Exception)　　　　■ ■ Exception getException()

■ ■ **interface PrivilegedExceptionAction**
■ ■ abstract Object run() throws Exception

■ ■ **class ProtectionDomain**
■ ■ ProtectionDomain(CodeSource,PermissionCollection)　　■ ■ final CodeSource getCodeSource()
■ ■ ProtectionDomain(CodeSource,PermissionCollection,ClassLoader,　■ ■ final PermissionCollection getPermissions()
Principal[])　　　　　　　　　　　　　　　　　■ ■ final Principal[] getPrincipals()
■ ■ final ClassLoader getClassLoader()　　　　　■ ■ boolean implies(Permission)

■ ■ **abstract class Provider extends java.util.Properties**
■ ■ protected Provider(String,double,String)　　■ ■ String getName()
■ ■ String getInfo()　　　　　　　　　　　　　　■ ■ double getVersion()

■ ■ **class ProviderException extends RuntimeException**
■ ■ ProviderException()　　　　　　　　　　　　■ ■ ProviderException(String)

■ ■ **interface PublicKey extends Key**
■ ■ final static long serialVersionUID

■ ■ **class SecureClassLoader extends ClassLoader**
■ ■ protected SecureClassLoader()　　　　　　　■ ■ final protected Class defineClass(String,byte[],int,int,CodeSource)
■ ■ protected SecureClassLoader(ClassLoader)　■ ■ protected PermissionCollection getPermissions(CodeSource)

■ ■ **class SecureRandom extends java.util.Random**
■ ■ SecureRandom()　　　　　　　　　　　　　　■ ■ static SecureRandom getInstance(String,Provider) throws
■ ■ SecureRandom(byte[])　　　　　　　　　　　NoSuchAlgorithmException
■ ■ protected SecureRandom(SecureRandomSpi,Provider)　■ ■ final Provider getProvider()
■ ■ byte[] generateSeed(int)　　　　　　　　　　■ ■ static byte[] getSeed(int)
■ ■ static SecureRandom getInstance(String) throws　■ ■ final protected int next(int)
NoSuchAlgorithmException　　　　　　　　　　■ ■ void setSeed(byte[])
■ ■ static SecureRandom getInstance(String,String) throws
NoSuchAlgorithmException, NoSuchProviderException

■ ■ **abstract class SecureRandomSpi implements java.io.Serializable**
■ ■ SecureRandomSpi()　　　　　　　　　　　　■ ■ abstract protected void engineNextBytes(byte[])
■ ■ abstract protected byte[] engineGenerateSeed(int)　■ ■ abstract protected void engineSetSeed(byte[])

■ ■ **final class Security**
■ ■ static int addProvider(Provider)　　　　　　■ ■ static Provider[] getProviders(String)
■ ■ static java.util.Set getAlgorithms(String)　　■ ■ static Provider[] getProviders(java.util.Map)
■ ■ static String getProperty(String)　　　　　　■ ■ static int insertProviderAt(Provider,int)
■ ■ static Provider getProvider(String)　　　　　■ ■ static void removeProvider(String)
■ ■ static Provider[] getProviders()　　　　　　■ ■ static void setProperty(String,String)

■ ■ **final class SecurityPermission extends BasicPermission**
■ ■ SecurityPermission(String)　　　　　　　　　■ ■ SecurityPermission(String,String)

■ ■ **abstract class Signature extends SignatureSpi**
■ ■ protected Signature(String)　　　　　　　　　■ ■ static Signature getInstance(String,String) throws
■ ■ final String getAlgorithm()　　　　　　　　　NoSuchAlgorithmException, NoSuchProviderException
■ ■ static Signature getInstance(String) throws　　■ ■ static Signature getInstance(String,Provider) throws
NoSuchAlgorithmException　　　　　　　　　　NoSuchAlgorithmException
　　　　　　　　　　　　　　　　　　　　　　■ ■ final AlgorithmParameters getParameters()

■ ■ final Provider getProvider()
■ ■ final void initSign(PrivateKey) throws InvalidKeyException
■ ■ final void initSign(PrivateKey,SecureRandom) throws InvalidKeyException
■ ■ final void initVerify(Certificate) throws InvalidKeyException
■ ■ final void initVerify(PublicKey) throws InvalidKeyException
■ ■ final void setParameter(AlgorithmParameterSpec) throws InvalidAlgorithmParameterException
■ ■ final protected static int SIGN
■ ■ final byte[] sign() throws SignatureException

■ ■ final int sign(byte[],int,int) throws SignatureException
■ ■ protected int state
■ ■ final protected static int UNINITIALIZED
■ ■ final void update(byte[]) throws SignatureException
■ ■ final void update(byte[],int,int) throws SignatureException
■ ■ final void update(byte) throws SignatureException
■ ■ final protected static int VERIFY
■ ■ final boolean verify(byte[]) throws SignatureException
■ ■ final boolean verify(byte[],int,int) throws SignatureException

■ ■ **class SignatureException extends GeneralSecurityException**
■ ■ SignatureException()

■ ■ SignatureException(String)

■ ■ **abstract class SignatureSpi**
■ ■ SignatureSpi()
■ ■ protected SecureRandom appRandom
■ ■ Object clone() throws CloneNotSupportedException
■ ■ protected AlgorithmParameters engineGetParameters()
■ ■ abstract protected void engineInitSign(PrivateKey) throws InvalidKeyException
■ ■ protected void engineInitSign(PrivateKey,SecureRandom) throws InvalidKeyException
■ ■ abstract protected void engineInitVerify(PublicKey) throws InvalidKeyException
■ ■ protected void engineSetParameter(AlgorithmParameterSpec) throws InvalidAlgorithmParameterException

■ ■ abstract protected byte[] engineSign() throws SignatureException
■ ■ protected int engineSign(byte[],int,int) throws SignatureException
■ ■ abstract protected void engineUpdate(byte[],int,int) throws SignatureException
■ ■ abstract protected void engineUpdate(byte) throws SignatureException
■ ■ abstract protected boolean engineVerify(byte[]) throws SignatureException
■ ■ protected boolean engineVerify(byte[],int,int) throws SignatureException

■ ■ **final class SignedObject implements java.io.Serializable**
■ ■ SignedObject(java.io.Serializable,PrivateKey,Signature) throws java.io.IOException, InvalidKeyException, SignatureException
■ ■ String getAlgorithm()
■ ■ Object getObject() throws java.io.IOException, ClassNotFoundException

■ ■ byte[] getSignature()
■ ■ boolean verify(PublicKey,Signature) throws InvalidKeyException, SignatureException

■ ■ **abstract class Signer extends Identity**
■ ■ protected Signer()
■ ■ Signer(String)
■ ■ Signer(String,IdentityScope) throws KeyManagementException

■ ■ PrivateKey getPrivateKey()
■ ■ final void setKeyPair(KeyPair) throws KeyException

■ ■ **class UnrecoverableKeyException extends GeneralSecurityException**
■ ■ UnrecoverableKeyException()

■ ■ UnrecoverableKeyException(String)

■ ■ **final class UnresolvedPermission extends Permission implements java.io.Serializable**
■ ■ UnresolvedPermission(String,String,String,Certificate[])
■ ■ boolean equals(Object)
■ ■ String getActions()

■ ■ int hashCode()
■ ■ boolean implies(Permission)

999.3.8   java.security.acl

■ ■ **package java.security.acl**
■ ■ **interface Acl extends Owner**
■ ■ abstract boolean addEntry(java.security.Principal,AclEntry) throws NotOwnerException
■ ■ abstract boolean checkPermission(java.security.Principal,Permission)
■ ■ abstract java.util.Enumeration entries()
■ ■ abstract String getName()
■ ■ abstract java.util.Enumeration getPermissions(java.security.Principal)

■ ■ abstract boolean removeEntry(java.security.Principal,AclEntry) throws NotOwnerException
■ ■ abstract void setName(java.security.Principal,String) throws NotOwnerException
■ ■ abstract String toString()

■ ■ **interface AclEntry extends Cloneable**
■ ■ abstract boolean addPermission(Permission)
■ ■ abstract boolean checkPermission(Permission)
■ ■ abstract Object clone()
■ ■ abstract java.security.Principal getPrincipal()
■ ■ abstract boolean isNegative()

■ ■ abstract java.util.Enumeration permissions()
■ ■ abstract boolean removePermission(Permission)
■ ■ abstract void setNegativePermissions()
■ ■ abstract boolean setPrincipal(java.security.Principal)
■ ■ abstract String toString()

■ ■ **class AclNotFoundException extends Exception**
■ ■ AclNotFoundException()

■ ■ **interface Group extends java.security.Principal**
■ ■ abstract boolean addMember(java.security.Principal)
■ ■ abstract boolean isMember(java.security.Principal)

■ ■ abstract java.util.Enumeration members()
■ ■ abstract boolean removeMember(java.security.Principal)

■ ■ **class LastOwnerException extends Exception**
■ ■ LastOwnerException()

■ ■ **class NotOwnerException extends Exception**
■ ■ NotOwnerException()

■ ■ **interface Owner**
■ ■ abstract boolean addOwner(java.security.Principal, java.security.Principal) throws NotOwnerException

■ ■ abstract boolean deleteOwner(java.security.Principal, java.security.Principal) throws LastOwnerException, NotOwnerException
■ ■ abstract boolean isOwner(java.security.Principal)

■ ■ **interface Permission**
■ ■ abstract boolean equals(Object)

■ ■ abstract String toString()

999.3.9　java.security.cert

■ ■ **package java.security.cert**
■ ■ **abstract class Certificate implements java.io.Serializable**
■ ■ protected Certificate(String)
■ ■ abstract byte[] getEncoded() throws CertificateEncodingException
■ ■ abstract java.security.PublicKey getPublicKey()
■ ■ final String getType()
■ ■ abstract String toString()
■ ■ abstract void verify(java.security.PublicKey) throws
java.security.InvalidKeyException,
java.security.NoSuchAlgorithmException,
java.security.NoSuchProviderException, java.security.SignatureException,
CertificateException

■ ■ abstract void verify(java.security.PublicKey,String) throws
java.security.InvalidKeyException,
java.security.NoSuchAlgorithmException,
java.security.NoSuchProviderException, java.security.SignatureException,
CertificateException
■ ■ protected Object writeReplace() throws
java.io.ObjectStreamException

■ ■ **class Certificate.CertificateRep implements java.io.Serializable**
■ ■ protected Certificate.CertificateRep(String,byte[])

■ ■ protected Object readResolve() throws
java.io.ObjectStreamException

■ ■ **class CertificateEncodingException extends CertificateException**
■ ■ CertificateEncodingException()

■ ■ CertificateEncodingException(String)

■ ■ **class CertificateException extends java.security.GeneralSecurityException**
■ ■ CertificateException()

■ ■ CertificateException(String)

■ ■ **class CertificateExpiredException extends CertificateException**
■ ■ CertificateExpiredException()

■ ■ CertificateExpiredException(String)

■ ■ **class CertificateFactory**
■ ■ protected CertificateFactory(CertificateFactorySpi,
java.security.Provider,String)
■ ■ final Certificate generateCertificate(java.io.InputStream) throws
CertificateException
■ ■ final java.util.Collection generateCertificates(java.io.InputStream)
throws CertificateException
■ ■ final CertPath generateCertPath(java.io.InputStream) throws
CertificateException
■ ■ final CertPath generateCertPath(java.io.InputStream,String) throws
CertificateException
■ ■ final CertPath generateCertPath(java.util.List) throws
CertificateException

■ ■ final CRL generateCRL(java.io.InputStream) throws CRLException
■ ■ final java.util.Collection generateCRLs(java.io.InputStream) throws
CRLException
■ ■ final java.util.Iterator getCertPathEncodings()
■ ■ final static CertificateFactory getInstance(String) throws
CertificateException
■ ■ final static CertificateFactory getInstance(String,String) throws
java.security.NoSuchProviderException, CertificateException
■ ■ final static CertificateFactory getInstance(String,
java.security.Provider) throws CertificateException
■ ■ final java.security.Provider getProvider()
■ ■ final String getType()

■ ■ **abstract class CertificateFactorySpi**
■ ■ CertificateFactorySpi()
■ ■ abstract Certificate engineGenerateCertificate(java.io.InputStream)
throws CertificateException
■ ■ abstract java.util.Collection
engineGenerateCertificates(java.io.InputStream) throws
CertificateException
■ ■ CertPath engineGenerateCertPath(java.io.InputStream) throws
CertificateException

■ ■ CertPath engineGenerateCertPath(java.io.InputStream,String)
throws CertificateException
■ ■ CertPath engineGenerateCertPath(java.util.List) throws
CertificateException
■ ■ abstract CRL engineGenerateCRL(java.io.InputStream) throws
CRLException
■ ■ abstract java.util.Collection
engineGenerateCRLs(java.io.InputStream) throws CRLException
■ ■ java.util.Iterator engineGetCertPathEncodings()

■ ■ **class CertificateNotYetValidException extends CertificateException**
■ ■ CertificateNotYetValidException()

■ ■ CertificateNotYetValidException(String)

■ ■ **class CertificateParsingException extends CertificateException**
■ ■ CertificateParsingException()

■ ■ CertificateParsingException(String)

■ ■ **abstract class CertPath implements java.io.Serializable**
■ ■ protected CertPath(String)
■ ■ abstract java.util.List getCertificates()
■ ■ abstract byte[] getEncoded() throws CertificateEncodingException
■ ■ abstract byte[] getEncoded(String) throws
CertificateEncodingException

■ ■ abstract java.util.Iterator getEncodings()
■ ■ String getType()
■ ■ protected Object writeReplace() throws
java.io.ObjectStreamException

■ ■ **class CertPath.CertPathRep implements java.io.Serializable**
■ ■ protected CertPath.CertPathRep(String,byte[])

■ ■ protected Object readResolve() throws
java.io.ObjectStreamException

■ ■ **abstract class CRL**
■ ■ protected CRL(String)
■ ■ final String getType()

■ ■ abstract boolean isRevoked(Certificate)
■ ■ abstract String toString()

■ ■ **class CRLException extends java.security.GeneralSecurityException**
■ ■ CRLException()

■ ■ CRLException(String)

■ ■ **abstract class X509Certificate extends Certificate implements X509Extension**
■ ■ protected X509Certificate()
■ ■ abstract void checkValidity() throws CertificateExpiredException,
CertificateNotYetValidException
■ ■ abstract void checkValidity(java.util.Date) throws
CertificateExpiredException, CertificateNotYetValidException
■ ■ abstract int getBasicConstraints()
■ ■ java.util.List getExtendedKeyUsage() throws
CertificateParsingException

■ ■ java.util.Collection getIssuerAlternativeNames() throws
CertificateParsingException
■ ■ abstract java.security.Principal getIssuerDN()
■ ■ abstract boolean[] getIssuerUniqueID()
■ ■ javax.security.auth.x500.X500Principal getIssuerX500Principal()
■ ■ abstract boolean[] getKeyUsage()
■ ■ abstract java.util.Date getNotAfter()
■ ■ abstract java.util.Date getNotBefore()
■ ■ abstract java.math.BigInteger getSerialNumber()

■ ■ abstract String getSigAlgName()
■ ■ abstract String getSigAlgOID()
■ ■ abstract byte[] getSigAlgParams()
■ ■ abstract byte[] getSignature()
■ ■ java.util.Collection getSubjectAlternativeNames() throws
CertificateParsingException

■ ■ **abstract class X509CRL extends CRL implements X509Extension**
■ ■ protected X509CRL()
■ ■ abstract byte[] getEncoded() throws CRLException
■ ■ abstract java.security.Principal getIssuerDN()
■ ■ javax.security.auth.x500.X500Principal getIssuerX500Principal()
■ ■ abstract java.util.Date getNextUpdate()
■ ■ abstract X509CRLEntry getRevokedCertificate(java.math.BigInteger)
■ ■ abstract java.util.Set getRevokedCertificates()
■ ■ abstract String getSigAlgName()
■ ■ abstract String getSigAlgOID()
■ ■ abstract byte[] getSigAlgParams()
■ ■ abstract byte[] getSignature()
■ ■ abstract byte[] getTBSCertList() throws CRLException

■ ■ **abstract class X509CRLEntry implements X509Extension**
■ ■ X509CRLEntry()
■ ■ abstract byte[] getEncoded() throws CRLException
■ ■ abstract java.util.Date getRevocationDate()

■ ■ **interface X509Extension**
■ ■ abstract java.util.Set getCriticalExtensionOIDs()
■ ■ abstract byte[] getExtensionValue(String)

■ ■ abstract java.security.Principal getSubjectDN()
■ ■ abstract boolean[] getSubjectUniqueID()
■ ■ javax.security.auth.x500.X500Principal getSubjectX500Principal()
■ ■ abstract byte[] getTBSCertificate() throws
CertificateEncodingException
■ ■ abstract int getVersion()

■ ■ abstract java.util.Date getThisUpdate()
■ ■ abstract int getVersion()
■ ■ abstract void verify(java.security.PublicKey) throws
java.security.InvalidKeyException,
java.security.NoSuchAlgorithmException,
java.security.NoSuchProviderException, java.security.SignatureException,
CRLException
■ ■ abstract void verify(java.security.PublicKey,String) throws
java.security.InvalidKeyException,
java.security.NoSuchAlgorithmException,
java.security.NoSuchProviderException, java.security.SignatureException,
CRLException

■ ■ abstract java.math.BigInteger getSerialNumber()
■ ■ abstract boolean hasExtensions()
■ ■ abstract String toString()

■ ■ abstract java.util.Set getNonCriticalExtensionOIDs()
■ ■ abstract boolean hasUnsupportedCriticalExtension()

999.3.10   java.security.interfaces

■ ■ **package java.security.interfaces**
■ ■ **interface DSAKey**
■ ■ abstract DSAParams getParams()

■ ■ **interface DSAKeyPairGenerator**
■ ■ abstract void initialize(int,boolean,java.security.SecureRandom)   ■ ■ abstract void initialize(DSAParams,java.security.SecureRandom)

■ ■ **interface DSAParams**
■ ■ abstract java.math.BigInteger getG()   ■ ■ abstract java.math.BigInteger getQ()
■ ■ abstract java.math.BigInteger getP()

■ ■ **interface DSAPrivateKey extends java.security.PrivateKey , DSAKey**
■ ■ abstract java.math.BigInteger getX()   ■ ■ final static long serialVersionUID

■ ■ **interface DSAPublicKey extends java.security.PublicKey , DSAKey**
■ ■ abstract java.math.BigInteger getY()   ■ ■ final static long serialVersionUID

■ ■ **interface RSAKey**
■ ■ abstract java.math.BigInteger getModulus()

■ ■ **interface RSAPrivateCrtKey extends RSAPrivateKey**
■ ■ abstract java.math.BigInteger getCrtCoefficient()   ■ ■ abstract java.math.BigInteger getPrimeP()
■ ■ abstract java.math.BigInteger getPrimeExponentP()   ■ ■ abstract java.math.BigInteger getPrimeQ()
■ ■ abstract java.math.BigInteger getPrimeExponentQ()   ■ ■ abstract java.math.BigInteger getPublicExponent()

■ ■ **interface RSAPrivateKey extends java.security.PrivateKey , RSAKey**
■ ■ abstract java.math.BigInteger getPrivateExponent()

■ ■ **interface RSAPublicKey extends java.security.PublicKey , RSAKey**
■ ■ abstract java.math.BigInteger getPublicExponent()

999.3.11   java.security.spec

■ ■ **package java.security.spec**
■ ■ **interface AlgorithmParameterSpec**
■ ■ **class DSAParameterSpec implements java.security.interfaces.DSAParams , AlgorithmParameterSpec**
■ ■ DSAParameterSpec(java.math.BigInteger,java.math.BigInteger,   ■ ■ java.math.BigInteger getP()
java.math.BigInteger)   ■ ■ java.math.BigInteger getQ()
■ ■ java.math.BigInteger getG()

■ ■ **class DSAPrivateKeySpec implements KeySpec**
■ ■ DSAPrivateKeySpec(java.math.BigInteger,java.math.BigInteger,   ■ ■ java.math.BigInteger getP()
java.math.BigInteger,java.math.BigInteger)   ■ ■ java.math.BigInteger getQ()
■ ■ java.math.BigInteger getG()   ■ ■ java.math.BigInteger getX()

■ ■ **class DSAPublicKeySpec implements KeySpec**
■ ■ DSAPublicKeySpec(java.math.BigInteger,java.math.BigInteger,   ■ ■ java.math.BigInteger getP()
java.math.BigInteger,java.math.BigInteger)   ■ ■ java.math.BigInteger getQ()
■ ■ java.math.BigInteger getG()   ■ ■ java.math.BigInteger getY()

■ ■ **abstract class EncodedKeySpec implements KeySpec**
■ ■ EncodedKeySpec(byte[])   ■ ■ abstract String getFormat()
■ ■ byte[] getEncoded()

■ ■ **class InvalidKeySpecException extends java.security.GeneralSecurityException**
■ ■ InvalidKeySpecException()   ■ ■ InvalidKeySpecException(String)

■ ■ **class InvalidParameterSpecException extends java.security.GeneralSecurityException**
■ ■ InvalidParameterSpecException()　　　　　■ ■ InvalidParameterSpecException(String)

■ ■ **interface KeySpec**

■ ■ **class PKCS8EncodedKeySpec extends EncodedKeySpec**
■ ■ PKCS8EncodedKeySpec(byte[])　　　　　■ ■ final String getFormat()

■ ■ **class PSSParameterSpec implements AlgorithmParameterSpec**
■ ■ PSSParameterSpec(int)　　　　　■ ■ int getSaltLength()

■ ■ **class RSAKeyGenParameterSpec implements AlgorithmParameterSpec**
■ ■ RSAKeyGenParameterSpec(int,java.math.BigInteger)　　　　　■ ■ int getKeysize()
■ ■ final static java.math.BigInteger Fo　　　　　■ ■ java.math.BigInteger getPublicExponent()
■ ■ final static java.math.BigInteger F4

■ ■ **class RSAPrivateCrtKeySpec extends RSAPrivateKeySpec**
■ ■ RSAPrivateCrtKeySpec(java.math.BigInteger,java.math.BigInteger,　　　　　■ ■ java.math.BigInteger getPrimeExponentQ()
java.math.BigInteger,java.math.BigInteger,java.math.BigInteger,　　　　　■ ■ java.math.BigInteger getPrimeP()
java.math.BigInteger,java.math.BigInteger,java.math.BigInteger)　　　　　■ ■ java.math.BigInteger getPrimeQ()
■ ■ java.math.BigInteger getCrtCoefficient()　　　　　■ ■ java.math.BigInteger getPublicExponent()
■ ■ java.math.BigInteger getPrimeExponentP()

■ ■ **class RSAPrivateKeySpec implements KeySpec**
■ ■ RSAPrivateKeySpec(java.math.BigInteger,java.math.BigInteger)　　　　　■ ■ java.math.BigInteger getPrivateExponent()
■ ■ java.math.BigInteger getModulus()

■ ■ **class RSAPublicKeySpec implements KeySpec**
■ ■ RSAPublicKeySpec(java.math.BigInteger,java.math.BigInteger)　　　　　■ ■ java.math.BigInteger getPublicExponent()
■ ■ java.math.BigInteger getModulus()

■ ■ **class X509EncodedKeySpec extends EncodedKeySpec**
■ ■ X509EncodedKeySpec(byte[])　　　　　■ ■ final String getFormat()

999.3.12　java.text

■ ■ **package java.text**

■ ■ **class Annotation**
■ ■ Annotation(Object)　　　　　■ ■ Object getValue()

■ ■ **interface AttributedCharacterIterator extends CharacterIterator**
■ ■ abstract java.util.Set getAllAttributeKeys()　　　　　■ ■ abstract int getRunLimit(java.util.Set)
■ ■ abstract Object getAttribute(AttributedCharacterIterator.Attribute)　　　　　■ ■ abstract int getRunStart()
■ ■ abstract java.util.Map getAttributes()　　　　　■ ■ abstract int getRunStart(AttributedCharacterIterator.Attribute)
■ ■ abstract int getRunLimit()　　　　　■ ■ abstract int getRunStart(java.util.Set)
■ ■ abstract int getRunLimit(AttributedCharacterIterator.Attribute)

■ ■ **class AttributedCharacterIterator.Attribute implements java.io.Serializable**
■ ■ protected AttributedCharacterIterator.Attribute(String)　　　　　■ ■ final static AttributedCharacterIterator.Attribute LANGUAGE
■ ■ final boolean equals(Object)　　　　　■ ■ final static AttributedCharacterIterator.Attribute READING
■ ■ protected String getName()　　　　　■ ■ protected Object readResolve() throws
■ ■ final int hashCode()　　　　　java.io.InvalidObjectException
■ ■ final static AttributedCharacterIterator.Attribute
INPUT_METHOD_SEGMENT

■ ■ **class AttributedString**
■ ■ AttributedString(String)　　　　　■ ■ void addAttribute(AttributedCharacterIterator.Attribute,Object,int,
■ ■ AttributedString(String,java.util.Map)　　　　　int)
■ ■ AttributedString(AttributedCharacterIterator)　　　　　■ ■ void addAttributes(java.util.Map,int,int)
■ ■ AttributedString(AttributedCharacterIterator,int,int)　　　　　■ ■ AttributedCharacterIterator getIterator()
■ ■ AttributedString(AttributedCharacterIterator,int,int,　　　　　■ ■ AttributedCharacterIterator
AttributedCharacterIterator.Attribute[])　　　　　getIterator(AttributedCharacterIterator.Attribute[])
■ ■ void addAttribute(AttributedCharacterIterator.Attribute,Object)　　　　　■ ■ AttributedCharacterIterator
　　　　　getIterator(AttributedCharacterIterator.Attribute[],int,int)

■ ■ **abstract class BreakIterator implements Cloneable**
■ ■ protected BreakIterator()　　　　　■ ■ static BreakIterator getSentenceInstance(java.util.Locale)
■ ■ Object clone()　　　　　■ ■ abstract CharacterIterator getText()
■ ■ abstract int current()　　　　　■ ■ static BreakIterator getWordInstance()
■ ■ final static int DONE　　　　　■ ■ static BreakIterator getWordInstance(java.util.Locale)
■ ■ abstract int first()　　　　　■ ■ boolean isBoundary(int)
■ ■ abstract int following(int)　　　　　■ ■ abstract int last()
■ ■ static java.util.Locale[] getAvailableLocales()　　　　　■ ■ abstract int next()
■ ■ static BreakIterator getCharacterInstance()　　　　　■ ■ abstract int next(int)
■ ■ static BreakIterator getCharacterInstance(java.util.Locale)　　　　　■ ■ int preceding(int)
■ ■ static BreakIterator getLineInstance()　　　　　■ ■ abstract int previous()
■ ■ static BreakIterator getLineInstance(java.util.Locale)　　　　　■ ■ void setText(String)
■ ■ static BreakIterator getSentenceInstance()　　　　　■ ■ abstract void setText(CharacterIterator)

■ ■ **interface CharacterIterator extends Cloneable**
■ ■ abstract Object clone()　　　　　■ ■ abstract int getIndex()
■ ■ abstract char current()　　　　　■ ■ abstract char last()
■ ■ final static char DONE　　　　　■ ■ abstract char next()
■ ■ abstract char first()　　　　　■ ■ abstract char previous()
■ ■ abstract int getBeginIndex()　　　　　■ ■ abstract char setIndex(int)
■ ■ abstract int getEndIndex()

■ ■ **class ChoiceFormat extends NumberFormat**

■ ■ ChoiceFormat(double[],String[])
■ ■ ChoiceFormat(String)
■ ■ void applyPattern(String)
■ ■ StringBuffer format(double,StringBuffer,FieldPosition)
■ ■ StringBuffer format(long,StringBuffer,FieldPosition)
■ ■ Object[] getFormats()
■ ■ double[] getLimits()

■ ■ final static double nextDouble(double)
■ ■ static double nextDouble(double,boolean)
■ ■ Number parse(String,ParsePosition)
■ ■ final static double previousDouble(double)
■ ■ void setChoices(double[],String[])
■ ■ String toPattern()

■ ■ **final class CollationElementIterator**
■ ■ int getMaxExpansion(int)
■ ■ int getOffset()
■ ■ int next()
■ ■ final static int NULLORDER
■ ■ int previous()
■ ■ final static int primaryOrder(int)

■ ■ void reset()
■ ■ final static short secondaryOrder(int)
■ ■ void setOffset(int)
■ ■ void setText(String)
■ ■ void setText(CharacterIterator)
■ ■ final static short tertiaryOrder(int)

■ ■ **final class CollationKey implements Comparable**
■ ■ int compareTo(Object)
■ ■ int compareTo(CollationKey)

■ ■ String getSourceString()
■ ■ byte[] toByteArray()

■ ■ **abstract class Collator implements Cloneable , java.util.Comparator**
■ ■ protected Collator()
■ ■ final static int CANONICAL_DECOMPOSITION
■ ■ Object clone()
■ ■ int compare(Object,Object)
■ ■ abstract int compare(String,String)
■ ■ boolean equals(String,String)
■ ■ final static int FULL_DECOMPOSITION
■ ■ static java.util.Locale[] getAvailableLocales()
■ ■ abstract CollationKey getCollationKey(String)
■ ■ int getDecomposition()
■ ■ static Collator getInstance()

■ ■ static Collator getInstance(java.util.Locale)
■ ■ int getStrength()
■ ■ abstract int hashCode()
■ ■ final static int IDENTICAL
■ ■ final static int NO_DECOMPOSITION
■ ■ final static int PRIMARY
■ ■ final static int SECONDARY
■ ■ void setDecomposition(int)
■ ■ void setStrength(int)
■ ■ final static int TERTIARY

■ ■ **abstract class DateFormat extends Format**
■ ■ protected DateFormat()
■ ■ final static int AM_PM_FIELD
■ ■ protected java.util.Calendar calendar
■ ■ final static int DATE_FIELD
■ ■ final static int DAY_OF_WEEK_FIELD
■ ■ final static int DAY_OF_WEEK_IN_MONTH_FIELD
■ ■ final static int DAY_OF_YEAR_FIELD
■ ■ final static int DEFAULT
■ ■ final static int ERA_FIELD
■ ■ final StringBuffer format(Object,StringBuffer,FieldPosition)
■ ■ final String format(java.util.Date)
■ ■ abstract StringBuffer format(java.util.Date,StringBuffer,FieldPosition)
■ ■ final static int FULL
■ ■ static java.util.Locale[] getAvailableLocales()
■ ■ java.util.Calendar getCalendar()
■ ■ final static DateFormat getDateInstance()
■ ■ final static DateFormat getDateInstance(int)
■ ■ final static DateFormat getDateInstance(int,java.util.Locale)
■ ■ final static DateFormat getDateTimeInstance()
■ ■ final static DateFormat getDateTimeInstance(int,int)
■ ■ final static DateFormat getDateTimeInstance(int,int,java.util.Locale)
■ ■ final static DateFormat getInstance()
■ ■ NumberFormat getNumberFormat()
■ ■ final static DateFormat getTimeInstance()
■ ■ final static DateFormat getTimeInstance(int)
■ ■ final static DateFormat getTimeInstance(int,java.util.Locale)

■ ■ java.util.TimeZone getTimeZone()
■ ■ final static int HOUR0_FIELD
■ ■ final static int HOUR1_FIELD
■ ■ final static int HOUR_OF_DAY0_FIELD
■ ■ final static int HOUR_OF_DAY1_FIELD
■ ■ boolean isLenient()
■ ■ final static int LONG
■ ■ final static int MEDIUM
■ ■ final static int MILLISECOND_FIELD
■ ■ final static int MINUTE_FIELD
■ ■ final static int MONTH_FIELD
■ ■ protected NumberFormat numberFormat
■ ■ java.util.Date parse(String) throws ParseException
■ ■ abstract java.util.Date parse(String,ParsePosition)
■ ■ Object parseObject(String,ParsePosition)
■ ■ final static int SECOND_FIELD
■ ■ void setCalendar(java.util.Calendar)
■ ■ void setLenient(boolean)
■ ■ void setNumberFormat(NumberFormat)
■ ■ void setTimeZone(java.util.TimeZone)
■ ■ final static int SHORT
■ ■ final static int TIMEZONE_FIELD
■ ■ final static int WEEK_OF_MONTH_FIELD
■ ■ final static int WEEK_OF_YEAR_FIELD
■ ■ final static int YEAR_FIELD

■ ■ **class DateFormat.Field extends Format.Field**
■ ■ protected DateFormat.Field(String,int)
■ ■ final static DateFormat.Field AM_PM
■ ■ final static DateFormat.Field DAY_OF_MONTH
■ ■ final static DateFormat.Field DAY_OF_WEEK
■ ■ final static DateFormat.Field DAY_OF_WEEK_IN_MONTH
■ ■ final static DateFormat.Field DAY_OF_YEAR
■ ■ final static DateFormat.Field ERA
■ ■ int getCalendarField()
■ ■ final static DateFormat.Field HOUR0
■ ■ final static DateFormat.Field HOUR1
■ ■ final static DateFormat.Field HOUR_OF_DAY0

■ ■ final static DateFormat.Field HOUR_OF_DAY1
■ ■ final static DateFormat.Field MILLISECOND
■ ■ final static DateFormat.Field MINUTE
■ ■ final static DateFormat.Field MONTH
■ ■ static DateFormat.Field ofCalendarField(int)
■ ■ final static DateFormat.Field SECOND
■ ■ final static DateFormat.Field TIME_ZONE
■ ■ final static DateFormat.Field WEEK_OF_MONTH
■ ■ final static DateFormat.Field WEEK_OF_YEAR
■ ■ final static DateFormat.Field YEAR

■ ■ **class DateFormatSymbols implements java.io.Serializable , Cloneable**
■ ■ DateFormatSymbols()
■ ■ DateFormatSymbols(java.util.Locale)
■ ■ Object clone()
■ ■ String[] getAmPmStrings()
■ ■ String[] getEras()

■ ■ String getLocalPatternChars()
■ ■ String[] getMonths()
■ ■ String[] getShortMonths()
■ ■ String[] getShortWeekdays()
■ ■ String[] getWeekdays()

■ ■ String[][] getZoneStrings()
■ ■ void setAmPmStrings(String[])
■ ■ void setEras(String[])
■ ■ void setLocalPatternChars(String)
■ ■ void setMonths(String[])

■ ■ class DecimalFormat extends NumberFormat
■ ■ DecimalFormat()
■ ■ DecimalFormat(String)
■ ■ DecimalFormat(String,DecimalFormatSymbols)
■ ■ void applyLocalizedPattern(String)
■ ■ void applyPattern(String)
■ ■ StringBuffer format(double,StringBuffer,FieldPosition)
■ ■ StringBuffer format(long,StringBuffer,FieldPosition)
■ ■ DecimalFormatSymbols getDecimalFormatSymbols()
■ ■ int getGroupingSize()
■ ■ int getMultiplier()
■ ■ String getNegativePrefix()
■ ■ String getNegativeSuffix()
■ ■ String getPositivePrefix()

■ ■ void setShortMonths(String[])
■ ■ void setShortWeekdays(String[])
■ ■ void setWeekdays(String[])
■ ■ void setZoneStrings(String[][])

■ ■ String getPositiveSuffix()
■ ■ boolean isDecimalSeparatorAlwaysShown()
■ ■ Number parse(String,ParsePosition)
■ ■ void setDecimalFormatSymbols(DecimalFormatSymbols)
■ ■ void setDecimalSeparatorAlwaysShown(boolean)
■ ■ void setGroupingSize(int)
■ ■ void setMultiplier(int)
■ ■ void setNegativePrefix(String)
■ ■ void setNegativeSuffix(String)
■ ■ void setPositivePrefix(String)
■ ■ void setPositiveSuffix(String)
■ ■ String toLocalizedPattern()
■ ■ String toPattern()

■ ■ final class DecimalFormatSymbols implements java.io.Serializable , Cloneable
■ ■ DecimalFormatSymbols()
■ ■ DecimalFormatSymbols(java.util.Locale)
■ ■ Object clone()
■ ■ java.util.Currency getCurrency()
■ ■ String getCurrencySymbol()
■ ■ char getDecimalSeparator()
■ ■ char getDigit()
■ ■ char getGroupingSeparator()
■ ■ String getInfinity()
■ ■ String getInternationalCurrencySymbol()
■ ■ char getMinusSign()
■ ■ char getMonetaryDecimalSeparator()
■ ■ String getNaN()
■ ■ char getPatternSeparator()
■ ■ char getPercent()
■ ■ char getPerMill()

■ ■ char getZeroDigit()
■ ■ void setCurrency(java.util.Currency)
■ ■ void setCurrencySymbol(String)
■ ■ void setDecimalSeparator(char)
■ ■ void setDigit(char)
■ ■ void setGroupingSeparator(char)
■ ■ void setInfinity(String)
■ ■ void setInternationalCurrencySymbol(String)
■ ■ void setMinusSign(char)
■ ■ void setMonetaryDecimalSeparator(char)
■ ■ void setNaN(String)
■ ■ void setPatternSeparator(char)
■ ■ void setPercent(char)
■ ■ void setPerMill(char)
■ ■ void setZeroDigit(char)

■ ■ class FieldPosition
■ ■ FieldPosition(int)
■ ■ FieldPosition(Format.Field)
■ ■ FieldPosition(Format.Field,int)
■ ■ int getBeginIndex()
■ ■ int getEndIndex()

■ ■ int getField()
■ ■ Format.Field getFieldAttribute()
■ ■ void setBeginIndex(int)
■ ■ void setEndIndex(int)

■ ■ abstract class Format implements java.io.Serializable , Cloneable
■ ■ Format()
■ ■ Object clone()
■ ■ final String format(Object)
■ ■ abstract StringBuffer format(Object,StringBuffer,FieldPosition)

■ ■ AttributedCharacterIterator formatToCharacterIterator(Object)
■ ■ Object parseObject(String) throws ParseException
■ ■ abstract Object parseObject(String,ParsePosition)

■ ■ class Format.Field extends AttributedCharacterIterator.Attribute
■ ■ protected Format.Field(String)

■ ■ class MessageFormat extends Format
■ ■ MessageFormat(String)
■ ■ MessageFormat(String,java.util.Locale)
■ ■ void applyPattern(String)
■ ■ final StringBuffer format(Object[],StringBuffer,FieldPosition)
■ ■ final StringBuffer format(Object,StringBuffer,FieldPosition)
■ ■ static String format(String,Object[])
■ ■ Format[] getFormats()
■ ■ Format[] getFormatsByArgumentIndex()
■ ■ java.util.Locale getLocale()

■ ■ Object[] parse(String) throws ParseException
■ ■ Object[] parse(String,ParsePosition)
■ ■ Object parseObject(String,ParsePosition)
■ ■ void setFormat(int,Format)
■ ■ void setFormatByArgumentIndex(int,Format)
■ ■ void setFormats(Format[])
■ ■ void setFormatsByArgumentIndex(Format[])
■ ■ void setLocale(java.util.Locale)
■ ■ String toPattern()

■ ■ class MessageFormat.Field extends Format.Field
■ ■ protected MessageFormat.Field(String)

■ ■ final static MessageFormat.Field ARGUMENT

■ ■ abstract class NumberFormat extends Format
■ ■ NumberFormat()
■ ■ final String format(double)
■ ■ abstract StringBuffer format(double,StringBuffer,FieldPosition)
■ ■ final String format(long)
■ ■ abstract StringBuffer format(long,StringBuffer,FieldPosition)
■ ■ final StringBuffer format(Object,StringBuffer,FieldPosition)
■ ■ final static int FRACTION_FIELD
■ ■ static java.util.Locale[] getAvailableLocales()
■ ■ java.util.Currency getCurrency()
■ ■ final static NumberFormat getCurrencyInstance()
■ ■ static NumberFormat getCurrencyInstance(java.util.Locale)
■ ■ final static NumberFormat getInstance()

■ ■ static NumberFormat getInstance(java.util.Locale)
■ ■ final static NumberFormat getIntegerInstance()
■ ■ static NumberFormat getIntegerInstance(java.util.Locale)
■ ■ int getMaximumFractionDigits()
■ ■ int getMaximumIntegerDigits()
■ ■ int getMinimumFractionDigits()
■ ■ int getMinimumIntegerDigits()
■ ■ final static NumberFormat getNumberInstance()
■ ■ static NumberFormat getNumberInstance(java.util.Locale)
■ ■ final static NumberFormat getPercentInstance()
■ ■ static NumberFormat getPercentInstance(java.util.Locale)
■ ■ final static int INTEGER_FIELD

■ ■ boolean isGroupingUsed()
■ ■ boolean isParseIntegerOnly()
■ ■ Number parse(String) throws ParseException
■ ■ abstract Number parse(String,ParsePosition)
■ ■ final Object parseObject(String,ParsePosition)
■ ■ void setCurrency(java.util.Currency)

■ ■ void setGroupingUsed(boolean)
■ ■ void setMaximumFractionDigits(int)
■ ■ void setMaximumIntegerDigits(int)
■ ■ void setMinimumFractionDigits(int)
■ ■ void setMinimumIntegerDigits(int)
■ ■ void setParseIntegerOnly(boolean)

■ ■ **class NumberFormat.Field extends Format.Field**
■ ■ protected NumberFormat.Field(String)
■ ■ final static NumberFormat.Field CURRENCY
■ ■ final static NumberFormat.Field DECIMAL_SEPARATOR
■ ■ final static NumberFormat.Field EXPONENT
■ ■ final static NumberFormat.Field EXPONENT_SIGN
■ ■ final static NumberFormat.Field EXPONENT_SYMBOL

■ ■ final static NumberFormat.Field FRACTION
■ ■ final static NumberFormat.Field GROUPING_SEPARATOR
■ ■ final static NumberFormat.Field INTEGER
■ ■ final static NumberFormat.Field PERCENT
■ ■ final static NumberFormat.Field PERMILLE
■ ■ final static NumberFormat.Field SIGN

■ ■ **class ParseException extends Exception**
■ ■ ParseException(String,int)

■ ■ int getErrorOffset()

■ ■ **class ParsePosition**
■ ■ ParsePosition(int)
■ ■ int getErrorIndex()
■ ■ int getIndex()

■ ■ void setErrorIndex(int)
■ ■ void setIndex(int)

■ ■ **class RuleBasedCollator extends Collator**
■ ■ RuleBasedCollator(String) throws ParseException
■ ■ int compare(String,String)
■ ■ CollationElementIterator getCollationElementIterator(String)
■ ■ CollationElementIterator
getCollationElementIterator(CharacterIterator)

■ ■ CollationKey getCollationKey(String)
■ ■ String getRules()
■ ■ int hashCode()

■ ■ **class SimpleDateFormat extends DateFormat**
■ ■ SimpleDateFormat()
■ ■ SimpleDateFormat(String)
■ ■ SimpleDateFormat(String,DateFormatSymbols)
■ ■ SimpleDateFormat(String,java.util.Locale)
■ ■ void applyLocalizedPattern(String)
■ ■ void applyPattern(String)
■ ■ StringBuffer format(java.util.Date,StringBuffer,FieldPosition)

■ ■ java.util.Date get2DigitYearStart()
■ ■ DateFormatSymbols getDateFormatSymbols()
■ ■ java.util.Date parse(String,ParsePosition)
■ ■ void set2DigitYearStart(java.util.Date)
■ ■ void setDateFormatSymbols(DateFormatSymbols)
■ ■ String toLocalizedPattern()
■ ■ String toPattern()

■ ■ **final class StringCharacterIterator implements CharacterIterator**
■ ■ StringCharacterIterator(String)
■ ■ StringCharacterIterator(String,int)
■ ■ StringCharacterIterator(String,int,int,int)
■ ■ Object clone()
■ ■ char current()
■ ■ char first()
■ ■ int getBeginIndex()

■ ■ int getEndIndex()
■ ■ int getIndex()
■ ■ char last()
■ ■ char next()
■ ■ char previous()
■ ■ char setIndex(int)
■ ■ void setText(String)

999.3.13   java.util

■ ■ **package java.util**
■ ■ **abstract class AbstractCollection implements Collection**
■ ■ protected AbstractCollection()
■ ■ boolean add(Object)
■ ■ boolean addAll(Collection)
■ ■ void clear()
■ ■ boolean contains(Object)
■ ■ boolean containsAll(Collection)

■ ■ boolean isEmpty()
■ ■ boolean remove(Object)
■ ■ boolean removeAll(Collection)
■ ■ boolean retainAll(Collection)
■ ■ Object[] toArray()
■ ■ Object[] toArray(Object[])

■ ■ **abstract class AbstractList extends AbstractCollection implements List**
■ ■ protected AbstractList()
■ ■ void add(int,Object)
■ ■ boolean addAll(int,Collection)
■ ■ int indexOf(Object)
■ ■ Iterator iterator()
■ ■ int lastIndexOf(Object)
■ ■ ListIterator listIterator()

■ ■ ListIterator listIterator(int)
■ ■ protected int modCount
■ ■ Object remove(int)
■ ■ protected void removeRange(int,int)
■ ■ Object set(int,Object)
■ ■ List subList(int,int)

■ ■ **abstract class AbstractMap implements Map**
■ ■ protected AbstractMap()
■ ■ void clear()
■ ■ boolean containsKey(Object)
■ ■ boolean containsValue(Object)
■ ■ Object get(Object)
■ ■ boolean isEmpty()

■ ■ Set keySet()
■ ■ Object put(Object,Object)
■ ■ void putAll(Map)
■ ■ Object remove(Object)
■ ■ int size()
■ ■ Collection values()

■ ■ **abstract class AbstractSequentialList extends AbstractList**
■ ■ protected AbstractSequentialList()
■ ■ Object get(int)

■ ■ abstract ListIterator listIterator(int)

■ ■ **abstract class AbstractSet extends AbstractCollection implements Set**
■ ■ protected AbstractSet()

■ ■ **class ArrayList extends AbstractList implements java.io.Serializable, Cloneable, List, RandomAccess**
■ ■ ArrayList()

■ ■ ArrayList(int)

■ ■ ArrayList(Collection)
■ ■ Object clone()
■ ■ void ensureCapacity(int)

■ ■ **class Arrays**
■ ■ static List asList(Object[])
■ ■ static int binarySearch(byte[],byte)
■ ■ static int binarySearch(char[],char)
■ ■ static int binarySearch(double[],double)
■ ■ static int binarySearch(float[],float)
■ ■ static int binarySearch(int[],int)
■ ■ static int binarySearch(long[],long)
■ ■ static int binarySearch(Object[],Object)
■ ■ static int binarySearch(Object[],Object,Comparator)
■ ■ static int binarySearch(short[],short)
■ ■ static boolean equals(byte[],byte[])
■ ■ static boolean equals(char[],char[])
■ ■ static boolean equals(double[],double[])
■ ■ static boolean equals(float[],float[])
■ ■ static boolean equals(int[],int[])
■ ■ static boolean equals(long[],long[])
■ ■ static boolean equals(Object[],Object[])
■ ■ static boolean equals(short[],short[])
■ ■ static boolean equals(boolean[],boolean[])
■ ■ static void fill(byte[],byte)
■ ■ static void fill(byte[],int,int,byte)
■ ■ static void fill(char[],char)
■ ■ static void fill(char[],int,int,char)
■ ■ static void fill(double[],double)
■ ■ static void fill(double[],int,int,double)
■ ■ static void fill(float[],float)
■ ■ static void fill(float[],int,int,float)
■ ■ static void fill(int[],int)

■ ■ **class BitSet implements java.io.Serializable , Cloneable**
■ ■ BitSet()
■ ■ BitSet(int)
■ ■ void and(BitSet)
■ ■ void andNot(BitSet)
■ ■ int cardinality()
■ ■ void clear()
■ ■ void clear(int)
■ ■ void clear(int,int)
■ ■ Object clone()
■ ■ void flip(int)
■ ■ void flip(int,int)
■ ■ boolean get(int)
■ ■ BitSet get(int,int)

■ ■ **abstract class Calendar implements java.io.Serializable , Cloneable**
■ ■ protected Calendar()
■ ■ protected Calendar(TimeZone,Locale)
■ ■ abstract void add(int,int)
■ ■ boolean after(Object)
■ ■ final static int AM
■ ■ final static int AM_PM
■ ■ final static int APRIL
■ ■ protected boolean areFieldsSet
■ ■ final static int AUGUST
■ ■ boolean before(Object)
■ ■ final void clear()
■ ■ final void clear(int)
■ ■ Object clone()
■ ■ protected void complete()
■ ■ abstract protected void computeFields()
■ ■ abstract protected void computeTime()
■ ■ final static int DATE
■ ■ final static int DAY_OF_MONTH
■ ■ final static int DAY_OF_WEEK
■ ■ final static int DAY_OF_WEEK_IN_MONTH
■ ■ final static int DAY_OF_YEAR
■ ■ final static int DECEMBER
■ ■ final static int DST_OFFSET
■ ■ final static int ERA
■ ■ final static int FEBRUARY
■ ■ final static int FIELD_COUNT
■ ■ protected int[] fields
■ ■ final static int FRIDAY

■ ■ Object get(int)
■ ■ int size()
■ ■ void trimToSize()

■ ■ static void fill(int[],int,int,int)
■ ■ static void fill(long[],int,int,long)
■ ■ static void fill(long[],long)
■ ■ static void fill(Object[],int,int,Object)
■ ■ static void fill(Object[],Object)
■ ■ static void fill(short[],int,int,short)
■ ■ static void fill(short[],short)
■ ■ static void fill(boolean[],int,int,boolean)
■ ■ static void fill(boolean[],boolean)
■ ■ static void sort(byte[])
■ ■ static void sort(byte[],int,int)
■ ■ static void sort(char[])
■ ■ static void sort(char[],int,int)
■ ■ static void sort(double[])
■ ■ static void sort(double[],int,int)
■ ■ static void sort(float[])
■ ■ static void sort(float[],int,int)
■ ■ static void sort(int[])
■ ■ static void sort(int[],int,int)
■ ■ static void sort(long[])
■ ■ static void sort(long[],int,int)
■ ■ static void sort(Object[])
■ ■ static void sort(Object[],int,int)
■ ■ static void sort(Object[],int,int,Comparator)
■ ■ static void sort(Object[],Comparator)
■ ■ static void sort(short[])
■ ■ static void sort(short[],int,int)

■ ■ boolean intersects(BitSet)
■ ■ boolean isEmpty()
■ ■ int length()
■ ■ int nextClearBit(int)
■ ■ int nextSetBit(int)
■ ■ void or(BitSet)
■ ■ void set(int)
■ ■ void set(int,int)
■ ■ void set(int,int,boolean)
■ ■ void set(int,boolean)
■ ■ int size()
■ ■ void xor(BitSet)

■ ■ int get(int)
■ ■ int getActualMaximum(int)
■ ■ int getActualMinimum(int)
■ ■ static Locale[] getAvailableLocales()
■ ■ int getFirstDayOfWeek()
■ ■ abstract int getGreatestMinimum(int)
■ ■ static Calendar getInstance()
■ ■ static Calendar getInstance(Locale)
■ ■ static Calendar getInstance(TimeZone)
■ ■ static Calendar getInstance(TimeZone,Locale)
■ ■ abstract int getLeastMaximum(int)
■ ■ abstract int getMaximum(int)
■ ■ int getMinimalDaysInFirstWeek()
■ ■ abstract int getMinimum(int)
■ ■ final Date getTime()
■ ■ long getTimeInMillis()
■ ■ TimeZone getTimeZone()
■ ■ final static int HOUR
■ ■ final static int HOUR_OF_DAY
■ ■ final protected int internalGet(int)
■ ■ boolean isLenient()
■ ■ final boolean isSet(int)
■ ■ protected boolean[] isSet
■ ■ protected boolean isTimeSet
■ ■ final static int JANUARY
■ ■ final static int JULY
■ ■ final static int JUNE
■ ■ final static int MARCH

■ ■ final static int MAY
■ ■ final static int MILLISECOND
■ ■ final static int MINUTE
■ ■ final static int MONDAY
■ ■ final static int MONTH
■ ■ final static int NOVEMBER
■ ■ final static int OCTOBER
■ ■ final static int PM
■ ■ void roll(int,int)
■ ■ abstract void roll(int,boolean)
■ ■ final static int SATURDAY
■ ■ final static int SECOND
■ ■ final static int SEPTEMBER
■ ■ void set(int,int)
■ ■ final void set(int,int,int)
■ ■ final void set(int,int,int,int,int)
■ ■ final void set(int,int,int,int,int,int)

■ ■ void setFirstDayOfWeek(int)
■ ■ void setLenient(boolean)
■ ■ void setMinimalDaysInFirstWeek(int)
■ ■ final void setTime(Date)
■ ■ void setTimeInMillis(long)
■ ■ void setTimeZone(TimeZone)
■ ■ final static int SUNDAY
■ ■ final static int THURSDAY
■ ■ protected long time
■ ■ final static int TUESDAY
■ ■ final static int UNDECIMBER
■ ■ final static int WEDNESDAY
■ ■ final static int WEEK_OF_MONTH
■ ■ final static int WEEK_OF_YEAR
■ ■ final static int YEAR
■ ■ final static int ZONE_OFFSET

■ ■ **interface Collection**
■ ■ abstract boolean add(Object)
■ ■ abstract boolean addAll(Collection)
■ ■ abstract void clear()
■ ■ abstract boolean contains(Object)
■ ■ abstract boolean containsAll(Collection)
■ ■ abstract boolean equals(Object)
■ ■ abstract int hashCode()
■ ■ abstract boolean isEmpty()

■ ■ abstract Iterator iterator()
■ ■ abstract boolean remove(Object)
■ ■ abstract boolean removeAll(Collection)
■ ■ abstract boolean retainAll(Collection)
■ ■ abstract int size()
■ ■ abstract Object[] toArray()
■ ■ abstract Object[] toArray(Object[])

■ ■ **class Collections**
■ ■ static int binarySearch(List,Object)
■ ■ static int binarySearch(List,Object,Comparator)
■ ■ static void copy(List,List)
■ ■ final static List EMPTY_LIST
■ ■ final static Map EMPTY_MAP
■ ■ final static Set EMPTY_SET
■ ■ static Enumeration enumeration(Collection)
■ ■ static void fill(List,Object)
■ ■ static int indexOfSubList(List,List)
■ ■ static int lastIndexOfSubList(List,List)
■ ■ static ArrayList list(Enumeration)
■ ■ static Object max(Collection)
■ ■ static Object max(Collection,Comparator)
■ ■ static Object min(Collection)
■ ■ static Object min(Collection,Comparator)
■ ■ static List nCopies(int,Object)
■ ■ static boolean replaceAll(List,Object,Object)
■ ■ static void reverse(List)
■ ■ static Comparator reverseOrder()
■ ■ static void rotate(List,int)

■ ■ static void shuffle(List)
■ ■ static void shuffle(List,Random)
■ ■ static Set singleton(Object)
■ ■ static List singletonList(Object)
■ ■ static Map singletonMap(Object,Object)
■ ■ static void sort(List)
■ ■ static void sort(List,Comparator)
■ ■ static void swap(List,int,int)
■ ■ static Collection synchronizedCollection(Collection)
■ ■ static List synchronizedList(List)
■ ■ static Map synchronizedMap(Map)
■ ■ static Set synchronizedSet(Set)
■ ■ static SortedMap synchronizedSortedMap(SortedMap)
■ ■ static SortedSet synchronizedSortedSet(SortedSet)
■ ■ static Collection unmodifiableCollection(Collection)
■ ■ static List unmodifiableList(List)
■ ■ static Map unmodifiableMap(Map)
■ ■ static Set unmodifiableSet(Set)
■ ■ static SortedMap unmodifiableSortedMap(SortedMap)
■ ■ static SortedSet unmodifiableSortedSet(SortedSet)

■ ■ **interface Comparator**
■ ■ abstract int compare(Object,Object)

■ ■ abstract boolean equals(Object)

■ ■ **class ConcurrentModificationException extends RuntimeException**
■ ■ ConcurrentModificationException()

■ ■ ConcurrentModificationException(String)

■ ■ **final class Currency implements java.io.Serializable**
■ ■ String getCurrencyCode()
■ ■ int getDefaultFractionDigits()
■ ■ static Currency getInstance(String)

■ ■ static Currency getInstance(Locale)
■ ■ String getSymbol()
■ ■ String getSymbol(Locale)

■ ■ **class Date implements java.io.Serializable , Cloneable , Comparable**
■ ■ Date()
■ ■ Date(long)
■ ■ boolean after(Date)
■ ■ boolean before(Date)
■ ■ Object clone()

■ ■ int compareTo(Object)
■ ■ int compareTo(Date)
■ ■ long getTime()
■ ■ void setTime(long)

■ ■ **abstract class Dictionary**
■ ■ Dictionary()
■ ■ abstract Enumeration elements()
■ ■ abstract Object get(Object)
■ ■ abstract boolean isEmpty()

■ ■ abstract Enumeration keys()
■ ■ abstract Object put(Object,Object)
■ ■ abstract Object remove(Object)
■ ■ abstract int size()

■ ■ **class EmptyStackException extends RuntimeException**
■ ■ EmptyStackException()

■ ■ **interface Enumeration**
■ ■ abstract boolean hasMoreElements()

■ ■ abstract Object nextElement()

■ ■ **interface EventListener**
■ ■ **abstract class EventListenerProxy implements EventListener**
■ ■ EventListenerProxy(EventListener)
■ ■ EventListener getListener()

■ ■ **class EventObject implements java.io.Serializable**
■ ■ EventObject(Object)
■ ■ Object getSource()

■ ■ protected Object source

■ ■ **class GregorianCalendar extends Calendar**
■ ■ GregorianCalendar()
■ ■ GregorianCalendar(int,int,int)
■ ■ GregorianCalendar(int,int,int,int,int)
■ ■ GregorianCalendar(int,int,int,int,int,int)
■ ■ GregorianCalendar(Locale)
■ ■ GregorianCalendar(TimeZone)
■ ■ GregorianCalendar(TimeZone,Locale)
■ ■ final static int AD
■ ■ void add(int,int)
■ ■ final static int BC

■ ■ protected void computeFields()
■ ■ protected void computeTime()
■ ■ int getGreatestMinimum(int)
■ ■ final Date getGregorianChange()
■ ■ int getLeastMaximum(int)
■ ■ int getMaximum(int)
■ ■ int getMinimum(int)
■ ■ boolean isLeapYear(int)
■ ■ void roll(int,boolean)
■ ■ void setGregorianChange(Date)

■ ■ **class HashMap extends AbstractMap implements java.io.Serializable , Cloneable , Map**
■ ■ HashMap()
■ ■ HashMap(int)
■ ■ HashMap(int,float)

■ ■ HashMap(Map)
■ ■ Object clone()
■ ■ Set entrySet()

■ ■ **class HashSet extends AbstractSet implements java.io.Serializable , Cloneable , Set**
■ ■ HashSet()
■ ■ HashSet(int)
■ ■ HashSet(int,float)
■ ■ HashSet(Collection)

■ ■ Object clone()
■ ■ Iterator iterator()
■ ■ int size()

■ ■ **class Hashtable extends Dictionary implements java.io.Serializable , Cloneable , Map**
■ ■ Hashtable()
■ ■ Hashtable(int)
■ ■ Hashtable(int,float)
■ ■ Hashtable(Map)
■ ■ void clear()
■ ■ Object clone()
■ ■ boolean contains(Object)
■ ■ boolean containsKey(Object)
■ ■ boolean containsValue(Object)
■ ■ Enumeration elements()
■ ■ Set entrySet()

■ ■ Object get(Object)
■ ■ boolean isEmpty()
■ ■ Enumeration keys()
■ ■ Set keySet()
■ ■ Object put(Object,Object)
■ ■ void putAll(Map)
■ ■ protected void rehash()
■ ■ Object remove(Object)
■ ■ int size()
■ ■ Collection values()

■ ■ **class IdentityHashMap extends AbstractMap implements java.io.Serializable , Cloneable , Map**
■ ■ IdentityHashMap()
■ ■ IdentityHashMap(int)
■ ■ IdentityHashMap(Map)

■ ■ Object clone()
■ ■ Set entrySet()

■ ■ **interface Iterator**
■ ■ abstract boolean hasNext()
■ ■ abstract Object next()

■ ■ abstract void remove()

■ ■ **class LinkedHashMap extends HashMap**
■ ■ LinkedHashMap()
■ ■ LinkedHashMap(int)
■ ■ LinkedHashMap(int,float)

■ ■ LinkedHashMap(int,float,boolean)
■ ■ LinkedHashMap(Map)
■ ■ protected boolean removeEldestEntry(Map.Entry)

■ ■ **class LinkedHashSet extends HashSet implements java.io.Serializable , Cloneable , Set**
■ ■ LinkedHashSet()
■ ■ LinkedHashSet(int)

■ ■ LinkedHashSet(int,float)
■ ■ LinkedHashSet(Collection)

■ ■ **class LinkedList extends AbstractSequentialList implements java.io.Serializable , Cloneable , List**
■ ■ LinkedList()
■ ■ LinkedList(Collection)
■ ■ void addFirst(Object)
■ ■ void addLast(Object)
■ ■ Object clone()
■ ■ Object getFirst()

■ ■ Object getLast()
■ ■ ListIterator listIterator(int)
■ ■ Object removeFirst()
■ ■ Object removeLast()
■ ■ int size()

■ ■ **interface List extends Collection**
■ ■ abstract void add(int,Object)
■ ■ abstract boolean addAll(int,Collection)
■ ■ abstract boolean equals(Object)
■ ■ abstract Object get(int)
■ ■ abstract int hashCode()
■ ■ abstract int indexOf(Object)

■ ■ abstract int lastIndexOf(Object)
■ ■ abstract ListIterator listIterator()
■ ■ abstract ListIterator listIterator(int)
■ ■ abstract Object remove(int)
■ ■ abstract Object set(int,Object)
■ ■ abstract List subList(int,int)

■ ■ **interface ListIterator extends Iterator**
■ ■ abstract void add(Object)
■ ■ abstract boolean hasPrevious()
■ ■ abstract int nextIndex()

■ ■ abstract Object previous()
■ ■ abstract int previousIndex()
■ ■ abstract void set(Object)

■ ■ **abstract class ListResourceBundle extends ResourceBundle**
■ ■ ListResourceBundle()
■ ■ abstract protected Object[][] getContents()

■ ■ Enumeration getKeys()
■ ■ final Object handleGetObject(String)

■ ■ **final class Locale implements java.io.Serializable , Cloneable**
■ ■ Locale(String)
■ ■ Locale(String,String)
■ ■ Locale(String,String,String)

■ ■ final static Locale CANADA
■ ■ final static Locale CANADA_FRENCH
■ ■ final static Locale CHINA

- final static Locale CHINESE
- Object clone()
- final static Locale ENGLISH
- final static Locale FRANCE
- final static Locale FRENCH
- final static Locale GERMAN
- final static Locale GERMANY
- static Locale[] getAvailableLocales()
- String getCountry()
- static Locale getDefault()
- final String getDisplayCountry()
- String getDisplayCountry(Locale)
- final String getDisplayLanguage()
- String getDisplayLanguage(Locale)
- final String getDisplayName()
- String getDisplayName(Locale)
- final String getDisplayVariant()
- String getDisplayVariant(Locale)
- String getISO3Country()
- String getISO3Language()
- static String[] getISOCountries()
- static String[] getISOLanguages()
- String getLanguage()
- String getVariant()
- final static Locale ITALIAN
- final static Locale ITALY
- final static Locale JAPAN
- final static Locale JAPANESE
- final static Locale KOREA
- final static Locale KOREAN
- final static Locale PRC
- static void setDefault(Locale)
- final static Locale SIMPLIFIED_CHINESE
- final static Locale TAIWAN
- final String toString()
- final static Locale TRADITIONAL_CHINESE
- final static Locale UK
- final static Locale US

interface Map

- abstract void clear()
- abstract boolean containsKey(Object)
- abstract boolean containsValue(Object)
- abstract Set entrySet()
- abstract boolean equals(Object)
- abstract Object get(Object)
- abstract int hashCode()
- abstract boolean isEmpty()
- abstract Set keySet()
- abstract Object put(Object,Object)
- abstract void putAll(Map)
- abstract Object remove(Object)
- abstract int size()
- abstract Collection values()

interface Map.Entry

- abstract boolean equals(Object)
- abstract Object getKey()
- abstract Object getValue()
- abstract int hashCode()
- abstract Object setValue(Object)

class MissingResourceException extends RuntimeException

- MissingResourceException(String,String,String)
- String getClassName()
- String getKey()

class NoSuchElementException extends RuntimeException

- NoSuchElementException()
- NoSuchElementException(String)

class Observable

- Observable()
- void addObserver(Observer)
- protected void clearChanged()
- int countObservers()
- void deleteObserver(Observer)
- void deleteObservers()
- boolean hasChanged()
- void notifyObservers()
- void notifyObservers(Object)
- protected void setChanged()

interface Observer

- abstract void update(Observable,Object)

class Properties extends Hashtable

- Properties()
- Properties(Properties)
- protected Properties defaults
- String getProperty(String)
- String getProperty(String,String)
- void list(java.io.PrintStream)
- void list(java.io.PrintWriter)
- void load(java.io.InputStream) throws java.io.IOException
- Enumeration propertyNames()
- void save(java.io.OutputStream,String)
- Object setProperty(String,String)
- void store(java.io.OutputStream,String) throws java.io.IOException

final class PropertyPermission extends java.security.BasicPermission

- PropertyPermission(String,String)

class PropertyResourceBundle extends ResourceBundle

- PropertyResourceBundle(java.io.InputStream) throws java.io.IOException
- Enumeration getKeys()
- Object handleGetObject(String)

class Random implements java.io.Serializable

- Random()
- Random(long)
- protected int next(int)
- boolean nextBoolean()
- void nextBytes(byte[])
- double nextDouble()
- float nextFloat()
- double nextGaussian()
- int nextInt()
- int nextInt(int)
- long nextLong()
- void setSeed(long)

interface RandomAccess

abstract class ResourceBundle

- ResourceBundle()
- final static ResourceBundle getBundle(String)
- final static ResourceBundle getBundle(String,Locale)
- static ResourceBundle getBundle(String,Locale,ClassLoader)
- abstract Enumeration getKeys()
- Locale getLocale()
- final Object getObject(String)
- final String getString(String)
- final String[] getStringArray(String)
- abstract protected Object handleGetObject(String)
- protected ResourceBundle parent
- protected void setParent(ResourceBundle)

interface Set extends Collection

- abstract boolean equals(Object)
- abstract int hashCode()

■ ■ **class SimpleTimeZone extends TimeZone**
■ ■ SimpleTimeZone(int,String)
■ ■ SimpleTimeZone(int,String,int,int,int,int,int,int,int,int)
■ ■ SimpleTimeZone(int,String,int,int,int,int,int,int,int,int,int)
■ ■ SimpleTimeZone(int,String,int,int,int,int,int,int,int,int,int,int,int)
■ ■ int getOffset(int,int,int,int,int,int)
■ ■ int getRawOffset()
■ ■ boolean inDaylightTime(Date)
■ ■ void setDSTSavings(int)
■ ■ void setEndRule(int,int,int)
■ ■ void setEndRule(int,int,int,int)

■ ■ void setEndRule(int,int,int,int,boolean)
■ ■ void setRawOffset(int)
■ ■ void setStartRule(int,int,int)
■ ■ void setStartRule(int,int,int,int)
■ ■ void setStartRule(int,int,int,int,boolean)
■ ■ void setStartYear(int)
■ ■ final static int STANDARD_TIME
■ ■ boolean useDaylightTime()
■ ■ final static int UTC_TIME
■ ■ final static int WALL_TIME

■ ■ **interface SortedMap extends Map**
■ ■ abstract Comparator comparator()
■ ■ abstract Object firstKey()
■ ■ abstract SortedMap headMap(Object)

■ ■ abstract Object lastKey()
■ ■ abstract SortedMap subMap(Object,Object)
■ ■ abstract SortedMap tailMap(Object)

■ ■ **interface SortedSet extends Set**
■ ■ abstract Comparator comparator()
■ ■ abstract Object first()
■ ■ abstract SortedSet headSet(Object)

■ ■ abstract Object last()
■ ■ abstract SortedSet subSet(Object,Object)
■ ■ abstract SortedSet tailSet(Object)

■ ■ **class Stack extends Vector**
■ ■ Stack()
■ ■ boolean empty()
■ ■ Object peek()

■ ■ Object pop()
■ ■ Object push(Object)
■ ■ int search(Object)

■ ■ **class StringTokenizer implements Enumeration**
■ ■ StringTokenizer(String)
■ ■ StringTokenizer(String,String)
■ ■ StringTokenizer(String,String,boolean)
■ ■ int countTokens()
■ ■ boolean hasMoreElements()

■ ■ boolean hasMoreTokens()
■ ■ Object nextElement()
■ ■ String nextToken()
■ ■ String nextToken(String)

■ ■ **class Timer**
■ ■ Timer()
■ ■ Timer(boolean)
■ ■ void cancel()
■ ■ void schedule(TimerTask,long)
■ ■ void schedule(TimerTask,long,long)

■ ■ void schedule(TimerTask,Date)
■ ■ void schedule(TimerTask,Date,long)
■ ■ void scheduleAtFixedRate(TimerTask,long,long)
■ ■ void scheduleAtFixedRate(TimerTask,Date,long)

■ ■ **abstract class TimerTask implements Runnable**
■ ■ protected TimerTask()
■ ■ boolean cancel()

■ ■ long scheduledExecutionTime()

■ ■ **abstract class TimeZone implements java.io.Serializable , Cloneable**
■ ■ TimeZone()
■ ■ Object clone()
■ ■ static String[] getAvailableIDs()
■ ■ static String[] getAvailableIDs(int)
■ ■ static TimeZone getDefault()
■ ■ final String getDisplayName()
■ ■ final String getDisplayName(Locale)
■ ■ final String getDisplayName(boolean,int)
■ ■ String getDisplayName(boolean,int,Locale)
■ ■ int getDSTSavings()
■ ■ String getID()
■ ■ abstract int getOffset(int,int,int,int,int,int)

■ ■ int getOffset(long)
■ ■ abstract int getRawOffset()
■ ■ static TimeZone getTimeZone(String)
■ ■ boolean hasSameRules(TimeZone)
■ ■ abstract boolean inDaylightTime(Date)
■ ■ final static int LONG
■ ■ static void setDefault(TimeZone)
■ ■ void setID(String)
■ ■ abstract void setRawOffset(int)
■ ■ final static int SHORT
■ ■ abstract boolean useDaylightTime()

■ ■ **class TooManyListenersException extends Exception**
■ ■ TooManyListenersException()

■ ■ TooManyListenersException(String)

■ ■ **class TreeMap extends AbstractMap implements java.io.Serializable , Cloneable , SortedMap**
■ ■ TreeMap()
■ ■ TreeMap(Comparator)
■ ■ TreeMap(Map)
■ ■ TreeMap(SortedMap)
■ ■ Object clone()
■ ■ Comparator comparator()

■ ■ Set entrySet()
■ ■ Object firstKey()
■ ■ SortedMap headMap(Object)
■ ■ Object lastKey()
■ ■ SortedMap subMap(Object,Object)
■ ■ SortedMap tailMap(Object)

■ ■ **class TreeSet extends AbstractSet implements java.io.Serializable , Cloneable , SortedSet**
■ ■ TreeSet()
■ ■ TreeSet(Collection)
■ ■ TreeSet(Comparator)
■ ■ TreeSet(SortedSet)
■ ■ Object clone()
■ ■ Comparator comparator()
■ ■ Object first()

■ ■ SortedSet headSet(Object)
■ ■ Iterator iterator()
■ ■ Object last()
■ ■ int size()
■ ■ SortedSet subSet(Object,Object)
■ ■ SortedSet tailSet(Object)

■ ■ **class Vector extends AbstractList implements java.io.Serializable , Cloneable , List , RandomAccess**
■ ■ Vector()
■ ■ Vector(int)
■ ■ Vector(int,int)
■ ■ Vector(Collection)
■ ■ void addElement(Object)

■ ■ int capacity()
■ ■ protected int capacityIncrement
■ ■ Object clone()
■ ■ void copyInto(Object[])
■ ■ Object elementAt(int)

■ ■ protected int elementCount
■ ■ protected Object[] elementData
■ ■ Enumeration elements()
■ ■ void ensureCapacity(int)
■ ■ Object firstElement()
■ ■ Object get(int)
■ ■ int indexOf(Object,int)
■ ■ void insertElementAt(Object,int)
■ ■ Object lastElement()

■ ■ int lastIndexOf(Object,int)
■ ■ void removeAllElements()
■ ■ boolean removeElement(Object)
■ ■ void removeElementAt(int)
■ ■ void setElementAt(Object,int)
■ ■ void setSize(int)
■ ■ int size()
■ ■ void trimToSize()

■ ■ **class WeakHashMap extends AbstractMap implements Map**
■ ■ WeakHashMap()
■ ■ WeakHashMap(int)
■ ■ WeakHashMap(int,float)

■ ■ WeakHashMap(Map)
■ ■ Set entrySet()

999.3.14   java.util.jar

■ ■ **package java.util.jar**
■ ■ **class Attributes implements Cloneable , java.util.Map**
■ ■ Attributes()
■ ■ Attributes(int)
■ ■ Attributes(Attributes)
■ ■ void clear()
■ ■ Object clone()
■ ■ boolean containsKey(Object)
■ ■ boolean containsValue(Object)
■ ■ java.util.Set entrySet()
■ ■ Object get(Object)
■ ■ String getValue(String)

■ ■ String getValue(Attributes.Name)
■ ■ boolean isEmpty()
■ ■ java.util.Set keySet()
■ ■ protected java.util.Map map
■ ■ Object put(Object,Object)
■ ■ void putAll(java.util.Map)
■ ■ String putValue(String,String)
■ ■ Object remove(Object)
■ ■ int size()
■ ■ java.util.Collection values()

■ ■ **class Attributes.Name**
■ ■ Attributes.Name(String)
■ ■ final static Attributes.Name CLASS_PATH
■ ■ final static Attributes.Name CONTENT_TYPE
■ ■ final static Attributes.Name EXTENSION_INSTALLATION
■ ■ final static Attributes.Name EXTENSION_LIST
■ ■ final static Attributes.Name EXTENSION_NAME
■ ■ final static Attributes.Name IMPLEMENTATION_TITLE
■ ■ final static Attributes.Name IMPLEMENTATION_URL
■ ■ final static Attributes.Name IMPLEMENTATION_VENDOR

■ ■ final static Attributes.Name IMPLEMENTATION_VENDOR_ID
■ ■ final static Attributes.Name IMPLEMENTATION_VERSION
■ ■ final static Attributes.Name MAIN_CLASS
■ ■ final static Attributes.Name MANIFEST_VERSION
■ ■ final static Attributes.Name SEALED
■ ■ final static Attributes.Name SIGNATURE_VERSION
■ ■ final static Attributes.Name SPECIFICATION_TITLE
■ ■ final static Attributes.Name SPECIFICATION_VENDOR
■ ■ final static Attributes.Name SPECIFICATION_VERSION

■ ■ **class JarEntry extends java.util.zip.ZipEntry**
■ ■ JarEntry(String)
■ ■ JarEntry(JarEntry)
■ ■ JarEntry(java.util.zip.ZipEntry)

■ ■ Attributes getAttributes() throws java.io.IOException
■ ■ java.security.cert.Certificate[] getCertificates()

■ ■ **class JarException extends java.util.zip.ZipException**
■ ■ JarException()

■ ■ JarException(String)

■ ■ **class JarFile extends java.util.zip.ZipFile**
■ ■ JarFile(java.io.File) throws java.io.IOException
■ ■ JarFile(java.io.File,boolean) throws java.io.IOException
■ ■ JarFile(java.io.File,boolean,int) throws java.io.IOException
■ ■ JarFile(String) throws java.io.IOException

■ ■ JarFile(String,boolean) throws java.io.IOException
■ ■ JarEntry getJarEntry(String)
■ ■ Manifest getManifest() throws java.io.IOException
■ ■ final static String MANIFEST_NAME

■ ■ **class JarInputStream extends java.util.zip.ZipInputStream**
■ ■ JarInputStream(java.io.InputStream) throws java.io.IOException
■ ■ JarInputStream(java.io.InputStream,boolean) throws
java.io.IOException

■ ■ Manifest getManifest()
■ ■ JarEntry getNextJarEntry() throws java.io.IOException

■ ■ **class JarOutputStream extends java.util.zip.ZipOutputStream**
■ ■ JarOutputStream(java.io.OutputStream) throws java.io.IOException

■ ■ JarOutputStream(java.io.OutputStream,Manifest) throws
java.io.IOException

■ ■ **class Manifest implements Cloneable**
■ ■ Manifest()
■ ■ Manifest(java.io.InputStream) throws java.io.IOException
■ ■ Manifest(Manifest)
■ ■ void clear()
■ ■ Object clone()

■ ■ Attributes getAttributes(String)
■ ■ java.util.Map getEntries()
■ ■ Attributes getMainAttributes()
■ ■ void read(java.io.InputStream) throws java.io.IOException
■ ■ void write(java.io.OutputStream) throws java.io.IOException

999.3.15   java.util.zip

■ ■ **package java.util.zip**
■ ■ **class Adler32 implements Checksum**
■ ■ Adler32()
■ ■ long getValue()
■ ■ void reset()

■ ■ void update(byte[])
■ ■ void update(byte[],int,int)
■ ■ void update(int)

■ ■ **class CheckedInputStream extends java.io.FilterInputStream**
■ ■ CheckedInputStream(java.io.InputStream,Checksum)

■ ■ Checksum getChecksum()

■ ■ **class CheckedOutputStream extends java.io.FilterOutputStream**
■ ■ CheckedOutputStream(java.io.OutputStream,Checksum)

■ ■ Checksum getChecksum()

■ ■ **interface Checksum**
■ ■ abstract long getValue()
■ ■ abstract void reset()

■ ■ **class CRC32 implements Checksum**
■ ■ CRC32()
■ ■ long getValue()
■ ■ void reset()

■ ■ **class DataFormatException extends Exception**
■ ■ DataFormatException()

■ ■ **class Deflater**
■ ■ Deflater()
■ ■ Deflater(int)
■ ■ Deflater(int,boolean)
■ ■ final static int BEST_COMPRESSION
■ ■ final static int BEST_SPEED
■ ■ final static int DEFAULT_COMPRESSION
■ ■ final static int DEFAULT_STRATEGY
■ ■ int deflate(byte[])
■ ■ int deflate(byte[],int,int)
■ ■ final static int DEFLATED
■ ■ void end()
■ ■ final static int FILTERED
■ ■ protected void finalize()
■ ■ void finish()

■ ■ **class DeflaterOutputStream extends java.io.FilterOutputStream**
■ ■ DeflaterOutputStream(java.io.OutputStream)
■ ■ DeflaterOutputStream(java.io.OutputStream,Deflater)
■ ■ DeflaterOutputStream(java.io.OutputStream,Deflater,int)
■ ■ protected byte[] buf

■ ■ **class GZIPInputStream extends InflaterInputStream**
■ ■ GZIPInputStream(java.io.InputStream) throws java.io.IOException
■ ■ GZIPInputStream(java.io.InputStream,int) throws java.io.IOException
■ ■ protected CRC32 crc

■ ■ **class GZIPOutputStream extends DeflaterOutputStream**
■ ■ GZIPOutputStream(java.io.OutputStream) throws
java.io.IOException

■ ■ **class Inflater**
■ ■ Inflater()
■ ■ Inflater(boolean)
■ ■ void end()
■ ■ protected void finalize()
■ ■ boolean finished()
■ ■ int getAdler()
■ ■ int getRemaining()
■ ■ int getTotalIn()
■ ■ int getTotalOut()

■ ■ **class InflaterInputStream extends java.io.FilterInputStream**
■ ■ InflaterInputStream(java.io.InputStream)
■ ■ InflaterInputStream(java.io.InputStream,Inflater)
■ ■ InflaterInputStream(java.io.InputStream,Inflater,int)
■ ■ protected byte[] buf

■ ■ **class ZipEntry implements Cloneable , ZipConstants**
■ ■ ZipEntry(String)
■ ■ ZipEntry(ZipEntry)
■ ■ Object clone()
■ ■ final static int DEFLATED
■ ■ String getComment()
■ ■ long getCompressedSize()
■ ■ long getCrc()
■ ■ byte[] getExtra()
■ ■ int getMethod()
■ ■ String getName()
■ ■ long getSize()

■ ■ **class ZipException extends java.io.IOException**
■ ■ ZipException()

■ ■ **class ZipFile implements ZipConstants**
■ ■ ZipFile(java.io.File) throws java.io.IOException
■ ■ ZipFile(java.io.File,int) throws java.io.IOException
■ ■ ZipFile(String) throws java.io.IOException
■ ■ void close() throws java.io.IOException
■ ■ java.util.Enumeration entries()
■ ■ protected void finalize() throws java.io.IOException
■ ■ ZipEntry getEntry(String)

■ ■ abstract void update(byte[],int,int)
■ ■ abstract void update(int)

■ ■ void update(byte[])
■ ■ void update(byte[],int,int)
■ ■ void update(int)

■ ■ DataFormatException(String)

■ ■ boolean finished()
■ ■ int getAdler()
■ ■ int getTotalIn()
■ ■ int getTotalOut()
■ ■ final static int HUFFMAN_ONLY
■ ■ boolean needsInput()
■ ■ final static int NO_COMPRESSION
■ ■ void reset()
■ ■ void setDictionary(byte[])
■ ■ void setDictionary(byte[],int,int)
■ ■ void setInput(byte[])
■ ■ void setInput(byte[],int,int)
■ ■ void setLevel(int)
■ ■ void setStrategy(int)

■ ■ protected Deflater def
■ ■ protected void deflate() throws java.io.IOException
■ ■ void finish() throws java.io.IOException

■ ■ protected boolean eos
■ ■ final static int GZIP_MAGIC

■ ■ GZIPOutputStream(java.io.OutputStream,int) throws
java.io.IOException
■ ■ protected CRC32 crc

■ ■ int inflate(byte[]) throws DataFormatException
■ ■ int inflate(byte[],int,int) throws DataFormatException
■ ■ boolean needsDictionary()
■ ■ boolean needsInput()
■ ■ void reset()
■ ■ void setDictionary(byte[])
■ ■ void setDictionary(byte[],int,int)
■ ■ void setInput(byte[])
■ ■ void setInput(byte[],int,int)

■ ■ protected void fill() throws java.io.IOException
■ ■ protected Inflater inf
■ ■ protected int len

■ ■ long getTime()
■ ■ boolean isDirectory()
■ ■ void setComment(String)
■ ■ void setCompressedSize(long)
■ ■ void setCrc(long)
■ ■ void setExtra(byte[])
■ ■ void setMethod(int)
■ ■ void setSize(long)
■ ■ void setTime(long)
■ ■ final static int STORED

■ ■ ZipException(String)

■ ■ java.io.InputStream getInputStream(ZipEntry) throws
java.io.IOException
■ ■ String getName()
■ ■ final static int OPEN_DELETE
■ ■ final static int OPEN_READ
■ ■ int size()

■ ■ **class ZipInputStream extends InflaterInputStream implements ZipConstants**
■ ■ ZipInputStream(java.io.InputStream)
■ ■ protected ZipEntry createZipEntry(String)
■ ■ void closeEntry() throws java.io.IOException
■ ■ ZipEntry getNextEntry() throws java.io.IOException

■ ■ **class ZipOutputStream extends DeflaterOutputStream implements ZipConstants**
■ ■ ZipOutputStream(java.io.OutputStream)
■ ■ void setComment(String)
■ ■ void closeEntry() throws java.io.IOException
■ ■ void setLevel(int)
■ ■ final static int DEFLATED
■ ■ void setMethod(int)
■ ■ void putNextEntry(ZipEntry) throws java.io.IOException
■ ■ final static int STORED

999.3.16   javax.microedition.io

□ ■ **package javax.microedition.io**
□ ■ **interface CommConnection extends StreamConnection**
□ ■ abstract int getBaudRate()
□ ■ abstract int setBaudRate(int)

□ ■ **interface Connection**
□ ■ abstract void close() throws java.io.IOException

□ ■ **class ConnectionNotFoundException extends java.io.IOException**
□ ■ ConnectionNotFoundException()
□ ■ ConnectionNotFoundException(String)

□ ■ **class Connector**
□ ■ static Connection open(String) throws java.io.IOException
□ ■ static java.io.InputStream openInputStream(String) throws java.io.IOException
□ ■ static Connection open(String,int) throws java.io.IOException
□ ■ static Connection open(String,int,boolean) throws java.io.IOException
□ ■ static java.io.OutputStream openOutputStream(String) throws java.io.IOException
□ ■ static java.io.DataInputStream openDataInputStream(String) throws java.io.IOException
□ ■ final static int READ
□ ■ final static int READ_WRITE
□ ■ static java.io.DataOutputStream openDataOutputStream(String) throws java.io.IOException
□ ■ final static int WRITE

□ ■ **interface ContentConnection extends StreamConnection**
□ ■ abstract String getEncoding()
□ ■ abstract String getType()
□ ■ abstract long getLength()

□ ■ **interface Datagram extends java.io.DataInput , java.io.DataOutput**
□ ■ abstract String getAddress()
□ ■ abstract void setAddress(String) throws java.io.IOException
□ ■ abstract byte[] getData()
□ ■ abstract void setAddress(Datagram)
□ ■ abstract int getLength()
□ ■ abstract void setData(byte[],int,int)
□ ■ abstract int getOffset()
□ ■ abstract void setLength(int)
□ ■ abstract void reset()

□ ■ **interface DatagramConnection extends Connection**
□ ■ abstract int getMaximumLength() throws java.io.IOException
□ ■ abstract Datagram newDatagram(int) throws java.io.IOException
□ ■ abstract int getNominalLength() throws java.io.IOException
□ ■ abstract Datagram newDatagram(int,String) throws java.io.IOException
□ ■ abstract Datagram newDatagram(byte[],int) throws java.io.IOException
□ ■ abstract void receive(Datagram) throws java.io.IOException
□ ■ abstract Datagram newDatagram(byte[],int,String) throws java.io.IOException
□ ■ abstract void send(Datagram) throws java.io.IOException

□ ■ **interface HttpConnection extends ContentConnection**
□ ■ final static String GET
□ ■ final static int HTTP_EXPECT_FAILED
□ ■ abstract long getDate() throws java.io.IOException
□ ■ final static int HTTP_FORBIDDEN
□ ■ abstract long getExpiration() throws java.io.IOException
□ ■ final static int HTTP_GATEWAY_TIMEOUT
□ ■ abstract String getFile()
□ ■ final static int HTTP_GONE
□ ■ abstract String getHeaderField(int) throws java.io.IOException
□ ■ final static int HTTP_INTERNAL_ERROR
□ ■ abstract String getHeaderField(String) throws java.io.IOException
□ ■ final static int HTTP_LENGTH_REQUIRED
□ ■ abstract long getHeaderFieldDate(String,long) throws java.io.IOException
□ ■ final static int HTTP_MOVED_PERM
□ ■ final static int HTTP_MOVED_TEMP
□ ■ abstract int getHeaderFieldInt(String,int) throws java.io.IOException
□ ■ final static int HTTP_MULT_CHOICE
□ ■ abstract String getHeaderFieldKey(int) throws java.io.IOException
□ ■ final static int HTTP_NO_CONTENT
□ ■ abstract String getHost()
□ ■ final static int HTTP_NOT_ACCEPTABLE
□ ■ abstract long getLastModified() throws java.io.IOException
□ ■ final static int HTTP_NOT_AUTHORITATIVE
□ ■ abstract int getPort()
□ ■ final static int HTTP_NOT_FOUND
□ ■ abstract String getProtocol()
□ ■ final static int HTTP_NOT_IMPLEMENTED
□ ■ abstract String getQuery()
□ ■ final static int HTTP_NOT_MODIFIED
□ ■ abstract String getRef()
□ ■ final static int HTTP_OK
□ ■ abstract String getRequestMethod()
□ ■ final static int HTTP_PARTIAL
□ ■ abstract String getRequestProperty(String)
□ ■ final static int HTTP_PAYMENT_REQUIRED
□ ■ abstract int getResponseCode() throws java.io.IOException
□ ■ final static int HTTP_PRECON_FAILED
□ ■ abstract String getResponseMessage() throws java.io.IOException
□ ■ final static int HTTP_PROXY_AUTH
□ ■ abstract String getURL()
□ ■ final static int HTTP_REQ_TOO_LONG
□ ■ final static String HEAD
□ ■ final static int HTTP_RESET
□ ■ final static int HTTP_ACCEPTED
□ ■ final static int HTTP_SEE_OTHER
□ ■ final static int HTTP_BAD_GATEWAY
□ ■ final static int HTTP_TEMP_REDIRECT
□ ■ final static int HTTP_BAD_METHOD
□ ■ final static int HTTP_UNAUTHORIZED
□ ■ final static int HTTP_BAD_REQUEST
□ ■ final static int HTTP_UNAVAILABLE
□ ■ final static int HTTP_CLIENT_TIMEOUT
□ ■ final static int HTTP_UNSUPPORTED_RANGE
□ ■ final static int HTTP_CONFLICT
□ ■ final static int HTTP_UNSUPPORTED_TYPE
□ ■ final static int HTTP_CREATED
□ ■ final static int HTTP_USE_PROXY
□ ■ final static int HTTP_ENTITY_TOO_LARGE
□ ■ final static int HTTP_VERSION

☐ ■ final static String POST
☐ ■ abstract void setRequestMethod(String) throws java.io.IOException

☐ ■ abstract void setRequestProperty(String,String) throws java.io.IOException

☐ ■ **interface HttpsConnection extends HttpConnection**
☐ ■ abstract SecurityInfo getSecurityInfo() throws java.io.IOException

☐ ■ **interface InputConnection extends Connection**
☐ ■ abstract java.io.DataInputStream openDataInputStream() throws java.io.IOException

☐ ■ abstract java.io.InputStream openInputStream() throws java.io.IOException

☐ ■ **interface OutputConnection extends Connection**
☐ ■ abstract java.io.DataOutputStream openDataOutputStream() throws java.io.IOException

☐ ■ abstract java.io.OutputStream openOutputStream() throws java.io.IOException

☐ ■ **interface SecureConnection extends SocketConnection**
☐ ■ abstract SecurityInfo getSecurityInfo() throws java.io.IOException

☐ ■ **interface SecurityInfo**
☐ ■ abstract String getCipherSuite()
☐ ■ abstract String getProtocolName()

☐ ■ abstract String getProtocolVersion()
☐ ■ abstract javax.microedition.pki.Certificate getServerCertificate()

☐ ■ **interface ServerSocketConnection extends StreamConnectionNotifier**
☐ ■ abstract String getLocalAddress() throws java.io.IOException

☐ ■ abstract int getLocalPort() throws java.io.IOException

☐ ■ **interface SocketConnection extends StreamConnection**
☐ ■ final static byte DELAY
☐ ■ abstract String getAddress() throws java.io.IOException
☐ ■ abstract String getLocalAddress() throws java.io.IOException
☐ ■ abstract int getLocalPort() throws java.io.IOException
☐ ■ abstract int getPort() throws java.io.IOException
☐ ■ abstract int getSocketOption(byte) throws java.io.IOException

☐ ■ final static byte KEEPALIVE
☐ ■ final static byte LINGER
☐ ■ final static byte RCVBUF
☐ ■ abstract void setSocketOption(byte,int) throws java.io.IOException
☐ ■ final static byte SNDBUF

☐ ■ **interface StreamConnection extends InputConnection , OutputConnection**

☐ ■ **interface StreamConnectionNotifier extends Connection**
☐ ■ abstract StreamConnection acceptAndOpen() throws java.io.IOException

☐ ■ **interface UDPDatagramConnection extends DatagramConnection**
☐ ■ abstract String getLocalAddress() throws java.io.IOException

☐ ■ abstract int getLocalPort() throws java.io.IOException

999.3.17 javax.microedition.pki

☐ ■ **package javax.microedition.pki**
☐ ■ **interface Certificate**
☐ ■ abstract String getIssuer()
☐ ■ abstract long getNotAfter()
☐ ■ abstract long getNotBefore()
☐ ■ abstract String getSerialNumber()

☐ ■ abstract String getSigAlgName()
☐ ■ abstract String getSubject()
☐ ■ abstract String getType()
☐ ■ abstract String getVersion()

☐ ■ **class CertificateException extends java.io.IOException**
☐ ■ CertificateException(String,Certificate,byte)
☐ ■ CertificateException(Certificate,byte)
☐ ■ final static byte BAD_EXTENSIONS
☐ ■ final static byte BROKEN_CHAIN
☐ ■ final static byte CERTIFICATE_CHAIN_TOO_LONG
☐ ■ final static byte EXPIRED
☐ ■ Certificate getCertificate()
☐ ■ byte getReason()
☐ ■ final static byte INAPPROPRIATE_KEY_USAGE

☐ ■ final static byte MISSING_SIGNATURE
☐ ■ final static byte NOT_YET_VALID
☐ ■ final static byte ROOT_CA_EXPIRED
☐ ■ final static byte SITENAME_MISMATCH
☐ ■ final static byte UNAUTHORIZED_INTERMEDIATE_CA
☐ ■ final static byte UNRECOGNIZED_ISSUER
☐ ■ final static byte UNSUPPORTED_PUBLIC_KEY_TYPE
☐ ■ final static byte UNSUPPORTED_SIGALG
☐ ■ final static byte VERIFICATION_FAILED

999.3.18 javax.security.auth.x500

■ ■ **package javax.security.auth.x500**
■ ■ **final class X500Principal implements java.io.Serializable , java.security.Principal**
■ ■ X500Principal(byte[])
■ ■ X500Principal(java.io.InputStream)
■ ■ X500Principal(String)
■ ■ final static String CANONICAL
■ ■ byte[] getEncoded()

■ ■ String getName()
■ ■ String getName(String)
■ ■ final static String RFC1779
■ ■ final static String RFC2253

999.4 Changes

The following section detail the changes in the changed execution environments. A + indicates a new declaration, a - indicate a deprecated declaration, and ~ means a modification. Classes that are modified are marked with (~).

999.4.1 Changes for ee.minimum from 1.1.3 to 1.2.0

999.4.1.1 New Packages

java.math
java.security.acl
java.security.interfaces
java.security.spec

java.text
java.util.jar
javax.security.auth.x500

999.4.1.2 New Classes and Interfaces

java.io.CharArrayReader
java.io.CharArrayWriter
java.io.FileFilter
java.io.FilenameFilter
java.io.FilterReader
java.io.FilterWriter
java.io.LineNumberReader
java.io.PipedInputStream
java.io.PipedOutputStream
java.io.PipedReader
java.io.PipedWriter
java.io.PushbackReader
java.io.SequenceInputStream
java.io.StreamTokenizer
java.lang.AssertionError
java.lang.Character$Subset
java.lang.Character$UnicodeBlock
java.lang.CharSequence
java.lang.Compiler
java.lang.Package
java.lang.StackTraceElement
java.lang.StrictMath
java.lang.UnsupportedClassVersionError
java.net.DatagramSocketImplFactory
java.net.Inet4Address
java.net.Inet6Address
java.net.InetSocketAddress
java.net.NetworkInterface
java.net.PortUnreachableException
java.net.SocketAddress
java.net.SocketTimeoutException
java.net.URI
java.net.URISyntaxException
java.security.AlgorithmParameterGenerator
java.security.AlgorithmParameterGeneratorSpi
java.security.AlgorithmParameters
java.security.AlgorithmParametersSpi
java.security.cert.CertificateExpiredException
java.security.cert.CertificateFactory
java.security.cert.CertificateFactorySpi
java.security.cert.CertificateNotYetValidException
java.security.cert.CertificateParsingException
java.security.cert.CertPath
java.security.cert.CertPath$CertPathRep
java.security.cert.CRL
java.security.cert.CRLException
java.security.cert.X509Certificate
java.security.cert.X509CRL
java.security.cert.X509CRLEntry

java.security.cert.X509Extension
java.security.Certificate
java.security.DigestException
java.security.DigestInputStream
java.security.DigestOutputStream
java.security.DomainCombiner
java.security.Identity
java.security.IdentityScope
java.security.InvalidAlgorithmParameterException
java.security.KeyFactory
java.security.KeyFactorySpi
java.security.KeyManagementException
java.security.KeyPair
java.security.KeyPairGenerator
java.security.KeyPairGeneratorSpi
java.security.KeyStore
java.security.KeyStoreException
java.security.KeyStoreSpi
java.security.MessageDigest
java.security.MessageDigestSpi
java.security.PrivateKey
java.security.ProviderException
java.security.SecureRandom
java.security.SecureRandomSpi
java.security.Signature
java.security.SignatureSpi
java.security.SignedObject
java.security.Signer
java.security.UnrecoverableKeyException
java.util.BitSet
java.util.Currency
java.util.EventListenerProxy
java.util.IdentityHashMap
java.util.LinkedHashMap
java.util.LinkedHashSet
java.util.Observable
java.util.Observer
java.util.RandomAccess
java.util.Timer
java.util.TimerTask
java.util.TooManyListenersException
java.util.zip.Adler32
java.util.zip.CheckedInputStream
java.util.zip.CheckedOutputStream
java.util.zip.Deflater
java.util.zip.DeflaterOutputStream
java.util.zip.GZIPInputStream
java.util.zip.GZIPOutputStream
java.util.zip.ZipOutputStream

999.4.1.3 Modified Classes and Interfaces

java.io.ByteArrayOutputStream
+ java.lang.String toString(java.lang.String) throws
java.io.UnsupportedEncodingException

java.io.File
+ File(java.net.URI)
+ static java.io.File createTempFile(java.lang.String, java.lang.String)
throws java.io.IOException
+ java.io.File getAbsoluteFile()
+ java.io.File getCanonicalFile() throws java.io.IOException
+ boolean isHidden()

+ java.lang.String[] list(java.io.FilenameFilter)
+ java.io.File[] listFiles(java.io.FileFilter)
+ java.io.File[] listFiles(java.io.FilenameFilter)
+ boolean setReadOnly()
+ java.net.URI toURI()

java.io.FileOutputStream
+ FileOutputStream(java.io.File, boolean)java.io.FileNotFoundException

java.io.FileWriter
+ FileWriter(java.io.File, boolean)java.io.IOException

java.io.ObjectInputStream
+ java.lang.Object readUnshared() throws java.io.IOException,
java.lang.ClassNotFoundException

java.io.ObjectOutputStream
+ void writeUnshared(java.lang.Object) throws java.io.IOException

java.io.ObjectOutputStream$PutField
- void write(java.io.ObjectOutput) throws java.io.IOException

java.io.ObjectStreamField
+ ObjectStreamField(java.lang.String, java.lang.Class, boolean)

java.io.PrintStream
+ PrintStream(java.io.OutputStream, boolean,
java.lang.String)java.io.UnsupportedEncodingException

java.lang.Boolean
+ static java.lang.String toString(boolean)

+ static java.lang.Boolean valueOf(boolean)

java.lang.Byte
+ static java.lang.Byte decode(java.lang.String)
+ static java.lang.String toString(byte)

+ static java.lang.Byte valueOf(java.lang.String)

java.lang.Character
+ static byte DIRECTIONALITY_ARABIC_NUMBER
+ static byte DIRECTIONALITY_BOUNDARY_NEUTRAL
+ static byte DIRECTIONALITY_COMMON_NUMBER_SEPARATOR
+ static byte DIRECTIONALITY_EUROPEAN_NUMBER
+ static byte DIRECTIONALITY_EUROPEAN_NUMBER_SEPARATOR
+ static byte DIRECTIONALITY_EUROPEAN_NUMBER_TERMINATOR
+ static byte DIRECTIONALITY_LEFT_TO_RIGHT
+ static byte DIRECTIONALITY_LEFT_TO_RIGHT_EMBEDDING
+ static byte DIRECTIONALITY_LEFT_TO_RIGHT_OVERRIDE
+ static byte DIRECTIONALITY_NONSPACING_MARK
+ static byte DIRECTIONALITY_OTHER_NEUTRALS
+ static byte DIRECTIONALITY_PARAGRAPH_SEPARATOR
+ static byte DIRECTIONALITY_POP_DIRECTIONAL_FORMAT
+ static byte DIRECTIONALITY_RIGHT_TO_LEFT
+ static byte DIRECTIONALITY_RIGHT_TO_LEFT_ARABIC
+ static byte DIRECTIONALITY_RIGHT_TO_LEFT_EMBEDDING
+ static byte DIRECTIONALITY_RIGHT_TO_LEFT_OVERRIDE
+ static byte DIRECTIONALITY_SEGMENT_SEPARATOR

+ static byte DIRECTIONALITY_UNDEFINED
+ static byte DIRECTIONALITY_WHITESPACE
+ static byte FINAL_QUOTE_PUNCTUATION
+ static byte INITIAL_QUOTE_PUNCTUATION
+ static byte getDirectionality(char)
+ static int getNumericValue(char)
+ static boolean isDefined(char)
+ static boolean isISOControl(char)
+ static boolean isIdentifierIgnorable(char)
+ static boolean isJavaIdentifierPart(char)
+ static boolean isJavaIdentifierStart(char)
+ static boolean isMirrored(char)
+ static boolean isTitleCase(char)
+ static boolean isUnicodeIdentifierPart(char)
+ static boolean isUnicodeIdentifierStart(char)
+ static java.lang.String toString(char)
+ static char toTitleCase(char)

java.lang.Class
+ boolean desiredAssertionStatus()

+ java.lang.Package getPackage()

java.lang.ClassLoader
+ void clearAssertionStatus()
+ java.lang.Package definePackage(java.lang.String, java.lang.String,
java.lang.String, java.lang.String, java.lang.String, java.lang.String,
java.lang.String, java.net.URL)
+ java.lang.Package getPackage(java.lang.String)

+ java.lang.Package[] getPackages()
+ void setClassAssertionStatus(java.lang.String, boolean)
+ void setDefaultAssertionStatus(boolean)
+ void setPackageAssertionStatus(java.lang.String, boolean)

java.lang.Double
+ static int compare(double, double)

+ static long doubleToRawLongBits(double)

java.lang.Error
+ Error(java.lang.String, java.lang.Throwable)

+ Error(java.lang.Throwable)

java.lang.Exception
+ Exception(java.lang.String, java.lang.Throwable)

+ Exception(java.lang.Throwable)

java.lang.Float
+ static int compare(float, float)

+ static int floatToRawIntBits(float)

java.lang.Integer
+ static java.lang.Integer getInteger(java.lang.String, java.lang.Integer)

java.lang.Long
+ static java.lang.Long decode(java.lang.String)
+ static java.lang.Long getLong(java.lang.String)
+ static java.lang.Long getLong(java.lang.String, java.lang.Long)

+ static java.lang.Long getLong(java.lang.String, long)
+ static java.lang.String toOctalString(long)
+ static java.lang.Long valueOf(java.lang.String)

java.lang.Runtime
+ void addShutdownHook(java.lang.Thread)
+ int availableProcessors()
+ java.lang.Process exec(java.lang.String, java.lang.String[], java.io.File)
throws java.io.IOException
+ java.lang.Process exec(java.lang.String[], java.lang.String[], java.io.File)
throws java.io.IOException

+ void halt(int)
+ long maxMemory()
+ boolean removeShutdownHook(java.lang.Thread)
+ void traceInstructions(boolean)
+ void traceMethodCalls(boolean)

java.lang.RuntimeException
+ RuntimeException(java.lang.String, java.lang.Throwable)

+ RuntimeException(java.lang.Throwable)

java.lang.SecurityManager
- void checkMulticast(java.net.InetAddress, byte)

java.lang.Short
+ static java.lang.Short decode(java.lang.String)
+ static java.lang.String toString(short)

+ static java.lang.Short valueOf(java.lang.String)

java.lang.String (-)

+ boolean contentEquals(java.lang.StringBuffer)
+ static java.lang.String copyValueOf(char[])

+ static java.lang.String copyValueOf(char[], int, int)
+ java.lang.CharSequence subSequence(int, int)

java.lang.StringBuffer (-)
+ java.lang.StringBuffer append(java.lang.StringBuffer)
+ int indexOf(java.lang.String)
+ int indexOf(java.lang.String, int)
+ java.lang.StringBuffer insert(int, char[], int, int)
+ int lastIndexOf(java.lang.String)

+ int lastIndexOf(java.lang.String, int)
+ java.lang.StringBuffer replace(int, int, java.lang.String)
+ java.lang.CharSequence subSequence(int, int)
+ java.lang.String substring(int)

java.lang.System
+ static void load(java.lang.String)

+ static java.lang.String setProperty(java.lang.String, java.lang.String)

java.lang.Thread
+ Thread(java.lang.ThreadGroup, java.lang.Runnable, java.lang.String, long)
+ void destroy()

+ static void dumpStack()
+ static int enumerate(java.lang.Thread[])
+ static boolean holdsLock(java.lang.Object)

java.lang.ThreadGroup
+ void interrupt()

java.lang.Throwable
+ Throwable(java.lang.String, java.lang.Throwable)
+ Throwable(java.lang.Throwable)
+ java.lang.Throwable getCause()

+ java.lang.StackTraceElement[] getStackTrace()
+ java.lang.Throwable initCause(java.lang.Throwable)
+ void setStackTrace(java.lang.StackTraceElement[])

java.net.Authenticator
+ java.lang.String getRequestingHost()

+ static java.net.PasswordAuthentication requestPasswordAuthentication(java.lang.String, java.net.InetAddress, int, java.lang.String, java.lang.String, java.lang.String)

java.net.ContentHandler
+ java.lang.Object getContent(java.net.URLConnection, java.lang.Class[]) throws java.io.IOException

java.net.DatagramPacket
+ DatagramPacket(byte[], int, int, java.net.SocketAddress)java.net.SocketException
+ DatagramPacket(byte[], int, java.net.SocketAddress)java.net.SocketException

+ java.net.SocketAddress getSocketAddress()
+ void setSocketAddress(java.net.SocketAddress)

java.net.DatagramSocket
+ DatagramSocket(java.net.DatagramSocketImpl)
+ DatagramSocket(java.net.SocketAddress)java.net.SocketException
+ void bind(java.net.SocketAddress) throws java.net.SocketException
+ void connect(java.net.SocketAddress) throws java.net.SocketException
+ boolean getBroadcast() throws java.net.SocketException
+ java.net.SocketAddress getLocalSocketAddress()
+ java.net.SocketAddress getRemoteSocketAddress()
+ boolean getReuseAddress() throws java.net.SocketException
+ int getTrafficClass() throws java.net.SocketException

+ boolean isBound()
+ boolean isClosed()
+ boolean isConnected()
+ void setBroadcast(boolean) throws java.net.SocketException
+ static void setDatagramSocketImplFactory(java.net.DatagramSocketImplFactory) throws java.io.IOException
+ void setReuseAddress(boolean) throws java.net.SocketException
+ void setTrafficClass(int) throws java.net.SocketException

java.net.DatagramSocketImpl
+ void connect(java.net.InetAddress, int) throws java.net.SocketException
+ void disconnect()
+ void joinGroup(java.net.SocketAddress, java.net.NetworkInterface) throws java.io.IOException

+ void leaveGroup(java.net.SocketAddress, java.net.NetworkInterface) throws java.io.IOException
+ int peekData(java.net.DatagramPacket) throws java.io.IOException

java.net.HttpURLConnection
+ boolean instanceFollowRedirects
+ boolean getInstanceFollowRedirects()

+ void setInstanceFollowRedirects(boolean)

java.net.InetAddress (-)
+ static java.net.InetAddress getByAddress(byte[]) throws java.net.UnknownHostException
+ static java.net.InetAddress getByAddress(java.lang.String, byte[]) throws java.net.UnknownHostException
+ java.lang.String getCanonicalHostName()
+ boolean isAnyLocalAddress()
+ boolean isLinkLocalAddress()
+ boolean isLoopbackAddress()

+ boolean isMCGlobal()
+ boolean isMCLinkLocal()
+ boolean isMCNodeLocal()
+ boolean isMCOrgLocal()
+ boolean isMCSiteLocal()
+ boolean isSiteLocalAddress()
- InetAddress()

java.net.JarURLConnection
+ java.util.jar.Attributes getAttributes() throws java.io.IOException
+ java.security.cert.Certificate[] getCertificates() throws java.io.IOException
+ java.util.jar.JarEntry getJarEntry() throws java.io.IOException

+ java.util.jar.JarFile getJarFile() throws java.io.IOException
+ java.util.jar.Attributes getMainAttributes() throws java.io.IOException
+ java.util.jar.Manifest getManifest() throws java.io.IOException

java.net.MulticastSocket
+ MulticastSocket(java.net.SocketAddress)java.io.IOException
+ boolean getLoopbackMode() throws java.net.SocketException
+ java.net.NetworkInterface getNetworkInterface() throws java.net.SocketException
+ void joinGroup(java.net.SocketAddress, java.net.NetworkInterface) throws java.io.IOException

+ void leaveGroup(java.net.SocketAddress, java.net.NetworkInterface) throws java.io.IOException
+ void setLoopbackMode(boolean) throws java.net.SocketException
+ void setNetworkInterface(java.net.NetworkInterface) throws java.net.SocketException
- void send(java.net.DatagramPacket, byte) throws java.io.IOException

java.net.ServerSocket
+ ServerSocket()java.io.IOException

+ void bind(java.net.SocketAddress) throws java.io.IOException

java.net.Socket
+ void bind(java.net.SocketAddress, int) throws java.io.IOException
+ java.net.SocketAddress getLocalSocketAddress()
+ int getReceiveBufferSize() throws java.net.SocketException
+ boolean getReuseAddress() throws java.net.SocketException

+ boolean isBound()
+ boolean isClosed()
+ void setReceiveBufferSize(int) throws java.net.SocketException
+ void setReuseAddress(boolean) throws java.net.SocketException

java.net.Socket
+ void bind(java.net.SocketAddress) throws java.io.IOException
+ void connect(java.net.SocketAddress) throws java.io.IOException
+ void connect(java.net.SocketAddress, int) throws java.io.IOException
+ boolean getKeepAlive() throws java.net.SocketException
+ java.net.SocketAddress getLocalSocketAddress()
+ boolean getOOBInline() throws java.net.SocketException
+ java.net.SocketAddress getRemoteSocketAddress()
+ boolean getReuseAddress() throws java.net.SocketException
+ int getTrafficClass() throws java.net.SocketException
+ boolean isBound()
+ boolean isClosed()

+ boolean isConnected()
+ boolean isInputShutdown()
+ boolean isOutputShutdown()
+ void sendUrgentData(int) throws java.io.IOException
+ void setKeepAlive(boolean) throws java.net.SocketException
+ void setOOBInline(boolean) throws java.net.SocketException
+ void setReuseAddress(boolean) throws java.net.SocketException
+ void setTrafficClass(int) throws java.net.SocketException
+ void shutdownInput() throws java.io.IOException
+ void shutdownOutput() throws java.io.IOException
- Socket()

java.net.SocketImpl
+ void connect(java.net.SocketAddress, int) throws java.io.IOException
+ void sendUrgentData(int) throws java.io.IOException
+ void shutdownInput() throws java.io.IOException

+ void shutdownOutput() throws java.io.IOException
+ boolean supportsUrgentData()

java.net.SocketOptions
+ static int IP_MULTICAST_IF2
+ static int IP_MULTICAST_LOOP
+ static int IP_TOS

+ static int SO_BROADCAST
+ static int SO_KEEPALIVE
+ static int SO_OOBINLINE

java.net.URL
+ java.lang.Object getContent(java.lang.Class[]) throws
java.io.IOException

+ int getDefaultPort()

java.net.URLClassLoader
+ java.lang.Package definePackage(java.lang.String, java.util.jar.Manifest,
java.net.URL)

java.net.URLConnection
+ void addRequestProperty(java.lang.String, java.lang.String)
+ java.lang.Object getContent(java.lang.Class[]) throws
java.io.IOException

+ java.util.Map getHeaderFields()
+ java.util.Map getRequestProperties()
- static java.lang.String guessContentTypeFromName(java.lang.String)

java.net.URLDecoder
+ static java.lang.String decode(java.lang.String, java.lang.String) throws
java.io.UnsupportedEncodingException

- static java.lang.String decode(java.lang.String)

java.net.URLEncoder
+ static java.lang.String encode(java.lang.String, java.lang.String) throws
java.io.UnsupportedEncodingException

- static java.lang.String encode(java.lang.String)

java.security.AccessControlContext
+ AccessControlContext(java.security.AccessControlContext,
java.security.DomainCombiner)

+ java.security.DomainCombiner getDomainCombiner()

java.security.Policy
+ java.security.PermissionCollection
getPermissions(java.security.ProtectionDomain)

+ boolean implies(java.security.ProtectionDomain,
java.security.Permission)

java.security.ProtectionDomain
+ ProtectionDomain(java.security.CodeSource,
java.security.PermissionCollection, java.lang.ClassLoader,
java.security.Principal[])

+ java.lang.ClassLoader getClassLoader()
+ java.security.Principal[] getPrincipals()

java.security.Security
+ static java.util.Set getAlgorithms(java.lang.String)

java.util.ArrayList (-)

java.util.Calendar
+ int getActualMaximum(int)
+ int getActualMinimum(int)
+ int getGreatestMinimum(int)
+ int getLeastMaximum(int)
+ int getMaximum(int)

+ int getMinimum(int)
- int get(int)
- long getTimeInMillis()
- void set(int, int)
- void setTimeInMillis(long)

java.util.Collections
+ static int indexOfSubList(java.util.List, java.util.List)
+ static int lastIndexOfSubList(java.util.List, java.util.List)
+ static java.util.ArrayList list(java.util.Enumeration)

+ static boolean replaceAll(java.util.List, java.lang.Object, java.lang.Object)
+ static void rotate(java.util.List, int)
+ static void swap(java.util.List, int, int)

java.util.GregorianCalendar
+ int getGreatestMinimum(int)
+ int getLeastMaximum(int)

+ int getMaximum(int)
+ int getMinimum(int)

java.util.Locale
+ Locale(java.lang.String)

java.util.Properties
+ void list(java.io.PrintWriter)

+ void save(java.io.OutputStream, java.lang.String)

java.util.SimpleTimeZone
+ static int STANDARD_TIME
+ static int UTC_TIME

+ static int WALL_TIME

+ SimpleTimeZone(int, java.lang.String, int, int, int, int, int, int, int, int, int, int)   + void setDSTSavings(int)

java.util.TimeZone
+ static int LONG
+ static int SHORT
+ int getDSTSavings()
+ java.lang.String getDisplayName()
+ java.lang.String getDisplayName(boolean, int)

+ java.lang.String getDisplayName(boolean, int, java.util.Locale)
+ java.lang.String getDisplayName(java.util.Locale)
+ int getOffset(long)
+ boolean hasSameRules(java.util.TimeZone)

java.util.Vector (-)

java.util.zip.ZipFile
+ static int OPEN_DELETE
+ static int OPEN_READ

+ ZipFile(java.io.File, int)java.io.IOException

999.5   References

[1]   *The Java Virtual Machine Specification*
Tim Lindholm and Frank Yellin, Addison Wesley, ISBN 0-201-63452-X

[2]   *Downloadable Execution Environments*
http://www.osgi.org/download

[3]   *J2ME, Java 2 Micro Edition*
http://java.sun.com/j2me

[4]   *CDC, Connected Device Configuration*
http://java.sun.com/products/cdc

[5]   *CLDC, Connected Limited Device Configuration*
http://java.sun.com/products/cldc

[6]   *Foundation Profile*
http://java.sun.com/products/foundation. This external specification is © Copyright 2000 Sun Microsystems, Inc.